Mountain Building Processes

Mountain Building Processes

Edited by

K.J.Hsü

Geologisches Institut
Eidgenössische Technische Hochschule
Zürich, Switzerland

1982

ACADEMIC PRESS

A Subsidiary of Harcourt Brace Jovanovich, Publishers

London   New York
Paris   San Diego   San Francisco
São Paulo   Sydney   Tokyo   Toronto

ACADEMIC PRESS INC. (LONDON) LTD.
24/28 Oval Road
London NW1

United States Edition published by
ACADEMIC PRESS INC.
111 Fifth Avenue
New York, New York 10003

Copyright © 1983 by
ACADEMIC PRESS INC. (LONDON) LTD.
Second printing 1984

British Library Cataloguing in Publication Data

Mountain building processes.
1. Mountains—Congresses   2. Geology,
Structural—Congresses
I. Hsu, K.J.
551.4'32   GB501.2

ISBN 0-12-357980-5

Printed in Great Britain by
The Alden Press,
Oxford

Contributors

Ben-Avraham, Z. Prof., Dept. of Geophysics, Stanford Univ., Stanford, CA 94305, USA
Bernoull, D. Prof., Geol.-Pal. Inst. der Univ., Bernoullistrasse 32, CH-4056 Basel
Caron, Ch. Prof., Inst. de Géol., Perolles, CH-1700 Fribourg
Chen, W.-P. Dr., Earth & Planet. Sci., M.I.T., Cambridge, MA 02139, USA
Dietrich, V. Dr., Inst., f. Krist. und Petr. ETH, CH-8092 Zürich
England, P. Dr, Dept. of Geol. Sci., Harvard Univ., 20 Oxford St., Cambridge, MA 02138, USA
Ernst, W.G. Prof. Dept. of Earth and Space Science, 3806 Geology Building, UCLA, Los Angeles, CA 90024
Gansser A. Prof., Geol. Inst. ETH, CH-8092 Zürich
Gill, J. Prof., Dept. of Geology, Univ. California, Santa Cruz, CA 95060, USA
Homewood P. Dr, Inst. de Géol., Perolles, CH-1700 Fribourg
Honegger, K. Mr., Inst., f. Krist. und Petr. ETH, CH-8092 Zürich
Hsü, K.J. Prof., Geol., Inst., ETH, CH-8092 Zürich
Karig, D.E. Prof., Dept. Geol. Sci., Cornell Univ., Ithaca, NY 14853, USA
Kaufman, S. Prof., Kimball Hall, Cornell Univ., Ithaca, NY 14853, USA
Laubscher, H.P. Prof., Geol.-Pal. Inst. der Univ., Bernoullistrasse 32, CH-4056 Basel
Le Pichon, X. Prof., Inst. Physique du Globe, 4 Place Jussieu, F-75005 Paris
Molnar, P. Prof., Earth & Planet. Sci., M.I.T., Cambridge, MA 02139, USA
Mueller, S. Prof., Inst. f. Geophysik ETH, CH-8093 Zürich
Nur, A. Prof., Dept. of Geophysics, Stanford Univ., Stanford, CA 94305, USA
Oxburgh, R. Prof., Dept. of Earth Sci., Downing Street, Cambridge CB2 3EQ, U.K.
Pitcher, W. Prof., Dept. Geol., Univ. Liverpool, Liverpool L69 3XB, U.K.
Ramsay, J.G. Prof., Geol. Inst. ETH, CH-8092 Zürich
Rodgers, J. Prof., Dept. of Geol., Yale University, New Haven, CT 06520, USA
Schmid, S. Dr., Geol. Inst. ETH, CH-8092 Zürich
Trommsdorff, V. Prof., Inst., f. Krist. und Petr. ETH, CH-8092 Zürich
Trümpy, R. Prof. Geol. Inst. ETH, CH-8092 Zürich
Turcotte D. Prof., Kimball Hall, Cornell Univ., Ithaca, NY 14853, USA

Augusto Gansser

Rudolf Trümpy

Mountain Building Processes: An Introduction

As a young man I was amazed by the audacity of the paleontologist Davidson Black, who named a hominid species *Pithecanthropus pekinensis* on the basis of a couple of molar teeth. Later on I admired the brilliance of Marcel Bertrand, who recognized the true nature of the Glarus Overthrust without ever having set foot on the soil of the Canton Glarus. The secret of their successes lies in their comprehension of comparative anatomies. Anatomical analyses are not purely geometrical. A successful reconstruction does not always depend on a full recovery of skeletons nor on the complete preservation of structures, but upon an understanding of the physiology of living creatures or of the processes that build a mountain. As John Rodgers aptly titled his article in this volume,—the life history of a mountain range—mountains live and die like a vital organism. We cannot always rely only on what we could find, or what we could observe; we have to fill out the missing parts, using our knowledge of the functional utilities of the various indispensable units. In other words, a sound theoretical knowledge is a prerequisite for a correction reconstruction, be it an animal or a mountain.

The geosynclinal theory of orogeny dominated our thinking for a century. James Hall proposed the theory because he was under the influence of earlier speculations that mountain building was triggered by the pressure and heat at the bottom of a thick pile of sediments. R.D. Dana started a "chicken-and-egg" type of argument when he proposed that geosynclinal depressions did not cause, but were created by, compressional forces in an early stage of mountain building. Nevertheless, both Hall and Dana, and their followers saw geosynclines as precursors of mountain building. Alfred Wegener, with his theory of continental drift, started a rebellion that found its victory in the revolution of the sixties. While he was denounced as a heretic in America, he did find followers on the continent of Europe, especially in Switzerland, where Emil Argand and Rudolf Staub anticipated the new global tectonics with their mobilistic theories: mountain building was envisioned as an expression of the oceanic resistance to continental drift, or as a consequence of continental collision.

Schooled by American conservative masters, I myself had tended to adopt a skeptical attitude, until I was finally faced with the necessity of having to accept the postulate of seafloor-spreading. The plate-tectonics theory, innovated by geophysicists such as Jason Morgan, Dan McKenzie, Bob Parker, Xavier LePichon, among others, and developed by geologists like John Dewey, Alan Smith, Warren Hamilton, and their co-workers, has proven its usefulness in providing a unifying set of explanations to many facets of the complicated mountain building processes. After more than a decade of intensive investigations, the time is ripe for a comprehensive review; we would like to look back to evaluate the degrees of successes achieved by the plate-tectonics in explaining orogeny.

According to the new theory, tectonic processes are expressions of plate interactions. The plates can be either oceanic or continental; there could be continent–continent, ocean–continent, or ocean–ocean interactions. The resulting movements could be compressional, extensional, or lateral. Continent–continent interaction in an extensional environment forms rift valley or Germano-type of mountains. Ocean–ocean extension produces sea-floor-spreading and mid-ocean ridges. Extension on or near continent–ocean boundary generates marginal or back-arc basins. Ocean–ocean compression makes submarine elevations such as the Mediterranean Ridge. Compression of an oceanic against a continental lithosphere leads to subduction, typical of the circum-Pacific mountains. Continent–continent collision gives rise to mighty deformed belts, such as the Alps and the Himalayas. Lateral movements between oceanic plates produce aseismic ridges such as the Ninety-east Ridge of the Indian Ocean. Such movements form continental borderland such as that offshore Southern California, as a result of ocean–continent interaction. Where a strike-slip fault (e.g. the San Andreas) separates two continental plates, the tectonic style is characterized by pull-apart basins and sharp folds such as the California style of Cenozoic tectonics. The articles in this volume will discuss all aspects of the various plate-interactions, with particular emphasis on the collision-type of orogeny.

The first part includes articles which deal with tectonic processes associated with, or leading to, mountain building. An article by the editor entitled *Geosynclines in plate-tectonic settings* discussed the causes of subsidence which permitted the accumulation of various types of sediments now found in the mountains; it was an attempt to translate the classical nomenclature of geosynclinal theories into the modern jargon of plate-tectonicists. The paper by James Gill on *Mountain building and volcanism* gave a brief review of the petrological characteristics of volcanic rocks found in deformed belts during different stages of their development. Wallace Pitcher related *Granite type and tectonic environment*. Peter Molnar and W.P. Chen wrote on *Seismicity and mountain building*; they noted that seismicity places an important constraint on the physical processes occurring during mountain building. Dan Karig contributed a paper on *Deformation in the forearc*. Using actualistic examples, he demonstrated that the deformation is strongly concentrated toward the base of the trench slope, forming folds, thrusts, or subduction mélanges. Amos Nur and Zvi Ben-Avrahan emphasized the importance of *Displaced terranes and mountain building*. Oceanic rises, underlain by thicker than normal oceanic crust, are fated to collide with continents at active margins in the future, leading to collision-type orogeny and accretion of continents. The next four papers of Part I took into consideration the rheological properties of the crust and mantle in evaluating mountain building processes. E.R. Oxburgh presented a model of *Heterogeneous lithospheric stretching in early history of orogenic belts*. He believed that such stretching controls the pattern of vertical movements, the subsequent closure of sedimentary basins, and the distribution of ophiolitic and other detached basement fragments in mountain belts. John Ramsay elaborated on *Rock ductility and its influence on the development of tectonic structures in mountain belts*. Whereas basement fracturing and cover décollement are characteristic of the external zones, the initiation and propagation of mechanical instabilities are particularly important in the internal zones, where there is often a linkage between the structures developed in basement with those in the cover. Stephan Schmid explained the use of *Microfabric studies as indicators of deformation mechanisms and flow laws operative in mountain buildings*. He also discussed estimates of paleostress, significance of crystallographic preferred orientation, and mechanisms of strain-softening leading to localized deformation in shear zones. Philip England made *Some numerical investigations of large scale continental deformation*. He abandoned the concept of rigid plates, and assumed that lithospheric plates, on the million-year time-scale and hundred-km length-scale, are governed by a non-Newtonian rheology, which may be approximated by power-law creep. His study contributed notably to the understanding of the uplift of the Tibetan Plateau. The final paper in Part I by Don Turcotte is a succinct review of *Driving mechanisms of mountain building*.

While we took the mountains apart and analysed the process in Part I, the authors of Part II put the parts together and made a synthesis of several prominent orogenic belts as case-histories to illustrate the operations of the processes. Rudolf Trümpy examined again the *Alpine paleogeography*. His reappraisal interpreted the development of the Alpine geosyncline in terms of movements of lithospheric plates during the last few hundred million years. Peter Homewood and Christian Caron wrote on *Flysch of the Alps*, and speculated on the relationships between Flysch sedimentation and Alpine mountain building. Hans Laubscher and Daniel Bernoulli brought us up to date with their article on *History and deformation of the Alps*; they developed a variation on a consensus theme that the Alpine tectonics records the motions along the plate-boundary Africa–Europe, first sinistrally divergent, then dextrally convergent. Stephan Mueller summarized the most recent geophysical

and geodetic observations in his model of *Deep structure and recent dynamics in the Alps*. He further speculated that a south- and a northward dipping slab of lower lithosphere must have been subducted to a depth of 200 or 250 km during a plate-collision which produced the Alps. Xavier Le Pichon's paper on *Land-locked oceanic basins and continental collision* diverted our attention to the eastern Mediterranean. He believed that the subduction along the Hellenic Trench is responsible for the active extension north, and the active compression south, of the trench, producing the Aegean Sea and the Mediterranean Ridge respectively. Volkmar Trommsdorff, Volker Dietrich, and Kaspar Honegger carried us farther east to *The Indus Suture Zone*, and they evaluated the paleotectonic and igneous evolution in the Ladakh-Himalayas in terms of displacements of lithospheric plates. Augusto Gansser reminded us that there is *The morphogenic phase of mountain building*, illustrating his conclusions with examples from the Alps, the Himalayas, and the Andes. John Rodgers described *The life history of a mountain range—the Appalachians*; it was a story of divergence, followed by a convergence punctuated by three orogenic climaxes. Sid Kaufman filed a report of the COCORP Project on *Crustal faults in North America*. The deep reflection-profiling revealed the importance of crustal overthrusting. Gary Ernst concluded the volume with his article on *Mountain building and metamorphism: a case history from Taiwan*. Taiwan is a very small island, but this well exposed natural laboratory documents the complicated interrelationships among plate tectonics, mountain building and metamorphism.

The 21 contributions of this volume were presented orally in the *Symposium on Mountain Building*, held in July, 1981 at Zurich. We are indebted to the "Schweizerischer Nationalfonds" and the "Schweizerische Natuforschende Gesellschaft" for the financial support. The editor is particularly grateful to Dr Ueli Briegel who single-handedly organized the Symposium; Dr Briegel also helped in the chore of editing. Thanks are due to Barbara Das Gupta for her frequent assistance. Finally, the editor wishes to dedicate this collection of essays to his colleagues Augusto Gansser and Rudolf Trümpy, in recognition of their outstanding contributions to our understanding of The Mountain Building Processes.

August 1982   K. Hsü

Contents

Part 1

Processes

Geosynclines in Plate-tectonic Settings: Sediments in Mountains

K.J. Hsü

Swiss Federal Institute of Technology,
Zurich, Switzerland

Abstract

Sediments in mountains used to be considered geosynclinal, and geosynclinal subsidence considered a precursor of orogeny. Modern plate-tectonics theory interprets mountain building as the result of compressional tectonics along consuming or transform plate-boundaries, involving sediments deposited on continental or plate-margins as well as those in plate-interiors. The classical miogeosynclines are now commonly referred to as passive continental margins. Subsidence is related to crustal thinning, and to cooling of a lithospheric plate as it moves away from a thermal perturbation. The cause of crustal thinning could have been either supracrustal erosion, or lithospheric stretching. Recurrent superposition of deep-water sediments over shallow marine deposits on a continental margin gave rise to geosynclinal cycles. Such renewed subsidence of a miogeosyncline during later stages of its development may signify a change from a passive to an active continental margin when a shelf along the margin was dragged down by a newly initiated subduction movement. As a rule subduction is responsible for the genesis of trenches or back-arc basins for flysch-sedimentation at or near active plate-margins. However, flysch or other turbidite basins may also be formed by a "pull-apart" mechanism due to local extension along a curved, or *en echelon*, strike-slip fault zone. Eugeosynclinal rocks are now found mainly as tectonic mélanges, marking the position of subduction zones in circum-Pacific mountains, or suture zones in collision-type of orogens.

I. Introduction

The geosynclinal theories of mountain building, first innovated by James Hall (1859), have served geology for a century, and have gradually been replaced during the last decade by a new paradigm of plate-tectonics. If we overlook all the now seemingly petty debates and differences in opinions and search for a common denominator in the meaning of the word geosyncline, we are reduced to a simple definition that geosynclinal deposits are the rocks of the mountains. Expressed in this way, the statement that geosynclines are precursors of mountains acquires an aura of truth, while becoming tautological. All sedimentary basins, including the deepest abysses, in greater or less probability, are likely to be deformed and uplifted to form lofty peaks, and many have been. Geosynclinal sediments thus include oceanic accumulations as well as deposits of continental interiors, and they may have been deposited on passive continental margin, or on active, in rifted valleys prior to seafloor-spreading, or in pull-apart basins on transform plate-boundary. In these days at the beginning of a new dynasty, it may not be fashionable to beat the dead horse and to indulge in talking about a ghost, but if we look closely, we may perceive that only the name of the theatre for debate has been changed. We no longer worry about the origin of geosynclines, yet we carry on the old controversies under the new fashionable canopy that reads "origin of sedimentary basins". The problem stays with us, and the question on the cause of subsidence remains to be answered, regardless of whether the site is to be called a geosyncline, or a plate-margin. The one relevant difference lies in the fact that the plate-tectonics theory does provide us with acutalistic models to interpret the origin of ancient sedimentary basins, whereas the geosynclinal theories speculated, often dogmatically, on hypothetical processes for which we can find no counterparts in the real world. This paper is an attempt to summarize our knowledge to date of the origin of sedimentary basins which once hosted the bulk of the rocks of the mountains. I shall refer to old terminology and present new interpretations.

II. Crustal Thinning and Mantle-density Changes

In an attempt to demythicize the concept of geosynclines, I pointed out in a youthful opus (Hsü, 1958) that Airy's (1855) model of isostasy demands that sedimentary basins are underlain by a thinner crust. The causes of geosynclinal subsidence are thus to be sought in mechanisms of crustal thinning. Later on, when heterogeneity in the earth's upper mantle was discovered, I added that the relation of surface elevations to mantle-density must also be taken into account: subsidence could be caused by a decay of a thermal perturbation in the upper mantle (Hsü, 1965a). So, in addition to the Airy isostasy, "thermal isostasy" has been invoked (Oxburgh, this volume) to describe the relation between surface elevation and mantle density in response to changes in thermal state, — an idea anticipated by Pratt (1864) when he formulated his isostatic model.

We now recognize that the earth's crust is in a state of approximately isostatic equilibrium except along active plate margins where mountain building is going on. The subsidence of isostastically adjusted sedimentary basins has to be related to the Airy, or to the Pratt (thermal) isostasy, and the subsidence history interpreted in terms of crustal thinning or of mantle density changes.

III. Miogeosynclines on Passive Continental Margins

Typical miogeosynclinal sediments, such as the Paleozoic of the Valley and Ridge Province of the Appalachians, or the Mesozoic of the Helvetic and Southern Alps, have been identified as largely sedimentary accumulations on passive margins (Rodgers, this volume; Bernoulli and Jenkyns, 1974), and undeformed Mesozoic and Cenozoic sediments of the Florida–Bahama region and of the Atlantic Coast of North America are models for comparison (Hsü, 1973). The subsidence history of the Atlantic margins has been a subject of intensive investigations during the last decade. The seismic results indicate a thin crust on the continental margin, and the gravity data are best fitted with an assumption of regional isostasy (Fig. 1). A deep well COST B-2 has penetrated some 5 km of Cenozoic and Mesozoic sediments without reaching the basement, which lies at a depth of about 12·8 km (Schlee *et al.*, 1976). Since the first sediment was probably deposited upon an erosional surface near sea-level, the total subsidence of the basement should be well in excess of 10 km. A part of the subsidence is, of course, a consequence of isostatic adjustment in response to sedimentary loading, and can be separated from that resulting from other effects (Fig. 2). The residual subsidence due to tectonic forces can then be plotted against the square root of time, $\sqrt{t}$. The results from two wells (Oneida 0–25, and COST B-2), obtained by Watts and Steckler (1979) are shown by Fig. 3. As they pointed out, the tectonic subsidence was a linear

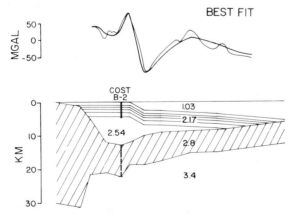

Fig. 1　Miogeosyncline on passive continental margin of eastern North America. Note the thin crust under thick sediments of the margin. The assumption of regional isostasy led to a best fit of the computed and observed gravity-data. (From Watts and Steckler, 1979.)

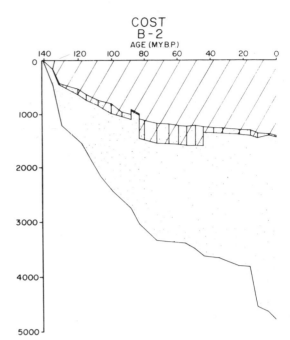

Fig. 2　Subsidence on passive continental margin, exemplified by COST B-2 well. The dotted region indicates that part of the subsidence was caused by sedimentary loading, and the hatched region was caused by other tectonic effects. The vertical line region indicates other complicating factors. (From Watts and Steckler, 1979.)

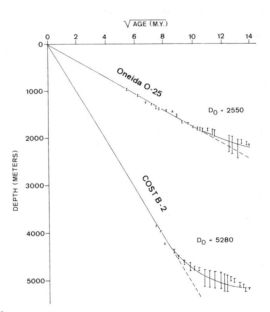

Fig. 3　Subsidence curve. Plot of tectonic subsidence against age for two wells on the Atlantic margin of North America. (After Watts and Steckler, 1979.)

function of $\sqrt{t}$, before the movement was arrested and decayed exponentially to an asymptotic value. This pattern is exactly the same as that predicted by Parsons and Sclater (1978) for the subsidence of the seafloor above a cooling lithospheric plate. Therefore, the general consensus today includes elements from both Airy's and Pratt's postulates: the subsidence of passive margins is related to contraction associated with cooling of regions underlain by a thin crust.

To change from the standard crust of continental interiors (30–40 km) to a thin crust under continental margins involves a process of thinning. The cause of crustal thinning is, however, a problem not yet resolved. Three possibilities

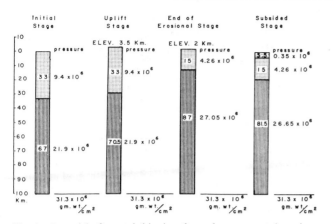

Fig. 4   A model of crustal thinning through supracrustal erosion. Thickness of crustal and mantle columns is shown by figures inside the pattern. Crustal density is 2·84 g/cm³, mantle densities vary between 3·27 and 3·11 g/cm³. (From Hsü, 1965.)

exist: supracrustal erosion, "necking" by crustal extension, or subcrustal changes.

Subcrustal models were popular a decade or two ago. One was to assume a shift of Moho through a conversion of basaltic crust into eclogitic mantle (Kennedy, 1959), but the hypothesis is no longer generally accepted because few geophysicists now believe that the Moho is a boundary of phase change. Another was to assume "basification" through subcrustal chemical processes (van Bemmeln, 1958; Beloussov, 1962; Falvey, 1974), but those ideas have remained largely idle speculations, for having failed to provide tests of validity. A third was to invoke "subcrustal" erosion (Gilluly, 1955). Such "erosion" might indeed be taking place where an oceanic plate descends under the inner wall of a trench (Scholl *et al.*, 1980), but the process is not applicable to the crustal thinning under passive margins.

I suggested a model of supracrustal erosion (Hsü, 1965a) on the basis of an observed pattern, first noted by Grabau (1924), that new sedimentary basins are commonly located on the ruins of old mountains. The exposure of high-grade plutonic rocks indicates a removal of many kilometres of overburden. Using the Great Basin of the western United States as an analogue, I envisioned supracrustal thinning when a continental crust was uplifted and eroded during an initial rifting stage (Fig. 4). This idea was subsequently developed by Sleep (1971) and is still one of the viable working hypotheses. However, the extent of supracrustal thinning may not have been everywhere sufficient to produce the thin

continental crust found in some regions of subsidence (McKenzie, 1978; Watts and Steckler, 1979).

Currently many geophysicists favour various models of lithospheric stretching (Oxburgh, this volume: Williams, 1981). The idea was originally proposed by Walter Bucher (1933): using the ductile "necking" of metals before failure as an analogue, Bucher envisioned isostastic subsidence as a consequence of crustal thinning under extension. Since isostastic adjustment is geologically instantaneous, the rate of subsidence should thus be a function of the rate of extensional strain. A modern, quantitative model by McKenzie (1978), however, assumes instantaneous deformation, so that the subsidence history is related to subsequent thermal changes within a stretched lithosphere. According to this analysis, the subsidence is a linear function of the square root of time as in the case of cooling lithospheric plates, except for the initial stage ($t < 16$ m.y.) Since we do not usually have a record of early subsidence we are rarely in a position to distinguish the effect of lithospheric stretching from that of supracrustal erosion.

While I am reluctant to discard my old idea, because supracrustal thinning is unavoidable where erosion is going on, I do accept the seismic evidence which clearly indicates, in some instances at least, lithospheric stretching. The passive margin of the Bay of Biscay, for example, has been shown to be underlain by half-grabens bounded by listic faults (Fig. 5; Montadert *et al.*, 1979). A similar structural pattern of low-angle normal faults in the Great Basin of the western United States has apparently inspired McKenzie to formulate his model.

The consequence of crustal thinning by lithospheric stretching is two-fold. The replacement of light crust by denser asthenosphere materials causes isostastic subsidence, which has also been referred to as "subsidence immediately after stretching" (Fig. 6) (Le Pichon and Sibuet, 1981), or "fault-controlled subsidence" (Christie and Sclater, 1980). I suggest that we use the term *Airy subsidence* to denote this component. The second consequence, results from the exponential decay of a thermal anomaly introduced by the emplacement of the asthenosphere material (see Oxburgh, this volume). This thermal subsidence under a stretched continental crust is similar to that experienced by an oceanic lithosphere as it moves away from the axis of seafloor-spreading (Sclater *et al.*, 1971). We may refer to it as the Pratt subsidence, in honour of the person who first postulated thermal isostasy.

The earliest sediments on present continental margins are mostly buried at great depth, not easily reached by drilling. Only mountain regions may offer an opportunity for a test of the various models. For example, the sediments deposited

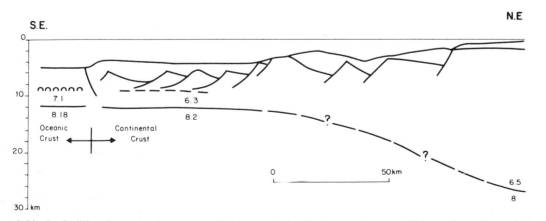

Fig. 5   Crustal thinning by lithospheric stretching, exemplified by a crustal section through the Bay of Biscay. (From Montadert *et al.*, 1979.)

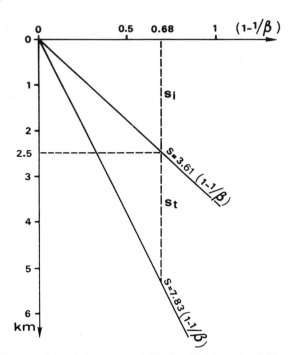

Fig. 6   Relation between crustal thinning $(1-1/\beta)$ and subsidence. The upper line is the relation immediately after an instantaneous stretching, the lower is the relation at time infinite. (From Le Pichon and Sibuet, 1981.)

on the southern margin of the Tethys are now exposed as parts of the Australpine nappes in the Swiss Alps. The stratigraphy of those formations provide some information on the Mesozoic subsidence there.

The carbonate platform of the Australpine Realm began to break up during the late Triassic when the Hauptdolomit formation was deposited. The dolomite deposits are typical sediments of a tidal flat complex, all laid down near the sea-level. Therefore, the thickness of the Hauptdolomite measures the total subsidence. The early Jurassic was a time

of extensional faulting and of rapid subsidence (Trümpy, 1960; this volume). When the Toarcian *ammonitico rosso* was first deposited at about 178 m.y. BP (Van Hinte's 1976 time scale), the seafloor was probably already 1000 to 1500 m deep (Bosselini and Winterer, 1975). By the time of Callovian-Oxfordian radiolarite-sedimentation at about 150 m.y. BP, the first ophiolite had already appeared in the Penninic Realm to the north of the Australpine (or southern Tethyan) margin. The site of pelagic sedimentation should have stood a little higher than the axial trough, therefore, I suggested a paleobathymetry of about 2000 m for the Jurassic radiolarite (Hsü, 1975). Subsidence continued through the Early Cretaceous. At about 100 m.y. BP, when the mid-Cretaceous black shales were deposited, the seabottom had sunk below the calcite-compensation-depth, which may have ranged from about 4000 to 5000 m (Bernoulli and Jenkyns, 1974; Bosellini and Winterer, 1975). Since the Alpine pelagic sediments are relatively thin ("leptogeosynclinal", Trümpy, 1960), the paleobathymetric figures cited above give an estimate of the subsidence.

Using the available stratigraphical data and the current paleobathymetrical interpretations, and making due corrections for subsidence under sedimentary load, I have attempted a reconstruction of the subsidence history for the Lower (more northerly) and Upper (more southerly) Australpine Realms (Fig. 7). Also shown is a theoretical curve for the Airy and Pratt subsidences of a region where the crust has been reduced to half of its original thickness ($\beta = 2$; McKenzie, 1978). I used the LePichon and Sibuet (1980) model to calculate the Airy subsidence, neglecting the errors involved because of the assumption that the subsidence took place during the first 20 million years of the Jurassic Period. The Pratt subsidence is approximated by the McKenzie model of instantaneous crustal stretching; the approximation should not introduce an error of more than 20% (Jarvis and McKenzie, 1980).

Figure 7 shows that the subsidence of the Lower Australpine could well all be caused by lithospheric stretching, involving a reduction of the thickness to about $\frac{1}{2}$ or $\frac{1}{3}$ of the original. However, a comparison of the Lower and Upper Australpine curves seems to argue against the hypothesis of

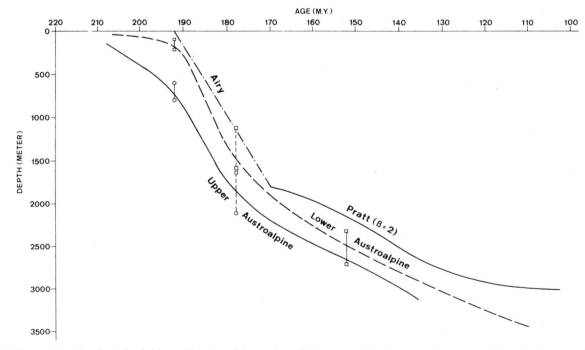

Fig. 7   Theoretical and estimated subsidence histories of the southern Tethyan margin (Upper and Lower Australpine Realms). See text for detailed explanation.

stretching. According to the "necking" concept, once a "neck" is initiated, the stress should be concentrated at the cross-section of a minimum area. The "neck" should have stayed at the same place which remained the site of maximum subsidence until failure ensued, when an axial valley of ocean-floor began to form in the middle of a pulled-apart "neck". The Lower Australpine Realm immediately south of the Pennine ophiolite-trough should have been closer to the place where the "neck" was; the Upper Australpine (Engadine Dolomite) realm was originally situated farther south, more distant from the Pennine axis. Consequently the "necking" model predicts that the crustal thinning and subsidence should always have been greater in the Lower Australpine. In fact, the stratigraphical data show the contrary: the Hauptdolomit are commonly a few hundred metres thick, or even less, very thin as compared to the sequences (>1000 m) of the Upper Australpine (Dössegger and Müller, 1976; Finger, 1978). Greater dolomite thickness indicates greater subsidence. It seems that the late Triassic axis of maximum subsidence was located closer to the Upper Australpine Realm, some distance away from the subsequent "neck" near the Lower Australpine. Perhaps we may have to apply a plate-cooling model (without "necking") to interpret the Triassic stratigraphy, while invoking crustal stretching to explain the Jurassic subsidence. It may seem an inelegant solution, but the geologic history of the Alps gives some support to such a suggestion: the Triassic signified the end of a long period of subsidence since the end of the Hercynian orogeny, while the Jurassic heralds the beginning of a new extensional tectonics (see Trümpy, this volume). The lithospheric stretching that gave birth to the Tethys may indeed have only started at the dawn of the Jurassic.

In summary we can conclude that we continue to seek answers to geosynclinal subsidence in crustal thinning and mantle-density changes, despite the great revolution that shook the foundation of the earth sciences. Isostasy is still the basic driving force for vertical movements, although lateral movements of lithospheric plates could lead to perturbations of isostastic equilibrium and cause readjustments, and thus lead indirectly to subsidence of passive continental margins to form miogeosynclines.

IV. Miogeosynclines on Active Continental Margins

The Airy subsidence of passive margin is geologically instantaneous. The Pratt subsidence decays exponentially and should reach an asymptotic limit after some 60 or 70 million years (McKenzie, 1978). When subsidence due to thermal isostasy becomes negligible, subsidence under sedimentary load could continue as long as sediment is being piled on top of the site of accumulation. However, the sedimentary load itself tends to fill up a basin: subsidence due to the load, combined with the effect of sedimentary fill should result in a water-depth about half as deep as that prior to the loading (Hsü, 1958). After the basin is filled up, subsidence under the load would also become negligible, so that no further sediments could be deposited. For example, the Bahama Platform on the south-eastern passive margin of the North American continent reached that stage during the Eocene. The subsidence started in the Jurassic and slowed down to a halt during the early Tertiary. Very little sediments younger than Eocene are present there (Sheridan *et al.*, 1966), and those were probably deposited during and after periods of relatively high stands of the sea-level. Nevertheless the stratigraphic records of many mountain regions give evidence of recurrent deepenings at sites of deposition: shallow-water carbonates are overlain by deep-water shales in many places.

Pettijohn (1957) used the expression "geosynclinal cycles"

to describe a repeatedly observed succession (in ascending of order) of carbonate-orthoquartzites (preorogenic), dark shales (euxenic), turbidite sandstones (flysch), and shallow-water clastics (molasse) (Fig. 8). Whereas the flysch–molasse sequence might represent filling of an initially deep basin accompanied by subsidence under sedimentary load, the deepening of the seabottom that changed the sedimentary environment from a carbonate-shelf to a slope for hemipelagic sedimentation indicates disturbances of isostastic equilibrium. I noticed a coincidence of timing of such "anti-isostastic" subsidences with that of orogenic deformations in nearby regions (Hsü, 1958). The sudden deepening of the Appalachian Miogeosyncline during the middle Ordovician and the middle Devonian are two notable examples: the older carbonate platforms were drowned at about the same time when the Taconic and Acadian Orogenies started. Going to the Alps, we found a similar story in the Helvetic nappes, which was once the northern margin of the Tethys Ocean. The subsidence there started with the opening of the Tethys in the Jurassic, and slowed down during the Early Cretaceous, when only shallow marine sediments were deposited (see Trümpy, this volume). However, the middle Cretaceous *Schrattenkalk*, a massive shelf-carbonate that now makes impressive cliffs in the Alps, is overlain by a deepening sequence, ending up in a pelagic limestone of the Turonian age (*Seewerkalk*). This rejuvenated subsidence of the Helvetic margin was approximately synchronous with the change from an extensional to a compressional phase of deformation in the western Alps. Later, with the "Paleocene Restoration" (Trümpy, this volume), shallow marine carbonates were again laid down in the Helvetic Realm. A second change to hemipelagic sedimentation took place during the Late Eocene, when the Nummulite Limestone was overlain by the Globigerina Marl, and the Late Eocene is well known as the time of continental collision when the meso-Alpine deformation was about to reach its conclusion (see Trümpy, this volume). The accelerated subsidences at times of orogenic deformation in the Appalachian and Alpine Geosynclines suggest that the change was brought about when passive continental margins were converted into active margins.

Subsidence of an active plate-margin has been investigated by the deep-sea drilling cruises Legs 56 and 57. Drilling a transect of holes across the Japan Trench, it was discovered that the inner-slope, now lying in thousands of metres depth,

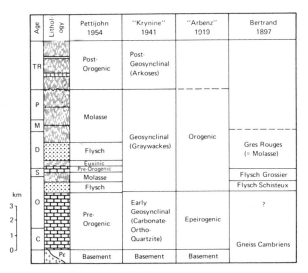

Fig. 8 Evolution of the concept of the Appalachian geosynclinal cycles. Note the recurrences of black shales (euxinic) above the sediments of carbonate-orthoquartzite (preorogenic) facies. (From Hsü, 1973.)

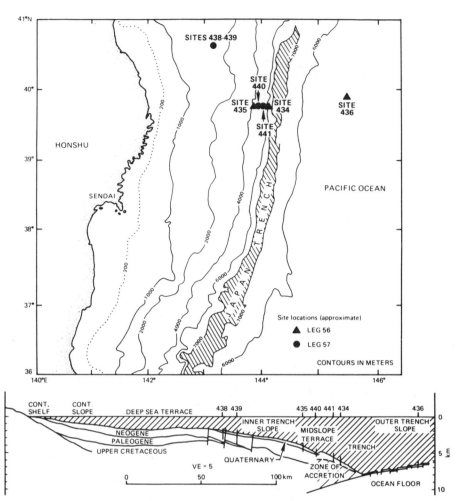

Fig. 9 Subsidence inner-trench slope of active continental margin. The Paleogene (Oligocene) sediments are largely terrestrial in origin, indicating thousands of metres of subsidence of the inner trench slope during the Neogene subduction. (From Scientific Party, 1980.)

was emergent during the Oligocene (Fig. 9). The continental margin there has apparently been dragged down by the Neogene subduction of the Pacific Plate (Scientific Party, 1980). The movement is largely compressional, disturbing the isostastic equilibrium of the margin, although crustal thinning by "subduction-erosion" may have contributed to the subsidence (Scholl *et al.*, 1980). To apply the model to the Alps, I envisioned a north-dipping Benioff-zone in the northern Tethyan margin during the Late Cretaceous (Hsü and Schlanger, 1971). The Cretaceous subsidence there may have been caused by the subduction of the Pennine Ocean under the Helvetic Shelf. The subduction direction was then flipped over and reversed after a continental collision in the Eocene. The foredeep containing the Globigerina Marl was formed when the Helvetic Margin was thrust southward under the on-coming Pennine and Australpine nappes. One might invoke the same idea to interpret the Appalachian history: the Middle Ordovician (Trenton) and the Middle Devonian (Portage) transgressions over subsided carbonate-platforms are quite comparable to that of the Globigerina-Marl transgression, when hemi-pelagic sediments were deposited on deep-sea slopes of "fore-deeps" in front of advancing nappes.

V. Flysch and Pull-apart Basins on Subduction or Transform Margins

The term *flysch* was originally used to designate a rock-stratigraphic unit in the Alps, ranging in age from Late Cretaceous to Eocene, but was later applied to designate a recurrent facies (Hsü, 1970). After the recognition of flysch sandstones as turbidite deposits, there was a tendency to consider flysch as a synonym for turbidite. The malpractice led to an outcry by my colleague, Rudolf Trümpy, who insisted that flysch was one Swiss product not intended for overseas export. After a historical review of the usages of the term, I came to share the view of my Swiss colleagues that flysch should not be made synonymous with turbidite, which only describes the mechanism of sediment transport of the deposit. Instead, we should consider the tectonic setting as a discriminating criterion, as to whether a particular turbidite should be called a flysch or not. What were the tectonic settings of the Alpine flysch?

Modern environments for turbidite-sedimentation include deep lakes, submarine fans of passive continental margins, oceanic abyssal plains, trenches, back-arc basins, continental borderland (California), etc. The first three alternatives can be excluded as the depositional environments of the Alpine flysch. We are thus left with trenches, back-arc and borderland basins.

I once compared the paleogeography of the Paleocene flysch basins of the Alps with the back-arc basin and trench, north and south, of the Cretan Island — Arc of the Eastern Mediterranean (Hsü and Schlanger, 1971). Although the site of the flysch basins is now believed to be located farther south than that which we originally proposed, the hypothesis of an island-arc-setting received some support after the finding of detritus of arc-volcanism in the Schlieren Flysch (see Homewood and Caron, this volume).

That some of the ancient flysch sediments were deposited under such tectonic settings has never been seriously questioned, because turbidites are encountered in trenches and back-arc basins during numerous cruises of the deep-sea drilling projects. However, the residence time of trench-sediments is relatively short if the direction of plate-subduction is normal to the trench axis.

A trench tens of kilometres in width, with its floor being subducted at the rate of centimetres per year, cannot host a continuous sedimentary sequence more than a few million years in age. Yet many flysch formations consist of conformable sequences more than 50 million years old. Bill Ryan was impressed by the long continuous deposition of some Cretaceous flysch, when he went on a field trip to the Austrian Alps. He then suggested to me that the direction of the plate-movement forming the trench there, should have been nearly parallel to the trench-axes, so that the subduction rate was negligible for several tens of million years. Studying the kinematics of the relative motion between Europe and Africa, the evidence indeed indicated that the Austrian Flysch-Trench probably was underlain by a transform fault to accommodate lateral plate-movements during the Cretaceous (Hsü, 1972).

The theme of sedimentation in oblique-slip mobile zones has become a theme of lively discussions (Ballance and Reading, 1980). Long and narrow ocean trenches hosting undeformed sediments, such as the Vema Fracture Zone of the Atlantic, are commonly found along major transform faults. In contrast, small-scale zones of extension and compression have been found along many wrench faults on land (Kingma, 1958; Quennell, 1959; Crowell, 1974). These are induced on account of the geometrical constraints of curvature along the fault, by the braiding of faults, or because of the side-stepping of *en echelon* branches (Fig. 10). Pull-apart basins are formed in zones of extension (Crowell, 1974; Rodgers, 1980).

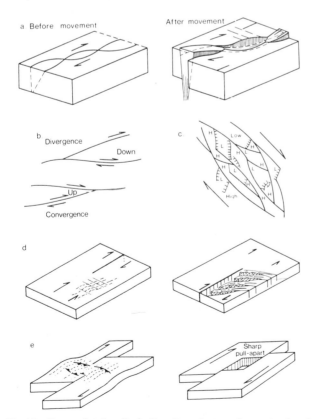

Fig. 10 Types of strike-slip fault pattern that produce extensional subsiding basins and compressional, uplifted blocks. (From Ballance and Reading, 1980.)

The recognition of the pull-apart basins provided an answer to a question which stopped me when I was taking my Ph.D. qualifying examination: are coastal and borderland basins of California geosynclinal or not? In my youthful inexperience I considered the sediments of those basins geosynclinal and compared them to the Alpine flysch (Hsü, 1958, 1960). I was chided by the late Emil Kündig, when he visited the Ventura Basin with me. To him the Ventura turbidites were not "geosynclinal" because they were deposited in a tectonic setting, and during a stage of tectonic development, quite different from that of the Alpine flysch-turbidites. I tend to agree with him, now that I have seen more of Switzerland: a trench or an island-arc may be the most common setting for the Alpine flysch. In contrast, the Neogene basins of California owed their origin to extension along strike-slip faults. The Ventura Basin should not be considered a geosyncline, if geosynclines are defined as precursors of the Alpino-type of mountains. If, however, we consider all sediments of the mountains geosynclinal, then the thick turbidite deposits of pull-apart basins should not be excluded. During a recent trip to Australia, I was impressed by the sedimentological and structural similarities of the lower Paleozoic graywackes of the Tasman Geosyncline to the Neogene turbidites of California. I did not object to the use of the term as long as no one insisted that the Tasman Geosyncline was an analogue of the Swiss Alps.

The "pull-apart" concept also helped answer the question concerning the cause of crustal thinning that initiated the tectonic (Airy) subsidence of California basins. The crust being pulled apart in the zone of extension of a transform margin, is stretched and thinned. Ultimately the continent is split apart to form a narrow oceanic gulf such as the Gulf of California, which is underlain largely by an oceanic crust. Kelts (1981) recently compared the Jurassic Pennine Trough of the Western Alps to the Gulf of California and this opinion is shared by many knowledgeable persons as well (see Trümpy, this volume). Turbidite basins of the Jurassic age were present in the Southern Alps and in Morocco. Since the movement of Africa was mainly lateral (sinistral) relative to Europe in those regions, we have to consider the role of "pull-apart" in the early development of the Southern Tethyan margins where the movement had a large strike-slip component.

VI. Eugeosynclines and Subduction Mélanges

I remember with nostalgia the time two decades ago when I started my work on the Franciscan rocks of the California Coast Range. The geology did not seem to make sense, and the mapping technique I learned as a student gave me little help. I could not define a single formation within the Franciscan, because I could not find a mappable unit. When I tried to trace a radiolarian chert, anticipating lateral continuity for this deep-sea deposit, I would find instead a graywacke a short distance away, butting right against the chert bed; or I might find a serpentinite, a glaucophane schist, or any one of the large variety of rocks which underlie the Franciscan terrane. The inch-to-four-mile maps of the California Division of Mines showed a number of scattered outcrops of various lithology amid what has been despairingly mapped as "undifferentiated Franciscan". Mapping at an inch-to-a-mile or larger scale only increased the number of mappable outcrops, but did little to help my understanding of the Franciscan geology. After roaming all over the hills behind Cayucos for several weeks, parched and fatigued by the Californian sun, I decided to take it easy for a day or two by looking over some coastal exposures on the beaches of San Simeon. My astonishment was great when I was able to see fresh and clean rocks where waves had washed away the debris of weathering and etched out sharp contacts. I realized suddenly that I could not find a mappable unit, because the bedding surfaces are broken everywhere by fractures and shears; the Law of Lateral Continuity is not applicable. I could not define a stratigraphic sequence, because rocks of various lithologies and diverse origins have been tectonically mixed; the Law of Superposition is not applicable. I could not determine the age of sedimentation of that mixture of blocks in a pervasively sheared matrix, because the blocks and matrix have not been mixed by sedimentary processes; the Law of Paleontological Dating is not applicable. The "undifferentiated Franciscan" terranes are not underlain by formations or by mappable units, but by a giant tectonic breccia, a chaotic mixture.

I showed my "discovery" to my friend and former mentor, John Crowell on a field trip. Crowell recognized that the tectonic processes responsible for the origin of the Franciscan had not been generally known, and he advised that I needed a new term to express a "new" idea. Heli Badoux who was then a guest professor at UCLA, suggested that I tried out the term *mélange*. Only later did I find a citation of Greenly (1919) in a paper by E.B. Bailey, and realize that I was rediscovering what had been wonderfully portrayed by the old master half a century ago. In fact, unbeknown to the Francophone Badoux, the term *mélange* came originally from Greenly.

My stories of the Franciscan mélange have been published in a series of articles during the 1960s (Hsü, 1965b, 1967, 1968). Using the *argille scagliose* of the Apennine as an analogue, I postulated gravity-sliding to account for the deformation of the mélange. I was, however, puzzled by the amount of bedding-plane shearing involved in the Franciscan. Restrained by the classical notion that the Franciscan rocks were deposited and deformed within the narrow confines of a eugeosynclinal trough, I had difficulty envisioning that exotic slabs could be displaced far enough to induce the pervasive shearing of the matrix. At about the same time, Fred Vine must also have been wondering about the same problem. He had to give an account of the missing eastern half of the Pacific Ocean, formed since the seafloor-spreading started there in the Jurassic. Several of my American friends on the West Coast, who had been more ready to accept the theory of seafloor-spreading, were quick to perceive that both puzzles could be resolved if the Franciscan mélange represents the remnants of the ancient Pacific Ocean floor, which had been welded onto the North American Plate during the subduction of the Pacific Plate

along an active plate-margin (Hamilton, 1969; Ernst, 1970), — a solution which I readily accepted after I had been converted to the new "faith" (Hsü, 1971).

During the last two decades, I have travelled far and wide to examine ancient eugeosynclines, from Anglesey (Precambrian) to Australia (Paleozoic), from Central Asia (Caledonian and Hercynian) to Turkey, Iran, and the Himalayas (Tethyan). I think few would now dispute the fact that eugeosynclinal rocks are ubiquitously present as tectonic mélanges in former subduction zones, which have become suture zones in places where continental collisions occurred. Eugeosynclinal ophiolites were the crust and upper mantle of former oceans. According to this view, the eugeosynclines were narrow, deep troughs, only during an early stage of rifting (Kelts, 1981). More commonly, eugeosynclinal ophiolites were the product of submarine volcanism on oceanic ridges or rises, along seamount-chains or in back-arc basins. To describe a broad expanse of ocean floor as a geosyncline would be misleading (see Fig. 11). There has been, therefore, a tendency recently to use a substitute *ophiolitic mélange* for the expression *"eugeosynclinal sequences"*, which are neither *synclinal* nor constitute a conformable *sequence*.

If we accept the plate-tectonic theory and consider ophiolites as relics of former ocean floor, the eugeosynclines are no longer a mystery. The origin of ocean crust on spreading ridges or in back-arc basins has been adequately explained by new theories (Vine and Matthews, 1965; Karig, 1970). The thermal subsidence of the ocean floor has been predicted theoretically (Sclater et al., 1971) and has been confirmed by the ample results of deep-sea drilling (Parsons and Sclater, 1978). Finally, when the seafloor is displaced close to an active continental margin, to receive abundant terrigenous detritus, subsidence under sedimentary load becomes an important factor.

Summary

Interpreted within the framework of the plate-tectonic theory, geosynclinal sediments refer to the thick accumulations on continental or plate-margins. Since those margins are likely to be deformed to form mountains, the original observation by Hall that geosynclinal deposits tend to be thicker than sediments of the same age on the craton has some validity. However, eugeosynclinal sediments of the mountains are not necessarily thicker. Pelagic sediments, having been laid down on ocean-bottom distant from land,

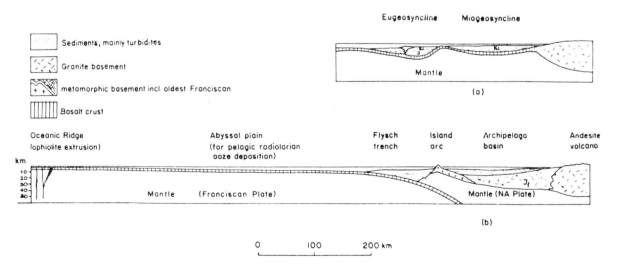

Fig. 11   Two different concepts of the Franciscan eugeosyncline. (a) The classical concept, with the eugeosyncline as the outer member of an eu-mio-geosynclinal couple. (After Bailey and Blake, 1969.) (b) Plate tectonic model. (After Hsü, 1971.)

are as a rule thinner than the sediments of the same age on cratons, as Suess (1875) pointed out more than a century ago. Thick "eugeosynclinal sequences", such as the Franciscan, are mostly tectonic mélanges. In view of our present knowledge of plate-tectonics, the idea of a eugeosyncline as a narrow, deep-water trough of submarine volcanism must be abandoned, unless one specifically refers to a tectonic setting such as the Gulf of California, or the Red Sea.

The geosynclinal theories of orogeny were based upon the postulates by Hall (1859) and by Dana (1873) that geosynclinal development led inevitably to mountain building. Those theories have not received support from many lines of new evidence, which favour plate-tectonic interpretations (Dickinson, 1970). The premise that the subsidence-history should be an integral part of an orogeny does not seem to have a theoretical basis. Mountain building takes place along consuming or transform plate-boundaries during or after continental collisions, involving sediments deposited on margins as well as those on cratons. Geosynclines are not necessarily precursors of mountains, unless we define geosynclinal deposits as the rocks of mountains. Such a definition, however, would reduce the term to a tautological expression.

Acknowledgement

The theme on the origin of geosynclines was presented in the very first talk I ever gave, 25 years ago in Zurich, at the invitation of Rudy Trümpy. Little did I suspect that I was to become a colleague of his and of Gansser's for the best part of my professional life, and to share this theme with them as one of our common interests. It is, therefore, most appropriate that I should select this topic to write an essay in this Gansser–Trümpy Festschrift. It seems, however, highly inappropriate that I should cite an inordinate amount of my own publications in the bibliography of a volume dedicated to their honour. This apparent immodesty is less motivated by an egomania than by the compulsion of writers to express themselves autobiographically. While engaging on various projects of geological research, I would from time to time write an article on the origin of sedimentary basins, *alias* geosynclines. Those articles are more of an essay, a review, or a term-paper by a student than an original research contribution. My understanding in 1958 that sedimentary basins are underlain by thin crust was made possible by the many geophysical researches in the forties and fifties, notably the marine seismic investigations of Maurice Ewing and his Lamont associates. My realization that thermal changes in the mantle might induce basinal subsidence was inspired by the seismic surveys and heat-flow measurements in the fifties and early sixties, and particularly so by the work by Lew Pakiser and his Crustal Studies Group of the U.S. Geological Survey. My representation of the Franciscan mélange as remnants of subducted ocean-floor was a direct outcome (by deduction) of my acceptance of Vine and Matthew's seafloor-spreading theory. My proposal that some Alpine Flysch may have been deposited along transform margins owed a suggestion from Bill Ryan and has been founded on the facts unearthed by several generations of Alpine geologists. Then, as now, I have always felt that I am a reporter, a writer, to convey and to communicate with a readable style. Only rarely, as I did in the case of studying the Franciscan, was I involved in the exciting game of first-hand data-gathering or fact-finding. I went through the series of my writings on the subject from 1958 to 1973 because I wanted to analyse my own progress, the evolution of my own thought-process, which has mirrored that of the profession at large. I cited them because they serve as historical annals that manifest our restless searches for meaning in the sediments of mountains. This long acknowledgement is written to express my indebtedness to those, too many to be included in the citations, who have helped me in musing over this interesting puzzle.

References

Airy, G.B. (1855). On the computation of the effect of the attraction of mountain masses disturbing the apparent astronomical latitude of stations in geodetic survey. *Roy. Soc. (London) Phil. Trans.* **145**, 101–104.

Bailey, E.H. and Black, M.C. (1969). Tectonic development of western California during the late Mesozoic. *Geotektonika* **3**, 17–30.

Ballance, P.F. and Reading, H.G. (1980). Sedimentation in *Oblique-Slip Mobile Zones*. *Int. Assoc. Sedim., Spec. Publ.* **5**, 265 pp.

Beloussov, V.V. (1962). "Basic Problems in Geotectonics". McGraw-Hill, New York. 820pp.

Bernoulli, D. and Jenkyns, H.C. (1974). Alpine, Mediterranean and central Atlantic Mesozoic facies in relation to the early evolution of the Tethys. *Soc. Econ. Paleont. Miner., Spec. Publ.* **19**, 129–160.

Bosellini, A. and Winterer, E.L. (1975). Pelagic limestone and radiolarite of the Tethyan Mesozoic, a genetic model. *Geology* **3**, 279–282.

Bucher, W.H. (1933). "The Deformation of the Earth's Crust". Princeton Univ. Press, Princeton. 518 pp.

Christie, P.A.F. and Sclater, J.G. (1980). An extensional origin for the Buchan and Witchground Graben in the North Sea. *Nature, London* **283**, 729–732.

Crowell, J.C. (1974). Origin of late Cenozoic basins in southern California. *Soc. Econ. Paleont. Miner., Spec. Publ.* **19**, 292–303.

Dana, R.D. (1873). On some results of the earth's contraction from cooling. *Am. J. Sci., Ser. 3* **5**, 423–443, **6**, 6–14, 104–115, 161–172.

Dässegger, R. and Müller, W.H. (1976). Die Sedimentserien der Engadiner Dolomiten und ihre lithostratigraphische Gliederung. *Eclogae geol. Helv.* **69**, 229–238.

Dickinson, W.R. (1970). Second Penrose conference: the new global tectonics. *Geotimes* **15, no. 4**, 18–22.

Ernst, G. (1970). Tectonic contact between the Franciscan mélange and the Great Valley sequence: Crustal expression of a Late Mesozoic Benioff Zone. *J. Geoph. Res.* **25**, 886–901.

Falvey, D.A. (1974). The development of continental margins in plate tectonic theory: *Am. Assoc. Petroleum Geol. Bull.* **58**, 95–106.

Finger, W. (1978). Die Zone von Samaden (Unterostalpine Decken, Graubünden) und ihre Jurassischen Brekzien. *Mitt. geol. Inst. ETH, Zürich, neue Folge* **224**, 141 pp.

Gilluly, J. (1955). Geologic contrast between continents and ocean basins. *Geol. Soc. Am., Spec. Paper* **62**, 7–18.

Grabau, A.W. (1924). Migration of geosynclines. *Geol. Soc. China Bull.* **3**, 207–349.

Greenly, E (1919). "The Geology of Anglesey". Great Britain Geol. Survey Mem., 980 pp.

Hall, J. (1859). Paleontology. *Geol. Surv. New York* **3** (1), 66–96.

Hamilton, W. (1969). Mesozoic California and the underflow of Pacific Mantle. *Geol. Soc. Am. Bull.* **88**, 2409–2430.

Homewood, P. and Caron, Ch. (this volume). Flysch of the Western Alps.

Hsü, K.J. (1958). Isostasy and a theory for the origin of geosynclines. *Am. J. Sci.* **256**, 305–327.

Hsü, K.J. (1960). Paleocurrent structures and paleogeography of the Ultrahelvetic Flysch basins, Switzerland. *Geol. Soc. Am. Bull.* **71**, 577–610.

Hsü, K.J. (1965a). Isostasy, crustal thinning, mantle changes, and the disappearance of ancient land masses. *Am J. Sci.* **263**, 97–109.

Hsü, K.J. (1965b). Franciscan rocks of Santa Lucia Range, California, and the *argille scagliose* of the Apennines, Italy — a comparison in style of deformation. *Geol. Soc. Am.* Abstracts for 1965, p. 210.

Hsü, K.J. (1967). Mesozoic geology of California Coast Ranges — a new working hypothesis. *In* "Etages Tectoniques" (Schaer, J., ed.). Neuchâtel, à la Baconnière, p. 279–296.

Hsü, K.J. (1968). Principles of mélanges and their bearing on the Franciscan–Knoxville paradox. *Geol. Soc. Am. Bull* **79**, 1063–1074.

Hsü, K.J. (1970). The meaning of the word Flysch — a short historical search. *Geol. Assoc. Canada, Spec. Paper* **7**, 1–11.

Hsü, K.J. (1971). Franciscan mélanges as a model for eugeosynclinal sedimentation and underthrusting tectonics. *J. Geoph. Res.* **76**, 1162–1170.

Hsü, K.J. (1972). Alpine Flysch in a Mediterranean setting. *Int. Geol. Congress, 24th Session, Montreal, Canada, Proc., Sec.* **6**, 67–74.

Hsü, K.J. (1973). The odyssey of Geosynclines. *In* "Evolving Concepts in Sedimentology", (Ginsburg, R.N., ed.). Johns Hopkins Univ. Press, Baltimore, pp. 66–92.

Hsü, K.J. and Schlanger, S.O. (1971). Ultrahelvetic Flysch sedimentation and deformation related to plate tectonics. *Geol. Soc. Am. Bull* **82**, 1207–1218.

Jarvis, J.G. and McKenzie, D.P. (1980). Sedimentary formation with finite extension rates. *Earth Planet. Sci. lett.* **48**, 42–52.

Karig, D. (1970). Ridges and basins of the Tonga-Kermadec Island Arc System. *J. geoph. Res.* **75**, 239–254.

Kelts, K. (1981). A comparison of some aspects of sedimentation and translational tectonics from the Gulf of California and the Mesozoic Tethys, Northern Penninic Margin. *Eclogae geol. Helv.* **73**, 317–338.

Kennedy, G.C. (1959). The origin of continents, mountain ranges, and ocean basins. *Am. Scientists* **27**, 491–504.

Kingma, J.T. (1958). Possible origin of piercement structures, local unconformities and secondary basins in the Eastern Geosyncline, New Zealand. *N.Z. J. Geol. Geoph.* **1**, 269–274.

LePichon, X. and Sibuet, J.-C. (1981). Passive margins: a model of formation. *J. Geoph. Res.* **86**, 3708–3720.

McKenzie, D.P. (1978). Some remarks on the development of sedimentary basins. *Earth Planet. Sci. Lett.* **40**, 25–32.

Montadert, L., De Charpal, O., Roberts, D.C., Guennoc, P. and Sibuet, J.-C. (1979). Northeast Atlantic passive margins: Rifting and subsidence processes. *In* "Deep Drilling Results in the Atlantic Ocean: Continental Margins and Paleoenvironment", Maurice Ewing Ser., Vol. 3 (Talwani, M. *et al.*, eds.). Am. Geoph. Union, Washington, D.C., pp. 164–186.

Oxburgh, R. (this volume). Heterogeneous lithospheric stretching in early history of orogenic belts.

Parsons, B. and Sclater, J.G. (1977). An analysis of the variation of ocean floor bathymetry and heat flow with age. *J. Geoph. Res.* **82**, 803–822.

Pettijohn, F.J. (1957). "Sedimentary Rocks". Harper, New York, 718 pp.

Pratt, J.H. (1864). Speculations on the Constitution of the Earth's Crust. *Proc. Royal Soc. (London)* **13**, 253–276.

Quennell, A.M. (1959). Tectonics of the Dead Sea Rift. *Int. Geol. Congress, 1956, Proc.* **20**, 385–405.

Rodgers, D.A. (1980). Analysis of pull-apart basin development produced by *en echelon* strike-slip faults. *Int. Assoc. Sedim. Spec. Publ.* **4**, 27–41.

Rodgers, J. (this volume). The life history of a mountain range.

Schlee, J. Behrendt, J.C., Grow, J.A., Robb, R.M., Mattick, R.E., Taylor, P.T. and Lawson, B.A. (1976). Regional geologic framework off north-eastern United States. *Am. Assoc. Petroleum Geol. Bull.* **60**, 926–951.

School, D.W., von Huene, R., Vallier, T.L. and Howell, D.G. (1980). Sedimentary masses and concepts about tectonic processes at underthrust ocean margins. *Geology* **8**, 564–568.

Scientific Party (1980). Initial Reports of the Deep Sea Drilling Project, Vol. **56**, Washington, U.S. Government Printing Office, 629 pp.

Sclater, J.G., Anderson R.N. and Bell, M.L. (1971). The elevation of ridges and the evolution of the central eastern Pacific. *J. Geoph. Res.*, **76**, 7888–7915.

Sheridan, R.E., Dranke, C.L., Nafe, J.E. and Hennion, J. (1966). Seismic refraction study of continental margin east of Florida. *Am. Assoc. Petroleum Geol. Bull.* **50**, 1972. 1991.

Sleep, N.H. (1971). Thermal effects of the formation of Atlantic continental margins by continental break-up. *Geoph. J. Royal Astron. Soc.* **24**, 325–350.

Suess, E. (1875). "Die Entstehung der Alpen". W. Braumüller, Wien, 168 pp.

Trümpy, R. (1960). Paleotectonic evolution of the central and western Alps. *Geol. Soc. Am. Bull.* **71**, 843–908.

(this volume). Alpine paleogeography, a reappraisal.

van Bemmelen, R.W. (1958). Stromingstelsels in de silicaatmantel. *Geol. Mijnb., n.s.* **20**, 1–17.

van Hinte, J.E. (1976). A Jurassic time scale. *Am. Assoc. Petroleum Geol. Bull.* **60**, 489–497.

Vine, F.J. and Matthews, D.M. (1963). Magnetic anomalies over ocean ridges. *Nature* **199**, 947–949.

Watts, A.B. and Steckler, M.S. (1979). Subsidence and isostasy at continental margin off eastern North America. *In* "Deep Drilling Results in the Atlantic Ocean: Continental Margins and Paleoenvironment", Maurice Ewing Ser., Vol. 3, (Talwani, M. *et al.* eds.). Am. Geoph. Union, Washington, D.C., p. 218–234.

Williams, C. (1981). Origin of sedimentary basins. *Nature* **292**, 802.

Mountain Building and Volcanism

J.B. Gill

Earth Sciences Board, UCSC, Santa Cruz, CA, U.S.A.

Abstract

Volcanism primarily precedes collisional mountain building so that "orogenic andesite" rarely accompanies orogeny. No aspect of magma composition seems geochemically diagnostic of collision. Consequently, interest in the volcanic rocks of mountain belts largely focuses on the provenance of rocks which predate orogeny. Age, geometry, and lithologic arguments may identify site of volcanism, but rock composition, especially the relative elemental and isotopic composition of REE and HFS elements, may be necessary and can be sufficient evidence. Four kinds of subduction-related volcanics can be identified geochemically and utilized tectonically: extensive arc tholeiites indicate eruption above subduction of old, sediment-poor lithosphere which was rapidly consumed; decreasing silica-normalized Zr/Nb and increasing La/Yb ratios in coeval metavolcanics indicate increasing distance from the plate boundary; mafic shoshonites are drawn from mantle which had been metasomatized by subducting lithosphere within 2 m.y. of the volcanism; and extensive boninites accompany early stages of volcanic- or adjacent back-arc development. Calcalkaline andesitic volcanism also occurs along arc-terminating transform faults, resulting in strata which could be mistaken in mountain belts for ancient volcanic arcs.

The general assumption that volcanism plays an important role in mountain building is held for two reasons: the widespread occurrence of volcanic rocks in many old mountain belts, and the volcanic activity in the present American cordilleran mountains. Certainly volcanism at active continental margins usually is associated with high elevations, most notably in the Andes, due to low density material within the underlying mantle. But whether widespread volcanism is synchronous with the strong deformation and metamorphism which also are widely accepted as integral to mountain building is a different matter.

I. Temporal Relationships between Volcanism and Collision Events

Alpine-type mountains result from collisions between non-subductable crusts (continents, arcs, or ocean islands) and these collisions tenuate volcanism. Most of the European alps are notoriously bereft of volcanic rocks synchronous with deformation, and modern examples of collisions are accompanied by volcanic hiatuses or aberrations. For example, volcanism and seismicity abate and volcanic arcs are segmented or terminated where seamount chains intersect subduction zones (Vogt *et al.*, 1976). A similar abatement occurs in the volcanic arcs of the northern Molucca Sea region, Indonesia, where arc–arc collision is approaching completion (Morrice *et al.*, 1981). There, collision completion, as inferred from absence of shallow earthquakes,

development of backarc thrusts, and regional uplift, also is accompanied by cessation of arc volcanism. Impending cessation is accompanied magmatically by an increase in incompatible element concentrations, by an accompanying distribution of hornblende phenocrysts over a wider range of silica contents, and by anomalously high concentrations of elements or isotopes attributable to some incorporation of the large volume of sediment trapped during collision (e.g. Cs, Th, ^{207}Pb). Similar cessation preceded by sediment-influenced volcanism accompanied arc-continent collision north of Timor, eastern Indonesia (Whitford *et al.*, 1977).

In contrast, some volcanism accompanies collisions between continents, but even this is volumetrically minor, is usually scattered over a wide area (in contrast to the narrow strips of volcanic arcs), and is usually bimodal in composition (calcalkaline dacites to rhyolites, usually with a strong crustal signature, plus alkali basalts). Recent examples include north-eastern Turkey (Innocenti *et al.*, 1976), western Iran (Forster *et al.*, 1972), and Tibet (Deng, 1978). Collision in the New Guinea Highlands, PNG, is dominated by mafic shoshonites (Mackenzie, 1976), and microplate accretion in south-eastern Alaska has been accompanied by uncommonly voluminous basalts to high-K acid andesites with high Mg-numbers.

Although regional chronological and geochemical data are available for none of these recent examples, some tentative observations seem warranted nevertheless. Apparently there is nothing geochemically diagnostic of collision. While sediment recycling and crustal contamination occur, they are not restricted to collision sites. However, continental collision-related volcanism is predominantly basaltic or rhyolitic, or both, instead of andesitic, and usually is calcalkaline or alkaline instead of tholeiitic. Volcanism lies mostly on the previously overthrust plate but can postdate subcrustal earthquake activity. That is, volcanism overlies mantle beneath which ocean crust was once subducted, but is not restricted to zones 100 to 200 km above actively-subducting slabs.

Thus, at least today, volcanism plays a minor role during the creation of mountains due to collisions, and such volcanism as does accompany orogeny is diverse in kind and nondistinctive in composition. Consequently, volcanic rocks in mountain belts tell more about events which predate and set the stage for mountain building than about the grand finale itself.

II. Determining the Provenance of Volcanic Rocks in Mountain Belts

In principle, the volcanic rocks encountered in mountain belts could be fragments of ocean crust, accreted ocean islands, fragments of backarc basins, or volcanic arcs which in turn could be accreted or *in situ*, island or continental margin. (Transform fault volcanism is treated separately below). Four kinds of criteria inform the choice between these possibilities: stratigraphic, lithologic, mineralogic, and geochemical. Stratigraphic criteria include the thickness, relative ages, and map pattern of units. All are typically problematical in mountain belts due to subsequent deformation. Lithologic criteria can be diagnostic: voluminous tephra indicate an arc; and sheeted dikes within a few stratigraphic kilometers of pelagic sediments indicate ocean or backarc crust. Mineralogic criteria are most helpful in silicic rocks where they are least needed. Phenocrystal orthopyroxene or hornblende are traits of arc volcanics, as is lack of Fe-enrichment in the phenocrysts of intermediate rocks, or lack of Ti–Na enrichment in their groundmass pyroxenes (Garcia, 1978; Nisbet and Pearce, 1977).

Thus, the main, and frequently encountered problem concerns voluminous but tectonically-bounded mafic pillow lavas, commonly with greenschist mineralogy. Their birthplace could be any of the four options listed above.

Over the last decade several geochemical discriminants have been proposed to aid this choice. Use of these discriminants has accelerated as the extent of differences between ocean island (OIB) and mid-ocean ridge basalt (MORB) has become more fully known (e.g. Allègre *et al.*, 1980). However, most of these differences involve elements (e.g. volatiles and alkalies) which are mobile during metamorphism and therefore are useless as indicators of paleo-provenance of the metavolcanic rocks in mountain belts. The best of the metamorphism-resistant discriminants are the isotopic composition of Nd and Hf, both of which are more radiogenic in MORB than OIB (Patchett and Tatsumoto, 1980), and the relatively high concentrations of Ti and related elements in OIB. That is, in OIB the TiO_2 and Zr contents are higher relative to Mg-number or V than in MORB (Perfit *et al.*, 1980; Pearce and Cann, 1973; Shervais, 1981) whereas Zr/Nb and Hf/Ta ratios are lower (less than 17 and 5, respectively, in OIB).

Whether the above (and other, less metamorphism-resistant) differences in basalt composition reflect differences in source composition on a global scale is a subject of vigorous debate. Proponents (e.g. Sun and Hanson, 1975; Allègre *et al.*, 1980; Anderson, 1981) disagree on the nature and three-dimensional distribution of source regions but concur that different source regions (e.g. upper versus lower mantle versus subducted ocean crust) melt in different tec-

tonic environments. This interpretation, which would provide the firmest theoretical justification for geochemical discriminant analysis of paleo-provenances, cannot be properly reviewed here but is challenged by a shrinking minority who attribute the differences in basalt composition to differences in refractory mineralogy (e.g. Beswick and Carmichael, 1978) or small (not global) scale heterogeneities (e.g. Tarney *et al.*, 1980). Nevertheless, for whatever reasons, the empirical distinction between normal MORB and OIB is the cleanest currently available in igneous geochemistry. (Yet even it blurs between 33° and 45°N on the Atlantic seafloor, such as in the FAMOUS area, where basalts intermediate between the two categories [i.e. enriched MORB] occur. Some OIB, as along the Hawaii-Emperor chain, is also transitional in several respects [e.g. Pb isotopes, Ta/Hf ratios]. Blurring is also expected in small ocean basins, e.g. Tethys.)

Subduction-related volcanism can often be distinguished from both MORB and OIB in one or more of five ways (Gill, 1981): greater abundance of intermediate rocks and tephra in arcs; less Fe-enrichment; differences in volatiles (higher fO_2, H_2O/CO_2, Cl/K, Cl/S, and possibly Cl/H_2O); differences in trace elements (higher Ba and Sr and sometimes Th, U, and Pb relative to the light REE, but lower Nb and Ta, and lower Ti/V), and differences in detail from MORB and most OIB in Sr-Pb-Nd isotopes. Most or all of these differences reflect the presence of some recycled ocean crust in arc magmas. The *combination* of low relative Ti-group elemental concentrations (e.g. La/Ta $>$ 30, Ti/V $<$ 20) plus radiogenic Nd ($^{143}Nd/^{144}Nd$ $<$ 0·5131) and Pb ($^{207}Pb/^{204}Pb$ above the mantle array or $^{206}Pb/^{204}Pb$ $>$ 18·6, or both) is both unique to volcanic arcs and resistant to metamorphism.

Backarc basalts are either indistinguishable geochemically from MORB or intermediate between MORB and arc tholeiitic basalt. At present their identification in mountain belts depends more on stratigraphic or lithologic than geochemical criteria.

In conclusion, the 1970s encouraged rather than diminished hope of successful determination of the tectonic provenance of metabasalts. However, such determinations are likely to be statistical in nature (e.g. with a given database there is an $x\%$ chance of proper assignment), and to involve expensive analyses by high-precision mass spectrometry or neutron activation.

III. Characteristics of Subduction-related Volcanism which have Paleo-Tectonic Significance

By "subduction-related" I mean volcanism 100 to 200 km above underthrusting lithosphere. Such volcanism of necessity precedes collision-related mountain building, but may also accompany orogeny if the modern Andes or the Cretaceous of California provide appropriate models of orogeny sans collision. Such volcanism characteristically includes basalt, andesite, dacite, and rhyolite of both calcalkaline and tholeiitic affinity, plus more exotic things such as shoshonite and boninite.

After decades of dispute, there is now at least a growing consensus that most subduction-related magmas are low-pressure differentiates of mafic magma derived in large part, if not entirely, from the mantle wedge above subducted lithosphere (Gill, 1981; Thorpe, 1982). These mafic parents contain an unknown, and surely variable, mass fraction of material drawn from subducted ocean crust, either as a silicate melt or a silica-rich steam (IRS fluid). During ascent, magmas interact with crust as they differentiate, largely by crystal-liquid fractionation of clinopyroxene, olivine, spinel, plagioclase, orthopyroxene, magnetite, and hornblende. Current debate focuses most on the process and mass fraction of recycling, the agent of mass transfer, the process and extent of crustal interaction, and the mechanisms of differentiation (including magma mixing), little of which matters to mountain building. Consider instead, therefore, the tectonic context of different magma types within volcanic arcs.

Arc tholeiites (Jakeš and Gill, 1970) are characterized by low concentrations of K_2O and related elements, plus Fe-enrichment. There is room for ambiguity in both characteristics. Although over 2/3 of low-K arc rocks (see Gill, 1981, Fig. 1.2 for definition) also are Fe-enriched, the identity and level of depletion of "related elements" varies. Specifically, arc tholeiites from Vanuatu, Java, and northern Honshu all have higher Th/U ratios, flatter REE patterns, and lower Nd isotope ratios than do the tholeiites in oceanic arcs such as Tonga, Izu, or South Sandwich (e.g. Masuda and Aoki, 1978). (Indeed, tholeiitic-ness in the sense of high FeO*/MgO ratios is not particularly restricted to low-K suites.) However, arc rocks with Fe-enrichment, low K_2O, and light REE depletion are found throughout the Kermadec, Tonga, Izu, and South Sandwich arcs, along about half the volcanic front of New Britain, and at one extremity each of the western Bismarck (PNG), Sangihe (Indonesia), and Antillean arcs. The four arcs entirely characterized by arc tholeiites share these things: all are situated on ocean crust; all have high rates of plate convergence (>7 cm/yr); all subduct old lithosphere bearing little terrigenous sediment; all are associated with backarc spreading; and all lack very large earthquakes. Collectively this may indicate low coupling between over and underthrust plates and, consequently, either no fusion of subducted ocean crust or a high percent fusion of the overlying mantle wedge. In any case, regionally extensive arc tholeiites in mountains arguably indicate that a similar tectonic situation had prevailed at the time of the volcanism. Intriguingly, arc tholeiites are most abundant in the basement of oceanic arcs (e.g. Fiji, Mariana-Bonin, Greater Antilles, and possibly Cascades), passing upwards to rocks richer in incompatible elements but poorer in Fe. Similar up-section trends occur in Archean greenstone belts and some Phanerozoic and Mesozoic mountain belts. Reasons for such changes remain uncertain and probably variable (Gill, 1981).

Three criteria seem most useful for identifying arc tholeiitic greenschists in mountains. The first two essentially discriminate arc rocks from MORB, with which arc tholeiites can be easily confused. One is that arc tholeiite strata still contain abundant tephra and shallow-water sediments. The other is the coupling of low Ti-group element concentrations with radiogenic Nd and Pb isotopic compositions mentioned earlier. Indeed, arc tholeiites are distinguished by a pair of additional similar criteria. Ti in arc tholeiites is higher relative to Zr (Ti/Zr > 100) but lower relative to V (Ti/V = 10–20) than in MORB (Pearce and Cann, 1973; Shervais, 1981). Finally, once the issue of arc provenance of metavolcanics is itself somehow settled, the tectonically distinctive tholeiite subset is easily recognized by its otherwise MORB-like traits: La/Yb < 1.8; Zr/Nb > 25; Hf/Th > 3; Zr/Y < 3.

More abundant in currently active volcanic arcs are the calcalkaline suites which are the kind of arc rocks least likely to be mis-identified in mountain belts. In addition to indicating that subduction had occurred somewhere nearby during, or shortly before, the time of volcanism, the other tectonic utility of such rocks is that they change in composition away from the plate boundary. From such changes in composition one can infer the direction of previous subduction if one knows that the rocks being compared were contemporaneous. The most consistent across-arc geochemical changes which are resistant to metamorphic alteration are decreasing Zr/Nb and increasing La/Yb ratios away from the plate boundary (Gill, 1981).

Next, consider the alkaline, and sometimes silica-undersaturated rocks erupted within or near volcanic arcs. These can be roughly divided into suites which do, or do not, share with other arc volcanics the differences in volatiles, trace elements, and isotopes cited earlier. For example, those behind the andesitic volcanoes of New Zealand, south-west Japan, and Alaska do *not* share these characteristics, and should be considered near-arc but nevertheless continental alkali basalts. In contrast, shoshonitic rocks (i.e. basaltic rocks with $SiO_2 < 55\%$, $K_2O = Na_2O$, $< 1.3\%$ TiO_2) tend to share the distinctive arc traits to an extreme, having very high Ba/La, Sr/Nd, Rb/Zr, and La/Ta, but very low Ti/V ratios. Consequently the shoshonites may share a common source with conventional arc volcanics but represent smaller degrees of fusion and a higher recycled slab component than is usually observed.

Amongst Neogene to Recent arcs, shoshonites are found in one of two situations: volcanoes farthest from the plate boundary, or in areas of uplift following cessation of subduction. The principal utility of rear-of-the-arc shoshonites for paleo-tectonics is for determining the former direction of subduction, as noted above concerning calcalkaline rocks. In contrast, post-subduction shoshonites occur in Fiji and the New Guinea Highlands where they are associated with less voluminous, medium to high-K, genetically unrelated intermediate rocks but, apparently, not by subjacent, subducted lithosphere. For example, in Fiji, shoshonitic volcanism began at the same time as the region began to be separated from a subduction site, due to creation of intervening marginal basins 5 m.y. ago (Gill, 1976; Whelan and Gill, 1980). Shoshonitic volcanism continued for about 2 m.y. thereafter, in regions which have since experienced over 1 km of uplift. Initially the shoshonites had the greatest relative enrichment of alkalies, [87]Sr, and [206]Pb, and the greatest depletion of Ti-group elements, of any Fijian rocks before or since. Throughout this 2 m.y. period, shoshonitic volcanoes were flanked by smaller cones yielding less voluminous, less alkalic, more typical andesitic rocks. Shortly afterwards, however, shoshonitic volcanism dissipated, being replaced eventually by alkali olivine basalts which became similar in elemental composition to OIB but which remained similar in isotopic composition to the earlier subduction-related Fijian andesites. That is, arc-like geochemical traits initially were retained in the alkalic rocks, but some of these traits were lost throughout most of the area within 2 m.y. after the region was no longer adjacent to a convergent plate boundary.

A third and final kind of alkaline volcanism within arcs consists of non-shoshonitic alkali olivine basalts to basanites with arc-like geochemistry (e.g. low Nb/La, Ti/V, and high Ba/La, Sr/Nd). These rocks are restricted to point sources (not belts) within volcanic arcs and arguably are associated with tear faults in underlying subducting lithosphere (DeLong et al., 1975; Arculus, 1976; Foden and Varne, 1980). However, because differences between these rocks and shoshonites (or other high-K_2O, Al_2O_3 basalts) lie mostly in alkali-silica relationships and corresponding feldspar-feldspathoid mineralogy, the differences are likely to be lost amongst mountain belt metavolcanics.

Finally, boninitic rocks (alias high-Mg andesites) occur in some volcanic arcs. In a restrictive sense, these are vesicular pyroxene vitrophyres free of feldspar phenocrysts, having instead quench phenocrysts of bronzite + Cr-spinel $\pm$ clinoenstatite, olivine, and Mg-augite (Cameron et al., 1979). In a more general sense they include all low-TiO_2 ($< 0.5\%$), high-MgO ($> 6\%$), high-SiO_2 ($> 52\%$) ejecta (Meijer, 1980). Such rocks should become easily recognizable greenschists, such as already found in some ophiolites. Their occurrence apparently signals conditions appropriate to high degrees of fusion of hydrous but refractory peridotite. This may accompany new subduction beneath young lithosphere (Meijer,

Granite Type and Tectonic Environment

W.S. Pitcher

Department of Geology,
Liverpool L69 3BX, U.K.

Abstract

The thesis is developed that different types of granites, of different origin, typify different kinds of mobile belt. Because of the greater precision offered by several critical chemical parameters it is possible to define, at least within the Phanerozoic record, an M-type which includes the scanty plagiogranite of the oceanic island-arcs, and which grades into an I(Cordilleran)-type representing the voluminous gabbro-quartz diorite-tonalite assemblage of active continental plate edges. The latter is separate, however, from an $\bar{I}$(Caledonian)-type which represents the granodiorite and granite of the immediately post-orogenic, uplift regimes. In sharper contrast are an S-type incorporating the peraluminous granite assemblage of encratonic and continental-collision fold belts, and a unique A-type which includes the alkalic granites of both the stabilized fold belts and the swells and rifts of the cratons. This close relationship between granite type and geological context occurs because granite, in the widest sense, arises as the end-stage of several generative processes involving different source-rocks, each process and source being appropriate to a particular environment.

A review of the occurrence of granite in Phanerozoic mobile belts the world over supports this connection, with a particularly clear contrast apparent between the granitoids of the Mesozoic Andean, the Upper Palaeozoic Hercynian and the late-Caledonian regimes. Following this review a case is made for a general typological-environmental categorization of post-Lower Proterozoic granites as a whole, and the question is then posed as to how far back in time the connection holds.

I. Introduction

It has long been realized that there are different kinds of granites, as is likely to be so when the mineral paragenesis involving quartz, K-feldspar and plagioclase represents "petrogeny's residual system". Such residual magmas are possible products of the several different processes of crystal, liquid or gaseous differentiation in melts variously derived by the partial melting of either sediments, igneous rocks or mantle materials. They may also represent the end-stage of metamorphic processes involving granitization and the mobilization of the products. Nevertheless, simple though the mode of the resultant rocks may be, each genetic type should carry some special signature indicative of its source and, furthermore, each should relate to a specific geotectonic environment.

The most special signature is the very composition of granite itself. There are granites, strictly plagiogranites, which occur in relatively small volume in association with the basalts and gabbros of the island arcs of oceanic environments. However granitic rocks in any substantial volume are genetically associated with the continental crust, and are especially characteristic of mobile belts, but it is not easy to decide whether this is a direct consequence of the special composition of this crust or simply of the unique temperature-depth regimes established when continental crust is especially thickened in mobile belts. Whilst it is tempting to accept the former proposition, or even a compromise model, we can note the finding of Thorpe and Francis (1979) that crustal thickness largely determines the variation in Andean andesite compositions. If then, thickness is the essential factor in relation to their plutonic analogues, it explains why island arcs mature to the extent of supporting plutonism.

At present there is very active discussion on the degree of involvement of the mantle and crustal rocks in the origin of the granitoids, only bedevilled by the lack of a clear understanding of the nature of the deep crust and upper mantle. A consensus view is that mantle is rarely directly involved, granitoids representing remelts derived either from an earlier separated fraction underplating the crust or from igneous rocks or sediments within the crust itself. The approach has been largely geochemical (see references in Atherton and Tarney, 1979), the constraints being the data of melt experiments, the results from modelling of the physical conditions within the crust and mantle, and a knowledge of both the Rare Earth Element distribution and the isotope systematics of Sr, Nd and Pb. In this essay, in accepting this geochemical guidance, an attempt is made to refine the further constraints introduced by the geological context.

Following this theme I first comment on the classic time

and place relationship enshrined in the *Granite Series* of Read (1948), in which granites are envisaged as progressively changing in character during the structural history of a mobile belt. In retrospect this seems likely to apply to just one particular genetic type, and that Read's derivative concept that there are "granites and granites" is of much wider application because each geological context is characterized by a particular magma-tectonic series. This is another theme of this essay.

II. The Granite Types

The difficulty in the past has been to find sufficiently decisive parameters to define granite types. Most easily observed are significant differences in mineralogy and in mode, especially in the range of the latter, and with these variables can be coupled the nature of the xenoliths and unique textural characteristics. Thus it has long been recognized that there is a marked contrast between the compositionally expanded tonalite association, so characteristic of the Mesozoic mobile belts of the eastern Pacific, and the compositionally restricted, peraluminous granite association which dominates the Hercynian mobile belt of Europe. Not only does the biotite –hornblende and magnetite content of the former contrast with the two-mica and ilmenite content of the latter, but simple, even-grain textures also contrast with pegmatitic and megacrystic textures. Furthermore the association of calc-alkaline granitoids with Mo-skarns and Cu-porphyry deposits contrasts with the occurrence with peraluminous granites of tin-bearing greisens, tourmalinization and hydrothermal kaolinization.

Both these associations contrast in their turn with the alkali-amphibole and alkali-pyroxene-bearing peralkaline granites and syenites with their special richness in Rare Earth and fluorine-bearing accessories. These rocks characteristically appear either at the end of an orogenic cycle, or quite independently of the mobile belts and in the cratons.

That there are such different compositional types of granite has often been observed (e.g. Eskola, 1932; Didier and Lameyre, 1969), and these have been related to differences in mineralization by Russian-workers (e.g. Tauson, 1974). However, it is through the particular strength of the Australian school of research in this field (Chappell and White, 1974, 1977; Hine *et al.*, 1978; White, 1979) that a whole range of geochemical parameters have been utilized to define accurately specific granite types. Two are of particular importance: an I (igneous)-type, broadly corresponding to the biotite–hornblende tonalite association, and an S (sedimental)-type, broadly corresponding to the two-mica granite association (see p.29). The chemical differences stem from differences of source. Granitoids derived from an igneous parent will necessarily contrast with those derived from rocks which have previously passed through a weathering cycle — which must radically alter the ratios between the alkalis, between Ca and Al and also between Fe^{3+} and Fe^{2+}. Furthermore, according to Halliday *et al.* (1981) the development of peraluminous composition is frequently paralleled by isotopic evidence for melting and assimilation of crustal rocks.

This I–S classification has been extended (White, 1979) by adopting prefixes "A" (see Loiselle and Wones, 1979) for the anorogenic alkali granites and "M" for the most calc-alkaline plagiogranites. Of course "type" in this geochemical sense only identifies source rocks, but the provenance, once identified, must be a guide to geotectonic environment (Table 1).

Thus the M-type can be modelled as being derived from a parental magma derived directly from mantle or the subducted oceanic crust beneath volcanic arcs, whilst the similar I-type is more likely to be derived, in a two-stage process, from such derived material first underplating the continental crust at ocean–continental convergent plate margins and then being remelted. S-types characterize continental collision zones and also encratonic, ductile shear belts where, in both cases, the crust is sufficiently tectonically thickened to cause the temperatures at depth to rise and so promote crustal remelting. A-types represent both the rift-associated magmatism of shield areas *and* the final plutonic event in orogenic belts and may be modelled by derivation from impoverished lower crustal material melted above mantle diapirs.

III. The Geochemical Parameters

Those parameters which Chappell and White have found most useful in distinguishing granite types are the total range of SiO_2, the Na and Ca depletion as revealed by the ratios $K/(Na+K)$ and Mol. $Al/(Na+K+Ca/2)$, and oxidation state as expressed by $Fe^3/(Fe^2+Fe^3)$. The latter turns out to be the least specific, presumably because the f_{O_2} is not simply a function of the original oxidization state of the source rocks (Beckinsale, 1971, p. 37), further changes inevitably occurring during the subsequent magmatic evolution — a comment which must also apply to the $\delta^{18}0$ values. Furthermore, an alternative division of granitoids by Ishihara (1977; Takahashi *et al.*, 1980) into magnetite-bearing and ilmenite-bearing types, which is presumably a consequence of differences in oxidation, is not wholly consonant with a division based fundamentally on the degree of sedimentary differentiation.

Well worth noting at this juncture is a sophisticated method of discriminating the major element data derived by La Roche (1979, La Roche *et al.*, 1980) and Debon and Le Fort (in press). It offers the possibility of an even more specific recognition of granite-types (or associations) in relation to source-rocks than that referred to above. For example whilst types equivalent to I and S are clearly recognized — as cafemic and aluminous associations respectively, so too is a monzonitic-type of granite — as an aluminous-cafemic association which is common in post-kinematic situations.

Differences in source may also be detected utilizing the varied concentration of rare-earth elements (REE), e.g. neodymium, or the isotope ratios, especially the initial $^{87}Sr/^{86}Sr$ ratios which are modelled as being relatively higher (>0.706) in rocks derived from a cycled source than those of igneous parentage (<0.706). Even so there is a range of alternatives, including rather extreme cases where otherwise geochemically established S-types exhibit relatively low initial ratios (e.g. Flood and Shaw 1977), or I-types show high ratios (Richards, 1980).

We must expect such apparent inconsistencies because source rocks, even if crustal in the strict sense, will vary in igneous content and degree of sedimentary maturity. The I–S categorization can only be a first order subdivision of a great number of granite types based on source-rock characteristics (White and Chappell, in press). Furthermore differences in the degree of partial melting will naturally diversify the nature and volume of the product and, then again, the more highly "evolved" rocks of the different types are necessarily going to converge in composition and so be less identifiable with the parental types.

Despite these complications there are clearly defined examples, world-wide, of the several granite types, the characteristics of which are outlined in Table I. It must be admitted, however, that there are few localities where, as yet, the distinctive character and the sedimental origin of S-types in the strict sense have been so well documented and demonstrated as in the Lachlan belt of south-east Australia (White and Chappell, 1974; Hine *et al.*, 1979, and see p. 29). In fact

Table I Granite-types, their character and geological environments

M-type	I- (Cordilleran) type	I- (Caledonian) type	S-type	A-type
Plagiogranite subordinate to gabbro	Tonalite dominant but broad compositional spectrum — diorite to monzonite — with wide SiO_2-range. Major association with gabbro	Granodiorite-granite in *contrasted* association with minor bodies of hornblende diorite and gabbro	Granites with high but narrow range of SiO_2. Leucocratic monzogranites predominate but granitoids with high biotite content locally important	Biotite granite in evolving series with alkalic granite and syenite. Highly contrasted acid–basic relationship
Hornblende and biotite; pyroxene	Hornblende and biotite; magnetite, sphene	Biotite predominates; ilmenite and magnetite	Muscovite and red biotite; ilmenite, monazite, garnet, cordierite.	Green biotite. Alkali amphiboles and pyroxenes in alkalic types, astrophyllite.
K-feldspar interstitial micrographic	K-feldspar interstitial and xenomorphic	K-feldspar generally interstitial and invasive. Often quartz-rich	K-feldspar often as megacrysts with protracted history. Autometasomatic variants	Perthites
Basic igneous xenoliths	Dioritic xenoliths; may represent restitic material	Mixed xenolith populations	Metasedimentary xenoliths predominant	Cognate xenoliths, also basic magma blebs
Typical initial $^{87}Sr/^{86}Sr$ ratios <0·704	$Al/\left(Na+K+\dfrac{Ca}{2}\right)<1\cdot1$ (often <1) <0·706	$Al/\left(Na+K+\dfrac{Ca}{2}\right)$ $ca.$ 1 >0·705 <0·709	$Al/\left(Na+K+\dfrac{Ca}{2}\right)>1\cdot05$ >0·708	Peralkaline, relatively rich in F. Considerable range, 0·703–0·712
Small, quartz diorite-gabbro composite plutons	Great multiple, linear batholiths with arrays of composite cauldrons	Dispersed, isolated complexes of multiple plutons and sheets	Multiple batholiths, plutons and sheets, less voluminous and more commonly diapiric than I-types	Multiple, centred, cauldron-complexes of relatively small volume
Associated island-arc volcanism	Associated with great volumes andesite and dacite	Sometimes associated basalt–andesite lava "plateaux"	Can be associated with cordierite-bearing lavas but characteristically lacking in voluminous volcanic equivalents	Associated with caldera centred alkalic lavas
Short, sustained plutonism	Very long-duration episodic plutonism	Short, sustained plutonism; postkinematic	Sustained plutonism of moderate duration; syn- and post-kinematic	Short-lived plutonism
Oceanic island arc	Andinotype marginal continental arc	Caledonian-type post-closure uplift	Hercynotype continental collision. Also encratonic ductile shear-belts	Post-orogenic or anorogenic situations
Open folding: burial-type metamorphism	Vertical movements, little lateral shortening; burial-type metamorphism	Dip-slip and strike-slip faulting: retrograde metamorphism	Much shortening; low-pressure metamorphism in slate belts; part of a *Granite Series*	Doming and rifting
Porphyry-Cu, Au, mineralization	Porphyry-Cu, Mo, mineralization	Rarely strongly mineralized	Sn and W-greisen and vein-type mineralization	Columbite, cassiterite and fluorite

the S-types of the Lachlan belt are petrographically rather different from the common two-mica, leucocratic granites of the world, as exemplified by the Main Range batholith of Malaysia, and it remains to be proved whether or not the rocks of Lachlan and Main Range represent examples of a genetically connected S-type series — as they are considered so to be in this essay.

Furthermore I-types, as chemically defined, seem to occur in at least two distinct geological niches with corresponding differences in composition. For example the end-Silurian, Caledonian granites of the British Isles, I-types by chemical definition, contrast in composition and context with the more typical I-type granitoids of the Andes, so much so that they are shown in Table I, provisionally, as a separate sub-type, in some aspects intermediate between I and S.

This essay is concerned with these differences and with the potential of the typological concept in identifying magma-tectonic environments. In much of what follows the range of chemical criteria mentioned above have not always been applied (but see Takahashi *et al.*, 1980) and the identifications are based on modal composition and rock association. I first refer briefly to those granitoids occurring in oceanic volcanic arcs.

IV. Granitoids in Oceanic Volcanic-Arcs

As noted in the introduction quartz diorites and tonalites occur in oceanic island-arc magmatic sequences, though in small volume relative to basic volcanic and plutonic associates. As an example, in the Aleutian arc (Perfit *et al.*, 1980) gabbros form the peripheries of zoned, quartz diorite plutons and the geochemistry of these augite-bearing, plagioclase-rich, quartz diorites, with low initial $^{87}Sr/^{86}Sr$ ratios (0·70299 to 0·70377) and low δO^{18} values ($\leqslant 6\cdot0$), is entirely comparable to those of the associated volcanic rocks. Indeed the granitoids are likely to have been derived by fractional crystallization of the same high-Al basaltic parental material which provided the comagmatic lavas, with the gabbros representing the cumulate. For such a geochemically primitive parent a mantle source is likely.

Of great interest is the finding that even in this situation (cf. p. 31), the initial ratios vary within a single pluton (Perfit and Lawrence, 1979), suggesting that such variations were inherited from their source.

Similar associations of primitive quartz diorites and tonalites are found wherever there is sufficiently deep erosion in ocean arcs, e.g. in the Kurile Islands (Viacheslav, personal communication, 1980), the Caribbean (Kesler, 1975), the Philippines (Wolfe *et al.*, 1978) and the Solomon Islands (Chivas 1978) — commonly in association with gold-bearing porphyry-copper deposits.

Such granitoids of oceanic arcs might usefully be distinguished, as an M(mantle)-type (White, 1979), from the I-type of continental margins even though the modal and geochemical parameters totally overlap: M-types are, however, uniformly low in silica. Nowhere is this apparent transition better demonstrated than in a comparison of the plutonic rocks of the New Guinea mobile belt, with its clearly identifiable I-type assemblage, and the adjacent North New Guinea New Britain arc, with its geochemically more primitive assemblage (Mason and McDonald, 1978). Genetically these granitoids of the oceanic arcs are important in showing that intermediate granitoids can be generated without the intervention of continental crust.

V. Silicic Plutonism in Phanerozoic Mobile Belts

Within the Phanerozoic great volumes of granite rocks characterize all types of mobile belt except the Alpine. In a survey of the special relationship between the type of granite and its tectonic environment a start is made by examining the setting of the Mesozoic batholiths of the circum-Pacific regions. The reason for doing so is threefold. First because the cordilleran granitoids of the Circum-Pacific borderlands provide a young, and therefore a near actualistic basis for a discussion of the geolocial environment. Secondly the cordilleran granites have an especially distinctive compositional and environmental signature, and thirdly the Pacific mobile belts show well a duality of plutonic belts which is of great genetic significance.

A. Granitoids of the Andean Mobile Belt

1. *Western Cordillera of the Central Andes: the Coastal Batholith*

In the Peruvian-north Chilean sector of the Andes (Fig. 1), during the Mesozoic and Cenozoic, the American Continental Plate abutted directly against the Nazca Oceanic Plate with the virtual absence of an accretionary wedge (Cobbing

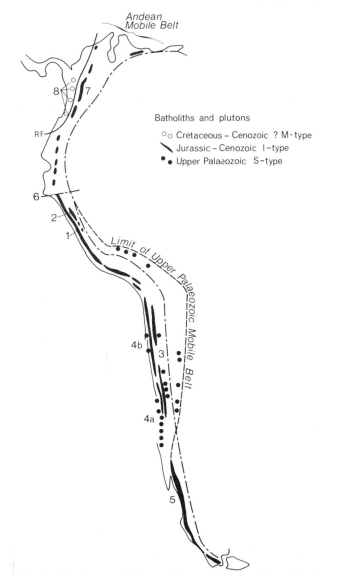

Fig. 1 The Mesozoic-Cenozoic, I-type batholiths of the Andean mobile belt. A line of possible M-type plutons is shown to the west of the Romeral suture (RF) in Colombia. The outer limit of the Upper Carboniferous mobile belt is shown to indicate the super-position of the Andean on the Eohercynian belt. The important belts of U. Palaeozoic granitoids are indicated. Numbers refer to items in the text.

et al., 1981). Long-standing subduction of the oceanic crust is thought to have provided the energetics for the episodic production of a vast volume of magma, possibly in response to varying rates of seafloor-spreading (Frutos and Samaniego, 1980). During this time the continental lip was progressively thickened by some kind of underplating, tectonic shortening being at a minimum.

The voluminous granitoids and their associated dyke swarms were intruded through an ancient crystalline crust and emplaced into a cover composed of the flows and debris of a marginal continental arc. This volcanic material had been collected in fault-controlled, back-arc basins, and was but little deformed and metamorphosed before the granitoids were emplaced. Intrusion was permissive, largely effected by stoping, with a remarkable degree of brittle structure control on all scales (Pitcher and Bussell, 1975). Furthermore the intrusions are located within major plutonic lineaments which exactly parallel the plate-edge.

The granitoids of the western cordillera of Peru provide a prime example (Pitcher, 1978). They are assembled in the form of a great linear, multiple batholith (1, Fig. 1), spanning 100 to 30 Ma in age, in which the rock types are dominated by tonalite, though with a broad compositional spectrum extending from gabbro to syenogranite — all magnetite-bearing. The several component magma suites (super-units) are characteristically I-types, and a remarkable space–time constancy in the initial $^{87}Sr/^{86}Sr$ ratio is suggestive of derivation from a very homogeneous source (Pitcher and Taylor, 1979) — which can be modelled as earlier mantle-derived material underplating the continental lip.

The close temporal and spatial relationship between the granitoids and the extrusive andesites forming the marginal arc is emphasized by the presence of sub-volcanic centred ring-complexes forming an integral part of the batholith (Bussell *et al.*, 1976) and also by the ubiquitous syn-plutonic features of swarms of dykes which probably represent the volcanic feeders. Finally, of all the characteristics of these I-type granitoids in Peru none is more important than the association with Mo-skarns and disseminated Cu-veins (Hudson, 1979; Agar, 1979).

At this point it is pertinent to refer to a general characteristic of cordilleran plutonism — the migration of plutonic locus with time, a process usually coupled with change in composition. In Peru the locus representing the Coastal Batholith remained fixed from between 100 and 30 Ma, seemingly an exceptional happening, and only in the mid-Tertiary did it move eastwards to provide both an eastern string of small plutons (Cobbing *et al.*, 1981) and the considerable batholith of the Cordillera Blanca (2, Fig. 1) (Egeler and De Booy, 1956). The latter is dominantly composed of biotite granites, locally muscovite-bearing and generally peraluminous, with initial $^{87}Sr/^{86}Sr$ ratios appreciably higher (at *ca.* 0·705) than those of the Coastal Batholith to the west (W. McCourt, unpublished data), and so approaches an S-type in composition. Such a plutonic migration is more evident in north and central Chile (3, Fig. 1) (Aguirre *et al.*, 1974; McNutt *et al.*, 1975; but see Zeil *et al.*, 1980) where the Andean plutonic rocks and their environment are otherwise exactly as in Peru. The eastward migration again parallels a change in composition, with the Cenozoic granitoids of Chile being more monzonitic than those of earlier age to the west.

What can be seen very clearly in Chile is the superposition of this Mesozoic Andinotype tectono-magmatic belt upon another of upper Palaeozoic age and of a totally contrasted, Hercynotype, geological environment (Fig. 1): a matter we return to later in this essay.

2. *Southern Andes*

In the Southern Andes (Fig. 1) the generally extensional tectonics so characteristic of the Mesozoic Andean led, as in Peru, to the development of back-arc basins which, in southern Chile, probably opened sufficiently to permit the formation of oceanic-related rocks (Dalziel *et al.*, 1974). Occupying a boundary between two such basins is a batholith (5, Fig. 1) composed of much the same I-type rocks as in Peru, and of even longer standing, i.e. 155-25 Ma, and here again without evidence of lateral migration (Halpern and Fuenzalida, 1978). Characteristically this batholith is also associated with marginal continental-arc type volcanism.

3. *Northern Andes*

In the northern Andes, despite a clear change in the overall geological context from that of the central Andes, the I-type plutonic lineament of Peru, still with a continental-crustal base, continues across the Huancabamba deflection of northern Peru (6, Fig. 1) into the Cordillera Central of Colombia (Iving, 1975) (7, Fig. 1). There, it is represented by an equally impressive chain of multiple batholiths accompanied, to the east, by a parallel line of plutons consisting of slightly peraluminous granites — yet another example of a transversal change.

However in this northern segment of the Andes, west of the Romeral Suture (RF, Fig. 1), the western cordillera of Columbia may represent an accreted oceanic volcanic arc of Mesozoic to Cenozoic age. In it a thick sequence of flyschoid volcaniclastic rocks, basaltic pillow-lavas, hyaloclastites and cherts, play host, not only to basic and ultrabasic intrusions, but to a linear array of tonalitic plutons varying in age from 91 to 16 Ma (8, Fig. 1). Little is yet known of their details and they could be simple I-types related to a young subduction zone (Stibane, 1981) but I suspect that these rocks may turn out to be candidates for the M-types, and it is thus of the greatest interest to observe that they are associated with a gold-quartz mineralization (Stibane, 1980), in just the same way as are the M-types within the Caribbean arcs (see p. 22).

B. Mesozoic Granitoids of Western North America

The Mesozoic batholiths of western North America (Fig. 2) provide a well documented example of plutonic magmatism straddling a continental-oceanic plate boundary. A general feature is an eastward change in composition and isotopic signature, especially in the initial $^{87}Sr/^{86}Sr$ ratio (Kistler and Peterman, 1978; Armstrong *et al.*, 1977), which has been interpreted in terms of location of the constituent plutons east or west of the leading edge of a continental shield.

1. *California: the Peninsular Ranges and Sierra Nevada Batholiths*

The linear array of plutons making up the mid-Cretaceous *Peninsular Ranges Batholith* (1, Fig. 2) of southern and Baja California was emplaced along the boundary between a belt of andesitic volcanic and volcaniclastic rocks, representing the debris of a mid-Cretaceous volcanic arc, and the mudstone–sandstone miogeosynclinal sequence, of Carboniferous to Jurassic age, which represent the proximal deposits of a continental lip (Gastil *et al.* 1974, 1975). Ductile shear-zones, probably representing deep-reaching faults, characterize this boundary (Todd and Shaw, 1979), a situation which might represent the environment of the Central Andes seen at a deeper level. Movement in these zones overlapped the time of emplacement of the early plutons, the latter comprising rocks with the familiar gabbro—quartz diorite—tonalite association; rocks which are themselves closely related in time, place and composition to their volcanic associates. On the western flank of the batholith, particularly in Baja California, the rocks are poor in potassium, have low initial ratios (see below), and are so clearly related to oceanic arc-type volcanic rocks that they approach M-types

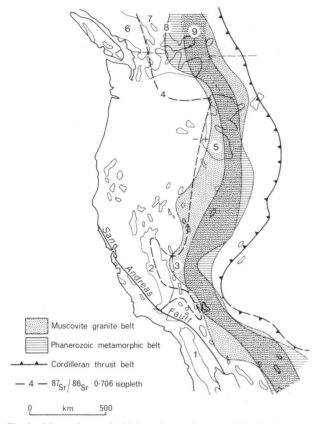

Muscovite granite belt

Phanerozoic metamorphic belt

Cordilleran thrust belt

— 4 — $^{87}Sr/^{86}Sr$ 0.706 isopleth

0   km   500

Fig. 2 Mesozoic granitoid intrusions of western North America (open outcrops) to show the relation of the belt of muscovite-bearing, peraluminous, S-type plutons to the belt of coeval metamorphism, to the Cordilleran thrust belt, and to the initial $^{87}Sr/^{86}Sr$ isopleth (after Miller and Bradfish, 1980). Numbers refer to locations mentioned in the text.

in character. In contrast, on the eastern flank of the batholith, there is a distinctive sequence of leucocratic tonalite and granodiorite plutons.

Within this I-type rock association studies of geographical variations in Rb and Sr, initial $^{87}Sr/^{86}Sr$ ratios, oxygen isotope abundances and REE patterns have revealed strong west–east geochemical asymmetries (e.g. initial ratios of 0.703 to 0.708, $\delta^{18}O$ from 7.0 to 13.0) that are largely independent of rock type (for references see Taylor and Silver, 1978; Silver and Taylor, 1979), changes which are not so much progressive as stepped-up eastwards across a medial line separating terranes of differing structural style and so possibly representing one of the major shear-zones.

Silver and Taylor are rightly cautious in their interpretation of these changes, but one possibility is that to the west the source was oceanic lithosphere, providing the M-types, whilst to the east it was material underplating the continental lip, providing the I-types.

Though there are many parallels with the situation in the Central Andes there are important differences. Thus in southern California and Baja there is no great volume of late-stage granite; there is a greater overall paucity in potassium feldspar, and a greater transverse variation in the geochemical parameters. It is tempting to attribute this to the absence of the very thick understory of crystalline basement which is so evident in Peru, but the problem remains whether the contrast is due to differences in crustal contribution or to differences in crustal thickness.

The great, multiple intrusion of the *Sierra Nevada Batholith* (Bateman and Clark, 1974) (2, Fig. 2) occupies a similar time-tectonic position to the Peninsular Ranges

Batholith except that it may represent emplacement a little farther eastwards into the lip of the continental crust. Here the change of facies between a Mesozoic arc-type "eugeosynclinal" belt and the Upper Palaeozoic, shelf-type "miogeosynclinal" belt, is now marked by the Melones Fault line, a major strike-slip, ductile shear-zone, located on the western flank of the batholith.

The compositionally expanded, magnetite-bearing I-types of the Sierra occur, as in Peru, in time separate suites, but in the former location the locus of intrusion migrated eastwards throughout the Cretaceous. This is marked by a progressive increase in K-feldspar and overall change in the composition of the rocks, the older and more dioritic of which, together with gabbros, outcrop in the west, whilst the younger and more granodioritic outcrop in the east, and so farther into the assumed ancient continental edge — as is possibly indicated by the location of the plutons in relation to the 0.706 isopleth (4, Fig. 2). Indeed the Sierra Nevada batholith could well be regarded as comprising two compositionally distinct batholiths lying in parallel juxtaposition! The chemical parameters naturally reflect this situation, not least the contrast in the extreme values of the initial $^{87}Sr/^{86}Sr$ ratios — 0.7034 in the west and 0.708 in the east (Bateman, 1980).

Eastwards of the Sierra Nevada, plutons satellitic to the batholith proper occur in the White, Ingo, Argus and Slate Ranges (3, Fig. 2) where they are accompanied by plutons of alkali granite (Sylvester *et al.*, 1978).

Still farther to the east and extending from northern Sonora (in Mexico), through Arizona and northwards as far as south-east British Columbia, is a well-defined belt of two-mica granites and granodiorites (Fig. 2) (Miller and Bradfish, 1980). These are peraluminous, with initial $^{87}Sr/^{86}Sr$ ratios ranging from 0.7086 to 0.733, and in most respects are to be regarded as leucocratic S-types — the Idaho batholith is a good example (5, Fig. 2). Characteristically these mid-Mesozoic to early Cenozoic plutons are associated in time and place with a belt of strong deformation involving major thrusts, and regional, low-pressure metamorphism involving the formation of migmatitic rocks. This change of tectonic style has been related to the ductility contrast to be expected between zones of such different magmatic, and therefore thermal histories (Coney, 1972).

In summary, leaving out the complication of translations on great strike-slip faults, the Mesozoic plutonic environment of western North America is one of a trench-type greywacke-flysch melange (the Franciscan) with its contemporary ultrabasic and basic plutonics, but lacking granitoid intrusions, lying oceanwards of a continent marginal arc with its pile of volcaniclastics and volcanics, itself flanking a shelf-type sequence of clastics, the boundary being straddled by M- to I-type granitoids. Within the continent, A-type, alkalic granites overlap in space with the more "evolved" I-types and then, within an inner zone of deformed, marginal basin-type deposits, S-type granites appear.

2. *The Coast Range Plutonic Complex and the Eastern Cordillera*

Western Canada presents an enigma in the sense that, geologically, the Coast Ranges seem to be out of context and so may represent an exotic micro-plate transposed from the far south (Irving *et al.*, 1980). Within them the Coast Range Plutonic Complex (6, Fig. 2) (Roddick and Hutchison, 1974) exposes a deeper level of erosion into a belt of Cordilleran type plutonic rocks than in most other locations around the Pacific margin. One interpretation is that an ancient gneiss complex, along with its volcaniclastic flyschoid cover, was metamorphically reactivated during the Mesozoic (Woodsworth, 1979), when tonalitic plutons were emplaced both syn-tectonically, as near solid diapirs, and post-tectonically, in a more mobile form. The genetic model presented by

Lappin (1976, in Harrison and Clarke, 1979) is one of 50–60% partial melting of the gneiss with varying amounts of amphibolite incorporation, providing quartz-diorites, tonalites and granodiorites, the homogenization of which produced I-type rocks which are in no way different from those of Peru, California and other Cordilleran sites. It is possible that in the Coast Range complex we are seeing an erosion level not far removed from the zone of anatexis where meta-igneous rocks underwent partial remelting to yield typical I-type granitoids.

To the west of this Coast Range complex, the Eastern Cordillera of British Columbia reveals a complicated history of granite emplacement extending from the Upper Triassic to the Palaeogene (Gabrielse and Resor, 1974).

The several age groups of intrusion have distinctive tectonic settings. The earliest are quartz diorites and granodiorites of I-type aspect (7, Fig. 2), having the familiar association with coeval volcanic rocks and Cu-mineralization. These high-level, sub-volcanic plutons occur within a western belt for which a marginal continental arc-type environment can be envisaged. Farther eastwards (8, Fig. 2), into a zone representing the distal part of a Palaeozoic miogeosynclinal apron overlying the lip of the North American craton, lie plutons of somewhat younger age consisting of coarse-grained, hornblende-biotite granodiorite and granite. Thus is seems that a cordilleran-type eastward change of rock type — and isotopic composition according to Le Couteur and Tempelman-Kluit (1976) — is discernible. Sizeable batholiths were emplaced post-kinematically (in the regional sense) yet strongly subject to local fault control. In the same interior position a group of biotite granites of early to mid-Cretaceous age (9, Fig. 2) is followed by a group of coarse-grained K-megacrystic granites, aged late-Cretaceous to Palaeocene, and both groups are thought to be of crustal origin. Latest of all are the small dioritic stocks associated with coeval, explosive volcanism and porphyry-copper deposits.

The geochemical studies necessary to typify these rocks, particularly those of younger ages, remain to be done, but the latter groups do seem to have a composition intermediate between I and S, only moving clearly into the S-type category in plutons to the far east of the cordillera.

3. *South-western Alaska*

In southern Alaska the transform-fault system of the western Americas turns into the complex east–west trending zone of subduction and accretion. Within this broad zone, up to 400 km in width, eight curvilinear plutonic belts have been recognized (Hudson, in press), variously either just within or just without the lip of the continental plate, and with ages ranging from early Jurassic to Palaeogene. These plutonic belts are spatially distinct and no neat order of migration is apparent. Most lie within, and parallel to, the continental lip, and the majority are tonalite batholiths with an extended spectrum of composition, including the ubiquitous gabbro. Again most rock assemblages belong to an I-type association consonant with their continental edge-subduction environment and, appropriately, there is clear evidence in most belts of coeval volcanicity of continental margin arc-type. In the Alaska Range belt, as a particular example, many plutons are clearly sub-volcanic in character and closely associated with cogenetic, subaerial volcanic rocks. A special feature, however, is the strong foliation recorded in many of the intrusives, a deformation which suggests the importance of the deep-fault control of intrusion, whereby plutons are located along strike-slip fault zones, and within which they are deformed during resurgent fault movement.

In contrast to this compositional generality are the rocks of the 2000 km long, Sanak-Baranot belt with its intrusives of Palaeocene age. Sharply discordant plutons of biotite granodiorite and granite intrude strongly deformed flyschoid rocks of Mesozoic and Palaeogene age (Plafker *et al.*, 1977). Such metasediments, immediately adjacent to the Pacific margin, would seem to represent a Tertiary accretionary prism within which the plutonic association seems out of context and in sharp contrast to Alaskan intrusives as a whole. This is a situation we shall meet again in considering the granitoids of south-east Japan.

C. Mesozoic-Cenozoic Granitoids of the Soviet Far East

In the Far East of the U.S.S.R. there exists a plexus of mobile belts of Phanerozoic age, the earlier members of which lie squeezed between several independent ancient megablocks. It is upon this great complex that are accreted the volcano-plutonic arcs now margining the Pacific (Shilo, 1979; Shilo and Milov, 1977*a*).

An example of these mobile belts is provided by the Yana-Kolyma fold system, which wraps around the Omelon massif (1, Fig. 3), and which probably overlies the thinned continental crustal lip of the latter. This has had a continuous history of sedimentation from the late Precambrian to the Jurassic, a long life ended by an Upper Jurassic deformation event, with the production of synclinoria and anticlinoria with strong axial cleavage, and accompanied by a low grade of low-pressure metamorphism. Within the resulting slate belts there are three major north-west-trending lines of batholiths said to be located along the contacts of belts with different geological histories (Sobolev and Kolisnighenko, 1979; Sobolev, 1980). That particular plutonic lineament which borders the Omelon massif on its south-west flank (2, Fig. 3) consists of a line of great lenticular bodies, constituting the Kolimsky Complex, of a late Jurassic age of emplacement. Its intrusions lie elongated and concordant within the fold trend, though with sharp contacts and narrow, superposed aureoles. Potassic, peraluminous leucocratic granites with aplitic, late-stage phases predominate, and in these muscovite accompanies an iron-rich biotite, ilmenite is present and the K-feldspar occurs as megacrysts. These rocks surely represent the S-type of granite, and in confirmation there is a strong cassiterite-tourmaline mineralisation.

A parallel chain of batholiths, of Lower Cretaceous age, lies to the south-west and farther from the Omelon massif (3, Fig. 3), and is duplicated by yet another batholithic lineament to the north-east of the latter (4, Fig. 3). These batholiths are more cross-cutting and less concordant in structural character, and their linearity has suggested to Vashekilov (1963) that emplacement was controlled by deep-seated faults. The constituent granodiorites and granites, though still with K_2O exceeding Na_2O, are more normally calc-alkaline. They lack muscovite, but contain hornblende along with a low-iron biotite; and ilmenite, sphene and zircon are accessory. In this plutonic lineament tin is now only one element in a polymetallic mineralization. In many respects their rock types resemble, as we shall see, those of the I-types of the Caledonian of Scotland.

It is important to note that none of these batholithic complexes is accompanied by coeval volcanism.

Set structurally astride (5, Fig. 3) the above north-west trending plexus of mobile belts is the north-east trending, 3000 km long, Okhotsk-Chukotka volcano-plutonic belt of late Jurassic and Palaeogene age (Shilo *et al.*, 1977*a*). This is interpreted as having been constructed within a continental lip and is comparable in almost every aspect with the central Andean situation (Beliy, 1978; Parfenov, 1978). As in the central Andes elongate troughs collected the waste of an eroding, continental margin volcanic arc, and into the resulting volcaniclastic flysch troughs, were stoped considerable batholiths (Milov, 1971, 1975).

Within this volcano-plutonic belt an external zone (Pacific

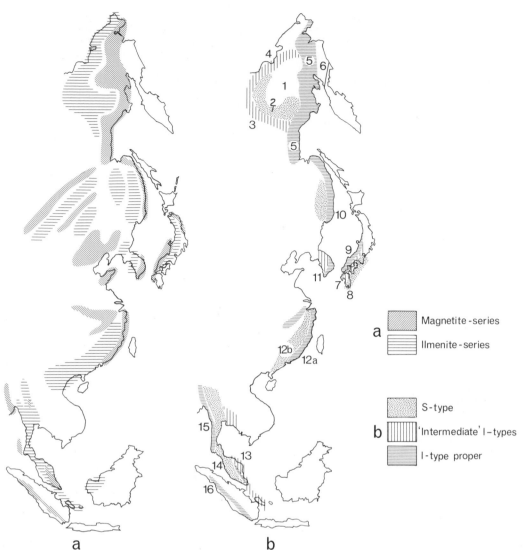

Fig. 3   Inferred distribution of (a) magnetite-series/ilmenite-series rocks, and (b) S- and I-type granitoids, in the Mesozoic and early Cenozoic orogenic belts of eastern Asia. (Modified from Takahashi *et al.*, 1980). Numbers refer to locations mentioned in the text.

side), of Lower Cretaceous age, comprises multiple intrusions of gabbro, diorite and tonalite, having all the features of magnetite-bearing, I-type granitoids of the western cordillera of the Andes. In a belt, internal to the latter, of early to late Cretaceous age, great linear batholiths include arrays of epizonal plutons, in which magnetite-bearing granodiorites prevail. At least three separate sequences are represented, all clearly in comagmatic relationship with coeval volcanics (Shilo *et al.*, 1977*b*), the latest represented by granites cutting silicic ignimbrites. The parallelism with the Andean situation is confirmed by the occurrence of a third, internal belt of later granitic stocks, and by a Cu and Mo mineralization.

It must be emphasized that Russian workers (as noted in Shilo *et al.*, in press) have long recognized the environmental significance of granitoid associations: that a granodiorite-granite association, with initial ratios >0·709 and not associated with gabbros or coeval volcanics, is located within internal miogeosynclines; but that a gabbro-diorite-granodiorite association, with coeval volcanics and with initial ratios <0·707, occupies the totally different environment of the eugeosynclinal belts of continental margins. These two associations, as noted above, are likely to represent the S- and I- of the Australian authors (see Takahashi *et al.*, 1980, p. 15), but it is important to point out

that Shilo *et al.* (in press) also recognize that there is a class of rather uniform granitic batholiths, less extreme in composition than either of the above, which seem to be of a class of their own, and which have been likened by Shilo and his co-workers to a Donegal Granite type — i.e. a Caledonian type.

The above is, of course, only part of the fascinating picture being pieced together by Soviet geologists. In brief the importance of the environmental control is further exemplified by the intrusives occurring within the Anakyr-Koryak wedge of mid-Cretaceous eugeosynclinal sediments (6, Fig. 3) accreted onto the Pacific side of the Ikhotsk-Chukotka belt: here only small bodies of gabbro and plagiogranite occur along with Alpine-type ultramafics. The younger plagiogranites of the younger external arcs have already been referred to.

One last point, both within the internal massifs themselves and also during the late stage of development of the Andinotype orogen, small volumes of alkali-granites appear bearing columbite, and representing the characteristic environmental position of the A-type granite.

D. Mesozoic-Cenozoic Granitoids of Japan

Granites of Mesozoic to Palaeogene age make up the bulk of

the acid intrusives of the Japanese Islands (Tanaka and Nozawa, 1977) and their ages show a zonal arrangement approximately corresponding to the tectonic divisions (Shibata, 1968). In south-western Japan a significant fault, the Median Tectonic Line, running generally parallel to the present Japanese arc, separates zones of very different geological context, viz. an Inner Zone (the Sea of Japan side) representing the ancient continental margin during the Cretaceous and Palaeogene, and an Outer Zone (the Pacific Ocean side) representing an accretionary wedge during that time.

1. Granitoids of the Inner Zone of south-west Japan

Within the Inner Zone (7, Fig. 3) immediately north of the Median Line and within the low-pressure metamorphic zone of the Ryoke belt, there are early gneissic granodiorites of syn- or late-kinematic character which clearly form an integral part of a magma-tectonic cycle: some of these rocks carry muscovite and garnet but their chemical characteristics are not well known other than that they are generally peraluminous (Ishihara and Terashima, 1977). Much better known are the numerous plutons of granodiorite and monzogranite, of late Cretaceous to Palaeogene age, which occur throughout the three structural belts comprising the Inner Zone — plutons which are wholly post-kinematic except for certain early representatives lying closest to the Medial Line and within the Ryoke belt. Despite differences in age, the plutonism and its associated coeval volcanism show a compositional coherence studied by many authors (references in Murakami, 1979; Takahasi et al., 1980). The granites have a generally I-type, calc-alkaline composition, and show overall a progressive change in isotopic ratios and in Fe-oxidation as is reflected by a south to north change over from ilmenite to magnetite-bearing rocks. A progressive north-westward decrease in both the initial $^{87}Sr/^{86}Sr$ ratio (from range 0·708–0·710 to range 0·704–0·706) and in δ ^{18}O values (10 to 8) is reminiscent of the cordilleran situation, though it is in the reverse order in relation to the thickness of the continental crust and its presumed margin (Murakami, 1979, p. 7). The associated mineralization is polymetallic in character, but is best known for its tungsten and molybdenum deposits.

2. Miocene granitoids of the Outer Zone, and of the Green Tuff Belt

South of the Median Tectonic Line, in the Outer Zone of south-west Japan, there is a belt of granodioritic and monzogranitic plutons of Miocene age (8, Fig. 3), plutons which are of high-level and post-tectonic type (Oba, 1977, 1978), associated with ring-dyke formation, and carrying xenoliths apparently derived from a "granulite basement".

The rocks carry ilmenite, they are sometimes cordierite bearing and, according to Takahashi et al. (1980), their chemistry, although spanning the S/I boundary, is predominantly that of a peraluminous S-type granite, though with initial $^{87}Sr/^{86}Sr$ ratios of ca. 0·706. There is a well marked association with a greisen-type cassiterite-wolfram mineralization.

These granites were emplaced into a thick, eugeosynclinal sequence representing the deposits of a southward migrating trough, representing the Shimanto Belt, initiated in the Upper Carboniferous and lasting until the uppermost Palaeogene. This apparently continental-margin accretionary wedge, strongly deformed during the Honsho tectogenesis and suffering a progressive metamorphism leading to blue schists, is hardly the expected environment of an S-type granite association, even though these Miocene granites significantly post-date the magma-tectonic system of the accretionary wedge. It seems that in this completely post-accretion and post-kinematic environment, temperatures in

the base of this thick wedge might have risen sufficiently high to effect melting during Miocene uplift; indeed the presence of such granites with their granulite xenoliths might even reveal the existence of an old sialic basement under this part of Japan (Oba, 1977; Shibata and Ishihara, 1979).

Remarkably these outer zone granites are coeval with the continental margin, arc-type magmatism of Miocene age, represented by the felsitic volcanism and tonalitic plutons of the Green Tuff Belt (9, Fig. 3) (Aramaki et al., 1977). This latter tonalite association, with its coeval gabbros and low initial ratios (0·7046 to 0·7050), is rather clearly of I-type both from the points of view of composition and environment.

3. I- and S-types in Japan: certain enigmas

Thus in the most general terms the plutonic history of south-west Japan reveals that during the Cretaceous and Palaeogene, an Andean-type marginal continental plutono-volcanic arc was established, characterized by I-type granitoids, showing a transverse progression of composition the reverse of that in the cordilleras of western America. The contiguous and coeval accretionary wedge was intruded by basic and ultrabasic magmas, rarely granitoids.

Upon this Cretaceous-Palaeogene base was superposed, in the Neogene, another Andean-type arc. This was remarkably and rather inexplicably margined, on its oceanic side, by a belt of sub-volcanic S-type plutonics; a finding which does not accord well with the general thesis as presently developed.

E. Mesozoic Granitoids of the Mainland of Eastern Asia: An Overview

An overview of the distribution of granitoid types throughout eastern Asia (Fig. 3) is provided by Takahasi and others (1980). Parallel belts of magnetite (largely I-type) and ilmenite (largely S-type)-bearing granitoids extend from the Sikhote-Alin region (10, Fig. 3) of the Soviet Far East, through South Korea (11, Fig. 3) (Lee, 1977) and along the coastal zone of China (Nanjing University, 1974). As an example, in Sikhote-Alin (Martinyuk and Ignatjev, personal communication, 1980), there is an internal zone (in relation to the Japan Sea) where S-type, two-mica granites of Lower Cretaceous age intrude a strongly-cleaved, green schist belt of flyschoid rocks: there is no clear association with volcanic rocks, the local cordierite-bearing ignimbrites being of Upper Cretaceous age. A special characteristic is the association with wolfram-bearing skarns. In contrast, an external, coastal belt, of volcano-plutonic type and of Upper Cretaceous to late Palaeogene age, is of the familiar continental-edge, andinotype, with its close interrelation in time, space and chemistry between the sub-volcanic plutons and the coeval andesites.

This dual belt is again well represented in the coastal region of China (12, Fig. 3). The Cretaceous to Palaeogene, late Yanshanian of China (12a) comprises a great thickness of andesite and silicic ignimbrite which characterise a block-faulted, continental-edge environment, again reminiscent of that of the central Andes. The associated tonalite batholiths are described as being sub-volcanic with granitoids involved in caldera-like complexes just as in the Andes. The accompanying mineralization is characterised by Mo, Pb and Zn, with some Cu. Internally to these batholiths, and well within a continent stabilized since the Upper Palaeozoic, a belt of early Yanashanian granites (12b) represents several overlapping ages of plutonism, all generally lacking volcanic representatives. Those of Jurassic age are ilmenite-bearing, biotite, two-mica granites associated with one of the world's richest zones of tungsten deposits. The latter, together with tin and a range of other metals, form zones peripheral to plutons in a situation reminiscent of that in Cornwall (Yan et al., 1980). Clearly this is a long-standing W, Sn province in which the constituents of the source rocks have been repeatedly mobilized by granites of all ages.

This dualism of the two types of plutonic environment, especially as expressed by the S- and I-type granitoids and the associated Sn or Cu mineralization, is a feature of the Mesozoic geology of the circum-Pacific regions. It is an expression of location in relation to the continental plate edge and, as we shall see below, it is a general feature of the tectonics of convergent plate margins. It is too easy to generalize, but it may be that the hinterland zone of a compressional tectonic regime represents the natural percursor in the establishment of a marginal volcano-plutonic arc.

Takahasi and others (1980) have remarked on the fact that this asymmetric distribution of plutono-tectonic belts is differently expressed on the opposite shores of the Pacific. However this is not absolutely true because the Andinotype environment, with its I-type association, can now be traced around the western Pacific border as far as south China, and an S-type belt lies internal to the American cordillera. But the volumetric contrast remains, and the superabundance of tin-associated, S-type granitoids within the western borderlands of the Pacific can be particularly well demonstrated in Malaysia and Thailand.

F. Granitoids of south-east Asia: The Tin Girdle

1. The Thai-Malay Peninsula and Sumatra

One of the most notable features of the Thai-Malay Peninsula is the abundance of granitic rocks disposed in three major belts: two of which, an eastern and central (13, 14, Fig. 3), of Permo-Triassic age, are best documented in Malaya (Hutchison, 1977; Hutchison and Taylor, 1978; Bignall and Snelling, 1977), whilst the western belt, of Lower Cretaceous age (Beckinsale et al., 1979), is only exposed in western Thailand and Burma (15, Fig. 3). According to the synthesis of Mitchell (1977) the former two belts are associated with Permo-Triassic continental collision along a suture now dividing the two belts, whilst the latter belt is associated with the much younger, eastward subduction of the oceanic Indian plate.

It is the central and eastern belts (in the regional sense) which are represented in Malaya, where the granites range from clearly recognizable S-types in the Main Range Batholith of western Malaya, to granodiorites with I-type characteristics disposed in a belt of separated plutons in the eastern part of the peninsula (14 and 13, respectively, Fig. 3). The western batholith is an elongate, multiple body emplaced within a clastic slate-belt of Lower Palaeozoic age (14, Fig. 3), and representing an encratonic environment of deposition (Hutchinson, 1977). Biotite granites predominate, though commonly bearing muscovite and tourmaline, and the rocks are often strongly K-feldspar megacrystic, and also pegmatitic. They have the geochemical features of leucocratic S-type granites (Beckinsale, 1979) including initial $^{87}Sr/^{86}Sr$ ratios of ca. 0·710 and a strongly developed tin association. The favoured interpretation is that they resulted from the crustal melting brought about by tectonic thickening of the continental crust during the collision process. Thus the entire situation including a virtual lack of coeval volcanics is very much like that of the Hercynian of Europe.

In the metamorphic core of the Peninsula there is a belt of seemingly I-type, hornblendic granitoids associated with a Cu–Au mineralization. Then to the east lies a broad belt of plutons intruding the little deformed, Upper Palaeozoic and Triassic clastic, volcaniclastic and volcanic rocks of eastern Malaya. Within these plutons there is a range of composition, the biotite granites supporting minor hornblende-bearing tonalitic and dioritic variants. In so far as they have been studied these granites appear to be more Ca-rich than those of western Malaya, show lower initial $^{87}Sr/^{86}Sr$ (ca. 0·708), but are still ilmenite-bearing in the main, and are still associated with a tin mineralization.

Hutchison and Taylor (1978) consider that this east coast belt has the features of a subduction related, slightly eroded volcano-plutonic arc, marginal to a continental edge during the Triassic, an environment thought to be reminiscent of the Andean, though the volcano-plutonic association is not of the same measure. I would, however, hesitate to identify these granitoids as I-types in the cordilleran sense, though they might equate, compositionally, with the most evolved, continental-based, eastern facies of the American cordilleran belt, or with the granites of the Caledonian of the British Isles: this is a theme already introduced in connection with the granitoids in the Soviet Far East, and which will be repeatedly returned to in this essay.

At this juncture I refer briefly to the plutonic association of the converging plate-margin, of Cretaceous age, which touches the western coastlands of Thailand, skirts the Peninsula and enters Sumatra (16, Fig. 2). This island provides an example of the subduction of the Indian oceanic plate beneath a continental lip, and although there is some likeness to the overall situation in the northern Andes (Cobbing 1979), it seems that oblique convergence — the transduction of Page et al (1979) — which is expressed as major transcurrent faulting, is more important than in Columbia (p. 23), and certainly much more so than in the central Andes. Perhaps this explains why the volume of rocks of the I-type, tonalite association is so much less in Sumatra (Cobbing loc cit, p. 584) — it is simply that less material was subducted!

G. Granitoids Flanking the Himalayan Indus Suture

Yet another example of the duality of S and I belts, though of different origin than those of the American cordilleran situation, is that provided by the conspicuous belts of granite intrusions running parallel to the Indus-Tsanpo Suture of the Himalayas. Such granites have been little studied but the opinion that the Transhimalayas, north of the Suture, represents a Mesozoic Andinotype margin of the Eurasian plate (Dewey and Burke, 1973) is supported by the presence of a chain of great, discordant batholiths of Andean-type (Fig. 4). Thus the Ladakh batholith (1, Fig. 4) has the characteristic compositional range of I-type granitoids and is near identical in its geochemical signatures with Andean batholiths, (Gansser, 1978; Dietrich et al., personal communication, 1981). Furthermore it is associated with gabbroic rocks of primitive composition and with basic lavas and volcaniclastic rocks of arc-type — the Dras (Indus) volcanics.

This situation contrasts strongly with that south of the Suture where, in the Higher Himalayas, the Neogene Kangdese granites (2, Fig. 4) are represented by great sheets of aluminous, muscovite and tourmaline-bearing leucogranite (Le Fort, 1973, 1975) lying within strongly deformed and migmatized, metasedimentary belts. Such rocks are syn- and post-kinematic in relation to that deformation within the Indian plate connected with the Cenozoic closure event: they are likely therefore to be leucocratic S-type granites, presumably of anatectic origin generated by crustal melting in response to crustal thickening.

A third belt of cordierite-bearing granites (3, Fig. 4) of Cambrian age, outcrops within the Lesser Himalayas (Le Fort et al., 1979). The rocks have all the characteristics of S-types proper (in the Lachlan sense, see p. 29) and must be of prime importance in interpreting the ancient history of the Himalayas.

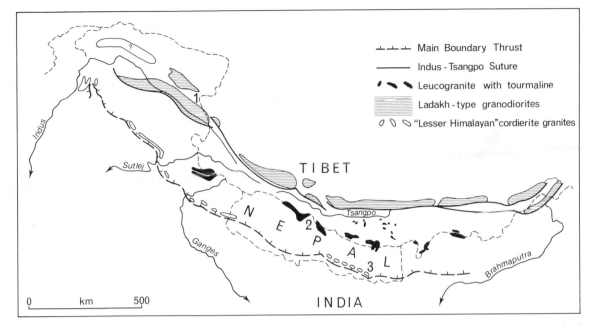

Fig. 4 Granitoids of the Himalayas. (After Gansser, 1976; Le Fort, 1973; Le Fort *et al.*, 1980). Main central thrust omitted.

H. Granitoids in the Tasman Mobile Belt

We move out of the Mesozoic-Cenozoic time-band to examine the plutonism associated with some important mobile belts of Palaeozoic age, the first to be discussed being that of the Tasman Mobile Belt of eastern Australia (Fig. 5), in a sense a type area of granite typology, and certainly an example of this duality of S-I plutonic belts.

1. *Lower Palaeozoic Lachlan Belt*

Granites are especially abundant in this Tasman zone, the mobile belt which fringes the Australian plate. In one of the constituent fold belts, the Lachlan belt (1, 2, Fig. 5), they have been studied by White, Chappell and coworkers (White *et al.*, 1974; White and Chappell, 1977*a, b*, in press; Chappell, 1978; Hine *et al.*, 1978). Multiple batholiths of Silurian and early Devonian age were emplaced into a Lower Palaeozoic slate belt, for the most part after the regional deformation, and dating at *ca.* 420 Ma in the west of the belt and 390 Ma in the east.

As noted above the constituent granitoids have been categorized into S- and I- types on the basis of a rich assemblage of geochemical data. There is a regional distribution into a western province with mainly, but not exclusively, S-types (1, Fig. 5), and an eastern province with wholly I-type rocks (2, Fig. 5), the former being peraluminous, two-mica granites with accessory ilmenite, cordierite or garnet; the latter calc-alkaline, hornblende-biotite, magnetite and sphene-bearing granodiorites and tonalites. Of an impressive number of discriminative parameters only the ranges in initial $^{87}Sr/^{86}Sr$ ratios and $\delta^{18}O$ values are mentioned here as > 0.708 and *ca.* 10 in the S-type, and from 0.704 to 0.706 and between 8 and 9, respectively, in the I-type.

It cannot be too strongly emphasized that the S-type granitoids of the Lachlan belt, the locality of the original definition, are predominantly cordierite-bearing, and can sometimes be so loaded with biotitic restite that the rocks assume a dioritic aspect, albeit always with a high quartz content. Certainly, their origin as partial melts of a sedimental source can hardly be in doubt. But these characteristics, coupled with a "dryness" recorded by the lack of pegmatites, aplites, and mineral veins, contrast with those of

peraluminous, two-mica granites generally elsewhere in the world, which are pegmatitic, aplitic and mineralized leucogranites. Also the S-types of the Lachlan belt are locally associated with cordierite-bearing silicic volcanic rocks (Wyborn, 1978) contrary to both general experience elsewhere and even expectation (Pitcher, 1979, p. 654). But the data are too incomplete in too many regions to follow up this point of apparent contrast.

The I–S boundary (Fig. 5) in the Lachlan belt is locally marked by a major, deep-seated fracture which may represent the ancient eastern edge of the "sialic" continental crust. The deep-seated rocks to the east of the fracture can be envisaged as representing an underplate of dioritic material, the age of which can be estimated (Compston and Chappell, 1979). The different granite types are modelled as partial melts emanating from these different sources, the S-type from deep, "sialic" continental crust, the I-type from a relatively old "subcreted" underplate. In the elegant "restite model" of White, Chappell and their coworkers the individual rock units are envisaged as representing different degrees of "unmixing" of such partial melts.

Concerning in particular the I-type rocks of the Lachlan belt, there are many similarities with their cordilleran analogues, especially in the distribution of their rocks in well-marked suites within their batholiths. There is also a west to east change in the overall range of composition, with the Lachlan rocks becoming more "cordilleran" in aspect, i.e. increasing in area of outcrop of diorites and gabbros (Griffin *et al.*, 1978). However, there are some significant contrasts; the Lachlan rocks are distinctly richer in model quartz, and lack important dyke swarms and coeval andesite lavas — though the latter fact might be attributable to greater depth of erosion. More important, perhaps, is the fact that the whole Lachlan belt of granitoids is distributed over a much wider belt, some 800 km, than in any possible circum-Pacific Mesozoic analogue. Again the best analogue is with the Caledonian plutonism of the British Isles.

2. *Upper Palaeozoic Belts of New England and Queensland*

The eastern sector of the Tasman mobile belt involves rocks of Upper Palaeozoic age stretching from New England to Northern Queensland. Batholithic arrays of plutons post-

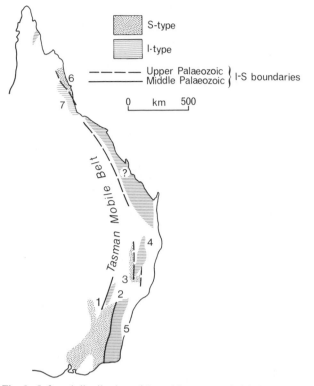

Fig. 5   Inferred distribution of S- and I-type granitoids in eastern Australia (After White and Chappell, 1977; Flood and Shaw, 1975; Richards, 1980). S–I boundary lines, of different age significance, shown tentatively.

date the slate-belt-type deformation of the several flyschoid basins and, as an example, the New England batholith (3, 4, Fig. 5) provides another case history of the division into S- and I-types. It has recently been shown (Flood and Shaw, 1977, Korsch and Harrington, in press) that an eastern belt of I-type granitoids (4, Fig. 5), the New England batholith *sensu stricto*, is flanked by two belts of plutons (3, Fig. 5) of earlier date of emplacement and of generally S-type plutons. The latter two differ in that one (in the west) is of a wider compositional range than the other, lacking muscovite, even bearing hornblende locally, and with garnet instead of cordierite as an accessory: this illustrates the range of modal parameters apparently acceptable within the S-type category.

In New England the I–S separation is a representation of the contrast between different environments, the S-type granitoids proper being associated with a clastic sedimentary sequence, the I-types with a volcanic cover sequence. The S-types are modelled as representing melting at the base of continental crust thickened by major under-thrusting, a tectonic phase which may have been the precursor to the establishment of a marginal, plutono-volcanic arc with its I-type plutonic associates.

In northern Queensland (Richards, 1980) (6, 7, Fig. 5) an even wider range of granite types is represented. Here an eastern belt of leucocratic S-type granites, again intruded into an Upper Palaeozoic slate-belt (the Hodgkinson), is temporally and spatially distinct from an array of I-type granite cauldrons outcropping within a time-equivalent shelf-facies (of the western, Chillagoe Shelf, 7, Fig. 5). Thus another I–S line is defined, but with a pattern hardly in accord with a cordilleran type model, at least not with an assumed plate edge lying to the east of the Hodgkinson basin (Henderson, 1980). Of particular interest in northern Queensland is the abundance of monzogranites which, though they may represent I-types in the general sense, are

highly evolved members of their respective suites, enriched in F-rich volatiles and with cassiterite concentrated in the late-stage differentiates.

Both in Queensland and elsewhere, particularly in south-eastern Australia (5, Fig. 5), Palaeozoic plutonism ended with the intrusion of sub-volcanic cauldrons and ring-complexes often involving peralkaline granites: these represent the A-type granite in its characteristic stable and wholly post-tectonic regime. Such magmas may have been derived from underplated material deplenished by the previous remelting episodes — an hypothesis consonant with their late appearance in the plutonic cycle (White and Chappell, in press).

Having outlined the type example of geochemical granite typology we move on to discuss the analogous belts in Europe and the western U.S.A.

I. Appalachian-Caledonian Plutonism of Europe and North America

The Appalachian-Caledonian mobile belt of eastern North America and Western Europe (Fig. 6) records the approach of the continents of Laurasia and Africa, their oblique collision during the mid-Ordovician, a continuation of inter-plate movement by sinistral shear during the late Silurian, and the final uplift of the suture-zone at the beginning of the Devonian. As we shall see the plutonic history closely reflects this tectonic evolution but I comment especially on the plutonic rocks of the relaxation, uplift stage, as these seem to have a special character of their own.

1. *The Caledonian Plutonism of Caledonia*

In the area of traditional Caledonia the tectonic history is rather less complicated than in the Appalachians because the late Cambrian to early Ordovician tectonic event is distinct from the end-Silurian event, and few complications resulted from the Hercynian overprint. Nevertheless a considerable range of granite type and age of emplacement is represented within the Caledonides of Scotland and Ireland; a particular contrast of environment, even of composition, depending on whether the plutons outcrop north-west (1, Fig. 6) or south-east (2, Fig. 6) of a major tectonic line represented by the Highland Border Fault, i.e. within the metamorphic Grampian block or within the non-metamorphic L. Palaeozoic slate-belt, respectively.

(a) Granites of the Grampians.
In the Grampians the earliest granites are migmatitic S-types, syn-kinematic in relation to the earliest and most intense deformational event at *ca.* 500 Ma. These were followed by a post-kinematic group of S-type, two-mica granites of mid-Ordovician age (Van Breeman and Bluck, 1980), and these peraluminous rocks, characterized by relatively high initial $^{87}Sr/^{86}Sr$ ratios (Brown and Hennessy, 1978), possibly represent a significant degree of fusion of a Proterozoic crystalline basement. By analogy with the circum-Pacific terranes it is possible that this latter group represents an internal, hinterland belt in relation to a mid-Ordovician subduction system, but there is very little evidence of the complementary, coeval, marginal cordilleran belt of I-type tonalites (see Fig. 3, Van Breeman and Bluck, *op. cit.*).

Be that as it may, the bulk of the granites intruding the Grampian block — representing the end-Silurian "Newer Granites" with ages between 430 and 380 Ma — clearly post-dates all the regional metamorphic and deformation events. These granites are associated in time with a post-orogenic period of uplift, and their emplacement was controlled by an important system of sinistral faults (Leake, 1978; Hutton, 1981): all events which long post-dated the mid-Ordovician oblique closure of the Iapetus ocean and the connected

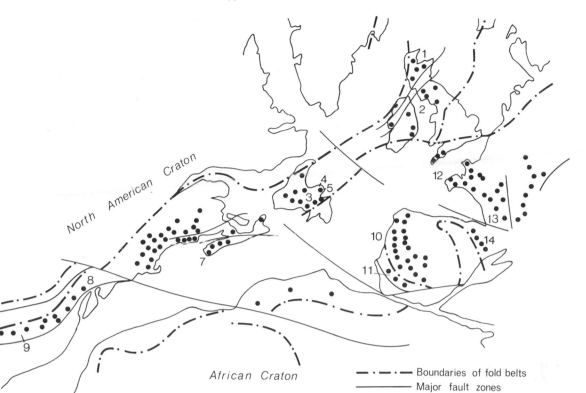

Fig. 6   Palimspastic sketch map of the Hercynian and Caledonian mobile belts and their associated belts of granite plutons. Numbers refer to locations noted in the text.

subduction. Furthermore the constituent plutons are widely scattered and fail to show the progressive space-time compositional changes characteristic of cordilleran granitoids.

There is an extensive literature and seemingly considerable variation but, generalising, the most abundant rock-types are biotite granite and granodiorite with hornblende-bearing variants, often in a zonal relation within single plutons. A special character is the close space–time relationship with small bodies of pyroxene-biotite-hornblende diorite and hornblende gabbro — the appinite suite (Pitcher and Berger, 1972).

Within the Newer Granites there has been some attempt to make a clear separation, structurally and geochemically, between a younger (*ca.* 400 Ma) group of permitted plutons and an older (*ca.* 420 Ma) group of forcefully intruded plutons, but there are clear anomalies and obvious juxtapositions in space (e.g. in the Donegal granite complex, Pitcher and Berger, 1972); and the differences may simply be a reflection of style and depth of emplacement. Nevertheless, despite little overall variation in the initial $^{87}Sr/^{86}Sr$ ratio (*ca.* 0·7060) (Pankhurst, 1979), a division has been made on the basis of variations in ratios such as Rb/Sr, K/Rb, the REEs etc. (Brown *et al.*, 1980).

Of particular interest is the recognition that some of the late, discordant group are sub-volcanic cauldrons associated in time with flows of olivine-basalt, dacite and rhyolite, though such volcanic rocks represent a quite separate magma type (Groome and Hall, 1974).

(b) Granites of the non-metamorphic Caledonides. There are more real, if subtle, petrological differences between these Newer Granites of the Grampian block and those of similar end-Silurian age intruded into the Lower Palaeozoic slate belt lying to the south (2, Fig. 6); a contrast best demonstrated by the presence of inherited 1600 Ma zircons in the former but not in the latter (Pigeon and Aftalion, 1978).

Also, particularly within those single plutons outcropping in the slate belt, there is evidence of a progressive crustal contamination of the magmas during their upwelling (Halliday *et al.*, 1980). The difference is modelled as a contrast in the nature and the degree of involvement of the crustal rocks — the ancient crystallines of the Grampians as against the Lower Palaeozoic greywackes (Brown and Locke, 1979).

From the location of this southern group of granites within a thick clastic sedimentary prism and the fact that their emplacement cannot long post-date the end-Silurian deformation of their country rocks, we might expect that their composition should have some affinity with S-types proper. However, with possible exceptions, such as the Fleet pluton (Halliday *et al.*, 1979), this is not so, their chemistry being more compatible with I-types but with an origin involving the incorporation of sedimentary material as a subordinate process.

(c) A post-collision, uplift environment. I believe that we must consider these New Granites, overall, as a coherent group genetically independent of subduction-related processes: that is if they have not been juxtaposed by great strike-slip movement! Although many of these granites, especially those of the Grampians, bear the geochemical signature of I-types, they do not really resemble Cordilleran types (cf. Brown, 1979, p. 648) — at least not the rocks of the western Cordilleras. They have neither the spectrum nor spread of composition, the association with gabbro, nor are they so rich overall in calcium, nor have they the uniformly low initial $^{87}Sr/^{86}Sr$ ratios (see Harman and Halliday, 1980). In fact, they are very much like the I-types of the Lachlan belt of south-east Australia and, as in that location, they lack economically significant mineralization. As noted above, their environment, that of post-collision uplift, also differs from that of the American cordilleras: it was never that of continental marginal type and indeed the granitoids vary from those of the cordilleran type in just the same way as do the Acadian granitoids (Wones, 1980, and see this page).

The presence of inherited zircons, also trace element and Pb isotope studies (Blaxland *et al.*, 1979; Pankhurst, 1979), indicate a substantial crustal component and so support a model of a mixed parental source, whereby melts derived from mantle, or lower crust, were mixed with remelts of different crustal rocks at higher levels. A possible model is that partial melts derived from such crustal or subcrustal rocks were produced during adiabatic decompression consequent on the end-Silurian uplift and erosion, and at a time when such rocks were rapidly elevated into low pressure zones (Hall, 1971). Melting was concentrated in the pressure-release zones provided by deep-faults, which might also have brought hot mantle rocks into juxtaposition with cooler crustal rocks. Such deep faults permitted vapour-enriched, basic cumulates, representing the appinite suite, to rise at the same time.

I have already expressed the view that this post-collision uplift phase of plutonism is worth separately identifying, because it seems to be characterized by granitoids with a special rock association.

2. The Acadian of the Appalachians

It requires extreme generalization to summarize the granite geology of the Appalachians, especially to treat separately Acadian events from those of the earlier, Avalonian and Taconic, and later Hercynian events. Also it seems, once again, that major strike-slip displacements have resulted in plutonically unrelated regions being juxtaposed.

(a) **Newfoundland.** The Gander zone of Newfoundland illustrates the long history of Palaeozoic plutonism (3, Fig. 6) (e.g. Strong, 1980). An early, plate-consuming environment is recorded in the flanks of this orogenic belt by a compositionally-expanded, tonalite association with comagmatic, arc-type volcanic equivalents. Plagiogranite of true oceanic island-arc type may also be represented, e.g. by the rocks of the Twillingate Granite (4, Fig. 6) (Williams and Payne, 1975).

Post-closure events are recorded both in the flanks and metamorphic core of the belt — a belt likely to be everywhere underlain by Precambrian basement — by three types of granite, all of a rather restricted range of composition. The most abundant is a coarse-grained, often microcline-megacrystic, biotite granite, sometimes in a highly contrasted association with gabbro but lacking coeval volcanics and metal-ore concentrations. A feature of this granite is the *apparent* wide range of age both in absolute terms (Bell *et al.*, 1977), i.e. from Upper Silurian to Devonian, even Carboniferous (see p. 33), and in relation to Acadian deformation, though most plutons are clearly post-kinematic (Neale and Pajari, 1972). Although the initial $^{87}Sr/^{86}Sr$ ratios are relatively low they have high K_2O contents and Rb/Sr ratios more consistent with a continental crustal derivation (Bell *et al.*, 1977). Associated in space with these biotite granites, but less abundant, are peraluminous, two-mica, garnetiferous leucogranites, of which good examples, still of Acadian age, occur in the Carmanville Ordovician slate belt (5, Fig. 6) (Currie and Pajari, 1981). Finally, restricted to the margins of the orogenic belt are belts of relatively late, alkaline-peralkaline granite plutons, locally associated with comagmatic volcanics.

Strong (1980, p. 763) argues against an I- and S-type designation for the granitoids of Newfoundland, which he also claims are not simply related to crustal melting in different tectonic environments, but to different degrees of melting in relation to the water concentration.

(b) **New Hampshire, Maine and Nova Scotia.** Farther to the south-west, in New Hampshire, the conventional division of the plutonic history based on time-relationship relative to deformation, has not been confirmed by radiometric dating: it is the several ages of deformation which are being measured. However, in Maine (6, Fig. 6) it is possible to observe, at least locally, the separation of Acadian granitoids in space (Loiselle and Ayuso, 1980). There is, for example, a great contrast across the Norumbega fault zone, so that the post-kinematic, coarse-grained, pegmatitic leucogranites, outcropping to the south-east of the fault, contrast with the hornblende-biotite granite and granodiorite outcropping immediately to the north-west. Farther to the north-west a rather homogeneous, medium- to fine-grained, biotite granite prevails. Thus it would seem that here each one had a different source, related to location in different fault-blocks.

Wones (1980) has contrasted the hornblende-biotite granites and granodiorites with those of the Cordilleras of the western U.S.A. Whilst the hornblendic granitoids, which have the widest spectrum of composition, have geochemical similarities to typical I-types, they are nevertheless distinct from cordilleran rocks in being more leucocratic, richer in K and often more aluminous; they are also less rich overall in Ca, and show no discernible regional compositional gradients. In fact they relate more nearly to the most "evolved" end-members of the Cordilleran composition range, as represented in the eastern sector of the Sierra Nevada batholith and by the plutons located east of it in the White Mountains which, it will be recalled, lie well within the continental crustal plate. The recognition of this contrast by Wones is important.

The coarse-grained, biotite leucogranite is reminiscent of that same type in Newfoundland and again it is rarely sufficiently strongly peraluminous to develop much muscovite, garnet, cordierite or aluminosilicate; neither does it have high initial ratios.

The granites which do develop these minerals are those of the Meguma Belt of Nova Scotia (7, Fig. 6) (Smith, 1979), lying to the south-east on the far side of yet another major transcurrent fault zone: an example is the South Mountain Batholith, 367 Ma in age (Reynolds *et al.*, 1981). Intruded into a slate belt these granites have most of the characteristic features of the S-type, even an association with a cassiterite-wolframite mineralization, perhaps the only uncharacteristic feature being the variable K_2O/Na_2O ratio, which is thought to be a consequence of different degrees of partial melting of the metagreywacke source rocks.

3. The Appalachian Piedmont

Farther south-west, within the Piedmont Province, the evolution of the granitoids within the outer Piedmont of Maryland (8, Fig. 6) shows a general composition change with age (Sinha *et al.*, 1980), and this may provide the clue to a general model. Thus there is a tonalite association of Cambrian age which seems to be of typical Cordilleran type, as it is in Newfoundland. In contrast the granodiorites of Ordovician-Silurian age are like those of Maine, and rocks of this "evolved" type are common within the outer Piedmont of the Carolinas, where they contrast in their turn with the muscovite-bearing Hercynian granites of the inner Piedmont (p. 33). Sinha and his co-authors suggest that this evolution indicates the increasing involvement of crustal rocks with time, which is consonant with a history of the collapse of an early established plutonic-volcanic arc during continental collision, followed by compression — and so presumably thickening — of the crust consequent on oblique collision and succeeding wrench movements.

J. Alleghenian, Hercynian and Eohercynian Plutonism of the U.S.A., Europe and the Andes

The Hercynides of Europe, the eastern U.S.A. and the Andes stand in strong geological contrast with the Pacific Cordilleran and Atlantic Caledonian, especially in the overall character of the associated plutonic rocks. I now consider the plutonic environment, rock association and types of this continental-collisional type mobile belt (or belts) at key sections along its length.

1. *Appalachians*

In the southern Appalachians a widespread penetrative deformation and metamorphism of late Palaeozoic age represents a compressive regime resulting from sliding between the Laurasian and African Plates, and representing a dextral megashear which extends from the south-western U.S.A. into central Europe (Arthaud and Matte, 1977). There is a clear implication in many studies of this belt that everywhere old crystalline rocks form a basement to Hercynian terranes. Thickening of such crust during collision and compression may well have provided the mechanism for granite production (Dewey and Burke, 1973, but see Zwart and Dornsrepen, 1978), though the halting of the presumed convection cell would have also lead to the build up of heat (Dennis and Jacoby, 1980). Everywhere intrusion is closely associated with important structural lineaments, often deep-seated, strike-slip fault systems.

In the southern Appalachians (9, Fig. 6), K-feldspar megacrystic, biotite leucogranites with relatively low initial ratios are both syn- and post-kinematic in relation to the latest deformation episode (Fullagar and Butler, 1979; Snoke *et al.*, 1980). These are associated with a more peraluminous, two-mica granite with high initial $^{87}Sr/^{86}Sr$ ratios and high $\delta^{18}O$ values (Wenner *et al.*, 1970) which, in this part of the Appalachians, completes the history of Palaeozoic plutonism.

Strangely in the northern Appalachians there are very few post-Devonian granites (Rast and Grant, 1977) in contrast both to the situation in the south and also in Europe.

2. *Western Europe, Iberia*

The character of Hercynian plutonism in Europe can be best viewed in western Iberia (10, Fig. 6) where, within the framework of a two-phase history of deformation, granitoids are emplaced pre-, syn- and post the second phase, dated at *ca.* 280 Ma, which involved strong compression with the production of penetrative cleavages, upright folds, and steep thrust faults. Of these granites, an early group of biotite granodiorites is more calc-alkaline than a later, and the most voluminous, group of muscovite-biotite granites, and the latest, post-tectonic phase is represented by a return to the more calc-alkaline type (Capdevilla and Floor, 1970; Den Tex, 1977; Corretage *et al.*, 1977, Ribeiro *et al.*, 1979).

It is the second group which comprises the most characteristic rock type of the Iberian Hercynian, perhaps of all the interior plate situations of the Hercynides of Europe. Characteristically associated with metamorphic belts it includes all the terms of the *Granite Series* of Read. Furthermore it is not associated with any great volume of coeval acid volcanic rocks — though it can be argued that the exceptional uplift and erosion to be expected in collision-thickened belts must commonly lead to destruction of any volcanic equivalents. A common rock-type is a strongly peraluminous, low calcium, two-mica granite, often bearing cordierite, garnet, sillimanite and tourmaline, and yielding high initial $^{87}Sr/^{86}Sr$ ratios. Texturally K-feldspar megacrystic and pegmatitic varieties are common. This is, of course, a typical S-type granite assemblage and is associated with the characteristic cassiterite-wolfram mineralization. Furthermore it is patently of crustal derivation.

The more calc-alkaline associates, though they bear the same petrological and textural stamp, are less aluminous, predominantly biotite-bearing, and exhibit lower initial ratios: a difference attributed by Capdevilla (1969) to crustal melting under more anhydrous conditions than those of peralkaline type — perhaps this represents the "Caledonian" I-type referred to above.

In southern Portugal and south-west Spain (11, Fig. 6) and separated by a major deep fracture zone from the continent-based rocks of the Meseta, a very different regime exists in the Ossa-Morena Zone (Aparicio *et al.*, 1977). There a sub-volcanic, gabbro-diorite-tonalite-granodiorite assemblage may represent an Andean-type situation, yet it seems to be superimposed in time and space on a syn-kinematic ophiolite complex; an assemblage representing, perhaps, an obducted island arc and its oceanic basement?

3. *Western Europe, France*

In the Variscan chain of France the plutonism is clearly of ensialic and post-collision character (Orsini, 1979*a*). In confirmation of this there are no tonalite batholiths of western cordilleran type or their associated andesites. Instead the geochemical characteristics of the granites strongly suggest participation of lower crustal material, with the different types resulting from the varying characteristics of the continental crust at source at the time of generation including composition, thickness and the thermal regime (Vidal in La Roche *et al.*, 1980*b*).

There are, as in Portugal, two contrasted groups of granitoids as is well demonstrated in both Brittany (La Roche *et al.*, 1980*b*) and the Massif Central (Didier and Lameyre, 1969; Duthou, 1977). A group of biotite granodiorites and monzogranites of general calc-alkaline affinity, show initial $^{87}Sr/^{86}Sr$ ratios of between 0·705 and 0·706, but more characteristic of Hercynian terranes is another group of megacrystic, peraluminous, two-mica granites with initial ratios ranging from 0·706 to 0·717 i.e. a typical S-type.

In *Brittany* (12, Fig. 6) these two groups are separately distributed in two belts of plutons aligned along major fractures — ductile shear zones — that not only located intrusion but may also, during their movement, have triggered the remelting process (Strong and Hanmer, 1981). Compositionally a southern belt of what are very clearly S-type granites contrasts with a northern belt of the less aluminous, biotite-granites, the rock-type of which has been recognized (Orsini, 1979*a*) as a separate Margeride sub-type, though still compositionally an S-type in the strictest sense. It is this sub-type which appears as a distinct compositional field when plotted by the method proposed by La Roche (1979). We can note that the granites of Cornwall and Devon probably belong in this category (see Hawkes and Dangerfield, 1978).

Everywhere these Hercynian granites are related to late-stage fluorite-lithionite granites and tourmaline greisens, also a tin, tungsten and uranium mineralization, and complex though the latter may be (Bromely, 1975; Chauris, 1977) it is unlikely to be genetically modelled on a simple subduction-type thesis.

In the *Massif Central* (13, Fig. 6) Didier and Lameyre (1969, esp. p. 225, Fig. 7) have also contrasted the characteristics of the leucogranites with those of the hornblende-biotite granodiorites and monzogranites, recognizing those very distinctions which constitute the basis of the S–I classification, and attributing the differences to variations in the depth and to the degree of partial melting of crustal rocks. Contemporary basic magmas are thought to be the source of the extra heat required for producing the calc-alkaline remelts.

Locally other types are important (Orsini, 1979*b*) as, for example, the strongly potassic syenogranites of both Corsica and the north coast of Brittany that, with associated horn-blende gabbros and diorites, could be related to zones of particularly great thickening where continental crustal blocks have over-ridden one another.

Finally, the Hercynian plutonism in the *Pyrenees* (14, Fig. 6) is characterized in its late stages by numerous concentrically-zoned diapirs (e.g. Debon, 1980), in which leucocratic, often cordierite-bearing, monzogranites form the cores, and various quartz-diorites and gabbrodiorites the peripheries. Dark, mafic inclusions are unbiquitous. According to Debon (*op. cit.*) the origin of this highly contrasted association is due to hybridization between basic magmas and silicic crustal melts produced during the intrusion of the former.

In conclusion the granitoids of the Hercynian belt, right across Europe, exemplify the types to be expected in en-cratonic zones where thick sedimentary sequences, possibly to be modelled as extensional basin deposits, are further thickened by compression. In such belts sedimentary source rocks will preponderate in the crustal prism and so therefore will the peraluminous, S-type granites which arise from them. But not exclusively so, as there still remains a crustal basement of contrasted composition to provide an alter-native source for the calc-alkaline, I-type granodiorites (of Lachlan or Caledonian sub-type — Table I).

4. *Central Andes*

As mentioned above the Mesozoic tectono-magmatic belt of the Andes is superimposed on a Upper Palaeozoic fold belt strikingly similar to those constituting the Hercynian mobile belt of Europe and the U.S.A. The general outlines of this Eohercynian belt of the Central Andes has been recently well documented by Dalmayrac *et al.* (1980) in Peru, and the associated plutonism described, in Chile, by Aguirré (in press). In essence a Palaeozoic slate belt, characterized by low-pressure metamorphism, is invaded by a granite series involving syn-kinematic, migmatitic granites and post-kinematic, discordant granites of Lower Carboniferous to Upper Permian age.

The Coastal Range batholith of Central Chile is a prime example (4a, Fig. 1) being a multiple body (Mercado, 1978) with a considerable range of rock types, mostly leucocratic, but so generally K-feldspar poor as to be technically tonalites and granodiorites. Coarseness of grain and richness in quartz, coupled with paucity in biotite and the sporadic occurrence of muscovite, are other characteristics of these generally peraluminous rocks. This batholith seems to have played a direct role in the generation of the high tempera-ture, low-pressure, regional metamorphism of its country rocks.

Where such late Palaeozoic plutons have been described in detail, as for example those around Chañaral (4b, Fig. 1) (Zeil *et al.*, 1980), it is recorded that the coarse, megacrystic monzogranites carry two micas, sphene and ilmenite — they are in fact rather typical S-types, as is confirmed by the high initial $^{87}Sr/^{86}Sr$ ratios.

Of particular interest is the finding that in the eastern cordillera of north-central Chile, Argentina and Peru, there are simple biotite monzogranite plutons, now wholly discor-dant and of Permian age, which are thought to have been intruded during a post-tectonic period of distension and uplift. Such plutonics are temporally and spatially associated with acid volcanic rocks and a red-bed molasse.

Thus in the Eohercynian of the Andes, as elsewhere, S-type granites, in a Granite Series, relate to an intra-cratonic mobile belt, the later relaxation stage of which is characterized by the intrusion of a rather uniform biotite granite.

K. The Lack of Alpine Plutonism

The difference between the Alpine and Hercynian mobile belts in Europe has often been commented on (e.g. Zwart, 1967, Zwart and Dornsiepen, 1978). The contrast is, respec-tively, between low-angle and high-angle thrusting, between high-pressure and low-pressure metamorphism and the paucity and abundance of granite. It is the latter difference which is the most remarkable — there are only a few sizeable bodies of granite of Alpine age. In the Swiss and Italian Alps for example — leaving aside some S-type migmatites and sheet complexes within the belt of Pennine nappes — there are only the Bergell and Ademello plutons, which are biotite granodiorites, perhaps of I-type, closely associated with the Insubric fault line.

This lack of silicic magmatism in the European Alpine belt suggests that little subduction was involved, or if it were then it was of limited duration. Furthermore crustal thickening could not have been so considerable and sustained a process as in the Hercynian where the necessary heat for remelting was probably generated by such thickening.

The Alpine belt is, of course, not the only accretionary wedge to lack acid plutonism, and other examples are the Franciscan of California and the Anadyr Koryak belt of the Soviet Far East. If granitoids are present in supposed accretionary wedges, e.g. in the Palaeozoic belt of the Scot-tish Southern Uplands, and the Shimanto belt of Japan, then it seems likely that continental-type crust had intervened, at least by the time of the granite-producing event.

VI. Granite Types and Precambrian Mobile Belts

Whilst the nature of the plutonism seems clearly to depend on the tectonic character of the mobile belt it also seems that no one mobile belt and its associated magmatism is exactly like another: each is unique within its geological time slot. Nevertheless the rather precise relationship between type and environment so far established might encourage the use of granitoids in unravelling ancient global tectonic histories.

This would surely be so in the younger Precambrian. For example the Cadomian (600 Ma) of Western Europe con-tains an I-type, "cordilleran" plutonic association which may help to identify a marginal continental, Andean type situation. On the other hand, the Brazilian orogenic cycle (1000–450 Ma), includes a variety of granitoids which seem to be more typical of ensialic mobile belts (Wernick and Penalva, 1978). However one must enter the reservation that the full gamut of granite types of the Phanerozoic is unlikely to be recognized earlier than the uppermost Proterozoic if only because possible sedimentary source-rocks would have passed through a different type of chemical weathering cycle: also the thermal regime and the isotopic composition of derived melts would have been different (Allegre and Oth-mann, 1980). Nevertheless, as reported below, S- and I-types have been recognized in mobile belts as old as 1700 Ma, where their presence has been taken to indicate the operation of plate tectonic processes.

The late-Precambrian Pan-African of north-east Africa and Arabia provides an example of this kind of reasoning. In what appears to be a continental crustal environment granitoids in great volumes were intruded into eruptive rocks and volcaniclastic sediments. Three such episodes have been identified (Gass, 1977) at 900, 900–600 and 600 Ma, each including a complete cycle of events and each involving both syn- and post-kinematic plutonism. Throughout the entire history the magmatic products became progressively more silicic with time. In each episode the granitoids are strongly calc-alkaline with low Nb concentrations and low initial $^{87}Sr/^{86}Sr$ ratios, and their common association with coeval andesite and dacite together suggest to Gass and others (e.g. Engel *et al.*, 1980) that, at least in the oldest episode, and by analogy with existing Andean-type regions, such magmatism lay at a plate margin and above an inclined subduction zone. This appears to be confirmed by the presence of narrow, discontinuous zones of ophiolite identifying the original oceanic tracts, yet palaeomagnetic studies and geological correlations across the belts indicate that little or no rotation, or relative displacement, took place. Perhaps the openings represent little more than incipient stages of the Wilson cycle of plate tectonics, when, however, we should expect the episodes of plutonism to be short-lived.

Yet another example of the method has been its recent use to unravel the history of the Protoerozoic of Sweden (Wilson, 1980). There, granitoids of several age groups have the geochemical characteristics of, separately, I- or S-types. A particularly well documented case (Nyström, 1982) is that of the I-type tonalitic batholiths of mid-Proterozoic age, and post-orogenic in relation to the Svecokarelian (*ca.* 1700 Ma). In full measure these record an Andinotype orogenic environment including the familiar volcanic association and the fracture control of the high-level emplacement of the plutons. It is a reasonable conceptual step to draw the conclusion that this identifies an ocean-continental, convergent-plate juncture, active between *ca.* 1700 and 1600 Ma (Gorbatschev, 1980). It would surely be worth searching for the corresponding hinterland belt of S-type granites!

Amongst the non-I-types in Sweden there are the anorogenic rapakivi granites which, though having the high initial $^{87}Sr/^{86}Sr$ and the high K/Na ratios expected of granitoids of crustal source, are not peraluminous and have the high feric/ferrous iron ratio more typical of I-types. Furthermore, they have a highly contrasted relationship to coeval gabbros. These rapakivi granites are thought to have been generated by magmatism initiated in the mantle during periods of tension (Kornfält, 1976), and involved crustal contributions during upwelling in a tensional regime. That such a hypothesis can be reasonably entertained reminds us to be aware of the alternative model for all encratonic magmatism — the possibility that deep-faults trigger crustal and sub-crustal melting (Leake 1978 and see p. 32).

The method of identifying actualistic counterparts, as used in Sweden, is not new, and a number of studies have compared granitoid composition, plutonic sequence and volcanic association in ancient mobile belts with the Cordilleran situation; e.g. Bridgwater, Esher and Watterson (1973) compare the Proterozoic Ketilidian mobile belt with that of the Andean and its granitoid batholiths, whilst Hietanen (1975) identifies a cordilleran-type marginal-arc situation in the mid-Proterozoic of Finland. Both take the conceptual step of identifying a plate juncture. What we may hope for is that the more precise use of the chemical criteria of Chappell and White (loc. cit., p. 20) will refine these comparative studies by identifying the several components of the plutonic association in ancient mobile belts just as is being done for the Phanerozoic.

For example Dalziel and De Wit (1976) present cogent arguments for regarding the "Rocas Verdes" marginal basin in South Chile as a modern counterpart of Archaean greenstone belts, and part of their case rests on recognizing the similitude of the granitoid association at these very different times in earth history. However, there is likely to be a compositional contrast between the tonalite-trondhjemite association (see Barker, 1979) of the Achaean and the tonalite-granodiorite association of the Cordilleran Mesozoic, as is indeed indicated by contrasts in isotopic composition (Allegre and Othman, 1980) and also by the K/Na ratios, which remain low in the former but increase in the latter during the evolution of respective rock suites.

Conclusions

Several themes thread this essay. One has been illustrated by the frequent reference to the fault control of intrusion. Within the detail of the outcrop, fractures and their intersections have often been shown to have focused intrusion and located contacts (e.g. Pitcher and Bussell, 1977) whilst, on the regional scale, major lithologic and structural boundaries clearly locate entire batholiths. Some of the major faults have been envisaged as so deeply penetrating the crust as to focus the upwelling of magma, even to promote the very melting itself by uplifting and juxtaposing rocks from different thermal levels (Leake, 1978).

Furthermore the field evidence is particularly strong that granite intrusion is often associated with the tensional stage in orogenesis and the concomitant uplift. As noted above, the Caledonian of Scotland and Ireland provides a clear example where the uplifting of fault-blocks, and the consequent rapid erosion, has been associated with an important, if short-lived episode of granite intrusion — all post-closure in plate-tectonic terms.

If high angle, deep-faults are important in granite emplacement, low-angle thrusting is probably more so, though largely from the point of view of providing one of the mechanisms of thickening the continental crust than providing conduits for magma. It is this thickening that leads inescapably to uplift and erosion and the deep exposure of Hercynotype belts (but see Zwart and Dornsiepen, 1978, p. 65).

It is just those mobile belts, which have been thickened by transverse shortening to provide the slate-belts with their low-pressure metamorphism, that are characteristically associated with S-type granites; witness the examples quoted above from localities as widely separated in time and place as the Yana-Kolyma belt of the Soviet Far East, the Hodgkinson Basin of Queensland, and the inner Piedmont of the Appalachians. How else than by such thickening are we to explain the build up of sufficient heat in the lower crust to produce regional metamorphism and the associated Granite Series to which S-types ultimately belong — and far away from the influence of active ocean-continent subduction zones?

Quite another type of crustal thickening occurs in mobile belts which have not been greatly shortened transversally: the central Andes provides a prime example (Cobbing *et al.*, 1981). The Andean orogenic root is likely to consist of underplated material of igneous aspect, derived from either subducted oceanic crust or mantle wedge. The true "sialic" crust is not necessarily very thick under the Andes so that there may never have been metasedimentary material available for melting in this situation, only the isotopically uniform, dioritic rocks of the "subcreted" underplate.

Returning to the main theme, this survey indicates that the granite-types, as rather over-simply designated above, can be widely recognized and do indeed relate to specific geological environments. Of course the relationship is not absolute, and it will have been noted that the S- and I-types, for example, are not wholly spatially exclusive. Nevertheless, I-type granitoids of the Andinotype orogenic environment are less likely to be accompanied by coeval S-types, than the latter are to be with I-types in the Hercynotype context. Such a finding is in accord with the expectation that, in marginal plutono-volcanic arcs, the material of the underplate will be a more important source of melts than the over-lying "sialic" crust, while real thickening of the continental crust in Hercynotype belts ensures that a variety of crustal components are available as source rocks.

Where I- and S-types do so occur together, and where there is some separation in time, it has been surmised that the S-type magmas were "wetter" and less hot than those of the associated I-types. This has been given a theoretical respectability by Clemens and Wall (1981) who point out that it reflects the lower stability range of biotite — in the quartz-bearing peraluminous source rocks of S-type melts — relative to that of hornblende — in the intermediate to basic source-materials of I-type melts. Clearly metasediments will melt at lower temperatures than meta-volcanics and will be the richer in water content.

Furthermore, in such examples of coexistence, as in Portugal and France, the I-types concerned are rarely so calc-alkaline or so expanded compositionally as those of the Cordilleran association proper. This was confirmed by Wones (1980) in reporting his contrast of the granitoids of the Sierra Nevada and New England (U.S.A.), the different geological contexts of which have already been remarked on. Despite the fact that the compositional latitude permitted by a general thesis involving the remelting of a variety of source rocks goes far to explain the observed variation in granitoid types, I restate my belief that these New England rocks, like those of Caledonia proper, need to be separately identified (Table I). This is not only because of the strong environmental contrast with that of the American cordillera on the one hand, and the Caledonides of Europe on the other, but the rocks are also different, being rather silica-rich, biotite granites with a narrow compositional range (Table I), though with a remarkably contrasted compositional relationship with lesser bodies of hornblende gabbro and diorite. Initial $^{87}Sr/^{86}Sr$ ratios tend to vary within single plutons, but only within the range 0·705 to 0·707. Of considerable interest is the finding that such granitoids in their special environment are not often associated with economic concentrations of ore metals.

In short, this "Caledonian-type" is to be regarded as a sub-type of I-type granitoids, and typical of the late, uplift stage of the orogenic process.

It cannot be surprising that granite types reflect their environment and that their rock assemblages and chemical compositions provide one of the determinant characteristics of mobile belts (Fig. 7) (Pitcher, 1979). A simplified model follows.

First it should be noted that under the conditions of the low heat flow to be expected in an accretionary wedge, in an Alpinotype mobile belt, melting of the new crustal rocks cannot be expected. When, as in the Outer Belt of south-west Japan or in the Southern Uplands of Scotland (see Brown et al., 1979), or in the Sanak-Baranot belt of Alaska, granites do appear in such a wedge, then it would seem likely that the latter had been obducted over a sliver of old continental crust.

In the oceanic environment of volcanic arcs, plagiogranites appear, though in small volume, when mature arcs develop a sufficiently thick crust to permit remelting and recycling above a subduction zone.

At continental margins whenever subduction energetics increase to the extent of providing sufficient heat and water to trigger remelting of underplate material, great volumes of relatively hot, dry, I-type magmas are produced, isotopically uniform, but with a wide range of bulk composition dependent on the degree of partial melting. Though episodic, such magmatism is of long overall duration. Rock sequences are built up with a progressive change in composition in relation to time, and also distance from the plate edge in response to increasing crustal thickness.

Farther inside the continent extensional basins, in which great thicknesses of sediment have been trapped, close by collision. A combination of the stopping of the convection cell (Dennis and Jacoby, 1980) and thickening due to compression leads to heat being impounded, so that S-type magmas are generated by crustal fusion, often as terms in a Granite Series, and with a close temporal and spatial connec-

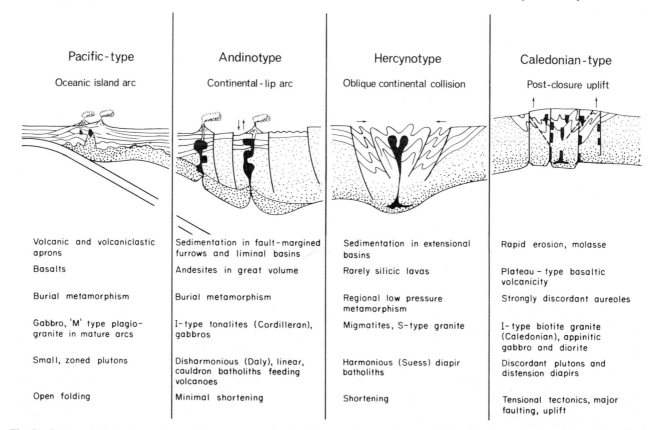

| Pacific-type | Andinotype | Hercynotype | Caledonian-type |
Oceanic island arc	Continental-lip arc	Oblique continental collision	Post-closure uplift
Volcanic and volcaniclastic aprons	Sedimentation in fault-margined furrows and liminal basins	Sedimentation in extensional basins	Rapid erosion, molasse
Basalts	Andesites in great volume	Rarely silicic lavas	Plateau - type basaltic volcanicity
Burial metamorphism	Burial metamorphism	Regional low pressure metamorphism	Strongly discordant aureoles
Gabbro, 'M' type plagio-granite in mature arcs	I-type tonalites (Cordilleran), gabbros	Migmatites, S-type granite	I-type biotite granite (Caledonian), appinitic gabbro and diorite
Small, zoned plutons	Disharmonious (Daly), linear, cauldron batholiths feeding volcanoes	Harmonious (Suess) diapir batholiths	Discordant plutons and distension diapirs
Open folding	Minimal shortening	Shortening	Tensional tectonics, major faulting, uplift

Fig. 7   Cartoon depicting the various geological environments of Phanerozoic granitic rocks. Notional changes in composition of the crust above an assumed Moho are indicated by density of the stipple, and under the continental lip the denser stipple represents underplated material. In the Andinotype model a wedge of lithospheric mantle is presumed to overlie the subduction zone.

tion with regional deformation and metamorphism. As might be expected, such relatively "wet" and low-temperture magmas are not often expressed by volcanic assemblages. Neither may plutonism be so long lasting, or as voluminous, as in marginal arcs.

After closure, cessation of lateral movement and compression will lead to relaxation, even tensional tectonics, and rapid uplift. The latter leads to melting within the ancient crystalline basement of the crust and the production of highly siliceous magmas — of the type characteristic of the latter stages of the evolution of the Caledonian mobile belt. Such melting may result from adiobatic decompression but doubtless sub-crustal, basic magmas are also instrumental in locally introducing heat into the crust along major fault lines: these are represented by the small bodies of wet basaltic magma crystallizing as hornblende gabbro and diorite (the appinite suite), and sometimes by considerable volumes of basic lava.

The final act in the plutonic cycle in these continental orogenic environments is represented by the intrusion of A-type, alkali-granite, in small volume but connected with localized volcanicity. The late appearance of such highly evolved magmas might suggest that they are derived by some process of localized remelting of still hot, but now depleted lower crustal rocks, in response to mantle diapirs rising into the stabilizing but deeply faulted crust.

Though much of the above typology may turn out to be a philosophical abstraction it does point some direction in dealing with the vast amount of regional geological research, and with the geochemical follow-up which needs to be completed before we can fully understand the separate genesis of the several types of granite, the relation between these and the different metal-ore concentrations and the changing role of the granite types in geological history. Not least it may represent the only way of discovering the nature of the continental lower crust.

Acknowledgement

My education in matters concerning granite has been greatly advanced by attendance at the various meetings of the Circum-Pacific Plutonism Project, IGCP Project 30, organized by Dr Paul Bateman of the U.S. Geological Survey: to him my sincere thanks.

References

Agar, R. (1979). La mineralización de cobre y la super-unidad Linga del Batolito de la Costa. *Bol. Geol. Soc. Perú* **62**, 45–62.

Aguirre, L. (In Press). Granitoids of Chile. *In* "Circum-Pacific Plutonic Terranes" (Roddick, J.A., ed.) *Spec. Pap. Geol. Soc. Am.* **193**.

Aguirre, L., Charrier, R., Davidson, J., Mpodozis, A., Rivano, S., Thiele, R., Ridy, E., Vergara, M. and Vincente, J.C. (1974). Andean magmatism: its paleogeographic and structural setting in the central part (30°–35°S) of the southern Andes. *Pacific Geol.* **8**, 1–38.

Allegre, C.J. and Othman, D.B. (1980). Nd–Sr isotopic relationship in granitoid rocks and continental crust developments: a chemical approach to orogenesis. *Nature, London* **286**, 335–342.

Aparicio, A., Barrera, J.L., Casquet, C., Peinado, M. and Tinao, J.M. (1977). Caracterización geoquímica del plutonismo postmetamorphico del sul del macizo hespérico. *Studia Geologica* **12**, 9–36.

Aramaki, S., Takahashi, M. and Nozawa, T. (1977). Kumano acidic rocks and Okueyama complex; two examples of the granitic rocks in the outer zone of Japan. *In* "Plutonism in Relation to Volcanism and Metamorphism" (Yamada, N., ed.). Circum-Pacific Plutonism Project, Toyama, Japan.

Armstrong, R.L., Taubeneck, W.H. and Hales, P.O. (1977). Rb–Sr and K–Ar geochronology of Mesozoic granitic rocks and their Sr isotopic composition, Oregon, Washington and Idaho. *Bull. geol. Soc. Am.* **88**, 397–411.

Arthaud, F. and Matte, P.L. (1977). Late Palaeozoic strike-slip faulting in southern Europe and northern Africa: results of a right-lateral shear zone beween the Appalachians and the Urals. *Bull. geol. Soc. Am.* **88**, 1305–1320.

Atherton, M.P. and Tarney, J. (1979). "Origin of granite batholiths: geochemical evidence". Shiva Publishing, Orpington, Kent, 148p.

Barker, F. (1979). Trondhjemite: definition, environment and hypothesis of origin. *In* "Trondhjemites, Dacites and Related Rocks", (Barker, F., ed.) Dev. in Petrol. Elsevier, Amsterdam, 6, 1–12.

Bateman, P.C. (1980). Geologic and geophysical constraints on models for the origin of the Sierra Nevada Batholith, California. *In* "The geotectonic development of California" (Ernst, W.G., ed.). Prentice Hall, London, pp. 71–86.

Bateman, P.C. and Clark, L.D. (1974). Stratigraphic and structural setting of the Sierra Nevada Batholith, California. *Pacific Geol.* **8**, 79–90.

Beckinsale, R.D. (1979). Granite magmatism in the tin belt of Southeast Asia. *In* "Origin of Granite Batholiths: Geochemical Evidence" (Atherton, M.P. and Tarney, J. eds). Shiva Publishing, Orpington, Kent, pp. 34–44.

Beckinsale, R.D., Suensilpong, S., Nakapadongrat, S. and Walsh, J.N. (1979). Geochronology and geochemistry of granite magmatism in Thailand in relation to a plate tectonic model. *J. geol. Soc. London* **136**, 529–540.

Beliy, V.F. (1978). "Formation and tectonics of the Okhotsk-Chutkotka volcanic belt". "Nauka", Moscow, 212 pp. (in Russian).

Bell, K., Blenkinsop, J. and Strong, D.F. (1977). The geochronology of some granitic bodies from eastern Newfoundland and its bearing on Appalachian evolution. *Can. J. Earth Sci.* **14**, 456–476.

Bignell, J.D. and Snelling, N.J. (1977). Geochronology of Malayan granites. *Overseas Geol. miner. Resour. London* **47**, 71 pp.

Blaxland, A.B., Aftalion, M. and van Breemen, O. (1979). Pb isotopic composition of feldspars from Scottish Caledonian granites, and the nature of the underlying crust. *Scott. J. Geol.* **15**, 139–151.

Bridgwater, D., Esher, A. and Watterson, J. (1973). Tectonic displacements and thermal activity in two contrasting Proterozoic mobile belts from Greenland. *Phil. Trans. R.Soc. Lond.* **A273**, 513–533.

Bromley, A.V. (1975). Tin mineralization of western Europe: is it related to Crustal Subduction? *Trans. Inst. Min. Metall.* **84**, B28-30.

Brown, G.C. (1979). Geochemical and geophysical constraints on the origin and evolution of Caledonian granites. *In* "The Caledonides of the British Isles — Reviewed" (Harris, A.L. *et al.*, eds). Scottish Academic Press, Edinburgh, pp. 645–651.

Brown, G.C. and Hennessy, J. (1978). The initiation and thermal diversity of granite magmatism. *Phil. Trans. R. Soc. Lond. A.* **288**, 631–643.

Brown, G.C. and Locke, C.A. (1979). Space-time variations in British Caledonian granites: some geophysical correlations. *Earth Planet. Sci. Lett.* **45**, 67–79.

Brown, G.C., Plant, J.A. and Thorpe, R.S. (1980). Plutonism in the British Caledonides: space, time and geochemistry. *In* "The Caledonides in the U.S.A." *In* (Wones, D.R., ed.) *Mem. Virginia Poly. Inst. State Univ.* **2**, 157–166.

Bussell, M.A., Pitcher, W.S. and Wilson, P.A. (1976). Ring complexes of the Peruvian Coastal Batholith: a long standing subvolcanic regime. *Can J. Earth Sci.* **13**, 1020–30.

Capdevila, R. (1969). Le metamorphisme régional progressif et les granites dans le segment hercynien de Galice Nord oriental. Thèses, Univ. Montpellier, 430 pp.

Capdevilla, R. and Floor, P. (1970). Les différents types des granites hercynians et leur distribution dans le nord-ouest de l'Espagne. *Bol. Geol. Min. Inst. Geol. Min. España.* **81**, 101–111.

Chappell, B.W. (1978). Granitoids from the Moonbi District, New England Batholith, Eastern Australia. *J. geol. Soc. Aust.* **25**, 267–284.

Chauris, L. (1977). Les associations paragenetiques dans la metallogenie varisque du massif Amoricain. *Mineral Deposita (Berl.)* **12**, 353–371.

Chivas, A.R. (1978). Porphyry-Copper mineralisation at the Koloula Igneous Complex, Guadalcanal, Solomon Islands. *Econ. Geol.* **73**, 645–677.

Clemens, J.D. and Wall, V.J. (1981). Origin and crystallisation of some peraluminous (S-type) granite magmas. *Canad. Mineral.* **19**, 111–131.

Cobbing, E.J. (1979). Comparison between Sumatra and the Andes. *J. geol. Soc. London.* **136**, 583–585.

Cobbing, E.J., Pitcher, W.S., Wilson, J.J., Baldock, J.W., Taylor, W.P., McCourt, W. and Snelling, N.J. (1981). "The geology of the Western Cordillera of northern Peru". *Overseas Mem. Inst. Geol. Sci.* **No.5**, 143 pp.

Compston, W. and Chappell, B.W. (1979). Sr-isotope evolution of granitoid source rocks. *In* "The Earth: Its Origin, Structure and Evolution" (McElhinny, M.W., ed.). Academic Press, London and New York, pp. 377–426.

Coney, P.J. (1972). Cordilleran tectonics and North American plate motion. *Am. J. Sci.* **272**, 603–628.

Corretge, J.M., Uqidos, J.M. and Martinez, F. (1977). Les séries granitiques varisques du secteur Centre-Occidental espagnol. *In* "La Chaîne Varisque d'Europe Moyenne et Occidentale". *Col. Intern. C.N.R.S. Paris* **No. 243**, 453–462.

Currie, K.L. and Pajari, G.E. (1981). Anatectic peraluminous granites from the Carmanville area, northeastern Newfoundland. *Canad. Mineral.* **19**, 147–161.

Dalmayrac, B., Laubacher, G. and Marocco, R. (1980). Charactères généraux de l'évolution géologique des Andes perviennes. *Trav. Doc. O.R.S.T.O.M. Paris,* **No. 122**, 501 pp.

Dalziel, I.W.D., de Wit, M.J. and Palmer, K.F. (1974). A fossil marginal basin in the southern Andes. *Nature, London* **250**, 291–294.

Debon, F. (1980). Genesis of three concentrically-zoned granitoid plutons of Cauterets-Panticasta (French and Spanish Western Pyrenees). *Geol. Rundshau* **69**, 107–130.

Debon, F. and Le Fort, P. (In Press). A chemical-mineralogical classification of granitoid rocks and associations.

Denis, J.G. and Jacoby, W.R. (1980). Geodynamic processes and deformation in orogenic belts. *Tectonophysics* **63**, 261–273.

Den Tex, E. (1977). Le socle poly-cyclique et son rôle dans (evolution de la chaîne varisque en Galice (Espagne du N.W.). *In* "La chaîne vasisque d'Europe Moyenne et occidentale". Coll. intern. C.N.R.S. *Paris* **243**, 441–451.

Dewey, J.F. and Burke, K.C.A. (1973). Tibetian, Variscan, and Precambrian basement reactivation: products of continental collision. *J. Geol.* **81**, 683–692.

Didier, J. and Lameyre, J. (1969). Les granites du Massif Central francais: étude comparée des leucogranites et granodiorites. *Contr. Mineral Petrol.* **24**, 219–238.

Didier, J. and Lameyre, J. (1969). Les granites du Massif Central francais: étude comparée des leucogranites et granodiorites. *Contr. Mineral Petrol.* **24**, 1–6.

Dietrich, V., Honegger, K. and Trommsdorff, V. (1981). Magmatism, metamorphism and mountain-building in the Ladakh-Himalayas. *In* "Symposium on Mountain-Building", Zurich 1981 (Abs).

Duthou, J.L. (1977). Géochronologie Rb/Sr et géochimie de granitoïdes d'un segment de la chaîne varisque. Relation avec le metamorphisme: le Nord-Limousin (Massif Central Francais). *Ann. Scient. Univ. Clermont-Ferrand* **63**, 244p.

Egeler, G.C. and De Booy, R. (1956). Geology and petrology of part of the southern Cordillera Blanca, Peru. *Verh. K. Ned. Geol. Minjnb. Genoot. Geol. Ser.* **17**, 11–86.

Engel, A.E.J., Dixon, T.H. and Stern, R.J. (1980). Late Precambrian evolution of Afro-Arabian crust from ocean arc to craton. *Bull. geol. Soc. Am.* **91**, 699–706.

Eskola, P.E. (1932). On the origin of granitic magmas. *Mitt. Mineral. Petrog.* **42**, 455–81.

Flood, R.H. and Shaw, S.E. (1977). Two "S-type" granite suites with low initial $^{87}Sr/^{86}Sr$ ratios from the New England Batholith, Australia. *Contr. Mineral. Petrol.* **61**, 163–173.

Frutos, J. and Samaniego, A. (1980). Andean mineralisation episodes related to the sea-floor spreading-rate variations. Geowissenschaffliches Lateinamerika Kolloquium, Heidelberg, 1980 (Abs), 32.

Fullagar, P.D. and Butler, J.R. (1979). 325 to 265 m.y.-old post metamorphic granitic plutons in the Piedmont of the southeastern Appalachians. *Am. J. Sci.* **279**, 161–185.

Gabrielse, H. and Reesor, J.E. (1974). The nature and setting of granitic plutons in the central and eastern parts of the Canadian Cordillera. *Pacific Geol.* **8**, 109–38.

Gansser, A. (1976). The great suture zone between Himalaya and Tibet: a preliminary account. In "Ecologie et Géologie de l'Himalaya", *Colloques internationaux du C.N.R.S.* **No. 268**, 181–191.

Gass, I.G. (1977). The evolution of the Pan African crystalline basement in N.E. Africa and Arabia. *J. geol. Soc. Lond.* **134**, 129–138.

Gastil, R.G., Krummenacher, D., Doupont, J. and Bushes, J. (1974). The batholith belt of Southern California and Western Mexico. *Pacific Geol.* **8**, 73–78.

Gastil, R.G., Phillips, R.P. and Allison, E.C. (1975). Reconnaissance geology of the State of Baja California. *Mem. geol. Soc. Am.* **140**, 170 pp.

Gorbatschev, R. (1980). The Precambrian development of southern Sweden. *Geol. Foren. Stockholm. Forh.* **102**, 2, 129–136.

Groome, D.R. and Hall, A. (1974). The geochemistry of the Devonian Lavas of the northern Lorne Plateau, Scotland. *Mineralog. Mag.* **39**, 621–40.

Hall, A. (1971). The relationship between geothermal gradient and the composition of granitic magmas in orogenic belts. *Contr. Mineral. Petrol.* **32**, 186–192.

Halliday, A.N., Aftalion, M., van Breeman, O. and Jocelyn, J. (1979). Petrogenetic significance of Rb and U-Pb isotope systems in the 400 Ma-old British Isles granitoids and their hosts. *In* "The Caledonides of the British Isles — reviewed" (Harris, A.L. *et al.*, eds). Scottish Academic Press, Edinburgh, pp. 653–662.

Halliday, A.N., Stephens, W.E. and Harmon, R.S. (1980). Rb–Sr and O isotopic relationships in three zoned Caledonian granite plutons, Southern Uplands, Scotland: Evidence for varying sources and hybridisation of magmas. *J. geol. Soc. Lond.* **137**, 329–348.

Halliday, A.N., Stephens, W.E. and Harmon, R.S. (1981). Istotopic and chemical constraints on the development of peraluminous Caledonian and Acadian granites. *Can. Mineral.* **19**, 205–216.

Halpern, M. and Fuenzalida, R. (1978). Rubidium-Strontium geochronology of a transect of the Chilean Andes between latitudes 45° and 46°S. *Earth Plant. Sci. Lett.* **41**, 60–66.

Harmon, R.S. and Halliday, A.N. (1980). Strontium and oxygen isotopic relationships in the British late Caledonian granites. *Nature, London,* **283**, 21–35.

Harrison, M.T. and Clarke, G.K. (1979). A model of the thermal effects of igneous intrusion and uplift as applied to Quottoon pluton, British Columbia. *Can. J. Earth Sci.* **16**, 411–420.

Hawkes, J.R. and Dangerfield, J. (1978). The Variscan granites of south-west England: a progress report. *Proc. Ussher Soc.* **4**, 158–171.

Henderson, R.A. (1980). Structural outline and summary geological history for northeastern Australia. *In* "The Geology and Geophysics of Northeastern Australia" (Henderson, R.A. and Stephenson, P.J. eds). *Geol. Soc. Aust. (Qd. Div.), Brisbane,* 1–26.

Hietanen, A. (1975). Generation of potassium-poor magmas in the Northern Sierra Nevada and the Svecofennian of Finland. *J. Res. U.S. geol. Surv.* **3**, 631–645.

Hine, R., Williams, I.S., Chapell, B.W. and White, A.J.R. (1979). Contrasts between I- and S-type granitoids of the Kosciusko batholith. *J. geol. Soc. Austr.* **25**, 219–234.

Hudson, C. (1979). Zoneamiento de la melalogenia Andina del Perú. *Bol. Soc. Geol. Perú* **60**, 61–72.

Hudson, T. (In Press). Calc-alkaline plutonism along the Pacific rim of southern Alaska. *In* "Circum-Pacific Plutonic Terranes" (Roddick, J.A., ed.). *Spec. Pap. geol. Soc. Am.* **193.**

Hutchison, C.S. (1977). Granite emplacement and tectonic subdivision of Peninsular Malaysia. *Bull. geol. Soc. Malaysia* **9**, 187–208.

Hutchison, C.S. and Taylor, D. (1978). Metallogenesis in S.E. Asia. *J. geol. Soc. London* **135**, 407–428.

Hutton, D. (1981). The main Donegal Granite: lateral wedging in a syn-magmatic shear zone. *J. Struct. geol.* **3**, 93.

Irving, E.M. (1975). Structural evolution of the northernmost Andes, Colombia. *U.S. geol. Surv. Prof. Pap.* **846**, 47 pp.

Irving, E., Monger, J.W.H. and Yole, R.W. (1980). New paleomagnetic evidence for displaced terranes in British Columbia. *In* "The Continental Crust and its Mineral Deposits" (Strangway, D.W., ed.). *Spec. Pap. Geol. Assoc. Canada.* **20**, 441–456.

Ishihara, S. (1977). The magnetite-series and ilmenite-series granitic rocks. *Mining Geol. (Japan)* **27**, 293–305.

Ishihara, S. and Terashima, S. (1977). Chemical variation of the Cretaceous granitoids across southwestern Japan: Shirakawa-Toki-Okazaki transection. *J. geol. Soc. Japan* **83**, 1–18.

Kesler, S.E., Jones, L.M. and Walker, R.L. (1975). Intrusive rocks associated with porphyry copper mineralisation in island arc areas. Econ. Geol. **70**, 515–526.

Kistler, R.W. and Peterman, Z.E. (1978). Reconstruction of crustal blocks of California on the basis of initial strontium isotopic compositions of Mesozoic granitic rocks. *Prof. Pap. U.S. Geol. Surv.* **1071**, 1–17.

Kornfält, K.A. (1976). Petrology of the Ragunda rapakivi massif, central Sweden. *Sveriges geologiska undersökning C725*, 1–111.

Korsch, R.J. and Harrington, H.J. (In Press). Granite belts in the New England orogen, Eastern Australia.

La Roche, H, de (1977). Granites' chemistry through multicationic diagrams. *Sciences de la Terre, Série Informatique Geologique* **13**, 65–88.

La Roche, H. de, Leterrier, J., Grandclaude, P. and Marchal, M. (1980). A classification of volcanic and plutonic rocks using $R_1 R_2$ diagrams and major element analyses. Its relation with current nomenclature. *Chem. Geol.* **29**, 183–210.

La Roche, H. de, Stussi, J.M. and Chauris, L. (1980b). Les granites à deux micas hercyniens Francois. *Sci. de la Terre, Nancy* **24**, 5b–121.

Leake, B.E. (1978). Granite emplacement: the granites of Ireland and their origin. *In* "Crustal Evolution in Northwestern Britain and Adjacent Regions" (Bowes, D.R. and Leake, B.E., eds). *Spec. Iss. Geol. J.* **10**, 221–48.

Lee, D.S. (1977). Chemical compositions of petrographic assemblages of igneous and related rocks in South Korea. *In* "Plutonism in Relation to Volcanism and Metamorphism" (Nozawa, T. and Yamada, N., eds). Toyama, Japan pp. 297–298.

Le Couteur, P.C. and Tempelman-Kluit, D.J. (1976). Rb/Sr ages and a profile of initial $^{87}Sr/^{86}Sr$ ratios for plutonic rocks across the Yukon Crystalline Terrane. *Can. J. Earth Sci.* **13**, 319–330.

Le Fort, P. (1973). Les leucogranites à tourmaline de l'Himalaya sur l'example du granite du Manaslu (Népal central). *Bull. geol. Soc. Fr.* **15**, 5–6, 555–61.

Le Fort, P. (1975). Himalayas: the collided range. Present knowledge of the continental arc. *Amer. J. Sci.* **275–A**, 1–44.

Le Fort, P., Debon, F. and Sonet, J. (1980). The "Lesser Himalayan" cordierite granite belt, topology and age of the pluton of Manserah (Pakistan). *Spec. issue, Geol. Bull. Univ. Peshawar* **13**, 51–61.

Loiselle, M.C. and Ayuso, R.A. (1980). Chemical characteristics of granites across the Merrimack synclinorium, eastern and central Maine. *In* "The Caledonides in the U.S.A." (Wones, D.R., ed.). *Dept. Geol. Sci. Virginia Poly. Inst. Mem.* **2**, 117–122.

Loiselle, M.C. and Wones, D.R. (1979). Characteristics of anorogenic granites. *Abstr. with programs geol. Soc. Am. A.G.M.* **1979**, 539.

Mason, D.R. and McDonald, J.A. (1978). Intrusive rocks and porphyry-copper occurrences of the Papua New Guinea–Solomon Islands region: a reconnaissance study. *Econ. Geol.* **73**, 857–877.

McNutt, R.H., Crocket, J.H., Clark, A.H., Caelles, J.C., Farrar, E., Haynes, S.J. and Zentilli, M. (1975). Initial $^{87}Sr/^{86}Sr$ ratios of plutonic and volcanic rocks of the Central Andes between latitudes 26° and 29°S. *Earth Planet. Sci. Lett.* **27**, 305–313.

Mercado, M. (1978). Cordillera de la Costa entre Chañaral y Caldera. Carta Geologica de Chile No. 27, *Inst. Invest. Geol. Chile.*

Miller, C.F. and Bradfish, L.J. (1980). An inner belt of muscovite-bearing plutons. *Geology* **8**, 412–416.

Milov, A.P. (1971). On the influence of tectonic conditions on the peculiarities of Late Mesozoic granitoidal magmatism of Chukotka. *In* "Mesozoic Tectonogenesis". Magadan pp. 291–295 (in Russian).

Milov, A.P. (1975). "Later Mesozoic granitoidal formations of Chukotka". "Nauka", Novosibirsk, 134 pp. (in Russian).

Mitchell, A.H.G. (1977). Tectonic settings for emplacement of Southeast Asian tin granites. *Bull. geol. Soc. Malaysia* **9**, 123–140.

Murakami, N. (1979) (ed.) "Mesozoic Acid Igneous Activity in Japan". *Mem. geol. Soc. Japan* No. 17, 302 pp.

Murakami, N. (1979). Outline of the longitudinal variation of late Mesozoic to Paleogene acid igneous rocks in eastern Chugoku, Southwest Japan. *In* "Mesozoic Acid Igneous Activity in Japan" (Murakami, N., ed.). *Mem. geol. Soc. Japan* No. 17, 3–18.

Nanjing University (1974). Granitic rocks of different geological periods of southeastern China and their genetic relations to certain metallic deposits. *Sci. Sinica* **17**, 55–72.

Ncalc, E.R.W. and Pajari, G. (1972). *In* "The Appalachian Structural Province: Granite Intrusions". (Williams, H., Kennedy, M.J. and Neale, E.R., eds). *Geol. Assoc. Canada Spec Paper* **11**, 181–262.

Nyström, J.O. (1982). Post-Svecokarelian Andinotype evolution in central Sweden. *Geol. Rdsch.* **71**, 141–157.

Orsini, J.B. (1979a). Existence de trois associations magmatiques dans les granitoïdes post viséen moyen (groupe des granodiorites — monzogranites) de la chaîne vasisque francaise. *C.R. Acad. Sc. Paris* **289–D**, 981–984.

Orsini, J.B. (1979b). Existence d'une zonation spatiale de la chaîne varisque francaise aux temps carbonifères à l'aide de marquers plutoniques. Implications géodynamiques. *C.R. Acad. Sc. Paris* **289 D**, 1109–1112.

Oba, N. (1977). Emplacement of granitic rocks in the outer zone of southwest Japan and geological significance. *J. Geol.* **85**, 383–393.

Oba, N., Tomita, K. and Yamamoto, M. (1978). Geologic environments of granitic rocks in the outer zone of southwest Japan. *Proc. 3rd Regional Conference Geol. Mineral Resources Southeast Asia, Bangkok 1978*, 275–279.

Page, B.G.N., Bennett, J.D., Cameron, N.R., Bridge, D.McC., Jeffery, D.H., Keats, W. and Thaib, J. (1979). A review of the main structural and magmatic features of northern Sumatra. *J. geol. Soc. Lond.* **136**, 569–579.

Pankhurst, R.J. (1979). Isotope and trace element evidence for the origin and evolution of Caledonian granites in the Southern Highlands. *In* "Origin of Granite Batholiths: Geochemical Evidence" (Atherton, M.P. and Tarney, J., eds). Shiva Publishing Limited, pp. 18–33.

Parfenov, L.M., Voinova, I.P., Natal'in, B.A. and Semenov, D.F. (1978). Geodynamics of the north-eastern Asia in Mesozoic and Cenozoic time and the nature of volcanic belts. *J. Phy. Earth* **26**, Suppl. 503–525.

Perfit, M.R. and Lawrence, J.R. (1979). Oxygen isotope evidence for meteoric water interaction with the Captains Bay pluton, Aleutian Island. *Earth Planet. Sci. Lett.* **45**, 16–22.

Perfit, M.R., Brueckner, H., Lawrence, J.R. and Kay, R.W. (1980). Trace element and isotope variations in a zoned pluton and associated volcanic rocks, Unalaska Island, Alaska: a model for fractionation in the Aleutian calc-alkaline suite. *Contrib. Mineral. Petrol.* **73**, 69–87.

Pigeon, R.T. and Aftalion, M. (1978). Cognetic and inherited zircon U-Pb systems in granites: Palaeozoic granites of Scotland and England. *In* "Crustal Evolution in Northwestern Britain and Adjacent Regions" (Bowes, D.R. and Leake, B.E., eds). *Geol. J. Spec. Issue* **10**, 183–248.

Pitcher, W.S. and Berger, A.R. (1972). "The Geology of Donegal: a study of Granite Emplacement and Unroofing". Wiley Interscience, London, 4–35 pp.

Pitcher, W.S. and Bussell, M.A. (1977). Structural control of batholith emplacement in Peru: a review. *J. geol. Soc. London* **133**, 249–56.

Pitcher, W.S. and Taylor, W.P. (1979). The episodic generation of magma sequences in the Coastal Batholith of Peru. Abs with Programs. *Geol. Soc. Am. A.G.M. San Diego* **92**, 496.

Pitcher, W.S. (1978). The anatomy of a batholith. *J. geol. Soc. Lond.* **135**, 157–182.

Rast, N. and Grant, R. (1977). Variscan-Appalachian and Alleghenian Deformation in the Northern Appalachians. In "La chaîne varisque d'Europe moyenne et occidentale". *Coll. intern. C.N.R.S. Rennes,* No. 243, 583–586.

Read, H.H. (1948). Granites and granites. *In* "Origin of Granite" (Gilluly, J.C., ed.). *Mem. geol. Soc. Am.* **28**, 1–19.

Reynolds, P.H., Zentilli, M. and Muecke, G.K. (1981). K–Ar and $^{40}Ar/^{39}Ar$ geochronology of granitoid rocks from southern Nova Scotia: its bearing on the geological evolution of the Meguma Zone of the Appalachians. *Cand. J. Earth Sci.* **18**, 386–394.

Ribeiro, A. *et al.* (1979). "Introduction à la géologie générale du Portugal". Serv. Geol. Portugal Lisbon, 114 pp.

Richards, D.N.G. (1980). Palaeozoic granitoids of northeastern Australia. *In* "Geology and Geophysics of Northeastern Australia" (Henderson, R.A. and Stephenson, P.J., eds). *Geol. Soc. Aust. Qd. Div. Brisbane*, 229–246.

Roddick, J.A. and Hutchinson, W.N. (1974). Setting of the Coast Plutonic Complex, British Columbia. *Pacific Geol.* **8**, 91–108.

Rogers, J.J.W. and Greenberg, J.K. (1981). Trace elements in continental margin magmatism: Part III. Alkali granites and their relation to cratonization: summary. *Bull. geol. Soc. Am.* **92**, 6–9.

Sharma, K.K. and Kumar, S. (1978). Contributions to the geology of north-western Himalaya. *Himalayan Geology* **8**, 252–287.

Shibata, K. (1968). K–Ar age determinations on granitic and

metamorphic rocks in Japan. Rept. *Geol. Surv. Japan* No. 227, 71 pp.

Shibata, K. and Ishihara, S. (1979). Initial $^{87}Sr/^{86}Sr$ ratios of plutonic rocks from Japan. *Contrib. Mineral. Petrol.* **70**, 381–390.

Shilo, N.A. (1979). (ed.). General problems of intrusive magmatism and its relation to tectonics. Abs. Papers XIV Pacific Science Congress, Sec. VIB, Khabarovsk, 163 pp. (in English).

Shilo, N.A. and Milov, A.P. (1977a). Late Mesozoic granitic magmatism in the geological structures of the U.S.S.R. North-East. *Bull. geol. Soc. Malaysia* **9**, 117–122.

Shilo, N.A., Kotlyap, I.N. and Milov, A.P. (1977b). Fundamental features of chemistry and some problems of the relationship between volcanic and plutonic rocks in Okhotsk-Chukotka volcanic belt. *In* "Plutonism in relation to volcanism and metamorphism" (Nozawa, T. and Yamada, N., eds). Toyama, Japan, pp. 297–8.

Shilo, N.A., Milov, A.P. and Sobolev, A.P. (in press). Mesozoic granitoidal magmatism in northeast Asia. *In* "Circum-Pacific Plutonic Terranes" (Roddick, J.A., ed.). *Spec. Pap. geol. Soc. Am.* **193**.

Sinha, K.A., Hanan, B.B., Sans, J.R. and Hall, S.T. (1980). Igneous rocks of the Maryland Piedmont: indicators of crustal evolution. *In* "The Caledonides in the U.S.A." (Wones, D.R., ed.). *Mem. Virginia Poly. Inst. State Univ.* **2**, 131–135.

Smith, T.E. (1979). The geochemistry and origin of the Devonian granitic rocks of southwest Nova Scotia: Summary. *Bull. geol. Soc. Am.* **90**, 424–426.

Snoke, A.W., Kish, S.A. and Secor, D.T. (1980). Deformed Hercynian granitic rocks from the Piedmont of South Carolina. *Am. J. Sci.* **280**, 1018–1034.

Sobolev, A.P. and Kolisnishenko, P.P. (1979). "Mesozoic Granitic Complexes of the South Yana-Kolimsky Fold System". "Nauka", Moscow, 197 pp.

Stibane, F. (1980). Tectonic de los Andes Septentrionales. *In* "Nuevos resultados de la investigación geocientífica alemana en Latinomamérica". Deutsche Forschungs gemeinschaft, Bonn, pp. 91–97.

Stibane, F.R. (1981). K/Ar-Alter von Tonaliten der Cordillera Occidental Kolumbiens und ihre tektonische Deutung. *Zentralbl. Geol. Paläont.* **1**, 3/4, 252–259.

Strong, D.F. (1980). Granitoid rocks and associated mineral deposits of eastern Canada and western Europe. *In* "The Continental Crust and its Mineral Deposits" (Strangway, D.W., ed.). *Geol. Assoc. Canada, Spec. Pap.* **20**, 741–769.

Strong, D.F. and Hanmer, S.K. (1981). The leucogranites of southern Brittany: origin by faulting, frictional heating, fluid flux and fractional melting. *Can. Mineral.* **19**, 163–176.

Sylvester, A.G., Miller, C.F. and Nelson, C.A. (1978). Monzonites of the White-Inyo Range, California and their relation to the calc-alkalic Sierra Nevada batholith. *Bull. geol. Soc. Am.* **89**, 1677–1687.

Takahashi, M., Aramaki, S. and Ishihara, S. (1980). Magnetite-series/Ilmenite-series vs. I-type/S-type granitoids. *In* "Granitic Magmatism and Related Mineralisation" (Ishihara, S. and Takenouchi, S., eds). *Mining Geol. Japan Spec. Iss.* **8**, 13–28.

Tanaka, K. and Nozawa, T. (1977). "Geology and Mineral Resources of Japan". *Geol. Surv. Japan*, Hisamoto, Japan.

Tarney, J., Dalziel, I.W.D. and De Wit, M.J. (1976). Marginal basin "Rocas Verdes" complex from S. Chile: a model for Archaean greenstone belt formation. *In* "The Early History of the Earth" (Windley, B.F., ed). Wiley, London, pp. 131–146.

Tauson, L.V. (1974). The geochemical types of granitoids. *In* "Symposium: Metallisation associated with Acid Magmatism" (Stemprok, M. ed.). *Sb. geol. Ved. Praha*, 221–27.

Taylor, H.P. and Silver, L.T. (1978). Oxygen isotope relationships in the plutonic igneous rocks of the Peninsular Ranges batholith, southern and Baja California. *In:* "Short papers of the fourth international conference, geochronology, cosmochronology, isotope geology" (Zartman, R.E., ed.). *Open File report, U.S. geol. Surv.* 78–701, 423–26.

Thorpe, R.S. and Francis, P. (1979). Variations in Andean andesite compositions and their petrogenetic significance. *Tectonophysics* **67**, 53–70.

Todd, V.R. and Shaw, S.E. (1979). Structural, metamorphic and intrusive framework of the Peninsular Ranges Batholith in southern San Diego County, California. *In* "Mesozoic Crystalline Rocks" (Abbot, P.L. and Todd, U.R., eds). Publ. Dept. Geol. Sci. San Diego State University.

Van Breemen, O. and Bluck, B. (1981). Episodic granite plutonism in the Scottish Caledonides. *Nature, London* **291**, 113–117.

Vashchilov, Y.Y. (1963). Deep-seated faults in the southern Yana-Kolyma fold-belt and the Okhotsk-Chukchi volcanic belt and their role in the emplacement of granitic intrusions. *Sov. Geol.* No. 4 (in Russian).

Wernick, E. and Penalva, F. (1978). Contribuição ao conhecimento das rochas granitóides do sul do Brasil. *Revista Brasileira de Geociências* **8**, 113–133.

White, A.J.R. (1979). Sources of granite magmas. Abstr. with programs. *Geol. Soc. Am. An. Gen. Meet., 1979*, p. 539.

White, A.J.R. and Chappell, B.W. (1977a). Ultrametamorphism and granitoid genesis. *Tectonophysics* **43**, 7–22.

White, A.J.R. and Chappell, B.W. (In Press). Granitoid types and their distribution in the Lachlan fold-belt, south east Australia. *In:* "Circum-Pacific Plutonic Terranes" (Roddick, J.A., ed.). *Spec. Pap. Geol. Soc. Am.* **193**.

White, A.J.R., Chappell, B.W. and Cleary, J.R. (1974). Geologic setting and emplacement of some Australian Palaeozoic batholiths and implications for intrusive mechanisms. *Pacific Geol.* **8**, 159–171.

White, A.J.R., Beams, S.D. and Cramer, J.J. (1977b). Granitoid types and mineralisation with special reference to tin. *In* "Plutonism in Relation to Volanism and Metamorphism" (Nozawa, T. and Yamada, N., eds). Toyama, Japan, pp. 89–100.

Whitney, J.A., Jones, L.M. and Walker, R.L. (1976). Age and origin of the Stone Mountain granite, Lithonia district, Georgia. *Bull. geol. Soc. Am.* **87**, 1067–1077.

Williams, H. and Payne, J.G. (1975). The Twillingate granite and nearby volcanic groups: an island arc complex in northeast Newfoundland. *Can. J. Earth Sci.* **12**, 982–995.

Wilson, M.R. (1980). Granite types in Sweden. *Forh. geol. Foren. Stockholm* **102**, 167–176.

Wolfe, J.A., Manuzon, M.S. and Divis, A.F. (1978). The Taysan porphyry copper deposit, southern Luzon Island, Philippines. *Econ. Geol.* **73**, 608–617.

Woodsworth, G.J. (1979). Metamorphism, deformation and plutonism in the Mount Raleigh pendant, Coast Mountains, British Columbia. *Bull. geol. Surv. Cand.* **295**, 58 pp.

Wones, D.R. (1980). A comparison between granite plutons of New England U.S.A. and the Sierra Nevada batholith, California. *In* "The Caledonides in the U.S.A." (Wones, D.R., ed.). *Dept. Geol. Sci. Virginia Poly. Inst. Mem.* **2**, 123–130.

Wyborn, D. (1979). The mineralogical and chemical relationships of Siluro-Devonian volcanics and granitoids in the Canberra Region (abs.). *In* "Crust and Upper Mantle of Southeast Australia" (Denhan, D. (compiler). *Rec. Bur. Miner. Resour. Aust. 1979/2*, p. 103.

Yan, M.Z., Wu, Y.L. and Li, C.Y. (1980). Metallogenetic systems of tungsten in southeast China and their mineralisation characteristics. *In* "Granite Magmatism and Related Mineralisation". *Min. Geol. Spec. Issue* No. **8**, 215–222.

Zeil, W., Damm, K.W. and Pichowiak, S. (1980). Los plutones de la Cordillera de la Costa al norte de Chile. *In* "Neuvos Resultados de la Investigación Geocientífica Alemana en Latinoamérica", pp. 112–122, Deutsche Forshungsgemeinschaft, Bonn.

Zwart, J.H. (1967). The duality of orogenic belts. *Geol. Mijnbouw* **46**, 283–309.

Zwart, H.J. and Dornsiepen, U.F. (1978). The tectonic framework of central and western Europe. *Geol. Mijnb.* **57**, 627–654.

Seismicity and Mountain Building

Peter Molnar and Wang-Ping Chen

Department of Earth and Planetary Sciences,
Massachusetts Institute of Technology
Massachusetts, U.S.A.

Abstract

We summarize some basic aspects of the seismicity of several individual mountain belts and of much of eastern Asia, with the point of view that seismicity places an important constraint on the physical processes occurring during mountain building. Much of the seismicity of the Himalaya seems to indicate that at present the India plate slides beneath the Himalaya as a coherent entity along a shallow plane. Although some seismicity beneath the Himalaya suggests internal deformation of the overlying mountains or of the region beyond the zone where the India plate remains coherent, at present there does not seem to be active detachment of a crystalline nappe from India, as seems to have occurred earlier at the Main Central and Main Boundary faults. In the Zagros, the seismicity indicates a shortening of the basement beneath the overlying, probably detached, sedimentary cover. If Arabia is sliding beneath Iran along a shallow dipping fault, it does so aseismically. The Tien Shan experiences north–south shortening by thrust faulting and strike-slip faulting caused by the convergence of the Tarim basin to the south and the Paleozoic platform to the north. Seismicity and deformation occur throughout the belt, with the stable areas north and south of it underthrusting the mountain belt. Seismicity in the Peruvian Andes concentrates on the flanks of the mountains. As in the Tien Shan, the belt is two-sided and experiences thrust faulting on both the east and west flanks. Moreover, in both areas fault planes are steep, suggesting greater similarity to the Colorado and Wyoming Rocky Mountains in the early Tertiary than to either the Himalaya at present or the Canadian Rockies and the Sevier belt in the western U.S. in the late Cretaceous. Active normal faulting at high altitudes in the Andes, however, makes them differ from the Tien Shan. The normal faulting is probably a result of buoyancy forces acting on the elevated areas. The north–west Himalaya, Pamir and Hindu Kush in Pakistan, Tadjikistan and Afghanistan show yet more varied and more complicated deformation than the belts described above. A spectrum of types of faulting and widespread seismicity and deformation characterize the region. In many ways it seems to be a miniature version of eastern Asia as a whole.

The seismicity of eastern Asia indicates active deformation in a region 1000 to 3000 km wide between the more stable, essentially aseismic Indian and Eurasian plates. Some of this seismicity and associated deformation is simply and directly attributable to the convergence of these plates. The thrusting in the Himalaya is clearly a result of this convergence, and that in the Tien Shan can also be interpreted as a consequence of it. Seismicity north and east of Tibet indicates a spectrum of fault types that include strike-slip and even normal faulting. Nevertheless the relatively consistent orientations of P and T axes over large areas are consistent with a stress field generated by India's penetration into Eurasia, and accordingly the seismicity can be considered a direct consequence of this penetration. The scattered earthquakes in Tibet, as well as the Quaternary faulting, indicate active normal faulting with east–west extension. This style of deformation probably results from buoyancy forces acting on the elevated and thickened crust of Tibet. Thus the active tectonics of Tibet are due to the penetration of India into Eurasia that caused the high elevations and thick crust, but this crustal shortening seems to have stopped except on the flanks of Tibet.

A study of depths of foci of earthquakes shows that most events occur in the cold outer 15 km of the crust. Deeper events seem to occur in older, colder, more stable shields, in belts where thrust faulting and crustal thickening have advected cold material down, or in the underlying mantle. The lower crust, however, seems usually to be aseismic and probably deforms ductilely. We infer that it is weaker than the region above and below it.

The seismicity of mountain belts is clearly more widespread and deformation is more varied than in oceanic regions. Several simple and obvious factors contribute to the greater complexity of continental regions and to the difficulty in gaining a quantitative description analogous to that of plate tectonics in oceanic regions. One surely is the inadequacy of the historic record of seismicity in portraying the long term seismicity. A second is the large lateral variations in strength due both to lateral variations in temperature and rheology and to inherited zones of weakness. A third is the effect of different strengths of the minerals abundant in the crust and mantle, which may introduce a zone of low strength between the middle crust and uppermost mantle in continental but not oceanic regions. Finally the stresses that balance the gravitational body forces must vary from regions of high to low elevation and of thin to thick crust, thus perturbing the regional stress field. While it is easy to recognize these sources of complexity, our problem for the future is to obtain data that constrain them quantitatively.

I. Introduction

In keeping with the basic geologic doctrine that "the present is the key to the past", our understanding of mountain building is likely to grow rapidly with the study of active belts. At the same time a thorough understanding requires a knowledge of the deep structure and of the processes that occur there. Although much of this information is provided by detailed studies of exhumed belts, we view seismicity as a link between geologic studies of active faulting and those of deeper structure by providing information about the active processes occurring beneath the earth's surface.

For us the word seismicity includes all geologic aspects of earthquakes — not only where and how frequently they occur but also the orientation, extent and amount of faulting involved in particular earthquakes. In Appendix A we give a general discussion of uncertainties and pitfalls in the interpretation of seismic data. As on occasion there has been misuse of seismic data, we think that it is useful to give the reader some simple rules for the cautious use of published seismic data.

This paper is concerned only with those mountain belts that are due directly or indirectly to large-scale convergence of continental masses. We do not discuss the seismicity of the continental rift zones, such as in east Africa, which although mountainous are not related to convergent plate margins. Similarly, our attention is not directed towards those subduction zones where one slab of oceanic lithosphere underthrusts another. There are two main differences between the seismicity of subduction zones and that of continental convergent zones. At subduction zones, usually there is a thin, shallow dipping ($\sim 10°$–$30°$) planar zone of shallow seismicity ($h < 70$ km) that defines a major thrust fault along which underthrusting takes place. Then at greater depths the planar seismic zone gradually steepens, usually to about $45°$, but sometimes to $90°$. These intermediate and deep focus earthquakes, however, occur *within* the subducted oceanic lithosphere, not on its upper boundary (e.g., Isacks and Molnar, 1971). Generally, seismicity is more diffuse in continental regions and there is no zone of intermediate and deep focus earthquakes like those at island arcs. The shallow seismicity often includes a spectrum of fault plane solutions and shows a much more complicated pattern of deformation than the simple underthrusting at island arcs. The few inclined zones of intermediate and deep focus seismicity within continental areas (in the Pamir-Hindu Kush, Burma, and the Carpathians) are usually cited as evidence for subduction of oceanic lithosphere in the last 10 to 20 m.y. Recently, intermediate depth seismicity has been recognized in other active convergent zones, but this activity seems to be part of the diffuse deformation of continental convergent zones at depth and does not reflect subduction of oceanic lithosphere (Chen et al., 1981; Chen and Molnar, 1981, 1983; Chen and Roecker, 1980; Hatzfeld and Frogneux, 1981).

Below, we first discuss the seismicity of several active mountain ranges, beginning with the Himalaya, which seems to us to be one of the simplest. Then we consider broad convergent zones and we give a brief discussion of possible variations in seismicity during the development of mountain belts. Finally, before giving a brief summary, we discuss the relevance of depth of earthquakes to the crustal and mantle rheology.

II. Linear Mountain Ranges and Convergent Plate Boundaries

Often plate boundaries in continental regions are marked by long, narrow mountain ranges. These ranges (and boundaries) do not necessarily separate two essentially rigid plates, but instead they often mark the boundary of one plate with a broader zone of deformation that separates that plate from its nearest neighbour. Two clear active examples of such belts are the Himalaya and Zagros, which bound the Indian and Arabian shields on the north and north-east. These belts are relatively narrow and the style of deformation changes little along strike. The Tien Shan and the Peruvian Andes are somewhat broader zones of deformation but separate two essentially rigid converging blocks or plates. Finally the north-western Himalaya, the Hindu Kush, and the Pamir in Pakistan, Afghanistan and Tadjikistan comprise a yet broader zone with little evidence of linearity. We discuss each of these individually and make comparisons as each new belt is discussed.

A. The Himalaya

Among the mountain belts discussed here, the Himalaya, from its north-east corner of Assam to Kashmir, is probably the simplest. Seismicity located teleseismically follows the range and most of it lies between the Main Central Thrust and the Main Boundary Fault (Fig. 1) (see Gansser, 1964, 1977; or LeFort, 1975, for geologic background). Most fault plane solutions show underthrusting either along shallow planes dipping north beneath the mountains or along steep planes dipping south (Figs 1 and 2) (e.g. Armbruster et al., 1983; Fitch, 1970; Molnar et al., 1973, 1977). In accordance with the dips of geologically mapped thrust faults in the Himalaya, the northerly dipping planes are probably the fault planes, and the earthquakes reflect northward convergence between the Indian shield and the Himalaya. The shallow dipping nodal planes dip north at angles of $15°$ or less in eastern Nepal and Assam, but some dip more steeply ($\sim 30°$) in western Nepal and further west (e.g., Armbruster et al., 1983; Molnar et al., 1977). Thus, in the east the solutions seem to imply a coherent underthrusting of India beneath the Himalaya (Molnar et al., 1977). Some of those farther west seem to indicate internal deformation of the Himalayan crust (Armbruster et al., 1983; Seeber et al., 1981).

Unfortunately, we are not aware of any detailed studies

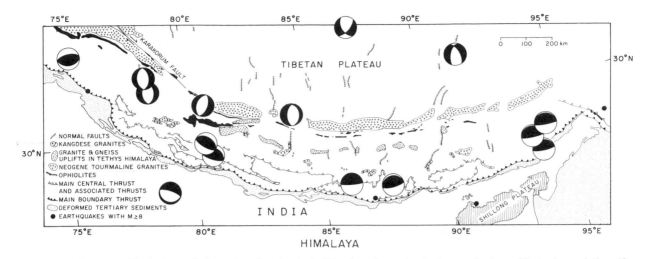

Fig. 1 Neotectonic map and fault plane solutions of earthquakes in the Himalaya. Lower hemisphere projections of fault plane solutions (from Armbruster *et al.*, 1983; Molnar *et al.*, 1977; Molnar and Tapponnier, 1978) of earthquakes between 1963 and 1976, which are large enough to study with the WWSSN, are plotted with blackened quadrants containing compressional first arrivals. When two events occurred at nearly the same location, only one is shown. Black dots are epicentres of major historical earthquakes. Faults in the Himalaya are from Gansser (1977), and those in the Tibetan plateau are from Molnar and Tapponnier (1978).

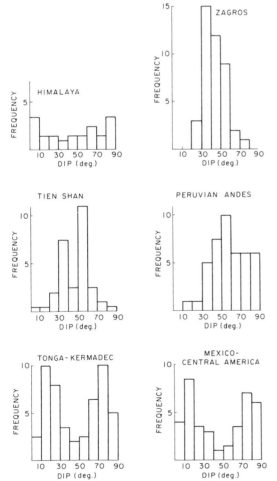

Fig. 2 Histograms showing dips of nodal planes for two subduction zones and four intracontinental mountain belts. Data are from Isacks *et al.* (1969) and Johnson and Molnar (1972) for Tonga-Kermadec, from Molnar and Sykes (1969) for Mexico and Central America, from Molnar *et al.* (1977) and Molnar and Tapponnier (1978) for the Himalaya, from Jackson and Fitch (1981) and McKenzie (1972) for the Zagros, from Tapponnier and Molnar (1979) for the Tien Shan, and from Suárez *et al.* (1983) for the Peruvian Andes.

using local networks of particular portions of the Himalaya between Kashmir and Assam. Consequently, the depth distribution of earthquakes is poorly known. A study of some of the larger events, however, shows that they occur at shallow depths, 10–20 km (Armbruster *et al.*, 1983). These depths and the shallow dipping planes are consistent with the events, at least in the eastern part of the range, occurring along the interface between the underthrusting Indian shield and the overriding mountain mass (Fig. 3).

The historic seismicity of the Himalaya includes four major events ($M > 8$) in the last 100 years (Fig. 1). The fault associated with one, the 1897 Assam earthquake (Oldham, 1899; Richter, 1958), however, probably underlies the Shillong plateau but not the Himalaya. Moreover, controversy surrounds the 1950 Assam earthquake. Whereas we suspect the important displacement occurred along a shallow, north dipping plane (Chen and Molnar, 1977), Ben-Menahem *et al.* (1974) inferred slip on a north–north-west striking plane. Unfortunately, little is known about the slip associated with either the 1905 Kangra earthquake or the 1934 Bihar–Nepal earthquake. From the fault plane solutions of nearby events, and from the intensity distributions associated with them, it is likely that those two events resulted from low angle underthrusting of India beneath the Himalaya (Armbruster *et al.*, 1983; Molnar *et al.*, 1977; Seeber *et al.*, 1981). The occurance of four major events in the last 100 years attests to important continuing tectonic activity in the region, but too little is known about any of these events to alter or verify the simple interpretation deduced from the focal depths and fault plane solutions discussed above.

The tectonic setting at the Himalaya is very similar to that of an island arc (e.g., Molnar *et al.*, 1977). The Indian plate bends down in front of the Himalaya and forms a deep basin, the Ganga basin. One event beneath it, in fact, shows normal faulting with a T axis perpendicular to the range (Molnar *et al.*, 1973, 1977; Fig. 1). This event is presumably analogous to those beneath deep sea trenches (e.g., Chapple and Forsyth, 1979; Stauder, 1968) and therefore is probably due to flexing of the Indian plate as it bends down in front of the Himalaya. The flexed Indian plate supports some of the excess mass in the Himalaya and maintains parallel belts of negative and positive isostatic anomalies over the Ganga basin and the Himalaya (Lyon-Caen and Molnar, 1983;

(i.e., within the last 50 years) (see also Simpson *et al.*, 1981), but the clear Quaternary displacements make it unwise to conclude that their activity has ceased. The orientation and sense of slip along these faults is consistent with a north–south or north–north-west — south–south-east maximum compressive stress, and with the idea that the Tien Shan is experiencing shortening with approximately the same orientation throughout the belt.

D. The Peruvian Andes

The close proximity of a subduction zone makes the Andes different from the other mountain ranges considered here. Yet, because of their tectonic similarity to intracontinental belts (e.g., Audebaud *et al.*, 1973), discussion of them here seems appropriate.

On the west side, active subduction of the Nazca plate creates most of the features typical of island arc structures. Fault plane solutions attest to eastward subduction (Stauder, 1975), and an inclined seismic zone dips at a shallow angle beneath the Andes (e.g., Barazangi and Isacks, 1976, 1979). The Andes, however, differ from most other subduction zones by the presence of a range of high mountains along the zone.

The origin of the Andes is controversial, but at least part of the high elevations and thick crust (see James, 1971; Ocola and Meyer, 1973) is surely due to east–west crustal shortening of the western margin of South America. Folding and thrust faulting in the Andes have dominated the structural

evolution, at least since the late Cretaceous (e.g., Audebaud *et al.*, 1973; Dalmayrac *et al.*, 1981; Mégard, 1978). Mesozoic and Paleozoic sediments in the high Andes reflect this deformation and Pliocene and Quaternary sediments in the sub-Andes, on the eastern flanks of the range, are folded and overthrusted one upon another.

The seismicity along the flanks of the Andes corroborates the suggestion of continued crustal shortening. Earthquakes seem to be shallow and most seem to occur in the crust between 10 and 25 km depth (Chinn and Isacks, 1981; Suárez et al., 1983). Two events have focal depths between 35 and 40 km and could have occurred in the uppermost mantle (Suárez *et al.*, 1983), as in the Tien Shan. There is no record of earthquakes with large magnitudes ($M > 7\frac{1}{2}$) in the sub-Andes, and therefore individual faults are probably quite short. Fault plane solutions indicate primarily thrust faulting with east–west trending P axes (Fig. 6; Suárez *et al.*, 1983). The dips of the planes are generally between 30° and 60° (Fig. 2). We presume that in most cases the west dipping plane is the fault plane so that the Brazilian shield under-thrusts the Andes to the west. Most of the mapped faults on the east side of the Andes dip west (e.g., Audebaud *et al.*, 1973), but there is no direct evidence that any of these faults were activated by the earthquakes that have been studied. In any case, a summation of the seismic moments shows that if the present rate of seismicity were typical of the last 80 m.y., the Andes could have been built solely by thrust faulting and crustal shortening (Suárez *et al.*, 1983).

The rather steep dips of the west dipping planes from the

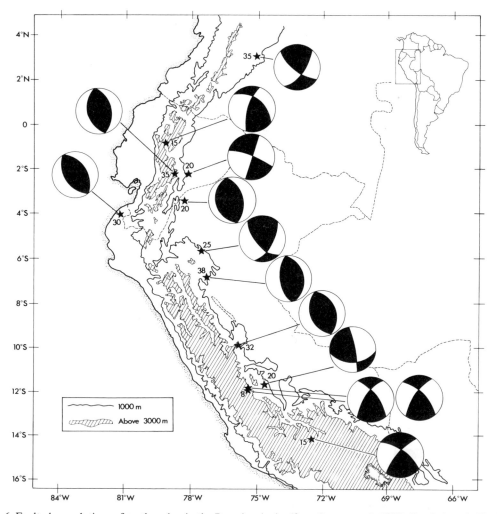

Fig. 6 Fault plane solutions of earthquakes in the Peruvian Andes (from Suarez *et al.*, 1983). Symbols as in Fig. 1.

fault plane solutions and the depths of these events suggests that the basement is involved in the deformation and that if low angle decollement as in the Canadian Rockies in the late Cretaceous occurs, it does so aseismically, at least in this portion of the Andes. If the tectonics of western North America in the late Cretaceous and early Tertiary were similar to those of the Peruvian Andes now, then the deformation in the sub-Andes would seem to be more similar to that of the Rocky Mountains in the early Tertiary (Laramide) than to that of the Sevier belt or Canadian Rockies in the late Cretaceous.

The active tectonics of the high Andes, as revealed by studies of Quaternary faulting and folding, show greater variability than that in the sub-Andes. In central Peru, Quaternary gravels are folded in response to east–west or north-east–south-west shortening (Dollfus and Mégard, 1968; Mégard, 1978). Moreover, the fault plane solutions and surface deformation associated with the 1969 Parian-huanca earthquakes show reverse faulting, with a north-east–south-west trending P axis (Philip and Mégard, 1977; Stauder, 1975; Suárez *et al.*, 1983). This sequence of events is unusual both because of the steep dip of the fault plane and because it occurred in a region of high altitudes. Most of the large events on the flanks of the Andes occurred beneath regions with elevations less than approximately 1000 m.

Whereas the high Andes of central Peru seems to be experiencing crustal shortening perpendicular to the range, north and south of this area there is evidence of normal faulting and crustal extension perpendicular to the range. This evidence includes observations of recent fault scarps that cut glacial moraines (Dalmayrac, 1974; Dalmayrac and Molnar, 1981; Mercier, 1981; Suárez *et al.*, 1983) and of both surface faulting and the fault plane solution of the 1946

Ancash earthquake (Hodgson and Bremmer, 1953; Richter, 1958; Suárez *et al.*, 1983). We doubt that the normal faulting involves a large amount of extension, but it does imply a different stress distribution from that in the central Andes at high altitudes or that in the sub-Andes (Dalmayrac and Molnar, 1981).

Thus, the seismicity of the Andes is in some ways similar to that of the Tien Shan in that it indicates crustal shortening and basement involvement. It differs by being bounded by a subduction zone and by the presence of normal faulting in some parts of the belt.

E. The North-western Himalaya, the Pamir, and the Hindu Kush

The discussion above is meant to present a sequence from a linear mountain belt with simple underthrusting of one continent beneath it (the Himalaya) to another linear belt, with deformation of the basement instead of simple underthrusting (the Zagros), to a two-sided linear belt experiencing crustal shortening and thickening with basement involvement (the Tien Shan) to another linear belt (the Andes) similar in some ways to the last but with greater variation along strike. In this respect the north-western Himalaya, Hindu Kush and Pamir represent a further step from the simplicity of the Himalaya. Although linear ranges can be identified within the region, on the whole it shows little linearity. In parts it seems to be two-sided, with northward underthrusting beneath the Himalaya and southward underthrusting beneath the northern edge of the Pamir (Fig. 7). Yet with strike-slip faulting and even some normal faulting, and with inclined zones of intermediate depth earthquakes, the region is clearly more complex than the others discussed above. Our

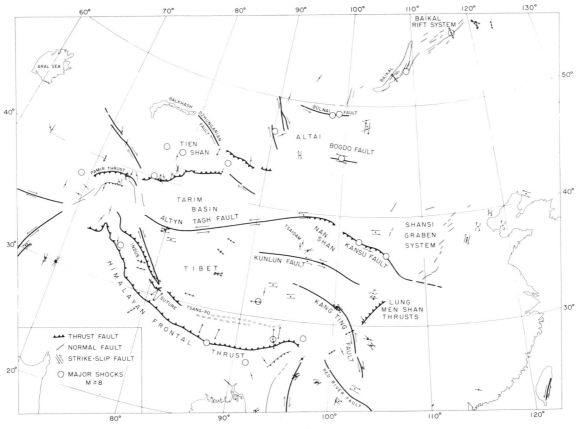

Fig. 7 Recent faults, and fault plane solutions of Central and Eastern Asia. Epicentres of major historical earthquakes (large dots) and earthquakes with known fault plane solutions (small dots) are shown, together with orientations of the P⊖(—) and T⊖axis (↔) for thrust and normal faulting events, slip vector (→) of low angle thrusts, and relative motion along the fault plane (⇌) for strike slip events (dashed when one of the nodal planes is arbitrarily chosen as the fault plane).

purpose here is not to ignore or minimize this complexity but to isolate aspects of it and discuss them separately.

First, the discussions of the seismicity of the regions described above are based primarily on the study of teleseismically located events. Much of the key information comes from the study of a small number of events: the largest events since 1962 when the WWSSN began operating. Few such shallow earthquakes have occurred in the north-western Himalaya, Hindu Kush or Pamir and most of what we know about the seismicity of this region is provided by studies of small earthquakes or microearthquakes using local networks. We suspect that similar studies of other areas will reveal complexities not apparent with only teleseismic data, but nevertheless we doubt that the difference in complexity for instance between the Himalaya in Nepal and in Pakistan will vanish with more data from studies of microearthquakes.

Studies of earthquake sequences or microearthquakes in the northern Pamir (Jackson *et al.*, 1979; Kieth *et al.*, 1982; Wesson *et al.*, 1976), in northern Pakistan (Armbruster *et al.*, 1978; Jacob *et al.*, 1979; Seeber and Armbruster, 1979; Seeber and Jacob, 1977), and in north-eastern Afghanistan (Prevot *et al.*, 1980) all show a spectrum of fault types and orientations. In all three areas, the crust seems to experience complicated deformation on planes with different strikes and dips. Although there clearly are major strike-slip faults, which accommodate large displacements, they are not obvious from the seismicity and are either aseismic or have been quiescent for their recorded history. Except for a large event in 1505 near Kabul (Heuckroth and Karim, 1970; Quittmeyer and Jacob, 1979), there is little seismic activity on the portions of the major strike-slip faults in this area — the Chaman (Lawrence and Yeats, 1979; Yeats *et al.*, 1979; Wellman, 1966), Darvaz-Karakul (Kuchai and Trifonov, 1977), Aksu-Murgab (Ruzhentsev, 1963), and other faults. There may also be major thrust (or normal) faults that are not defined by the seismicity. Instead, the seismicity scatters throughout much of the area, defining few linear trends. Yet within this complexity there appears to be a consistent north–south to north–north-west — south–south-east orientation of P axes of fault plane solutions. Despite some exceptions, this pattern suggests that the crust is undergoing north–south or north–north-west — south–south-east crustal shortening, presumably in response to the convergence of India and Eurasia. The variety of fault plane solutions and the widespread seismicity implies more homogeneous deformation than in the regions discussed above. We cannot exclude the possibility that a longer history of seismicity will reveal concentrated deformation on faults that bound relatively aseismic blocks. Nevertheless, it is clear that the tectonics of this region cannot be described easily by plate tectonics, unless one wants to use tens or hundreds of small plates.

The Hindu Kush and Pamir are particularly unusual in that they are underlain by a belt of intermediate depth events. We think that in fact there are two zones: one dipping north under the Hindu Kush and the other dipping south or southeast beneath the Pamir (Chatelain *et al.*, 1980; Roecker *et al.*, 1980). Seismicity extends to 300 km depth, and between about 150 km and 300 km it is confined to a rather narrow zone (Billington *et al.*, 1977; Chatelain *et al.*, 1980; Roecker *et al.*, 1980). The fault plane solutions show some variability, but for events deeper than about 150 km, the T axes lie in the plane of seismicity and plunge steeply. This similarity with seismicity at island arcs suggests that within the last 10 to 20 m.y., oceanic lithosphere was subducted beneath the Hindu–Kush and Pamir. Chatelain *et al.* (1980) inferred that two separate basins were subducted, one northwards beneath the Hindu–Kush and the other southward beneath the Pamir, and that one or both may have been interarc basins, like those in the western Pacific.

The seismicity between 70 and about 150 km depth shows some peculiarities atypical of subduction zones. First, seismicity shallower than about 70 km, within the thickened crust, is very low. This suggests that if deformation occurs in the crust, it is aseismic. The seismic zone between 70 and 150 km depth occurs over a broader zone and the fault plane solutions are much more variable than at greater depths. In general these fault plane solutions are consistent with north–south shortening of the region, but neither is the T axis consistently parallel to the dip direction of the seismic zone nor is the seismicity aligned with one of the nodal planes for each of the solutions. In any case, Roecker's (1982) inference that these earthquakes occur in subducted continental crust, possibly modified by high pressure phase changes, renders peculiarities in the seismicity a likely occurrence, even if we cannot at this time predict the nature of the peculiarities.

Thus, the seismicity of the north-west Himalaya, Pamir and Hindu–Kush differs in two ways from that of the regions discussed above. First, it is yet more complicated, with a mixture of thrust, strike-slip and even normal faulting and with diffuse deformation over a broad area. Second, the presence of inclined zones of intermediate depth seismicity in an intracontinental region suggests that there has been recent subduction of oceanic lithosphere. Although there may be some temptation to relate these differences to one another, we suspect that they are unrelated. The complicated deformation of the north-west Himalaya, Pamir and Hindu–Kush region make it resemble a miniature example of the broader zones between converging continents, such as in the vast region east of it, where intermediate depth seismicity is rare.

III. Intracontinental Convergent Zones on a Large Scale

Most of the belts described are only portions of broad zones of deformation between converging continental plates. Whereas most, if not all, of the deformation occurring in these broad zones seems to be due to such convergence, the deformation is often more complicated and more varied than that described above for the individual ranges within these zones. Several factors contribute to this complexity. One is the inadequacy of the historic record of seismicity. To discuss consistent patterns in the tectonics requires a combination of seismic data with those from different sources relating to Quaternary faulting. Together these data allow a qualitative description of the tectonics. Unlike in oceanic area, however, where seismicity occurs on narrow belts (plate boundaries) for which estimates of average rates of slip can be made, in continents the earthquakes and recent faulting are often dispersed over a broad area. Correspondingly deformation is not concentrated in a small number of intercontinental narrow zones, and it is difficult to determine rates of deformation.

Faulting in continental areas often includes a spectrum of fault types and orientations. In some, and perhaps in most cases, active faults develop along older zones of weakness. These inherited zones of weakness introduce a second important source of complexity to the active tectonics of continental regions generally absent in oceanic areas. Deformation in continents is diffuse, but zones of concentrated deformation are not completely absent. In particular, movement along large strike-slip faults seems to accommodate an important fraction of the convergence both between Arabia and Eurasia (McKenzie, 1972) and between India and Eurasia (Molnar and Tapponnier, 1975; Tapponnier and Molnar, 1976, 1977, 1979). Parts of many of these strike-slip faults seem to follow older faults, sutures, or other zones of intense deformation. Accordingly, whereas the deformation of continents is probably better approximated by the response of a continuum to external stresses than by the relative motion of rigid blocks (e.g., Tapponnier and Molnar, 1976), only some aspects can be approximated by a continuum with uniform properties.

Despite the complications due to inherited zones of weakness, large areas between converging continents often seem to be deforming in response to a relatively uniform stress field. Usually the P axes of fault plane solutions show a uniform orientation over a large area, and when they do not, usually the T axes are consistent. These axes are generally consistent with the direction either of crustal shortening or of crustal extension implied by the orientations of folds and faults and by the senses of motion on the faults. The consistency of these data implies a coherent regional stress field over large areas. In general the inferred regional stress fields change gradually over a broad region, but not always. In particular where there are large changes in mean elevation and in crustal thickness the vertical stress can change from the maximum to the minimum compressive stress. Consequently, the concept of a regional stress field is limited in applicability and must be used cautiously.

To illustrate how these factors lead to complexity in the tectonics of continents, let us consider central and eastern Asia between India and Siberia.

Above we discussed the underthrusting of India and the creation of the Himalaya. Let us discuss Tibet below. North of Tibet, the Tien Shan experience crustal shortening, by thrust and strike-slip faulting, in an approximately north–south direction, parallel to the convergence between India and Eurasia. The seismicity in the last 20 years has been very low in the Nan Shan, north-east of Tibet (Fig. 7), but studies of Quaternary faulting indicate north-east–south-west shortening (e.g. Tapponnier and Molnar, 1977). East of Tibet, the predominance of thrust faulting seems to give way to strike-slip faulting, consistent with east–west crustal shortening. This rotation of the orientations of the P axes of fault plane solutions and directions of crustal shortening seems to be a characteristic feature of continental deformation. Such a rotation is predicted by calculated stress fields for continuous media indented by or stressed on particular boundaries (e.g. England and McKenzie, 1982; Tapponnier and Molnar, 1976), and it militates against interpretations in terms of a small number of rigid plates.

This gradual change in orientations of P, T, and B axes of fault plane solutions and in the orientation of the axes of principal strain (or stress) can also be seen further north-east. The predominance of thrust faulting in the Tien Shan and Nan Shan seems to pass into predominantly conjugate strike-slip faulting with north-east–south-west P axes and north-west–south-east T axes in Mongolia and north-central China (Fig. 7). Further north-east and east, a large component of normal faulting dominates the strike-slip component in the Baikal Rift System, the Shansi Graben, and the region between them. The gradual change in the style of deformation and the orientation of strain implies that the stress field changes gradually across the region. The widespread deformation does not allow well defined plate boundaries to be drawn except in restricted areas.

The seismicity of Mongolia illustrates the inadequacy of the historic record of seismicity. Fault plane solutions of earthquakes in the last 18 years (four solutions) are wholly inadequate to justify the inference of important strike-slip faulting. Yet the surface deformation associated with several major earthquakes and Quaternary faulting seen both on the ground (Tikhonov, 1974) and on the Landsat imagery (Tapponnier and Molnar, 1979) demonstrate large-scale conjugate faulting. In particular, two major events ($M \sim 8\cdot5$) in 1905 in northern Mongolia ruptured an east–west zone

370 km long causing several metres of left-lateral slip (Florensov and Solonenko, 1965; S.D. Khilko, personal communication, 1974). In 1957, another major earthquake ($M \sim 8\cdot3$) ruptured a 270 km long east–west zone in southern Mongolia, again causing several metres of left-lateral motion (Florensov and Solonenko, 1965). Then in 1967, a smaller earthquake ($M \sim 7\frac{3}{4}$) caused between 1 and 2 m of right-lateral slip along a 40 km fault that trends north–south (Natsag-Yum *et al.*, 1971). Moreover, in 1931 a major event in China just west of Mongolia caused several metres of right-lateral slip in a north–north-west — south–south-east trending fault (Deng Qidong, personal communication, 1981). Thus, although the seismicity in the last 20 years has been too low to define a pattern, the large earthquakes, which ruptured long faults, corroborate the inference of conjugate faulting seen on the satellite imagery (Tapponnier and Molnar, 1979).

The Baikal Rift Zone and the Shansi Graben also illustrate the difficulties with the historic seismic record. The Baikal system is clearly active, both with large events and microearthquakes (e.g. Golonetskii, 1975). Fault plane solutions of earthquakes with $M \sim 6$ (Misharina, 1967; Tapponnier and Molnar, 1979) and with $M \sim 4$–5 (Misharina and Solonenko, 1972), as well as surface faulting associated with recent earthquakes (Solonenko *et al.*, 1966a, 1966b, 1968) attest to active normal faulting. Seismicity in the Shansi Graben, however, has been essentially non-existent since the turn of the century (Lee *et al.*, 1978). There are no fault plane solutions for earthquakes within it, although there are for several events to the east. Yet the Chinese catalogue of earthquakes lists two events with $M \sim 8$ and another four with $M \sim 7$ for this region, prior to 1800 (e.g. Lee *et al.*, 1976). One must conclude that the graben is active, even if there has been negligible seismicity for nearly 200 years.

These portions of eastern Asia illustrate several different styles of deformation, but we think that all of them can be related to the penetration of India into Eurasia. This penetration causes thrust faulting and the creation of high mountains near the suture zone and strike-slip and normal faulting further from the suture. Crudely India seems to squash (and to have squashed) Eurasia directly in front of it and further away to wedge it apart. Nevertheless, if the seismicity and active deformation of Mongolia, Baikal and Shansi seem only indirectly related to the collision between India and Eurasia, there is one other portion of eastern Asia in which this relationship is even less apparent — Tibet.

Although Tibet lies directly in front of India, at present it experiences normal faulting and east–west extension instead of north–south shortening and thrusting (Chen *et al.*, 1981; Molnar and Tapponnier, 1975; 1978; Ni and York, 1978). Some 15 fault plane solutions, including one for an event at 90 km depth (Chen *et al.*, 1981), show this extension (Figs 1 and 7), which is corroborated both by the analysis of satellite imagery (Molnar and Tapponnier, 1975, 1978; Ni and York, 1978) and by observations made on the ground (e.g. Bally *et al.*, 1980). Note that this style of deformation calls for a major change in the "regional stress field" from that in the Himalaya or Nan Shan and Tien Shan. We relate this extension and change in "regional stress field" to the gravitational buoyancy forces acting on the high elevation and thick crustal root of Tibet (Molnar and Tapponnier, 1978). To balance the gravitational body force, either horizontal compressive stresses applied in the surrounding areas of low elevations or the strength of the elevated (and thickened) crust must hold the area together, preventing the collapse and spreading apart of the mountains. Apparently India's convergence with Eurasia provides the necessary north–south compressive stress, but neither the east–west compressive stress on the flanks of Tibet nor the strength of Tibet are adequate to prevent it from extending in an east–west direction.

We presume that this extension began recently and that the amount of extension is quite small. At the same time the variation in the direction of underthrusting from north-east in the north-western Himalaya to north–north-west in the eastern Himalaya implies a rate of extension across Tibet of about 1 cm/yr (Armbruster *et al.*, 1983). In 5 to 10 m.y., extension would amount to 50 to 100 km, which would indicate a small amount of strain (~ 5%) within the plateau compared with that which probably occurred during crustal thickening (~ 100%).

The active tectonics of eastern Asia illustrate a variety of fault types and fault orientations. The pattern of deformation is not simple at any scale. Yet, we think that all of this deformation can be related to India's collision with and penetration into Eurasia. In some regions the relationship is simple: India pushes on Eurasia and causes crustal shortening and thrust faulting. In other areas, relatively strong blocks are pushed as rigid bodies, causing deformation on their edges. The eastward motion of such blocks with respect to Eurasia probably contributes in part to the opening of the Baikal rift system and the Shansi Graben zone. The relationship to the collision is even less direct in Tibet. There the present strain field and style of tectonics owe their existence more to the previous tectonic history, during which the plateau was formed probably by north–south crustal shortening, than to the continued penetration of India into Eurasia. This less direct relationship suggests that during the evolution of a belt, the seismicity and active tectonics of a mountain belt can pass through phases as crustal shortening causes crustal thickening and increases the vertical normal stress that in turn resists further thrust faulting (Tapponnier and Molnar, 1976).

IV. Depths of Focus

We separate the discussion of depths of focus in order to call attention to what appears to be a simple pattern: in continental regions, seismicity usually is confined to the shallower part of the crust but occasionally occurs also in the uppermost mantle, just below the Moho. The lowermost crust, however, in general seems to be aseismic (see Chen and Molnar, 1981, 1983, for more details).

Most intermediate and deep focus earthquakes occur at subduction zones and are assumed to occur in downgoing slabs of lithosphere. Those that occur in continental settings are often attributed to recent subduction of oceanic lithosphere. It is now becoming clear that there are intermediate depth events* that cannot be associated with subduction of oceanic lithosphere and that there are numerous other shallower, subcrustal events that also cannot. Chen and Molnar (1981, 1983) compiled a list of depths of well-located events not associated with subduction zones and found the majority to be in the upper 15 km. In stable shields and platforms depths as great as 25 km were noted. Greater depths also were encountered where thrust faulting and crustal shortening actively occur. In those regions, the colder temperatures of the shallow crust are transported down by underthrusting. In a few areas, earthquakes have been precisely located in the mantle at depths from 45 km to 100 km, and apparently even 150 km in the High Atlas Mountains (Hatzfeld and Frogneux, 1981). Yet, in general, the lower crust, however thick the crust may be, seems to be devoid of seismicity.

These observations can be taken to indicate the following:

Earthquakes in the crust occur in material with temperature less than about 350°C (± 100°C). Crustal

---

* Strictly speaking, intermediate depths are usually defined to be between 70 and 300 km.

material with higher temperature probably flows and does not fracture suddenly. Earthquakes in the mantle, however, probably occur where the material is colder than about 800°C (± 200°C) (Chen and Molnar, 1981, 1983; Chen *et al.*, 1981; Molnar *et al.*, 1979). Olivine is probably much stronger than most crustal minerals at the same temperature, and there may be a low strength zone in the lower crust (although not necessarily at the Moho) (Fig. 8). Crystalline nappes are likely to detach within this low strength zone.

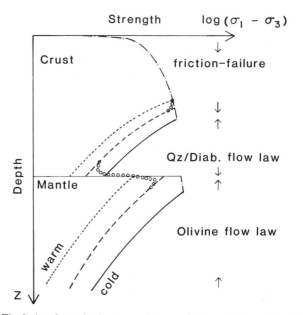

Fig. 8 A schematic diagram of the variation of the mechanical strength of the crust and uppermost mantle with respect to depth for cold (solid curve), intermediate (dashed curve) and warm (dotted curve) geotherms. The upper part of the curve is based on linear relationship between the shear stress and normal stress to represent stick-slip or brittle failure behaviour. The strength in the lower crust and upper mantle is bounded by flow laws of crustal and mantle materials, respectively. The open circles are smoothed to indicate possible gradual changes of strength in the brittle-ductile transition zone and the crust-mantle boundary (from Chen and Molnar, 1983).

Summary

Unlike island arc structures, the seismicity of mountain belts exhibits considerable variability. There is no typical mountain belt exemplifying characteristics common to all other belts. Instead, different belts exhibit different styles of deformation that probably result from different earlier tectonic histories and from different stages of evolution in their present development.

The seismicity of the Himalaya implies that India is sliding beneath the Himalaya along a shallow dipping fault near, if not along, the top surface of the Indian Shield. The seismicity gives no evidence of active detachment of a crystalline nappe from the top of the Indian Shield, but sediments deposited in the Ganga Basin could be experiencing decollement (Seeber *et al.*, 1983; Seeber and Armbruster, 1981).

The seismicity of the Zagros is different in that at present there is no clear *seismic* evidence for decollement. Instead the earthquakes seem to occur in the basement beneath the thick evaporite and carbonate layers. The basement seems to be deforming not by low-angle faulting but along steeper faults (30–60°). Jackson (1980b) suggests that ancient normal faults that formed in an earlier rifting phase are reactivated as reverse faults.

The Tien Shan is a broader belt with active seismicity showing thrust faulting throughout. The belt is two-sided.

On the north the Siberian platform underthrusts southwards and on the south the Tarim basin underthrusts northwards. Thrust faults seem to dip steeply (30–60°), so that simple decollement, or detachment of thin crystalline sheets does not seem to be occurring unless the faults change dip at greater depths. In addition, there are prominent strike-slip faults in the Tien Shan for which there is no seismic evidence for recent activity, but which show clear evidence of movement in the Quaternary. The sense of strike-slip movement is consistent with a north–north-west — south–south-east maximum compressive stress inferred from the fault plane solutions.

Westward underthrusting of the west Brazilian craton beneath the Andes also occurs on faults dipping steeply (30–45°) into the basement. Depths of focus require that the larger events occur within the basement, not in the sedimentary cover. Thus the active tectonics revealed by the seismicity more closely resembles that of the western United States during the early Tertiary (Laramide) than that of the Sevier belt or the Canadian Rockies in the late Cretaceous. The active tectonics of the high Andes shows either normal or reverse faulting, depending upon the locality along the zone.

The seismicity of the north-west Himalaya, Pamir and Hind–Kush shows greater variety than that of the other belts. Although strike-slip faults, clearly active during the Quaternary, bound the region on its east and west, and although clear thrust faulting occurs on the northern and southern edges of the region, the seismicity suggests diffuse deformation with a spectrum of fault plane solutions.

The north-west Himalaya, Pamir and Hindu–Kush region is in many ways a microcosm of the broader region further east or west between Eurasia and India or Arabia. In these regions, deformation also includes a spectrum of fault types and fault orientations. Strike-slip faulting, in particular, seems to play a crucial role in displacing material and allowing convergence of continental masses to continue without building mountains with limitless elevations. In general the orientation and sense of motion on the strike-slip faults is consistent with a regional stress field resulting from convergence between the major continental plates. More problematic is the evidence for normal faulting in portions of these broad convergent zones. We think that this extension nevertheless is attributable to the collision process. Some normal faults may result from buoyancy forces acting on regions of high elevation and compensating crustal roots (Tibet) and others (Baikal and Shansi Grabens) may result from wedging apart of Asia by movement of relatively rigid blocks past one another.

Several factors contribute to the greater complexity in continental convergent zones than at subduction zones. One factor is the inadequacy of the seismic record. Whereas the rate of convergence at subduction zones is usually several cm/year, rates of mm/year are likely to characterize individual fault zones in a continental region. Thus, seismicity alone is likely to be lower on such continental fault zones than on plate boundaries in oceanic regions. In addition, the role of fault creep is clearly important in some continental regions, and in others (like Mongolia) a substantial amount of deformation occurs during very large earthquakes. This variation both in the frequency and the maximum size of earthquakes and in the importance of fault creep from region to region is an obvious but poorly understood phenomenon in continental seismicity.

A second factor contributing to the complexity of continental seismicity is the variation in strength of the earth's crust in continents compared with the more homogeneous oceanic lithosphere. Variations in strength result both from differences in temperature profiles (e.g., Molnar and Tapponier, 1981) and from inherited zones of weakness. For instance, the major strike-slip faults of the Tien Shan seem to have been active in the late Paleozoic, and the existence of large relatively rigid blocks, like the Tarim Basin, cause a concentration of deformation on their margins. An eastward motion of cold, strong blocks relative to Eurasia may contribute to the opening of the Baikal and Shansi grabens. Thus the variation in strength both causes stress concentrations and alters the orientation of stress in continental regions.

Another phenomenon that alters the stress field is the variation in crustal thickness (e.g., Artyushkov, 1973; Dalmayrac and Molnar, 1981; Frank, 1972; Molnar and Tapponnier, 1978). In the equations of equilibrium the gravitational body force, which varies from regions of high and low elevation and of thicker and thinner crust, must be balanced by variations in the stress field. In particular, regions of thick crust are likely to experience horizontal extension. Surrounding regions of thinner crust and lower elevations are more prone to horizontal compression. Thus, differences in the style of deformation and in the seismicity are likely between regions of high and low elevation, as can be seen in Tibet and the neighbouring Himalaya and Nan Shan or in portions of the Andes.

If the buoyancy of continental crust does perturb the stress field, one can imagine that during the history of a continental convergent zone, a mass of rock might first experience rapid thrust faulting while crustal thickening occurs, and then reverse faulting at a lower rate while the area being deformed grows in size. Later strike-slip or normal faulting might develop when the convergence or the movement of surrounding material change in some way so as to relax the horizontal compressive stress in one or all horizontal directions (Tapponnier and Molnar, 1976). The observed differences in the seismicity of different belts may exist partly because each is at a different stage in its development

One other factor probably contributes to the greater complexity of continental seismicity than that of subduction zones. Laboratory studies show that olivine is much stronger than typical crustal rocks and minerals at the same temperature. Thus oceanic lithosphere, which consists mostly of mantle material, probably can withstand much larger stresses than continental lithosphere can. Continental lithosphere consists of thick crustal layer, and consequently does not contain the thick zone of cold mantle (T < 500°) that characterizes oceanic lithosphere. A study of depths of earthquakes (Chen and Molnar, 1981, 1983) supports the inference that the continental lithosphere may contain a weak zone in lower crust. The lower crust appears to be aseismic, while most seismicity occurs at shallow depths in the crust. In some regions the mantle lithosphere is also seismically active. We infer that the lower crust deforms by aseismic (ductile) flow and may be weaker than the overlying brittle crust and underlying uppermost mantle. Crystalline nappes may detach along this zone in the lower crust.

Although the seismicity and tectonics of continental regions are more complicated than those of subduction zones, we think that this complexity owes its existence to relatively simple physical phenomena. A key problem for the future is to evaluate quantitatively the relative importance of these phenomena. Clearly a continued and even expanded interaction of geologists from different disciplines will be necessary to bring about a quantitative understanding of continental tectonics that is comparable to that of plate tectonics in oceanic regions. It is also clear that we seismologists still have many unresolved problems that must be addressed before we will have done our part.

References

Aki, K. (1966). Generation and propagation of G waves from the Niigata earthquake of June 16, 1964, 2, Estimation of earthquake moment, radiated energy and stress-strain drop from the G wave spectrum. *Bull. Earthq. Res. Inst., Tokyo Univ.* **44**, 73–88.

Aki, K. (1967). Scaling law of seismic spectrum. *J. Geophys. Res.* **72**, 1217–1231.

Anderson, J.G. (1979). Estimating the seismicity from geological structure for seismic-risk studies. *Bull. Seism. Soc. Am.* **69**, 135–158.

Armbruster, J., Seeber, L. and Jacob, K.H. (1978). The northwestern termination of the Himalayan mountain front: active tectonics from microearthquakes. *J. Geophys. Res.* **83**, 269–281.

Armbruster, J., Baranowski, J., Seeber, L. and Molnar P. (1983). In preparation.

Artyushkov, E.V. (1973). Stresses in the lithosphere caused by crustal thickness inhomogeneities. *J. Geophys. Res.* **78**, 7675–7708.

Audebaud, E., Capdevila, B., Dalmayrac, B., Debelmas, J., Laubacher, G., Le Fevre, C., Marocco, R., Martinez, C., Mattauer, M., Megard, F., Paredes, J. and Tomasi, P. (1973). Les traits géologiques essentiels des Andes Centrales (Pérou-Bolivia). *Revue de Géographie Physique et de Géologie Dynamique* Vol. **XV**, fasc. 1–2.

Bally, A.W., Allen, C.R., Geyer, R.B., Hamilton, W.B., Hopson, C.A., Molnar, P., Oliver, J.E., Opdyke, N.D., Plafker, G. and Wu, F.T. (1980). Notes on the geology of Tibet and adjacent areas — Report of the plate tectonics delegation to the People's Republic of China. *U.S. Geological Survey Open File Rept. 80–501*, 100 pp., Washington, D.C.

Barazangi, M. and Isacks, B. (1976). Spatial distribution of earthquakes and subduction of the Nazca plate beneath South America. *Geology* **4**, 686–692, 1976.

Barazangi, M. and Isacks, B. (1979). Subduction of the Nazca plate beneath Peru: evidence from spatial distribution of earthquakes. *Geophys. J.R. Astr. Soc.* **57**, 537–555.

Ben-Menahem, A., Aboudi, E. and Schild, R. (1974). The source of the great Assam earthquake and interplate wedge motion. *Phys. Earth Plan.Int.* **9**, 265–289.

Billington, S., Isacks, B.L. and Barazangi, M. (1977). Spatial distribution and focal mechanisms of mantle earthquakes in the Hindu Kush-Pamir region: A contorted Benioff zone. *Geology* **5**, 699–704.

Bogdanovitch, K.I., Kark, I.M., Korolkov, Ya.B. and Mushketov, D.I. (1914). Earthquake in the northern districts of the Tien Shan, 22 December 1910 (4 January 1911) (in Russian). Commission of the Geology Committee, Leningrad, U.S.S.R.

Brune, J.N. (1968). Seismic moment, seismicity, and rate of slip along major fault zones. *J. Geophys. Res.* **73**, 777–784.

Burtman, V.S. (1961). On the Talasso-Fergana strike-slip fault (in Russian). *Bull. Acad. Sci. USSR Geol. Soc.* **12**, 37–48.

Burtman, V.S. (1963). The Talasso-Fergana and San Andreas strike slip faults (in Russian). In Faults and Horizontal Movements of the Earth's Crust. *Tr. Geol. Inst. Akad. Nauk SSSR* **80**, 128–151.

Burtman, V.S. (1975). Structural geology of the Variscan Tien Shan. *Am. J. Sci.* **275A**, 157–186.

Chapple, W.M. and Forsyth, D.W. (1979). Earthquakes and bending of plates at trenches. *J. Geophys. Res.* **84**, 6729–6749.

Chatelain, J.L., Roecker, S.W., Hatzfeld, D. and Molnar, P. (1980). Microearthquake seismicity and fault plane solutions in the Hindu Kush region and their tectonic implications. *J. Geophys. Res.* **85**, 1365–1387.

Chen, W.P. and Molnar, P. (1977). Seismic moments of major earthquakes and the average rate of slip in central Asia. *J. Geophys. Res.* **82**, 2945–2969.

Chen, W.P. and Molnar, P. (1981). Depth distribution of earthquake foci and its possible implications for the rheological structure of the crust and upper mantle (abstract). *E+S Trans. AGU* **62**, 397.

Chen, W.P. and Molnar, P. (1983). The depth distribution of intracontinental and intraplate earthquakes and its implications for the thermal and mechanical properties of the lithosphere, submitted to *J. Geophys. Res.*, **88**.

Chen, W.P. and Roecker, S.W. (1980). Regional variation of the focal mechanism of intermediate depth earthquakes and seismicity in the Karakorum-East Hindu Kush area (abstract). *E⊕S Trans. AGU* **61**, 1031.

Chen, W.P., Nábělek, J.L., Fitch, T.J. and Molnar, P. (1981). An intermediate depth earthquake beneath Tibet: Source characteristics of the event of September 14, 1976. *J. Geophys. Res.* **86**, 2863–2876.

Chinn, D. and Isacks, B. (1981). In preparation.

Cleary, J. (1967). Azimuthal variation of the Longshot source term. *Earth Planet. Sci. Lett.* **3**, 29–37.

Dalmayrac, B. (1974). Un exemple de tectonique vivante: les failles sub-actuelles du pied de la Cordillère Blanche (Pérou). *Cah. ORSTROM, sér. Géol.* **VI(1)**, 19–27.

Dalmayrac, B. and Molnar, P. (1981). Parallel thrust and normal faulting in Peru and constraints on the state of stress. *Earth Plan. Sci. Lett.* **55**, 473–481.

Dalmayrac, B., Laubacher, G. and Marocco, R. (1980). Géologie des Andes péruviennes: Caractères généraux de l'évolution géologique des Andes péruviennes. *Trav. et Documents ORSTROM* **No. 122**, Paris.

Dewey, J.F. and Şengör, A.M.C. (1979). Aegean and surrounding regions: complex multiplate and continuum tectonics in a convergent zone. *Bull. Geol. Soc. Amer.* **90**, 84–92.

Dollfus, D. and Mégard, F. (1968). Les formations quaternaires du bassin de Huanuco et leur néotectonique (Andes Centrales péruviennes). *Rev. Géogr. Phys. Géol. Dyn.* **X**, fasc. 5, 429–440.

Engdahl, E.R., Sleep, N.H. and Lin. M.T. (1977). Plate effects in north Pacific subduction zones. *Tectonophysics* **37**, 95–116.

England, P.C. and McKenzie, D.P. (1982). A thin viscous sheet model for continental deformation. *Geophys. J. Roy. Astr. Soc.* **70**, 295–320.

Fitch,, T.J. (1970). Earthquake mechanisms in the Himalayan, Burmese and Andaman regions and continental tectonics in Central Asia. *J. Geophys. Res.* **75**, 2699–2709.

Florensov, N.A. and Solonenko, V.P. (1965). *The Gobi-Altai Earthquake*, Nauka, Moscow, 1963. (English translation available from U.S. Dept. of Commerce, Springfield, Va., 1965).

Frank, F.C. (1972). Plate tectonics, the analogy with glacier flow and isostasy. *In* "Flow and Fracture of Rocks." *Geophys. Monograph* **16** (H.C. Heard, I.Y. Borg, N.L. Carter, and C.B. Raleigh eds). Amer. Geophys. Un., Washington, D.C., pp. 285–292.

Gansser, A. (1964). "The Geology of Himalayas." Interscience Publ., London, 289.

Gansser, A. (1977). The great suture zone between Himalaya and Tibet: A preliminary account, *Colloque Internationaux du CNRS, Himalaya: Sciences de la Terre.* Éditions du Centre National de la Recherche Scientifique, Paris, 181–192.

Geological Staff of the Iran Oil Company (1957). "Geological Map of Iran." National Iranian Oil Company.

Golonetskii, S.I. (1975). Earthquakes in Pribaikalia (in Russian). *In* "Earthquakes in the U.S.S.R.". Nauka, Moscow, pp.110–123.

Hatzfeld, D. and Frogneux, M. (1981). Evidence of intermediate depth earthquakes around the Gibraltar area. *Nature, London*, **292**, 443–445.

Helwig, J. (1976). Shortening of continental crust in orogenic belts and plate tectonics. *Nature, London* **260**, 768–770.

Heuckroth, L.E. and Karim, R. (1970). "Earthquake history, seismicity and tectonics of the regions of Afghanistan." Seismological Center, Faculty of Engineering, Kabul University, Kabul, Afghanistan.

Hodgson, J.H. and Bremner, P.C. (1953). Direction of faulting in the Ancash, Peru, earthquake of November 10, 1946, from teleseismic evidence. *Bull. Seismol. Soc. Am.* **43**, 121–125.

Isacks, B. and Molnar, P. (1972). Distribution of stresses in the descending lithosphere from a global survey of focal mechanism solutions of mantle earthquakes. *Rev. Geophys.* **9**, 103–174.

Isacks, B. Sykes, L.R. and Oliver, J. (1969). Focal mechanism of deep and shallow earthquakes in the Tonga-Kermadac region and the tectonics of island arcs. *Geol. Soc. Am. Bull.* **80**, 1443–1470.

Jackson, J.A. (1980a). Errors in focal depth determination and the depth of seismicity in Iran and Turkey. *Geophys. J. Roy. Astr. Soc.* **61**, 285–301.

Jackson, J.A. (1980b). Reactivation of basement faults and crustal shortening in orogenic belts. *Nature, London* **283**, 343–346.

Jackson, J. and Fitch, T. (1981). Basement faulting and the focal depths of the larger earthquakes in the Zagros Mountains (Iran). *Geophys. J. Roy. Astr. Soc.* **64**, 561–586.

Jackson, J., Molnar, P., Patton, H. and Fitch, T. (1979). Seismotectonic aspects of the Markansu Valley, Tadjikistan, earthquake of August 11, 1974. *J. Geophys. Res.* **84**, 6157–6167.

Jacob, K.H., Pennington, W.D., Armbruster, J., Seeber, L. and Farhatulla, S. (1979). Tarbela reservoir, Pakistan: A region of compressional tectonics with reduced seismicity upon initial reservoir filling. *Bull. Seismol. Soc. Am.* **69**, 1175–1192.

James, D.E. (1971). Andean crustal and upper mantle structure. *J. Geophys. Res.* **76**, 3246–3271.

Johnson, T. and Molnar, P. (1972). Focal mechanisms and plate tectonics of the southwest Pacific. *J. Geophys. Res.* **77**, 5000–5032.

Kieth, C., Simpson, D.W. and Soboleva, O.V. (1982). Induced

seismicity and deformation style at Nurek reservoir. Tadjik SSR, *J. Geophys. Res.* **87**, 4609–4624.

Kostrov, B.V. (1974). Seismic moment and energy of earthquakes, and the seismic flow of rock. *Izv. Acad. Sci. USSR, Phys. Solid Earth*, 23–40 (English trans. 13–21).

Kuchai, V.K. and Trifonov, V.G. (1977). A young left-lateral displacement in the Darvaz-Karakul fault zone. *Geotektonika* **11** (English trans.), 218–226.

Lawrence, R.D. and Yeats, R.S. (1979). Geological reconnaissance of the Chaman fault in Pakistan. *In* "Geodynamics of Pakistan" (A. Farah and K. De Jong, eds). Geol. Surv. Pakistan, Quetta, Pakistan, pp. 351–357.

Lee, W.H.K., Wu, F.T. and Jacobson, C. (1976). A catalog of historical earthquakes in China compiled from recent Chinese publications. *Bull. Seismol. Soc. Am.* **66**, 2003–2016.

Lee, W.H.K., Wu, F.T. and Wang, S.C. (1978). A catalog of instrumentally determined earthquakes in China (magnitude ⩾ 6) compiled from various sources. *Bull. Seismol. Soc. Am.* **68**, 383–398.

LeFort, P. (1975). Himalayas: the collided range: Present knowledge of the continental arc. *Am. J. Sci.* **275–A**, 1–44.

Lyon-Caen, H. and Molnar P. (1983). Constraints on the structure of the Himalaya from an analysis of gravity anomalies and a flexural model of the lithosphere, submitted to *J. Geophys. Res.* **88**.

McKenzie, D.P. (1972). Active tectonics of the Mediterranean region. *Geophys. J. Roy. Astr. Soc.* **30**, 109–186.

Mégard, F. (1978). "Etude Géologique des Andes du Pérou Central." Contribution a L'Etude Géologique des Andes No. 1. Memoires ORSTROM No. 86, Paris.

Mercier, J.L. (1981). Extensional/compressional tectonics associated with the Aegean Arc: comparison with the Andean Cordillera of South Peru-North Bolivia. *Phil. Trans. Roy. Soc. London* **A300**, 337–355.

Misharina, L.A. (1967). "Stresses in the Earth's Crust in Rift Zones" (in Russian). Nauka, Moscow, 1967.

Misharina, L.A. and Solonenka, N.V. (1972). On the stresses of weak earthquakes of Pribaikalia (in Russian). *Izv. Acad. Sci. USSR, Phys. Solid Earth* **4**, 24–36.

Molnar, P. and Sykes, L.R. (1969). Tectonics of the Caribbean and Middle America regions from focal mechanisms and seismicity. *Geol. Soc. Am. Bull.* **80**, 1639–1684.

Molnar, P. and Tapponnier, P. (1975). Cenozoic tectonics of Asia: Effects of a continental collision. *Science* **189**, 419–426.

Molnar, P. and Tapponnier, P. (1978). Active tectonics of Tibet. *J. Geophys. Res.* **83**, 5361–5375.

Molnar, P. and Tapponnier, P. (1981). A possible dependence of the tectonic strength on the age of the crust in Asia. *Earth Planet. Sci. Lett.* **52**, 107–114.

Molnar, P., Fitch, T.J. and Wu, F.T. (1973). Fault plane solutions of shallow earthquakes and contemporary tectonics of Asia. *Earth Planet. Sci. Lett.* **16**, 101–112.

Molnar, P., Chen, W.P., Fitch, T.J., Tapponnier, P., Warsi, W.E.K. and Wu, F.T. (1977). Structure and tectonics of the Himalaya: A brief summary of relevant geophysical observations, *Colloque Internationaux du CNRS, Himalaya: Sciences de la Terre*, Éditions du Centre National de la Recherche Scientifique, Paris, 267–294.

Molnar, P., Freedman, D. and Shih, J.S.F. (1979). Lengths of intermediate and deep seismic zones and temperatures in downgoing slabs of lithosphere. *Geophys. J. Roy. Astr. Soc.* **56**, 41–54.

Natsag-yum, L., Balzhinnyam, I. and Monkho, D. (1971). Earthquakes in Mongolia (in Russian). *In* "Seismic Regionalization of Ulan-Bator." Nauka, Moscow, pp. 54–82.

Ni, J. (1978). Contemporary tectonics in the Tien Shan region. *Earth Planet. Sci. Lett.* **41**, 347–355.

Ni, J. and York, J.E. (1978). Cenozoic extensional tectonics of the Tibetan Plateau. *J. Geophys. Res.* **83**, 5377–5384.

Niazi, M., Asudeh, I., Ballard, G., Jackson, J., King, G. and McKenzie, D. (1978). The depth of seismicity in the Kermanshah region of the Zagros Mountains (Iran). *Earth Planet. Sci. Lett.* **40**, 270–274.

North, R.G. (1974). Seismic slip rates in the Mediterranean and Middle East. *Nature, London* **252**, 560–563.

Ocola, L. and Meyer, R.P. (1973). Crustal structure from the Pacific Basin to the Brazilian Shield between 12° and 30° South Latitude. *Geol. Soc. Am. Bull.* **84**, 3387–3404.

Oldham, R.D. (1899). Report on the great earthquake of 12th June 1897. *Mem. Geol. Surv. India* **29**, 1–379.

Philip, H. and Mégard, F. (1977). Structural analysis of the superficial deformation of the 1969 Pariahuanca Earthquakes (Central Peru). *Tectonophysics* **38**, 259–278.

Prevot, R., Hatzfeld, D., Roecker, S.W. and Molnar, P. (1980). Shallow earthquakes and active tectonics in eastern Afghanistan. *J. Geophys. Res.* **85**, 1347–1357.

Quittmeyer, R.C. and Jacob, K.H. (1979). Historical and modern seismicity of Pakistan, Afghanistan, northwestern India, and southeastern Iran. *Bull. Seismol. Soc. Am.* **69**, 773–823.

Richter, C.F. (1958). "Elementary Seismology." W.H. Freeman and Co., San Francisco, 768.

Ricou, L.-E., Braud, J. and Brunn, J.H. (1977). Le Zagros. *In* "Livre à la Mémoire de Albert F. de Lapparent, Recherches Géologiques dans les Chaînes Alpines de l'Asie du Sud-Ouest." *Mém.* **No. 8**, *Soc. Géol. Fr.* 33–52.

Roecker, S.W. (1982). Velocity structure of the Pamir-Hindu Kush region: Possible evidence of subducted crust. *J. Geophys. Res.* **87**, 945–960.

Roecker, S.W., Soboleva, O.V., Nersesov, I.L., Lukk, A.A., Hatzfeld, D., Chatelain, J.L. and Molnar, P. (1980). Seismicity and fault plane solutions of intermediate depth earthquakes in the Pamir-Hindu Kush region. *J. Geophys. Res.* **85**, 1358–1364.

Romanovicz, B. (1981). Depth resolution of earthquakes in central Asia by moment tensor inversion of long period Rayleigh waves: Effects of phase velocity variations across Eurasia and their calibration. *J. Geophys. Res.* **86**, 5963–5984.

Ruzhentsev, S.V. (1963). Strike slip faults of the southeastern Pamir (in Russian). *In* "Faults and Horizontal Movements of the Earth's Crust." *Tr. Geol. Inst. Akad. Nauk SSSR* **80**, 113–127.

Seeber, L. and Armbruster, J.G. (1979). Seismicity of the Hazara arc in northern Pakistan: Décollement vs. basement faulting. *In* "Geodynamics of Pakistan" (A. Farah and K.A. De Jong, eds). *Geol. Surv. Pakistan* 131–142.

Seeber, L. and Armbruster, J.G. (1981). Great detachment earthquakes along the Himalayan arc and long-term forecasting. *In* "Earthquake Prediction: an International Review, Maurice Ewing Series IV" (D.W. Simpson and P.G. Richards, eds) pp. 259–279. Am. Geophys. Un., Washington, D.C.

Seeber, L., Armbruster, J.G. and Quittmeyer, R.C. (1981). Seismicity and continental subduction in the Himalayan arc. Interunion Commisson in Geodynamics, Working Group 6 Volume. *Zagros, Hindu Kush, Himalaya Geodynamic Evolution, Geodynamic Series Volume 6*, Amer. Geophys. Un., Washington, D.C. and Geol. Soc. Amer., Boulder, Colo., 215–242.

Shirokova, E.I. (1967). General regularities in orientation of principal stresses in the foci of earthquakes of the Mediterranean-Asiatic seismic belt (in Russian), *Izv. Acad. Sci. USSR Phys. Solid Earth* **1**, 22–36.

Shirokova, E.I. (1974). Detailed study of the stresses and fault planes at earthquake foci of Central Asia (in Russian). *Ivz. Acad. Sci. USSR Phys. Solid Earth* **11**, 22–36.

Simpson, D.W., Hamburger, M.W., Pavlov, V.D. and Nersesov, I.L. (1981). Tectonics and seismicity of the Toktogul reservoir region, Kirgizia, USSR. *J. Geophys. Res.* **86**, 345–358.

Solomon, S.C. and Julian, B.R. (1974). Seismic constraints on ocean-ridge mantle structure: anomalous fault plane solutions from first motions. *Geophys. J. Roy. Astr. Soc.* **38**, 265–285.

Solonenko, V.P., Kurushin, R.A. and Khilko, S.D. (1966a). Strong earthquakes (in Russian). *In* "Recent Tectonics, Volcanoes, and Seismicity of the Stanovoy Upland." Nauka, Moscow, pp. 145–171.

Solonenko, V.P., Kurushin, R.A. and Pavlov, O.V. (1966b). Seismogenic structures of the Udokan system of activated faults (in Russian). *In* "Recent Tectonics, Volcanoes, and Seismicity of the Stanovoy Upland." Nauka, Moscow, pp. 187–205.

Solonenko, V.P., Khromovskikh, V.S., Pavlov, O.V., Kurushin, R.A., Khilko, S.D., Shmotov, A.P. and Zhilkin, V.M. (1968). Epicentral areas of early (preseismostatistical) earthquakes (in Russian). *In* Seismotectonics and Seismicity of the Rift System of Pribaikalia". Nauka, Moscow, pp. 7–59.

Stauder, W. (1968). Tensional character of earthquake foci beneath the Aleutian Trench with relation to sea-floor spreading. *J. Geophys. Res.* **73**, 7693–7702.

Stauder, W. (1975). Subduction of the Nazca plate under Peru as evidenced by focal mechanism and by seismicity. *J. Geophys. Res* **80**, 1053–1064.

Stöcklin, J. (1977). Structural correlation of the Alpine ranges between Iran and Central Asia. *In* "Livre à la Mémoire de Albert F.

de Lapparent, Recherches Géologiques dans les Chaînes Alpines de l'Asie du Sud-Ouest." *Mém. No. 8, Soc. Géol. Fr.* pp. 333–353.

Suárez, G., Molnar, P. and Burchfiel, B.C. (1983). Seismicity, fault plane solutions, depth of faulting and active tectonics of the central Andes, submitted to *J. Geophys. Res.* **88.**

Takin, M. (1972). Iranian geology and continental drift in the Middle East. *Nature, London* **235,** 147–150.

Tapponnier, P. (1977). Évolution tectonique du système alpin en Méditerranée: poinçonnement et écrasement rigide-plastique. *Bull. Soc. Géol. Fr.* **XIX,** 437–460.

Tapponnier, P. and Molnar, P. (1976). Slip-line field theory and large-scale continental tectonics. *Nature, London* **264,** 319–324.

Tapponnier, P. and Molnar, P. (1977). Active faulting and tectonics of China. *J. Geophys. Res.* **82,** 2945–2969.

Tapponnier, P. and Molnar, P. (1979). Active faulting and Cenozoic tectonics of the Tien Shan, Mongolia and Baykal Region. *J. Geophys. Res.* **84,** 3425–3459.

Tikhonov, V.I. (1974). Faults (in Russian). *In* "Tectonics of the Mongolian People's Republic." Nauka, Moscow, pp. 196–209.

Trifonov, V.G. (1978). Late Quaternary tectonic movements of western and central Asia. *Bull. Geol. Soc. Am.* **89,** 1059–1072.

Utsu, T. (1967). Anomalies in seismic wave velocity and attenuation associated with a deep earthquake zone (I). *J. Fac. Sci., Hokkaido Univ., Series VII (Geophys.)* **3,** 1–25.

Vilkas, A. (1981). In preparation.

Voitovich, V.S. (1969). Nature of the Dzungarian deep fault (in Russian). *Tr. Geol. Inst. Akad. Nauk SSSR* **183,** 189 pp.

Warsi, W.E.K. and Molnar, P. (1977). Plate tectonics and gravity anomalies in India and the Himalaya. *Colloques Internationaux du CNRS, Himalaya: Sciences de la Terre,* Éditions du Centre National de la Recherche Scientifique, Paris, 463–478.

Wellman, H.W. (1966). Active wrench faults of Iran, Afghanistan and Pakistan. *Geol. Rundschau* **55,** 716–735.

Wesson, R.L., Leonova, V.G., Maksimov, A.B., Nersesov, I.L. and Fisher, F.G. (1976). Results of field seismological investigations in 1975 in the region of the Peter I Range. *In* "Sbornik: Soviet-American work on the Prediction of Earthquakes, I," Book 1, Donish, Dushanbe, USSR, pp. 43–69.

Yeats, R.S., Lawrence, R.D., Jamil-Ud-Din, S. and Hassan Khan, S. (1979). Surface effects of the 16 March 1978 earthquake, Pakistan-Afghanistan border. *In* "Geodynamics of Pakistan" (A. Farah and K. De Jong, eds). Geol. Surv. Pakistan, Quetta, Pakistan, pp. 359–361.

Appendix A

Methods, Uncertainties, and Philosophy in Interpreting Seismic Results

A. Locations of Earthquakes

Locating earthquakes reliably is a deceptively difficult process. Obtaining a location is relatively easy; usually one seeks a location and origin time that minimize the differences in observed and calculated arrival times of P and sometimes S phases at various stations. Numerous computer programs for different station-source geometries exist and are routinely implemented. The major difficulty is estimating an uncertainty in the location, particularly in the depth of focus. The effects of different seismic wave velocity structures, station distributions, and uncertainties in arrival times on computed locations are often difficult to evaluate without simply making numerous tests with both real and synthetic data, with different velocity structures, and with various randomly added errors to the data. Some simple rules of thumb do exist, but we caution readers to pay careful attention to the discussions of uncertainties in published studies.

Both the U.S. Geological Survey (and formerly the U.S. Coast and Geodetic Survey and the National Oceanic and Atmospheric Administration) and the International Seismological Center routinely locate earthquakes using P wave arrival times reported by stations distributed throughout the world. During the last 20 years the number of stations used, the number of earthquakes located, and the quality of the locations have all increased. These locations provide basic data sets that have been very useful for seismic studies of all kinds. Nevertheless, blind acceptance of these locations can lead to erroneous inferences. One must filter the reported locations by removing those with poor station distributions and with large residuals between observed and calculated arrival times. The uncertainties of the most reliable epicentres are probably at least 10 km, and systematic errors of as much as 20 km are known for well recorded and precisely located events (e.g. Cleary, 1967; Utsu, 1967). By careful examination of the distribution of stations used to locate the events and having small residuals, one can produce a list of events with uncertainties in epicentres generally less than 20 km. Such lists generally include only $\frac{1}{3}$ to $\frac{1}{4}$ of the locations reported by the USGS or ISC (e.g. Barazangi and Isacks, 1976, 1979; Billington *et al.*, 1977; Isacks and Molnar, 1971; Molnar *et al.* 1973). The uncertainties in relative locations can be reduced by determining the locations relative to a nearby master event, but it is our opinion that relocations of individual events that occurred in the last 10 years using the same data that the USGS or ISC used are not likely to be significantly better than the locations reported by those agencies.

Depths of foci are considerably more uncertain than epicentral coordinates. Depths can be well constrained if phases reflected from the earth surface above the earthquake (pP and sP) are well recorded. Such phases are often clear for events deeper than about 70 km but rarely so for shallower events. If there are stations closer to the epicentres than the focal depth, depths can be reliably obtained, but this is rarely the case for shallow events. Consequently all reported depths less than about 70 km for events located teleseismically should be viewed with suspicion, unless other information is used to support the reported depth.

Recently there has been considerable progress using synthetic seismograms to constrain depths of shallow events. Using the known fault plate solution one calculates theoretical seismograms for P or S phases (including sP and sP or pS and sS) for different depths and compares them with observed seismograms. The method works best for simple events, whose dimensions are sufficiently small and for which the slip on the fault is sufficiently abrupt that the source can be adequately modeled as point source. With synthetic seismograms, the uncertainties in depths can usually be reduced to less than 5 km.

For earthquakes recorded by local networks, locations can be more accurate than when only teleseismic data are used. For earthquakes occurring within the network, both epicentres and depths can be precise within a few km. Depths depend upon the distances to the nearest stations. Depths rapidly become unreliable the more the epicentral distance to the nearest station exceeds the focal depth. For events outside the network, uncertainties in both depths and epicentres can be very large, and generally we do not trust such locations unless special studies have been made to examine the uncertainties.

Once locations and their uncertainties have been determined, geologic inference can include the spectrum of seemingly conflicting possibilities. Whereas the occurrence of earthquakes attests to current tectonic activity, the absence of earthquakes can mean tectonic stability, merely temporary quiescence, or aseismic, but possibly rapid, deformation. Clearly geologic inference in the absence of other geologic information can be risky, if not simply subjective. An often asked question is whether a given distribution of earthquakes that occurred during a finite time interval is representative of the long term seismicity. It is our belief that in most regions thousands of years of data will be necessary to establish the long term average characteristics of the seismicity. If this is so, then one is safer posing questions for which a detailed knowledge of the long term seismicity is not important. Thus, while we can use seismicity to study aspects of the active tectonics of selected regions, we must recognize that there are both aseismic processes and discontinuous processes about which our short record of earthquakes can tell us little or nothing.

B. Fault Plane Solutions

Most fault plane solutions are determined using only the initial motions of P waves, but solutions can be improved using initial motions or polarizations of S waves, the complex spectra or amplitudes of surface waves, or the wave forms of body waves. It is our opinion that the orientations of the nodal planes determined in fault plane solutions with P wave initial motions are rarely more certain than $\pm 10°$. The other techniques mentioned above can improve the precision of the solutions, but because lateral variations in earth structure can alter the ray paths substantially and distort the solutions (e.g. Engdahl *et al.*, 1977; Solomon and Julian, 1974), we still think that 10° is a safe lower bound for the uncertainty.

With teleseismic data, the most precisely determined solutions are those for strike-slip faulting on vertical planes. Both nodal planes are vertical and the data usually constrain them tightly (Fig. A1). The poorest determined solutions are for dip slip faulting on planes dipping at 30° to 60°. Most of the data come from stations far enough away from the source and for which the take-off angles of the rays are steep so that first motions of only one sign cluster in the centre of the focal sphere (Fig. A1). There is no doubt about the type of faulting — normal or thrust — but the orientations of the nodal planes are not constrained. Moreover, because of both lateral variations in and an inadequate knowledge of the earth's upper mantle structure, the direction of P waves leaving the source to stations closer than about 30° is very uncertain. Unfortunately fault plane solutions of earthquakes in continents are often of this type and therefore are poorly constrained (Fig. A1).

When local networks are used, the uncertainties in the ray paths are even greater and can depend strongly on the assumed velocity structure. Whereas the location of an earthquake might be insensitive to whether rays leave the source upwards or are refracted by deeper layers before returning to the surface, the fault plane solutions depend critically on an accurate knowledge of the directions the rays leave the source. In some cases, particularly for strike-slip faulting, the solutions are not very sensitive to the assumed velocity structure, but in others, it can be impossible to determine a solution because of this dependence. Accordingly sometimes it is very difficult to estimate the uncertainty of the parameters describing a fault plane solution, because one cannot evaluate the uncertainties in the directions that the ray paths leave the source. The best measure of the quality of the solution is probably given by the number of reliable readings. Solutions based on only 8 or 10 first motions are less reliable than those based on 15 or 20. Often to increase the number of data, composite fault plane solutions are determined, using many different earthquakes. It is our opinion that composite fault plane solutions are useful only when the data from events in a small volume are very consistent with only one pair of nodal planes. We do not put much faith in composite solutions for which data from neighbouring regions of diffuse seismicity give different solutions and with 10% or more of the readings inconsistent with the inferred solutions. One good solution for one event is more valuable than several composite solutions. Moreover, solutions for bigger events are probably more representative of the large-scale deformation than those of small events.

For published discussions of fault plane solutions, the rules of thumb are (1) if a stereographic projection of the focal sphere is not shown or not readily available in the referenced literature, it is often safer to ignore the reported solution than to believe it; and (2) if the data are presented

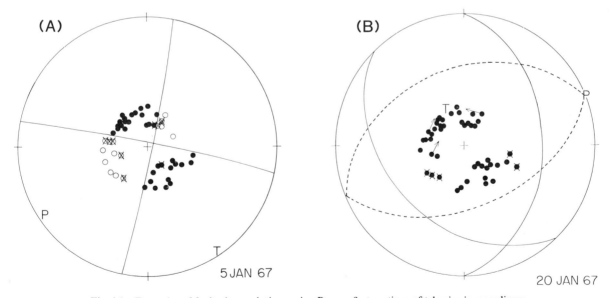

(A) P T 5 JAN 67

(B) T P 20 JAN 67

Fig. A1 Examples of fault plane solutions using P wave first motions of teleseismic recordings:
(a) A well-constrained solution for a vertical strike-slip event where the nodal planes are primarily determined by the azimuthal distribution of data points.
(b) A poorly-constrained solution for a thrust event where the position of the nodal planes are primarily determined by the distances of the data points from the centre of the projection (the take-off angles). The solid curves are the preferred solution based on the observed strike of the surface rupture and the S wave polarization angles (arrows). Note the dotted curves arbitrarily drawn are also consistent with the first motions. Solid circles indicate compressional first motions (away from the source), the open circles for dilatational first motions (towards the source). The dip-slip event is an aftershock and occurred about 40 km to the south of the strike-slip event (main shock) in southern Mongolia in 1967. Data taken from Tapponnier and Molnar (1979).

and plotted reliably, it is an easy matter for anyone familiar with stereographic projections to examine how consistent the P wave initial motions are and how well they define two orthogonal planes. When additional data (S waves, surface waves, etc.) are used, it can be more difficult for the nonseismologist to obtain an appreciation of the uncertainty in the solution, but in some cases the authors do address this question directly.

Once one has a fault plane solution there is some uncertainty in how to interpret it. The solution is defined by two nodal planes. One is the fault plane, and the normal to the other, the slip vector, gives the direction of relative motion on the fault plane. From the fault plane solution alone, one cannot choose which of the nodal planes is the fault plane. Additional information is needed to resolve this ambiguity — mapped faults, planes or belts of seismicity, etc. Sometimes the ambiguity cannot be resolved. Clearly, if we can identify the strike of the fault plane from other geologic information, the fault plane solution can be used to give the dip of the plane and the direction of slip on it. But even when this is not the case, solutions often provide useful information about the active tectonics in the area.

Fault plane solutions can be uniquely described by the strikes and dips of the two nodal planes or by the plunges and azimuths of the normals to these planes. They also can be described by the orientations of the P, T, and B axes. The P and T axes lie at 45° to the two nodal planes in the quadrants with dilatational and compressional initial motions, respectively. The B axis is parallel to the line of intersection of the two planes. The P, B, and T axes crudely, but often inaccurately, approximate the directions of the maximum, intermediate and least compressive stresses. The solution can be described by any two of the planes or axes, and in fact requires only three angles for its complete description, for instance, the strike and dip of one nodal plane and the direction of slip in that plane. Thus, the axes and planes are not unique quantities. Which among them are physically important and which are merely consequences of the others are subjective questions whose answers are not universally agreed upon. We give some opinions below.

Along well defined faults or fault zones such as plate boundaries, the important parameters seem to be the orientations of the planes and slip vectors. The P, T, and B axes do not seem to be quantities worthy of discussion. For instance where spreading centres and transform faults intersect, the horizontal components of the slip vector do not change, but the T axis rotates 45° and P and B axes change by 90°. If the regional stress field changed by this much in such a short distance, then the concept of a regional stress field would not be very useful. Similarly the consistent orientation of the P axes for earthquakes along major strike-slip faults or at underthrust zones of island arcs is merely a consequence of the directions of motion along the faults. The stress field is likely to change along the faults, but because it is a zone of weakness, the fault controls the response of the region to the local stress field.

In regions with numerous faults, however, slip will occur on those with orientations most suitably oriented with respect to the stress field. In such a case, one can expect slip on nearby planes with different orientations. The slip vectors and nodal planes might scatter widely, but either the P or the T axis might be consistent among these solutions. For instance, in the western Basin and Range province of North America, both strike-slip and normal faulting are common, but the T axes are usually oriented north-west–south-east. This suggests that the region is being stretched in a north-west–south-east direction.

The simple rule of thumb with fault plane solutions for many earthquakes in a region is that the consistent parameter is the important one. If the nodal planes are paral-

lel, then probably there is slip on one, or several parallel faults, because of translation of one block (or plate) past another. If the nodal planes are not parallel but either the P or the T axis is consistent in orientation, then the orientation of that axis is probably the important parameter obtained from the analysis.

C. The Seismic Moment, Dimensions of Faults, and Rates of Deformation

A major step forward was made in seismology 15 years ago when Aki (1966, 1967) recognized that the amplitudes of long period seismic waves are proportional to the product $\mu A \bar{u}$, which he called the seismic moment, M_0. In this expression μ is the shear modulus in the volume surrounding the earthquake, A is the rupture area, and $\bar{u}$ is the average displacement over the faulted area. The theory behind this relationship is beyond the scope of this paper, but estimating M_0 is sufficiently easy that it has become a part of nearly all seismologists' repertoire. Uncertainties in M_0 are rarely discussed, but in general they probably are less than a factor of 2. For older events, for which the data are relatively poor, the uncertainty may be larger. Also for shallow events with one shallow dipping nodal plane, the estimated value of M_0 becomes very sensitive to the dip and increasingly uncertain for shallower and shallower dips. For strike-slip faults or for solutions with planes dipping at 30° to 60°, the uncertainty of a factor of 2 is probably a reasonable upper bound.

To estimate either of A or $\bar{u}$ one must independently determine the other. One may estimate $\bar{u}$ from measurements of surface displacement when surface faulting is observed. A can be estimated from (and assumed to be equal to) the area of the aftershock zone. Often one can estimate a fault length, from surface faulting or from the length of the aftershock zone. Then one may estimate $\bar{u}$ using plausible values of the fault width. Clearly the uncertainties in all of M_0, A and $\bar{u}$ are comparable.

We can use the seismic moments of earthquakes to estimate the rate of deformation in a region. Brune (1968) showed that when only one fault plane is active, one can estimate the average rate of slip, v, by adding the seismic moments of earthquakes occurring in a reasonable length of time, t:

$$v = \sum_{i=1}^{n} M_{0i}/\mu A t = \sum_{i=1}^{n} \bar{u}_i/t$$

Here, A is the area of the entire fault under consideration. Kostrov (1974) generalized this for faults of different orientations and gave a similar expression for the strain rate in a volume (see also Anderson, 1979; Chen and Molnar, 1977). The uncertainty in the rate of slip or in the strain rate consists of four parts. One is related to the estimates of the moments and again is approximately a factor of two. A second enters with the assumed area of the fault or volume of the region. Usually we know well ($\pm$ a few percent) the fault length or the area of the region in which we calculate the slip or strain rate, but the depth involved in deformation by earthquakes is less certain. This uncertainty (of about a factor of 2) arises both from our ignorance of the depths of earthquakes and brittle deformation and from the likely gradual brittle ductile transition. Another uncertainty arises from our ignorance of how much deformation occurs by fault creep instead of by earthquakes, and cannot be estimated easily yet. Finally there exists the (very likely) possibility that the time, t, is too short to make the present value of v a reliable estimate of long term seismic slip. Clearly Brune's and Kostrov's methods are too crude to corroborate rates of slip on deformation determined using marine magnetic anomalies and plate tectonics. Their value comes in placing constraints on the thickness of the zone of brittle deformation, on the importance of fault creep, or on the possibility that a large event is imminent. A low rate of seismic slip, compared with that obtained from plate motions, can be attributed to an unusually thin layer of brittle deformation, a large fraction of fault creep or aseismic slip, an unrepresentative seismic history, or a recent change in plate motions. Deciding which is correct requires the consideration of other data.

Acknowledgments

This paper contains results from numerous studies that at the time of this writing are not yet completed. Accordingly we would like to use these acknowledgments as a platform to encourage the reader to seek out these relevant but unfinished papers. In particular, J. Armbruster, J. Baranowski, and L. Seeber did most of the work that will be contained in Armbruster *et al.* (1983) on the Himalaya. A. Vilkas has not yet completed her study of the Tien Shan, and neither G. Suárez nor D. Chinn and B. Isacks had finished writing their papers on the Andes when this paper was first assembled. Moreover, we have appreciated continuous interaction with D. Hatzfeld on the seismicity of the Atlas region and with P. Tapponnier on the tectonics of Asia in general. Finally, without a close interaction with W.F. Brace, B. Evans, and C. Goetze, the discussion of depths of foci would not have evolved to its present state. This research was supported by the National Science Foundation Grant #EAR 79–26349 and #EAR 80–18705, and NASA Grant #NAG 5–41 and #NAG 5–19.

Deformation in the Forearc: Implications for Mountain Belts

D.E. Karig

Department of Geological Sciences
Cornell University
New York, U.S.A.

Abstract

Most mountain belts display complexes of highly deformed deep marine sediments and oceanic crustal rocks that accumulated beneath the forearc of an arc-trench system. However, variations in the response of these rocks to subduction and the causes of those variations are only beginning to be understood. The flow patterns of material entering trenches appear to be more the functions of near surface geological parameters and relative plate motions than of deep seated factors or absolute plate motions. Sediments tend to be accreted where they form a thick cover and have internal horizons with shear strength minima. Thin sediments with high basement relief may favour intermittent accretion of oceanic crustal slices, but these conditions have also been postulated as favourable for tectonic erosion. Subduction of part of the sediment cover is well documented, but there is growing evidence that some of this subducted sediment is subcreted to the base of the upper plate.

Forearc deformation is strongly concentrated toward the base of the trench slope, but under some conditions, zones of arc-directed thrusting may develop along the rear of the trench slope break. Deformation may occur as folding, thrusting or more complete disruption with either seaward or arcward vergence. A thrust geometry with seaward vergence appears to be most common and bears remarkable similarities to that of foreland thrust belts, despite the great differences in sediment type and degree of lithification. Concentration of deformation near the trench precludes large scale turbulence within the accretionary prism to explain mixed and exotic lithologies in subduction complexes. Arguments about the tectonic vs. sedimentary origin of highly disrupted strata may be answered by studies of more local processes on trench slopes. Detailed surveys and submersible observations reveal canyon-fed fans on trench floors that could contain far-transported exotics and that are quickly involved in thrusting. The thrusts themselves may develop extensional zones which merge with rubble fronts lying in depositional contact on trench sediments. Continued thrusting could then impart shear dislocations in material just subjected to bedding-parallel extension and soft sediment slumping.

I. Introduction

For almost a century island arcs have been suspected of having a consanguinity with mountain belts, although the nature of that relationship has been perceived quite differently over this period. The plate tectonic paradigm identifies both island arcs and mountain belts as effects of plate convergence, but each of these two groups is too variable to permit construction of simple correlations. It is generally felt that many or most mountain belts result from collision events, and, as such, include elements of active arc systems. From this premise, it would appear critical to explore the characteristics of island arc elements and the processes responsible for them, so that more reliable interpretations of arc remnants in mountain belts can be made. Only after these interpretations become reliable can grander orogenic syntheses leave the realms of speculation.

The recent rapid expansion in knowledge of arc systems precludes any overall review within the constraints of this paper. I have chosen to concentrate this discussion on structural aspects of the forearc region where most of the deformation associated with convergence occurs. In mountain belts, the rocks deformed in forearcs probably account for many subduction-accretion terranes and flysch belts, as well as some ophiolites. The relatively widespread acceptance of this correlation is undoubtedly a large factor for the current interest in and excitement generated by forearc structures. Although there is acceptance of this correlation, there is much less understanding of and agreement about the variations in material response to subduction and of the causes of these variations. Because of the paucity of relevant data, much of which is still unpublished, I have blatantly drawn heavily on data from studies in which I have participated and have stressed those structural aspects in which I am most familiar.

II. Trajectories of Materials at Convergent Plate Margins

Geological and marine geophysical studies as well as deep-sea drilling results in active arcs have clearly demonstrated that there is a wide range in mechanical response of both sediments and deeper crustal units to plate convergence. The sediment cover entering a trench may be accreted to the base of the trench slope or it may be subducted to deeper levels, where it might either be subcreted to the base of the upper plate or returned to the mantle, partly to be recycled by magmatic processes. At other trenches, pieces of igneous rocks from the descending oceanic lithosphere may be transferred to the upper plate, either as thrust slices or as large coherent sheets (ophiolites). There are also trenches in which evidence supports the tectonic erosion of material from the leading edge of the upper plate and its subsequent subduction.

III. Deep vs. Shallow Causes for Variations in Response

Basic for the understanding of variations in mechanical response and of the ultimate fate of materials entering a trench is the determination of the relative importance of deeper level processes, such as the motion of the plates involved with respect to the subjacent asthenosphere, and of shallow geological processes.

A. Deep Seated Causes

Some workers (e.g. Wilson and Burke, 1972; Uyeda and Kanamori, 1979) propose basically different mechanical responses in arc systems that depend upon whether the arc-bearing plate is moving trenchward or rearward with respect to the underlying mantle. Uyeda and Kanamori (1979) suggest that, in arcs moving trenchward, strong interplate coupling would cause compression, leading to accretion and widespread deformation within the upper plate whereas retreat of the upper plate would lead to weak coupling and a greater tendency for total subduction or even tectonic erosion. Other workers suggest that, alternatively or in addition, the overall stress regime of an arc is a function of the age of the descending lithosphere. Molnar and Atwater (1978) postulate that older, denser lithosphere would lead to lower compression or even extension across the plate boundary whereas subduction of young buoyant lithosphere would favour "Cordilleran" tectonics, with broad zones of deformation and high mountains.

It is quite reasonable that the stress conditions at depth, between the rigid parts of the two plates, are affected by their age and motions with respect to the mantle, but several lines of reasoning argue against extending the effects of these stresses to the forearc region. First of all, there is evidence to suggest that the interplate stress field at shallow depth, beneath the forearc, is not highly dependent upon the deeper level stress behaviour. The descending lithosphere beneath arcs describes a two-part geometry, with a flatter shallow section and a steeper deep section, separated by a hinge zone of maximum curvature (Fig. 1; Karig et al., 1976) where deformation is probably plastic (McAdoo et al., 1978). The width of the upper section correlates closely with the width of the forearc in most arcs, suggesting an evolutionary relationship (Karig et al., 1976). Because the geometry of broader examples of upper seismic sections can be successfully modeled as elastic slabs loded under the weight of the forearc, we concluded that deeper stresses in the descending plate are only partly transmitted through the hinge zone.

This hinge zone, located beneath the upper part of the

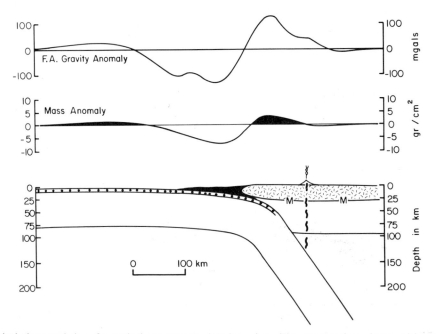

Fig. 1.   Some mechanical characteristics of a typical convergent plate boundary. The cross-section, shown without vertical exaggeration, illustrates the plate interface, separated into two sections by a hinge zone at 20–50 km depth. Most of the vertical span of interplate contact occurs below this hinge. The mass anomaly (after Grow, 1973; Grow and Bowin, 1975) is determined from seismic refraction and gravity data and indicates that interplate compression is maintaining a dynamic elevation of the frontal arc. This is also expressed by large positive free-air gravity anomaly over most frontal arcs (e.g. Talwani, 1970).

inner slope, has been interpreted to be approximately fixed during arc evolution (Karig *et al.*, 1976) and to mark the original mechanical contact between the two plates when subduction began (e.g. Westbrook, 1975). Thus it is plausible that the major interplate mechanical coupling occurs between the hinge zone, which begins at depths of 20–30 km, and the base of the upper plate (Fig. 1). Such mechanical coupling ought to be manifested by dynamic elevation of the frontal arc above its isostatic equilibrium position. This condition can be shown to exist in several frontal arcs where crustal structure, defined by seismic refraction profiles, can be converted to mass columns and compared to standard ocean basin sections known to be in isostatic equilibrium (e.g. Grow, 1973; Grow and Bowin, 1975). Much of the large free-air gravity anomalies over most frontal arcs (e.g. Talwani, 1970) very likely also reflect this dynamic elevation.

Deeper stress conditions might also affect the response to material entering forearcs through their effects on the geometry of the descending lithosphere beneath and seaward of the trench, and on the resultant development of normal faults on the outer trench slope (Jones *et al.*, 1978; Bodine and Watts, 1979). The relief developed by this faulting is one of the factors that will be suggested to be important in controlling material response to convergence, but a close correlation between the curvature of the outer trench slope (and thus development of extensional faults) and the width of accretionary prism indicated that the load this element imposes on the descending lithosphere plays the dominant role in shaping the geometry of the outer trench slope (Karig *et al.*, 1976).

Another reason for doubting the efficacy of deeper level stresses in controlling forearc structure is the apparent poor correlation between variations in these two parameters (Fig. 2). For example, tectonic erosion has been postulated in a range of arcs, from those which move strongly seaward with respect to the mantle to those moving rapidly to the rear; forearc responses seems equally insensitive to the age of the descending lithosphere.

B. Shallow Level Factors Affecting Accretion and Subduction

Shallow level geologic and kinematic factors appear to exert a dominant influence on the trajectory of material landward of the trench. Influencing factors that can be identified or are suspected include the thickness and mechanical properties of the sedimentary cover on the descending plate, the local relief of basement on this plate, and the rate and direction of subduction.

Thick sediment covers correlate well with large accretionary prisms. There does not, however, appear to be a linear relationship between sediment thickness and the amount of accretion; that is, the percentage of the incoming sediment that is accreted to the base of the trench slope varies widely. The thickness of accreted sediment appears to be controlled by the presence of zones within the sediment section having local porosity maxima and shear strength minima (Karig, 1974; Moore, 1975). These zones can develop in clay-rich sediments that are sandwiched between coarser clastic sequences, or near the top of slowly deposited clay-rich sections that are overlain by rapidly deposited coarse clastics. The most common site for the prospective shear zones that propagate at the base of the trench slope is near the base of the relatively coarse grained trench-fill turbidites, where the porous material can be the youngest basin sediments or the hemipelagic fringe of the trench wedge. Rapid sedimentation promotes elevated pore pressures in these zones of low permeability. Thrusting at the base of the trench slope employs this zone as a decollement, which, after tectonic loading, develops even greater pore pressure-lithostatic pressure ratios and further reduces its residual strength.

Recent high-quality seismic reflection profiles illustrate quite a consistent correlation between accretion and the character of the incoming sediment section over a broad range of sediment geometries (Fig. 3). Where relatively thick trench turbidites overlie a thin pelagic basin cover, as in the Cascade arc, most of the sediment column appears to be

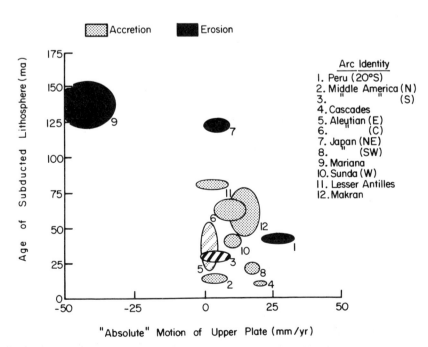

Fig. 2 Plot of the age of subducted lithosphere vs. "absolute" motion of the upper plate with respect to a deeper mantle that is assumed nearly stationary, showing a lack of correlation between either of these and the material response at trenches. Data from Uyeda and Kanamori (1979), Chase (1978), and Molnar and Atwater (1978).

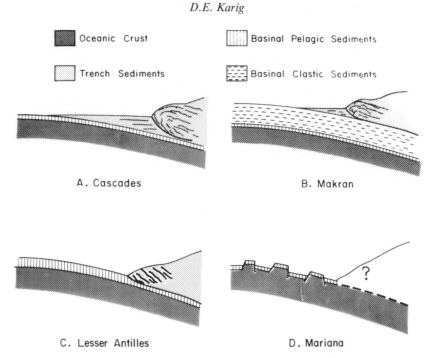

Fig. 3 Modes of accretion at trenches as a function of the character of the sediment cover on the descending plate. The fraction of sediments accreted to the lower slope is dependent on the existence, occurrence and position of a zone of relatively high porosity and low shear strength within sediment columns. Such zones commonly occur near the transition from basinal to trench sediments (A, B). Monotonic upward increase in porosity favours accretion of little or no sediments at the base of the slope (C). Thin sediment cover and high basement relief has been assumed to produce either tectonic erosion or accretion of crustal slices (D).

involved in thrusting at the base of the trench slope (Seeley et al., 1974; Snavely et al., 1980). In contrast, of the more than 6 km of sediment on the floor of the Arabian Sea that enters the Makran Trench, only the upper 2 to 2·5 km, comprising a broad trench wedge, are initially accreted (White and Klitgord, 1976; White, 1981). Where no significant trench fill exists, but the oceanic crust has a moderate to thick pelagic section, as in the Lesser Antilles Arc, the uppermost pelatic sediment appears to be accreted (Bijou-Duvall et al., 1981). As the pelitic cover on the incoming crust thins, the forearc response becomes more uncertain and/or variable. Minor accretion, lack of any material transfer across the plate interface, or tectonic erosion has been suggested for the Japan (Scientific Party, 1980), south-eastern Middle America (Von Huene et al., 1980), Peru–Chile (Kulm et al., 1977; Hussong et al., 1976), and Mariana trenches (Hussong and Uyeda, 1981).

A reduction in thickness of the sedimentary cover may also be paralleled by an increased involvement of oceanic crustal and even mantle fragments in the accretion. This relationship is deduced primarily from the mapping of tectonic blocks or thrust slices of these igneous rocks in the shallow structural levels of accretionary prisms where structural position is constrained by the preservation of overlying slope sediments. Particularly clear examples of crustal involvement are the early Miocene accretionary complex on Nias Island of the Sunda Arc (Moore and Karig, 1980), and the early Tertiary Shimanto complex of south-west Japan (Taira et al., 1980). Unfortunately, deep-sea drilling has not yet succeeded in documenting this type of material flow pattern.

Accretion of igneous rocks may correlate with thin sediment covers but it might more directly reflect an increased importance of the nature of the oceanic basement entering trenches, in particular, its local relief. The relief of the oceanic basement entering trenches is a function not only of the rate of spreading that created it but also of the intensity of normal faulting resulting from the flexure of oceanic lithosphere seaward of the trench. In the most highly flexed crust, this horst graben relief may exceed 500 m, with

displacements exceeding the total sediment thickness (Jones et al., 1978).

Karig and Sharman (1975) proposed that protuberances on oceanic basement, including horsts and seamounts, might on occasion be sheared off and intermittently or temporarily be accreted to the inner slope. This possibility is supported by the identification of basement ridges which apparently have been displaced with respect to the descending plate in the Peru–Chile (Kulm et al., 1973) and Mariana (Karig and Sharman, 1975) trenches. Alternatively, Schweller and Kulm (1978) and Jones et al. (1978), among others, have proposed that the horst blocks act as rigid teeth, not only protecting the sediments in the grabens from accretion, but even tectonically eroding the leading edge of the upper plate.

Perhaps relief on the descending plate could result in both accretion and erosion. It should be pointed out, however, that the upper few hundred metres of the basaltic ocean crust consists of a heterogeneous mixture of volcanic flows, breccias, and even sediments (e.g. Aumento et al., 1977) rendering it significantly weaker than massive basalt. Although horsts and seamounts may be more rigid than an accretionary toe of semi-consolidated sediments, it is not at all obvious that they would resist the shear forces exerted by the leading edge of a prism of lithified sediment or igneous rocks, as would be developed by previous tectonic erosion.

IV. Subcretion

Until recently, it was commonly assumed that the deeper sections of the sediment cover, carried beneath the toe of the inner trench slope, were subducted to mantle depths. In part, this was because crustal sections and cartoons were generally drawn with high vertical exaggeration. The resulting distortion gave the impression that the oceanic lithosphere dives sharply near the trench. In fact, the oceanic plate descends at angles generally less than 10° beneath most of the forearc area (Fig. 1), which may be from 50 to more than 300 km wide. Across this zone the descending plate is still at crustal depths and has not yet penetrated the mantle of the upper plate. Evidence is now accumulating that material can be transferred from the lower to the upper plate, or subcreted, beneath much of the forearc region (Karig and Kay, 1981; Watkins *et al.*, 1982).

Unfortunately, indirect evidence for subcretion has so far proved more convincing than direct evidence. Oceanic basement subducted in trenches with thick pelagic or clastic sediment covers can be traced up to 50 km inboard on highly processed seismic reflection profiles (e.g. Beck and Lehner, 1974). Relief on this subducted basement has been interpreted on some reflection profiles as the result of thrust faulting (e.g. von Huene, 1979) but such structural relief cannot now be reliably differentiated from the relief impressed at the spreading ridge or on the outer trench slope. The subducted sediment section loses its acoustic coherence much closer to the trench than does basement, but effects of subcretion cannot be distinguished from attenuation effects of the seismic signal.

Calculations comparing the influx of sediment to the trench with growth of the accretionary prism have often been used to argue the fate of the sediment cover (e.g. von Huene, 1972; Karig and Sharman, 1975; Shipley *et al.*, 1980; Watkins *et al.*, 1982), but the boundary conditions are generally poorly constrained. Sediment feed rates cannot often be extrapolated reliably back in time, determinations of the volume decrease in the accretionary prism due to dewatering are imprecise, and the definition of a rear boundary to the accreted parcel involves a large degree of assumption. A calculation for the Sunda arc at Nias, where some constraints are offered by the emergence of the trench slope break, indicates that all incoming sediment over the past 13 m.y. can be accommodated within the accretionary prism, but does not distinguish between accreted and subcreted material (Karig *et al.*, 1980). A similar approach, but with a higher assumed porosity for the accreted sediment, has been used to indicate subcretion in the Middle America Trench (Watkins *et al.*, 1982).

The origin of most protoliths in the metamorphic aureoles beneath ophiolite sheets and in high P/T metamorphic sequences as oceanic basalts and ocean floor sediments strongly supports subcretion (Karig and Kay, 1981). Those data also suggest an increase in the proportion of pelagic sediments and mafic igneous rocks, at the expense of clastic trench fill, with increasing pressure (depth of subcretion). If real, this progression would imply the removal of most sedi-

ment from the descending plate at crustal depths (less than 30 km). Depths along the plate interface beneath the arc corresponding to the pressures deduced from mineral phase assemblages (e.g. Ernst, 1973) point to subcretion at least as far back as the trench slope break and along almost all the flatter upper section of the plate interface.

Some idea of the percentage of the accretionary prism that might be subcreted is afforded by the data set for the Sunda Arc at Nias. The structural geometry of slope sediments on the emergent trench slope break (Moore and Karig, 1980), coupled with reflection profiles across the lower trench slope indicates that less than 10% of the interplate convergence is accommodated by deformation more than 20 km from the base of the trench slope (Karig *et al.*, 1980). This horizontal shortening corresponds to, at most, a doubling in the thickness of the accretionary prism between 20 and 80 km from the trench. However, multichannel reflection profiles (Moore *et al.*, 1980) and refraction data (Kieckhefer *et al.*, 1980) show that the accretionary prism thickens almost twice as rapidly as can be explained by lateral structural shortening over this region (Fig. 4). The additional thickening is most logically the result of subcretion.

V. Tectonic Erosion

Tectonic erosion (subduction erosion of Scholl *et al.*, 1980) is another possible response of material to plate convergence. This process, in contrast to subcretion, would transfer material from the upper to lower plates at shallow depths. Tectonic erosion is visualized as being favoured by descending plates with very thin sediment covers (Kulm *et al.*, 1977) and with high basement relief (Jones *et al.*, 1980). Sections of the Peru–Chile Trench are suggested to provide an optimal setting (Kulm *et al.*, 1977; Hussong *et al.*, 1976). Evidence used to infer tectonic erosion include very narrow forearcs with missing morphotectonic elements (Scholl *et al.*, 1970), subsidence and normal faulting of the inner trench slopes (Scientific Party, 1980), and paleogeographic reconstructions requiring removal of continental masses once existing seaward of the present arc (Hussong *et al.*, 1976). As is the case for subcretion, direct evidence for tectonic erosion has been elusive. No in situ continental basement has yet been recovered from the lower part of the inner slope, and definitive shallow structural patterns in this setting have not been resolved.

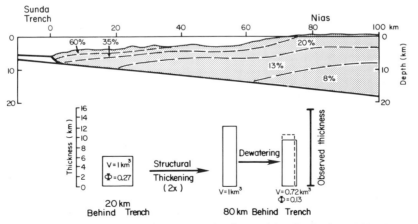

Fig. 4 Cross-section of the lower trench slope off Nias, Sunda Arc, showing porosity distribution within the accretionary prism (stippled pattern), from seismic and gravity data (Kieckhefer *et al.*, 1980, 1981) and parameters used to document the need for subduction of material. The structural thickening is from Karig *et al.* (1980). Porosity was obtained using density-seismic velocity relationships of Ludwig *et al.* (1970). The alternative shapes of the dewatered volume at 80 km assume that all volume loss is in the vertical dimension (solid) or is equal in both dimensions (dashed).

VI. Relative Plate Motions

Both the magnitude and direction of the subduction vector might affect the trajectory of material entering the trench. The magnitude of the convergence vector has been suggested to affect the style of deformation (Karig and Sharman, 1975; Moore, 1979), but it may also affect material trajectories because the thickness of the trench wedge is inversely proportional to the subduction rate if the subduction zone geometry and sediment source remain constant (Helwig and Hall, 1974; Moore et al., 1975).

The direction of the relative convergence vector may also be important because there is often a vector component parallel to the arc, producing strike-slip faults along that trend (e.g. Fitch, 1972). Large strike-slip faults along the interior of arc systems have been recognized for some time, but other such faults, some probably splays from the major trend have been identified in the forearc of the Sunda arc (Karig et al., 1980b). The possible juxtapositon of material with different lithologies and metamorphic grade resulting from these faults (Karig, 1980) may be responsible for some of the exotic terranes and microcontinental blocks now being recognized along ancient convergent margins in western North America (e.g. Blake and Jones, 1978).

VII. Temporal Changes in Material Trajectories

Temporal changes in the material flow patterns at convergent margins have now been documented in several arc systems and are to be expected in most. Not only might the apparent ratio of accreted to subcreted material change with time, but there may also be shifts from crustal growth to destruction at the leading edge of the upper plate. These latter changes may be responsible for the apparently discrete pulses of accretion, shown by the division of accretionary terranes into units separated by major discontinuities in age and lithologies of material (e.g. Kodiak, Connelly et al., 1977). Some of these accretionary episodes might correspond to periods or pulses of plate convergence (Sunda, Karig et al., 1980a; Watkins et al., 1981, Mexico) or major plate reorganizations, but global plate kinematic reconstructions indicate that such a solution is not sufficient. Changes in the geologic factors discussed above are likely to be more important.

VIII. Distribution of Deformation Across the Forearc

There is an abundance of data demonstrating that deformation resulting from plate convergence is concentrated in the forearc area (e.g. Seely et al., 1974; Karig 1974; Moore et al., 1979). Backarc thrusting and other forms of intra-arc deformation occur sparsely, as in the Andes (e.g. Burchfiel and Davis, 1976) and possibly in the Banda Arc (Hamilton, 1977), but these reflect much less total shortening than occurs in the forearc and generally at much slower rates of deformation.

Perhaps the most important source of information concerning the distribution of deformation in the forearc is the sediment cover deposited over material previously emplaced or existing in that region. With caution this carapace of sediment can be viewed as a passive strain marker for the deformation of the material beneath. The application of this tool, however, is not a trivial operation, because it is often quite difficult to differentiate slope from accreted sediments, both in the rock record and on seismic reflection profiles. In emergent subduction-accretion complexes, lithologic ranges of the two units may be very similar, and diagnostic structural criteria may involve circular reasoning. On seismic reflection profiles, the apparent base of the slope strata might represent the level where deformation can no longer be acoustically resolved, rather than the true base of the slope carapace.

Despite these hazards, there are several emergent sections of accretionary prisms in active arc systems where slope and trench sediments are relatively easily differentiated by their distinctive lithologies and by gross geometric patterns (Karig, 1980, and references therein). In each of these cases there is a rapid decrease in the intensity of deformation upward from the base of the slope sediment section, despite large differences in style and intensity of disruption among the various accretionary prisms. For example, in Barbados, mildly folded and faulted slope sediments of the Oceanic Group overlie highly deformed, but structurally coherent, trench and/or oceanic basin turbidites with complex and disputed contact relationships (Pudsey and Reading, in press; Speed, 1981). On Nias, the slope sediments are nearly as highly deformed as are the Barbados trench sediments but trend downward to a complex of extremely disrupted sediments and oceanic igneous rocks (Oyo mélange of Moore and Karig, 1980).

This rapid upward decrease in deformation of slope sediments, implying concentration of the compressional effects of plate convergence toward the base of the trench slope (Moore and Karig, 1976) is supported by the lateral changes in the gross geometry of slope carapaces as revealed by seismic reflection profiles. Most carapaces thin trenchward, often becoming too thin to resolve near the base of the slope. The arcward increase in thickness is attributed to both an increasing duration of deposition and increasing sedimentation rates toward the arc. Some carapaces form an apron or blanket in which thicknesses change relatively gradually, whereas others develop sizable slope basins. The slope basin style has been extensively described off central Sumatra (Moore and Karig, 1976, 1980; Karig et al., 1981), but it would equally apply to the Makran arc (White and Klitgord, 1976; Farhoudi and Karig, 1977; White, 1981). Slope basins are generally smaller and more highly deformed closer to the trench. The southern section of the Middle America arc (Ladd et al., 1978; Ibrahim et al., 1979) and the Lesser Antilles arc (Westbrook, 1975) display slope aprons. The difference in style apparently reflects whether or not that deformation which does occur higher on the trench slope is concentrated into larger reverse faults, forming slope basins, or is more uniformly distributed.

A combination of the marine and land data from the Nias transect of the Sunda Arc led to the conclusion that most of the larger-scale deformation of that slope carapace is a result of compression related to convergence (Moore and Karig, 1980; Karig et al., 1980). Larger scale gravitational features are rare and concentrated at the base of the slope, where the carapace is thin and accreted sediments are least consolidated (Karig et al., 1980). The landward increase in depth to significant deformation in slope sediments recovered by drilling across the inner slope of the Middle America Trench (Moore et al., 1979) similarly was cited as evidence for distributed deformation that was skewed strongly toward the base of the slope. The possibility that this deformation could reflect either tectonism or gravitational processes was recognized, but its distribution implied that gravitational processes would also have been active principally near the base of the slope.

Although large scale gravitational structures involving both slope sediments and the underlying material are rare, smaller gravitational structures and other forms of downslope remobilization of slope sediments appear to be extremely common. Mass flow deposits and redeposited turbidites from hemipelagic slope sediments, as mapped on Nias (Moore et al., 1980), are probably responsible for the acous-

Fig. 5   Heads of small slumps in slope sediments on the inner slope of the Hellenic Trench. The headwall scarps are about 20 cm high. Photo from dive 4 of the HEAT project (Le Pichon *et al.*, 1981).

tically diffuse and irregular surficial reflectors on seismic reflection profiles across the inner slope (Karig *et al.*, 1980b).

During submersible operations in the Hellenic Trench (Le Pichon *et al.*, 1981) we observed abundant, thin (0·2-3 m) slide sheets (Fig. 5). Gross morphologic patterns have been cited in support of large gravity-induced normal faults on this slope (Le Pichon *et al.*, 1981), but there was no evidence of displacements with the requisite sense of slip; only a few high-angle reverse faults were actually seen.

Drilling results in the northern Middle American Arc (Moore *et al.*, 1979) have basically supported the concept of a slope carapace that is relatively undeformed except near its base. In contrast, drilling results from the slope carapace in the Japan Arc revealed numerous small scale structural complexities at very shallow depths, leading scientists involved in this drilling program to favour large slumps and a high degree of deformation within the slope carapace (Scientific Party, 1980). However most of the observed folding was not associated with paleontologically resolvable stratal repetition and could have been a result of shallow slumping. The pronounced fracturing and veining noted at shallow depths (Arthur *et al.*, 1980) bears little resemblance to deformational fabrics described in emergent subduction complexes (e.g. Cowan, 1978; Hsü, 1974). Upward migration of water, driven from the more highly tectonized regions below (Arthur *et al.*, 1980), could produce these hydraulic fracturing features in passive slope sediments. In any case, the larger scale coherence of the slope carapace, both seismically and stratigraphically (Scientific Party, 1980) require that the amount of shortening in this unit be at least one order of magnitude less than the total interplate convergence rate.

Seismic reflection profiles across the offshore Makran Arc and reconnaissance observations on the Chaman-Ornach Nal transform system that bounds the arc system to the east have led White (1981) amd Lawrence (1981) to suggest that much more deformation is occurring far from the trench than is defended in the previous paragraphs. The question

remains unresolved without better quantified displacements on the transforms and by processed multichannel seismic profiles across the uppermost continental slope, where White suggests major displacement, but there are several reasons to question this interpretation.

There clearly are a number of active or very young reverse faults across the Makran Ranges (Hunting Survey Corporation, 1960; Kazmi, 1979; Lawrence, 1981). These separate broad open synclines of Pliocene to Quaternary deposits, which comprise the upper sections of slope basins. Thus, active crustal shortening is constrained almost entirely to movement on these fault zones. Although impressive tilting of fluvial deposits can be observed on some of these high angle reverse faults (Hunting Survey Corporation, 1960; Karig, 1978, personal observations), horizontal slip during the past few m.y. cannot exceed several km. Total shortening on these faults over the past 2–4 m.y. can only account for a small fraction of the 50 km/m.y. convergence rate. On the other hand, the rapid downward increase in intensity of deformation near the base of the pre-Pliocene slope strata of these basins (Hunting Survey Corporation, 1960; Karig, personal observation, 1978), is very similar to the deformational patter in other slope carapaces and logically reflects a similar distribution of deformation.

Infaulting, of "kneading" of slope sediments into the underlying material has been assigned a large role in the deformation models of Hamilton (1977), Scholl *et al.* (1980), Cowan and Silling (1978) and others. Thrust faulting and structural repetition certainly occurs upslope from the concentrated deformation at the base of the inner slope but, as discussed earlier, at a much slower rate. Where slope sediments are observed in emergent subduction-accretion complexes they are neither extensively mixed with "basement" nor converted into melanges (Karig, 1980, and references therein).

The rapid downward increase in lithification within the material beneath the inner trench slope, documented by drilling (e.g. Moore and Karig, 1976) and by models using integrated gravity and seismic velocity data sets (e.g. Kieckhefer *et al.*, 1980, 1981) would not favour major mechanical decoupling between the slope carapace and the deeper rocks. A downward increase in density coupled with the concentration of deformation near the slope base, in turn argues against the possibililty of large scale diapirism or other circulation of mass within the accretionary prism beneath a cap of less deformed slope sediments. Although diapirism is common in forearc settings, only shallow and volumetrically insignificant shale bodies are involved (Karig, 1980; White, 1981). There thus appears to be only very limited opportunity for material underlying the slope carapace to be exposed and to be recycled to the trench (Karig *et al.*, 1980).

Exceptions to the pattern of forearc deformation favoured above are to be expected; a few can already be identified. In the Sunda arc a zone of large arc-directed structures has developed along the rear flank of the trench slope break. These structures are expressed as flexures at shallow depths but change downward into high angle reverse faults, and possibly flatten at even greater depths (Karig *et al.*, 1980). They developed during the late Pliocene in sediments of the forearc basin and the accretionary prism that had been structurally quiescent since the mid-Miocene, and account for only several km of horizontal shortening. We have suggested that this deformational episode occurred in response to increased stress, of indeterminate origin, along the base of the accretionary prism.

A more pronounced example of this sort of rejuvenated deformation may be occurring along the Banda arc where it is colliding with the Australian continent. North of Savu, a small island west of Timor, arc-directed thrusting has been noted on a published industrial reflection profile (Crostella and Powell, 1976; Hamilton, 1977). Similar thrusting may be responsible for the intense recent uplift of Timor (Tjokrosapoetro, 1978) and for part of the collapse of the forearc basin implied by Bowin *et al.* (1980).

The arc-continent collision occurring in Taiwan has proceeded to the stage of a west-directed foreland thrust belt; the arc morphology has been destroyed, and arc structures are strongly uplifted. This collision event is credited with having produced not only arc-vergent thrusts behind the trench slope break, as in the Sunda example, but also an associated melange unit containing blocks of oceanic crustal lithologies (Page and Suppe, 1981). This melange has depositional contacts with the remnants of the forearc basin sediments and is interpreted as a slump deposit at the toe of the thrust, but it also displays a pervasively sheared deformational fabric, which suggests tectonic overprinting.

IX. Styles of Deformation in Accreted Forearcs

Delineation of structural style on trench slopes remains one of the most important unfulfilled objectives of current arc research because the nature of the structural elements and their distribution provides the strongest evidence of and constraints for the kinematics of the forearc region. Our present understanding of structural style in the forearc is fragmentary because of the dearth of detailed information from this region. Structural patterns in arcs where sediments are accreted are most completely understood because accreted sediments carry spatial and temporal markers that can be resolved by reflection profiling and by drilling.

Semi-quantitative modelling of accretion in the western Sunda arc indicated that seaward verging, tabular slices of the sediment cover, 1–1·5 km thick and 6–9 km wide, are sheared off the descending plate at intervals of several 10^5 years (Karig *et al.*, 1980). Although it is clear that these thrust sheets must suffer internal deformation, a correlation bet-

ween the number of major thrusts needed to balance the gross geometry and the number of ridges on the lower slope, as well as the occurrence of several relatively coherent slices imbedded well up the slope support the idea that most of the displacement is concentrated in zones between the thrust slices. Large scale folding of these slices occurs primarily as a geometrical necessity, where slices ride up over the ramps of the underlying thrust units.

Very little folding appears to precede or accompany the initial thrusting. Any folds that develop along the thrust surface must be smaller and tighter than the resolving power of the reflection profiles. Rather, the thrusts propagate seaward along a decollement near the base of the sediment section. Modern processed multichannel seismic reflection profiles across lower trench slopes, most of which are still unpublished, suggest to me that this style of thrusting is the most common response of accreted sediment.

In some arcs, however, perhaps best illustrated by the Makran, folding can precede thrusting. In that arc, the uppermost 2–2·5 km of the 6 km sediment cover, which constitutes a very broad trench wedge, is selectively accreted in seaward verging folds (White, 1981). However, these mild open folds account for only a few percent of the 50 mm/yr convergence rate before they are largely replaced by thrust faults that cut upward across the shorter limbs. Both reflection profiles (White, 1981) and field mapping ashore suggest that thrusting dominates the structural style further upslope and modifies the folds to complex antiformal zones consisting of highly sheared sediments (Falcon, 1974).

Accretion with an arcward vergence has been identified in the Cascades (Silver, 1972), and along sections of the eastern Aleutian (Seely, 1977; Moore and Allward, 1980), Sunda (Karig *et al.*, 1980) and Hellenic arcs (Le Pichon *et al.*, 1981). This style is attributed by Seely (1977) to more complete mechanical decoupling at the base of the accreted section. Several questions arise concerning the evolutionary pattern of arcward vergent structures. They cannot propagate in the vergence direction as do seaward facing structures. Where, then, do the incipient folds or thrusts begin relative to the trench floor? Do they form seaward of the base of slope and trap sections of trench floor in front of them as suggested by the observations in the Hellenic Trench (Le Pichon *et al.*, 1981)? Do the initially arcward vergent structures remain active across the inner slope, or are they overprinted by seaward vergent structures?

Less coherent styles of accretion, producing totally disrupted fabrics (melanges) and/or slices of igneous rocks from the descending plate cannot be distinguished on reflection profiles and have yet to be drilled. Mapping in emergent subduction-accretion complexes suggests that, although melange can constitute large percentages of a complex (e.g. Oyo complex of Moore and Karig, 1980; Uyak complex of Connelly *et al.*, 1977), they may also form bands associated with structural highs or major fault zones as in the Makran (McCall and Kidd, 1982). This distribution suggests a genetic relationship to tectonic faulting, but this does not preclude a sedimentary component, as is discussed in the following section.

Inclusion of larger slices of oceanic crust and mantle defines another structural style of accretion. The detachment of basaltic crustal slices from the descending plate is reasonably well documented in the Peru–Chile Trench (Kulm *et al.*, 1973), but the subsequent fate of these bodies is unclear. A lack of definable accretionary ridges on that inner trench slope suggested that most of these slices are later subducted (Schweller *et al.*, 1981).

Even larger ridges of oceanic crust and mantle appear to underlie much of the inner slope in the southern Mariana Trench (Karig and Sharman, 1975; Karig and Ranken, in press). The largest of these ridges stands more than 1 km

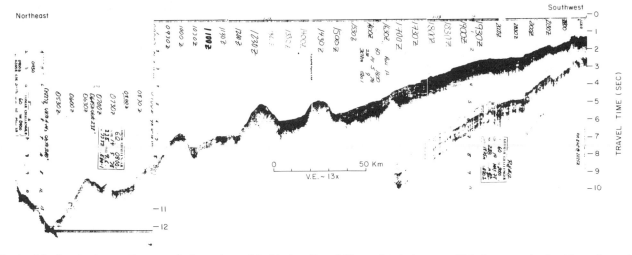

Fig. 6 Seismic reflection profile across the inner slope of the Mariana Trench illustrating the basement highs interpreted to be ridges of oceanic crust and mantle (from Karig and Ranken, in preparation). This profile from DSDP leg 60 crosses the slope obliquely from North of Guam to the trench near 18°N, which produces a lower apparent vertical exaggeration than is noted. Note the lack of structural activity on those ridges buried beneath the upper slope apron.

above the general slope and can be traced for more than 50 km along the base of the slope (Fig. 6). Ridges higher on the inner slope have less relief and, where mantled by the slope apron, are demonstrably inactive. The interpretation of this basement relief that is most compatible with all available data is that slices of the oceanic crust have intermittently been sheared off the descending plate and accreted to the base of the inner slope. The occurrence of a small accretionary prism seaward of the ridges leads us to speculate that between accretion episodes, a part of the incoming sediment may also be accreted, perhaps to be removed during emplacement of the subsequent oceanic slice.

Under what circumstances crustal slices could be transferred to the upper plate remains unknown. High basement relief, such as seamounts or horst blocks were suggested by Karig and Sharman (1975). Nicolas and Le Pichon (1980) speculated that high compressive stresses near the base of young oceanic lithosphere beneath the outer swell could lead to through-plate thrusting and the sequential accretion of large units of oceanic lithosphere (ophiolites). The slices interpreted to exist in the Mariana arc are smaller and would be made of very old oceanic lithosphere. Moreover, these thrusts and those of Kulm et al. (1973) in the Peru–Chile Trench are located well arcward of the outer swell. Hussong et al. (1976) have suggested a large thrust on the outer swell of the Peru–Chile Trench on the basis of a rapid change in crustal structure, but this thrust does not produce the expected near-surface displacements (Schweller et al., 1981).

Styles of deformation produced by tectonic erosion are conjectural because only the inferred results of the process are available. The material removed presumably thins and narrows the forearc. Several structural patterns have been envisaged which could accomplish this.

Murauchi and Ludwig (1980) propose that the material be removed from the upper plate in a series of thrust slices of indeterminate size. These slices would be similar in geometry to those involved in accretion except that they would continue to move arcward along the plate interface. The effect on the near-surface morphology and structure of this process is not discussed. A cartoon of Schweller et al. (1981) implies that smaller increments of the upper plate might be removed at the base of the slope. Hussong et al. (1976) used the constraints of reflection and refraction data across the Peru–Chile Trench near 12°S to develop a model in which material of the upper plate was removed along faults further

up the slope, behind a small mass of accreted oceanic sediments. The faults proposed had normal displacements at the surface but inverted to thrusts at depth. Thrust faults masked by surficial gravity slumps would appear more plausible and accomplish the same mass transfer, but why should material be accreted trenchward of that being removed?

Not only in the Peru–Chile Trench but also in the Japan (Scientific Party, 1980), Mariana (Mrozowski et al., 1981), and southern Middle America trenches (Ibrahim et al., 1979), all prime candidates for tectonic erosion, the base of the inner slope is underlain by low velocity, semi-transparent material which is interpreted as having been accreted. This accreted material, although sufficient to account for only a fraction of the incoming sediment, places constraints on models in tectonic erosion. These bodies could be transient features (Scholl et al., 1980), but the limited data set suggests that they are usually present. They might instead by steady state features, with material constantly circulating through them. If so, this flow should be reflected in the structural pattern of the accreted sediments, and still would require some form of surficial shortening within the older slope material as recognized by Hussong et al. (1976).

Deeper seated flow patterns could be masked by slumping on the lower slope but documentation of such slumps has yet to be presented. Slope aprons are not seismically defined on the lowermost slopes of the four trenches presumed to be eroding, either because they are too thin or too disturbed to be recorded. If they are too thin it would undermine the case for long-term erosion, which would imply an apron that was more nearly continuous across the forearc and truncated sharply along their trenchward margins.

Subcretion as a process is itself poorly documented, so speculation on a resultant structural style is perhaps unwarranted. Nevertheless, it is important to keep before us the likelihood that both structural style and lithologic character in accretionary prisms change as functions of depth. If we assume that the shallow sections of sediment are selectively transferred to the upper plate at the trench, then a higher percentage of pelagic sediments and igneous rocks will be in contact with the plate interface beneath the prism. At higher confining pressures, lower porosities, and perhaps lower values of hydrostatic/lithostatic pressure ratios, a more ductile or diffuse deformational style could be generated. The high degree of shearing in the metamorphics and related material of subophiolitic aureoles (e.g. Williams and Smyth,

1978) provides observational evidence in support of this idea. Highly sheared ophiolitic melange in the structural highs of the deeply eroded northern Makran Complex (McCall and Kidd, 1982) and the schistose to gneissic fabrics of the highest grade bluechists in the Franciscan complex (e.g. Coleman and Lanphere, 1971) may provide more information concerning the structural response of subcreted material.

X. Some Detailed Observations of Structures on Trench Slopes

More detailed characterization of structures and structural processes on the trench slope have only recently become possible with the introduction of techniques such as multi-element bathymetric sounding arrays, near-bottom remote controlled instruments, submersibles, and deep-sea drilling. Features outlined by this scale of study bear directly on the interpretation of outcrop and locality scale geology in mountain belts.

The base of the trench slope, when deformation is concentrated and, where sediments are relatively unconsolidated, is a critical setting for the development of structures preserved in mountain belts. These conditions also imply that the interaction between structural and gravitational processes should be much stronger at the base of the slope than in most other settings. What are not clear, however, are the local framework of morphology and distribution of deformation, and the sequence of events that generate the critical relationships cited by field geologists for their interpretations of processes that were once active in emergent subduction-accretion terrances.

One semi-detailed study of processes at the base of the inner slope was undertaken during our project in the Sunda Trench off Nias (Karig et al., 1980, in preparation). At the foot of the basal thrust slice small sediment fans and aprons are superimposed on the flat trench floor. The fans and aprons consist of acoustically layered sediments (dominantly turbidites) which become progressively more reflective (and presumably more coarse-grained) toward their apices. The apical areas of these fans and aprons consist of acoustically chaotic material with a lobey surface that is steeper than the more distal sections of the aprons. This material also forms linear mounds that extend almost to the periphery of the fans. Sediment with similar acoustic characteristics elsewhere have been shown by coring to consist of debris flows (e.g. Embley, 1976; Jacobi and Mrozowski, 1979). The acoustic character and distribution of these depositional features suggests that they result from the slumping and disaggregation of still poorly consolidated sediments that had been rapidly uplifted by the basal thrust.

No such fans or aprons were observed along the bases of scarps that form behind slope basins further upslope. Apparently progressive dewatering and lithification of accreted sediments prevents or greatly reduces this slumping further upslope and restricts the gravitational instability to the slope cover (Karig et al., 1980). These observations, and a similar set on the Makran slope (White and Louden, in press) suggest again to us that gravitational structures involving accreted material are primarily found at the base of the trench slope. It also suggests that even in this setting, the amount of material involved in gravitational structures is very small in comparison to the size of the thrust sheets.

Quite a different interpretation of slumping in the Japan (Scientific Party, 1980) and eastern Aleutian (Piper et al., 1973) trenches was reached, using more widely spaced seismic profiles. These proposed slumps are very much larger masses, with highly irregular surfaces and steep, blunt toes. They more closely resemble the gently dipping basal section

of the inner slope of the Lesser Antilles Trench, which consists of stacked thrusts (Moore, Biju-Duval et al., in press).

Some melanges are interpreted as olistostromes, in which clasts are depositionally mixed into a fine-grained matrix, and subsequently sheared. Observations in the Sunda Trench suggest that such olistostromes are likely to be represented by the acoustically chaotic material at the base of the inner slope, which are very quickly involved in thrusting in the forearc. Exotic clasts in these units can reasonably be derived from mass flow units transported to the trench down large submarine canyons from sources on the shelf or along the canyon walls (Underwood and Karig, 1980), and subsequently exposed on the basal scarp.

A much closer look at the deformational style at the base of the trench slope was afforded during submersible operations in the Hellenic Trench (Le Pichon et al., 1981). There, arc-directed thrusts at the base of the outer trench slope are expressed as rubble-fronted ramps in which deformation is remarkably well delineated by a manganese-stained calcareous crust. From a flat and relatively undeformed terrace forming the upper thrust block, deformation often begins as a smooth arching or downflexing, producing many extensional cracks. Closer to the thrust toe, the slope steepens and extension increases until the material loses coherence and slumps to the sediment floor of the lower plate.

The stiff marl and landward vergence on the outer slope of the Hellenic Trench may be unusual, but they suggest a more general model which may explain some of the intimately mixed and apparently contradictory relations between sedimentary and structural features of melange units. In this model (Fig. 7), semi-consolidated material of the upper thrust plate is stretched over the thrust toe and later slumps to the base of the scarp, where it lies in depositional contact on trench floor sediments. With continued thrusting, the rubble is overridden, and a shear component is superimposed on material previously subjected to bedding plane extension, or more completely disrupted by gravitational, soft sediment deformation. The overriding of rubble might have similarities with "forethrust debris" described along several subaerial thrusts (e.g. Brock and Engelder, 1977). Underthrusting of sheared or brecciated material from the base of the upper thrust plate could cause the continued oversteepening and collapse of the thrust toe. Thus, a mixture of deformational fabrics, reflecting both sedimentary or gravitational, and tectonic processes would be preserved in the same or closely positioned outcrops, but all would form part of a tectonically generated thrust boundary. It is also possible that series of thrust slivers comprising oceanic crust might develop depositional aspects at the toe of the thrust ridge, which would create the impression that these rootless bodies of igneous rocks were slide blocks.

Conclusions

Forearcs are the repository of most of the compression related to plate convergence. They vary in geometry, lithologic composition, and in mechanical response to incoming material, but, despite current stress placed on this variety, there do appear to be systematic controls for the response of forearc material. Most of these controls are shallow-seated factors that affect the mechanical properties of the uppermost part of the descending plate. Deep-seated, intraplate stresses very likely have a dominant effect on the mechanical response of intra- and backarc regions, but appear to have little affect on the forearc. Nor does gravitational tectonism seem to be a major factor in shaping larger structures or in material transport processes.

The character of the carapace of sediments deposited on the inner trench slope, and the mapping of emergent

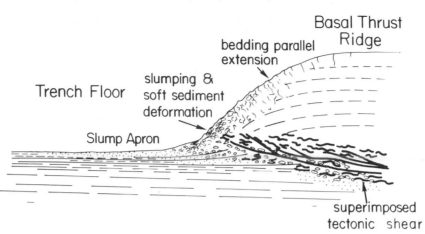

Fig. 7 Model of thrust front at the base of the trench slope, generalized from thrusts observed in the Hellenic Trench (Le Pichon *et al.*, 1981) and slump aprons observed in the Sunda Arc (Karig *et al.*, 1980). "Soft sediment" gravitational deformation is spatially and temporally closely related to shearing along the thrust zone.

subduction-accretion complexes in which much of carapace is preserved, strongly indicate that tectonic deformation is concentrated near the base of the trench slope, and further suggest that what gravitational structures do occur are also concentrated there. The base of the slope is critical as well in preserving structural patterns that can document and calibrate the range of material response, from accretion to tectonic erosion.

The history of interpretations of mountain belts would suggest that outcrop geology has not been very successful in elucidating the processes that shape forearcs and forearc structures. This, in part, results from the complex and locally heterogeneous character of forearcs, but it also seems to stem from the difficulty in envisaging instantaneous regional morphologies and dislocation patterns from outcrop or local observations. It is quite clear that the most important objective now in the study of forearcs is the in situ delineation of structural features and of their formative processes on a very local scale.

References

Arthur, M.A., Carson, B. and von Huene, R. (1980). Initial tectonic deformation of the hemipelagic sediment at the leading edge of the Japan convergent margin. *In Scientific Party, Initial Reports of the Deep Sea Drilling Project* **56, 57,** *pt. 1,* Washington, D.C. (U.S. Government Printing Office), pp. 569–614.

Aumento, F., Melson, W.G., *et al.* (1977). *Initial Reports of the Deep Sea Drilling Project* **37,** Washington, D.C. (U.S. Government Printing Office), 1008 pp.

Beck, R.H. and Lehner, P. (1974). Oceans, new frontiers in exploration. *Am. Assoc. Petroleum Geologists Bull.* **58,** 376–395.

Blake, M.C., Jr. and Jones, D.L. (1978). Allochthonous terranes in northern California? — a reinterpretation. Mesozoic Paleogeography of the Western United States, Pacific Section Soc. Econ. Paleontol. and Mineral. Pac. Coast Paleogeography Symposium, pp. 397–400.

Bodine, J.H. and Watts, A.B. (1979). On lithospheric flexure seaward of the Bonin and Mariana Trenches. *Earth Planet. Sci. Lett* **43,** 132–148.

Bowin, C., Purdy, G.M., Johnston, C., Shor, G., Lawver, L., Hartono, H.M.S. and Jezek, P. (1980). Arc-continent collision in the Banda Sea region. *Am. Assoc. Petroleum Geologists Bull.* **64,** 868–915.

Brock, W.G. and Engelder, T. (1977). Deformation associated with the movement of the Muddy Mountain overthrust in the Buffington window, southeastern Nevada. *Geol. Soc. Amer. Bull.* **88,** 1667–1677.

Burchfiel, B.C. and Davis, G.A. (1976). Compression and crustal shortening in Andean-type orogenesis. *Nature, London* **260,** 693–695.

Chase, C.G. (1978). Extension behind island arcs and motions relative to hot spots. *J. Geophys. Res.* **83,** 5385–5387.

Coleman, R.G. and Lanphere, M.A. (1971). Distribution and age of high-grade blueschists, associated eclogites, and amphibolites from Oregon and Washington. *Geol. Soc. Amer. Bull.* **82,** 2397–2412.

Connelly, W., Hill, M., Hill, B.B. and Moore, J.C. (1977). The Uyak complex, Kodiak Island, Alaska: A subduction complex of early Mesozoic age. *In* "Island Arcs, Deep Sea Trenches and Back-arc Basins" (M. Talwani and W.C. Pitman III, eds). Maurice Ewing Series v. 1, *Am. Geopys. Union,* 465.

Cowan, D.S. (1978). Origin of blueschist-bearing chaotic rocks in the Franciscan Complex, San Simeon, California. *Geol. Soc. Amer. Bull.* **89,** 1415–1423.

Cowan, D.S. and Silling, R.M. (1978). A dynamic, scaled model of accretion at Trenches and its implications for the tectonic evolutions of subduction complexes. *J. Geophys. Res.* **83,** 5389–5396.

Crostella, A. and Powell, D.E. (1976). Geology and hydrocarbon prospects of the Timor area. *Indonesian Petroleum Assoc. Proc.* **4,** 149–171.

Embley, R.W. (1976). New evidence for occurrence of debris flow deposits in the deep sea. *Geology* **4,** 371–374.

Ernst, W.G. (1973). Blueschist metamorphism and P-T regimes in active subduction zones. *Tectonophysics* **17,** 255–272.

Falcon, N.L. (1974). An outline of the geology of the Iranian Makran. *Geograph. J.* **140,** 284–291.

Farhoudi, G. and Karig, D.E. (1977). Makran of Iran and Pakistan as an active arc system. *Geology* **5,** 664–668.

Fitch, T.J. (1972). Plate convergence, transcurrent faults and internal deformation adjacent to southeast Asia and the western Pacific. *J. Geophys. Res.* **77,** 4432–4460.

Grow, J.A. (1973). Crustal and upper mantle structure of the central Aleutian Arc. *Bull. Geol. Soc. Amer.* **84,** 2169–2192.

Grow, J.A. and Bowin, C.O. (1975). Evidence for high density crust and mantle beneath the Chile Trench due to the descending lithosphere. *J. Geophys. Res.* **80,** 1449–1458.

Hamilton, W. (1977). Subduction in the Indonesian region. *In* "Island Arcs, Deep Sea Trenches and Back-arc Basins" (M. Talwani and W.C. Pitman, eds). *Maurice Ewing Series* **1,** 15–32.

Helwig, J. and Hall, G.A. (1974). Steady-state trenches? *Geology* **2,** 309–316.

Hsü, K.J. (1974). Melanges and their distinction from olistostromes. *In* "Modern and Ancient Geosynclinal Sedimentation" (R. Dott and R. Sharer, eds). *Soc. Econ. Paleontologists and Mineralogists, Sp. Pub.* **19,** 321–332.

Hunting Survey Corporation (1960). "Reconnaissance survey of part of West Pakistan". Maracle Press, Toronto.

Hussong, D.M. and Uyeda, S. (1981). Tectonics in the Mariana Arc: Results of recent studies, including DSDP Leg 60. *Oceanologica Acta* **4** (suppl.), 203–212.

Hussong, D.M., Edwards, P.B., Johnson, S.H., Campbell, J.F. and Sutton, G.H. (1976). Crustal structure of the Peru-Chile Trench: 8°–12°S latitude. *In* "The Geophysics of the Pacific Ocean Basin and Its Margin" (G. Sutton, M. Manghani, and R. Moberly, eds). *Geophys. Mono.* **19**, AGU, Washington, D.C.

Ibrahim, A.K., Latham, G.V. and Ladd, J. (1979). Seismic refraction and reflection measurements in the Middle America Trench offshore Guatamala. *J. Geophys. Res.* **84**, 5643–5649.

Jacobi, R.D. and Mrozowski, C.L. (1979). Sediment slides and sediment waves in the Bonin Trough, Western Pacific. *Marine Geology* **29**, M1–M9.

Jones, G.M., Hilde, T.W.C., Sharman, G.F. and Agnew, D.C. (1978). Fault patterns in outer trench walls and their tectonic significance. *J. Phys. Earth* **26**, 585–5101.

Karig, D.E. (1974). Evolution of arc systems in the Western Pacific. *Ann. Rev. Earth Planet. Sciences* **2**, 51–75.

Karig, D.E. (1980). Material transport within accretionary prisms and the "knocker" problem. *J. Geol.* **88**, 27–39.

Karig, D.E. and Kay, R.W. (1981). Fate of sediments on the descending plate at convergent margins. *Phil. Trans. Roy. Soc. London, Ser. A*, **301**, 233–.

Karig, D.E. and Ranken, B. (in press.). Marine geology of the forearc region, southern Mariana Island Arc. *AGU Geophys. Mono.* 26.

Karig, D.E. and Sharman, G.F. (1975). Subduction and accretion in trenches. *Geol. Soc. Amer. Bull.* **86**, 377–389.

Karig, D.E., Caldwell, J.G. and Parmentier, E.M. (1976). Effects of accretion on the geometry of the descending lithosphere. *J. Geophys. Res.* **81**, 6281–6291.

Karig, D.E., Lawrence, M.B., Moore, G.F. and Curray, J.R. (1980a). Structural framework of the forearc basin, northwest Sumatra. *J. Geol. Soc. London* **187**, 77–91.

Karig, D.E., Moore, G.F., Curray, J.R. and Lawrence, M.B. (1980b). Morphology and shallow structure of the lower trench slope off Nias Island, Indonesia. *In* "Tectonic and geologic evolution of Southeast Asian seas and islands" (D.E. Hayes, ed.). *Amer. Geophys. Union Geophys. Mono.* **23**, 179–208.

Kazmi, A.H. (1979). Active fault systems in Pakistan. *In* "Geodynamics of Pakistan" (A. Farah and K. deJong, eds). *Geol. Survey of Pakistan, Quetta*, 285–294.

Kieckhefer, R.M., Shor, Jr., G.G. and Curray, J.R. (1980). Seismic refraction studies of the Sunda Trench and forearc basin. *J. Geophys. Res.* **85**, 863–889.

Kieckhefer, R.M., Moore, G.F., Emmel, F.J. and Sugiarta, W. (1981). Structure of the Sunda forearc region west of central Sumatra from gravity data. *J. Geophys. Res.* **86**, 7003–7012.

Kulm, L.D., Scheidegger, K.F., Prince, R.A., Dymond, J., Moore, T.C., Jr. and Hussong, D.M. (1973). Tholeiitic basalt ridge in the Peru Trench. *Geology* **1**, 11–14.

Kulm, L.D., Schweller, W.J. and Masias, A. (1977). A preliminary analysis of the subduction processes along the Andean continental margin, 6° to 45°S. *In* "Island Arcs, Deep Sea Trenches, and Back-arc Basins" (M. Talwani, ed.), pp. 285–301.

Ladd, J.W., Ibrahim, A.K., McMillen, K.J., Latham, G.V., von Heune, R.E., Watkins, J.S., Moore, J.C. and Worzel, J.L. (1978). Tectonics of the Middle America Trench offshore Guatamala. International Symposium of the Guatamala 4 February Earthquake and Reconstruction Process, Guatamala City, May 1978, v. **1**.

Lawrence, R.D., Khan, S.H., deJong, K.A., Farah, A. and Yeats, R.S. (1981). Thrust and strike-slip fault interaction along the Chaman Transform zone, Pakistan. *In* "Thrust and Nappe Tectonics". (K.R. McClay and N.J. Price eds). *Geol. Soc. Land. Sp. Publ.* **9**, 363–370.

Le Pichon, X., Huchon, P., Angelier, J., Lyberis, N., Boulin, J., Bureau, D., Cadet., J.P., Decourt, J., Glacon, G., Got, H., Karig, D., Mascle, J., Ricou, L.E. and Thiebault, F. (1982). Active tectonics in the Hellenic Trench. *In* "Trench and Forearc Sedimentation and Tectonics" (J.K. Leggett, ed.). *Geol. Soc. Lond., Sp. Pub.* **10**, 319–334.

Ludwig, W.J., Nafe, J.E. and Drake, C.L. (1970). Seismic refraction. *In* "The Sea", Vol. 4, Part 1 (M.N. Hill, ed.), pp. 53 84. Interscience, New York.

McAdoo, D.C., Caldwell, J.G. and Turcotte, D.L. (1978). On the elastic-perfectly plastic bending of the lithosphere under generalized loading with application to the Kuril trench. *Geophys. J.R. Astron. Soc.* **54**, 11–26.

McCall, G.J.H. and Kidd, R.G.W. (1982). The Makran, southern Iran: The anatomy of a convergent plate margin active from Cretaceous to present *In* "Trench and Forearc Sedimentation and Tectonics" (J.K. Leggett, ed.). *Geol. Soc. Lond., Sp. Pub.* **10**, 387–397.

Molnar, P. and Atwater, T. (1978). Interarc spreading and cordilleran tectonics as alternates related to the age of subducted oceanic lithosphere. *Earth Planet. Sci. lett.* **41**, 330–340.

Moore, G.F. and Karig, D.E. (1976). Development of sedimentary basins on the lower trench slope. *Geology* **4**, 693–697.

Moore, G.F. and Karig, D.E. (1980). Structural geology of Nias Island, Indonesia: implications for subduction zone tectonics. *Amer. J. Sci.* **280**, 193–223.

Moore, G.F., Caldwell, J.G. and Karig, D.E. (1975). Steady-state trenches? Comment. *Geology* **3**, 221–222.

Moore, G.F., Billman, H.G., Hehanussa, P.E. and Karig, D.E. (1980). Sedimentology, and paleobathymetry of Neogene Trench slope deposits, Nias Island, Indonesia. *J. Geology* **88**, 161–180.

Moore, J.C. (1975). Selective subduction. *Geology* **3**, 530–532.

Moore, J.C. (1979). Variation in strain and strain rate during underthrusting of trench deposits. *Geology* **7**, 185–188.

Moore, J.C. and Allwardt, A. (1980). Progressive deformation of a Tertiary trench slope, Kodiak Islands, Alaska. *J. Geophys. Res.* **85**, 4741–4756.

Moore, J.C. and Karig, D.E. (1976). Sedimentology, structural geology, and tectonics of the Shikoku subduction zone, southwest Japan. *Geol. Soc. Amer. Bull.* **87**, 1259–1268.

Moore, J.C. *et al.* (1979). Progressive accretion in the Middle America Trench, southern Mexico. *Nature, London* **281**, 638–642.

Moore, J.C., Biju-Duval, B. *et al.* (In press). Offscraping and underthrusting at the deformation front of the Barbados Ridge: Results from Leg 78 A DSDP. *Geol. Soc. Amer. Bull.*

Mrozowski, C.L., Hayes, D.E. and Taylor, B. (1981). Multi-channel seismic reflection surveys of Leg 60 sites. *In* (D.M. Hussong, S. Uyeda, *et al.*). Initial Reports of the Deep Sea Drilling Project, **60**. U.S. Government Printing Office, Washington D.C.

Murauchi, S. and Ludwig, J.J. (1980). Crustal structure of the Japan Trench: the effect of subduction of ocean crust. *In* "Scientific Party, Initial Reports of the Deep Sea Drilling Project, **56, 57**, part. 1, 463–470. U.S. Government Printing Office, Washington D.C.

Nicolas, A. and Le Pichon, X. (1980). Thrusting of young lithosphere in subduction zones with special reference to structures in ophiolitic peridotites. *E.P.S.L.* **46**, 397–406.

Page, B.M. and Suppe, J. (1981). The Pliocene Lichi melange of Taiwan: its plate tectonic and olistostromal origin. *Am. J. Sci.* **281**, 193–227.

Piper, D.J.W. (1973). Late Quaternary sedimentation in the active eastern Aleutian Trench. *Geology* **1**, 19–22.

Pudsey, C.J. and Reading, H.G. (1982). Sedimentology and structure of the Scotland group, Barbados. *In* "Trench and Forearc Sedimentation and Tectonics" (J.K. Leggett, ed.). *Geol. Soc. Lond., Sp. Pub.* **10**, 291–308.

Scholl, D.W., Christensen, M.N., von Huene, R. and Marlow, M.S. (1970). Peru-Chile Trench sediments and sea floor spreading. *Geol. Soc. Amer. Bull.* **81**, 1339–1360.

Scholl, D.W., von Huene, R., Vallier, T.L. and Howell, D.G. (1980). Sedimentary masses and concepts about tectonic processes at underthrust ocean margins. *Geology* **8**, 564–568.

Schweller, W.J. and Kulm, L.D. (1978). Extensional rupture of oceanic crust in the Chile Trench. *Marine Geology* **28**, 271–291.

Schweller, W.J., Kulm, L.D. and Prince, R.A. (In press). Tectonics, structure, and sedimentary framework of the Peru-Chile Trench. *Geol. Soc. Amer. Mem.*

Scientific Party (1980). Initial Reports of the Deep Sea Drilling Project, **56, 57**. U.S. Government Printing Office, Washington D.C.

Seely, D.R. (1977). The significance of landward vergence and oblique structural trends on inner/slopes. *In* "Island Arcs, Deep Sea Trenches and Back-Arc Basins" (M. Talwani, W.C. Pitman, III, eds). AGU Maurice Ewing Series, **1**, 187–198.

Seely, D.R., Vail, P.R. and Walton, G.G. (1974). Trench slope model. *In* "The Geology of Continental Margins" (C.A. Burk and C.L. Drake eds). pp. 249–260. Springer-Verlag, New York.

Shipley, T.H., McMillen, K.J., Watkins, J.S., Moore, J.C., Sandoval-Ochoa, J.H. and Worzel, J.L. (1980). Continental margin of Guerrero and Oaxaca, Mexico. *Marine Geology* **35**, 65–82.

Silver, E.A. (1972). Pleistocene tectonic accretion of the continental slope off Washington. *Marine Geology* **13**, 239–249.

Snavely, P.D., Jr., Wagner, H.C. and Lander, D.L. (1980). Geologic cross section of the central Oregon continental margin. *Geol. Soc. Amer. Map and Chart Series,* MC27J.

Speed, R.C. (1981). Geology of Barbados: implication for an accretionary origin. *Oceanologica Acta* **4** (suppl.), 259–265.

Taira, A., Tashiro, M., Okamura, M. and Katto, J. (1980). The geology of the Shimanto Belt in Kochi Prefecture, Shikoka, Japan. *In* "Geology and Paleontology of the Shimanto Belt" (A. Taira and M. Tashiro, eds). Rinya-Kosaikai Press, Kochi, Japan, pp. 319–389.

Talwani, M. (1970). Gravity. *In* "The Sea" (A.E. Maxwell, ed.), Vol. 4, part 1, pp. 251–298.

Tjokrosapoetro, S. (1978). Holocene tectonics on Timor Island, Indonesia. *Bull. Geol. Survey Indonesia* **4**, 49–63.

Underwood, M.B. and Karig, D.E. (1980). Role of submarine canyons in trench and trench slope sedimentation. *Geology* **8**, 432–436.

Uyeda, S. and Kanamori, H. (1979). Back-arc opening and the mode of subduction. *J. Geophys. Res.* **84**, 1049–1062.

von Heune, R. (1972). Structure of the continental margin and tectonism of the eastern Aleutian Trench. *Bull. Geol. Soc. Amer.* **83**, 3613–3626.

von Heune, R. (1979). Structure of the outer convergent margin off Kodiak Island, Alaska, from multichannel seismic records. *In* Geological and Geophysical Investigations of Continental Margins". *Am. Assoc. Petroleum Geol. Mem.* **29**, 261–272.

von Heune, R., Abouin, J. *et al.* (1980). Leg 67: The Deep Sea Drilling Project Mid-America Trench transect off Guatamala. *Geol. Soc. Amer. Bull.* **pt. 1, 91,** 421–432.

Watkins, J.S., McMillen, K.T., Bachman, S.R., Shipley, T.H., Moore, J.C. and Angevine, C. (1982). Tectonic synthesis, leg 66 DSDP transect and vicinity. *In (*J.C. Moore, J.S. Watkins, *et al.* eds). Initial Reports of the Deep Sea Drilling Project, **66.** U.S. Government Printing Office, Washington D.C.

Westbrook, G.K. (1975). The structure of the crust and upper mantle in the region of Barbados and the Lesser Antilles. *Geophys. J.R. Astr. Soc.* **43**, 201–242.

White, R.S. (1982). Deformation of the offshore Makran accretionary sediment prism. *In* "Trench and forearc sedimentation and tectonics in modern and ancient subduction zones" (J.S. Leggett, ed.). *Geol. Soc. Lond., Sp. Pub.* **10**, 357–372.

White, R.S. and Klitgord, K. (1976). Sediment deformation and plate tectonics in the Gulf of Oman. *Earth and Planet. Sci. Lett.* **32**, 199–209.

White, R.S. and Louden, K.E., (In press). The Makran margin: structure of a thickly sedimented convergent plate boundary. *Am. Assoc. Petroleum Geol. Mem.*

Displaced Terranes and Mountain Building

A. Nur and Z. Ben-Avraham

Department of Geophysics
Stanford University, Ca., U.S.A.

Abstract

Numerous oceanic rises, several of which are submerged continental fragments, are embedded in the earth's oceanic plates and are fated to be consumed at active margins in the future. Some of these buoyant rises are presently being consumed, causing gaps in active volcanic chains, disordering the normal seismic pattern associated with subduction of oceanic crust, emplacing ophiolites, and possibly creating marginal seas. Some past oceanic rises have become accreted terranes, now found in ancient active margins. We suggest that some of these accreted, or allochthonous terranes resulted from the break-up of Gondwana and led to the growth by accretion of other continents. From Permian fragments in southern Europe to present Arabia and Somalia, a host of continental slivers, microcontinents, and related rises have migrated from Gondwana to be accreted into Europe and Asia. Orogenic deformation has resulted, well before full continent–continent collision took place.

Numerous accreted continental and noncontinental rises, have been identified also in the Cordillera of western North America, Alaska, east Siberia, Japan and south-east Asia, also involving extensive orogenic deformation, usually without full continent–continent collision. Many of these Pacific terranes have migrated across open oceans, coming from older continental masses. One possible source is Pacifica, an extension of Gondwana beyond New Zealand and Australia. Just as fragments of northern Gondwana and Africa are found today in the Alpine–Himalaya Chain, so are fragments of eastern Gondwana — possibily Pacifica — found in the northern and western circum Pacific.

I. Introduction

In a recent paper (Ben-Avraham *et al.*, 1981) we have presented ideas concerning the tectonic complexities in the large cordilleran chains of the world. Although some appear to be the results of large plate collisions, many of these mountain chains are known to be composed of numerous juxtaposed slivers with dramatically different tectonic and stratigraphic histories. Some of these slivers, often termed "allochthonous terranes", are separated from adjacent terranes by bounding faults, and have come to their present resting places from distant origins. We have reviewed evidence for example, that large parts of the mountainous regions of western North America are composed of such allochthonous terranes, some of which migrated thousands of kilometres to be added by accretion.

We have suggested that modern analogues of many allochthonous terranes may be the topographic rises, or plateaus which comprise about 10% of the floor of today's oceans (Fig. 1). These plateaus, now in migration with the oceanic plates in which they are embedded, are fated to be accreted to continents adjacent to the subduction zones. This process provides direct links between plate tectonics in the oceans and orogenic tectonics on land, links involving several important aspects of continental tectonics: volcanism and its gaps at active margins, the seismicity at active margins, the emplacement of ophiolites, orogenic deformation, continental growth by accretion, entrapment of marginal basins, and the fragmentation of continents.

Oceanic plateaus (Fig. 1), the anomalous rises above the sea floor, which are not parts of known continents, active volcanic arcs, or active spreading ridges, may rise thousands of metres above their surrounding sea floor to above sea level, such as the Seychelles Bank, or to 1500 to 2000 m below sea level, such as the Ontong Java Plateau. We have pointed out that many plateaus have crustal thicknesses between 20 km and 40 km, much greater than usual oceanic crust (Fig. 2). Many of these thick plateaus have an upper 10–15 km crust with compressional wave velocities of 6·0–6·3 km/sec., typical of granitic rocks in the continental crust. The Ontong Java Plateau and the Seychelles Bank (Fig. 2) could thus be submerged continental fragments similar to the Continental Rockall Plateau. Continental affinities are indicated also by the granitic basement exposed in the Seychelles Island, in the Paracel Islands and the Agulhas Plateau (Ben-Avraham *et al.*, 1981).

Those plateaus which are continental slivers must have originated from edges of continents, transported either along

Fig. 1 World-wide distribution of the present day's oceanic plateaus (hatchured). Many of these plateaus may be continental fragments in spite of their situation well within oceanic plates. Others are of different origins, such as extinct arcs and hot spot traces (after Ben-Avraham et al., 1981).

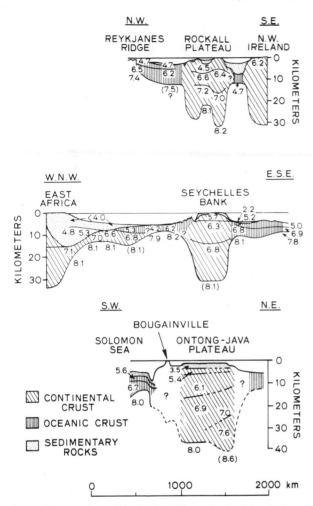

Fig. 2 Cross sections of the Rockall Plateau in the Atlantic Ocean, Seychelles Bank in the Indian Ocean (both after Scrutton, 1976), and Ontong-Java Plateau in the Pacific Ocean. The numbers are compressional wave velocities in km/sec. All three plateaus may be composed in part of continental crust (after Ben-Avraham, 1981).

strike slip faults, such as Baja California, or as separated fragments involving complex rifting and ridge jumping, such as envisioned for the Seychelles, Madagascar, the Broken Ridge in the Indian Ocean (McKenzie and Sclater, 1973). Generally, oceanic plateaus do not exhibit significant isostatic anomalies, implying isostatic compensation. Consequently, these elevated plateaus must have fairly deep, light roots underneath. These plateaus, whether continental slivers or oceanic basaltic piles, are more buoyant than normal oceanic lithosphere. This buoyancy may prevent, or diminish, their tendency to be subducted.

II. Oceanic Plateaus at Active Margins

The few plateaus which are presently being consumed at subduction zones, cause profound geological effects such as reduced seismicity and shifts in volcanic activity (Nur and Ben-Avraham, 1981). The best examples are the collisions of the Juan Fernandez and Nazca Ridges with the western margins of South America, resulting in a remarkable variety of combinations of seismicity, volcanism, and morphology (Vogt *et al.*, 1976; Barazangi and Isacks, 1976 and 1979; Isacks and Barazangi, 1977). In particular a 1500 km gap in active volcanism exists north of the collision point with the Nazca Ridge. In addition, the dip of the seismic plane is

anomalously shallow. A similar volcanic gap is present just north of the collision with the Juan Fernandez Chain.

We have suggested that the volcanic gaps and the associated shallow dips of the seismic planes are closely related to the oblique consumption of the ridges, and that similar effects may exist in general where anomalously buoyant oceanic crust is being consumed. The oblique Juan Fernandez and Nazca Ridge (Fig. 3) which meet the trench complex at the southern ends of their associated volcanic gaps, have probably already been partially consumed either by subduction or by collision. Because the ridges are oblique, the point at which they meet the continent moves with time along the boundary with a sweep velocity w:

$$w = v \cdot \tan\phi$$

where v is the plate convergence rate and as the angle between the direction of plate motion and ridge. For the Nazca Ridge, $v \sim 10\,\text{cm/year}$, $\phi \sim 45°$ and hence the sweep rate $w = 10\,\text{cm/year}$. Thus about 15 m.y. are required to sweep the 1500 km gap. For the Juan Fernandez ridge, $v = 10\,\text{cm/year}$, $\phi \sim 15°$ and the w sweep velocity is $w = 3\,\text{cm/year}$. To sweep the 500 km gap requires about 17 m.y., similar to the time for the Nazca gap.

The Marcus Necker Ridge and the Magellan Seamounts in the western Pacific are also colliding with their respective trenches (Fig. 3), with volcanic gaps extending north of their points of collision. Both ridges sweep the collision zone from north to south. The volcanic gap in the Ryukyu chain can

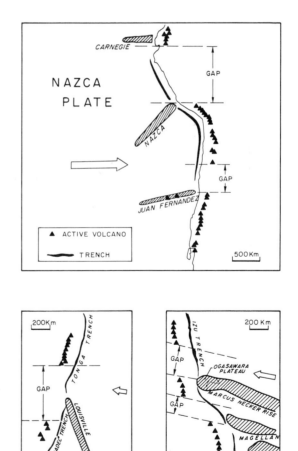

Fig. 3 The oblique consumption of the Nazca and Juan Fernandez Ridges in the eastern South Pacific and the Marcus-Necker and Louisville Rises in the Western Pacific is associated with volcanic gaps, possibly due to disruption of the subduction process. These gaps are temporarily trailing behind the moving contact between the ridge and the overriding plate (Nur and Ben-Avraham, 1981).

similarly be associated with the approach of the Oko-Daito Ridge in the Phillipine Sea.

Direct evidence for the buoyancy of accreted ridges is found at the Michelson Ridge south of Japan, which crosses the Bonin trench without down-warping as would be anticipated if it were firmly attached to the subducting oceanic plate (Smoot, 1981).

The disrupted slab in South America is associated with gaps in deep seismic activity (Fig. 4). We suggest that these deep seismic gaps may be the remnant effect of the accreted parts of the plateaus or rises. A gap has also been observed in the Hellenic Arc (Fig. 4) where it was also associated with an accreted terrane (Rotstein and Kafka, 1981).

Another important effect of the arrival of plateaus at active margins is the entrapment of marginal seas. For example, the *Arctic Ocean Basin* could have originated by the entrapment of a part of the proto-Pacific (Kula?) Plate. As the northern Atlantic opened in the Jurassic, the convergence of the Siberian and Russian Platforms and the North American Plate separated Alaska-Chukotka from Siberia. The continuation of the northward motion of the Kula and Kolyma Plates resulted in the collision and suturing of Alaska-Chukotka with Eurasia and the isolation of part of the Kula Plate creating the Arctic Basin (Churkin and Trexler, 1980).

The *Bering Sea* may also be a trapped portion of the Kula Plate (Cooper *et al.*, 1976) which prior to the formation of the Aleutian Arc in early Tertiary, was subducted along the present day continental margin of the Bering Sea. Ben-Avraham and Cooper (1981) suggest that the encroachment of the Umnak Plateau at this margin caused subduction to jump southward, forming the Aleutian Arc.

The *Sea of Okhotsk*, underlain by continental crust (Burk and Ghibidenko, 1977; Sovostin *et al.*, 1981), is probably a microcontinental block of unknown origin (Den and Hotta, 1973; Dickinson, 1978) which collided with the eastern margin of Eurasia during early Cenozoic time and which caused the subduction along the Kurile Ridge. The continental fragment lodged in the Okhotsk Sea is now submerged.

III. Accreted Fragments Round the Pacific Rim

One of the most extensive records of the consumption of former rises or plateaus which have migrated as parts of oceanic plates comes from the northern rim of the Pacific Ocean in Mexico, western North America, Alaska, Siberia, and Japan.

The evidence for the migration comes from magnetic inclination measurements. Data for several terranes in Alaska and north-east Asia show migrations of several thousand kilometres over periods of tens of millions of years. (Hillhouse, 1977; Stone, 1977). Paleomagnetic azimuths and declinations are often anomalous, suggesting that many terranes have also undergone substantial rotations (Cox, 1980).

The nature, history, and character of allochthonous terranes along the Pacific margin are best understood in the northern Cordillera of western North America (Fig. 5). Some of these allochthonous terranes, such as the Cache Creek Terrane (Monger, 1977), are clear candidates for ancient oceanic plateaus now incorporated into the continental framework (Ben-Avraham *et al.*, 1981). The presence of Tethyan Permian fusulinids led to the early recognition of this terrane as allochthonous (Monger and Ross, 1971).

Several terranes in the circum Pacific margins show continental affinities. For example, some of the allochthonous terranes in north-west America, which were clearly separate microcontinents at one time (Coney *et al.*, 1980), are thought

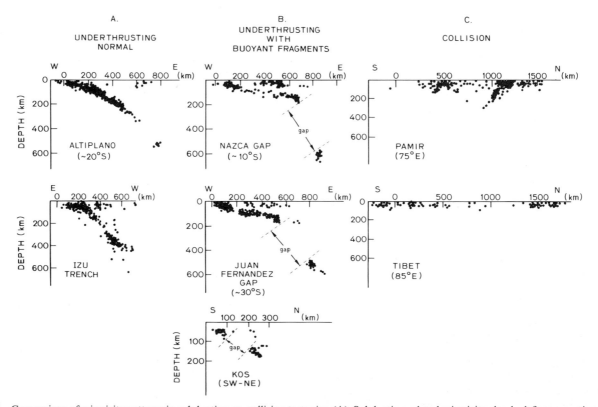

Fig. 4   Comparison of seismicity patterns in subduction vs. collision tectonics: (A) Subduction related seismicity clearly defines a continuous and coherent slab which contains shallow and deep earthquake, with systematic fault plane solutions. (B) Seismicity in "mixed" cases, where normal subduction is disrupted by a ridge, such as Nazca or Juan Fernandez, or a continental fragment, such as in the Hellenic arc, near the Island of Kos (Rotstein and Kafka, 1981). (C) Collision related earthquakes are mostly shallow, show mixed fault plane solutions, are widely scattered and typically define relatively short faults.

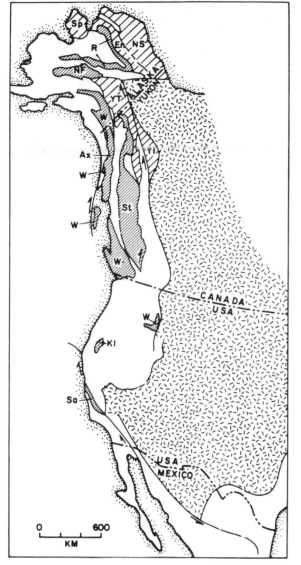

Fig. 5   Accreted terranes in western North America with clear continental origins of affinities (D. Jones, personal communication). Wide hatchures indicate accreted terranes which have possibly been derived from the North American craton itself. Fine hatchures indicate allochthonous terranes which have originated at other continents, definitely at more southern latitudes. The North American craton is indicated by pattern. NS = North Slope, EN = Endicott, R = Ruby, SP = Seward Peninsula, NF = Nixon Fork, YT = Yukon-Tananer, W = Wrangellia, AX = Alexander, ST = Stikine, KL = Klamath Mountains, SA = Salinia.

to be underlain by a continental crust (Fig. 5). These microcontinents or continental fragments include the Nixon Fork, Ruby and Klamath Mountains. One of the best documented terranes is Wrangellia, which is characterized by an enormous accumulation of Middle to Upper Triassic *subaerial* basalts over an upper Paleozoic volcanic arc assemblage (Jones *et al*, 1977). These subaerial basalts probably represent rifting of the Wrangellia block from southern paleolatitudes (Hillhouse, 1977).

In Central America, Gose and Swartz (1977) have suggested that a Honduras Continental terrane was situated far in the Pacific Ocean during Cretaceous times. The Chiapas Masif and the Yucatan platform are also of unknown origins. That large migration took place is also supported by the 1000–1500 km displacement inferred for the Motague fault zone (Pinet, 1972; MacDonald, 1976a, b). C. Rangin

(personal communication, 1980) suggests that an accreted terrane or terranes, similar to Salinia, can be identified also in north-western Mexico.

In north-east Siberia (Fig. 6), the Kolyma composite microcontinent (Churkin and Trexler, 1980; Fujita, 1978) probably separated from the Kula Plate as indicated by paleomagnetic date (McElhinny, 1973). Other microcontinents have also been involved in a series of accretion-type collisions until the end of the Mesozoic when the accreted terranes became firmly embedded in the Asian Plate (Markov *et al*., 1980).

Paleomagnetic studies show that southern parts of Japan (Hattori and Hirooka, 1979) were at equatorial latitude in the late Paleozoic, after rifting from an unknown continent (Harata *et al*., 1978) possibly Pacifica (Nur and Ben-Avraham, 1977). Collisions have been suggested also for the older Maizuru and Tamba belts in Japan, in late Paleozoic or early Mesozoic (Shimizu *et al*., 1978), the younger Miura Belt (Ogawa and Horiuchi, 1978) and the Quaternary collision of the Izu Peninsula with central Honshu (Matsuda, 1978; Ben-Avraham and Cooper, 1981).

Late Paleozoic Australian fauna in the Kitakami Mountains, Japan (Saito and Hashimoto, 1982) and the ancient suture zone between the west Hokkaido extension of Honshu and the east Hokkaido extension of the Okhotsk Plate (S. Uyeda, personal communication) also suggest collisions. The inferred Oyashio land mass off Honshu (von Huene *et al*., 1980) which served as a sediment source in late cretaceous times has probably moved north with the Kula Plate leaving behind small continental fragments on the Japanese Islands.

The Sikhote Alin Complex (McElhinny, 1973; Hamilton, 1970), parts of Korea (Kawai *et al*., 1969) and the northern and southern China platforms (e.g. Terman, 1973; McElhinny, 1973) appear also to have accreted from the south or south-east, possibly as fragments of a Pacifica land mass (Nur and Ben-Avraham, 1978).

Several microcontinents are found in south-east Asia including Sundaland, (Powell and Johnson, 1980) and offshore including the Reed Bank area west of Palawan, northern Palawan, Calamian Islands, Cuyo Shelf, the Paracel Islands and Macclesfield Bank (Ludwig *et al*., 1979; Taylor and Hayes, 1980), the Tantum Massif in eastern Vietnam, the Banggai-Sula and the Buton microcontinents near Celebes (Hamilton, 1979), the Halmahera fragments where Precambrian or Paleozoic continental rocks are exposed on islands,

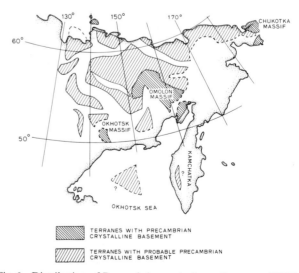

Fig. 6   Distribution of Precambrian rocks in north-eastern USSR (after Khain and Seslavinsky, 1979). Several have originated in more southern latitudes, as suggested by paleomagnetic evidence (McElhinny, 1973).

the Seram and Buru region where Precambrian rocks are exposed, and the Sumba Island continental fragment (Hamilton, 1979).

The late Paleozoic and Mesozoic tectonic evolution of New Zealand also involves collisions such as with the Torlesse terrane (Howell, 1980; Kamp, 1980; and Pirajno, 1980), which has been associated with a large unknown continent, possibly Pacifica (Kamp, 1980). This continent could have served as a source for the sediments for the Canterbury Suite.

Unquestionably, many other Precambrian and Paleozoic continental fragments of unknown origins, in part unexposed, must exist in the circum Pacific margins (e.g. Hattori and Hirooka, 1979). The collisions and accretion of all these fragments have probably played a crucial role in the orogenic evolution of these margins.

IV. Accreted Fragments in the Alpine–Himalaya Chain

Accreted terranes play a leading role in orogenic deformation not only in the Andean-type margins of the north and west Pacific but also in the Alpine–Himalaya Chain. In Table I, we list some of the evidence for the *extent* of incorporation of microplates, many of which were involved with orogenic deformation and continental growth. The list shows that numerous terranes have indeed been incorporated in most segments of the chain well before full continental collision have occurred (Fig. 8). Included are the Calabria, Adria, and Toscana microplates (e.g. Kruezer *et al.*, 1979), now part of Italy; the Paikon, Paleogonian, and Gavrono platforms (e.g.

Biju-Duval, 1977; Giese *et al.*, 1979) and the Apulian, Moesian, and Rhodopian fragments (Burchfield, 1980) which may be responsible for the Carpathians and Balkan orogenic belts; the central Anatolian Massif with the Sakaraya microcontinent (Sengor and Yilmaz, 1981); the transcaucasus median mass (Khain, 1977); the Rezaiyd microcontinent of northern Iran (e.g. King, 1973); and the Lut Block in central Iran (e.g. Gealy, 1977). Many Gondwana fragments which were accreted over a wide span of time have been recognized (Fig. 7) further east (Boulin, 1981) such as the Herat and Panjchir zones in Afghanistan (Mattauer *et al.*, 1980), the Helmand block (Gansser, 1980a,b), the Pamir block (Gealy, 1977), the accreted blocks in the Altyn Tagh and Kun Lun sutures in Tibet (e.g. Burke *et al.*, 1980; Gansser, 1980) including the Tsaidam block, Chang Thang, north and south Tibet platforms (Chang and Cheng, 1973). Sundaland (e.g. Powell, 1979), containing several massifs, e.g. the Tantum Massif in Vietnam, was probably accreted in Cretaceous times (Klompe, 1957). Finally, the South China platform (Terman, 1978) and Sikhote Alin originated also as separate terranes. Sikhote Alin has migrated approximately 30 degrees northward since Permian time (McElhinny, 1973). Very recent paleomagnetic results (McElhinny *et al.*, 1981) suggests that fragments in east China originated in southern latitudes as well, possibly as parts of a Pacifica mass.

Many of these continental fragments are thought to have rifted away from Gondwana, moved across the proto-Tethys and accreted into northern continents, causing extensive deformation and thrusting without actual collisions between two full-sized continents. Indeed, it is questionable whether

Table I Continental fragments in the Alpine Orogenic deformation

Western and Central Mediterranean	Host of continental blocks and arcs, coalescing into present day Italy and European platform: Calabria, Adria, Toscana, etc. Deformation in Appenines (e.g. Kreuzer *et al.*, 1979).
Hellenides	Coalescence of "African" fragments, e.g. Paikon platform, Pelagonian platform, Gavrono platform (e.g. Biju-Duval, 1977; Giese *et al.*, 1979).
Carpathian/ East Europe	At least three fragments of continental crust which lay between Europe and Africa accreted since Jurassic time, Apulian, Moesian, and Rhodopian fragments (Burchfield, 1980).
Turkey	Central Anatolian Massif with Sakaraya/Cimmerian microcontinents (Sengor and Yilmaz, 1981) divided Tethyes into northern and southern parts. Coalesced with Pontides in mid-Miocene. The Erathosthenes Block is colliding with Cyprus (Ben-Avraham *et al.*, 1982).
Caucasus	The transcaucasian median mass, composed of Precambrian basement and Paleozoic rocks. The mass probably closed an ocean basin in mid to late Mesozoic time (e.g. Khain, 1977).
Arabia	Colliding at present with the collages of Turkey and Iran.
Iran	The Rezaiyeh-Esfandgeheh microcontinental complex in northern Iran, probably separated from Gondwana after Permian time (King, 1973; Stocklin, 1974).
Afghanistan	Accretion of Gondwana (?) fragments into the Eurasian margin along the Herat and Panjchir Sutures (e.g. Mattauer *et al.*, 1980). The origin of the Helmand Block is established by paleomagnetic measurements (Krumsiek, 1976). The Pamir Block originated also at the same time (e.g. Gealy, 1977).
Tibet	The accretion of a series of Gondwana fragments, or microcontinents beginning in Permian times. The Tarim Block collided with Kazakhatan in Early Permian (Burtman and Porshiakov, 1973); the Tsaidam Block, Chang Thang, the N. Tibet platform and S. Tibet platform (e.g., Chang and Cheng, 1973). The Altyn Tagh and Kun Lun Lines define the sutures of the latter ones (e.g. Burke *et al.*, 1980; Gansser, 1980a, b).
South-east Asia	Sundaland composed of several continental domains. Was separated from South China in the Cretaceous (Powell and Johnson, 1980). Some of the blocks, e.g. the Tantum Massif (e.g. Klompe, 1957) old continental basement rocks. The Massif was accreted from the east (?) (Powell, 1979).
China	The South China continental platform (Terman, 1973) has probably originated as a separate fragment. Paleomagnetic data (McElhinny, 1973) suggests an origin 30° to the south.

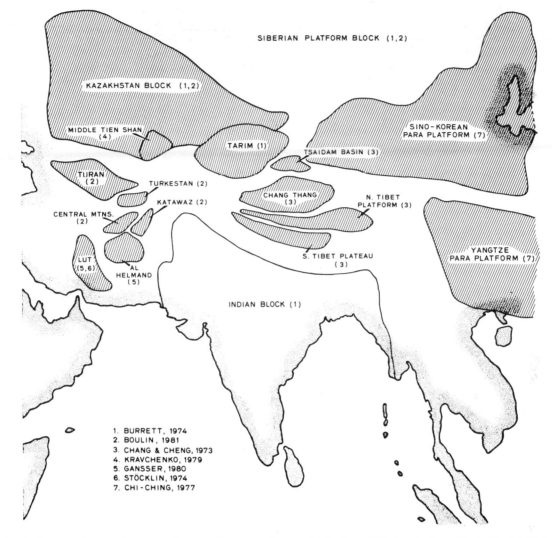

Fig. 7   A sketch of proposed accreted microcontinents and fragments in central Asia since mid-Paleozoic times. Most of the late Paleozoic and Mesozoic terranes are generally believed to have originated from Gondwana.

a full collision between Africa and Europe, presumably responsible for the development of the European Alps, actually occurred. Recent seismic refraction results in the eastern Mediterranean (Ben-Avraham *et al.*, 1979) reveal that the crust is oceanic, clearly separating the central Anatolian Massif from Africa where it is assumed to have originated. In fact, most of the microcontinents in Table I were distinctly separate from Africa when they collided with Europe. Even at present, the Arabia sub-plate, now being accreted by collision to Asia, is separated from Africa by oceanic crust in the spreading Red Sea. We suggest that much of the orogenic complexity in the Alpine Chain is due to the consumption of the separate fragments and not necessarily due to massive continent–continent collision.

In Fig. 8 we show a majority of the known accreted terranes in the world's Mesozoic–Cenozoic orogenic belts, the alpine as well as the circum Pacific ones (Nur and Ben-Avraham, 1982). Clearly the accretion of terranes is a very general aspect of these orogenic belts and, by inference, older ones as well.

V. The Emplacement of Ophiolites

Ophiolite emplacement by continental collision is fairly well understood (Oxburgh, 1972; Mattauer *et al.*, 1980). How-

ever, emplacement of ophiolite in zones which are not associated with continental collision is less clear. Around the Pacific margins, the emplacement of ophiolites is often thought to involve young or hot oceanic lithosphere (Dewey, 1976; Coleman, 1977) interacting with the subduction zone. The accretion of microplates and continental fragments may provide another potent mechanism for ophiolite emplacement. This process has been recognized in the Alpine system where emplacement can often be associated with the accretion of relatively small microplates (Burchfield, 1980) well before full continental collision. Ophiolites may, therefore, represent the arrival of fragments at subduction zones rather than closing marginal basins or large ocean basins (Church, 1980; Ben-Avraham *et al.*, 1982).

Several emplaced ophiolites can indeed be associated with plateaus at present and allochthonous fragments in the past (Ben-Avraham *et al.*, 1982):

Cyprus. Newly completed seismic refraction results (Ben-Avraham *et al.*, 1979) show that the crust in the eastern Mediterranean south of Cyprus is oceanic, thus ruling out full continental collision as the mechanism for the emplacement of the Troodos ophiolite complex (Coleman, 1977; Gass, 1963; Moores and Vine, 1971; Gass and Mason-Smith, 1963; Vine *et al.*, 1973). Instead, the collision of Cyprus with the prominent Eratosthenes

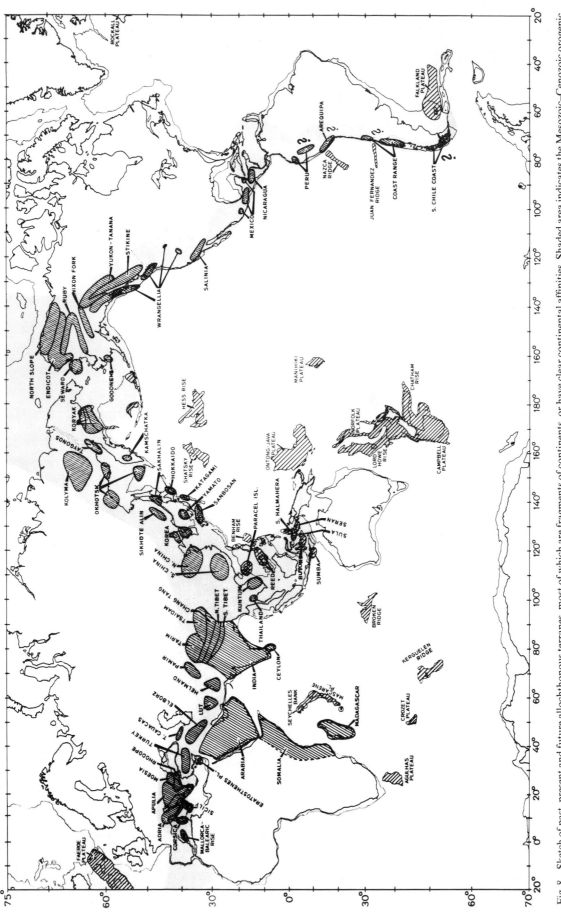

Fig. 8 Sketch of past, present and future allochthonous terranes, most of which are fragments of continents, or have clear continental affinities. Shaded area indicates the Mesozoic–Cenozoic orogenic belts. Allochthonous terranes within the belt are most likely parts of Gondwana, which have migrated towards and collided with Europe, S.E. Asia, and the Pacific margins. Oceanic plateaus, some of which are shown, are moving towards consuming boundaries, possibly to become accreted allochthonous terranes. Several fragments of Africa (e.g. Madagascar, Somalia) will probably collide with the Euroasian Plate in the future (after Nur and Ben-Avraham, 1982).

Seamount, south of Cyprus, may be responsible (Ben-Avraham *et al.*, 1982).

Bahama Bank, Cuba and Hispaniola. The ophiolites in Hispaniola and Cuba could have been emplaced via the collision between the Cuban Arc and the Bahama Platform and Banks (Gealy, 1980).

Papua. The causes for the emplacement of the Papua ophiolite, and shifts in subduction history (Davies, 1980; Parrot and Dugas, 1980) may well be the approach of the Trobriand Platform, with crustal thickness of 24 km (Finlayson *et al.*, 1977), now located just north of eastern Papua.

Solomon Islands. The arrival of the Ontong Java Plateau (Parrot and Dugas, 1980) could have obducted the Solomon Island ophiolites and caused subduction to flip to the south side of the Solomon Islands.

Luzon. The arrival of the Benham Rise on the east side of Luzon during the Miocene may have caused the emplacement of ophiolites in the Sierra Madre Range and the change in subduction to the Manila Trench. The ophiolites on the western side of Luzon were possibly emplaced later by collisions of seamounts (Hawkins, 1980).

Sula Platform. The arrival of the Sula continental fragment from New Guinea (Hamilton, 1979) could have caused the emplacement of the ophiolite complex on the eastern side of Celebes.

Shimanto Terrane (Japan). This ophiolite could have been emplaced by the collision of the northward moving Izu Bonin Ridge.

Coast Range (California). This ophiolite (Bailey *et al.*, 1970; Hopson *et al.*, 1980) is the largest, most continuous, and best studied ophiolitic suite in North America. The continuous accretion of a package of large seamounts and small plateaus into the subduction zones is a possible explanation for emplacement of the ophiolite. The Yolla Bolly Terrane considered to be allochthonous of unknown origin (Blake and Jones, 1974) may contain the remains of these rises.

The mechanism for ophiolite emplacement may thus be one and the same in both the Alpine- and Andean-type orogenes: in both cases obduction of oceanic lithosphere onto the continental lithosphere is caused by the convergence of light buoyant bodies in the form of oceanic plateaus, continental slivers, island arc, or old hot spot traces. Without such light material, obduction may not occur.

VI. Speculations on the Origins of Continental Fragments

Most of the accreted continental blocks in the Alpine chain probably originated from Gondwana since the Permian and through the present. The sizes of fragments range from small slivers such as in Italy to large ones such as India and Arabia. In Fig. 9 we returned, cartoon fashion, the allochthonous blocks of Fig. 8 into one hypothetical origin configuration, with the South European and Near Eastern blocks situated near North Africa and Arabia, the Iran and Afghanistan blocks off East Africa (Gealy, 1977), and the Tibet-Himalaya blocks off India (see Powell, 1979, for summary).

The circum Pacific continental accreted terranes may have a similar source in a Pacifica which might be also an extended Gondwana domain (Fig. 9). Unlike more westerly parts of the northern rim of Gondwana, Pacifica faced a vast ocean so that its fragments, if they existed, became more widely dispersed over much greater distances.

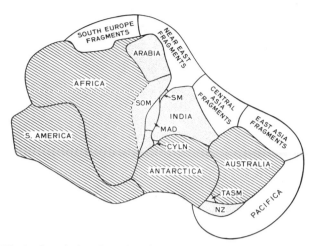

Fig. 9 Speculation about the origin of many of the accreted allochthonous terranes in the Alpine and Pacific Mesozoic–Cenozoic orogenic belts. Possibly, the fragmentation of Gondwana, and particularly its margins gave rise to a host of large and small fragments, which have become embedded in oceanic plates, moving towards subduction zones along the boundaries of other continental masses (after Nur and Ben-Avraham, 1982).

The model of Fig. 9 thus suggests that Gondwana's northern and eastern margins were repeatedly fragmented by some unknown process at least since Premian times. This fragmentation, which is still active today, supplied numerous continental fragments to the oceanic plates, fragments which have been or will be accreted by collision into active continental margins.

VII. The Andes and the Andean- vs. Collision-Type Orogenies

The orogenic deformation in the northern Pacific rim may indeed have required collisions with accreted fragments and arcs and is not simply due to normal subduction of oceanic lithosphere. Fragment collisions are responsible also for orogenic deformation in the Alpine–Himalaya chain, not necessarily requiring two coherent continents. Consequently, both orogenic systems may have a single mechanical origin: collisions with fragments. Whether this is true for all orogenic belts depends on the nature of the Andean chain, which is, after all, the classical example of a noncollision orogenic system.

The geological data for western South America is as yet insufficient to determine whether allochthonous terranes are present now, or were present in the past. Nevertheless, evidence suggests that the orogenic history of the Andes is not as simple as that expected for simple subduction. For example, the Andes are made up of several tectonically and stratigraphically distinct geologic assemblages, possibly allochthonous terranes, which have been welded together over a wide range of geological time (Zeil, 1979). Many Paleozoic and early Mesozoic structures run obliquely to the overall north–south structural trend of the Andes, including regions with penetrative deformation in continental basement rocks of late Paleozoic age.

Continental basement rocks are exposed along the western coast from Tierra del Fuego to Peru, between the trench and the young Andean Cordillera, with ages ranging from 1·8 m.y. BP to 300 m.y. BP. These basement rocks have been greatly deformed in Paleozoic and early Mesozoic times but only mildly since then. Furthermore, several investigators suggest that continental sources to the west of Andes fed

voluminous late Paleozoic and early Mesozoic conglomerates and sandstones now found in the Andean chain.
Arc terranes incorporated from the west have also been invoked by geophysicists to explain the presence of old continental basement off the Peru coast.

These observations suggest that allochthonous terranes
may have played a role in the Andean orogenic belt. In fact,
given the abundance of these terranes and their impact
elsewhere in the circum Pacific, it would be puzzling not to
find accreted terranes in the Andean chain. Consequently,
we believe that the concept of Andean orogeny, which means
orogeny produced by subduction of normal oceanic crust
beneath a continent, may be open to question. In other
words, it may turn out that a single process is responsible for
orogenic deformation everywhere on earth: namely,
collision.

Conclusions

Numerous oceanic rises, several of which are submerged
continental fragments, are presently embedded in the earth's
oceanic plates and are fated to be consumed at active margins
in the future. A few of these buoyant rises are at present being
consumed, causing gaps in active volcanic chains, disordering the normal seismic pattern associated with subduction of
oceanic crust, emplacing ophiolites, and possibly creating
marginal seas. Many past oceanic rises have become accreted
terranes, now found in ancient active margins.

We suggest that the continental fragments now found as
accreted or allochthonous terranes resulted from the break-
up of Gondwana and led to the growth by accretion of other
continents. The break-up of northern and eastern Gondwana, continuing through the more recent break-up of
Africa, illustrate the persistence and continuity of this
process. From Permian fragments in southern Europe to
present Arabia and Somalia, a host of continental slivers,
microcontinents, and related rises have migrated from the
southern continental centres to be accreted into Europe and
Asia. Substantial orogenic deformation has resulted from
the accretion of these bodies, well before full
continent–continent collision took place.

Numerous accreted continental fragments, as well as a
variety of noncontinental rises, have been identified also in
the Cordillera of western North America, Alaska, east
Siberia, Japan and south-east Asia. As in the Alpine chain,
the accretion of these allochthonous terranes involve extensive orogenic deformation, without full continent–continent
collisions. Although the sources of these Pacific terranes
remain unknown, many have migrated across open oceans,
coming from older continental masses which underwent
fragmentation processes such as Gondwana in the past and
Africa more recently. One possible source configuration is
Pacifica, an extension of Gondwana beyond New Zealand
and Australia. Just as fragments of northern Gondwana and
Africa are found today in the Alpine–Himalaya chain, so are
fragments of eastern Gondwana — possibly Pacifica —
found in the northern and western circum Pacific.

If the deformational role of fragments can also be
established for the Andes, then an important generalization
may be made. The accretion of continental fragments is the
main cause for orogenic deformation. Subduction of normal
oceanic crust is insufficient to cause such deformation,
whereas full continental collision is unnecessary.

Acknowledgement

This study was supported by a grant from the Geophysics
Program, Division of Earth Sciences, U.S. National Science
Foundation.

References

Bailey, R.H., Blake, M.C., Jr and Jones, D.L. (1970). On-land
    Mesozoic oceanic crust in California and coast ranges. *U.S. Geol.
    Surv., Prof. Pap. 700–C*, C70–81.
Barazangi, M. (1979). Subduction of the Nazca plate beneath Peru:
    Evidence from spatial distribution of earthquakes. *R. Astron.
    Soc., Geophys. J.* **57**, 537–555.
Barazangi, M. and Isacks, B. (1976). Spatial distribution of earth-
    quakes and subduction of the Nazca plate beneath South
    America. *Geology* **4**, 686–692.
Ben-Avraham, Z. (1981). The movement of continents. *Amer. Sci.*
    69, 285–299.
Ben-Avraham, Z. and Cooper, A.K. (1981). Early evolution of the
    Bering Sea by collision of oceanic rises and north Pacific subduc-
    tion zones. *Geol. Soc. Am. Bull.*, Pt. **1**, 92, 485–495.
Ben-Avraham, Z., Behle, A., Makris, J., Ginsburg, A., Geise, P.,
    Steinmetz, L. and Whitmarch, R.B. (1979). Crustal structure of
    the eastern Mediterranean: A seismic refraction profile from
    Israel to Cyprus (abs.), *Trans. Am. Geophys. Union* **60**, 886–887.
Ben-Avraham, Z., Nur, A., Jones, D. and Cox, A. (1981). Continent-
    al accretion and orogeny: From oceanic plateaus to allochthonous
    terranes. *Science* **213**, 47–54.
Ben-Avraham, Z., Nur, A. and Jones, D. (1982). The emplacement
    of ophiolites by collision. *J. Geophys. Res.* **87**, 3861–3867.
Biju-Duval, B., Dercourt, J. and Le Pichon, X. (1977). From the
    Tethys Ocean to the Mediterranean Seas: A plate tectonic model
    of the evolution of the western alpine system. *In* "Int. Symposium
    on the Structural History of the Mediterranean Basins, Split
    (Yugoslavia)", 25–29 Oct. 1976, (B. Biju-Duval and L. Mon-
    dadert, eds). Editons Technip, Paris, pp. 143–164.
Blake, M.C., Jr. and Jones, D.J. (1974). Origin of Franciscan
    mélanges in northern California. *In* Modern and Ancient Geosyn-
    clinal Sedimentation. *Society of Economic Paleontologists and
    Mineralogists, Spec. Pub.* **19**, 345–357.
Boulin, Jean (1981). Afghanistan structure, greater India concept
    and eastern tethys evolution. *Tectonophysics* **72**, 261–287.
Burchfield, B.C. (1980). Eastern European alpine system and the
    Carpathian orocline as an example of collision tectonics. *Tec-
    tonophysics* **63**, 31–61.
Burk, C.A. and Gnibidensko, H.S. (1977). The structure and age of
    acoustic basement in the Okhotsk Sea. *In* "Island Arcs, Deep Sea
    Trenches, and Back Arc Basins" (Manik Talwani and W.C. Pit-
    mann, III, eds). *Am. Geophys. Union Maurice Ewing Ser.* **1**,
    451–461.
Burke, K., Dewey, J., Kidd, W.S.F. and Sengor, A.M.C. (1980). The
    Alpine–Himalayan zone of continental collision and collision as
    a stage in continental evolution. *In* "Proceedings of Symposium
    on Quinghai-Xizang (Tibet) Plateau, Beijing, China", May–June,
    Organizing Committee Symposium on Quinghai-Xizang (Tibet)
    Plateau, Academia Sinica, pp. 72–73.
Burtman, V.S. and Porsniakov, G.S. (1973). Tectonics of variscides
    of Tien Shan and Kyzyl Kum, In "Developmental Stages of
    Folded Belts and the Problem of Ophiolites III", *Acad. Sci. USSR
    Geol. Inst., Moscow*, p. 61.
Chang, C. and Cheng, H. (1973). Some tectonic features of the Mt.
    Polmo Lungma area, southern Tibet, China. *Sci. Sinica* **16**,
    257–265.
Church, W.R. (1980). Late Proterozoic ophiolites. *In* "Orogenic
    mafic and ultramafic association" (C. Allegre and J. Aubouin,
    eds). *Coll. Inter. Centre National de la Recherge Scientifique, Paris*
    272, 105–117.
Churkin, M., Jr and Trexler, J.H. (1980). Circum-arctic plate
    accretion-isolating part of a Pacific plate to form the nucleus of
    the Arctic Basin. *Earth Planet. Sci. Lett.* **48**, 356–361.
Coleman, R.G. (1977). "Ophiolites, ancient oceanic lithosphere?".
    Springer-Verlag, Berlin, p. 229.
Coney, P.J., Jones, D.L. and Monger, J.W.H. (1980). Cordilleran
    suspect terranes. *Nature, London* **288**, 329–333.
Cooper, A.K., Scholl, D.W. and Marlow, M.S. (1976). Mesozoic
    magnetic lineations in the Bering Sea marginal basin. *J. Geophys.
    Res.* **81**, 1916–1934.
Cox, A. (1980). Rotation of microplates in western North America.
    In "The Continental Crust and its Mineral Deposits" (D.W.
    Strangway, ed.). *Can., Geol. Surv., Spec. Pap.* **20**, Toronto,
    Canada, 305–321.
Davies, H.L. (1980). Crustal structure and emplacement of ophiolite
    in south-eastern Papua New Guinea. *In* "Orogenic mafic and

ultramafic association" (C. Allegre and J. Aubouin, eds). *Coll. Inter. Centre National de la Recherche Scientifique, Paris* **272**, 17–33.

Den, N. and Hotta, H. (1973). Seismic refraction and reflection evidence supporting plate tectonophysics in Hokkaido. *Meterol. Geophys. Pap.* **24**, 31–54.

Dewey, J.G. (1976). Ophiolite obduction. *Tectonophysics* **31**, 93–120.

Dickinson, W.R. (1978). Plate tectonic evolution of north Pacific rim. *J. Phys. Earth Suppl.* **26**, S1–19.

Finlayson, D.M., Drummong, E.J., Collins, C.D.M. and Connely, J.B. (1977). Crustal structures in the region of the Papuan ultramafic belt. *Phys. Earth Planet. Inter.* **14**, 13–20.

Fujita, K. (1978). Pre-Cenozoic tectonic evolution of northeast Siberia. *J. of Geol.* **86**, 159–172.

Gansser, A. (1980a). The timing and significance of orogenic events and the Himalaya. *In* "Proceedings of Symposium on Quinghai-Xizang (Tibet) Plateau, Beijing, China", May–June 1980, Organizing Committee Symposium on Quinghai-Xizang (Tibet) Plateau, Academia Sinica, 69–70.

Gansser, A. (1980b). The Peri-Indian suture zone. *In* "Geology of the Alpine chains born of the tethys". 26th Int. Geol. Con., June 7–17, Paris, pp. 140–148.

Gass, I.G. (1963). Is the Troodos Massif of Cyprus a fragment of Mesozoic ocean Floor? *Nature, London* **220**, 39–42.

Gass, I.G. and Masson-Smith, D. (1963). The geology and gravity anomalies of the Troodos Massif, Cyprus. *R. Soc. Lond., Philos. Trans.* A–**255**, 417–467.

Gealey, W.K. (1977). Ophiolite obduction and geological evolution of the Oman Mountains and adjacent areas. *Geol. Soc. Am., Bull.* **88**, 1183–1191.

Gealey, W.K. (1980). Ophiolite obduction mechanism. *In* "Ophiolites" (A. Panayiotu, ed.). Cyprus Geol. Surv. Dept., Cyprus, pp. 228–243.

Giese, P., Gorler, K., Jacobshagen, V. and Reutter, K.J. (1979). Geodynamic evolution of the Apennines and Hellenides. *In* "Mobile Earth" (M. Closs, ed.). Inter. Geodyn. Proj., Final Report of the Federal Republic of Germany, Boppard, pp. 71–87.

Gose, W.A. and Swartz, D.K. (1977). Paleomagnetic results from cretaceous sediments in Honduras: Tectonic implications. *Geol.* **5**, 505–508.

Hamilton, W. (1970). The Uralides and the motion of the Russian and Siberian platform. *Geol. Soc. Am., Bull.* **81**, 2553–2576.

Hamilton, W. (1979). Tectonics of the Indonesian region. *U.S. Geol. Surv., Prof. Pap.* **1078**, 346.

Harata, T., Hisatomi, K., Kumon, F., Nakazawa, K., Tateishi, M., Suzuki, H. and Tokuoka, T. (1978). Shimanto geosyncline and Kuroshio paleoland. *J. Phys. Earth Suppl.* **26**, S357–366.

Hattori, I. and Hirooka, K. (1979). Paleomagnetic results from Permian greenstones in central Japan and their geologic significance. *Tectonophysics* **57**, 211–235.

Hawkins, J.W., Jr. (1980). Petrology of back-arc basins and island arcs: their possible role in the origin of ophiolites. *In* "Ophiolites" (A. Panayiotou, ed.), Cyprus Geol. Surv. Dept., Cyprus, pp. 244–254.

Hillhouse, J.W. (1977). Paleomagnetism of the Triassic Nikolai greenstone, McCarthy quadrangle, Alaska. *Can. J. Earth Sci.* **14**, 2578–2992.

Hopson, C.A., Mattinson, J.M. and Pessagno, E.A., Jr. (1980). Coast range ophiolite, western California. *In* "The Geotectonic Development of California" (W.G. Ernst, ed.). Prentice-Hall, New Jersey, pp. 419–510.

Howell, D.G. (1980). Mesozoic accretion of exotic terranes along the New Zealand segment of Gondwanaland. *Geology* (Boulder) **8**, 487–491.

Isacks, B.L. and Barazangi, M. (1977). Geometry of Benioff zones: Lateral segmentation and downwards bending of the subducted lithosphere. *In* "Island Arcs, Deep Sea Trenches and Back-arc Basins" (M. Talwani and W.C. Pitman III, eds). *Am. Geophys. Union Maur. Ewing Ser.* **1**, 99–114.

Jones, D.G., Silberling, N.J. and Hillhouse, J. (1977). Wrangellia — a displaced terrane in northwestern North America. *Can. J. Earth Sci.* **14**, 2565–2577.

Kamp, P.J.J. (1980). Pacifica and New Zealand: Proposed eastern elements in Gondwanaland's history. *Nature, London* **288**, 659–664.

Kawai, N., Hirooka, K. and Nakajima, T. (1969). Paleomagnetic and Potassium-Argon age information supporting Cretaceous-Tertiary hypothetic bend of the main island Japan. *Paleogeogr. Paleoclimatol. Paleoecol.* **6**, 277–282.

Khain, V.W. and Seslavinsky, K.B. (1979). Comments and reply on "the Siberian connection: A case for Precambrian separation of the North American and Siberian Cratons'. *Geology* (Boulder) **7**, 466–467.

King, L. (1973). An improved reconstruction of Gondwanaland. In "Implications of Continental Drift to the Earth Sciences" (D.H. Tarling and S.K. Runcorn, eds). Academic Press, London and New York, pp. 853–863.

Klompé, Th. H.F. (1957). Pacific and Variscan orogeny in Indonesia: A structural systhesis, *Indones. J, Nat. Sci.* **113**, 43–89.

Kreuzer, H., Moreani, G. and Roeder, D. (1979). Geodynamic evolution on the eastern Alps along a geotraverse. *In* "Mobil Earth" (M. Closs, ed.). Int. Geodyn. Proj., Final Report of the Federal Republic of Germany, Boppard, pp. 51–64.

Krumsiek, K. (1976). Zur Bewegung der Iranisch-Afganischen Platte. *Geol. Rundsch.* **65**, 909–929.

Ludwig, J.W., Windish, C.C., Houtz, R.E. and Dwing, J.I. (1979). Structure of Falkland Plateau and offshore Tierra del Fuego, Argentina. In "Geological and Geophysical Investigations of Continental Margins" (J.S. Watkins, L. Montadert, and P.W. Dickerson, eds). Tulsa, Oklahoma, *Am. Assoc. Petrol. Geol.*, Memoir, **29**, 125–127.

MacDonald, W.D. (1976a). Cretaceous-Tertiary evolution of the Caribbean. *Caribb. Geol. Conf., Trans.* **7**, 69–78.

MacDonald, W.D. (1976b). The importance of Central America to the tectonic evolution of the Caribbean, Guatamala, C.A. *Pub. Geol. del ICAITA* **5**, 23–50.

Markov, M.S., Yu, M., Pushcharovsky, M. and Tilman, S.M. (1980). Active continental margins of the northwest Pacific. *Tectonophysics* **70**, 1–8.

Matsuda, T. (1978). Collision of the Izu-Bonin Arc with central Honshu: Cenozoic tectonics of the fossa magna, Japan. *J. Phys. Earth Suppl.* **26**, S409–421.

Mattauer, M., Proust, F. and Tapponnier, P. (1980). Tectonic mechanism of obduction, in relation with high pressure metamorphism. *In* "Orogenic, Mafic and Ultramafic Association" (C. Allegra and J. Aubouin, eds). Coll. Inter., Centre National de la Recherche Scientifique, Paris, **272**, 197–201.

Mattauer, M., Tapponier, P. and Proust, F. (1980). Some analogies between the tectonic histories of Afghanistan and Tibet. *In* "Proceedings of Symposium on Quinghai-Xizang (Tibet) Plateau, Beijing China", May–June 1980, Organizing Committee Symposium on Quinghai-Xizang (Tibet) Plateau, Academia Sinica, 62.

McElhinny, M.W. (1973). "Paleomagnetism and Plate Tectonics". Cambridge Univ. Press, p. 358.

McElhinny, M.W., Embleton, B.J.J., Mz, X.H. and Zhang, Z.K. (1981). Fragmentation of Asia in the Permian, *Nature*, **293**, 212–216.

McKenzie, D.P. and Sclater, J.G. (1973). The evolution of the Indian Ocean. *Sci. Am.* **288**, 62–72.

Monger, J.W.H. and Ross, C.A. (1971). Distribution of fusulinaceans in the western Canadian cordillera. *Can. J. Earth Sci.* **8**, 259–278.

Monger, J.W.H. (1977). Upper Paleozoic rocks of the western Canadian Cordillera and their bearing on Cordilleran evolution. *Can. J. Earth Sci.* **14**, 1832–1859.

Moores, E.M. and Vine, F.J. (1971). The Troodos Massif, Cyprus and other ophiolites as oceanic crust: Evaluation and implications. *R. Soc. Lond., Philos. Trans.* A–**268**, 443–460.

Nur, A. and Ben-Avraham, Z. (1977). Lost Pacifica continent. *Nature, London*, **270**, 41–43.

Nur, A. and Ben-Avraham, Z. (1978). Speculations on mountain building and the lost Pacifica continent. *J. Phys. Earth Suppl.* **26**, S21–37.

Nur, A. and Ben-Avraham, Z. (1981). Volcanic gaps and the consumption of aseismic ridges in South America. *Geol. Soc. Am.*, Memoir, **154**, 729–740.

Nur, A. and Ben-Avraham, Z. (1982). Oceanic plateaus, the fragmentation of continents and mountain building. *J. Geophys. Res.*, **87**, 3644–3661.

Ogawa, Y. and Horiuchi, K. (1978). Two types of accretionary fold belts in central Japan. *J. Phys. Earth Suppl.* **26**, S321–336.

Oxburgh, E.R. (1972). Flake tectonics and continental collision. *Nature, London*, **239**, 202–204.

Parrot, J.F. and Dugas, F. (1980). The disrupted ophiolitic belt of the south-west Pacific: Evidence of an Eocene subduction zone. *Tectonophysics* **66**, 349–372.

Pinet, P.R. (1972). Diapir like features offshore Honduras. *Geol. Soc. Am., Bull.* **83**, 1911–1922.

Pirajno, F. (1980). Origin of the eastern geotectonic domain of New Zealand and a Pacifica continent. *Geol. Soc. New Zealand, Newsletter* **49**, 19–21.

Powell, C.McA (1979). Speculative tectonic history of Pakistan and surroundings; some constraints from the Indian Ocean. *In* "Geodynamics of Pakistan" (Farah and DeJong, eds). *Geol. Surv. Pakistan, Quetta*, 5–24.

Powell, C.McA. and Johnson, B.D. (1980). Constraints on the Cenozoic position of Sundaland. *Tectonophysics* **63**, 91–109.

Rotstein, Y. and Kafka, A.L. (1981). Seismotectonics of the Levant Basin, eastern Mediterranean. *EOS* **52**, 404.

Saito, Y. and Hashimoto, M. (1982). South Kitakami region: An allochthonous terrain in Japan. *J. Geophys. Res.*, in press.

Scrutton, R.A. (1972). The crustal structure of Rockall Plateau microcontinent. *R. Astron. Soc., Geophys. J. 27*, 181–241.

Sengor, A.M.C. and Yilmaz, Y. (1981). Tethyan evolution of Turkey: A plate tectonic approach. *Tectonophysics* **75**, 181–241.

Shimizu, D., Imoto, N. and Musahino, M. (1978). Permian and Triassic sedimentary history of the Honshu geosyncline in the Tamba Belt, southwest Japan. *J. Phys. Earth Suppl.* **26**, S337–344.

Smoot, N.C. (1981). Multi-beam survey of the Michelson Ridge at the Bonin trench (abstract). *Symposium on Convergence and Subduction*, Texas A & M University.

Sovostin, L., Zonenshayn, L. and Baranov, B. (1981). Geology and plate tectonics of the Sea of Okhotsk, Geodynamics Series. *Final Reports of the International Geodynamics Program*, in press.

Stocklin, J. (1974). Possible ancient continental margins in Iran. *In* "Geology of Continental Margins" (Burke and Drake, eds). Springer, New York, pp. 873–887.

Stone, D.B. (1977). Plate Tectonics, Paleomagnetism and the Tectonic history of the N.E. Pacific. *Geophys. Surv.* **3**, 3–37.

Taylor, B. and Hayes, D. (1980). The tectonic evolution of the South China Basin. *In* "The tectonic and Geologic Evolution of Southeast Asian Seas and Islands" (D.E. Hayes, ed.). *Am. Geophys. Union, Washington, D.C., Geophys. Mono.* **23**, 89–104.

Terman, M.J. (1973). Tectonic map of China and Mongolia. *Geol. Soc. Am., Boulder, Co., Map and Chart Series, MC–4*.

Tucholke, B.E., Houtz, R.E. and Barrett, D.M. (1981). Continental crust beneath Agulhas plateau, southwest Indian Ocean. *J. Geophys. Res.* **86**, 3791–3806.

Vine, F.J., Poster, C.K. and Gass, I.G. (1973). Aeromagnetic survey of the Troodos igneous massif. Cyprus. *Nature Phys. Sci.* **244**, 34–38.

Vogt, P.R., Lowrie, A., Bracey, D.R. and Hey, R.H. (1976). Subduction of aseimic ridges: Effects on shape, seismicity, and other characteristics of consuming plate boundaries. *Geol. Soc. Am., Spec. Pap.* **172**, 59.

Von Huene, R., Langseth, M. and Nasu, N. (1980). Summary, Japan trench transect. *In* "Initial Reports of the Deep Sea Drilling Project, leg", **56–57** (M. Lee and L. Strout, eds). National Science Foundation and University of California, Scripps Inst. of Oceanograhy, Washington, D.C., pp. 473–488.

Zeil, W. (1979). The Andes — a geological review, Gebruder Borntraeger, Berlin. *Beitrage zur Regionalen Geologie der Erde* **13**, 260.

Heterogeneous Lithospheric Stretching in Early History of Orogenic Belts

E.R. Oxburgh

Department of Earth Sciences,
Cambridge, U.K.

Abstract

Continental lithosphere comprises a relatively thin cap of continental crust upon a zone of mechanically coupled mantle material of poorly constrained and probably variable thickness but of the order of several hundred kilometres thick. The mechanical properties of continental lithosphere are dependent upon temperature, pressure and chemical composition. Although this dependence is not well understood, it is highly likely that the M-discontinuity is a zone of weakness and that strength varies strongly with depth within both crustal and mantle components. During deformation the lithosphere will behave as a multilayer body and the accommodation of strain will occur on different wavelengths in the different layers. In particular the crustal stretching that commonly occurs in the early history of certain orogenic belts (e.g. Alpine) is likely to have been associated with heterogeneous mantle stretching which controlled both the pattern of vertical movements, the subsequent closure of the basin, and the distribution of ophiolitic and detached basement fragments.

1. Introduction

It is now widely recognized that the thermal evolution of an orogenic belt is inextricably interwoven with its deformational history and that an understanding of one is probably impossible without an understanding of the other. Heat is available to the crust in an orogenic zone both from the underlying upper mantle and from the decay of heat producing elements within it. Heat is also contributed by the conversion of mechanical work to heat during episodes of deformation or translation. The distribution of *temperature* within the crust, however, depends not only on the relative magnitudes and distribution of these heat sources but on the balance of rate of heat loss at the surface against the rate of heat supply. And this in turn depends on what processes of heat transfer dominate in different parts of the crust at different times.

The effect of straining the crust either by a ductile stretching or shortening, or by moving one part against or over another along a fault zone is, almost invariably, to modify rapidly the crustal temperature distribution. This is because the rates of diffusion of heat within rocks are small by comparison with common geological rates of strain.

On the other hand the mechanical properties of rocks have an important dependence on temperature, and the mechanical response of the lithosphere to differential stress must in part be determined by the temperature structure within it at the onset of deformation. During deformation therefore

there is a continuing, subtle and complex relationship between thermal and deformational events.

In this paper we examine some of the consequences of this relationship for the evolution of orogenic belts.

II. The Influence of Movements on Temperature

It is convenient at this point to review in a qualitative way the principal consequences of various kinds of deformational process on the temperature structure of the crust and upper mantle. We consider the same starting condition in each case, a slab of lithosphere capped by continental crust in conductive thermal equilibrium with the underlying mantle. The boundary within the mantle between the lithosphere and the asthenosphere is taken to be an isotherm. The warmer material lying below the isotherm is regarded as fluid on the time-scales of interest, and that above as ductile solid.

Four idealized situations are shown in Figs 1 and 2. At this stage we ignore the effects of radiogenic heat production within the lithosphere, the dependence of thermal conductivity on temperature and pressure, and heat transfer by non-conductive processes. It is also assumed that in each case the deformation occurs rapidly by comparison with the rates of conductive transfer of heat. Figure 1a shows the consequences of crustal stretching. This is precisely the model proposed by McKenzie (1978) for the formation of certain kinds of sedimentary basin. Immediately after the

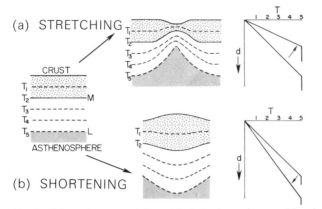

Fig. 1 Schematic representation of the behaviour of compositional boundaries and isotherms during stretching and shortening of the lithosphere; crust, dashed ornament; M — mohorovicic discontinuity; mantle part of the lithosphere — blank; asthenosphere — dark tone; isotherms, dashed lines, $T_1 < T_2$ etc.; d, depth.

deformation the temperatures at the top and bottom of the lithosphere are the same as they were before but in the thinned part of the lithosphere, the isotherms are bunched, and the thermal gradient and surface heat flow, therefore, higher. As discussed by McKenzie, subsequent conductive relaxation and cooling of the thinned zone allow the lithosphere to approach its pre-deformational thickness by the freezing on of asthenospheric material. The crustal part of the lithosphere, however, remains permanently thinned, and the stretched zone remains the locus of surface subsidence until the underlying lithosphere achieves full thickness.

The situation represented in Fig. 1b is the reverse of that shown in Fig. 1a. The lithosphere is imagined to have been rapidly shortened and the crust thickened. Again, it is taken that isostatic equilibrium is maintained throughout. In the zone of thickening the isotherms are spread and the thermal gradient within the crust is lowered. Conductive relaxation in this case brings about a thinning by conductive warming of the lithosphere that had been previously shortened and thickened. The crust in such regions remains permanently thickened apart from the effects of surface erosion (see Houseman and McKenzie, 1981, for other possible consequences).

A rather different situation is shown in Fig. 2a. This is the overthrusting situation discussed by Oxburgh et al. (1971) and Oxburgh and Turcotte (1974) and subsequently, in more detail, by many others. If lithosphere is thickened not by homogeneous shortening but by movement of one part of the lithosphere over an adjacent region along a low angle thrust

fault, a saw-tooth thermal gradient is set up as the warm, lower part of the overriding block comes to rest on the cold upper surface of the lower block. Once movement has ceased, the inverted thermal gradient rapidly decays and is replaced by a low but positive gradient which steepens with time during the return to thermal equilibrium. In this case too, the consequences of thickening the lithosphere should be slow, and sustained uplift should be associated with the thermal decay of the lithospheric root.

From a petrological point of view this process offers the important possibility of a high pressure – low temperature metamorphic environment immediately under the overriding sheet for a short period during and after emplacement. Whether high pressure – low temperature metamorphic rocks are ever formed in this environment is at present not clear, but it is possible that the eoalpine blueschists of the Eastern Alps formed in this way.

A further aspect of this means of thickening the lithosphere concerns the distribution of crustal radioactivity and its effect on thermal gradients and crustal temperatures. Radioactive heat sources tend to be concentrated in the upper part of the crust (e.g. Birch et al., 1968; Lachenbruch, 1968; Hawkesworth, 1974). Such a distribution of radioactivity has the effect of minimizing the mean conductive thermal gradient through the crust, and the temperatures in the crust and underlying upper mantle. A consequence of the large-scale overthrusting process described above may be the tectonic burial of crust rich in radioactive components that was previously close to the surface. Buried in this way the radioactivity has a major effect on the thermal structure of the region and ultimately as conductive equilibrium is approached may give rise to a zone of partial fusion.

The fourth major scenario in which there is an important interplay between thermal structure and tectonics is shown in Fig. 2b. If an area begins to undergo uplift and erosion at rates of more than a millimetre or so per year, the effect on the thermal structure of the region is a "beheading" of the thermal gradient; rocks which until recently had been buried at a depth of several kilometres and at a temperature appropriate to that depth may be exposed at the surface and cooled rapidly to surface temperature. The underlying rocks have time to equilibrate only partially to the new situation and the result is that the near surface thermal gradient is much enhanced and there is in consequence a transient high surface heat flow. This effect of erosion on temperature and heat flow was first thoroughly explored by Clark and Jaeger (1969). The degree of enhancement depends on the rate of

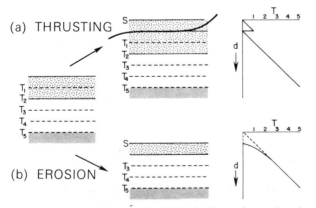

Fig. 2 Cartoons illustrating the thermal effects of over-thrusting and erosion; symbols as in Fig. 1; S, surface.

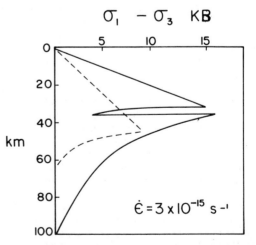

Fig. 3 The strength of continental lithosphere (after Molnar and Tapponnier, 1981). The stress difference ($\sigma_1 - \sigma_3$) required to maintain a deformation rate ($\dot{\varepsilon}$) of $3 \times 10^{-5} sec^{-1}$, plotted against depth. The base of the crust is taken at 35 km.

uplift and will diminish as soon as uplift ceases. In regions with a history of episodic uplift, the near surface thermal gradient and heat flow values based on it, may be very difficult to interpret.

It should be noted that although normal processes of weathering and erosion may have a very marked effect on heat flow (Oxburgh and England, 1980), the most dramatic effects are associated with tectonic erosion, e.g. the sliding away of a series of cover rocks in a region of "thin-skinned" tectonic activity.

For completeness mention should be made of a fifth situation, one which is complementary to that just described and which is reasonably well understood. This is the situation in which sediment is deposited in a basin so rapidly that conductive thermal equilibrium cannot be maintained throughout the pile; in this case a rather low thermal gradient is set up through the rapidly deposited sequence of sediments (Grossling, 1959).

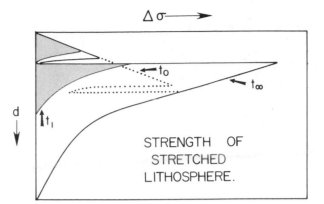

Fig. 4 The strength of continental lithosphere: pre-stretching (t_0 dotted; immediately after stretching, (t_1) toned profile; after cooling to equilibrium (t_∞) solid line. See text for discussion. In all profiles the strength minimum corresponds to the base of the crust.

III. Thermal Structure and Deformational Properties

All the movements discussed in the previous section lead to changes both in the thickness and in the temperature regime within the crust, and in the lithosphere as a whole. In consequence mechanical properties of the lithosphere having a dependence on temperature, pressure and composition, must be changed also, and must continue to change during the whole period of thermal relaxation.

Although knowledge of the rheology of crust and mantle rocks is imperfect it is possible to deduce the general character of the changes in the properties of the lithosphere that result from the processes described.

We consider the continental lithosphere as comprising two parts: an upper part which is the continental crust and a lower part which is a poorly constrained thickness of mechanically coupled upper mantle material. The mantle part of the lithosphere is believed to be mechanically coherent and independent of the "fluid" mantle beneath because it is a little cooler and therefore stronger.

When stretching of the lithosphere occurs (Fig. 1) "fluid" mantle must well up into the necked zone and, in the absence of other tectonic activity, will cool with time and become incorporated in the lithosphere until ultimately the isotherms return to their original position and the lithosphere acquires its full thickness once more. The only permanent change that results from the stretching, therefore, is the thinning of the continental crust, and that may in part be compensated by the deposition of sediments at the surface.

Molnar and Tapponnier (1981) have guardedly modelled the strength of the continental lithosphere using the rheological properties of quartz to place bounds on the strength of the crust and those of olivine to model the mantle portion. As shown in Fig. 3 this gives two strength maxima in the lithosphere, one in the middle part of the crust and the second at the top of the mantle. A qualitatively similar result would have resulted from an assumption that strength was proportional to homologous temperature (T/Tm, the ratio of the absolute temperature of the material to its melting temperature) and that the temperature of beginning of melting of the mantle is several hundred degrees higher than that of the lower crust at any particular depth.

Molnar and Tapponnier were concerned with possible long term changes in the strength of the continental lithosphere as its thermal structure changed with increasing age. The changes in thermal structure resulting from the processes described in the previous section are much more drastic and should have a very marked effect on the strength of the lithosphere. Figure 4 shows the character of these

changes in lithosphere which has been stretched. The mantle portion of the profiles was calculated from the data of Ashby and Verrall (1978) for the deformation of olivine; the crustal part follows Molnar and Tapponnier (1981). No scales are given because the assumptions involved are so large that the curves have only qualitative significance. The dotted curve shows a possible strength profile through the lithosphere before the onset of stretching; the strength of the lithosphere is largely determined by that of the uppermost part of the mantle. Immediately after stretching the strength profile has the form indicated by the shaded zone and strength is reduced by more than half. With time, as the thermal effects of stretching die away, the lithosphere returns to its pre-stretching thickness and the strength profile approaches that indicated by the heavy line. In so far as the crust has been permanently thinned, the mantle component of the lithosphere is thickened. This additional thickness makes a disproportionately large additional contribution to the strength of the lithosphere because the upper part of the mantle is shallower, cooler and therefore stronger than previously. The lithosphere as a whole is somewhat stronger than lithosphere which had never been stretched. It will, however, require some hundreds of millions of years for this to come about.

To summarize, lithosphere which undergoes a rapid 50% extension is likely to experience an immediate strength reduction of the same order, or slightly more. After a long period of thermal equilibration, however, the lithosphere returns to full thickness and may even be somewhat stronger than before, although it takes a very long time to reach that state.

IV. Evidence for Lithospheric Stretching

In the following section it will be argued that if stretching is a general mode of lithospheric deformation, it has a number of important implications for a number of tectonic processes. We therefore consider the evidence that stretching does in fact occur.

Perhaps one of the clearest examples is provided by Karig's (1970, 1974) study of crustal extension behind the island arcs of the Western Pacific. On the evidence both of the sea-floor topography and of the patterns of sedimentation, he was able to show clear heterogeneous rifting and stretching of the oceanic crust. The loci of recent stretching were recognized as deep troughs free from all but the most recent sediment, while earlier basins were characterized by their thicker sedimentary fill and the age of the oldest sediments contained within them.

Using very different lines of evidence, namely crustal

thicknesses and mesoscopic strain markers observable in the field, Le Pichon and Angelier (1979, 1981) have demonstrated inhomogeneous stretching of the crust in the Aegean area. Their interpretation is supported by observations of Mercier (1981) in the same area.

One of the most instructive studies of stretching and rupture of the continental lithosphere has been published by Montadert *et al.* (1979a,b) in the Bay of Biscay. Although the kinematics of the opening of the Bay of Biscay are not well understood, the authors show that the continental crust thins westward from a full 30 km thickness under western France over a distance of some 150 km to about 8 km thick. At this point a clear magnetic signature is observed and it appears that there is a transition to oceanic crust. It appears that the continental crust thins by different mechanisms at different depths; the upper 8 km or so seems to have stretched by sliding on listric normal faults while below that depth the crust has deformed by apparently homogeneous, ductile stretching (Fig. 5a,b).

To the evidence of these regional studies that seem to indicate that the lithosphere may be stretched, should be added the general success of the lithospheric stretching model in predicting the thermal and subsidence behavior of sedimentary basins (e.g. Sclater and Christie, 1980; Steckler and Watts, 1978; Jarvis and McKenzie, 1980; Wood, 1981).

The causes of such stretching are still a matter for speculation, but the supporting evidence from other tectonic situations where the evidence has not been obscured by complex subsequent deformation leaves little doubt that it is a plausible mode of lithospheric behaviour.

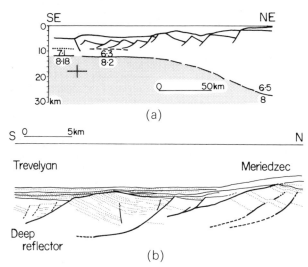

(a)

(b)

Fig. 5 Profiles of the crust on eastern flank of the Bay of Biscay after Montadert *et al.* 1979a. Figure 5a: detail of the listric normal faults upon which upper crustal slices have rotated; Fig. 5b: profile of the whole crust thinning from east to west, the upper part by listric faulting, the lower part apparently by ductile flow.

V. Stretching of a Two-layer Lithosphere

If the arguments presented in the two preceding sections are correct, extension of continental lithosphere should be considered as the stretching of a two-layer body floating on a fluid medium. The two layers could well be separated by a strength minimum at the *M*-discontinuity but would in any case have different physical properties. Physically the situation is not unlike that on a smaller scale when a series of rock units with contrasting properties undergoes boudinage. The main differences are that the stretching occurs at a free surface, presumably in isostatic equilibrium, and that temperature and pressure gradients across individual layers are important.

The most important aspect of the stretching of a heterogeneous multilayer is that the stretching is not uniformly distributed between the layers and that the more brittle units stretch relatively little before breaking, while in the intervening ductile layers the strain is more uniformly distributed along their length. We should predict therefore that if the continental lithosphere is stretched, the strain should be differently distributed in the crustal and mantle parts of the lithosphere, and indeed it should be differently distributed within those parts as a result of the gradients in properties across them. There is observational evidence to support this latter suggestion from the studies in the Bay of Biscay already discussed, where the upper part of the crust appears to extend by a faulting mechanism and the lower part by ductile extension.

There is an overall requirement that mass be conserved but beyond this, there is no requirement that different layers

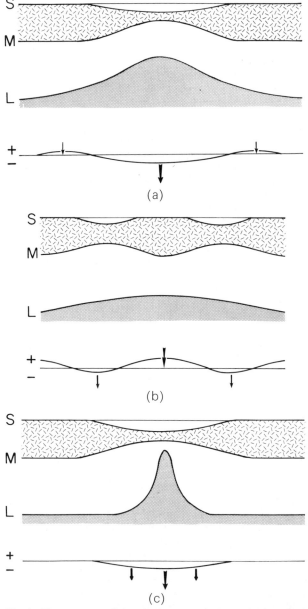

Fig. 6 Heterogeneous lithospheric stretching. (a) Strain in crust more narrowly confined than in the mantle, (b) mantle strain more narrowly confined than in the crust, (c) multiple necking of the crust corresponding to a zone of distributed mantle necking; in each case the heavy solid line below shows the expected surface deflection after stretching, and the arrows the relative amount of subsidence and its lateral distribution during thermal relaxation.

should deform on the same wavelength, i.e. that in cross-section the strain in different layers should be distributed over the same horizontal distance. For example, a particular well defined zone of extension in the crust might correspond to a much broader zone of stretching in the mantle part of the lithosphere with a lower average degree of strain. Similar ideas have been suggested by Sclater and Christie (1980) and Royden and Sclater (1981).

Figure 6 shows how the differences in mechanical properties between crustal and mantle parts of the lithosphere could result in their accommodating the same amount of extension rather differently. At one extreme, short-wavelength crustal necking could correspond to a broad zone of mantle extension which was many times wider. At the other extreme the mantle zone could be narrower than that observed in the crust. On the assumption that isostatic equilibrium was maintained in both cases, the near surface expression in terms of differential subsidence or uplift would be very different. These differences are considered in more detail below.

A further implication of two-layer stretching is that where stretching goes sufficiently far for separation of the continental crust to occur, it is not necessarily true that separation of crust and separation of the underlying mantle part of the lithosphere will occur simultaneously.

VI. Some Geological Consequences of Heterogeneous Stretching

We now explore some of the consequences of the model described above. If we first consider the "Bay of Biscay model" for stretching, it is clear that one possible mode of crustal extension is for the upper part of the crust to stretch by listric normal faulting and the lower part by macroscopic ductile flow. This suggests that any piece of middle or lower crust which has been extended in this way should show the regional development of an "early" stretching fabric. Such fabrics may today be hard to recognize insofar as they are likely to have undergone a number of subsequent deformations. One expression of such a stretching fabric might be the development of a subhorizontal regional foliation which obliterated earlier fabrics and formed a new reference surface destined to be folded and otherwise deformed in the later history of the zone. The alternative to the development of a regional penetrative stretching fabric might be crustal extension by means of deep zones of ductile shear. There is now direct observational evidence (Smithson *et al.*, 1978) that fault-like zones may persist into the lower crust, and that has in any case been the implication of the distribution of crustal earthquakes for many years. Which of these modes was followed in any particular situation would presumably depend on the crustal temperature distribution, the composition of the crust and the rate of extension.

A further consequence of thinning the continental crust in this way is that lower crustal rocks are brought relatively close to the surface. At the temperatures to be expected in lower crust at normal depths (Oxburgh, 1981) micas are unlikely to be able to retain the radiogenic daughter products of unstable isotopes. If, however, these rocks are brought relatively close to the surface they will cool, and the stretching event that elevated them will be recorded as a "thermal event" in the geochronological history of the basement. This is probably the case in the Ivrea zone of the Central Alps (see below).

Probably the most important consequence of heterogeneous stretching of the continental lithosphere is its implications for regional vertical movements of the crust. If stretching were homogeneous all vertical movements should essentially be restricted to the zone of surface subsidence. If the zones of stretching in crust and mantle are not the same the range of tectonic possibilities is very wide. Some of these are illustrated in Fig. 6. In Fig 6a the stretching of the mantle part of the lithosphere extends outside the zone of crustal stretching. If we take as a standard of comparison a model in which the two zones exactly correspond, in this model a surface sedimentary basin will form with a slightly smaller initial depth (because there has been a little less lithospheric thinning beneath it); on the other hand the unstretched crust on the flanks of the basin will tend to rise (because the underlying mantle lithosphere has been somewhat thinned). After these initial vertical movements all areas underlain by stretched lithosphere should subside as cooling occurs within the stretched zone and the lithosphere slowly thickens. Maximum subsidence will occur in the zone of crustal necking and the previously elevated margins of the basin will subside to their former elevation except insofar as they may in the meantime have been modified by erosion. The rate of subsidence of the central sedimentary basin will also be somewhat modified insofar as the bunching of the isotherms in the mantle lithosphere is less than in the reference model, and thus the rate of cooling and lithospheric thickening will be affected.

Another extreme possibility is shown in Fig. 6b where the zone of mantle stretching is narrower than that in the crust. In this case subsidence is restricted to the area of crustal stretching but the central part of the sedimentary basin will have deeper initial subsidence and the flanks less. During subsequent cooling and thickening of the lithosphere after stretching, there will be less subsidence on the flanks and more in the centre than in the reference model.

Figure 6c shows a situation in which multiple necking in the crust corresponds to a single larger-scale thinning of the mantle lithosphere. The subsidence and elevation history of such a region may be readily understood from the discussion of Fig. 6a. It is interesting to compare this sketch with Fig. 7. This shows NNW–SSE cross-sections across the central Alps for both Lower Jurassic and Lower Cretaceous times as deduced from sedimentary facies, thicknesses and faunas. This evidence leaves little doubt that pelagic sediments were deposited during Cretaceous times in part on top of areas that had previously been the site of epicontinental deposits, and in part between such regions (which appear formerly to have been contiguous) on recently formed oceanic crust. It appears that heterogeneous stretching of the crust occurred during the Mesozoic in the Alpine realm, giving rise to the "ribbon continents" of Trümpy. We have no means today of knowing how strain was distributed in the mantle part of the lithosphere beneath the separated crustal strips, but it is unlikely, for the reasons given earlier, to have mirrored precisely that observed in the crust.

The zones of deep water and pelagic deposition (e.g. the Piemont and Valais troughs of the Central Alps and the Flysch zone of the Eastern Alps) are of considerable interest. The pelagic rocks deposited in them are now for the large part strongly deformed and thrust over the adjacent continental areas and their evidence is somewhat obscured. It is, however, likely that these basins were not everywhere fully oceanic in the sense of having spreading centres at which normal oceanic crust was formed.

When the stretching of the crust is sufficient, presumably crustal separation occurs and new ocean floor begins to be formed in between. In the Bay of Biscay it seems that separation occurred when the continental crust had thinned to about 8 km. It is not, however, obvious that the conditions which need to be satisfied in the mantle for the development of a spreading centre and the extrusion of basaltic liquids to form "normal" oceanic crust, are necessarily met at the precise moment that the continental crust finally separates.

E.R. Oxburgh

NNW

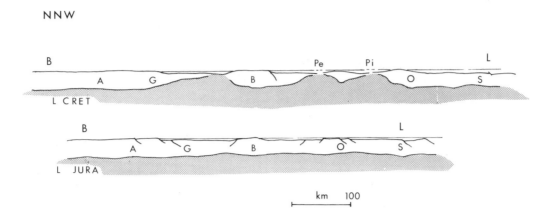

Fig. 7 The deduced extension of the central alpine crust between early Jurassic and early Cretaceous times; crust white, mantle tone; A = Aar massif, G = Gotthard, B = Basel, O = Austroalpine, S = Southern Alps, L = Lugano, Pe = External part of Piemont, Pi = Internal part of Piemont. (After Trümpy, 1980.)

The formation of a ridge and the onset of ridge volcanism depends on the necking and final separation of the mantle part of the lithosphere as well. It is therefore possible that in the earliest stages of continental separation the floor of the new ocean has no igneous crust and that pelagic sediments are deposited directly on upper mantle tectonites. Ocean floor formed in this way would therefore carry no magnetic signature (and would presumably pass rapidly oceanward into floor with normal crust).

It is therefore possible to visualize a setting for the Alpine basin in which the ribbon continents were separated by basins which were several thousand metres deep and with a character that varied along strike; in some places the continental crust may have been very thin but not separated; elsewhere lenticular gaps may have opened within which mantle tectonite was briefly exposed at the sea floor before being covered directly with terrigenous debris; elsewhere fully organized spreading centres may have existed, as in the Red Sea today. Such a pattern of "oceans" may help to explain the apparent over-representation of ultramafic rocks in the Alpine ophiolite suite by comparison with rocks which could be reasonably attributed to the oceanic crust; and to explain the virtual absence of ophiolitic rocks from such regions of pelagic deposition as the Flysch Zone of the Eastern Alps. Other explanations are, of course, possible for all of these observations.

Another feature which is characteristic of many orogenic belts is that the tectonic grain of the belt is established very early in its history; the geometry of the early patterns of sedimentary deposition is reflected in the geometry of the nappe pile developed in the later stages of its evolution. This is particularly evident in the Alps where particular elements in the tectonic pile are characterized by their own original sedimentary facies. Such an early and persistent imprint of tectonic grain is more readily understood in terms of the model of heterogeneous lithospheric stretching outlined earlier. In the early extensional phase, the continental lithosphere acquires zones of weakness, the loci of crustal stretching, which both form sites of sedimentary deposition and zones where the whole lithosphere is relatively weak for periods of some hundreds of millions of years. The external massifs of the Central and Western Alps, and indeed almost every major tectonic unit in the Alps, have features which show that they were tectonically distinct from their neighbouring units even from earliest times.

Several authors (e.g. Jackson, 1980; Helwig, 1976) have made the general point that in many collision type orogenic belts where there is evidence for extensive shortening of the sedimentary cover and where there is today insufficient continental basement to provide an area of deposition for the cover sequence, the continental crust is not abnormally thick. It is not therefore possible to explain the discrepancy between cover and basement by shortening of the crust *unless* either the pre-depositional basement was originally anomalously thin, or deposition was preceded by a phase of crustal stretching, so that in either case considerable subsequent shortening generated a crust which was little thicker than normal. Jackson (1980) applied these ideas to the Zagros mountains but they also have obvious applicability in the Alps.

Most of the analysis of lithospheric stretching models in terms of basin subsidence has been concerned with their long-term subsidence behaviour and it has generally been assumed for computational convenience that the stretching itself took place instantaneously. Jarvis and McKenzie (1980) showed that this makes negligible difference to the calculation of the long term behaviour provided that the stretching takes less than about 20 million years. They argue that because the subsidence pattern of many sedimentary basins is well matched by the instantaneous stretching assumption, that stretching is in most cases very rapid. If such stretching is rapid and isostatic equilibrium is maintained during stretching, it provides a mechanism for the very rapid rates of subsidence for which there is occasional evidence in the stratigraphic record. Jenkyns (1970) identified a late Triassic–early Jurassic episode of widespread but diachronous extensional deformation in the Tethys, his "disintegration of the carbonate platforms" in which a relatively shallow water regime was overtaken by pelagic sedimentation. More recently Schlager (1981) has referred to "the paradox of drowned reefs and carbonate platforms". He shows that the growth potential of Jurassic reefs was at least 1 mm/yr, about four times faster than the maximum known rates of normal basin subsidence. Yet even so there are times when reefs have clearly been drowned and this drowning has not been the result of eustatic sea level rise. Taking the profiles of Montadert *et al.* (1979) for the Bay of Biscay and assuming a stretching rate > 1 cm/yr, gives a mean subsidence rate at the continental margin of > 0.6 mm/yr. This is clearly of the right order to explain the evidence of regional, rapid basin subsidence.

We conclude that a marriage of the ideas of an extensional origin for sedimentary basins with ideas of pre-orogenic extension of continental margins, with ideas of heterogenous distribution of the stretching strain through the lithosphere, begins to provide a tectonic framework in which a great many diverse features of the early history of orogenic belts form part of a single coherent picture.

VII. **The Shortening of Heterogeneously Stretched Lithosphere**

The most important characteristic of stretched lithosphere has already been mentioned in the previous section, namely that stretching affects the thermal and thus the mechanical, properties of the whole lithosphere and that these zones of mechanical weakness are expected to persist for hundreds of millions of years. They are therefore highly likely to control the largest scale patterns of crustal deformation in the later phases of orogeny when shortening and/or collision occurs.

In detail, the closure patterns of zones of former stretching are both diverse and complex as evidenced in the Alps. In all of them, however, it is to be expected that along the axis of maximum thinning, formerly deeply buried crustal rocks such as granulites (or even blueschists which had been mechanically accumulated by subduction processes against the base of the crust) are brought relatively close to the surface. If basin closure occurs at crustal levels not by ductile shortening but in asymmetrical fashion along major thrust faults or zones, with the thinned crust of one flank being thrust over the other, this may provide the opportunity for rocks of the lower crust such as granulites to be emplaced near the surface (Fig. 8). The implication of such a process if it existed would be that the presence of very high pressure terrains at the surface today in regions such as the Northwest highlands of Scotland where Lewisian granulites are exposed would not necessarily provide evidence for previous great crustal thickness in those areas. Hans Laubscher (this volume) has independently pointed out that a process of this kind can explain the long-standing problem of the Ivrea Zone; in this case, however, not only the crust but some of

the mechanically coupled upper mantle was transported upwards over the adjacent thinned crust.

A further possible consequence of the closing of a stretched basin may be deduced from the studies in the Bay of Biscay where the upper part of the crust is broken into prism-shaped slices by listric normal faults (Fig. 5a,b). The length of the slices along strike is variable but seems to be of the order of some tens of kilometres; their other horizontal dimension is a few kilometres and they are perhaps 10 km high. In many cases it is to be expected that they would be largely made up of rocks of the metamorphic basement. During any subsequent shortening deformation affecting the stretched zone as a whole, the motion on the faults bounding these prisms would presumably be reversed. It is, however, unlikely that shortening of the basin would occur by simple reversal of the stretching strain path. Not only would the mechanical properties of both crust and lithosphere have changed since the stretching, but the basin might also have accumulated a sedimentary fill. If, as seems likely in the case of some of the Alpine basins, the closure involved the development of thrust or fold nappes, the previously detached basement prisms could be carried along as part of the sub-thrust complex forming allochthonous basement slices within the overlying sedimentary sequences. Thin and laterally discontinuous basement slices of this kind have long presented a problem within both the Pennine and Lower East Alpine Zones of the Eastern Alps, e.g. the Twenger Kristallin (Tollman, 1963) or the Mölltal gneiss lamellae (Exner, 1962). It is also possible that such basement slices could form the cores of nappe-like folds. The gneissic cores of the major alpine nappes, however, seem to be too large to have formed in this way.

There are also clearly important thermal considerations associated with the closure of stretched basins. In their earliest stages shortly after opening, the heat flow is high and temperatures are higher than in adjacent regions. During the asymmetrical closure of such a basin, major perturbations of the thermal field are inevitable. This problem has been discussed by Oxburgh and Turcotte (1974) in a much simplified form but the boundary conditions are likely to be somewhat different from those considered by them.

Conclusions and Discussion

This article has touched on only a few of the implications of the tectonic model it advocates. Some of these are at present being investigated in a quantitative way and require much more detailed study. It is, however, hard to avoid the three main conclusions:

(1) that stretching of the continental crust is an important process in the early history of many orogenic belts;
(2) that stretching of the crust necessarily involves stretching of the whole lithosphere which may be many times thicker than the crust;
(3) that the variation of rheological properties with depth within the lithosphere both because of gradients of composition and of temperature, makes it very unlikely that the distribution of lithospheric strain will be homogeneous.

If this third conclusion is true on anything but a trivial and local scale, there are important implications for regional vertical movements. Similarly the distribution and character of post-stretching horizontal movements must be strongly influenced by the lateral strength heterogeneities introduced by stretching.

These major considerations are likely to be modulated in various ways by factors which have not been considered above. It has for example been assumed that the subcon-

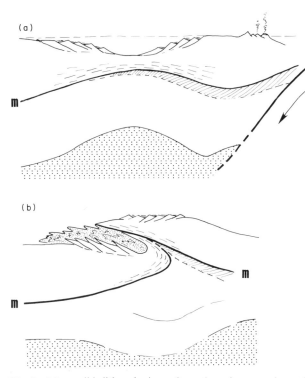

Fig. 8   (a) possible lithospheric configuration after crustal stretching: ornament of long dashes — stretching fabric; oblique hatched area — possible subcrustal accretion complex associated with subduction on the right hand side of the diagram; M, M-discontinuity; asthenosphere, dotted.
(b) asymmetrical closure of stretched basin; motion on listric faults is reversed and some fault bounded blocks become involved in the fold complex formed by the sediments deposited in the basin.

tinental mantle component of the lithosphere has the same composition as the asthenosphere and that the rheological difference between them is entirely attributable to temperature effects. This is unlikely to be true (e.g. Jordan, 1978; Oxburgh and Parmentier, 1977) and subcontinental lithospheric mantle may in part have a significantly different density and composition from that of average asthenosphere, affecting both its rheology and the isostatic behaviour of a region where it occurs.

Similarly the effects of phase changes have been ignored. As discussed by Richardson and England (1979), the inversion of the lower continental crust to high density mineral assemblages is highly likely under certain circumstances, in which case there will be an important effect on the magnitude, timing and rate of vertical movements.

One of the greatest uncertainties is associated with the chemical composition of the lower crust and the extent to which lateral variations in composition introduce important variations in rheology. The overriding consideration is likely to be the water content of the lower crust and the immediately adjacent upper mantle.

In the discussion above, considerable weight was given to the expected difference in rheological properties between the mantle and crustal components of the lithosphere. Whereas this difference is very likely to be real, even to the extent of making the M-discontinuity a potential zone of delamination within the lithosphere, it may be that this contrast in properties is less important than that which occurs *within* the mantle part of the lithosphere. The uppermost mantle (Fig. 4) may well be very strong indeed (but sensitive to water content) and could dominate the large scale tectonic behaviour of the lithosphere.

This article has been highly speculative and represents a tentative approach towards understanding those processes which, although in a sense secondary to the large scale motions of the plates, are extremely important in controlling the thermal and mechanical phenomena for which evidence is found in the field. It is the immense corpus of careful field observations and regional geological synthesis to which Augusto Gansser and Rudi Trümpy have contributed massively in the past (and show no signs of ceasing!), that makes it possible to constrain and to begin to understand the deeper tectonic processes which determine which rocks we find at the Earth's surface and how they are arranged.

References

Ashby, M.F. and Verrall, R.A. (1977). Micromechanisms of flow and fracture, and their relevance to the rheology of the upper mantle. *Phil. Trans. Roy. Soc. Lond.* **288**, 59–95.

Birch, F., Roy, R.F. and Decker, E.R. (1968). Heat flow and thermal history in New England and New York. *In* "Studies of Appalachian geology, northern and maritime" (Zen, E., White, W.S., Hadley, J.B. and Thompson, J.B., eds). Interscience Publishers, New York, pp.437–452.

Bodine, J.H., Steckler, M.S. and Watts, A.B. (1981). Observations of flexure and the rheology of th oceanic lithosphere: *J. Geoph. Res.* **86**, 3695–3707.

Clark, S.P. Jr., and Jäger, E. (1969). Denudation rate in the Alps from geochronologic and heat flow data. *Am. J. Sci.* **267**, 1143–1160.

Exner, C. (1962). Sonnblicklamelle und Mölltalline. *Jahrbuch der Geologischen Bundesanstalt, Vienna* **105**, 273–286.

Frisch, W. (1979). Tectonic progradation and plate tectonic evolution of the Alps. *Tectonophysics* **60**, 121–139.

Grossling, B.F. (1959). Temperature variations due to the formation of a geosyncline. *Bull. Geol. Soc. Am.* **70**, 1253–1282.

Hawkesworth, C.J. (1974). Vertical distribution of heat production in the basement of the Eastern Alps. *Nature, London* **249**, 435–436.

Haxby, W.F., Turcotte, D.L. and Bird, J.M. (1976). Thermal and mechanical evolution of the Michigan basin. *Tectonophysics* **36**, 57–75.

Helwig, J. (1976). Shortening of continental crust in orogenic belts and plate tectonics. *Nature, London* **260**, 768–770.

Houseman, G.A. and McKenzie, D.P. (1981). Convective instability of a thickened boundary layer and its relevance for the thermal evolution of continental convergent belts. *J. Geophys. Res.* **86**, 6115–6132.

Jackson, J.A. (1980). Reactivation of basement faults and crustal shortening in orogenic belts. *Nature, London* **283**, 343–346.

Jarvis, G.T. and McKenzie, D.P. (1980). Sedimentary basin formation with finite extension rates. *Earth Planet. Sci. lett.* **48**, 42–52.

Jenkyns, H.C. (1970). Growth and disintegration of a carbonate platform. *Neues Jahrbuch für Geologie und Palaeontologie, Stuttgart, Monatshefte*, pp.325–344.

Jenkyns, H.C. (1980). Tethys: past and present. *Proc. Geol. Assoc.* **91**, 107–118.

Jordan, T.H. (1978). Composition and development of the continental tectosphere. *Nature, London* **274**, 544–548.

Karig, D.E. (1970). Ridges and basins of the Tonga–Kermadec Island Arc System. *J. Geophys. Res.* **75**, 239.

Karig, D.E. (1974). Evolution of arc systems in the Western Pacific. *Ann. Rev. Earth Planet. Sci.* **2**, 51–75.

Lachenbruch, A.H. (1968). Preliminary geothermal model of the Sierra Nevada. *J. Geophys. Res.* **73**, 6977–6989.

Le Pichon, X. and Angelier, J. (1981). The Aegean Sea. *Phil. Trans. Roy. Soc. Lond. A* **300** 357–372.

Le Pichon, X. and Sibuet, J.-C. (1981). Passive margins: a model of formation. *J. Geophys. Res.* **86**, 3708–3720.

McKenzie, D.P. (1978). Some remarks on the development of sedimentary basins. *Earth Planet. Sci. lett.* **40**, 25–32.

Mercier, J.L. (1981). Extensional-compressional tectonics associated with the Aegean Arc: comparison with the Andean Cordillera of south Peru — north Bolivia. *Phil. Trans. Roy. Soc. Lond. A* **300**, 337–355.

Molnar, P. and Tapponnier, P. (1981). A possible dependence of tectonic strength on the age of the crust in Asia. *Earth Planet. Sci. lett.* **52**, 107–114.

Montadert, L., Roberts, D.G., De Charpal, O. and Guennoc, P. (1979a). Rifting and subsidence of the Northern Continental Margin of the Bay of Biscay. *Init. Rep. Deep Sea Drilling Proj.* **48**, 1025–1060.

Montadert, L., De Charpal, O., Roberts, D.G., Guennoc, P. and Sibuet, J.-C. (1979b). Northeast Atlantic passive margins: rifting and subsidence processes. *In* "Deep drilling results in the Atlantic ocean: continental margins and paleoenvironment" (Talwani, M., Hay, W.W., and Ryan, W.B.F., eds). Maurice Ewing Series, Vol. 3, AGU, Washington, D.C., pp. 164–176.

Oxburgh, E.R. (1981). Heat flow and differences in lithospheric thickness. *Phil. Trans. Royal. Soc. Lond. A* **301**, 337–346.

Oxburgh, E.R. and England, P.C. (1980). Heat flow and the metamorphic evolution of the Eastern Alps. *Eclogae Geologicae Helvetiae, Lausanne* **73**, 379–398.

Oxburgh, E.R. and Parmentier, E.M. (1977). Compositional and density stratification in oceanic lithosphere — causes and consequences. *J. Geol. Soc.* **133**, 343–355.

Oxburgh, E.R. and Turcotte, D.L. (1974). Thermal gradients and regional metamorphism in overthrust terrains with special reference to the Eastern Alps. *Schweizerische Mineralogische und Petrographische Mitteilungen* **54**, 641–662.

Oxburgh, E.R., Norris, R.J. and Cliff, R.A. (1971). Conclusions. *In* "Structural, metamorphic and geochronological studies in the Reisseck and Southern Ankogel groups, the Eastern Alps" (Cliff, R.A., Norris, R.J., Oxburgh, E.R., and Wright, R.C., eds). *Jahrbuch der Geologischen Bundesanstalt, Vienna* **114**, 248–255.

Richardson, S.W. and England, P.C. (1979). Metamorphic consequences of crustal eclogite production in overthrust orogenic zones. *Earth Planet. Sci. Lett.* **42**, 183–190.

Royden, L. and Sclater, J.G. (1981). The Neogene intra-Carpathian basins. *Phil. Trans. Roy. Soc. Lond. A* **300**, 373–381.

Schlager, W. (1981). The paradox of drowned reefs and carbonate platforms. *Bull. Geol. Soc. Am. I* **92**, 197–211.

Sclater, J.G. and Christie, P.A.F. (1980). Continental stretching: an explanation of the post-Mid-Cretaceous subsidence of the central North Sea basin. *J. Geophys. Res.* **85**, 3711–3739.

Smithson, S.B., Brewer, J., Kaufman, S., Oliver, J. and Hurich, C. (1978). Nature of the Wind River thrust, Wyoming, from

COCORP deep-reflection data and from gravity data. *Geology* **6**, 648–652.

Steckler, M.S. and Watts, A.B. (1978). Subsidence of the Atlantic-type continental margin off New York, *Earth Planet. Sci. lett.* **41**, 1–13.

Tollman, A. (1963). "Ostalpensynthese". *Deuticke, Vienna,* 256 pp.

Trümpy, R. (1980). Geology of Switzerland: a guide-book. Part A: An outline of the geology of Switzerland. *Schweizerische Geologische Kommission,* ed., Wepf & Co., Basel and New York, 104 pp.

Wood, R.J. (1981). The subsidence history of Conoco well 15/30–1, central North Sea. *Earth Planet. Sci. lett.* **54**, 306–312.

Microfabric Studies as Indicators of Deformation Mechanisms and Flow Laws Operative in Mountain Building

S.M. Schmid

Geologisches Institut ETH,
Zürich, Switzerland

Abstract

After an introduction into the major deformation mechanisms the following applications to tectonic studies are discussed:
(i) Paleostress estimates based on the extrapolation of experimentally determined flow laws and based on the size of dynamically recrystallized grains; (ii) the significance of crystallographic preferred orientation work; and (iii) mechanisms of strain softening leading to localized deformation in shear zones.

I. Introduction

In discussions with field oriented geologists an experimental geologist sometimes notes criticism with regard to the applicability of the results of experimental rock deformation to the study of naturally deformed rocks. The critics often point out that the experiments were performed under such simple conditions (co-axial strain path, constant stress or strain rate, homogeneous monomineralic rocks) that they are inadequate to throw light on the more complex processes in natural environments. However, any laboratory study must begin with well defined boundary conditions so that the influence of a great number of variables on rock creep can be recognized. Also it is necessary to learn as much as possible about the physics and the mechanisms of rock deformation in order to avoid erroneous extrapolations from the laboratory into the geological situation.

It is the study of the microfabric in both experimentally and naturally deformed rocks which permits direct comparisons to be made between nature and experiment. The microfabric records the active mechanisms of deformation and its study therefore helps to close the gap between experiment and field observation.

Some of the complexities of natural tectonic situations can be modelled much more easily by using analytical or numerical methods or by using readily deformable analogue materials than by an attempt to perform more complex experiments on natural rock specimens. In this case it is important however to know as much as possible about the rheology of rocks which depends on the active deformation mechanisms recorded in the microfabric.

This contribution will specifically discuss some selected applications to tectonic studies. Thereby some of the goals of microfabric studies are illustrated within the framework of tectonic studies in general. In order to do so it was felt necessary first to introduce the non-specialist reader into some basic concepts of flow laws and deformation mechanisms.

II. Some General Remarks on Flow and Deformation Mechanisms

A rock loaded under a constant differential stress σ (classical creep test) will immediately shorten elastically. Later it will undergo a permanent change of shape at a strain rate $\dot{e} = de/dt$ which is dictated primarily by three factors according to a flow law of the general form:

$$\dot{e} = \dot{e}\,(\sigma, e, T)$$

where the stress difference σ $(= \sigma_1 - \sigma_3)$ (informally referred to as "stress"), the strain e and the temperature T are the most important quantities determining the resulting strain rate. Strictly, such a flow law is only valid as long as other factors such as confining pressure, water content or partial pressure, grain size etc. are held constant or can be assumed to have no major influence on the rheological properties.

Confining pressure is usually assumed to be of minor importance in the ductile field, once frictional processes (cataclasis) can be ruled out (Paterson, 1978). Water can have a "mechanical" effect through the well known pore pressure effect (Hubbert and Rubey, 1959), again in the brittle and cataclastic fields, or it may have an influence on the nature of atomic bonding in silicates, influencing the resistance to deformation by crystal plasticity, a phenomen known as hydrolitic weakening (Griggs, 1967). In the latter case there is evidence that pressure enhances the solubility of water in quartz and therefore, that pressure strongly influences the rock strength outside the cataclastic field as well (Tullis et al., 1979; Paterson and Kekulawala, 1979). The influence of grain size will be discussed in more detail in the next section.

During the first stages of deformation the strain rate strongly depends on strain (primary creep); after a few percent strain the rate of deformation usually decreases to a constant value. The rock is then said to deform in steady state. Ideally, strain has no influence on the strain rate any more. We will see later that rocks may eventually soften at high strains causing the strain rate to increase again. At this point it is important to say that the concept of steady state is used here to merely imply flow at constant stress and strain rate.

In the case of a constant strain rate experiment the stress may rise with increasing strain (strain hardening), it may stay constant (steady state) thereafter, or it may eventually decrease with increasing strain (strain softening).

For thermally activated creep one can empirically derive flow laws from a series of experiments on the same rock, valid for steady state flow only. They are usually presented in the form of:

$$\dot{e} = \dot{e}_0 \exp -H/RT \; f(\sigma) \tag{1}$$

where $\dot{e}_0$ is a material dependent constant, H is the apparent activation energy for creep and R is the Gas Constant. The stress dependence can adequately be described in most cases by either:

$$f(\sigma) = \exp \sigma/\sigma_0 \quad \text{(exponential creep law)} \tag{2}$$

or

$$f(\sigma) = \sigma^n \quad \text{(power creep law)} \tag{3}$$

where the constants σ_0 and n determine the stress sensitivity of the strain rate. Because in most cases the parameter n is found to be greater than unity, rocks usually deviate from linear viscous behaviour.

There is no single flow law for all conditions of stress and temperature, simply because the deformation mechanism is a function of stress and temperature as well. Associated with each of these deformation mechanisms is a different flow law. It is usual to subdivide the stress-temperature space into different fields by means of a deformation mechanism map (Ashby and Verrall, 1978 and Fig. 1). Within each of these fields a particular mechanism is dominant.

Such deformation mechanism maps are normally calculated from first principles by assuming specific microdynamical models. Experiments often merely provide numbers for the various material dependent constants in the theoretical flow laws.

The primary aim of these deformation mechanism maps is to outline the expected conditions of appearance of given deformation mechanisms outside the range of $\dot{e}$–σ–T–conditions accessible to the experimentalist. The main problem in the application of the laboratory data is the enormous gap between geological strain rates of the order of 10^{-10}s^{-1} to 10^{-15}s^{-1} (involving time spans of between 30 and 3 million years for 10% shortening strain) and the laboratory strain rates usually between 10^{-2} and 10^{-7}s^{-1}. As can be seen in Fig. 1 one has a high chance of crossing a boundary between deformation mechanism fields by extrapolating down to lower strain rates and consequently to lower stresses at any given temperature. Therefore a flow law observed at high stresses under laboratory strain rates can only be extrapolated over a limited range of strain rates and stresses. In order to explore the flow behaviour at low stresses the experimentalist is forced to elevate the temperature beyond the range of temperatures expected under natural conditions

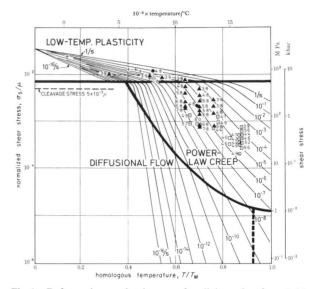

Fig. 1   Deformation mechanism map for olivine, taken from Ashby and Verrall (1978, Fig. 14). The map is constructed for a grain size of 100 μm and for zero confining pressure. The solid lines delineate deformation mechanism boundaries, superimposed are the constant strain rate contours. The various symbols indicate the position of experimental data on this map.

(Paterson, 1976). Thus, elevated temperatures are essentially used as a "trade off" for unattainably slow geological strain rates. Once a flow law has been established at high temperatures and low stresses the geologist has to extrapolate down to lower temperatures, along a path which is less likely to cross deformation mechanism boundaries.

There are some problems with the concept of steady state creep and the associated concept of flow laws and deformation mechanisms:

(i)   Strain may alter the microstructure and this in turn causes strain hardening or strain softening (see section VI). In these cases the situation can no longer be described in terms of a single deformation mechanism map which assumes constant microstructure and steady state creep.

(ii)   As will be discussed in the next section, there is a subtle difference between the deformation mechanism accounting for all or most of the total strain in the rock and the concept of a rate controlling step which contributes only a small part of the total strain (such as dislocation climb in power law creep).

(iii)   Strictly a deformation mechanism map only applies to a particular mineral in a rock and it is rather difficult to talk about the deformation mechanism of a polymineralic rock. Many mylonites offer good examples for crystal plastic flow accompanied with recrystallization within quartz domains while the feldspars deform by cataclastic processes.

With these general remarks in mind we shall now review the major modes of deformation more specifically. This will allow us to discuss some geological applications such as paleostress estimates, crystallographic preferred orientation work and finally strain softening mechanisms.

III.   Deformation Regimes

Different approaches towards the problem of deformation mechanisms are possible. The physicist wants to be very exact about the processes on an atomic level and it is possible to theoretically postulate specific microdynamical models. There is a great number of such models and for a comprehensive review the reader is referred to Poirier (1976).

Here we will follow a more empirical approach. The experimentalist often derives empirical flow laws from a series of experiments and it is rarely clear what the exact mechanisms of deformation are. In such cases it is useful to talk about deformation regimes, defined by empirical flow laws and associated diagnostic microstructural imprints.

A. Cataclastic Flow

The term "cataclastic" refers to a mode of deformation where fracture and subsequent loss of cohesion may occur on all scales. The brittle-ductile transition does not necessarily coincide with the transition from cataclastic to non-cataclastic processes. If intra- and intergranular fracture occurs along a dispersed network of microcracks, the bulk deformation of the rock may still be ductile in the sense that considerable amounts of permanent strain can be taken up without the typical stress drop associated with localized faulting, characteristic for the brittle field (Paterson, 1969).

Cataclastic flow is made possible by rolling and sliding of grains and crystal fragments of a cataclastically granulated rock. Since frictional resistance between the fragments depends on the magnitude of normal stress across cohesionless surfaces, this mechanism is strongly dependent on confining pressure and, in the presence of fluids, on the effective pressure, i.e. the difference between lithostatic and fluid pressure (Hubbert and Rubey, 1959).

Because to a first approximation deformation by cataclastic flow is not thermally activated, temperature and strain rate have little influence on the strength of the rock.

Figure 2 illustrates the microstructure typical for cataclastic flow within an experimentally produced fracture zone: grain size reduction by cataclastic processes produces a wide spectrum of angular fragments with a wide range of grain sizes. This type of grain size reduction should not be con-

fused with the mechanism of grain size reduction by dynamic recrystallization, typical for mylonites (White *et al.*, 1980). Since the pioneering work of Carter *et al.* (1964) it is clear that mortar quartz in mylonites is the product of dynamic recrystallization during power law creep and that mylonites should not be referred to as cataclastic rocks (Higgins, 1971).

At more elevated temperatures and pressures crystal plastic deformation will successfully compete with fracturing because elevated temperatures promote the ease of glide within crystals and because higher pressures prohibit cataclastic processes associated with volume increases and frictional processes.

B. Low Temperature Plasticity

Within this regime strain in the rock is largely achieved by the conservative motion of dislocations through the crystal lattice (i.e. the dislocations propagate strictly within crystallographic planes), or, on a larger scale of observation, by glide on slip systems defined by slip plane and direction. The resistance to glide is not controlled by friction and thus independent of confining pressure. There is a resistance to glide caused by either the necessity of breaking atomic bonds as a dislocation moves or by obstacles such as impurities, other dislocations or grain boundaries (lattice resistance versus obstacle controlled plasticity, Ashby and Verrall, 1978).

The resistance to dislocation glide is the rate controlling factor during deformation and usually an exponential stress dependence of strain rate (equation 2) is observed. The motion of dislocations is thermally activated, the apparent activation energy for creep is usually smaller than for the lattice self-diffusion. Thus, stress, temperature and strain rate become interrelated in the form of a pseudoviscous flow law (Fig. 1).

The fact that grain boundaries are obstacles to the free propagation of slip (and twinning in the case of calcite) into the neighbouring grain is reflected by the observation that the yield stress of fine-grained materials is generally higher than that of coarse-grained materials. This grain size depen-

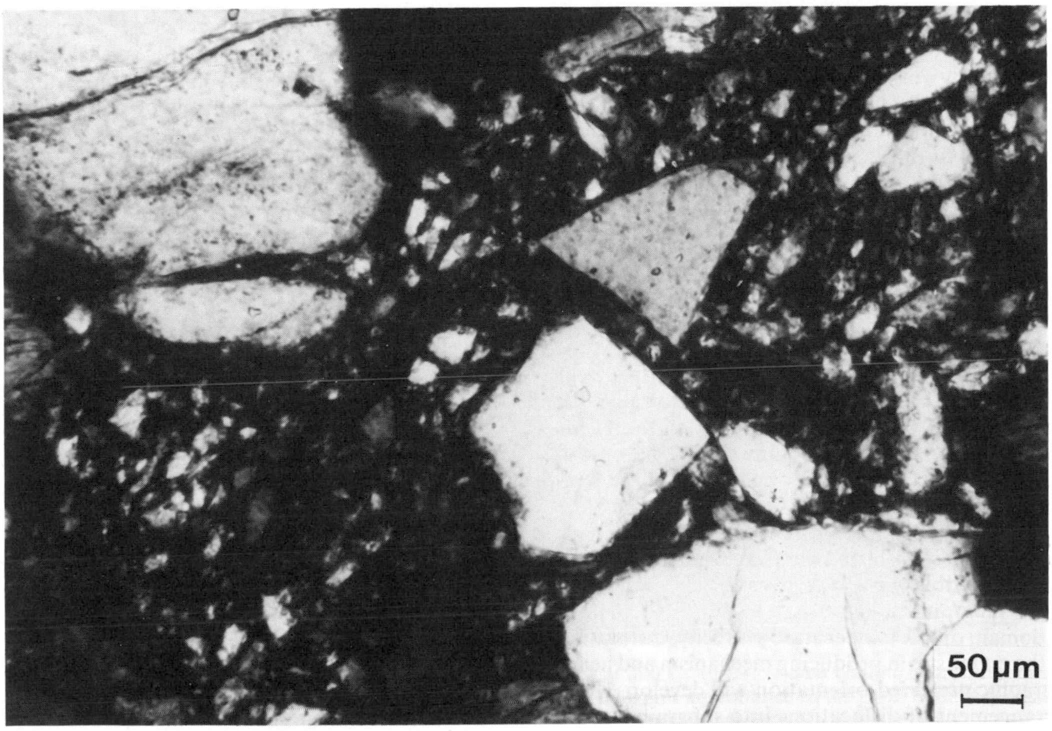

Fig. 2 Grain size reduction by fracturing within a shear fracture zone in experimentally deformed quartzite. Note the angular shape and the wide spectrum of grain sizes of the crystal fragments.

pressure solution) or by sliding along grain boundaries of essentially rigid crystallites (superplasticity).

Diffusional flow in the solid state via migration of point defects along a stress gradient is known as Nabarro-Herring or Coble creep, depending on whether diffusion occurs through the lattice in the grain interior or near grain boundaries. For strain compatibility reasons, sliding at grain boundaries has to occur but the grain boundary shear stresses are so low that diffusion remains the rate controlling step during deformation (Beeré, 1978). The strain rate can be calculated from first principles by considering the stress dependence of the equilibrium density of point defects (for a simple derivation see Poirier, 1976). It has the form:

$$\dot{e} = C\, D_{eff}\sigma\Omega/kTd^2 \tag{5}$$

where C is a geometrical constant, D_{eff} is the effective diffusion coefficient, Ω is the atomic volume and d is the grain size. The effective diffusion coefficient is made up of two components: the lattice diffusion component dominating in Nabarro-Herring creep and the grain boundary diffusion component dominating in the Coble creep field. In the latter case the effective diffusion coefficient is inversely proportional to the grain size and thus the exponent b in equation 4 is equal to 3.

There is as yet no experimental evidence for solid state diffusional flow in rock materials. Diffusional flow is likely to occur at very low stresses and high temperatures only.

Pressure solution, involves diffusional mass transport in an aqueous environment via solution and redeposition of material (Fig. 6). It is a widespread mode of deformation in low grade rocks (Durney, 1972) but hard to observe under laboratory conditions because it is expected to dominate at low temperatures and stresses and at very slow strain rates only (Rutter, 1976). Rutter (1976) derived a constitutive equation for pressure solution on the domain of individual grains (Fig. 6) whose formalism is analogous to the equation for Coble creep: instead of a gradient in the equilibrium concentration of vacancies along the grain boundary there is a difference in solubility in the fluid films at the grain boundaries. The rate of deformation also depends on the grain boundary diffusivity in the presence of a fluid film.

The situation becomes more complex however if the solution transfer occurs over much larger distances as, for example, from a stylolite to a calcite vein (Durney and Ramsay, 1973). Such a situation can no longer be described in terms of a microdynamical model.

Another kind of grain size sensitive creep, likely to operate at low stresses and small grain sizes, is grain boundary sliding leading to *superplastic flow*. In this case grain boundary sliding acts as the prime strain producing mechanism and it is not just a consequence of strain compatibility problems as is the case during diffusional creep. Also the grains are now free to rotate and to switch neighbours after high amounts of strain (Edington et al., 1976). Microdynamical models for superplastic flow usually assume that the strain rate is not controlled by the viscous resistance to gliding at grain boundaries but by the slowest event during sliding, namely the minor changes in shape the grains have to undergo in order to slide past each other. Ball and Hutchinson (1969) proposed that dislocations pile up at unfavourably oriented grain boundaries and that these dislocations escape by climbing into the grain boundaries. An alternative model by Ashby and Verrall (1973) proposes local diffusional mass transfer along grain boundaries.

In contrast to diffusional creep and pressure solution, a non-linear strain rate vs. stress relationship is observed, but the value of the exponent n in equation 3 is always smaller than 3. The grain size exponent b in equation 4 is usually found to lie between 2 and 3.

There is some ambiguity about the term superplasticity. In a wider sense, the notion of superplastic flow is a phenomenological one and just implies extreme ductility during an extension experiment, a common mode of testing metals. Ductility is a measure of resistance to necking in a tensile test and not directly related to a specific mechanism. In geology, the term superplastic in this wide sense can be used for any rock which is highly strained, such as any mylonite.

Fig. 6   Pressure solution on the scale of individual grains in a crinoidal limestone. Solution took place along horizontally oriented stylolites, the white redeposition areas grow in crystallographic continuity over the dark grey impure original single crystals of calcite.

High ductility and resistance to necking are however related to the deformation mechanism indirectly through the value of the parameter n in equation 3. If $n = 1$ necks do not propagate (Gittus, 1978) and therefore materials deforming by diffusional creep can be referred to as being superplastic too in this wide sense.

In a more restricted sense however superplasticity implies that:

(i) grain boundary sliding is the major strain-producing mechanism,

(ii) that the microstructure remains stable, i.e. that the grains remain equiaxed even after large amounts of strain and

(iii) that the stress sensitivity of strain rate in terms of the parameter in equation 3 is between 1 and 3.

All these criteria do not apply in the case of diffusional creep, so here the term superplasticity will be used in this narrow sense.

Superplastic flow in rock materials has only recently been reported (Bouiller and Gueguen, 1975; Schmid *et al.*, 1977). It is difficult however to find direct evidence for grain boundary sliding in naturally deformed rocks and a stable microstructure can also be explained by dynamic recrystallization during power law creep. It is only the absence of a strong crystallographic preferred orientation which can indicate that grain boundary sliding may be the dominant strain producing mechanism.

IV. Paleostress Estimates

A. Estimates Based on the Extrapolation of Flow Laws

Ideally, the magnitude of differential stress can be estimated by extrapolation of laboratory determined flow laws into geological conditions on the basis of a deformation mechanism map, provided that there are independent estimates of strain rate and temperature. These extrapolations heavily rely on the accuracy of the deformation mechanism maps used, and thus also on the reliability of the theoretically calculated flow laws for regimes outside the range of experimental conditions accessible to the experimentalist.

Most of the experimentally determined flow laws apply to the mechanisms of low temperature plasticity and power law creep (for reviews see Carter, 1976; Tullis, 1979). Stresses operating during brittle fracture and cataclastic flow can be estimated through the well known Mohr-Coulomb criterion. Flow laws for grain size sensitive creep are available only for superplastically deformed calcite and olivine (Schmid *et al.*, 1977; Twiss, 1977 on the basis of data by Post, 1973, 1977).

Figure 7 is a graphical synopsis of some of the laboratory derived flow laws on various monomineralic rocks in the coordinates of a deformation mechanism map (compare Fig. 7). Possible transitions into cataclastic flow at high stresses (depending on confining pressure) and into grain size sensitive creep laws at low stresses are not considered in this figure because of the lack of experimental data (except for fine-grained limestone, deforming superplastically at low stresses). The curves are drawn for geologically realistic strain rates by simple extrapolations of empirical flow laws and they exhibit a more or less drastic drop in strength at vastly different temperatures. The relative strength of these materials corresponds nicely to the relative competence of these rocks in the field.

The slope at constant strain rate, as derived from a power law relationship (equation 3) is given by:

$$d \log \sigma / dT = - \frac{H}{2 \cdot 3 \, R n T^2} \qquad (6)$$

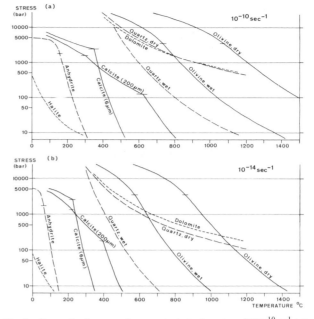

Fig. 7 Synoptic diagrams for constant strain rates of $10^{-10} \mathrm{s}^{-1}$ (a) and $10^{-14} \mathrm{s}^{-1}$ (b) illustrating the relative strength of different rock types as a function of temperature. The constant strain rate contours are based on experimentally determined flow laws for polycrystalline aggregates of halite (Heard, 1972), anhydrite (Müller and Briegel, 1980), fine-grained limestone (Schmid *et al.*, 1977), coarse-grained marble (Schmid *et al.*, 1980), wet and dry quartz (Parrish *et al.*, 1976), dolomite (Heard, 1976) and dunite (Post, 1977).

and depends not only on the apparent activation energy for creep but also on the value of the stress exponent n.

It is readily seen that accurate stress estimates are difficult because temperature estimates are usually not too precise. Also there are dependencies on water content in the case of the silicates and the limestone data emphasize the importance of grain size (note the reversal in relative strength of the two calcite rocks from the high stress area into the low stress area). On top of these difficulties come some of the problems discussed in the previous chapters.

Figure 7 however illustrates the vast differences in flow stress to be expected between different materials under conditions of constant strain rate. In reality, these differences are relaxed by inhomogeneous deformation and salt, anhydrite and limestone in particular are good decollement horizons at moderate temperatures, where dolomite and the silicates remain essentially brittle. Müller and Hsü (1980) showed by numerical modelling that the decollement of the Swiss Jura mountains including the Swiss molasse basin is compatible with the experimentally determined flow laws for anhydrite (Müller *et al.*, 1981), a major constituent within the Triassic evaporites.

At somewhat more elevated temperatures calcite may become an important decollement horizon provided that it deforms by superplastic flow. Based on the flow law for superplastically deformed limestone, the flow stress at the base of the Glarus overthrust and within a thin calc-mylonite layer (Schmid, 1975) can be estimated to be lower than 100 bar at the estimated temperatures and strain rates. New microfabric work on this mylonite horizon produced evidence that grain boundary sliding is the operative deformation mechanism (Schmid *et al.*, 1981).

The relative strength of decollement horizons and thrust blocks also has a major influence on the questions of gravity spreading versus active tectonic push at the rear of a thrust based numerical models. There is a vast amount of texture data in the geological literature, but in many cases interpretations of the pole figures have remained highly speculative and sometimes nebulous.

The work of Lister and co-authors (Lister *et al.*, 1978; Lister and Paterson, 1979; Lister and Hobbs, 1980) in particular made it very clear that texture development is governed by three main factors:

1. *The particular set of glide systems active during deformation*. This produces characteristic patterns from which we can learn about the stress, strain rate and temperature conditions during deformation (Lister and Paterson, 1979). Experimental work on single crystals provides important input parameters for these numerical models in providing information on the relative magnitudes of the critical resolved shear stresses needed to operate particular glide systems as a function of the environmental parameters.

2. *Finite strain*. With the same set of active glide systems the type of finite strain (flattening, constriction, plane strain etc.) produces different pole figure patterns (Lister and Hobbs, 1980). In the case of texture development through glide-induced lattice rotations, as modelled by Lister and co-authors, it is difficult to estimate the magnitude of strain. For an alternative mechanism, such as the passive rotation of sheet silicates in a ductile matrix, attempts have been made to relate the strength of the texture to the strain magnitude (March, 1932).

3. *The strain path or the kinematic framework*. The influence of these on the final texture pattern has been studied by Lister and Hobbs (1980) and Etchecopar (1977). Starting with a random texture and excluding complex multiphase strain histories, an asymmetry of the pole figures in respect to the macroscopic fabric axes (foliation, lineation) is indicative for a non-coaxial strain path with a large component of simple shear and the sense of the asymmetry reflects the sense of shear.

   It is still not clear how much and in exactly which way intracrystalline slip occurring in low temperature plasticity and power law creep determines the lattice rotations of individual grains. Many rocks with a strong texture are dynamically recrystallized and dynamic recrystallization was not considered by the model work of Etchecopar (1977) and Lister *et al.* (1978).

Figure 10, taken from Casey *et al.* 1978, is a good example for how the deformation mechanisms and the set of active glide systems influence the texture in the case of calcite. The type 1 textures (Fig. 11) are indicative of twinning, known to be the easiest glide system at low temperatures. The type 2 textures occur in the absence of twinning and Lister (1978) simulated this texture remarkably well by activating slip mainly on the rhombs r and f. The type 3 textures are comparatively weak and the transition from type 2 into type 3 exactly coincides with the change in deformation mechanism form power law creep into superplastic flow (Schmid *et al.*, 1977; Casey *et al.*, 1978). The fact that a weak texture does develop indicates that some intracrystalline slip takes place during grain boundary sliding.

Usually the laboratory experiments produce uniaxially deformed specimens and, as a consequence of this, the pole figures exhibit rotational symmetry around the compression axis (this is the reason for using inverse pole figures for details; see Bunge, 1969). The experimental work of Kern (1971) is the only example of a more complex type of coaxial strain and he experimentally demonstrated how the type of strain influences the texture.

Experiments in simple shear are very difficult to perform

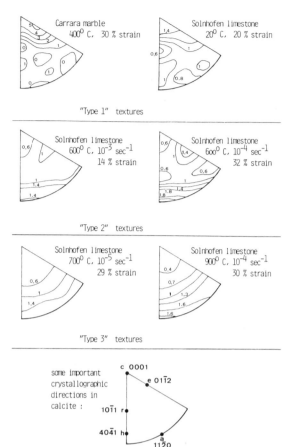

Fig. 10   Inverse pole figures for experimentally deformed calcite rocks, contoured in multiples of a uniform distribution, taken from Casey *et al.* (1978).

and here we rely on model work and on the interpretation of textures in naturally deformed rocks. Nature provides independent evidence for shearing deformation and for the sense of shear in many shear zones (Ramsay, 1980; Simpson, 1980).Figure 11 illustrates the texture of a quartz mylonite within such a shear zone. X-ray texture goniometry allows the determination of a set of pole figures and we do not rely only on the pole figure for the c-axis in quartz, as is the case in optical U-stage measurements (Schmid *et al.*, 1981b). In addition, the calculation of the orientation distribution function (Bunge, 1969), Bunge and Wenk. 1977; Casey, 1981) allows ideal crystal orientations in terms of all crystallographic axes to be determined from a set of pole figures for different crystallographic directions. Figure 12 plots the

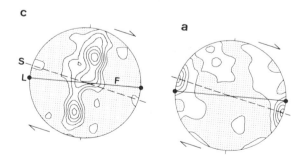

Fig. 11   X-ray determined pole figures for the quartz c-axis and the a-direction (1120) in quartzite taken from a shear zone (Schmid *et al.*, 1981b). The countours are given in multiples of a uniform distribution. The orientation of foliation (F) and lineation (L) are labelled together with the shear zone boundary (S). The arrows indicate the sense of shear inferred from the shear zone geometry.

most likely orientation of a quartz grain in case of the specimen presented in Fig. 11. The a-direction (normal to the second order prism in quartz), an important glide direction, is aligned with the inferred shear direction within the shear zone. In addition, the position of the c-axis suggests that the positive rhombs prefer to be aligned with the shear zone boundary and this is confirmed in Fig. 12. This is a stable orientation for easy glide on the rhomb planes and in the following chapter the rheological consequences of such a stable end-orientation will be discussed.

Figure 13 illustrates that this same specimen dynamically recrystallized, probably by a rotation mechanism. Dynamic recrystallization did not destroy the texture, which can still be readily interpreted in terms of intracrystalline slip. There is thus no need to invoke separate models of texture development for dynamically recrystallized grains, such as the Kamb model (see discussion in Nicolas and Poirier, 1976).

An immediate application of such asymmetries lies in the determination of shear sense, not known in many geological settings, and in kinematic interpretation of lineations in terms of a- and b-lineations following Sanders terminology. In our case, the lineation is at a small angle to the shear direction and therefore represents a stretching lineation subparallel to the relative displacement of the shear zone boundaries (a-lineation). There are now numerous examples of the determination of shear sense using this principle (Eisbacher, 1970; Boucher, 1978; Burg and Laurent, 1978; Bouchez and Pecher, 1981). Systematic regional studies on the significance of lineations for inferring the direction of relative displacement of nappes or during internal deformation of gneissic bodies will certainly be of major geotectonic importance in the future.

VI. Strain Softening Mechanisms

Localized deformation in shear zones is an important mode of deformation in basement rocks (Ramsay, 1980) and ductile flow in mylonite layers accounts for large nappe translations. The formation of shear zones and mylonite horizons is a consequence of local shear instabilities. There is a variety

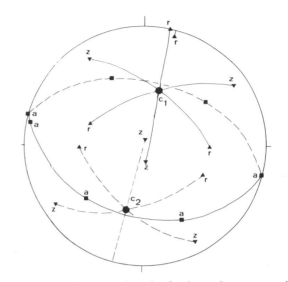

Fig. 12   Favoured crystal orientation for the specimen presented in Fig. 11. The c-axis position labelled c_1 and c_2 correspond to the positions of the c-axis maxima in Fig. 11, the positions of the poles to $(11\bar{2}0)$ are labelled a (second order prisms), the positions of the poles to $(10\bar{1}1)$ and $(01\bar{1}1)$ are labelled r and z (positive and negative rhombs respectively).

of possible mechanisms which can lead to strain softening (see reviews by Poirier, 1980 and White *et al.*, 1980) and hence to shear instabilities. Although shear heating (Brun and Cobbold, 1980; Fleitout and Froidevaux, 1980) probably is the most popular softening mechanism, we will only discuss two other possible mechanisms, because they relate closely to the topics discussed so far:

(1) Geometrical softening caused by the rotation of easy glide systems into orientations of high resolved shear stresses during texture formation and

(2) softening as a consequence of a change in deformation mechanism from power law creep into grain size sensitive

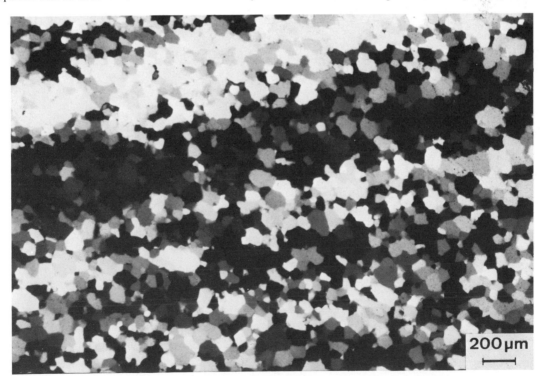

Fig. 13   Microstructure of the dynamically recrystallized quartzite specimen referred to in Fig. 11.

creep. The latter process can be induced by dynamic recrystallization.

Both these mechanisms rely on two aspects of the microfabric which are typical for mylonites: a strong crystallographic preferred orientation and dynamic recrystallization towards small grain sizes.

A. Geometrical Softening

In the previous chapter, the development of textures in shearing situations was discussed and it was demonstrated that a type of texture may develop which increases the average resolved shear stress on one or, in many other cases, on a few of the slip systems. In the case of quartz, a good alignment of the a-directions with the shear direction is observed in many cases (Bouchez, 1978; Schmid *et al.*, 1981).

In such a situation, the flow stress for intracrystalline slip will eventually drop to a minimum. Both Etchecopar (1977) and Lister and Hobbs (1980) simulated the development of such end-orientations in their models.

Experimental data by Burrows *et al.* (1979) suggests that the reorientation of the lattice may be assisted by dynamic recrystallization and many mylonites with a strong texture are dynamically recrystallized. The mechanism of grain boundary migration in particular offers a good empirical explanation for the enhancement of the rate of reorientation of the crystal lattice towards an end-orientation for easy glide. Those grains which are unsuitably oriented for easy glide will accumulate high levels of internal elastic strain energy through a high dislocation density and lattice distortions in the form of undulose extinction, kink bands, deformation bands etc. Grains oriented for easy glide on the other hand have a lower dislocation density and because they deform in compatibility with the bulk aggregate they store less elastic strain energy. This promotes the consumption of unsuitably oriented grains and hence strengthens the texture.

B. Softening by a Strain Induced Change in Deformation Mechanism

Dynamic recrystallization during power law creep effectively changes the grain size of the starting material as illustrated in Fig. 5 for experimentally deformed calcite. The same process of grain size reduction in the case of the calc-mylonite along the Glarus overthrust in the Helvetic nappes of Switzerland is illustrated in Figs 14, 15, 16. For Fig. 16 it is particularly obvious that the mechanism of dynamic recrystallization by subgrain rotation induces the change in grain size.

The new recrystallized grain size has been determined to be around 6–7 µm and according to the stress vs. grain size relationship of Fig. 9 this indicates paleostresses of around 700 bar during subgrain formation and recrystallization in power law creep. As the initial grain size is reduced, grain size sensitive creep may or may not take over depending on the size of the new grains and the position of the mechanism boundary between power law creep and grain size sensitive creep. This will now be discussed in some detail on the basis of Fig. 17, which shows a deformation regime map with grain size as a variable at constant temperatures. This graph was constructed for calcite aggregates by combining the constitutive equations for exponential and power law creep as observed in Carrara marble (Schmid *et al.*, 1980) with those for superplastic flow observed in Solnhofen limestone (Schmid *et al.*, 1977). Because superplastic flow is grain size dependent, the resulting deformation regime boundary is grain size dependent as well and separates a high stress — large grain size area of predominantly power law creep from a low stress — small grain size area of superplastic flow.

Superimposed on this deformation regime map is the curve of stress vs. the size of new grains recrystallizing by a rotation mechanism of dynamic recrystallization (see Fig. 9). Strictly speaking this curve should fall within the power law field because this recrystallization by subgrain rotation can only be brought about by power law creep and the notion of an "equilibrium grain size" is meaningless in the domain of

Fig. 14   Recrystallization concentrated along grain boundaries at the beginning stage of progressive mylonitization. Lochseiten mylonite, Glarus.

Fig. 15 Recrystallization to a new fine-grained aggregate in the matrix. Old grains (porphyroclasts) are heavily twinned. Lochseiten mylonite, Glarus.

superplastic flow (Etheridge and Wilkie, 1979). The stress vs. grain size curve however is superimposed on the deformation mechanism map solely for the purpose of demonstrating the following evolution with increasing strain:

A calcite aggregate deforms by a strain rate and under a stress indicated by the position of point A in Fig. 17. The position of this point A indicates that the material has a grain size which is larger than the size of the subgrains and recrystallized grains expected to form with increasing strain. The material deforming by dislocation creep at point A will eventually recrystallize to a grain size along a curve which comes to lie within the field of superplasticity. The paths to point B and C indicated in Fig. 17 indicate two extreme possibilities of what can hypothetically occur if the production of a new grain size by rotation recrystallization would

Fig. 16 Recrystallization went almost to completion. The new grains are free of optical strain features, the grain boundaries are well equilibrated (compare Fig. 18). Lochseiten mylonite, Glarus.

comparatively low, most crustal rocks generally deform elastically. This elastic energy may be stored in the rock, to be recovered at a later period of uplift and erosion, perhaps with the development of regular fracture or joint development related to the principal axes of stored stress. It is also possible that the stresses reach some critical value at which the elastic limit is passed, with the initiation of extensional fractures and shear faults. At depths greater than about 5 km, many crustal rocks undergo creeping flow with the development of non-recoverable deformations. The conditions at which flow takes place vary from rock type to rock type and the initiation and speed of this deformation depend upon which of the various possible deformation mechanisms are active in the minerals making up the rock in question. There has been much recent work aimed at discovering which particular flow law is in operation with a given set of environmental parameters and to express the various parameters in the form of rheological equations. Stefan Schmid's contribution in this volume is an excellent example of this type of approach linking the results of laboratory experiments with observations of the fabrics and textures of naturally deformed rocks. The main limitations of the applications of these results to orogenic belts is that most of the studies so far made have focused attention on monomineralic aggregates. As a logical approach to arrange experiments from simple to complex systems this is a correct working method, but there is still a long way to go before we will be in a position to formulate the relevant rheological equations for the polymineralic rocks that make up most of the Earth's crust. The approach of this paper is to see what we can learn from a study of the geometric forms of naturally deformed rocks, particularly with respect to understanding the relative flow properties of the commonest rock types. Such a study is complimentary to the experimental methods, and there is developing a valuable

cross fertilization of both types of approach, the critical link being an analysis of the mechanics of the instabilities arising during deformation.

Although we do not know the exact flow laws for the commonest crustal rock, an analysis of structural geometry in the light of mechanical predictions clearly indicates that at given environmental conditions some rocks flow more readily than others. In geological descriptions the expression *competence contrast* (Willis, 1893) has been used to describe these differences in ductility, and we can say that one type is more competent than another. The relationship expressed here is clearly only a relative one, but observations on rock systems comprised of several different rock types enable us to put the ductilities in a relative order of magnitude. The sections of this paper which follow will describe some of the practical methods whereby a ductility series can be established and how we can determine the characteristic behaviour of different rock types in different orogenic regions. If it is possible to make particular assumptions as to the rheological properties of a particular rock (e.g. linear viscous behaviour) there are methods available for giving numerical values to describe the competence contrasts (e.g. viscosity ratio in the case of linear viscous materials). Clearly the establishment of such a numerically defined scheme of flow parameters should be our long-term aim, but it is probably unwise at this stage of research to formulate lists with numbers of spurious mechanical significance.

II. Methods for Assessing Competence Contrast

A. Comparison of Finite Strain State

If two rocks undergo an identical stress history, then the most competent rock will develop less total or finite strain

Fig. 1 Deformed polymict conglomerate, Lebendun Nappe, Swiss Alps. The shapes of the deformed pebbles are variable as a result of ductility differences between the rock types comprising the pebbles. The pebbles of pale coloured, coarse grained feldspathic gneiss are more competent than pebbles of granite and aplite which are, in turn, more competent than the dark mica schist pebbles.

Fig. 2a Cleavage refraction in a graded calcareous sandstone (flysch), Wildhorn Nappe, Valais, Switzerland. The cleavage shows a curved form in the graded bed and a sudden change of orientation at the base of the graded unit. These changes in orientation are related to the changing strain state and to the differences of rock ductility.

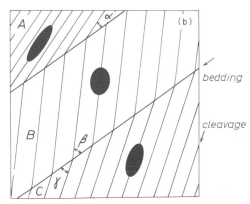

2b The significance of cleavage refraction in terms of changing shape and orientation of the finite strain ellipses in the different rock types. The magnitude of the angles between cleavage and bedding surfaces is $\beta \rangle \gamma \rangle \alpha$, implying a competence contrast $B \rangle C \rangle A$.

than the incompetent rock. In some naturally deformed rocks we have objects of known original shape (embedded fossils, oolites etc.) which enable us to measure the finite strain state (Ramsay, 1967) and by making an analysis of the shapes of these objects after deformation we can obtain some idea of the relative competence differences of different rock types. The main practical problem in employing this strain measurement technique is that we must be sure that the rocks are sufficiently closely located that they did suffer the same stress history. For example, it would be incorrect to compare the strain state of a rock in the hinge zone of a fold with that found in a layer of the same composition but located in the fold limb. Comparisons of finite strain should be made in different rock types where they are in contact along a constantly oriented planar interface.

Conglomerates are especially useful rocks for assessing competence contrasts of a variety of rock types. In many deformed conglomerates it is generally observed that the shapes of the individual deformed pebbles varies with pebble composition (Fig. 1). Two explanations are possible to account for this observation. The pebbles of different compositions could have had differing ductilities during deformation, or they could have had differing initial shapes in the undeformed sediment. There are various methods of analysis which enable us to assess the extent of variations in the initial pebble shape and initial orientation (Ramsay, 1967; Dunnet, 1969; Dunnet and Siddans, 1971) and so we can isolate the shape effects relating to the difference of ductility between pebbles from those features of the initial fabric.

B. Cleavage Refraction

A particularly useful and rapid method of assessing competence contrast can be used in rocks which show the development of tectonically induced planar fabrics such as cleavage and schistosity. These planar structures often change their orientation where they pass from one layer to the next, a feature known as cleavage refraction (Fig. 2) (Sorby, 1853; Furtak, 1961; Wilson, 1961). Cleavage and Schistosity are fabrics whose intensity and orientation depends upon the intensity of the finite strain and the orientation of the strain ellipsoid. Cleavage forms perpendicular to the direction of maximum total shortening (perpendicular to the Z-direction in strain ellipsoids with axes $X \geqslant Y \geqslant Z$) and the intensity of cleavage increases with the value of the ratio of lengths of the maximum and minimum axes of the strain ellipsoid X/Z. Changes in orientation of cleavage across an interface between two rock types imply that the magnitudes and orientations of the principal finite strains are also changing. When a mathematical analysis of the linkage of the finite strain ellipsoid on one side of the interface with that on the other side is carried out it can be shown that the greatest tectonic shortening occurs in the rock type where the cleavage makes the smallest angle with the contact surface. The angle between cleavage and lithological surfaces is always smaller in the less competent rocks than in the more competent rocks. At a locality where several parallel layers show cleavage refraction the competence contrasts can be evaluated from the changing refraction angles. In Fig. 2B the angles between cleavage and bedding are in order of magnitude $\beta > \gamma > \alpha$, a relationship which implies competence contrasts of the three rock types $B > C > A$.

Although observations of strain variation and cleavage geometry enable us to place the different rock types in order of competence contrast, it is more difficult to relate the actual values of finite strain or changes in refraction angles to arrive at numerical values for ductility contrast. This is because the concept of ductility contrast, although a most useful one for relating features of differential flow in different rock types, has no firm mathematical correspondence to the parameters describing material properties (whether the rock is plastic, viscous or undergoes power law creep). Another complicating factor is that many rocks undergo significant volume changes during deformation which influence values and orientations of the finite strain axes. These volume changes come about by complete or partial removal of initial porosity in sediments, and from chemical changes arising from mineral transformations and solution-transfer-deposition processes developed in specific metamorphic environments.

C. Boudinage

Boudinage is the structure that is developed in layered rocks of differing competence as the result of the growth of mechanical instabilities set up when the layers are mechanically stretched (Wegmann, 1932; Ramberg, 1955) (Fig. 3A). Especially high stresses are built up within the more competent layers at certain locations controlled by initial imperfections in the material and by the generation of high loads at the mid-points of previously initiated boudins (the fibre-loading process). These higher stresses give rise to higher than average strain rates, to accelerated thinning and eventually to physical rupture and separation of the boudins. It is well known that the presence of boudin structure can be used to tell which were the competent layers and which were the incompetent layers, but it is somewhat less well known that the shapes of individual boudins can be used to specify in more detail the relative differences of ductility of layers of differing composition (Fig. 4).

The cross-section shapes of boudins are the result of the primary competence differences that exist at the time of initiation of the boudin neck and the amount of extensive strain along the layer subsequent to initiation. Flow of the surrounding ductile material into the space arising from separation of the more competent layers often modifies the shape of the competent layer into a fishmouth cross-sectional form (Fig. 3A). The region between the separating parts of a boudinaged layer is often the site for the deposition of crystalline material derived from fluid phases in the rock during deformation. The composition of this material is often a very good indicator of the metamorphic grade and pressure–temperature conditions during the formation of the neck zone. Where deformation is prolonged over a considerable time this newly crystallized material may also exert a strong mechanical effect on the geometric forms of the boudins. Figure 3B illustrates an example of a boudinaged basic dyke in a matrix of less competent argillaceous slate. The neck zones of the early stages of boudinage were filled with quartz and chlorite, and with further extension (perhaps with a change in metamorphic conditions) this newly crystallized vein material proved to be more competent than both basic rock and the surrounding slate, and the greatest stretching of the dyke subsequently took place in the central parts of the previously formed boudins. Here is a good example to show how an analysis of the structural geometry of a deformed rock system can indicate features about the progressive behaviour of the system during the progress of deformation.

D. Fold Shapes

When alternating rock layers of differing competence are subjected to a contraction along the layering, mechanical instabilities are set up which lead to a sideways deflection of the incompetent layers into the less competent material and to the formation of buckle folds (Ramberg, 1963, 1964). In many layered rock systems these folds show a characteristic periodic wavelength (or several periodic polyharmonic wavelengths) controlled by competence contrasts and layer thicknesses. The shape variation of the buckled layers, as

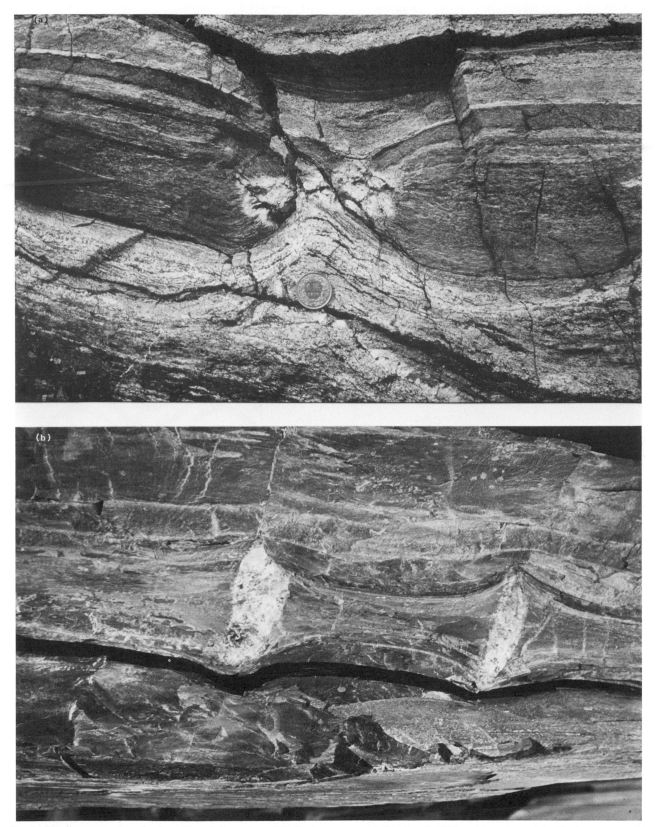

Fig. 3a Boudinage structure developed in a deformed amphibolite layer surrounded by banded feldspathic gneisses, Aiguilles Rouges Massif, Swiss Alps. The boudin ends in the neck zone show a characteristic fish mouth form, and the zone between the boudins has been a site for the crystallization of pegmatitic material.

3b Boudinaged dolerite dyke in a matrix of argillaceous slate, Dinorwic, North Wales, U.K. The boudin neck zones were initially filled with quartz and chlorite and, on further deformation, this material proved to be more competent than the basic dyke and strongly resisted the shortening taking place perpendicular to the dyke.

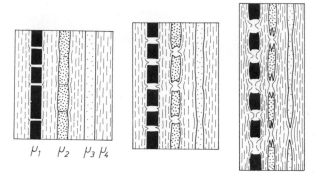

Fig. 4 Boudin shapes and competence contrasts. The form of the boudins is influenced by the ductility contrast between the competent layer being boudinaged and its surrounding more ductile material. Competence contrast $\mu_1 > \mu_2 > \mu_3 > \mu_4$.

recorded by changes in layer thickness and shapes of the interfaces between different layers, is also a function of competence contrast. Figure 5 illustrates the principal features of fold wavelength and geometry developed during the shortening of a single competent layer embedded in matrix of less competent material. Where competence contrasts are large (layer competence μ_1 in matrix μ_5, Fig. 5A), the folds which form show a large initial wavelength in comparison to competent layer thickness, whereas where these contrasts are small (layer competence μ_4 in matrix μ_5, Fig. 5D) the folds

have a short initial wavelength relative to competent layer thickness. There exists a whole range or spectrum of potential fold shapes between the so-called ptygmatic folds characteristic of high competence contrasts end member, and cuspate-lobate shaped folds characteristic of the low competence contrast end member (Fig. 5, A to D). The variations in fold shape go hand in hand with differing patterns of strain variations. The different folds show regions of high finite strain and low (perhaps zero) finite strain, and the distrbution of these high and low strain regions changes with competence contrast. We have previously noted that finite strain state is closely connected with the intensity and orientation of planar deformation fabrics known as cleavage and schistosity. It therefore follows that differences in competence between layer and matrix set up different types of cleavage patterns.

Multilayered rocks give rise to a more complicated range of wavelengths and fold shapes depending upon the various competence contrasts and layer thickness variations. Where the competent layers are relatively close to each other harmonic folds showing the same wavelength are developed and axial surfaces interconnect the individual competent layers (Fig. 6A). Where the competent layers are separated by considerable thickness of incompetent material either disharmonic folds form (Fig. 6B), or folds with several characteristic wavelengths (polyharmonic folds) are developed (Fig. 6C). The geometric features of these various types of

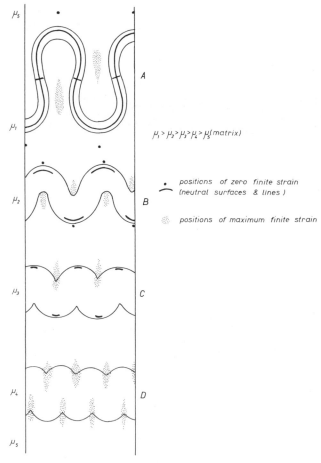

$\mu_1 > \mu_2 > \mu_3 > \mu_4 > \mu_5 \text{(matrix)}$

•   positions of zero finite strain (neutral surfaces & lines)

positions of maximum finite strain

Fig. 5 Changing fold shapes and strain distributions as a result of folding single layers of competent rock in a less competent matrix. Competence contrast $\mu_1 > \mu_2 > \mu_3 > \mu_4 > \mu_5$.

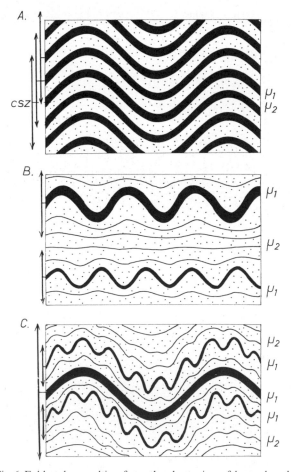

Fig. 6 Fold styles resulting from the shortening of layered rocks parallel to the direction of layering. Each competent layer (μ_1) deflects the surrounding incompetent material (μ_2) within its contact strain zone (csz). Where these zones overlap (A) harmonic folds are formed. If they do not overlap (B) disharmonic folds are formed. Systems with overlapping contact strain zones and with competent layers of differing thickness (C) produce polyharmonic folds.

folds basically accord with the principles discussed above with respect to single competent layers in a less competent host; first, as the thickness of a competent layer increases, the initial wavelength of folds in that layer becomes larger; second, as the competence contrast between a competent layer and its neighbours increases, so does the potential initial wavelength of the fold in that layer. The variations of the thicknesses of individual layers within a multilayered assemblage is a function of the variation in shapes of the interfaces between the competent and incompetent materials. At an interface between more and less competent rock the curvature of the boundary is always greatest where the incompetent material lies on the inside of a fold arc surrounded by more competent material, a feature which gives rise to periodic and successive alternations of cuspate and lobate fold shapes along the interface. This geometric feature leads to special geometric properties of the folds in individual layers; competent layers tend to show a more or less constant orthogonal layer thickness (convergent dip isogon folds, style 1B or 1C, Ramsay, 1967), whereas incompetent layers localized between competent layers show very marked increases of layer thickness in the hinge zone, and marked decreases of thickness in the limbs (divergent dip isogon folds style 3, Ramsay, 1967).

The type of alternating cuspate and lobate fold geometry is a feature of the interface between any two rock types of differing competence, and not only of folded layers (Ramsay, 1967; Dietrich and Onat, 1969). Figure 7 illustrates a contact between a quartzite and a calcareous schist metamorphosed to the lower amphibolite facies during deformation. The cuspate-lobate forms are very strongly developed and clearly show that the quartzite was more competent than the schist. These geometric features also occur along the interfaces of rock masses of differing competence on a regional scale. Basement and cover contacts often show a large scale geo-

metry of this type. Figure 8 illustrates a basement-cover contact in the Naukluft Mountains in South West Africa. The contact between underlying granitic rock and overlying sediments has been shortened, and the less competent cover strata now occupy the cores of tightly pinched synclines.

III. Competence Contrast Lists

When the geometric principles set out above are applied to a systematic study of relative rock ductility in a number of orogenic zones, consistent patterns of competence contrast emerge. Sedimentary rocks deformed under conditions of low grade or very low grade metamorphism can be arranged in list form with the most competent rocks at the head, and the least competent rocks below. A typical list is as follows:

1. Dolomite
2. Arkose
3. Quartzsandstone
4. Greywacke
5. Coarse grained limestone
6. Fine-grained limestone
7. Siltstone
8. Marl
9. Shale
10. Halite, anhydrite

Dolomite is extremely competent. In terrains where a competence relation between dolomite and crystalline metamorphic rocks can be investigated, as for example the basement-cover interface of the external massifs of the Alps, dolomite can be shown to be more competent than the underlying granitic and gneissic basement.

The ductility of crystalline basement rocks and of rocks deforming under metamorphic conditions is more complex

Fig. 7 Alternating cuspate and lobate folds formed along a contact between more competent quartzite (above) and less competent mica schist (below), indicating that the quartzite was more competent than the mica schist. Nufenenpass, Central Switzerland.

Fig. 8 Cuspate-lobate folds developed at a deformed basement-cover interface, Naukluft Mountains, S.W. Africa. The underlying basement consists of crystalline gneiss and massive igneous rock, whereas the cover consists of a basal arkose (mechanically attached to the basement at the unconformity) and overlying calcareous strata.

than the relationships set out above in the list of sediment ductility. The ductility depends to a great extent on the mineralogy and mineral transformation that take place under changing pressure and temperature conditions. In many terrains deformed under green schist or lower amphibolite facies conditions a typical competence list would be:

1. Metabasic rocks
2. Coarse-grained granite and granitic gneiss
3. Fine-grained granite and granitic gneiss
4. Banded quartz, two felspar mica gneiss
5. Quartzite
6. Marble
7. Mica schist

but many interesting and geologically significant changes of position of a rock type in this list can occur. For example the relative position of metabasic and granitic rocks depend upon the mineralogical composition of the basic rock, a feature which is related to the metamorphic grade and water content. Figures 9 and 10 illustrate examples of a basic (basaltic) dyke cutting through surrounding granite gneisses at two different localities in the pre-Cambrian Lewisian complex of north-west Scotland. The basic dykes were originally steeply dipping planar dykes cutting a pre-existing Archaean gneiss complex. As a result of the subsequent Laxfordian orogenic deformation both dykes and gneissic rocks became strongly strained, and the dykegneiss contacts became shortened and developed folds. At the locality shown in Fig. 9 the cuspate-lobate geometry along the dyke contacts indicates that the basic dyke was more competent than the surrounding granitic gneiss. In contrast, the dyke contact geometry of Fig. 10 is best interpreted as showing that the dyke was less

competent than the surrounding gneiss. There are significantly different geological differences between the rock mineralogy at the two localities that could account for the change over in relative ductilities between the two rock types. At the first locality the dyke consists mostly of pyroxene and plagioclase. At the second locality there is a strong imprint of new amphibolite grade mineralogy together with an increase in water content of the basic minerals, and the original pyroxene has been completely transformed to an aggregate consisting mostly of amphibole and biotite. These mineral transformations have led to a marked reduction in competence of the dyke rock, whereas the overall chemistry of the two rock types has been only slightly altered.

Another striking example of mineralogical control of rock competence is found in the deformed Triassic carbonates and calcareous shales from the envelope of the Adamello pluton of the Southern Alps. Figure 11 shows an outcrop of deformed carbonates (pale coloured) and marls (dark) a few kilometres from the pluton contact, and outside the thermal influence of the igneous mass. An analysis of the shapes of the folded layers and the boudinage geometry indicates that the limestone was more competent than the marl. Figure 12 shows rocks from the same formation, but from a locality quite close to the pluton contact where they have become involved in the thermal aureole. The limestones (pale layers) have become marmorized and the calcareous shales have become transformed into calc-silicate rocks (dark layers). The folded calc-silicate layers have sub-ptygmatic forms (Fig. 5A) with wavelengths in proportion to layer thickness, and it is clear from this geometry that they are more competent than the intervening marmorized limestone. Here we have an excellent example of the effect of mineral transformations on relative rock competence. The thermal

Fig. 9 Basic dyke and gneissic country rock folded together with the fold shapes indicating that the dyke was *more* competent than the gneiss Lewisian complex. North Uist, Outer Hebrides, Scotland.

Fig. 10 Folded basic dyke with cuspate-lobate contact indicating that the dyke was *less* competent than the surrounding gneiss (c.f. Fig. 9). Lewisian complex, Benbecula, Outer Hebrides, Scotland.

Fig. 11 Folded Triassic carbonates (limestone, marl) outside the influence of the Adamello pluton aureole. The fold shapes indicate the limestone was more competent than the marl.

Fig. 12 Folded Triassic carbonates (marble, calc-silicate rock) inside the influence of the Adamello pluton aureole. The calc-silicate layers (thermally metamorphosed marls) are now more competent than the marble (c.f. Fig. 11).

metamorphism has led to mineral changes which have resulted in a total reversal of the competence differences between the two rock types.

IV. Mechanical Instabilities Developed in Rocks without Initial Competence Variations

Some rock materials are statistically homogeneous and isotropic over quite large volumes, for example, many massive limestones, sandstones and plutonic igneous rocks can be categorized in this way. Although such rocks show little or no mechanically effective lithological layering or preferred alignments of their componental minerals, they can develop certain types of mechanical instability under stress. As study of such rocks in the field shows that the most common type of mechanical behaviour leads to the formation of subplanar zones of high deformation known as shear zones. Shear zones usually initiate in conjugate sets with right handed and left handed shear aspect oriented symmetrically to the principal stress axes (and incremental strain axes) at the time of their formation (Figs 13 and 14). The conjugate shear sets usually intersect along the direction of intermediate principal stress (σ_2) and the angles between the sets are bisected by the greatest and least principal stresses (σ_1 and σ_3) (Fig. 13). Although differential sideways displacement is the predominant geometric feature of these zones (hence the terminology shear zone) other types of differential displacement play subsidiary roles. For example, it is not uncommon to find volumetric changes localized along the shear zones, and in many terrains deformed in a very ductile environment the shear zones and intervening wall rock material are both affected by a more or less homogeneous bulk strain (Ramsay, 1980).

The mechanical reasons for the initiation of shear zones is

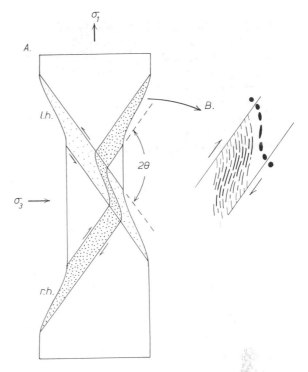

Fig. 13 The geometry of conjugate shear zones. The shear senses are either right handed (r.h.) or left handed (l.h.) and the angle (2θ) between the conjugate zones is bisected by the greatest compressive (or least tensile) stress σ_3. B illustrates the type of strain variation and resulting schistosity pattern in the right handed shear zone.

Fig. 14 Conjugate ductile shear zones cutting granites and aplite dykes in Alpinized Hercynian basement of the Maggia Nappe, Laghetti, Swiss Alps. The shear zone running from top left to bottom right has a left handed shear sense. That running along the bottom of the picture has a right handed shear sense and is clearly later than the left hand zone (c.f. Fig. 13). The angle between these conjugate zones is not the correct dihedral angle between the shear planes (2θ) as the outcrop surface is not a true profile.

not fully understood, but it seems likely that many arise from small localized imperfections and heterogeneities in the statistically isotopic rock. Once a small shear zone starts to form however, the deformation in the zone leads to changes in the properties of the rock in the zone, and further straining of the rock mass is concentrated along the already formed shear zone. Thus, although the starting material does not possess any special competence differences, the initiation of shear zones leads to the formation of deformation induced competence contrast. The rock in the shear zone becomes less competent than that in the walls, a feature which has been termed *strain softening* (Ramsay and Graham, 1970). The reasons for this reduction in competence vary in different regions and in different geological environments. The change in flow properties can be the result of changes in grain size of the component crystals, to deformation induced dilation leading to changes in fluid pressure, or to influx of fluids affecting the chemical stability of the rock. As deformation becomes more concentrated in the zone it is likely that deformation induced fabric anisotropy, such as the formation of planar schistosity, also plays an important mechanical role (Figs 15 and 16).

Shear zone formation is an especially important deformation mode in massive and mechanically rather homogenous gneisses and metaigneous rocks of many crystalline basement terrains. The deformation style leads to a highly characteristic overall regional deformation style: lozenge shapes areas of relatively undeformed rock are surrounded by zones of exceptionally highly strained and often strongly schistose products (Ramsay and Alison, 1979). The rock within the relatively undeformed blocks retains its initial structural and geometric characteristics and sometimes its original mineralogical and petrographic features. In contrast these features are more or less totally transformed and over-printed by a schistose fabric in the shear zone regions and initially unbanded parent rocks can be transformed into banded gneisses (Figs 15, 16). In regions where the shear zone deformation mode is dominant there are often strikingly rapid variations in rock fabric and metamorphic grade. For example, in parts of the Sesia zone of the Alps where amphibolite grade gneisses of Hercynian age have been subjected to repeated Alpine deformation under metamorphic conditions ranging from blueschist to green schist facies, it is not uncommon to find mineral assemblages indicative of these three differing P-T condition within a few metres of each other, with the two overprinted Alpine mineral assemblages localized in two sets of Alpine age shear zones. Shear zones developed in basement terrains which have undergone a later orogenic recycling can produce very large overall bulk strains and lead to very profound relative displacements across the later orogenic zone (Escher *et al.*, 1975; Beach, 1974).

In cover rocks the shear zone deformation mode is not as regionally important as in the underlying recycled basement, because the initial anisotropy of, for example, cover sediments tends to induce other types of deformational instability such as folding and boudinage. However, where the cover sediments consist of poorly bedded sedimentary packets, such as massive limestones and sandstones, shear zones may play an important deformation role. In these environments the sediments often contain entrapped pore fluids and high pore pressure may be developed locally in shear zones as a result of change of the porosity during deformation. The build up of a high fluid pressure often leads to the formation of brittle extension fractures in the shear zones and the transportation of the more soluble rock components into these progressively opening fractures often leads to the formation of en-echelon calcite- or quartz-filled vein arrays (Fig. 17).

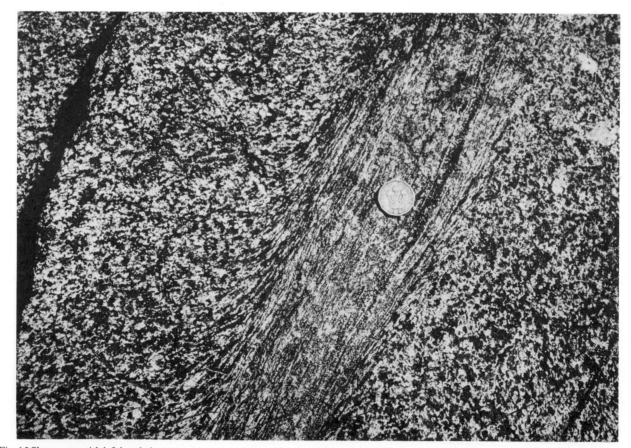

Fig. 15 Shear zone with left handed sense cutting an undeformed metagabbro. Note the characteristic sigmoidal shape of the schistosity induced by the deformation and the development of a banding in the gabbro, even though the parent rock shows no banding.

Fig. 16 A shear zone of Alpine age cutting a Hercynian granite containing an aplite dyke. The dyke has been reoriented with a reduction in width of X1/35, and the granite has been transformed into a strongly foliated granite gneiss. Laghetti, Swiss Pennine Alps.

Fig. 17 Conjugate shear zones with en-echelon calcite filled extension vein arrays in massive Upper Jurassic limestone (Malmkalk), Wildhorn Nappe, Melchtal, Switzerland. This surface is a true profile to the conjugate shear zones with a 2θ angle of about 60 degrees. The height of the cliff is about 20 m.

The structural characteristics of shear zones are observed to change with geological conditions in an orogenic zone. Ductile shear zones are found in the deeper parts of the orogen (greater than 10 km depth) and these pass upwards and outwards into semi-brittle and brittle shear zones (see Table I).

Table I shows that the angles between conjugate shear zones change as one passes from the deep seated ductile zones to the high level fault types. In ductile zones the maximum shortening direction bisects the obtuse angle between the conjugate shear sets, whereas in semi-brittle and brittle environments this direction bisects the acute angle between the sets. Several explanations have been put forward to account for these changing angular relationships. It has been suggested that the shear zone angles of ductile zones were initiated like those of brittle zones, with the acute angle facing the maximum compression and that, as a result of later ductile flow, the zones rotate away from the maximum compression direction to produce an obtuse angle. Although this is geometrically feasible, those studies of terrains where transitions can be seen between embryonic and fully developed shear zones do not show the changing spectrum of angles predicted by this theory (Escher *et al.*, 1975; Beach, 1974; Ramsay and Alison, 1979). More in accord with observations of naturally deformed shear zones are theories which postulate that the currently observed angle between the conjugate sets is close to the angle of zone initiation. Casey (1980) made an analysis of the stress conditions at the time of shear failure and showed how variations in the mean stress ($\overline{\sigma} = (\sigma_1 + \sigma_2 + \sigma_3)/3$) could control the angles between the shear zones and the principal stress directions. Situations where the mean stress is low lead to failure on shear planes oriented at less than 45 degrees to the maximum compression stress, whereas those of high mean stress should give rise to shear planes oriented at angles of more than 45 degrees to the maximum compressive stress. Durney (1979) has explained shear zone orientation using criteria based on deformational features and volume changes taking place during shear. He predicts that shear zones formed under simple shear without volume change and which have the principal maximum and minimum incremental strains oriented at 45 degrees to the shear zone walls should make angles of ± 45 degrees to the bulk incremental strain axes (Fig. 18C). Where the shear displacement is accompanied by a volume increase in the zone ($\delta\Delta +$) the directions of the maximum and minimum incremental strain axes take up angles of less than 45 degrees and greater than 45 degrees to the zone walls respectively (Fig. 18B). If there is a direct correspondence between the local strain axes of the shear zone and the bulk strain axes of the deformation system then conditions of strain compatibility necessitate that the shear zones form with an acute bisector parallel to the maximum regional shortening (Fig. 18B, x and X parallel). Shear zones with a positive dilatation are likely to correspond with those showing a strong development of extension veins. In contrast, this theory predicts that shear zones showing a volume decrease ($\delta\Delta -$) have their obtuse bisector parallel to the maximum regional shortening (Fig. 18D). Durney's hypothesis implies a range of geometric possibilities. At one end of the deformation spectrum, where the bulk strain is one of unidirectional extension, extensional veins without shear systems should occur. At the other end of the spectrum where the bulk strain is one of unidirectional shortening, the structures should indicate only contraction without shear effects, for example, the formation of pressure solution seams and tectonic stylolites. Between these end members there are a whole range of conjugate shear zone possibilities with varying angles of intersection and with varying development of extensional veins and volume loss structures depending on the overall regional changes arising from the values of the bulk strains (Fig. 18).

V. Change of Angular Relationships between Structural Components as a Result of Strain

Before orogenic deformation the individual rock layers and rock types possess characteristic angular relationships one with another. For example in crystalline basement gneisses cut by igneous plutons and dykes there is usually an angular discordance between the igneous rock contact and the lithological banding of the surrounding country rock. At the basement-cover interface there is commonly an angular unconformity and, in the sediments which overlie the basement, it is usual to find discordances on a range of scale from angular unconformities of regional extent to the smaller scale discordances of features such as cross bedding.

As a result of a tectonic strain during orogenesis the original angles along all discordances contained in the rock mass undergo modifications. The resulting geometry depends upon the initial orientation of the planar components and upon the intensity and orientation of the finite strains. The most commonly observed modification in regions of high strain is a reduction in the angles between initially oblique structural elements, because all lines and planes become rotated towards the XY principal plane of the finite strain ellipsoid, and towards the greatest finite extension X within this XY principal plane. In the highly strained central parts of orogens one often sees striking results of these geometric modifications. The initial angular unconformities and

Table I

Approximate depth	Metamorphic facies	Structural features of shear zones	2θ, angle between conjugate zones (see Figs 13 and 18)
>10 km	Granulite amphibolite blueschist	Ductile flow, strong sigmoidal schistosity in zones	120°–90°
5–10 km	Greenschist zeolite	Ductile to semibrittle. Localized schistosity. Enechelon vein arrays. Pressure solution features	90°–60°
0–5 km	Anchimetamorphism no metamorphism	Brittle. Fault breccia and clay gouge. Some pressure solution features	60°

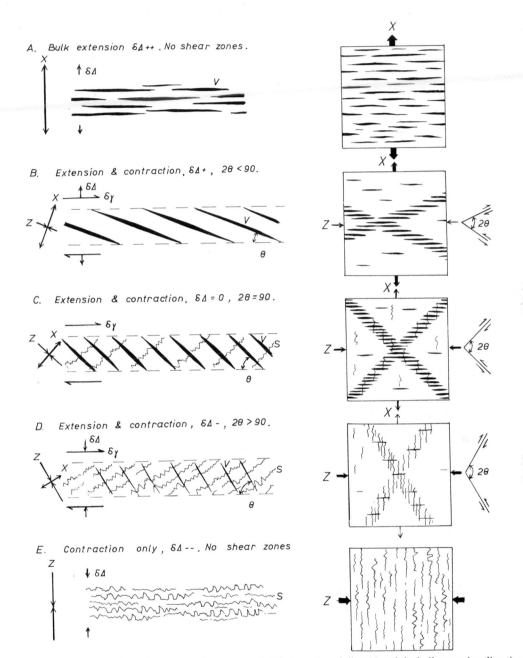

Fig. 18 The relationship between extension vein systems (v), pressure solution tectonic stylolites (s) and the bulk extension directions (maximum extension direction X, maximum shortening direction Z). The local maximum and minimum principal incremental strain axes which give rise to veins and stylolites have directions x and y. Shear zones develop with incremental shear (δ_γ) and incremental volume change ($\delta\Delta$), and the angles between the conjugate systems (2θ) is a function of the incremental volume change.

Fig. 19 Basic dyke with chilled margin cutting discordantly through banded granulitic gneisses, Archaen, West Greenland.

Fig. 20 Basic dyke and banded gneiss transformed structurally and metamorphically in the Nagssugtoqidian orogenic zone (c.f. Fig. 19), West Greenland).

disconformities clearly seen in the orogenic foreland become progressively more difficult to recognize when traced into more highly deformed regions, and locally may be almost impossible to detect. Dykes which were originally markedly oblique to the country rock structures become progressively more concordant and eventually sub-parallel to the lithological layering of the country rocks. Figures 19 and 20 illustrate a typical example of such modifications from the Nagssugtoqidian orogenic zone of West Greenland. Figure 19 shows a basic dyke with chilled margins cutting discordantly through banded granulitic gneisses and is typical of the Archaen Foreland region of the later orogen. Figure 20 shows the contact of a basic dyke from the same swarm but taken from a quite strongly deformed part of the later orogenic zone. Both dyke and country rocks have suffered a new amphibolite grade metamorphic overprint. The basic dyke has been transformed into a hornblende schist with a well developed schistosity, while the angle between gneissic banding and dyke has been greatly reduced, and the angular discordance is now less than 4 degrees (Escher *et al.*, 1975).

As a result of increasing internal deformation all the rocks from the undeformed Foreland become structurally modified towards the central parts of the orogen. Structures with a wide range of initial orientations become progressively more parallel. As a result of these modifications it is often quite a difficult matter to separate basement and cover, particularly when the increasing structural parallelism is accompanied by medium to high grade metamorphism perhaps with accompanying migmatisation and melting.

Conclusions

(1) The ductility of deformed rocks in mountain belts can be investigated by observing the characteristic geometric features of structures that have arisen as a result of the development of mechanical instabilities produced during deformation.

(2) Field observations of structural geometry can be used to establish relative ductilities between rocks of different composition, and it is possible to formulate, for any region, a list indicating the relative ductility or competence contrasts of the various rock types. These observations indicate that some current ideas of relative rock ductility need revision. For example, granitic rocks may be less competent than dolomite. Mineralogical changes taking place during metamorphism may lead to marked changes of relative ductility.

(3) The structures developed in cover rock sediments mostly arise from mechanical instabilities controlled by lithological variations. In contrast, the crystalline rocks of basement terrains are often mechanically rather homogeneous. Instabilities arise from shear zone formation. The progressive development of the shear zones themselves is the major factor in competence control, and an initially homogeneous rock can develop incompetent zones by the process of strain softening. Localized shear zones in the crystalline basement propagate upwards and outwards from the orogen centre and are often connected with the localization of some of the folds in the cover sediments.

Acknowledgement

Part of this work was carried out with support from the Schweizerischer Nationalfonds (Grant 2.824-0.80).

References

Beach, A. (1974). The measurement and significance of displacement on Laxfordian shear zones, North-West Scotland. *Proc. Geol. Assoc.* **85**, 13–21.

Casey, M. (1980). Mechanics of shear zones in isotropic dilatent materials. *J. Struct. Geol.* **2**, 143–147.

Dietrich, J.H. and Onat, E.T. (1969). Slow finite deformation of viscous solids. *J. Geoph. Res.* **74**, 129–154.

Dunnet, D. (1969). A technique of finite strain analysis using elliptical particles. *Tectonophysics* **7**, 117–136.

Dunnet, D. and Siddans, A.W.B. (1971). Non random sedimentary fabrics and their modification by strain. *Tectonophysics* **12**, 307–325.

Durney, D.W. (1979). Dilation in shear zones and its influence on the development of en-echelon fractures. Abstract, Shear Zone Conference Barcelona, pp. 30–31.

Escher, A., Escher, J.C. and Waterson, J. (1975). The reorientation of the Kangamiut dike swarm, West Greenland. *Can. J. Earth Sci.* **12**, 158–173.

Furtak, H. (1961). Die "Brechung" der Schiefrigkeit. *Geol. Mitt.* **12**, p. 177–196.

Ramberg, H. (1955). Natural and experimental boudinage and pinch and swell structure. *J. Geol.* **63**, 512–526.

Ramberg, H. (1963). Fluid dynamics of viscous buckling applicable to folding of layered rocks. *Bull. Am. Assoc. Petrol. Geol.* **47**, 484–515.

Ramberg, H. (1964). Selective buckling of composite layers with contrasted rheological properties, a theory for the simultaneous formation of several orders of folds. *Tectonophysics* **1**, 307–341.

Ramsay, J.G. (1967). "Folding and fracturing of rocks". McGraw Hill Book Co., New York, 568 pp.

Ramsay, J.G. (1980). Shear zone geometry: a review. *J. Struct. Geol.* **2**, 83–99.

Ramsay, J.G. and Alison, I. (1979). Structural analysis of shear zones in an alpinised Hercynian granite, Maggia Lappen, Pennine zone, Central Alps. *Schweiz. min. pet. Mitt.* **59**, 251–279.

Ramsay, J.G. and Graham, R.H. (1970). Strain variation in shear belts. *Can. J. Earth Sci.* **7**, 786–813.

Sorby, H.C. (1853). On the origin of slaty cleavage. *New Phil. J. Edinburgh* **55**, 137–148.

Wegmann, C.E. (1932). Note sur le boudinage. *Bull. Soc. Géol. France* **2**, 477–489.

Willis, B. (1893). The mechanics of Appalachian structure. U.S. Geol. Survey, 13th Ann. Rept., p.212–281.

Wilson, G. (1961). The tectonic significance of small scale structures, and their importance to the geologist in the field. *Ann. Soc. Géol. de Belg.* **84**, 423–548.

Some Numerical Investigations of Large Scale Continental Deformation

P. England

Department of Geological Sciences,
Harvard University,
Cambridge, Mass, U.S.A.

Abstract

The theory of plate tectonics cannot adequately account for the deformation of the continents: within the oceanic portions of the plates seismic deformation is seen to occur in belts only a few tens of kilometres wide, but seismic, topographic, gravity and field geology data all indicate that the continents are deforming (and have deformed for most of geological time) in zones that are hundreds to thousands of kilometres wide. Qualitatively, this difference in style of deformation may be attributed to the greater buoyancy and lesser strength of the continental lithosphere, but there has been little attempt to treat the process in a quantitative manner.

One approach is to abandon the concept of a rigid plate as far as the deforming continent is concerned, and to regard the continental lithosphere as a continuum of known rheology; in particular it is assumed here that the lithosphere is governed, on the million-year timescale and hundred-kilometre length scale, by a non-Newtonian rheology which may be approximated by power-law creep.

The deformation of such a medium may be investigated numerically, and it is found that this model provides reasonable quantitative agreement between theory and observation as to crustal thickness distribution and relative motions in the India–Asia collision zone, *provided* that the model lithosphere does not behave as a Newtonian fluid, and provided that it is capable of supporting deviatoric stresses of at least 100 to 300 bars. Notable features of the deformation include the development of along-strike extension in the region of thickest crust and significant deformation at distances of more than 1000 km from the collision zone. The style of deformation depends very strongly on the effective viscosity assumed for the lithosphere and on the driving forces available for continuing continental collision.

I. Introduction

Depending upon one's school of thought either it has been clear for some years or it has never been seriously in doubt that the deformation of the continents cannot adequately be described within the framework of plate tectonics. This is not to deny that plate motions are responsible for continental deformation, but the formation of orogenic belts cannot be understood solely in terms of the interactions of a few rigid plates (e.g. McKenzie, 1972, 1976; Tapponnier and Molnar, 1976, 1977).

The deformation of the oceanic portions of the plates appears to be relatively simple — it occurs almost entirely within belts a few tens of kilometres wide that take up the relative motion between otherwise rigid plates. However, the style of continental deformation is very different: regions like the Alpine-Himalayan belt and Western North and South America are deforming in zones hundreds to thousands of kilometres wide. Figure 1 shows the epicentres of earthquakes located by the ISC between 1964 and 1977 in the region of India and Central and Eastern Asia; only those earthquakes reported by more than 50 stations are included. Note the diffuse nature of the seismicity compared with the narrow linear or planar zones associated with mid-ocean ridges or subduction zones. Figure 1 also shows the topography of Central Asia, contoured at 1 km intervals; this indicates that appreciably thickened continental crust extends over 1000 km north of the Indus suture. (See the sparser crustal thickness data compiled by Soller *et al.* (1982)).

A common feature of conventional approaches to the diffuse style of deformation which characterizes the collison zones between two continental plates has been the assumption that, while large scale plate tectonics no longer applies, it must be possible to find some scale on which the deforma-

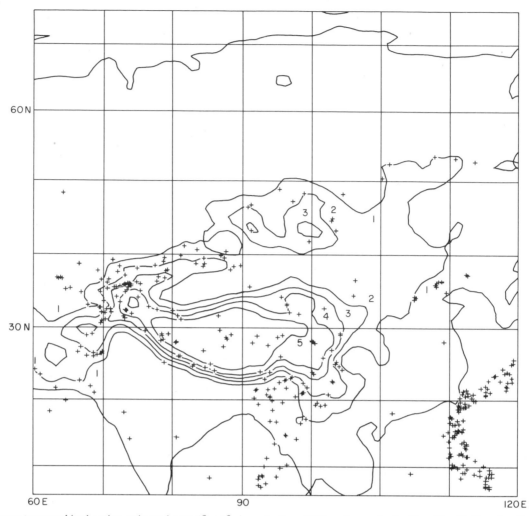

Fig. 1   Average topographic elevation estimated over 1° × 1° elements (Lee, 1966) and smoothed with a 2° × 2° Gaussian filter. The area between 5° and 65° N, and 60° E and 120° E is contoured from 0 to 5 km in steps of 1 km. The superimposed crosses indicate earthquakes reported by at least 50 stations in the interval 1961 to 1977. (Data from ISC Bulletins).

tion can be described in terms of plate motion. This leads to a view of continental deformation in which the strain is taken up by as many "microplates" as thought necessary, that move around in response to forces arising at their edges. The origin of these forces is usually unspecified or they are likened, by an appealing but unphysical analogy, to the forces acting on a melon seed squeezed between one's fingers.

It is the purpose of this paper to suggest that we may regard the deformation of the continents in terms of the response of a continuous viscous medium to forces applied on its edges by plate collisions and to forces within its interior arising from crustal thickness contrasts. This approach is capable of explaining the widespread deformation of the continental lithosphere, and permits us to make estimates of the forces required to deform the continents. A detailed treatment of this approach is given by England and McKenzie (1982, 1983).

Before proceeding to the details of this model for continental deformation it is necessary to discuss briefly the kinds of observation we hope to explain and to indicate why others — perhaps equally prominent — will not be treated in this simple approach.

The first problem concerns the relevance of a viscous continuum model to the continental lithosphere; the second — and related — problem concerns the interpretation of the surface geology in terms of the large scale forces which may

be responsible for continental deformation. Faults, and in particular strike-slip faults, are often outstanding features of the surface geological record, yet the approach to be outlined below involves treating the large scale deformation of the continents in terms of a continuum model which, by its very nature, cannot take account of faults. This is not such a serious drawback as it might at first appear; faults are certainly prominent indicators of plate deformation — in that they are often visible at the surface and are loci of earthquake activity — but the discontinuous nature of this deformation would only be important on the large scale of continental deformation (hundreds to thousands of kilometres, and millions to tens of millions of years) if the properties of the brittle layer were those that control the plate deformation. Unfractured crustal rock is certainly capable of supporting high deviatoric stresses at low strains or over short timespans, but the mechanical properties of the upper crust as a whole are governed by the many faults and planes of weakness it contains, and I shall be assuming that for the timespans and strains involved in continental deformation the outer 10 to 20 km of crust that make up the brittle zone follows passively the motion of the deeper portion of the lithosphere.

This assumption is certainly in accord with the low values of stress drops determined for near-surface earthquakes, but — and this leads us to the second problem — it is clear that major strike-slip faults play an important part in the present day near-surface deformation of Asia (Molnar *et al.*, 1973; Chen and Molnar, 1977; Molnar and Tapponnier, 1975, 1978; Tapponnier and Molnar, 1976, 1977). Nevertheless, the finite deformation that can be accommodated by a few strike-slip faults is limited, and it is self-evident that no amount of strike-slip faulting can account for the region of greatly thickened crust extending over 1000 km north of the Himalayas.

Probably at least part of discrepancy results from the ease with which large strike-slip faults may be identified on satellite imagery, but this example serves to show that neither a continuum model nor a "microplate" model is capable of explaining *all* the features of continental deformation.

An additional problem connected with the inference of large scale driving forces from observations of surface geology lies in the fact that the crust is highly heterogeneous on all scales; it may be anisotropic owing to fabrics defined by pre-existing faults or joints, and variations in its temperature or its intrinsic mechanical properties may be great enough to affect the geometry of deformation on a regional scale. An interesting discussion of the possible influence of regional temperature differences on the tectonic style of Asia is given by Molnar and Tapponnier (1981), but these — and the other inhomogeneities outlined above — may only be treated on an *ad hoc* basis.

For the reasons outlined above, this paper will be concerned to develop a relatively simple model for the deformation of the continental lithosphere as a whole, and to interpret this in terms of the general features which might be expected in the surface geology, rather than to attempt the reverse process. Thus, while faults are excluded in the treatment of the deformation of a continuous medium, we may infer thrust faulting as the likely mode of near-surface deformation in a region of the lithosphere which is undergoing thickening, and normal faulting as the mode of brittle failure in a region which is extending.

The principal observables to be predicted by this approach are the topographic height and the deviatoric stress, and these will be constrained by the information available from the India–Asia collision zone, and from independent estimates of intraplate stress and of the forces available to drive place motion.

II. Formulation

Figure 1 shows that the deformation of Asia, as indicated by seismic activity and surface elevation, extends between 1000 and 2000 km north of the Himalaya — a distance which is large compared to the thickness of the continental lithosphere. In addition we may assume that the upper and lower surfaces of the lithosphere are free of tractions: the upper surface is the land surface and the lithosphere is usually regarded as overlying an asthenosphere very much weaker than itself. (It may need emphasizing that in what follows the "lithosphere" is not regarded as rigid, merely as very much stronger than its substrate, and it would be defined in purely mechanical, not seismic or thermal terms.).

The assumptions that the lithosphere is thin compared to the wavelengths of the loads acting on it, and that it has traction-free base and top allow us to neglect, *on the large scale*, vertical gradients of horizontal velocity, so that the motion of the deforming medium may be described in terms of the horizontal components of velocity only; because the rocks are assumed to be incompressible, the deformation in the vertical (z) direction is given by:

$$\dot{\varepsilon}_{zz} = -(\dot{\varepsilon}_{xx} + \dot{\varepsilon}_{yy}) = -\left(\frac{\partial u_x}{\partial x} + \frac{\partial u_y}{\partial y}\right) \quad (1)$$

where u_x and u_y are the x- and y-components of velocity.

The x-y plane is taken as the earth's surface (curvature ignored) and in describing the results below the y axis will be taken as pointing north in order to avoid the inappropriate use of "top" and "bottom" when referring to horizontal planes.

In this formulation the line vertically beneath a point x, y on the surface will be moving with a constant velocity $u(x,y)$ and the deformation of the medium is governed by the vertically averaged stresses acting on it, and by its vertically averaged constitutive relation.

Note that although this formulation is in terms of horizontal velocity, it takes account of strain rates in the vertical direction that lead to variations in crustal thickness. The medium will therefore deform in response to whatever boundary conditions are imposed upon it (e.g. the collision of one continent with another) and to the forces arising within its interior, owing to contrasts in crustal thickness (e.g. the mountain belts resulting from the collision). It is the interaction of these two sets of forces which characterizes the deformation to be discussed below.

The buoyancy forces arising from crustal thickness contrasts arise in the following way: Consider two portions of lithosphere, thickness L, one having continental crust of thickness s_0 and the other with crust of thickness s; the density of the crust is ρ_c and of the mantle, ρ_m and the crust is in isostatic equilibrium (Fig. 2).

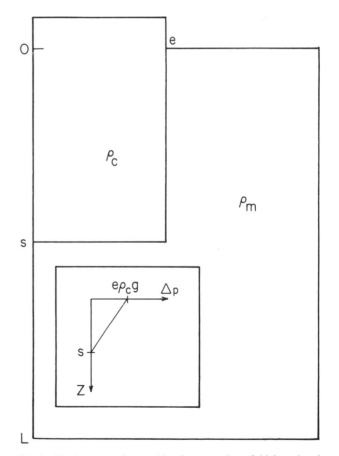

Fig. 2 The buoyancy force arising from a region of thickened and elevated crust: continental crust of thickness s and density ρ_m is in isostatic equilibrium with mantle of density ρ_m. Because of the elevation contrast between the two, the elevated region exerts a force on the lower region, indicated by the insert showing the difference in pressure between the two regions as a function of depth below the surface. In the formulation used here, the average of this pressure difference is taken as one of the driving forces for the deformation of a thin viscous sheet representing the continental lithosphere (Equation 2).

In static equilibrium, the average difference in pressure within these two units is:

$$\frac{1}{L}\int_0^L \Delta p \, dz = \frac{g\rho_c(1-\rho_c/\rho_m)(s^2-s_0^2)}{2L} \quad (2)$$

Studies of the deformation properties of earth materials at laboratory strain rates suggest that the steady state creep of many materials over a broad range of temperatures and applied pressures obeys a law of the form:

$$\dot{\varepsilon} = A(\sigma_1-\sigma_3)^n \exp(-Q/R\theta) \quad (3)$$

(e.g. Goetze, 1978); Ashby and Verrall, 1978), where θ is absolute temperature, R is the gas constant and A, Q and n are experimentally determined constants of the material. Unfortunately the values of these parameters are poorly known for most rock-forming minerals — let alone aggregates — but we are able to make a couple of simplifying assumptions that leave us with two free parameters governing the behaviour of the models for the continental lithosphere.

We assume that there is one portion of the lithosphere that dominates its vertically averaged strength, and that Q and n do not change with position in this region. This gives a relation between the vertically averaged strain rate and vertically averaged deviatoric stress of the form

$$\tau_{ij} = \eta_{eff}\dot{\varepsilon}_{ij}^{1/n} \quad (4)$$

where ε_{ij} and τ_{ij} are components of the strain rate and deviatoric stress tensors and η_{eff} is the effective viscosity of the medium, which is stress- and therefore position-dependent. Equation 4 is the constitutive equation for a Stokesian, or *power law*, material in which the strain rate is proportional to some power, n, of the applied deviatoric stress. When n is unity the material is Newtonian and strain rate is proportional to stress; for some earth materials in steady state creep n seems to be between 3 and 5 (e.g. Goetze, 1978). η_{eff} is a strong function of the temperature at the top of the layer and — for ranges of Q, θ and n that apply to the lithosphere — is only weakly dependent on the depth of, and the thermal gradient in, the layer. (This is discussed more fully by England and McKenzie, 1982.)

It is plausible on the basis of present day knowledge of the strength of rock-forming minerals, to suggest that this strong layer is the top of the upper mantle (being the coldest region in which olivine — the strongest mineral with a well-defined rheology — occurs); this point is discussed at greater length by Molnar and Tapponnier (1981). To fix ideas, we may think of the strong layer as "the top of the upper mantle" but it must be understood that our knowledge of the creep strength of rocks at geological strain rates is in its infancy, and this simplification may not be justified; the mathematical formulation refers only to a power-law material (Equation 4) and makes no geological judgement.

Equation 2 gives the vertically averaged buoyancy force acting on the lithosphere, and Equation 4 gives the vertically averaged rheology; because earth materials deform so slowly we may neglect accelerations of the material and demand

Table I Values of parameters used in the scaling of solutions to Equations 5 and 6.

$g = 9 \cdot 8 \, \text{m s}^{-2}$
$L = 100 \, \text{km}$
$u_0 = 50 \, \text{mm/yr}$
$\rho_c = 2 \cdot 9 \, \text{Mg m}^{-3}$
$\rho_m = 3 \cdot 3 \, \text{Mg m}^{-3}$

that pressure gradients in the medium are balanced by gradients in the viscous stresses involved in deforming the medium (which may be calculated from the rheology of Equation 4). Equating these forces leads to an equation for the velocity field in the lithosphere:

$$\frac{\partial}{\partial x_y}\left[\eta_{eff}\left(\frac{\partial u_i}{\partial x_j}+\frac{\partial u_j}{\partial x_i}\right)\right] + \frac{\partial}{\partial x_i}\left[2\eta_{eff}\frac{\partial u_k}{\partial x_k}\right] = Ar\, s\frac{\partial s}{\partial x_i} \quad (5)$$

where u_i, u_j are the x and y components of velocity and only horizontal derivatives are considered.

A fuller formulation is given by England and McKenzie (1982, 1983) and the main point of introducing Equation 5 here is to indicate that the nature of the flow depends only on Ar and on n (which appears through the effective viscosity (Equation 4).

The left hand side of Equation 5 contains the terms expressing the viscous forces involved in deforming the medium; these are of the form (effective viscosity × strain rate). Gradients of these stresses are balanced against gradients of the buoyancy forces, which appear on the right hand side of the equation.

When the material is Newtonian (n is unity in Equation 3) the effective viscosity is constant, but for most of the cases to be discussed here n is greater than one, and the effective viscosity is a function of strain rate, and therefore of position. Under these conditions the material exhibits the property known as "shear thinning" — that is, the effective viscosity decreases with increasing strain rate (or increasing deviatoric stress) and the deformation of the medium is concentrated into regions of highest stress.

The physical significance of Ar, which England and McKenzie have called the Argand number, is that it expresses the relative magnitudes of the buoyancy forces arising from crustal thickness contrasts and the forces required to deform the medium at the ambient strain rates. Another way of putting it is to say that the Argand number is a measure of the tendency of the lithosphere to strain in response to contrasts in crustal thickness.

If the Argand number is small — i.e. if the effective viscosity of the continental lithosphere is large at ambient strain rates — then the deformation of the lithosphere will be governed entirely by the boundary conditions. At the other extreme, if the Argand number is very large, the forces arising from crustal thickness variations will be dominant, and the medium will not be strong enough to support appreciable elevation contrasts.

III. Some Simple Geometries of Continental Deformation

England and McKenzie (1982, 1983) presents the means of solution of Equation 5, and the results of numerical experiments on the system for a variety of different values of Argand number and n.

The numerical experiments summarized below illustrate the influence exerted by the exponent, n, in the power law relation and by the effective viscosity of the medium — contained in the Argand number — on the type of deformation experienced by the medium. These numerical solutions were obtained in idealized geometries in order better to understand general principles of continental deformation: they are not intended to model (in the sense of reproducing closely) any real continental collision zone, although there will be fundamental similarities. In Section 4 these results will be interpreted in terms of their geological relevance. The geometry of the numerical experiments is shown in Fig. 3.

When Ar is zero the velocity field given by Equation 5 is independent of time, provided that the boundary conditions do not change, because even though the flow produces changes in the crustal thickness distribution according to the conservation relation:

$$\frac{\partial s}{\partial t} = \frac{\partial}{\partial x_j}(su_j) \qquad (6)$$

these changes do not affect the flow.

Figure 4 shows the flows resulting from the influx of material over the south-western corner of a portion of model lithosphere (see Fig. 3); Ar is zero and n is 1 (Newtonian material), 3 and 5 (power-law materials). The figure shows velocity vectors, indicating the speed and direction of the induced flow as a function of distance from the influx boundary, and contours of the instantaneous rate of thickening or thinning of the lithosphere.

This latter quantity is:

$$-(\dot{\varepsilon}_{xx}+\dot{\varepsilon}_{yy}) = \dot{\varepsilon}_{zz} = \frac{1}{s}\frac{Ds}{Dt} \qquad (7)$$

where Ds/Dt is the rate of change of crustal thickness "following the motion": i.e. it is the rate of change of crustal thickness that an observer fixed to a moving and deforming portion of the continental surface would observe, as opposed to the rate of change of crustal thickness at a position (x,y) fixed relative to the boundaries of the deforming medium. The latter quantity is given by Equation 6, and the importance of the distinction will become apparent later.

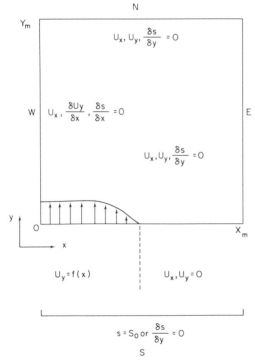

Fig. 3   Geometry of the numerical models described in the text. Finite difference solutions to Equation 5 are obtained on a mesh within this box subject to the boundary conditions shown. In the applications described in this paper $X_m = Y_m = 3200$ km and for convenience of description the points of the compass, as shown, are used for orientation when referring to the numerical solutions. The western boundary is an axis of symmetry and the other three boundaries are rigid.

Varying n from 1 to 3 to 5 changes the flow from a general divergence away from the influx boundary — as seen in Figs 4a and 4b, where velocities comparable to the influx velocity are seen at large distances from the southern boundary, and where contours of thickening and thinning rates are widely spaced — to flows which are progressively more concentrated around the influx boundary. Figures 4c and 4d show that the effect of a power law rheology is to concentrate the deformation into the regions of highest stress around the influx boundary, where the same rate of mass influx as in Figs 4a and 4b is now accommodated in a smaller region of higher strain rate. This compression of flow is further enhanced when n is 5 (Figs 4e and 4f) and the flow may be seen to be more or less independent of the confining effects of the distant boundaries, with nearly all the deformation occurring within 1000 km of the influx boundary.

The crustal thickness distribution resulting from the flows shown in Fig. 4 are illustrated in Fig. 5; the thickness is contoured at intervals of 5 km for 16 m.y. influx at a velocity of 5 cm/yr over the eastern portion of the southern boundary. The original crustal thickness was 35 km over the whole box and again the transition from Newtonian fluid to $n = 3$ and $n = 5$ results in increasingly concentrated deformation; the contours of crustal thickness mimic (but do not exactly follow, remembering the difference between Equations 6 and 7) the contours of Fig. 4, with the same amount of inflowing material being accommodated by progressively narrower zones of greater crustal thickness as n increases.

Note in Figs 4 and 5 that a region of net extension exists to the east of the influx boundary. The origin of this feature can best be seen in the velocity field for $n = 1$ (Fig. 4a), where an induced flow northwards is visible to the east of the influx boundary; this flow causes tension in the region of the fixed boundary to its south.

Figure 6 illustrates the influence of changing Ar for a medium whilst keeping the boundary conditions and n unchanged. The geometry is the same as in Fig. 3, except that there is zero gradient of crustal thickness at the southern boundary, not a constant crustal thickness; this change is for reasons of computational stability and does not affect the arguments which follow.

Figures 6a, d and g show contours of crustal thickness after 40 m.y. influx at 5 cm/yr, for a medium having Ar equal to 1, 3 and 10; Figs 6b, e and h show the corresponding contours of instantaneous rate of thickening or thinning, and Figs 6c, f and i show the velocity vectors.

Although Ar is defined above in terms of an effective viscosity of the lithosphere, there is no meaningful set of data to compare this quantity with, and it is preferable to characterize these models by deviatoric stress (Equation 4): — the maximum deviatoric stress in the flow illustrated in Figs 6a, b and c is 1040 bars (Ar = 1); in Figs 6d, e and f 320 bars (Ar = 3); in Figs 6g, h and i: 95 bars (Ar = 10).

An important difference between these solutions and those for zero Argand number is that the maximum crustal thickness does not increase appreciably between 30 m.y. and 40 m.y., except for the strongest lithosphere (Ar = 1). The reason for this is that in each case the buoyancy forces from crustal thickness contrasts have become large enough to counteract the flow imposed on the medium by the boundary conditions: the tendency for the crust to thicken in front of the influx boundary is now counterbalanced by a tendency of the already thickened crust to flow away.

The spreading of thickened crust can be seen in each of Figs 6b, e and h as minima in the thickening strain rate near the middle of the southern boundary of the boxes. In Figures 6e and h these minima are areas of net extension "following the flow" and we should expect to see extensional tectonics in any analogous position in the continental lithosphere.

(e.g. Molnar and Tapponnier, 1975). The stress exponent, n, has been fixed at 3 in these figures (but similar conclusions are reached if n is 5 — England and McKenzie, 1982) and the parameter that governs the deformation is the Argand number. In Figs 6a, b and c the maximum shear stress supported by the material is 1040 bars; in Figs 6d, e, f, it is 320 bars; x in Figs 6g, h, i, 95 bars.

Even when the maximum shear stress is 320 bars, the deformation reaches the morthern edge of the box, although the bulk of the deformation is near the influx boundary, but it is clear that a viscous medium supporting shear stresses as low as 100 bars (Figs. 6g, h, i) does not produce the kind of crustal thickness distribution seen in Central Asia.

The first conclusions, then, are that for a viscous sheet model to be able satisfactorily to account for the deformation of a region like Central Asia, the medium must have a non-Newtonian rheology and must be capable of supporting shear stresses of around 300 bars at strain rates typical of continental collision.

Let us now consider the type of deformation that occurs in a viscous sheet that satisfies these requirements, and the way in which it changes with time. Figure 7 shows the distribution of deformation as a function of time for the case where n is 3 and Ar is 3 (see Figs 6d, e). Four different types of deformation are illustrated, according to the relative magnitudes of the principal strain rates in the medium: the solid black areas (1) show regions in which both the principal horizontal strain rates are compressive — shortening is occurring in a fashion that lies between the extremes of uniaxial and homogeneous compression; the rectangularly cross-hatched areas (2) show regions in which only one principal horizontal strain rate is compressional and the other is extensional, but with less than half the magnitude of the compressional strain rate — shortening is occurring with a significant proportion of strike-slip motion; the dotted

areas (3) indicate regions where one principal strain rate is compressional, and the other tensional and the magnitude of the smaller strain rate is greater than one half that of the larger — this includes areas where the principal horizontal strain rates are equal and opposite (simple strike-slip) while in general, strike-slip motion is occurring with components of shortening (indicated by plus signs) and extension (minus signs); the diagonally cross-hatched areas (4) are the extensional analogues of (2) — extension is occurring with a significant component of strike-slip.

The orientations of the boxes are the same as in Figs 4 to 6 (influx of material over the bottom-left boundary) and the style of deformation is indicated only when the rate of deformation, given by the magnitude of the strain rate, is greater than $2 \times 10^{-16} s^{-1}$; the intensity of the cross-hatching and the dots is an indication of the local rate of deformation. There is an extensional equivalent to region (1) but it is deforming too slowly to be shown. Deformation is shown at 8, 16, 32 and 40 m.y. (Figs 7a, b, c, d).

The strong compression (1) in the south-east corner is nearly uniaxial, and is a feature of all the stages of deformation. It is surrounded initially by a region of intense shortening and a larger one of less intense shortening with a region of predominantly strike-slip motion to the east (Fig. 7a). With increasing time, the shortening leads to thickened crust in front of the influx boundary that generates its own eastward flux of material; this results in a component of predominantly strike-slip motion away from the elevated region which can be seen in an enlarging of the strike-slip regions from Figs 7a to 7c. Finally, after 32 m.y. the region of predominantly strike-slip motion has grown to surround the influx boundary entirely (Fig. 7d); it contains within it regions of appreciable thickening as well as regions of appreciable thinning (see also Figs 6d, e). A large amount of the deformation is now being accommodated by strike-slip motion behind the influx boundary, although there is still compression immediately in front of the influx boundary and the buoyancy of the thickened crust exerts a compressive stress on the region to the north of the zone of a strike-slip motion.

Before interpreting this deformation in terms of a geological history it is important to issue two caveats: first, Fig. 7 depicts only instantaneous strain-rate patterns and these cannot be interpreted to yield the total *strain* of any particular area — the crustal thickness gives the accumulated shortening strain that a region underwent in reaching its present location (Fig. 6e corresponds to Fig. 7d), but the other components of strain are not known. Secondly the instantaneous strain rate of the viscous medium need not relate exactly to the deformation of a brittle layer overlying it.

In fact, there are a number of similarities between the strain pattern shown in Fig. 7d, and the contemporary deformation of Eastern and Central Asia. Figure 8 is a sketch map of the distribution of tectonic styles in Asia (from Tapponnier and Molnar, 1976), based on focal mechanism determinations and on satellite imagery; the principal features are strong compression in the Himalaya, a large area of predominantly strike-slip movement to the north, that contains regions both of thrust faulting and normal faulting, and a large area of extension to the east in northern China and Eastern Siberia. With the exception of the latter feature these areas of different tectonic styles have their analogues in Fig. 7d. In both cases, while there is an area of strong compression immediately in front of the influx boundary, a large amount of deformation is being accommodated by strike-slip motion within and to the north of the area of thickest crust.

The present-day normal faulting in Tibet (Gansser, 1964; Fitch, 1970; Molnar et al., 1973; York et al., 1976; Tappon-

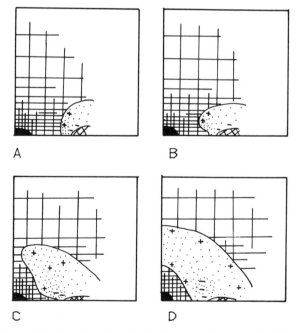

A   B

C   D

Fig. 7   The style of deformation in the thin viscous sheet with Ar = 3 and n = 3 after 8 m.y. (7a), 16 m.y. (7b), 32 m.y. (7c) and 40 m.y. (7d). The black areas indicate regions of compression; the vertically and diagonally hatched areas correspond respectively to regions of compression and regions of extension, both with a significant component of strike-slip; the dotted areas indicate regions of predominantly strike-slip motion with components of compression (+) and tension (−).

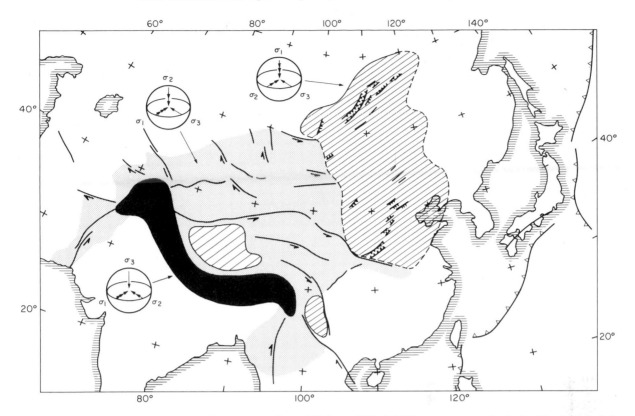

Fig. 8   Distribution of tectonic style in Asia (from Tapponnier and Molnar, 1976). Bold lines represent major faults. The dark shaded area indicates major crustal shortening; the dotted area — regions where strike-slip faulting occurs, and the hatched area — normal faulting and crustal thinning. Note the thrust faulting and the extension within the area of predominantly strike-slip faulting.

nier and Molnar, 1977; Molnar and Tapponnier, 1978; Ni and York, 1978) is of particular interest because it implies net extension immediately in front of a compressive plate boundary. This is a feature which also occurs in the viscous model for continental deformation (see Figs 6e and 7b) and its origin lies in the tendency to spread of the region of thickened, and therefore elevated, crust. Although this is not illustrated, the least principal horizontal stress in this region of extension in Figs 6e and 7d is approximately east–west (England and McKenzie, 1982, Fig. 13); this and the north-eastward motion of material to the east of the region of thickest crust (Fig. 6) provide a close parallel to late Cenozoic tectonics of Tibet, which involve east–west extension of the Tibetan plateau and the eastward motion of eastern Tibet and western China (Ni and York, 1978; Tapponnier and Molnar, 1977; Molnar and Tapponnier, 1978).

The results of the viscous models for continental deformation also have a bearing on the driving forces that are necessary to maintain orogenic processes. In the deformation described above the forces acting on the boundary must do work against gravity, in forming and maintaining regions of thickened crust and against viscous forces in deforming the medium.

The force per unit length of plate boundary may be calculated directly from the numerical solutions. The buoyancy force is proportional to the square of the elevation (Equation 2) and is about 1.5×10^{13} N m^{-1} for $Ar = 1$; 6×10^{12} N m^{-1} for $Ar = 3$ and 2×10^{12} N m^{-1} for $Ar = 10$, corresponding to maximum crustal thicknesses of 100 km, 70 km and 50 km. (It is assumed that the crustal thickness of the inflowing continental material is 35 km; thus s^2 in Equation 2 is replaced by s^2–(35 km^2).) The force necessary to overcome viscous dissipation is calculated to average about

2×10^{13} N m^{-1} when $Ar = 1$; 6×10^{12} N m^{-1} when $Ar = 3$ and 2×10^{12} N m^{-1} when $Ar = 10$.

Thus the net force resisting plate motion per unit length of collisional boundary is about 3.5×10^{13} N m^{-1} for models with $Ar = 1$; about 10^{13} N m^{-1} when $Ar = 3$ and about 4×10^{12} N m^{-1} when Ar is 10. These forces may be compared with those available to drive plate motion: the elevation of the ridges relative to the deep ocean basins provides a force of about 2×10^{12} N per metre of ridge and the negative buoyancy of the slabs may provide a maximum of around 2×10^{13} N per metre of trench (Richter and McKenzie, 1978). Note, however, that the negative buoyancy of the slabs must be counteracted to some extent by viscous dissipation in the mantle; independent estimates (Richter and McKenzie, 1978; McKenzie and Jarvis, 1980) suggest that there may be net resisting forces of as much as 8×10^{12} N per metre of trench. The net force available to drive plate motion may also be reduced because of compositional buoyancy in the slab (Oxburgh and Parmentier, 1977; England and Wortel, 1980) and because full negative buoyancy of a slab is not developed in a slowly converging subduction zone (Richter and McKenzie, 1978). Based on these considerations, England and Wortel (1980) have estimated that the average net driving force per unit length of subducting slab may be as low as 5×10^{12} N m^{-1} for the plates with major slabs (Indian and Pacific plates); if the average resistance to slab descent were half that suggested above — 4×10^{12} N m^{-1} — this raises the estimate of the average net slab pull to around 10^{13} N m^{-1}.

Clearly the resistance to plate motion that continental deformation provides is comparable in magnitude to the forces that are available to drive plate motion. We remember that the maximum crustal thickness attainable in the viscous models depends critically on the Argand number — that is, on the effective viscosity of the lithosphere. Provided the viscous model for continental deformation applies, the maximum crustal thickness that is supported in a collision zone permits us to make a good estimate of the effective viscosity of the medium; different boundary conditions would result in different geometries of deformation but it would require significantly different values of the effective viscosity to change the maximum crustal thickness that is supportable.

Consequently we may use the estimated values of crustal thickness in Tibet and the Himalaya to infer a value of Ar, and hence for the forces resisting plate motion at the India–Asia collision zone. The crust is around 70 km thick beneath Tibet and the Tibetan Himalaya (Krestnikov and Nersesov, 1964; Menke and Jacob, 1976; Chen and Molnar, 1977; Soller *et al.*, 1981) so a value of 3 for Ar and a net resisting force of 10^{13} N m^{-1} of plate boundary seem appropriate for the India–Asian collision.

This implies that the continuing orogeny in Asia, bounded by the 1500 km front of the Himalaya, requires the driving force of between 2500 and 5000 km of subducting slab or 12 000 km of ridge. These conditions are satisfied on the Indian plate: England and Wortel (1980) estimate that there are over 9000 km of slab on the Indian plate that have a negative buoyancy great enough to overcome a resisting force of 8×10^{12} N m^{-1}, and that the average net driving force from these is over 5×10^{12} N m^{-1} and Forsyth and Uyeda (1975) estimate that there is about 11 000 km of ridge on the plate which exerts a force in the direction of the plate motion. Either mechanism would be capable of driving the orogeny in Asia; although there are other forces that may resist the motion (traction on the plate base or on transform faults) there is no obvious shortage of driving force on the Indian plate. These forces are presumably balanced by a combination of edge and basal tractions acting on the Eurasian plate.

However, for an orogeny such as that in Central Asia, it is not sufficient that there should be a balance of forces at the present day; the collision of India with Asia occurred 30–40 m.y. BP and India has been moving northwards at approximately 4·5 cm/yr since then (McKenzie and Sclater, 1971; Molnar and Tapponnier, 1975). This has involved around 1500 km of convergence between India and Asia; as a slab that is exerting an effective driving force must continue to descend into the mantle, it is evident that the remnants of any slab that was attached to the northern edge of India must have ceased to play a significant role in driving the motion, once the continental collision had occurred.

It seems probable that the Java–Sumatra–New Hebrides trench systems, or their historical analogues, have been sites of subduction of old oceanic lithosphere since the early Tertiary, at least (McKenzie and Sclater, 1971; Harper *et al.*, 1981) and hence that the necessary balance of forces has been available for continental convergence between India and Asia since that time.

In contrast let us consider the balance of forces on the African plate: there is little, if any, oceanic slab attached to this plate that would be capable of driving its convergence with Europe, and there is a total effective ridge length of 3500 km (Forsyth and Uyeda, 1975).

We cannot be certain that this was always the case, but most plate reconstructions and palaeo-magnetic evidence suggest that the history of Africa's motion relative to Europe has been one of slow convergence with appreciable strike-slip motion (e.g. Biju-Duval *et al.*, 1977; Channell *et al.*, 1979) which suggests no major slab driving force even during the closing of western Tethys (compare India's northward motion at over 15 cm/yr in the late Mesozoic and early Tertiary: McKenzie and Sclater, 1971) and the geometry of plate boundaries since the early Tertiary rules out any major system of slabs attached to the African plate.

The force required to maintain continental deformation on the scale that is seen in Central and Eastern Asia today is comparable to the forces that are believed to be available to drive plate motion. One explanation for the contrast in styles between the Alpine–Mediterranean and the India–Asia continental collision zone could lie in the fact that the Indian plate has a large slab system attached to its northern edge which has been capable of driving the continued northward motion of India over the last 40 m.y. whereas no such system existed for the African plate during the Tertiary.

Conclusions

A viscous sheet model for the deformation of the continental lithosphere provides a framework for describing the distributed nature of the deformation in continental collision zones, and predicts crustal thickness distributions and deviatoric stresses that are in agreement with those inferred for the India–Asia collision zones when the viscous sheet has a non-Newtonian rheology and is capable of supporting deviatoric stresses of around 300 bars.

The dominant features of this model are that it treats the continental lithosphere as a power-law material, and that it takes account explicitly of the crustal thickness contrasts that are generated during the deformation. The buoyancy forces exerted by regions of thickened crust play an important part in the deformation of the continental lithosphere for most geologically plausible ranges of lithospheric strength; in particular they are responsible for transmitting the stresses arising from plate collision into the interior of continents.

The sequence of deformation in a continental collision zone may be expected in general to follow this pattern: initially the convergence of two regions of buoyant crust results in predominantly compressional deformation and crustal thickening close to the plate boundary. If collision proceeds the crust will thicken until it exerts a buoyancy force great enough to deform the surrounding regions; at this stage the region of thickest crust may be in net extension and much of the strain associated with collision will be taken up by predominantly strike-slip motion outside the region of thickest crust.

The large resistance to plate motion that is provided by continental collision means that a large-scale orogeny like the Tibetan–Himalayan one, where deformation has been occurring over several million square kilometres for about 30 m.y., requires a large driving force elsewhere on one of the participating plates — most plausibly a large slab system. A slab attached to one continental plate at the time of continental collision may provide enough driving force for smaller scale thickening of continental crust, but cannot provide a continuing driving force over tens of millions of years or thousands of kilometres convergence.

Although a viscous model for the continental lithosphere provides an improvement in understanding the large scale deformation of the continents, there are many problems still to be resolved; among the most important of these are the nature of the response of the inhomogeneous brittle layer of the lithosphere to the large scale forces acting upon it and how we may use surface observations on this layer to find out more about the deeper-seated processes.

Acknowledgements

I am grateful to Dan McKenzie for making several helpful comments on this manuscript. This work was supported by National Science Foundation grant EAR-81-07659.

References

Ashby, M.F. and Verrall, R.A. (1978). Micromechanisms of flow and fracture, and their relevance to the rheology of the upper mantle. In "The Creep of Engineering Materials, and of the Earth". Royal Society, London.

Biju-Duval, B., Dercourt, J. and Le Pichon, X. (1976). From Tethys to the Mediterranean seas: a plate tectonic model of the evolution of the Western Alpine system. In "Structural History of the Mediterranean Basins" (B. Biju-Duval and L. Montadert, eds). Editions Technip.

Channell, J.E.T., D'Argenio, B. and Horvath, F. (1979). Adria, the African Promontory. *In* "Mesozoic Mediterranean Paleogeography". Earth Sci. Rev. **15**, 213–292.

Chen, W.P. and Molnar, P. (1977). Seismic moments of major earthquakes and the average slip rate in Central Asia. *J. Geophys. Res.* **82**, 2945–2970.

England, P.C. and Wortel, M.J.R. (1980). Some consequences of the subduction of young slabs. *Earth Planet Sci. lett.* **47**, 403–415.

England, P.C. and McKenzie, D.P. (1982). A thin viscous sheet model for continental deformation. *Geophys. J. R. astr. Soc.* **70**, 295–321.

England, P.C. and McKenzie, D.P. (1983). Correction to: A thin viscous sheet model for Continental deformation. *Geophys. J. R. Astr. Soc.*

Fitch, T.J. (1970). Earthquake mechanisms in the Himalayan, Burman and Andaman regions, and continental tectonics in Central Asia. *J. Geophys. Res.* **75**, 2699.

Forsyth, D. and Uyeda, S. (1975). On the relative importance of the driving forces of plate motion. *Geophys. J. R. astr. Soc.* **43**, 163.

Gansser, A. (1964). "Geology of the Himalayas". Wiley-Interscience, London.

Goetze, C. (1978). The mechanisms of creep in olivine. *In* "Creep of Engineering Materials and of the Earth". Royal Society, London.

Harper, J.F., Hurley, A.M., Smith, A.G. (1981). Plate driving forces at anomaly 23 time. *Tectonophys.* **74**, 169–187.

Krestnikov, N.V. and Nersesov, L. (1964). Relations of the deep structure of Pamirs and Tien Shan to their tectonics. *Tectonophys.* **1**, 183.

McKenzie, D.P. (1972). Active tectonics of the Mediterranean system. *Geophys. J. R. astr. Soc.* **30**, 109–185.

McKenzie, D.P. (1976). Can plate tectonics describe continental deformation? *In* "Structural History of the Mediterranean Basins" (B. Biju-Duval and L. Montadert, eds). Editions Technip.

McKenzie, D.P. and Jarvis, G.T. (1980). The conversion of heat into work by mantle convection. *J. Geophys. Res.* **85**, 6093–6096.

McKenzie, D.P. and Sclater, J.G. (1971). The evolution of the Indian Ocean since the late Cretaceous. *Geophys. J. R. astr. Soc.* **24**, 437.

Menke, W.H. and Jacob, K.H. (1976). Seismicity patterns in Pakistan Northwestern India associated with continental collision. *Bull. Seismol. Soc. Am.* **66**, 1695.

Molnar, P. and Tapponnier, P. (1975). Cenozoic Tectonics of Asia: Effects of a Continental Collision. *Science* **189**, 419.

Molnar, P. and Tapponnier, P. (1978). Active tectonics of Tibet. *J. Geophys. Res.* **83**, 5361.

Molnar, P. and Tapponnier, P. (1981). A possible dependence of the tectonic strength on the age of the crust in Asia. *Earth Planet. Sci. lett.* **52**, 107–114.

Molnar, P., Fitch, T.J. and Wu, F.T. (1973). Fault plane solutions of shallow earthquakes, and contemporary tectonics of Asia. *Earth Planet. Sci. lett.* **16**, 101.

Ni, J. and York, J.E. (1978). Late Cenozoic Tectonics of the Tibetan Plateau. *J. Geophys. Res.* **83**, 5377.

Oxburgh, E.R. and Parmentier, E.M. (1977). Compositional and density stratification in oceanic lithosphere — causes and consequences. *J. Geol. Soc. Lond.* **133**, 343.

Richter, F.M. and McKenzie, D.P. (1978). Simple plate models of mantle convection. *J. Geophys.* **44**, 441.

Soller, D.R., Ray, R.D. and Brown, R.D. (1981). A Global Crustal Thickness Map. McClean, VA, Phoenix Corporation, 51 pp.

Tapponnier, P. and Molnar, P. (1976). Slip-line field theory and large-scale continental tectonics. *Nature, London* **264**, 319.

Tapponnier, P. and Molnar, P. (1977). Active faulting and tectonics in China. *J. Geophys. Res.* **82**, 2905.

York, J.E., Cardwell, R. and Ni, J. (1976). Seismicity and quaternary faulting in China. *Bull. Seismol. Soc. Am.* **66**, 1983–2001.

Driving Mechanisms of Mountain Building

D.L. Turcotte

Department of Geological Sciences
Cornell University, NY, U.S.A.

Abstract

Plate tectonics provides a general framework for understanding mountain building. The mid-ocean ridge system is a world-wide range of mountains. A quantitative theory can be given for the elevation of the ridge system and the resulting horizontal stress field. Topography in the continents is discussed in terms of crustal thickening (Airy isostasy) and thinning of the continental lithosphere (thermal isostasy). The resulting horizontal stress fields are derived. Although we have some knowledge of basic driving mechanisms of mountain building much remains to be learned.

I. Introduction

Mountain building requires energy. The source of this energy is the decay of radioactive isotopes within the earth and the secular cooling of the earth. The interior of the earth behaves as a fluid on geological time scales due to solid-state creep processes. The heat from the interior of the earth is lost to the surface, thus the near-surface rocks are cooler and are relatively more dense than the rocks at depth. This leads to a gravitational instability and the result is thermal convection. Holmes (1931) estimated the Rayleigh number for the interior of the earth and concluded that thermal convection of the solid mantle caused continental drifts. His result is generally accepted today.

One manifestation of mantle convection is plate tectonics. The surface plates (the lithosphere) are thermal boundary layers of mantle convection cells (Turcotte and Oxburgh, 1967). The forces that drive the motions of the surface plates can be determined with some accuracy. By studying the relative velocities of the surface plates Forsyth and Uyeda (1975) and Chapple and Tullis (1977) have established the relative magnitudes of the forces that drive the plate motions. Both sets of authors concluded that a force couple at subduction zones determines the velocities of oceanic plates with extensive trench systems. This force couple is a balance between the gravitational body forces driving the plates downward and the viscous retarding forces resisting the motion. As a result of this couple, subduction rates of about 10 cm/yr are common. It was also concluded that traction forces on the base of the plates are negligibly small. The reason for this conclusion is easily illustrated. The Cocas, Nazca, and Pacific plates are subducted at approximately equal rates. All three plates are oceanic and have extensive trench systems; however, the Pacific plate has a much larger surface area. If traction forces retard plate motion it would be expected that the Pacific plate would move more slowly than the other plates, if traction forces drive plate motion it would be expected that the Pacific plate would move more rapidly. The conclusion is that the resistance to the motion of oceanic plates is at the subduction zones. This is not surprising since the seismic attenuation of the asthenosphere indicates that it has a lower viscosity and is thus less resistive to motion than the mesosphere beneath. The existence of a low viscosity channel has been confirmed by studies of post-glacial rebound (Cathles, 1975).

The North and South American plates have extensive ridge systems at their margins but few trenches. The lower velocities of these plates can be attributed to the smaller forces exerted at ocean ridges. Gravitational sliding off ocean ridges contributes to the motion of these plates and results in compressional stresses in plate interiors.

An important conclusion from these qualitative studies is that the *surface plates act as stress guides*. The lack of deformation of plate interiors indicate that plates can transmit elastic stresses over large distances on geological time scales. Studies of the flexure of oceanic plates under loads (Caldwell and Turcotte, 1979; Watts *et al.*, 1980) and studies of the rheology of the oceanic lithosphere (Kirby, 1980; Minster and Anderson, 1981) indicate that kilobar level stresses can be transmitted through the elastic lithosphere. The elastic lithosphere is the upper part of the thermal lithosphere that has temperature less than about 400°C. At higher temperatures elastic stresses are relaxed by solid state creep processes.

Thus it is concluded that the horizontal forces that cause mountain building are primarily applied to the lithospheric plates at plate margins. In order to understand quantitatively how processes at accretional plate margins cause mountain building we first consider a typical mid-ocean ridge.

II. Mountain Building at Ocean Ridges

The mid-ocean ridge system is a world-wide range of mountains lying below sea level. The elevation of the ridges are about 3 km above the reference level of the ocean basins. Quantitative studies based on plate tectonics can explain the morphology of the ocean ridge system.

Due to sea-floor spreading hot mantle rock reaches the surface at the axis of an ocean ridge. This mantle rock cools due to heat loss to the sea floor. A rigid lithosphere plate forms which thickens with age. The base of the lithosphere is an isotherm which determines the boundary between cool rigid lithospheric rocks and hot viscous mantle rocks. The thermal structure of the oceanic lithosphere can be obtained by solving the equation for the one-dimensional transfer of heat:

$$\frac{\partial T}{\partial t} = \kappa \frac{\partial^2 T}{\partial y^2} \qquad (1)$$

where T is temperature, y is depth, t is the age of the lithosphere, and κ is the thermal diffusivity of the mantle rocks that make up most of the lithosphere. The required boundary conditions are $T = T_0$ [at $y = 0$ (T_0 the sea water temperature) and $T \to T_m$ as $y \to \infty$ (T_m the temperature of the hot mantle rock). The solution of (1) that satisfies these boundary conditions is:

$$\frac{T_m - T}{T_m - T_0} = \text{erfc}\,(y/2\sqrt{\kappa t}) \qquad (2)$$

where erfc is the complementary error function.

Assuming isostasy this temperature distribution can be used to determine the elevation of the ridge system as a function of age. The condition of isostasy relative to the crest of the ocean ridge requires that:

$$w = \frac{1}{(\rho_m - \rho_w)} \int_0^\infty (\rho - \rho_m)\, dy \qquad (3)$$

where w is the depth of the sea floor relative to the ridge crest, ρ_m is the density of hot mantle rock, ρ_w the density of water, and ρ the density within the lithosphere. The density within the lithosphere is related to the temperature by:

$$\rho - \rho_m = \rho_m \alpha (T_m - T) \qquad (4)$$

where α is the volumetric coefficient of thermal expansion. Substitution of (2) and (4) into (3) and integrating gives:

$$w = \frac{2\rho_m \alpha (T_m - T_0)}{(\rho_m - \rho_w)} \left(\frac{\kappa t}{\pi}\right)^{\frac{1}{2}}. \qquad (5)$$

This relation predicts the elevation of an ocean ridge as a function of age.

Taking $\rho_m = 3\cdot3$ gm/cm³, $\kappa = 10^{-2}$ cm/s², $\alpha = 3 \times 10^{-5}$ °K⁻¹, $T_m - T_0 = 1300$°K, and $\rho_w = 1$ gm/cm³ the predicted elevation is compared with the observed bathymetry (Parsons and Sclater, 1977) in Fig. 1. Good agreement is obtained although the subsidence of the sea floor is less than predicted for ages greater than about 80 m.y. If the one dimensional cooling model is applied to the continents, poor agreement is obtained. The older continents do not continue to subside. Heat input into the base of the continental lithosphere results in an equilibrium thickness for continental cratons older than about 100 m.y. In general, however, the simple isostatic model given above successfully predicts the morphology of the mid-ocean ridge system.

Although the morphology of mid-ocean ridges is primarily the result of vertical isostatic tectonics as described above, horizontal forces are also generated. These horizontal forces are equivalent to a gravitational sliding away from the ridge crest. They can also be thought of as a horizontal pressure gradient associated with the mantle convection cell at depth.

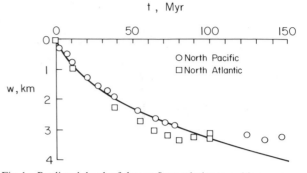

Fig. 1   Predicted depth of the sea floor relative to a ridge crest as a function of the age of the sea floor. The predicted dependence from (5) is compared with observed depths from the north Pacific and north Atlantic (Parsons and Sclater, 1977).

The elevation of the ridge is a hydrostatic head that is equivalent to a fluid pressure.

The horizontal force on the elastic lithosphere generated at an ocean ridge can be obtained by integration over the free-body diagram given in Fig. 2. A two-dimensional model is appropriate since a mid-ocean ridge is primarily a linear feature. All pressure forces are referenced to the ridge crest. The net horizontal pressure force on the upper surface of the lithosphere is:

$$F_2 = \tfrac{1}{2}\rho_w g w^2. \qquad (6)$$

The net horizontal force on the base of the lithosphere is:

$$F_1 = \tfrac{1}{2}\rho_m g (w + y_L)^2. \qquad (7)$$

The horizontal pressure force acting within the lithosphere is:

$$F_3 = \int_0^{y_L} \left(\rho_w g w + \int_0^y \rho g\, dy'\right) dy. \qquad (8)$$

The net horizontal force on the lithosphere adjacent to an ocean ridge F_R is given by:

$$F_R = F_1 - F_2 - F_3. \qquad (9)$$

This is the elastic force that is transmitted through the lithosphere. Substitution of (6) to (8) into (9), introducing (2) and (4), and integrating yields:

$$F_R = g\rho_m \alpha (T_m - T_0)\left[1 + \frac{2}{\pi}\frac{\rho_m \alpha (T_m - T_0)}{(\rho_m - \rho_w)}\right]\kappa t \qquad (10)$$

Taking the values for parameters given above with $g = 10^3$ cm/s² we find that the total ridge push on 100 m.y. old oceanic lithosphere is $F_R = 4\cdot2 \times 10^{15}$ dynes/cm. If the thickness of the elastic lithosphere, the fraction of the thermal lithosphere that can transmit elastic stresses over geological times, is 50 km the resulting compression stress in the oceanic elastic lithosphere is 840 bars. Gravitational sliding off the ridge crest causes a compressional stress in the

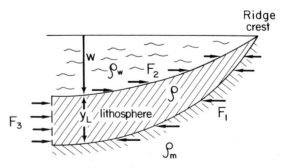

Fig. 2   Free body diagram used to determine the compressional body force generated by gravitational sliding off a ridge crest (ridge push).

adjacent oceanic lithosphere which has a magnitude of the order of a kilobar.

An example of where this ridge push could result in continental tectonics is the Red Sea. The axis of the Red Sea is a mid-ocean ridge crest. The forces determined above would be expected to act as compressional stresses on the adjacent plates.

III. Vertical Continental Tectonics

The relative roles of vertical and horizontal forces in building continental mountain belts has been a subject of considerable controversy. Clearly both types of forces must be important; we first consider vertical forces. It has long been known that major continental mountain belts are in near isostatic equilibrium, the excess mass of the topography has low density roots.

One explanation for a low density root is a thickening of the continental crust beneath the mountain belt; this is a form of Airy isostasy. If the density of the crustal root is ρ_c the thickness of the crust is related to the height of topography h by:

$$y_{cc} = y_{cco} + \frac{h\rho_m}{\rho_m - \rho_c} \qquad (11)$$

where y_{cco} is the original thickness of the continental crust. Taking $y_{cco} = 35$ km, $\rho_c = 2 \cdot 78$ g/cm^3, and $\rho_m = 3 \cdot 33$ g/cm P3 the dependence of h on y_{cc} is given in Fig. 3a.

Several mechanisms can be responsible for thickening the continental crust. One is extensive intrusive or extrusive volcanics. In mountain belts associated with subduction zones such as the Andes this mechanism may play an important role. The continental crust may also be thickened due to various compressional mechanisms. These will be discussed in a later section.

Thinning of the continental lithosphere can also lead to elevated topography. This is the same thermal compensation mechanism that was previously applied to ocean ridges. We assume that the continental lithosphere has reached a steady-state thermal structure. Thus a linear temperature distribution is a good approximation beneath the near-surface crustal layer containing high concentrations of radioactive isotopes. Therefore we take:

$$T = T_m - (T_m - T_0)\left(1 - \frac{y}{y_L}\right) \qquad (12)$$

This relation is also assumed to be valid after the lithosphere has been thinned. Using thermal isostasy the height of the additional topography can be related to the thickness of a thinned continental lithosphere according to:

$$h = \frac{1}{2} \frac{\rho_m \alpha (T_m - T_0) y_{LO}}{\rho_c} \left(1 - \frac{1}{\beta_L}\right) \qquad (13)$$

where y_{LO} is the initial thickness of the continental lithosphere and $\beta_L = y_{LO}/y_L$ is the lithospheric thinning factor. Taking $\rho = 2 \cdot 78$ g/cm^3 and $y_{LO} = 180$ km (Turcotte and McAdoo, 1979) the dependence of uplift on the thinning factor is given in Fig. 3b. It is seen that thinning a continental lithosphere that originally had a thickness of 180 km can lead to a maximum uplift of $4 \cdot 3$ km. This mechanism undoubtedly makes an important contribution to the topographic elevation in the western United States where the asthenosphere reaches the base of the crust in the basin and range province. It is likely to contribute to the elevation in many orogenic belts.

Several mechanisms have been proposed to explain the thinning of the continental lithosphere. If the lithosphere is stretched due to horizontal extension it will also be thinned; however, uniform stretching of the continental lithosphere also thins the continental crust. The thinning of the crust leads to subsidence and the formation of sedimentary basins rather than elevated topography (McKenzie, 1978). Alternative mechanisms have been proposed for the thinning of the lithosphere in the western United States. Lachenbruch (1978) has suggested that the heat transported by the upward migration of magma is responsible for the thinning of the lithosphere. Bird (1979) has hypothesized lithospheric delamination; in this hypothesis the lower part of the dense, unstable thermal continental lithosphere breaks away and founders into the asthenosphere. The cold rocks of the delaminated lithosphere are replaced by hot asthenospheric rock thus thinning the lithosphere.

Lithospheric thinning is an efficient mechanism for providing elevated topography. The energy required to provide the elevation is provided by the potential energy of the cold unstable continental lithosphere relative to the deep, hot mantle rocks.

IV. Horizontal Continental Tectonics

It was previously shown that lithospheric thinning at ocean ridges leads to large horizontal forces. We next consider how elevated topography in continents can also result in large horizontal forces. If the elevated topography is due to a thickening of the continental crust (Airy isostasy) the force balance problem is illustrated in Fig. 4a. Prior to thickening the thickness of the continental crust is y_{cco}, after thickening it is y_{cc}; the elevation h is related to y_{cco} and y_{cc} by (11).

The total horizontal body force in the mountain belt integrated to the base of the thickened continental crust (the assumed depth of compensation) is given by:

$$F_1 = \tfrac{1}{2}\rho_c g y_{cc}{}^2 \qquad (14)$$

The total horizontal body force integrated to the same depth for normal continental crust is:

$$F_2 = \rho_c g y_{cco}(y_{cc} - h - \tfrac{1}{2}y_{cco}) + \tfrac{1}{2}\rho_m g(y_{cc} - h - y_{cco})^2 \qquad (15)$$

The net horizontal force in the normal continental crust is:

$$F_R = F_1 - F_2. \qquad (16)$$

Substitution of (14) and (15) along with (11) gives:

$$F_R = \rho_c g h \left[y_{cco} + \frac{\rho_m h}{\rho_m - \rho_c} \right] \qquad (17)$$

Taking $\rho_c = 2 \cdot 78$, $\rho_m = 3 \cdot 33$, $y_{coo} = 35$ km, and assuming the elastic lithosphere to have a thickness of 50 km the resulting

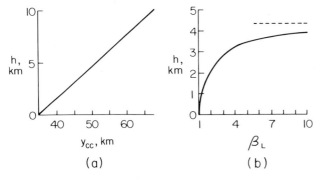

Fig. 3 (a) Height of elevated topography as a function of the thickness of the continental crust for Airy isostasy from (11). (b) Height of elevated topography as a function of the lithospheric thinning factor for thermal isostasy from (13). The dashed line is the elevation in the limit $\beta_L \to \infty$.

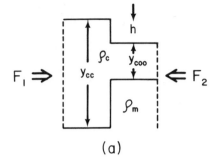

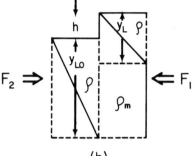

(a)

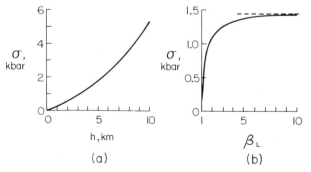

(b)

Fig. 4 (a) Free-body diagram used to determine the horizontal body forces associated with crustal thickening (Airy isostasy). (b) Free-body diagram used to determine the horizontal body forces associated with a thinned continental lithosphere (thermal isostasy). The linear temperature profiles in the normal and thinned lithospheres are shown.

compressional stress is given as a function of elevation in Fig. 5a. It is seen that kilobar level stresses can develop if the elevation is greater than about 3 km. Since a uniform horizontal stress can be added arbitrarily the topographic stresses are either compressional in the adjacent normal continental crust or tensional in the thickened crust.

Physically these stresses can be explained in terms of the stress required to maintain the topography. The equilibrium in the presence of a gravitational field is a surface of constant gravitational potential, i.e. constant elevation. Elevated topography results either in a deviatoric horizontal tensional stress within the region of elevated topography or a deviatoric compressional stress in the adjacent regions of lower topography. It is the latter that is given by (17).

We next obtain the horizontal stresses generated when the continental lithosphere is thinned. This problem is illustrated in Fig. 4b. It is assumed that the temperature profile is given by (12). The total horizontal body force integrated to the base of the normal continental lithosphere is:

$$F_2 = \int_0^{y_{LO}} \left(\int_0^y \rho(y') \, dy' \right) dy$$

$$= \int_0^{y_{LO}} \left[\rho_m g y + g \alpha \rho_m (T_m - T_0) \left(y - \frac{y^2}{2 y_{LO}} \right) \right] dy$$

$$= \rho_m g [\tfrac{1}{2} + \tfrac{1}{3} \alpha (T_m - T_0)] y_{LO}^2 \qquad (18)$$

where the temperature distribution in (12) has been used. The total horizontal body force to the same depth for the thinned and elevated continental lithosphere is given by:

$$F_1 = \int_0^{y_L} \left[\rho_m g y + g \alpha \rho_m (T_m - T_0) \left(y - \frac{y^2}{2 y_L} \right) \right] dy$$

$$+ \int_{y_L}^{y_{LO}+h} [\rho_m g y + \tfrac{1}{2} g \alpha \rho_m (T_m - T_0) y_L] \, dy \qquad (19)$$

$$= \tfrac{1}{2} \rho_m g [(y_{LO} + h)^2 + \alpha (T_m - T_0)(y_L y_{LO} + y_L h - \tfrac{1}{3} y_L^2)].$$

Utilizing (13) the net horizontal force in the normal continental lithosphere is:

$$F_R = F_1 - F_2 =$$

$$\tfrac{1}{6} \rho_m g \alpha (T_m - T_0)[1 + \tfrac{3}{4} \alpha (T_m - T_0)] y_{LO}^2 \left(1 - \frac{1}{\beta_L^2} \right). \qquad (20)$$

Assuming the elastic lithosphere to have a thickness of 50 km and taking the values of parameters used above the resulting compressional stress is given as a function of the thinning factor in Fig. 5b. A reduction in the lithosphere thickness of 50% or more results in stress levels of a kilobar or more.

Discussion

The main point made above is that thinning of the lithosphere can lead to significant horizontal stresses. One example of such a situation is illustrated in Fig. 6a. A rift valley in a continent will result in compressional stresses in the adjacent continental lithosphere. In the illustration the rift valley has developed to form a small sea with a median spreading centre. An example would be the Red Sea. Although tensional stresses and tectonics are associated with the ridge crest, large compressional stresses are developed in the adjacent continental lithosphere. If the lithosphere were sufficiently weak compressional tectonics would be expected.

In Fig. 6b a thermally elevated continental crust is illustrated. We have shown that tensional deviatoric stresses would be expected in the elevated terrane. This could lead to crustal extension and a horst and graben structure such as that found in the Basin and Range Province in the western United States. Our analysis predicts compressional tectonics in the adjacent continental lithosphere. It is interesting to speculate whether these compressional stresses are responsible for the elevation of the Colorado Plateau and the Sierra Nevada block in California.

So far we have avoided a quantitative discussion of stresses at subduction zones. The reason is that the required boundary value problem is poorly posed. As discussed earlier it is not clear whether the body forces on the subducted lithosphere result in a compressive or tensional stress in the subducting lithosphere at the ocean trench. A typical trench system is illustrated in Fig. 7a. This is a schematic representa-

Fig. 5 (a) Compressional stresses generated by thickened continental crust as a function of the topographic elevation. (b) Compressional stresses generated by thinning the continental lithosphere as a function of the thinning factor.

OCEAN
RIDGE

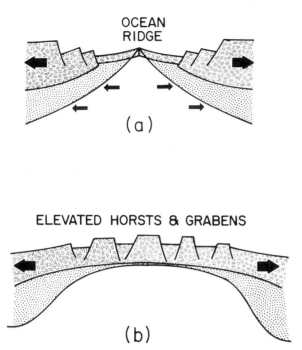

(a)

ELEVATED HORSTS & GRABENS

(b)

Fig. 6 Stresses generated by the thinning of the continental lithosphere. (a) Illustration of the horizontal compressional stresses generated at a median spreading centre in a small sea. (b) Thinned continental lithosphere leads to a region of elevated topography with tensional stresses. These stresses may lead to a horst and graben terrane.

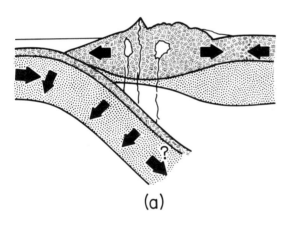

(a)

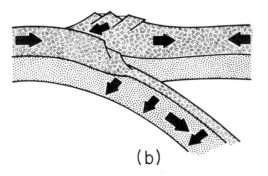

(b)

Fig. 7 (a) Illustration of a subduction zone adjacent to a continental margin. (b) Illustration of a continental collision.

tion of the Andes. The relative contributions of intrusive and extrusive volcanics and thinning of the lithosphere to the topography of the Andes is not clear. The elevation of the Andes is expected to lead to deviatoric tensional stresses within the mountain belt and deviatoric compressional stresses in the adjacent lithosphere. But is the ridge push from the Mid-Atlantic Ridge sufficient to reduce or eliminate the tensional stresses within the belt?

Subduction occurs because old oceanic lithosphere is gravitationally unstable with respect to the mantle. The resultant downward body force drives plate tectonics. However, in addition this body force will cause the trench to migrate seaward. This mechanism is referred to as lithospheric foundering. The result is a suction on the adjacent lithosphere. It has been suggested (Chase, 1978) that the resulting deviatoric tensional stresses leads to the formation of marginal basins.

Major mountain belts are often associated with continental collisions. Examples are the Himalayas and the Alps. Such collision zones generally involve regional compressive deviatoric stresses and tectonics. The origin of such stresses is unclear. A continental collision is illustrated schematically in Fig. 7b. Continental collision zones are generally associated with subduction zones that have closed an ocean. It is difficult, however, to understand how the gravitational body forces on the subducted lithosphere can contribute to compressional stresses in a collision zone. A more viable mechanism is that adjacent ocean ridges and/or continental rifts are driving the two continents together. Finite-element stress calculations for alternative models of the Zagros collision zone have been given by Bird (1978).

Conclusions

Plate tectonics has provided a framework for understanding many aspects of mountain building. However, other aspects are poorly understood. The tectonics of spreading centres can be understood qualitatively. Some aspects of subduction zones are well understood. The morphology of the descending lithosphere is reasonably well understood. However, the structure and stress distribution in the adjacent island arc or continental orogenic zone is poorly understood. Even the origin of the volcanic rocks that make up the associated volcanic line is a subject of considerable controversy.

Even less is understood about continental orogenic belts not associated with rifting or subduction. The mechanics of continental collision zones are poorly understood. An important unanswered question is the relationships between these collision zones and the subduction process. Clearly much work, both observational and theoretical, remains to be done.

Acknowledgements

This research has been supported by the Division of Earth Sciences, National Science Foundation, NSF Grant EAR 7919414. This is contribution 703 of the Department of Geological Sciences, Cornell University.

References

Bird, P. (1978). Finite element modelling of lithosphere deformation: The Zagros collision orogeny. *Tectonophysics* **50**, 307–336.
Bird, P. (1979). Continental delamination and the Colorado Plateau. *J. Geophys. Res.* **84**, 7561–7571.
Caldwell, J.G. and Turcotte, D.L. (1979). Dependence of the thickness of the elastic oceanic lithosphere on age, J. Geophys. Res., v. 84, p. 7572–7576.

Cathles, L.M. (1975). "The Viscosity of the Earth's Mantle". Princeton University Press, Princeton, NJ, 386 pp.

Chapple, W.M. and Tullis, T.E. (1977). Evaluation of the forces that drive the plates. *J. Geophys. Res.* **82**, 1967–1984.

Chase, C.G. (1978). Extension behind island arcs and motions relative to hot spots. *J. Geophys. Res.* **83**, 5385–5387.

Forsyth, D. and Uyeda, S. (1975). On the relative motion of the driving forces of plate motion. *Geophys. J. Roy. Astron. Soc.* **43**, 163–200.

Holmes,, A. (1931). Radioactivity and Earth Movements, XVIII. *Trans. Geol. Soc., Glasgow* **18**, 559–606.

Kirby, S.H. (1980). Tectonic stresses in the lithosphere: Constraints provided by the experimental deformation of rocks. *J. Geophys. Res.* **85**, 6353–6363.

Lachenbruch, A.H. (1978). Heat flow in the Basin and Range Province and thermal effects of extension. *Pure Ap. Geophys.* **117**, 34–50.

McKenzie, D. (1978). Some remarks on the development of sedimentary basins. *Earth Planet. Sci. Let.* **40**, 25–32.

Minster, J.B. and Anderson, D.L. (1981). A model of dislocation-controlled rheology for the mantle. *Phil. Trans. Roy. Soc. London* **229A**, 319–356.

Parsons, B. and Sclater, J.G. (1977). An analysis of the variation of ocean floor bathymetry and heat flow with age. *J. Geophys. Res.* **82**, 803–827.

Turcotte, D.L. and McAdoo, D.C. (1979). Geoid anomalies and the thickness of the lithosphere. *J. Geophys. Res.* **84**, 2381–2387.

Turcotte, D.L. and Oxburgh, E.R. (1967). Finite amplitude convection cells and continental drift. *J. Fluid Mech.* **28**, 29–42.

Watts, A.B., Bodine, J.H. and Ribe, N.M. (1980). Observations of flexure and the geological evolution of the Pacific Ocean basin. *Nature, London* **283**, 532–537.

Part 2

Case Histories

Alpine Paleogeography: a Reappraisal

R. Trümpy

Geologisches Institut der ETH,
Zürich, Switzerland

Abstract

Alpine evolution may be divided into five stages: gradual subsidence (mid-Permian to Middle Triassic), rifting and accelerated subsidence (Late Triassic to mid-Jurassic), spreading and transcurrent motions (mid-Jurassic to end of Early Cretaceous), subduction and transcurrent motions (Late Cretaceous to (?) Eocene) and collision (late Eocene to present). A long period of subsidence and rifting precedes the oceanic opening of the first Atlantic and of the Alpine oceans. The latter are ascribed to lateral shear movements rather than to orthogonal spreading. The importance of lateral movements from the spreading stage to the collisional stage casts some doubt on the method of reasoning along "geotraverses".

I. Introduction

About a quarter of a century ago, French geologists (Debelmas, 1957; Lemoine, 1953) and the author of this paper (1955, 1957) undertook a revision of some basic concepts of Alpine paleogeography. We stressed the existence of tensional faults during the Jurassic and Early Cretaceous, first recognized by Günzler-Seiffert (1942), and we insisted on the deep-sea origin of many Alpine sediments. This interpretation of oceanic deposits was not really new, but had been somewhat neglected in the "all-shallow" outlook of the 1930s and 40s (see, however, Steinmann, 1925; Tercier, 1939). While criticizing Argand's (1920) theory of compressional embryonic folds, which had assumed that future nappes were prefigured since the Jurassic or even the Late Paleozoic as compressional structures, we wholly accepted his mobilistic view.

If the three basic concepts — tensional Mesozoic paleotectonics, more or less oceanic character of Alpine troughs, mobilism — have stood the test of time, many of the views then expressed now look rather antiquated. We failed to understand the nature of ophiolites. Our interpretation of Alpine sedimentation lacked firm actualistic bases. We neglected the influence of lateral displacements during both the preparatory and the orogenic stage of Alpine folding, and we underestimated the importance of Cretaceous deformation. Plate tectonics and the study of recent deep-sea sediments have since brought solutions to many problems, by providing a new set of controls of possible hypotheses and by fitting the Alpine history into a much wider context.

In this paper, I intend to present a brief outline of Alpine paleotectonic phases, to discuss the relationship between the Late Paleozoic-Triassic (or Jurassic) Paleotethys and the Jurassic to Mid-Tertiary Tethys, to question the nature of the Alpine oceans, and to give a few words of warning against our accustomed reasoning along "geotraverses".

II. Paleotectonic Stages of the Alps

A. Variscan and Pre-Variscan (Precambrian to Early Carboniferous)

This long and still obscure pre-history of the Alps produced the basement complex of the future Helvetic and Penninic belts, the basement complex plus the feebly to strongly metamorphic Ordovician to Mississippian formations of the Eastern and Southern Alps.

The intensity of Variscan deformation and metamorphism decreases from north-west to south-east. A "Caledonian" (probably pre-Late Ordovician) event, is attested by numerous radiometric data. The nature of these Paleozoic deformations is still difficult to interpret. We may assume that the Variscan orogeny led to thickening and instability of the crust.

B. Late Variscan Rifting (Late Carboniferous and Early Permian)

Rifting in the aftermath of the main Variscan deformation produced graben- and half-graben-like structures, which were filled by continental detritus (Upper Carboniferous coal-bearing shales, sandstones and conglomerates; Lower Permian redbeds). Sedimentation was accompanied by bimodal volcanism. Several granitoid bodies were emplaced, especially K-rich granites, some of them of subvolcanic character. To the SE, where the Variscan folding had been least intensive, marine formations of the Paleotethys encroached upon the future Alps. The original direction of Late Carboniferous to Early Permian basins is generally SW–NE to WSW–ENE, subsequently (in Late Cretaceous and Tertiary times) rotated to almost S–N in the French Alps and in part of the Austroalpine nappes.

At first sight, the late Variscan deformations can be

ascribed to block-faulting in response to the crustal distur-bance caused by the main Variscan folding of ca. 310 m.y. But the deformations are in fact much more complicated. In the extra-Alpine areas west of the Alps, important transcur-rent faulting is probable (see Arthaud and Matte, 1975). Transcurrent movements can locally even give rise to thrust-ing, as in the small nappes east of the Cévennes.

The mid-Permian events, at the close of this epi-Variscan stage, involved a complete reorientation of the tectonic pat-tern, with the onset of "Mesozoic" paleogeography. They coincide in time with the definite constitution of Pangaea, through the last folding phases of the Appalachians and the Ural, and on a larger scale with the end of one plate-tectonics cycle (Late Precambrian to Early Permian) and the begin-ning of the next one (Late Permian to ?).

In spite of this break, part of the Variscan and especially late Variscan heritage is carried over into the "Mesozoic" paleogeography. Some Pennsylvanian to Lower Permian basins continued as sites of greater sediment accumulation during the Late Permian and the Triassic (see e.g. Cas-tellarin, 1972; Ellenberger, 1958). In how far Late Paleozoic transcurrent faults may have had an influence on the later history of the Alps remains a matter of speculation. Likewise, areas with a high concentration of Variscan granitoids, such as the Haut Dauphiné, Montblanc and Aar massifs, or the Lower Austroalpine belt of Switzerland, seem to have played a particular role during the time of Mesozoic sedimentation.

C. Gradual Subsidence with Local Rifting (Late Permian to Middle Triassic

While the Upper Carboniferous-Lower Permian interval still pertained to the Variscan cycle, the following stage marks the gradual onset of Alpine subsidence. The Variscan chain and its subsequent volcanoes had been worn down; sedimenta-tion was at first arenaceous and then carbonatic, with some evaporitic intervals.

The switch from detrital to carbonate deposition is heterochronous, becoming gradually younger from the south-eastern Paleotethys towards the west and north, and also, to a lesser degree, from the Germanic basin, which had originated during the mid-Permian reversal of paleogeography, towards the south and east. After a regression in the early Late Permian (Val Gardena sand-stones), the seas of Late Permian–Early Eotriassic age ad-vanced westwards to the Alto Adige (South Tyrol) region, those of Late Eotriassic age to the Ticino. By late Anisian time, the carbonate platform covered most of the future Alps.

In a general way, Triassic subsidence was slow and water depth remained very shallow, although several hundreds or even thousands of metres of sediment were accumulated. Relief of the platforms was very subdued, outside of a few areas in the Southern Alps, and paleogeographic trends are often distinct from those of Latest Triassic, Jurassic and Early Cretaceous times. The following realms can be distin-guished, especially for the Middle Triassic (see e.g. Mégard-Galli and Baud, 1977):

(a) Southern and eastern margin of the Germanic and Provence inland seas.

(b) A broad swell, with very little sedimentation, but presumably broken by shallow sea-ways in the Wes-tern Alps (mainly in the North Penninic nappes). Poss-ibly contiguous with the Vindelician High.

(c) The Paleo-Briançonnais basin, with up to 700 m of Middle Triassic carbonates.

(d) A swell with very much reduced sedimentation (ca. 100 m of Middle Triassic), on the site of the future Lower Austroalpine nappes and of the westernmost part of the Southern Alps.

(e) Basins of the eastern and central to eastern Southern Alps, belonging to the Paleotethys s.str. Strong vol-canism in the eastern part of the Southern Alps; vol-canic ash layers extending to the other parts of realm e as well as to realms d and c.

In the south-eastern part of the Alps, facies distribution is much more varied than in the other areas, with the well known carbonate "reefs" and intervening basins with vol-caniclastic, locally turbiditic sedimentation of the Dolomites. The significance of this late Middle Triassic vol-canic and tectonic activity is at present in dispute. Evidence of tensional structures is abundant (e.g. Assereto et al., 1973), while compressional features are rather uncertain. For most authors, the Middle Triassic volcanism is related to a phase of abortive rifting, but Castellarin et al. (1980) have recently even proposed a scenario involving island arcs, which seem rather surprising to most Alpine geologists.

There is no doubt that a major change of Alpine paleogeography occurred at the end of the Middle Triassic (Upper Ladinian and Lower Carnian). This crisis was also accompanied by an important phase of mineralization (Pb–Zn to the south-east, Cu to the NW). Within the future Alps, this rearrangement of the paleotectonic pattern did not lead to any major unconformities. The lower to middle Triassic events appear as an "abortive drama", in the pic-turesque language of Termier and Termier (1956). Whether this drama simply related to the progressive opening of the Paleotethys further to the south-east, or whether it has other implications, remains an open question.

D. Rifting and Accelerated Subsidence (Late Triassic to Early Middle Jurassic)

After the Ladinian-Carnian "event", carbonate platform sedimentation was re-established over most of the area of the future Alps. The Upper Triassic is again characterized by the existence of a virtually unbroken shallow-water platform, with continental influences to the north-west and somewhat deeper water, reminiscent of "Balkanic" (Dinaric-Hellenic) conditions, only in the Far East. Swells (b) and (d) of the Middle Triassic pattern (see above) are submerged but remain areas of reduced sediment thickness. The Briancon-nais rise, one of the most prominent features of Alpine paleogeography, becomes individualized in Late Triassic time. There is yet little indication of rifting.

Rifting begins locally in the latest Triassic and becomes general during the Early Jurassic. Early Jurassic faults are found all through the Helvetic, Penninic and Austroalpine–South Alpine realms. With the Middle Jurassic, the fault margins limiting the Piemont and Valais basins become more active (e.g. Finger, 1975; Trümpy, 1975). Where the Jurassic faults can be directly observed (which is rather exceptional, as they were generally transfor-med into thrusts or lags during the Cretaceous–Tertiary deformations), they show normal, often antithetic character, and relatively low dips (40–60°). En-échelon fault patterns possibly exist along the northern margin of the Alpine Liassic basins. The Alemannic Land of Early Jurassic time stands out as a sort of trough-shoulder to the north. The Lower Austroalpine rise may have had a similar role south of the Penninic basins, especially during the Middle Jurassic.

While tensional stresses are evident, there is as yet no cer-tain proof of transcurrent movements, which does not necessarily mean that they did not exist. According to the recent results of deep-sea drilling (Sheridan and Gradstein, 1981) it appears that the first oceanic opening of the Atlantic did not start around 180 m.y. ago, as previously suggested, but only around 165 or 160 m.y., i.e. in the middle of the Middle Jurassic. This would imply that the changeover from rifting to spreading regime in the Alps (ca. Bathonian?) coincided in time with the onset of spreading in the Atlantic. Important transcurrent movements, subordinate to the sinistral movement between Africa and Europe, should have begun only then.

The early to middle Jurassic faults are moderately inclined at the surface, and they may be assumed to flatten still further at depth. The overall effect is an extension and thinning of the crust (compare d'Argenio and Alvarez, 1980; Bott, 1976). Whether this mechanism of extension alone is sufficient to account for the accelerated subsidence during the Jurassic (compare Bally *et al.*, 1981), or whether other, somewhat mythical processes such as subcrustal erosion must be invoked, remains open to discussion. In the section of the Swiss Alps, the amount of pre-spreading (i.e. pre-late Middle Jurassic) stretching is difficult to evaluate; we guess it may have reached some 50 km.

In many of the Mediterranean basins, Upper Triassic to middle Lower Jurassic deep-sea (but not oceanic) sediments overlie shallow-water carbonates of Middle Triassic to early Lower Jurassic age. The onset of deep-sea sedimentation is marked by the appearance of monotonous, thick shales in those basins that served as receptacles for the European detritus (Dauphiné-Ultrahelvetic, Valais and possibly part of Piemont). Farther away from the European margin, marl shales and spongolitic limestones with turbidites appear in the basins, red cephalopod limestones under starved conditions. The onset of deep-sea conditions varies from place to place, generally progressing from the south-east, i.e. from the internal parts of the Paleotethys, to the north-west and west. In the Dinarides and in part of the highest Austroalpine nappes, it occurs already during the Triassic. In the western Mediterranean, Triassic and lower Liassic are quite generally of shallow-water character, and the deepening of the basins frequently begins with the Domerian (Upper Pliensbachian).

E. Spreading and Transcurrent Movements (Late Middle Jurassic to Late Lower Cretaceous)

The onset of truly oceanic conditions in the Alps is marked by a significant change in paleogeographic pattern. The rifting mechanism weakens, as new oceanic crust begins to be generated in several troughs. Many of the early to middle Jurassic faults become inactive, and sediments are draped in a more or less blanket-shaped manner over the horst- and graben-structures. This, of course, is a widespread feature along many passive continental margins (e.g. de Charpal *et al.*, 1978; Kent, 1977; Montadert *et al.*, 1977); the analogy has been stressed by several authors (e.g. Bernoulli and Lemoine, 1980; Bernoulli *et al.*, 1979; Bourbon *et al.*, 1977; de Graciansky *et al.*, 1979).

As far as can be established, Alpine spreading begins in mid-Jurassic (late Bajocian to Bathonian) times. Direct evidence is not very precise: the oldest ophiolites are overlain by radiolarian cherts, which are generally of late Middle Jurassic to early Upper Jurassic age (Decandia and Elter, 1972). Radiometric data on ophiolites (Bertrand and Delaloye, 1976) give a wide scatter of apparent ages, but all within the mid-Jurassic to mid-Cretaceous bracket. The latest basaltic flows or sills connected with ophiolite production are of Aptian to Albian age (Dietrich, 1970).

Circumstantial evidence allows a more precise dating of the first spreading. The breakdown of the Alemannic Land, which had served as a sort of trough-shoulder during the Lower Jurassic and which had received only scanty shallow-water sediments up to the Middle Bajocian, may be one indication. From the Late Bajocian to the Early Oxfordian, it was the site of hemipelagic condensed sedimentation

(Bircher, 1935; Dollfus, 1965), before becoming a relatively deep basin in which the subeuxinic Quinten limestones accumulated during the Upper Jurassic. Thus, the breakdown occurred between the Late Bajocian and the Oxfordian. In the Western Alps, the Dauphiné trough continued to gather thick pelitic deposits up to the Oxfordian.

In the Prealps (Briançonnais s.l.), a marked change of pattern took place around the Bajocian-Bathonian boundary (Furrer, 1979; P. Felber, personal communication). The deep-water Zoophycos shales were covered by shallow-water limestones or by a formation of redeposited limestones; on the Briançonnais platform itself, continental bauxites were followed by the brackish Mytilus beds.

Apparently, both the Valais and Piemont troughs originated during the Middle Jurassic. The Lower Jurassic, or at least its lower part, where present, is formed by thin shallow-water limestones. Bündnerschiefer sedimentation in the Valais belt has been dated by palynological evidence back to the Middle Jurassic or to the late Lower Jurassic (Pantić and Gansser, 1977; Pantić and Isler, 1978).

As already stated, Lower Jurassic rifting is found all over the area of the future Alps. With the Middle Jurassic, the site of fault-scarp breccia sedimentation shifts to the margins of the future oceans: Falknis breccias on the southern margin of the Valais trough (Gruner, 1982) and Lower Austroalpine breccias on the southern margin of the Piemont trough (Finger, in press). Within the Austroalpine and South-Alpine belt, i.e. along the Apulian "continental" margin, mid-Jurassic obsolescence of the early Jurassic fault pattern is also well expressed (e.g. Kälin and Trümpy, 1977).

Thus, the most plausible date for the oceanic opening of the small Alpine oceans can be assumed as mid-Jurassic, possibly late Bajocian or somewhat later. This coincides fairly well in time with the oceanic opening of the first Atlantic Ocean, according to the most recent information (Sheridan and Gradstein, 1981). The connection between the early Atlantic and the Alpine oceans followed the Maghrebine furrows of north-west Africa (Smith and Gilbert, 1971; Dewey *et al.*, 1973). The first indications of deep water in the Maghrebine trench (southernmost part of the internal zones; substratum of the Flysch nappes; external zones of the Rif) are also (late?) Middle Jurassic (Didon *et al.*, 1973; Wildi, 1981). Seen from the Mediterranean angle, a mid-Jurassic opening of the first Atlantic is more plausible than an early Jurassic one. The nature of the mid-Jurassic to mid-Cretaceous oceanic troughs will be discussed in a later chapter. Their origin is connected not only with transverse spreading, but also with important transcurrent movements. The Late Jurassic and the earliest Cretaceous is a time of carbonate sedimentation on the shallower platform, chert and pelagic limestone deposition on deeper platforms and in starved basins ("leptogeosynclinal phase", Trümpy, 1955, 1960). Apparently, only the Valais and external parts of the Piemont trough received thick Bündnerschiefer formations. During the remainder of the Early Cretaceous, sedimentation rates again increased, probably in connection with renewal of (largely transform?) fault activity.

F. Subduction and Transcurrent Movements (Mid-Cretaceous to (?) Early Eocene)

Around mid-Cretaceous time (ca. Albian), the production of new oceanic crust ceases and crustal shortening begins. Cretaceous deformations are accompanied by metamorphism, frequently of high pressure/low temperature character. No intrusions or major volcanism corresponding to the Cretaceous orogenies are known from the Alps. The Cretaceous events are quite generally ascribed to subduction of oceanic and some continental crust (e.g. Dal Piaz *et al.*, 1972; Debelmas, 1975; Dietrich, 1976), but the timing, nature and direction of these subductions are still rather obscure. Except in parts of the Austroalpine nappes (including Sesia-Dentblanche), Cretaceous (eo-Alpine) structures have been strongly overprinted by Tertiary deformations.

During this stage, the Penninic and Ultrahelvetic flysch basins came into existence, partly within the former "eugeosynclinal" furrows, partly on new sites. Relations between flysch and underlying formations are of three types: they lie unconformably on their substratum (these areas are rarely preserved), they follow conformably upon pelagic shales and limestones, or they develop gradually, via the ill-defined "pre-Flysch", out of Bündnerschiefer. At any rate, flysch sedimentation is contemporaneous with compressive and transcurrent deformation, so that tectonically "static" models cannot always be applied (see Homewood and Caron, 1982).

As flysch often occurs in detachment nappes, underlain only by tectonosedimentary mélanges or wildflysch (see Bayer, in press), it is difficult to assign a definite paleogeographic origin to each nappe. In the Swiss Alps and their vicinity, the following scheme has recently been proposed:

Ultrahelvetic Flysch (Tertiary) — north of a "marginal high" (Homewood, 1974).
Niesen Flysch (Maestrichtian to Lower Eocene) — south of the same high.
Prätigau Flysch (Upper Cretaceous to Lower Eocene) — south of an intra-Valais high (Adula rise?)
Rheno-Danubic Flysch (Cretaceous, in the east also Tertiary) — north of the Brianconnais rise.
Gurnigel-Schlieren Flysch (Maestrichtian to Lower Eocene) — external part of Piemont basin, south of a prolongation of the Acceglio rise?
Helminthoid and Simme Flyschs (Upper Cretaceous) — north of the Austroalpine/internal Piemont complex, consolidated and partly emerged during the Cretaceous folding.

This tentative scheme does not furnish an altogether satisfactory picture (see also p. 155). Some flysch units, such as the Feuerstätt nappe of western Austria (similar position to Niesen?) or the Wägital Flysch of central Switzerland (Valais or Piemont belt?) cannot be located in this simple paleogeographic pattern.

The position of the Rheno-Danubic Flysch of the Eastern Alps is fairly well established. Hesse (1973) has convincingly shown that its Aptian–Albian part was deposited immediately to the north of the Tasna nappe, i.e. of the northern slope of the Brianconnais rise. Similarities between younger terms of the Rheno-Danubic and the Helminthoid Flysch (Caron et al., 1981) are thus more probably due to a convergence of depositional mechanisms in two separate flysch basins. The Schlieren-Gurnigel Flysch, formerly regarded as Ultrahelvetic or North-Penninic, is almost certainly of more internal origin, at least from south of the Brianconnais rise (Caron, 1976; Caron et al., 1980). This, of course, raises the question of the importance and timing of Cretaceous deformation in the Piemont realm: if it did affect the entire basin, it must be of pre-Maestrichtian, possibly even of pre-Cenomanian age.

Other evidence points to a very early (Albian-Cenomanian) date of major thrusting. In the Cenomanian, the Northern Calcareous Alps were already lying upon (or next to) the south-Penninic Arosa Zone (Müller, 1973; Burger, 1978). However, the youngest sediments in the Lower Austroalpine nappes of the Upper Engadine are also of Cenomanian age (Roesli, 1946). Quite possibly, the Northern Calcareous Alps moved in from the east or southeast rather than from the south. Turonian (pre-Gosau) movements are of great importance in the Austroalpine nappes, possibly in the Piemont and even in the Valais belt;

they are also evident far to the west, in the Devoluy mountains.

Some radiometric data point to still older, Early Cretaceous (120–110 m.y.) events (Hanson et al., 1969). Their nature is still quite conjectural; it is not impossible that they relate to transcurrent rather than compressive movements. Other data, among others from high-pressure assemblages, give very late Cretaceous or even Paleocene (75–60 m.y.) apparent ages. Here also, many questions are open.

The Helvetic margin, deeply submerged from the Albian, i.e. from the beginning of crustal shortening, onwards, rose above sea-level at the end of the Cretaceous, to become again flooded by shallow seas from the south-east during the Upper Paleocene and the Eocene. Along with some other, rather circumstantial lines of evidence, the author (1973) has interpreted this regression as a sign of remission of subduction at the turn from the Cretaceous to the Tertiary ("Paleocene restoration"); this hypothesis needs further confirmation or rebuttal.

The direction of Cretaceous subduction is also under discussion. The main subduction zone, in the southern part of the Piemont belt, was almost certainly inclined to the south (dal Piaz et al., 1972; Trümpy, 1975). A north-dipping subduction north of the Gurnigel Flysch basin (then still regarded as "Ultrahelvetic") was postulated by Hsü and Schlanger, 1971); but there is little other evidence to corroborate this hypothesis.

The source areas for the Alpine flysch formations raise very thorny problems. Some remarks on this question will be made in the last chapter.

G. Collision (Mid-Eocene to Present)

This is the time of the meso-Alpine and neo-Alpine deformations, accompanied by basaltic-andesitic Taveyannaz volcanism, followed by metamorphism, emplacement of granitoid bodies, uplift and late transcurrent and dip-slip faulting. The correlated sediments are the latest flyschs, restricted to the northern margin of the deformed belt, and the molasse. They will not be discussed in this paper.

III. Paleotethys and Tethys

There is general agreement on the existence of a Paleozoic eastern Paleotethys, a vast gulf of Panthalassa. This ocean (if indeed it was a true ocean), or large parts of it, was consumed, presumably in a Paleocimmerian-Indosinian subduction scar. In the Jurassic, a new ocean or new oceans opened, along a new emplacement near the northern margin of Paleotethys (e.g. Sengör, 1979). This Jurassic–Cretaceous ocean has been called Tethys (in the strict sense, or Mesogea (Biju-Duval et al., 1977).

The relations between Paleotethys and Tethys are apparently rather complex. There is still some uncertainty as to when and where Paleotethys (or major parts of it) was subducted. The Major Caucasus appears to be a rather unlikely location for major Jurassic subductions: the tremendously thick Lower Jurassic to Bajocian shale formations, comparable to those of the Dauphiné belt, link the main range to the Swanetian massif and the latter to the Dziroula block (Paffengol'c, 1963). Northern Iran, the Lesser Caucasus and northern Anatolia are probably or possibly areas of major Eocimmerian shortening, but westwards the traces of late Paleozoic-early Mesozoic subduction become increasingly indistinct.

Looking at the problem from the side of the western Mediterranean area, there does not seem to be a major break between Paleotethys and Tethys stages, but rather a gradual evolution from the one to the other. Paleotethys (as a sea, not as an ocean) reached to the south-eastern part of the Alps, to Sicily and to Tunisia in the Early Permian; after a mid-Permian regression, Late Permian seas again advanced slightly further west. All during the Triassic, we witness continuous expansion of shallow seas, which finally reached westwards to the internal zones of the Betic Cordilleras. During the Early Jurassic, this vast carbonate belt was disintegrated by normal faulting, and the basins became wider and deeper.

As already stated, the Early Jurassic to early Middle Jurassic episode of rifting has many features in common with the early stages of passive continental margins. But it is a curious continental margin, as the Paleotethys ocean is very far away to the east (in Turkey?), and uncertain even there. On the whole the Early Jurassic Tethys (or Late Paleotethys?) appears as a wedge-shaped expanse of deep but not oceanic seas, possibly — as Daniel Bernoulli has suggested orally — comparable to the pre-oceanic stage of the Bay of Biscay (Montadert *et al.*, 1977), or, in the terminology of Carey (1958), to an incipient sphenochasm.

Thus, there is a very long preparatory, Paleotethys-oriented evolution before the mid-Jurassic opening of the oceanic, Atlantic-oriented Tethys. This oceanic spreading was largely discordant to the pre-oceanic paleogeographic pattern, but not entirely so: features like the Briançonnais rise or the Lower Austroalpine rise are inherited from the Triassic–Lower Jurassic structures and may themselves have been prefigured by much older, late Variscan trends.

Not only the Tethys, but the Atlantic as well has had a long preparatory history, going back to the earliest post-Pangaea rifting (mid-Permian origin of the East Greenland rift) and continuing with increasing rifting and non-oceanic subsidence both along the future Atlantic and in its offshoots such as the North Sea basins (see e.g. Ziegler, 1981).

When Tethys and the Atlantic finally became oceanic and joined, sometime in the middle of the Jurassic, both had gone through a long previous evolution. If we ascribe the pre-oceanic rifting phase of both Atlantic and Tethys to a continental-margin type of environment, it was a continental margin without an ocean (in the case of the Atlantic) or with a far-away, elusive ocean (in the case of Tethys Paleotethys). One might just as well simply talk of complex basins.

IV. The Nature of the Alpine Oceans

As already stated, oceanic crust was produced from mid-Jurassic to mid-Cretaceous time, over a span of some 60 m.y. The nature and extent of Alpine spreading is rather difficult to assess, as large parts of these oceanic basins were consumed by Tertiary and especially Cretaceous subductions.

There can be no doubt about the direct relation between the opening of the Atlantic and the opening of the Alpine oceanic troughs. The extent of Alpine spreading depends on the question whether the Atlantic opening was taken up entirely by the western oceanic areas (especially the Piemont-Ligurian ocean) or whether it was also compensated inth Dinaric-Hellenic troughs. The Atlantic history implies important, presumably sinistral, transcurrent movements during the mid-Jurassic to Cretaceous opening and also during its Cretaceous extension northward to the sphenochasm of the Bay of Biscay.

Thus, any reconstruction of the Alpine oceans has to take into account external evidence. In this paper, we simply want to assess the internal evidence furnished by Alpine paleogeography itself.

A spreading ridge has hitherto not been found in the Alps. This does not in itself exclude the former existence of such spreading axes, as they may have disappeared through subduction. At any rate, the existence of orthogonal, present-Atlantic type spreading is neither proved nor disproved.

Typical ophiolite sequences are rare in the Alps, except for some occurrences in the Western Alps. Generally, only isolated bodies of ultramafic and mafic rocks are found. They are interpreted as dismembered tectonic fragments or slivers of a once complete ophiolite suite. But this explanation may not hold in all instances. Statistically, there is an over-representation of serpentinites and an under-representation of pillow lavas and especially gabbros. Sheeted dikes have not been described, but may be difficult to recognize when affected by deformation and metamorphism.

On the other hand, there are thick Bündnerschiefer sequences with abundant intercalations of metabasalt (prasinite) and occasional gabbros. Most of these "greenstones" very probably represent sill-like intrusions into soft sediment, as suggested by Kelts (1981) in analogy to similar occurrences in the Gulf of California. Good descriptions were given by Nabholz (1945) and Loubat (1968). Formerly, these rocks were also subsumed under the term "ophiolites", but they lack the typical association and do not represent truly oceanic basement. We have called them "ophiolitoids". Emplacement of the ophiolitoids may have begun earlier (Early Jurassic) than the formation of true ophiolites (i.e. of new oceanic crust) and also seems to have stopped with the onset of compression. Bündnerschiefer with ophiolitoids overlie shallow-water Triassic and Lower Jurassic deposits, and were apparently deposited over thinned or anomalous (high-density) continental crust. They occur in the Valais trough and in the external part of the Piemont trough (e.g. Avers Bündnerschiefer).

Furthermore, the Alpine oceans are studded with "ribbon continents", with narrow rises of perhaps 20 to 100 km width, underlain by continental basement. The Briançonnais rise is the most prominent of these, but not the only one; others occur within the Valais belt (e.g. Adula rise) and within the Piemont belt (e.g. Margna rise). None of these rises represent volcanic arcs. Flysch with volcanic débris is also rare in the Alps.

Was there only one true ocean, the Ligurian-Piemont trough, in the Alps, or were there several? This is a matter of dispute, and almost of faith. A similar discussion is under way in the Hellenic chains. To the tenants of the "one-ocean" school (e.g. Laubscher, 1975; Laubscher and Bernoulli, 1977), the Valais belt is a mere marginal basin, a somewhat anomalous part of the European continental margin; it has even been linked, in spite of the great difference of geological history, to the Ultrahelvetic-Dauphiné trough.

Looking only at the Western Alps, this interpretation (though not the Valais-Dauphiné lumping) is defensible. Here, indeed, the margin of the Tethys seems to lie east of the Briançonnais platform (Bourbon *et al.*, 1977; Lemoine, 1975). In Valais, the Valais trough starts to widen; it contains ophiolitoids. Apparently, it developed only during the Lower Cretaceous.

In Graubünden, the Valais belt* has swollen to some 200 km and contains not only Cretaceous but also Jurassic Bündnerschiefer (Pantić and Gansser, 1977). True ophiolites appear in the most internal part of the belt (e.g. Ramoz Zone of the Lower Engadine window, Trümpy, 1972). Thus, the Valais belt becomes wider, older and more oceanic eastwards. By extrapolation, one is led to attribute the Bündnerschiefer of the Tauern window to the Valais rather than to the Piemont belt, if indeed the two were still separated by the

---

* "Valais belt" is here of course taken in its original sense (Haug, 1925), comprising the entire zone between the Ultrahelvetic and the Briançonnais s.l. The restriction of the term to only part of this belt (Nabholz, in Bolli *et al.*, 1980) is not justified.

Briançonnais rise that far east. The higher Bündnerschiefer nappes of the Tauern (Glockner zone) contain ophiolites, but one certainly cannot equate *a priori* oceanic character with the assignment to the Piemont realm. The Hochstegenkalk rise (Frisch, 1975), to the north of the Tauern Bündnerschiefer basins, may occupy a position comparable to the Adula rise (Probst, 1980).

A proposed connection between the formation of the Valais trough and the sinistral Pyrenean shear (Laubscher and Bernoulli, 1977; Frisch, 1977) does not appear to be probable, as the Valais basin already existed by Middle Jurassic or late Early Jurassic time. In our opinion, an eventual prolongation of the Pyrenean translation zone should be sought further to the south (Trümpy, 1976).

If the Valais trough widens eastwards, the Piemont trough, on the contrary, becomes narrower, though not necessarily less oceanic, in the same direction. Assuming an origin of the Schams nappes ($\pm$ Briançonnais) from below the Tambo nappe (Streiff, 1962), the Piemont realm would consist of three paleogeographic units in central Graubünden: the Avers Bündnerschiefer (with ophiolitoids) and the Malenco ophiolite complex to the north, the intraoceanic Margna rise, and the frankly oceanic Platta nappe to the south. If the Schams nappes were derived from the Margna swell, as upheld by many authors, the Piemont trough would be reduced to the Platta nappe alone. In the Lower Engadine, at any rate, the Piemont realm is only represented by a thin zone of mélange-type rocks, including ophiolites, between the Tasna nappe ($\pm$ Briançonnais) and the Austroalpine units.

One may wonder whether this apparent narrowing eastwards of the Piemont belt is a primary feature or whether it is simply due to increasing Cretaceous subduction in the east. The lack of nappes expelled from the subduction scar, the presence of Eocene rocks in the Lower Engadine window (Rudolf, in Oberhauser et al., 1980) and certain facies analogies between the Tasna nappe and the Austroalpine nappes (see below) are points in favour of the first hypothesis.

The Briançonnais ribbon continent is one of the most prominent features of Alpine paleogeography. In the Western Alps, its breadth was estimated at 50 km (Bourbon et al., 1977); but, together with its unknown western margin and its complex eastern margin (Acceglio zone) it may easily have measured 100 km across. There are considerable facies changes not only across but also along the strike. Nevertheless, the Briançonnais belt must have been fairly continuous from the Mediterranean to eastern Graubünenden, over a distance of 600 km, as attested by strong facies analogies from Liguria to the type Briançonnais, thence to the Vanoise mountains of Savoy, thence to the Prealps, thence to the klippen of central Switzerland and thence to the Sulzfluh nappe of northern Graubünden. The more northerly Falknis nappe, corresponding to the northern slope of the Briançonnais rise, also correlates closely to the Tasna nappe of the Engadine window. No certain equivalents are known from the Tauern window. In the Western Alps, the Briançonnais belt is certainly close to the European continental margin; but in eastern Graubünden it appears to be much closer to the Adriatic-Apulian margin. There are undoubted analogies between the pre-spreading (pre-Middle- Jurassic) rocks of the Tasna nappe and those of the Austroalpine units. For instance, the basement granites and rhyolites of the Tasna nappe and of the boulders in the Upper Jurassic of the Falknis nappe are very similar to the granitoids of the Lower Austroalpine Err nappe (Wenk, 1962; Gruner, 1982), and also the red Lower Jurassic limestones of the Tasna and Austroalpine nappes (H. Furrer, personal communication), are closely comparable. The post-spreading (Upper Jurassic and Cretaceous) formations of the Tasna-Falknis-Sulzfluh

nappes and of the Lower Austroalpine nappes are quite different from each other.*

Thus, the Briançonnais microcontinent ran obliquely to Alpine paleogeographic trends, and crossed most of the Alpine oceanic realm between the Savoy and the eastern Graubünden traverses, suggesting dextral shear at the time of birth of the oceanic basins (mid-Jurassic), in accordance with the views of Biju-Duval et al. (1977). Sinistral shear should be expected in later (Cretaceous) times, in connection with the Iberian rotation.

Dietrich (1976) and Lemoine (1980) have commented on the implications of transform faulting during the oceanic stage of Alpine evolution. The occurrence of serpentinite immediately associated with sediments, including serpentinite breccias and the large proportion of ophicalcite, both point to a very strong, indeed dominating, role of lateral translations, as opposed to orthogonal spreading, in the genesis of Alpine oceans. The widespread occurrence of radiolarian cherts overlying ophiolite complexes may also point in this direction; in the classical theory of ocean-floor spreading, one would expect pelagic limestones in this position. The lozenge-shaped Alpine oceanic basins (or "rhombochasms") can be largely interpreted as resulting from first dextral, then sinistral shear movements. The analogy with Gulf of California, as recently pointed out by Kelts (1981), is indeed striking. The Gulf of California model is of course far from perfect — lacking, for instance, the broad carbonate shelves around the Alpine basins — but it is far more realistic, at any rate, than the once-popular "present-Atlantic" model. The early Atlantic, contemporaneous with mid-Jurassic to mid-Cretaceous Alpine spreading, may have had a different nature yet.

We have recently tried to evaluate the amount of stretching and shortening in the Graubünden section (in Debelmas et al., in press), arriving at the following figures:

Initial breadth (Triassic)	420 km
Stretching during the rifting phase, plus "proven" spreading	+ 80 km
Additional spreading (mid-J to mid-K)	+ Q km
Shortening by Cretaceous deformations	− 80 + Q km
Shortening by Tertiary deformation	− 250 km
Present breadth	170 km

The great unknown, of course, is the value of Q — oceanic crust section lost by subduction. At present, we would suggest a rather moderate figure (100 to a few hundred km). Paleomagnetic data do not yet allow a certain assessment of the difference in paleolatitudes between the two margins of the Alps.

V. The Pitfalls of "Geotraverses"

The figures just quoted provide an example both of "pseudomatics" and of our time-honoured way of reasoning along "geotraverses", by drawing palinspastic sections along a line and trying to understand the facies relationships between the different paleogeographic units. This is a necessary and unavoidable exercise.

But it should not be forgotten that it may be fraught with a number of pitfalls. It neglects the lateral movements between continental and oceanic slivers, which may lead to juxtaposition of unrelated paleogeographic units, to cutting-out of paleogeographic belts in one geotraverse and duplication in another (such as the apparent duplication of the Penninic-Austroalpine margin in the traverse of Western

---

* Gruner's suggestion that the Falknis-Sulzfluh nappes might derive from the Lower Austroalpine belt is improbable, in view of their position below an ophiolite-bearing zone, the character of their post-Mesojurassic formations and especially the age of the youngest preserved sediments (Eocene in the Falknis and Sulzfluh nappes, Cenomanian in the Lower Austroalpine).

Switzerland, see Trümpy, 1976). Jurassic dextral and Cretaceous sinistral translations may have completely modified the original paleogeograhic pattern.

These transcurrent movements may also have a bearing on the difficult question of the flysch source areas. These source areas must have been large islands, composed of Mesozoic sediments but also sialic basement rocks. If we try to accommodate such islands in our palinspastic profiles, we arrive at impossible results, which would practically double the width of subducted or eroded continental basement. This would clash with the known volume of preserved sialic root (Müller *et al.*, 1980) and the volume of post-orogenic detrital sediments (Guillaume and Guillaume, 1982), even if we accounted for considerable thinning of sialic crust before subduction. Assuming considerable lateral displacements between depositional and source areas may provide a solution of the dilemma in some cases (see Crowell, 1974, for particularly striking examples from California). Thus, sinistral transcurrent movements may have transported the southerly source area of a flysch sequence far to the east of the present outcrop area of the flysch. These source areas were presumably welts consolidated and uplifted by tectonic deformation before and during flysch sedimentation.

Another source of error in palinspastic sections stems from aberrant transport direction of nappes. This applies especially to the Cretaceous (and later?) counterclockwise rotation of the Western Alps (Mattauer and Tapponier, 1978).

In spite of all these difficulties — without mentioning the disputed origin of many nappes — we must go on trying to unravel the early history of mountain chains, keeping open our minds and playing with multiple hypotheses. We must also try to understand Alpine paleogeography in the light of present-day models. But where should we take our models? Today's Atlantic will not do, the Gulf of California is not perfect. We should probably be looking to the Caribbean or to the seas around Indonesia.

Uniformitarianism at any price has its pitfalls too. We have been told that it was bad form to use the term geosyncline in these days. But in some cases it may be more honest to call a basin a geosyncline — pending its comparison with a present-day model and abstaining from mythical implications — than to assign it prematurely to some supposed actualistic equivalent with all the genetic consequences it may suggest.

References

Argand, E. (1920). Plissements précurseurs et Plissements tardifs des Chaînes de Montagnes. *Soc. Helv. Sci. Nat. Actes* **101**, sess., pt. 2, 13–39.

Arthaud, F. and Matte, P.H. (1975). Les décrochements tardihercyniens du sudouest de l'Europe, et essai de reconstruction des conditions de la déformation. *Tectonophysics* **25**, 139–171.

Assereto, R., Bosellini, A., Fantini Sestini, N. and Sweet, W.C. (1973). The Permian-Triassic boundary in the Southern Alps (Italy). *In* "Permian and Triassic Systems" (A. Logan and L.V. Hills, eds). Canad. Soc. Petroleum Geol., Calgary, pp. 176–199.

Bally, A.W., Bernoulli, D., Davis, G.A. and Montadert, L. (1981). Listric normal faults. Oceanol. Acta, 26me Congrès géol. int., Colloque géol. des marges continentales, 87–101.

Bayer, A. (in press). Untersuchungen im Habkern-Mélange ("Wildflysch") zwischen Aare und Rhein. *Beitr. z. Geol. Karle d. Schweiz.*

Bernoulli, D. and Lemoine, M. (1980). Birth and early evolution of the Tethys: the overall situation. *Mém. Bur. Rech. Géol. Min.* **115**, 168–179.

Bernoulli, D., Caron, C., Homewood, P., Kälin, O. and Van Stuijvenberg, J. (1979). Evolution of continental margins in the Alps. *Schweiz. Min. Petr. Mitt.* **59**, 165–170.

Bertrand, J. and Delaloye, M. (1976). Datation par la méthode K-Ar de diverses ophiolites du flysch des Gets (Haute-Savoie, France). *Eclogae geol. Helv.* **69/2**, 335–341.

Biju-Duval, B., Dercourt, J. and Le Pichon, X. (1977). From the Tethys Ocean to the Mediterranean Seas: a plate tectonic model of the evolution of the Western Alpine System. Int. Symp. Struct. Hist. of Mediterr. Basins, Split 1976. Technip. Paris, 143–164.

Bircher, W. (1935). Studien im oberen Bajocien der Ostschweiz (Glarnerund St. Galleralpen). Kairo (Diss. Univ. Zürich).

Bolli, H., Burri, M., Isler, A., Nabholz, W., Pantić, N. and Probst, Ph. (1980). Der nordpenninische Saum zwischen Westgraubünden und Brig. *Eclogae geol. Helv.* **73/3**, 779–797.

Bott, M.H.P. (1976). Formation of sedimentary basins of grabentype by extension of the continental crust. *Tectonophysics* **36**, 77–86.

Bourbon, M., Caron, J.M., De Graciansky, P., Lemoine, M., Megard-Galli, J. and Mercier, D. (1977). Mesozoic evolution of the Western Alps: birth and development of part of the spreading oceaic Tethys and of its European continental margin. *In* "Int. Symp. Structural Hist. of Mediterranean Basins, Split 1976" (B. Biju-Duval and L. Montadert, eds). Technip, Paris, pp. 19–34.

Burger, H. (1978). Arosa- und Madrisa-Zone im Gebiet zwischen dem Schollberg und der Verspala (Osträtikon). *Eclogae geol. Helv.* **71/2**, 255–266.

Carey, S.W. (1958). A tectonic approach to continental drift. *In* "Symposium on Continental Drift 1956, Hobart". Geol. Dept. Univ. Tasmania, pp. 177–349.

Caron, C. (1976). La nappe du Gurnigel dans les Préalpes. *Eclogae geol. Helv.* **69/2**, 297–308.

Caron, C., Homewood, P., Morel, R. and van Stuijvenberg, J. (1980). Témoins de la nappe du Gurnigel sur les Préalpes Médianes: une confirmation de son origine ultra-brianconnaise. *Bull. Soc. fribourg. Sci. nat.* **69/I**, 64–79.

Caron, C., Hesse, R., Kerckhove, C., Homewood, P., van Stuijvenberg, J., Tasse, N. and Winkler, L. (1981). Comparaison préliminaire des flyschs á Helminthoïdes sur trois transversales des Alpes. *Eclogae geol. Helv.* **74/2**, 369–378.

Castellarin, A. (1972). Evoluzione paleotettonica sinsedimentaria del limite tra "piattaforma veneta" e "bacino lombardo" a nord di Riva del Garda. *Giornale di Geologia* **2/38**, 11–212.

Castellarin, A., Lucchini, F., Rossi, P.L., Simboli, G., Bosellini, A. and Sommavilla, E. (1980). Middle Triassic magmatism in Southern Alps. II: a geodynamic model. *Riv. ital. Paleont. (Stratigr.)* **85**, 1111–1124.

de Charpal, O., Guennoc, P., Montadert, L. and Roberts, D.G. (1978). Rifting, crustal attenuation and subsidence in the Bay of Biscay. *Nature, London* **275/5682**, 706–711.

Crowell, J.C. (1974). Sedimentation along the San Andreas Fault in Southern California. *In* "Modern and Ancient Geosynclinal Sedim." (D.G. Howell, ed.) *S.E.P.M. Spec. Publ.* **19**, 292–303.

Dal Piaz, G.V., Hunziker, J. and Martinotti, G. (1972). La zona Sesia-Lanzo e l'evoluzione tettonico-metamorfica delle Alpi nordoccidentali interne. *Mem. Soc. geol. ital.* **11**, 433–460.

D'Argenio, B. and Alvarez, W. (1980). Stratigraphic evidence for crustal thickness changes on the southern Tethyan margin during the Alpine cycle. *Bull. geol. Soc. Amer.* **91/1**, 2558–2587.

Debelmas, J. (1957). Quelques remarques sur la conception actuelle du terme "Cordillère" dans les Alpes internes Francaises. *Soc. géol. France Bull. ser. 6* **7**, 463–474.

Debelmas, J. (1975). Les Alpes et la théorie des plaques. *Revue de géogr. Physique et de géologie dynamique* **17/3**, 195–208.

Decandia, F.A. and Elter, P. (1972). La "zona" ofiolitifera del Bracco nel settore compreso fra Levanto e la Val Graveglia (Appennino ligure). *Mem. Soc. geol. Ital.* **11**, 503–530.

Dewey, J.F., Pitman, W.C., Ryan, W.B.F. and Bonnin, J. (1973). Plate Tectonics and the Evolution of the Alpine System. *Bull. geol. Soc. Amer.* **84**, 3137–3180.

Didon, J., Durand-Delga, M. and Kornprobst, J. (1973). Homologies géologiques entre les deux rives du détroit de Gibraltar. *Bull. Soc. géol. France, (7)* **15**, 77–105.

Dietrich, V. (1970). Die Stratigraphie der Platta-Decke. Fazielle Zusammenhänge zwischen Oberpenninikum und Unterostalpin. *Eclogae geol. Helv.* **63/2**, 631–671.

Dietrich, V. (1976). Plattentektonik in den Ostalpen: eine Arbeitshypothese. *Geotekton. Forsch.* **50**, 1–84.

Debelmas, J., Escher, A. and Trümpy, R. (in press). Profiles through the Western Alps. Int. Geodynamics Project, Final report W.G. 9, subgroup 1.

Dollfus, S. (1965). Ueber den helvetischen Dogger zwischen Linth und Rhein. *Eclogae geol. Helv.* **58/1**, 453–554.

Ellenberger, F. (1958). Etude géologique du pays de Vanoise. *Carte géol. France mém.*, 561 pp.

Finger, W. (1975). Jurassic marine scarp breccias in the Lower Austroalpine belt of Julier Pass (Graubünden, Switzerland). IXme Congrés International de Sedimentologie, Nice, 119–124.

Finger, W. (in press). Zur Stratigraphie, Sedimentologie (insbes. der jurassischen Breccien) und Tektonik der Zone von Samedan.

Frisch, W. (1975). Hochstegen-Fazies und Grestener Fazies — ein eine Vergleich des Jura. *N. Jb. Geol. Paläont. Min.* **1975/2**, 82–90.

Frisch, W. (1977). Die Alpen im westmediterranen Orogen — eine plattentektonische Rekonstruktion. *Mitt. Ges. Geol. Bergbaustud. Oesterr.* **24**, 263–275.

Furrer, U. (1979). Stratigraphie des Doggers der östlichen Prélpes médianes. *Eclogae geol. Helv.* **72/3**, 623–672.

Graciansky, P.C. de, Bourbon, M., Charpal, O. de, Chenet, P.Y. and Lemoine, M. (1979). Genèse et evolutions comparées de deux marges continentales passives: marge ibérique de l'Océan Atlantique et marge européenne de la Téthys dans les Alpes Occidentales. *Bull. Soc. géol France (7)* **21**, 663–674.

Gruner, U. (in press). Die jurassischen Breccien der Falknis-Decke und altersäquivalente Einheiten in Graubünden. *Beitr. z. geol. K. d. Schweiz, N.F.* **154**.

Guillaume, A. and Guillaume, S. (1982). L'érosion dans les Alpes au Plio-Quaternaire et au Miocène. *Eclogae geol. Helv.*, **75/2**, 247–268.

Günzler-Seiffert, H. (1942). Persistente Brüche im Jura der Wildhorn-Decke des Berner Oberlandes. *Eclogae geol. Helv.* **34/2** (1941), 164–172.

Hanson, G.N., Grünenfelder, M. and Soptrayanova, G. (1969). The geochronology of a rechristallized tectonite in Switzerland — the Roffna gneiss. *Earth Planet. Sci. lett.* **5**, 413–22.

Haug, E. (1925). Contribution à une sythèse stratigraphique des Alpes Occidentales. *Bull. Soc. géol. France* **4/3**, 99–244.

Hesse, R. (1973). Flysch-Gault und Falknis-Tasna-Gault (Untere Kreide): Kontinuierlicher Uebergang von der distalen zur proximalen Flyschfazies auf einer penninischen Trogebene der Alpen. *Geologica et Palaeontologica* **SB 2**, 53 pp.

Homewood, P. (1974). Le flysch du Meilleret (Préalpes romandes) et ses relations avec les unités l'encadrant. *Eclogae geol. Helv.* **67/2**, 349–401.

Homewood, P. and Caron, C. (1982). Flysch of the Western Alps. Symposium on Mountain-Building Zurich/Switzerland, July 14–18, 1981.

Hsü, K.J. and Schlanger, S.O. (1971). Ultrahelvetic Flysch Sedimentation and Deformation related to Plate Tectonics. *Geol. Soc. America, Bull.* **82**, 1207–1218.

Kälin, O. and Trümpy, D.M. (1977). Sedimentation und Paläotektonik in den westlichen Südalpen: Zur triadisch-jurassischen Geschichte des Varesotto. *Eclogae geol. Helv.* **70/2**, 295–350.

Kelts, K. (1981). A comparison of some aspects of sedimentation and tectonics from the Gulf of California and the Mesozoic Tethys, Northern Penninic margin. *Eclogae geol. Helv.* **74/2**, 317–338.

Kent, P.E. (1977). The Mesozoic development of aseismic continental margins. *J. geol. Soc.* **134**, 1–18.

Laubscher, H.P. (1975). Plate boundaries and microplates in Alpine history. *Amer. J. Sci.* **275**, 865–876.

Laubscher, H. and Bernoulli, D. (1977). Mediterranean and Tethys. *In* "The Ocean Margins", Vol. 1 (A.E.M. Nairn, ed.), pp. 129–152.

Lemoine, M. (1953). Remarques sur les caractères et l'évolution de la paléogéographie de la zone briançonnaise au Secondaire et au Tertiaire. *Soc. géol. France bull., ser. 6* **3**, 105–120.

Lemoine, M. (1975). Mesozoic sedimentation and tectonic evolution of the Briançonnais Zone in the Western Alps — Possible evidence for an Atlantic-type margin between the European craton and the Tethys. 9ème Congrès international de sédimentologie, Thème 4, 211–215.

Lemoine, M. (1980). Serpentinites, gabbros and ophicalcites in the Piemont-Ligurian domain of the Western Alps: possible indicators of oceanic fracture zones and of associated serpentinization. *Archives Sci., Genève* **33/2–3**, 103–115.

Loubat, H. (1968). Etude pétrographique des ophiolites de la "Zone du Versoyen", Savoie (France), Prov. d'Aoste (Italie). *Archives Sci. Genève* **21/3**, 265–457.

Mattauer, M. and Tapponier, P.)1978). Tectonique des plaques et tectonique intra-continentale dans les Alpes franco-italiennes. *C.R. Ac. des Sciences, Paris* **287**, 899–902.

Mégard-Galli, J. and Baud, A. (1977). Le Trias moyen et supérieur des Alpes nord-occidentales et occidentales: données nouvelles et corrélations stratigraphiques. *Bull. B.R.G.M., Section* **IV/3**, 233–250.

Montadert, L., Roberts, D., Auffret, G., Bock, W., du Peuble, P., Hailwood, E., Harrison, W., Kagami, H., Lumsden, D., Muller, C., Thompson, R., Thompson, T. and Timofeev, P.P. (1977). Rifting and subsidence on passive continental margins in the North East Atlantic. *Nature, London* **268**, 305–309.

Müller, K. (1973). Das "Randcenoman" der Nördlichen Kalkalpen und seine Bedeutung für den Ablauf der ostalpinen Deckenüberschiebungen und ihrer Schubweiten. *Geol. Rundschau* **62/1**, 54–96.

Müller, S., Ansorge, J., Egloff, R. and Kissling, E. (1980). A crustal cross section along the Swiss Geotraverse from the Rhinegraben to the Po Plain. *Eclogae geol. Helv* **73/3**, 463–483.

Nabholz, W.K. (1945). Geologie der Bündnerschiefergebirge zwischen, Rheinwald, Valser- und Safiental. *Eclogae geol. Helv.* **38/1**, 122 pp.

Oberhauser, R. *et al.* (1980). Der Geologische Aufbau Oesterreichs. Springer Wien and New York, 699 pp.

Paffengol'c, K.N. (1963). Geologischer Abriss des Kaukasus. Berlin: Akademie-Verl. 1963, 351 S. Fortschritte der sowjetischen Geologie, Heft 5–6.

Pantić, N. and Gansser, A. (1977). Palynologische Untersuchungen in Bündnerschiefen. *Eclogae geol. Helv.* **70/1**, 59–81.

Pantić, N. and Isler, A. (1978). Palynologische Untersuchungen in Bündnerschiefern (II). *Eclogae geol. Helv.* **71/3**, 447–465.

Probst, Ph. (1980). Die Bündnerschiefer des nördlichen Penninikums zwischen Valser Tal und Passo di San Giacomo. *Beitr. geol. Karte Schweiz (N.F.)* **153**, 63 pp.

Roesli, F. (1946). Sedimentäre Zone von Samaden (Kt. Graubünden). *Eclogae geol. Helv.* **38/2**, 329–336.

Sengör, A.M.C. (1979). Mid-Mesozoic closure of Permo-Triassic Tethys and its implications. *Nature, London* **279**, 590–593.

Sheridan, R.E. and Gradstein, F.M. (1981). Early history of the Atlantic Ocean and gas hydrates in the Blake outer ridge. Results of the Deep Sea Drilling Project. *Episodes No. 2*, 16–22.

Smith, A. Gilbert (1971). Alpine Deformation and the Oceanic Areas of the Tethys, Mediterranean, and Atlantic. *Geol. Soc. Am. Bull.* **82**, 2039–2070.

Steinmann, G. (1925). Gibt es fossile Tiefseeablagerungen von erdgeschichtlicher Bedeutung? *Geol. Rundschau* **16/6**, 435–468.

Streiff, V. (1962). Zur östlichen Beheimatung der Klippendecken. *Eclogae geol. Helv.* **55/1**, 77–132.

Tercier, J. (1939). Dépôts marins actuels et séries géologiques. *Eclogae geol. Helv.* **32**, 47–100.

Termier, H. and Termier, G. (1956–1957). L'évolution de la lithosphère II. Orogénèse, 2 vol., 941 pp. Paris, Masson and Cie., 1956/1957.

Trümpy, R. (1955). Wechselbeziehungen zwischen Palaeogeographie und Deckenbau. *Vjschr. natf. Ges. Zürich* **100/4**, 218–231.

Trümpy, R. (1957). Quelques Problèmes de Paléogéographie Alpine. *Soc. géol. France Bull., sér 6* **7**, 443–461.

Trümpy, R. (1960). Paleotectonic evolution of the Central and Western Alps. *Geol. Soc. America Bull.* **71/6**, 843–908.

Trümpy, R. (1972). Zur Geologie des Unterengadins. *In* "Oekologische Untersuchungen im Unterengadin, Liefg. I/4". Eg. wiss. Unters. Schweiz. Nationalpark, Bd. 12, pp. 71–87.

Trümpy, R. (1973). Timing of orogenic events in the Central Alps. *In* "Gravity and Tectonics" (K.A. de Jong and R. Scholten, eds). John Wiley & Sons, New York, pp. 229–251.

Trümpy, R. (1975). Penninic-Austroalpine Boundary in the Swiss Alps: A Presumed Former Continental Margin and its Problems. *Amer. J. Sci.* **275–A**, 209–238.

Trümpy, R. (1976). Du Pèlerin aux Pyrénées. *Eclogae geol. Helv.* **69/2**, 249–264.

Wenk, E. (1962). Einige Besonderheiten des unterostalpinen Kristallins im Unterengadin. *Eclogae geol. Helv* **55/2**, 457–460.

Wildi, W. (1981). Le Ferrysch: cône de sédimentation détritique en eau profonde à la bordure nord-ouest de l'Afrique au Jurassique moyen à supérieur (Rif externe, Maroc). *Eclogae geol. Helv.* **74/2**, 481–527.

Ziegler, P.A. (1981). Evolution of sedimentary basins in North-West Europe. *In* "Petroleum Geol. of the Cont. Shelf of N.-W. Europe". Inst. of Petroleum, London, pp. 3–39.

Flysch of the Western Alps

P. Homewood and C. Caron

Institute of Geology,
Fribourg, Switzerland

Abstract

Flysch of the Western Alps is defined, cursorily described, and contrasted with older Alpine scarp breccias, wildflysch and younger Molasse deposits. The character of Flysch basins is deduced from hemipelagic shales and palaeogeography, whereas the nature of detrital sources is reconstructed from clast types. Oceanographical, sedimentological and tectonic controls of Flysch deposition are discussed, and the relationships between Flysch sedimentation and Alpine mountain building are speculated on.

I. Introduction

A. Alpine Flysch

Flysch formations of the Alps (Studer, 1827; Kerckhove, 1980; Trümpy, 1980) are invariably detrital, deep-marine (bathyal or abyssal) "turbidite" deposits (Matter *et al.* 1980). "Turbidite" is taken here in the wider sense of the word, including all the various types of accumulation deposited by sediment gravity flow processes. These include turbidity currents as one member (Middleton and Hampton, 1976). The turbidites, which are interbedded with thin hemipelagic marls or clays, generally contain clastics derived from exposed land areas. These generally lay adjacent to or within the Tethyan realm but a subordinate quantity of detritus came from intrabasinal sources.

Flysch, which are specific Late Cretaceous or Paleogene homotaxial formations within the Alps (Hsü, 1970), appear fairly late in the history of the Tethyan realm, by which time alpine diastrophism had led to the constriction or even elimination of previously formed oceanic basins.

It is significant that turbidite sequences related to the earlier stages of diastrophism (Trias-Early Cretaceous) which were characterized by extensional movements (rifting followed by spreading of oceanic crust, Trümpy, 1973; Argyriadis *et al.*, 1980) are not considered to be Flysch in the parlance of alpine geologists. Why? For geologists not acquainted with the Alps, or from a purely sedimentological point of view, this conundrum is most easily solved by the abandonment of the term Flysch (Stanley, 1979). However, the equation of Flysch with turbidites or deep-sea fans (a result in part of the use of *flysch* to designate a *turbidite facies*) is overly simplistic. The key to the problem resides in the nature of the sediments themselves – the particularity of facies was recognized by the early authors even though they lacked the tools required for interpretation.

The aim of our contribution, by means of a somewhat general review of the Flysch of the Western Alps, is to sketch out the basic characteristics of Flysch deposits. The nature of both source areas and depositional environments, as well as the presiding controls, can be deduced in part from the very same sediments; this information, combined with independent evidence from structural geology, metamorphic petrology, geochronology and regional geology, can provide some objective insight into the close relationship between alpine mountain building and the accumulation of Flysch. It is this relationship which governs the salient distinctions between Flysch and other turbidite sequences.

B. Flysch Units of the Western Alps

Flysch formations (see Table I for those mentioned in the text) occur in each of the main structural units or nappes. They may be the younger parts of cover sequences, or they may form décollement nappes. Flysch were therefore deposited virtually throughout the Tethyan realm at various times, although caution is required since palaeogeography underwent continuous modification, particularly during times of Flysch sedimentation (Trümpy, 1980, p. 30). As a corollary, Flysch formations are frequently referred to either by using the name corresponding structural units (e.g. Ultrahelvetic, Niesen, Médianes) or in a more general way by using a palaeogeographical term (Helvetic, Ultrahelvetic, Valais, Briançonnais, Piemont-Ligurian). The disadvantage of the latter usage obviously stems from the progressive modification of the palaeogeographical pattern already mentioned. In a more detailed manner, local formational names are used, but these are too numerous to be given here.

II. Alpine Turbidite Facies

A. Flysch

1. *Petrography*

All Flysch units contain turbidites with a wide spectrum of

Table I Flysch sequences referred to in the text

Palaeogeographic Zone	Flysch Units, French Alps		Flysch Units, Western Swiss Alps
Foreland Platform	Annot	Champsaur	Gres du Val d'Illiez (Cucloz, Goldegg, Spierberg)
Helvetic Platform — (Dauphinois)			Taveyanne
Ultrahelvetic Basin	Aiguilles d'Arves		Ultrahelvetic (Valerette, Orsay)
			(Sardona, Central Alps)
Valais Trough	Tarentaise		Niesen
Briançonnais Platform (Including Sub-Briançonnais)	Briançonnais		North Penninic Melange (Zone Submediane) Medianes
Piemont-Ligurian Ocean	Autapie, Parpaillon (With Crevoux Pic) Serenne		Voirons, Gurnigel, Schlieren Helminthoid Flysch Simme Flysch (Mocausa, Rodomonts) Gets Flysch

grain-size, from rudites to lutites, although most are characterized by fairly stable relative proportions of conglomerate, sandstone and shale. To some extent this is due to the post-depositional structural dismembering and separation of proximal from distal deposits. In other cases distinct relationships between grain-size, sediment type and pattern of fan growth suggests a greater individuality of Flysch units, the conglomeratic Niesen Flysch (Lombard, 1972) being a typical example.

Conglomerates, which are invariably polygenic (petromict orthoconglomerates, Pettijohn, 1975), not only delineate regional grain-size variations, but also provide a precise information on provenance. In some cases Variscan basement complexes and earlier Mesozoic cover sequences of "subsident margin" type have been reconstructed (Niesen and Ultrahelvetic Flysch, Homewood, 1974), whereas in others, composite clastic stocks are shown to derive from a mobile belt and an adjacent stable craton (Schlieren Flysch, Winkler, 1981b), or from within the mobile belt alone (Helvetic Flysch, Sawatzki, 1975). Particular microfacies or their associations suggest palaeogeographical provinces or parenthood of source areas for now widely dispersed allochthonous units (Apennines, Montferrat, Prealps; Simme Flysch, Elter *et al.*, 1966; Ultrahelvetic and Niesen Flysch, Homewood, 1974). In the case of the Niesen nappe, the addition through time of clasts from deeper stratigraphic horizons indicates progressive erosion in the source area.

Sandstones usually fall within the litharenite, feldspathic litharenite or lithic arkose classes of Folk (1968) (Fig. 1). Their compositions can in general be correlated with clast types in proximal conglomeratic facies. In some cases, however, for example the Sardona quartzite (Ruefli, 1959), composition does not follow this general rule, and it is evident that unusual terrigenous sources were occasionally tapped (this reasoning is taken further in Chapter 1-6).

Heavy mineral spectra vary widely from one Flysch unit to another, but remain constant within particular units at any given time. Four basic assemblages appear from comparison of the different Flysch sandstones. A chromite-dominated assemblage, related to ophiolite detritus, characterizes the early Flysch of the Simme nappe, Swiss Alps

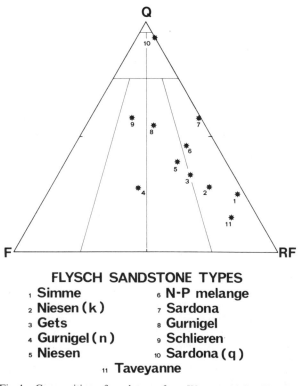

FLYSCH SANDSTONE TYPES

1 **Simme**   6 **N-P melange**
2 **Niesen (k)**   7 **Sardona**
3 **Gets**   8 **Gurnigel**
4 **Gurnigel (n)**   9 **Schlieren**
5 **Niesen**   10 **Sardona (q)**
11 **Taveyanne**

Fig. 1   Composition of sandstones from Western Alpine Flysch: 1. Simme, 2. Niesen (Cretaceous), 3. Gets, 4. Gurnigel (Niremont area), 5. Niesen (Tertiary), 6. North-Penninic mélange, 7. Sardona (Maastrichtian), 8. Gurnigel (Gurnigel area), 9. Schlieren, 10. Sardona quartzite, 11. Taveyanne.

(Flück, 1973), whereas the majority of Senonian and Palaeogene Flysch units are dominated by a Tourmaline-Zircon association, related to Variscan cratonic sources (Flück, 1973; Van Stuijvenberg, 1979; Morel, 1980; Winkler, 1981; T. Ackermann, personal communication). The Flysch of the Gets nappe, which overlies an ophiolite-bearing mélange formation (Perrières series, Caron, 1972) has no chromite, but contains abundant apatite. In the Schlieren Flysch (Winkler, 1981a) apatite predominance is related to volcanic input, but in the case of the Gets nappe it is problematical whether this spectrum is derived from volcanics or from metamorphic rocks. Finally, a TiO_2 group (Rutile, Anatase, Brookite) is related to abundant Permian volcanic clasts in the Niesen nappe (T. Ackermann, personal communication, 1981).

The study of light minerals has not yet allowed systematic comparison of Flysch sequences, but quartz grain thermoluminescence studies (Ivaldi, 1974) have pin-pointed likely source areas. The surface textures of quartz grains using the S.E.M. suggest various stages of pedogenesis, fluvial transport and shallow marine evolution before final deposition in deep-marine turbidites (Winkler, 1981b).

Turbiditic mudstones are either dark grey shales related to coarser detrital fractions, or are light grey calcilutites (lithified coccolith oozes in some cases) which were presumably derived from intrabasinal slopes and rises. During the Senonian period these light grey lime-mud turbidites were widespread, and in the case of the Helminthoid Flysch (Matter *et al.*, 1980; Caron *et al.*, 1981) they are the component common to Flysch units as widespread as the Apennines and the Western, Central and Eastern Alps.

Hemipelagic lutites are marls or clays of grey, green or ochre colour, depending on the proportions of carbonate, terrigenous clay and volcanic ash.

2. *Palaeontology*

Reworked fossils and bioclasts generally revealed an entirely normal shallow marine benthic community of molluscs, bryozoans, algae and foraminifers from the turbiditic sandstones, as well as numerous species of planktonic microfossils from the shales (Weidmann, 1967). The shale fractions have provided stratigraphically useful planktonic foraminifers, and both calcareous nannofossils and dinoflagellates have been widely used for accurate dating (Matter *et al.*, 1980).

Foraminiferal associations from hemipelagic clays or marls are quite different from those of the turbidites. Marls are characterized by planktonic species, whereas claystones contain associations of benthonic agglutinating species (Brouwer, 1965; Weidmann, 1967; Matter *et al.*, 1980). It remains debatable as to whether or not claystones with a "Rhabdammina" fauna may be interpreted as indicative of deposition below carbonate compensation depth (Moorkens, 1976; Gradstein and Berggren, 1981).

Trace fossils are abundant in Alpine Flysch deposits but, in contrast to the Carpathians (Kziazkiewicz, 1977) have not been the object of systematic study in the Western Alps. Recently, however, Crimes *et al.*, (1981) have revealed a dependence of trace fossil associations on local depositional environment, in the Gurnigel and Schlieren Flysch of Western and Central Switzerland. Higher energy, proximal sites (i.e. channels) are colonized by animals that make "shallow water" traces (*Arenicolites, Ophiomorpha, Pelecypodichnus* etc.). It is in the more distal, sandstone lobe or fan fringe environments that the spiral, meandering and network traces (e.g. *Paleodyction*), once considered to be the typical "deepwater" traces (Seilacher, 1967), predominate. It is not yet clear whether the animals whose traces are more widely known from shallow marine environments only "rode" the turbidity currents down to the proximal fan environments,

or whether they permanently colonized the substrate wherever higher energy conditions suited their way of life.

3. *Facies*

The various individual "Turbidite Facies" of Mutti and Ricci Lucchi (1975) are found in differing proportions in each of the Flysch sequences (Homewood, 1977; Matter *et al*., 1980): both organized and disorganized conglomerates and pebbly mudstones (Facies A_1 and A_2), cross-bedded sandstones (Facies B_2 and E), moderately thick sandstones with poor grading but frequent water-escape structures (Facies B_1), complete or top-missing Bouma cycles (Facies C_1 and C_2), and finally base-missing Bouma cycles (Facies D_1, D_2 and D_3).

These different facies are considered to have been deposited by sediment gravity flows (Middleton and Hampton, 1976). Lowe (1976a) has shown that the processes of fluidized flow, liquefaction and grain-flow should not be considered as important distributors of deep-sea sands, and many beds showing fluid escape structures are better considered as watery turbidites rather than as fluidized- or liquefied-flow deposits. According to LOWE (1976b) the process of grain-flow should also be considered with circumspection when interpreting sandstone and conglomerate beds.

The different turbidite facies occur in the same associations as outlined by Mutti and Ricci Lucchi (1972, 1975) and occasionally display the thinning and fining or thickening and coarsening cycles that can be related to progressive filling and abandonment of channels or to the progradation of sandstone lobes (Ricci Lucchi, 1975). Many Flysch sequences show well-arranged cyclic patterns in bed thickness, although not all of these are interpreted as due to progradation or channel filling (see Chapter 1-5). Whatever the cause of individual cyclic sequences, the general model for deep-sea fan facies and their distribution (Mutti and Ricci Lucchi, 1972, 1975; Walker, 1978; Nilsen, 1980) has provided the basis to describe and interpret the facies of Flysch sequences in the Alps.

B. Other Alpine Turbidites

1. *Jurassic scarp breccias*

In the Western Alps, the earlier stages of alpine diastrophism involved rifting and break-up of a wide, shallow platform initially overlying continental crust (Argyriadis *et al.*, 1980; Bernoulli and Lemoine, 1980; Lemoine, 1980). These stages of rifting and spreading created subsident margins with large blocks tilting and sinking along listric fault surfaces. Thus the sediments of the proximal north-Tethyan margin (Helvetics), of the distal north-Tethyan margin (Briançonnais and Pre-Piemontais) and of the distal south-Tethyan margin (preserved in the Southern Alps) all show local or more widespread occurrences of Jurassic scarp breccias. In these examples thick proximal mass-flow deposits accumulated in fairly deep marine environments grade basinward into typical turbidite sequences (Trümpy, 1975b; Kerchkhove, 1980; Weidmann, 1972; Hendry, 1969; Bernoulli *et al.*, 1979).

Jurassic scarp breccias are mostly litharenites, composed of detritus eroded from some Lower Jurassic limestones and shaly limestones, but mainly from Triassic platform carbonates and basal quartzites, together with a subordinate amount of clasts from the Variscan basement. Herein lies a major difference between the scarp breccias and the later Flysch turbidites. Flysch normally contains a higher proportion of clasts from Variscan basement complexes, but more significantly, abundant shale clasts (the smaller clasts often constituting a pseudomatrix) and mud from the erosion of Mid-Jurassic and younger mudstones deposited in the newly-formed basins.

Consequently, not only do these scarp-breccias occur at a different, earlier stratigraphic level than do the Flysch formations, but they also display a somewhat different petrography. Nevertheless, they constitute typical fan deposits and some of these are particularly well documented from the Brèche nappe of the Prealps (Lugeon, 1896, Hendry, 1969; Weidmann, 1972; Wicht, 1979).

2. *Oligocene Molasse*

There is no general transition from Flysch to Molasse in the Western Alps. As a rule, Flysch deposits were palaeogeographically restricted to the Tethyan realm, whereas Molasse deposits were deposited on the Alpine foreland. The only exception to this rule is the region of the "hinge" between the foreland on the one hand and the "geosyncline" on the other, where there is a gradual passage in both space and time from the youngest and northernmost Flysch (north-Helvetic Flysch; Vuagnat, 1952; Gasser, 1968; Siegenthaler, 1972; Matter *et al.*, 1980) to the southernmost Molasse deposits. The latter are now stacked up as imbricate thrust slices which make up the Subalpine Molasse (Trümpy 1980, Matter *et al.* 1980).

The lowermost formation of the French–Swiss "Subalpine Molasse" is the Lower Marine Molasse of Rupelian age, which has been studied near Annecy (Savoie, France, Rigassi, 1957), in the Swiss Val d'Illiez (Schroeder and Ducloz, 1955), near Vaulruz (Mornod, 1946) and near Lucerne (Matter *et al.*, 1980) as well as farther east in Switzerland. The Group is a regressive sequence in which wave-built shoreline sandstones (Bonneville, Carrières, Vaulruz and Horw Sandstones) prograde over shallow-marine mudstones with intercalated beds of storm sandstones (Homewood, 1978; Diem, 1981). Within the lower part of the shale sequence, turbiditic gravels, sands and muds filled channels and formed depositional lobes below wave base, but probably not much deeper. These are the Grès du Val d'Illiez, Cucloz, Goldegg and Spierberg Sandstones (Vuagnat, 1952; Mornod, 1946; Blau, 1966; Gasser, 1966; Matter *et al.*, 1980). The deposits are interpreted as delta-front turbidites, fed axially (SW to NE) to the residual, not-so-deep-marine seaway along the northern rim of the rising Alps (cf. Siegenthaler, 1972). From both palaeogeographical and sedimentological points of view, these sediments constitute the only transition from Flysch to Molasse.

C. Wildflysch

Wildflysch (Kaufmann, 1886 initiated the use of the term) designates chaotic formations comprising clasts of all sizes and any lithology, but often including turbidites, within a shaly matrix, the whole being tectonised to a variable degree. These formations are widespread throughout the Alps, both within the décollement nappes (Caron, 1966; Kerckhove, 1969) and within the Penninic zone (Caron, 1977; Marthaler, 1981), so there is not only one "Wildflysch" in the Alps any more than there is one "Flysch".

The décollement nappes of the French–Swiss Prealps provide the widest variety of wildflysch formations. These formations can be classified according to their present occurrence, and their origin or place of formation (many have been tectonically displaced subsequently). *Supra-Helvetic* wildflysch are the Plaine-Morte (Furrer, 1962; Homewood, 1976), Habkern (Kaufmann, 1886; Gigon, 1952) and some of those from the French Annes and Sulens Klippes (Caron *et al.*, 1967); *Infra-Prealpine* wildflysch are represented by the Chantemerle wildflysch (Matter *et al.*, 1980; Weidmann *et al.*, in preparation), the Bodevena wildflysch (Guillaume, 1957) and the Seligraben wildflysch (Van Stuijvenberg, 1979); *North-Penninic* wildflysch comprise the Zone Submédiane (Weidmann *et al.*, 1976) and probably the Gros Plané Zone

(Morel, 1976); *Mid-Penninic* wildflysch, overlying the Médianes and Brèche nappes are known as "wildflysch à lentilles de Couches rouges" (Caron, 1966; Badoux; 1962); *South-Penninic* wildflysch are located within the Simme and Gets nappes, making up part of the Manche and Perrières series (Caron, 1972).

Dating these formations has proved difficult. Individual rock-fragments (olistoliths, clasts or slices) show a wide spectrum of Mesozoic or Caenozoic ages. Presumed matrix often turns out to be a pseudo-matrix of shale clasts, older than some of the other clasts, or to be sterile.

Inventories of clasts types often suggest several incompatible combinations for a given age, indicating that different rock sequences have been broken up and mixed to form the resulting whole. In other cases the material is disrupted from one coherent original sequence. This allows a distinction between "heterogeneous" and "homogeneous" wildflysch types.

The debate about the possible sedimentary or tectonic origin of wildflysch is not restricted to alpine cases alone, but is extended to the "mélange" problem in general (Silver and Beutner 1980). Where we are concerned, it suffices to say that in the Alps an undeniable sedimentary origin can be demonstrated in a few cases (e.g. Kerckhove, 1969), whereas more generally, subsequent tectonic shearing has masked possible earlier relationships between clasts and matrix. In some other cases a very definite tectonic mixing produced the wildflysch (Weidmann *et al.*, 1976).

Grouping of the different wildflysch according to their content (homogeneous, heterogeneous), predominant process of formation (sedimentary, tectonic) and relationship with underlying rock units (stratigraphic, tectonic) provides two categories. The Supra-Helvetic and Mid-Penninic wildflysch are simple, homogeneous, predominantly sedimentary (sheared olisthostromes) and with their stratigraphic relationships to the underlying rock units preserved. The north-Penninic and south-Penninic wildflysch, on the other hand, are complex, heterogeneous, largely tectonic (at least during later phases of formation) and their relationships to the underlying rock units are tectonic. The Infra-Prealpine wildflysch fall within both categories.

III. Flysch Basins

A. Successive Flysch Basins of the Tethyan Ocean

Flysch considered to have been deposited in the Piedmont-Ligurian ocean (Trümphy, 1980; Kerckhove, 1980) range in age from Turonian (Simme Flysch) through Senonian (Gets and Helminthoid Flysch) up to Eocene (younger horizons of Gurnigel and Schlieren Flysch). The individual basins were apparently floored, at an earlier stage at least, by oceanic crust which had been accreted mainly during Jurassic spreading, according to isotopic ages of ophiolites from the Gets nappe (Fontignie *et al.*, 1980). However, much of this oceanic crust was probably already consumed, constricting the overall basin size, by Palaeogene times (see Chapter 1-7). Hemipelagic clays certainly indicate deposition below carbonate compensation depth for Helminthoid Flysch of both the French and Swiss Alps as well as for the Gurnigel and Schlieren Flysch, throughout their accumulation. In addition, chromite, presumed to be derived from ophiolites, is abundant in the Simme Flysch.

The extremely widespread occurrence of Helminthoid Flysch (Stanley, 1973; Caron *et al.*, 1981) suggests a wide basin interspersed with numerous intrabasinal rises and submerged banks, which must have been located above calcite compensation depth, and where pelagic carbonate mud accumulated. Such morphological features must be postulated to explain the origin of the lime-mud turbidites which are not accompanied by shallow carbonate platform material.

As these different Flysch units succeed each other in time, it is tempting to relate them to each other in an oversimplified vertical pile, with the Helminthoid Flysch overlying the Simme Flysch and with the Gurnigel and Schlieren sandstone fan facies overlying the Helminthoid Flysch. Indeed, the earlier Maastrichtian sequences of these otherwise "sandy" Flysch do closely resemble the Helminthoid Flysch facies (Caron *et al.*, 1981; Van Stuijvenberg, work in progress). The Gets Flysch would be an easterly (Swiss) equivalent to the French Crévoux Pic sandstones, a submarine fan facies more proximal to the "Helminthoid basin" margin than the typically basin plain type facies of the more classical Helminthoid Flysch. This simple vertical pile hypothesis is supported by the occurrence of conglomerates similar to those of the Simme Flysch within the Helminthoid Flysch of the Prealps (Colerin conglomerate, Caron *et al.*, 1981). Pebble types of these conglomerates are notably analogous to those of South-Alpine distal margin sequences, with clasts of radiolarian chert, Maiolica limestones and so on (Mocausa conglomerate, Elter *et al.*, 1966).

Whatever the original vertical or laterally adjacent disposition of these sequences, complex deformation must have preceded their present stacking, which seems to have shuffled any previous logical order.

B. Basins of the Northern Tethyan Margin

1. *Distal margin*

The Briançonnais and Pre-Piemontais palaeogeographical realms are currently compared with distal continental margins of the Atlantic Ocean (Bourbon, 1980; Graciansky *et al.*, 1980) Tensional movements with subordinate strike-slip (Caron *et al.*, 1976) governed morphology of tilted fault blocks up to Palaeocene times. Flysch was deposited over this area from early or middle Eocene times, when pelagic limestones and marls rich in planktonic foraminifers (indicating deposition above carbonate compensation depth) were swamped by influx of terrigenous clastics. These Flysch sequences accumulated at bathyal depths, but rapidly passed into olisthostrome deposits and wildflysch, confirming the late Eocene emplacement of an allochthon composed of more internal Flysch units (Gurnigel and Helminthoid Flysch).

2. *Intermediate Trough*

The Valais Trough, possibly originating by transform movements during the Jurassic (Homewood, 1977), accommodated Flysch deposits in one or several distinct basins during the early stages of the Late Cretaceous. These Flysch are now incorporated into the North-Penninic mélange (Weidmann *et al.*, 1976; Homewood, 1977). This mélange also contains Flysch sequences from various basins of Late Cretaceous and Palaeogene age. The Niesen Flysch (Lombard, 1972) of the Prealps and St Cristophe Flysch of the Tarentaise Zone (Antoine, 1972) are the best preserved sequences from the Valais trough in the Western Alps. The Niesen Flysch, at least, has hemipelagic clays indicating deposition below carbonate compensation depth, but these deep basins narrowed to the west and disappeared to the south-west in the French Alps. They widened however to the east, where small "Gulf of California"-type ocean crust floors may have existed (Kelts, 1981). No oceanic crust is considered to have been formed in these basins in the Western Alps (Trümpy, 1980), although extrusion of basic volcanics was widespread (Antoine, 1972).

3. *Proximal margin*

The North Tethyan proximal margin is formed by the Ultrahelvetic and Helvetic zones of the Swiss Alps, and the Dauphinois zone (including the so called ultra-dauphinois zone) of the French Alps. Flysch deposition began here in the Ultrahelvetic zone, as early as Maastrichtian (Sardona Flysch, Leupold, 1933) in the Central Alps, but generally not before Eocene times in the Western Alps.

The Aiguilles d'Arves Flysch (French Alps) and the Ultrahelvetic Flysch (Prealps) accumulated in bathyal environments, as a number of localized terrigenous deposits along the outer part of this proximal margin, brusquely limited to the south and east by their source areas in the rising Alps (Homewood, 1977). Flysch sedimentation spread north and west across the margin, reaching shallower, more proximal areas in the late Eocene (Helvetic Flysch; Taveyanne, Champsaur and Annot Sandstones) when concomitant volcanic activity supplied the only significant andesitic accumulations of the Alps. This ultimate phase of Flysch deposition died out at the base of the shallow Lower Marine Molasse sequence of the Alpine Foreland, during early Oligocene times, with the Grès du Val d'Illiez, the Cucloz and the Spierberg sandstones.

IV. **Detrital Sources**

A. Marginal Land Areas

The rapid uplift and emergence of portions of previously subsident margins created source areas at different times during the Late Cretaceous and Palaeogene.

The degree of rounding of pebbles (clasts were subjected to some stream transport) together with the admixture of contemporaneous shallow-water marine fossils, prove that these source areas were emergent and that they were fringed by extensive shallow marine environments.

Uplift was rapid in geological terms, as the age of younger clasts immediately predates the age of the Flysch itself. For example, there are Upper Cretaceous clasts in the Maastrichtian Niesen Flysch (Homewood, 1974) and in both the Maastrichtian Schlieren Flysch (Winkler, 1981b) and Gurnigel Flysch (Van Stuijvenberg, 1979), while there are Albian-Turonian clasts in the Turonian to early Senonian Simme Flysch (Elter *et al.*, 1966).

That these land areas, underlain by continental crust, had previously undergone progressive subsidence is shown by the microfacies of the pebbles which appear "*en bloc*". A wide variety of Variscan mica-schists, gneisses, amphibolites and granites showing either north-Alpine (Ultrahelvetics, Niesen) or south-Alpine (Gurnigel, Schlieren, Simme) affinities, portray the basement. Mesozoic microfacies comprise continental and shallow marine Triassic rock types, whereas Jurassic and Cretaceous facies are mainly neritic for north-Alpine stocks or predominantly pelagic for south-Alpine derived clasts.

B. Intrabasinal Sources

Subordinate detrital populations of significantly different grain-size and composition betray distinct, apparently intrabasinal sources.

1. *Ophiolites*

In the case of the Simme Flysch (Elter *et al.*, 1966) the coarser terrigenous fraction is mixed with ophiolite debris of sand grade. Further study should clarify the relationship between these two grain populations (J.M. Wicht, work in progress), but it would be reasonable to infer an intrabasinal source area from which ophiolite debris was eroded to provide this material.

2. *Intrabasinal lime-mud*

Lime-mud turbidites are common among Senonian Flysch, but apparently are not related to the subordinate amounts of bioclastic sand accompanying the terrigenous deposits. S.E.M. studies of some specimens show coccoliths together with or subordinate to equigranular carbonate crystals (Van Stuijvenberg, Winkler, personal communication). An independent origin is therefore postulated for this lime-mud, and it is suggested that intrabasinal slopes and banks, lying above carbonate compensation depth, accumulated considerable amounts of this sediment. Dilute turbidity currents, unrelated to fan development, would then have redeposited the lime-mud in the deeper basins which lay below the carbonate compensation depth.

C. Volcanic Sources

1. *Magmatic arc*

Winkler (1981a) has demonstrated the existence of two detrital populations within the Schlieren Flysch, each comprising conglomerate, sand and shale. One was fed along the elongated basin from an emergent land area to the west (source of the red granites), whereas the other, which was fed in from the south, is postulated to derive from a tonalitic-andesitic arc. The presence of numerous bentonites strongly suggests that the coarser volcanic clasts were eroded from a contemporaneous magmatic arc, although these pebbles have not been dated as yet.

2. *Deep fractures across the north-Tethyan margin*

The origin of the andesitic volcanics of the Helvetic Flysch remains unknown. These are the Champsaur and Taveyanne sandstones (Vuagnat, 1952; Beuf *et al.*, 1961; Martini, 1968; Sawatzki, 1975). The two hypotheses proposed to explain their petrography invoke either (a) the emplacement and erosion of a volcanic nappe which would have occupied the highest position of the alpine structure of late Eocene to early Oligocene times (Vuagnat, 1952), or (b) the reworking of contemporaneous volcanics related to a subduction zone underlying the Ultrahelvetics (Sawatzki, 1975). Neither hypothesis is satisfactory since there are no remnants of a volcanic nappe unit in the Western Alps, and there is no other evidence for a volcanic arc in the Ultrahelvetics.

There is, however, evidence that this volcanism was contemporaneous with the deposition of the Helvetic Flysch. A number of labile and fragile components preserved in the Taveyanne sandstones preclude extensive reworking (K. Crook, personal communication, 1978) and isotope dates obtained from clasts and minerals (Fontignie, 1980) indicate Eocene to Oligocene ages. The spectrum of dates found by Fontignie may also be due to the mixing of volcanic material from several different origins particularly when considered in the light of Winkler's (1981a) results.

Andesitic volcanics of Oligocene–Miocene age are recorded from the Nice area (Giraud and Turco, 1976) and in the French Subalpine chains (Arbey *et al.*, 1976) as well as in the Massif Central (Brousse, 1961). The two former occurrences are related to synsedimentary Oligocene graben formation and deep, north-trending fractures (Giraud and Turco, 1976; Baudoin *et al.*, 1977), so it is tempting to relate the Champsaur-Taveyanne volcanic activity to a structural regime with similar deep fractures affecting the autochthonous foreland basement (cf. Kerckhove, 1980).

D. Cordilleras

The notion that Flysch represents essentially deep-marine sediments that were deposited in structurally controlled basins and were derived from surrounding cordilleras was developed by Tercier (1948), and the magmatic arc providing one of the detrital populations of the Schlieren Flysch (Winkler, 1981, IV C above) would fit in very well with this type of source. The ophiolite source of the Simme Flysch might also be ascribed to an intrabasinal cordillera. Another example comes from the Annot Sandstones (Stanley and Bouma, 1964). Ivaldi (1974) has demonstrated, through analysis of quartz grain thermoluminescence, that these sandstones were fed from two distinct sources, namely a Corsica–Sardinia landmass to the south (a prolongation of the Maures-Estérel massif) and the Helminthoid Flysch to the south-east. The Helminthoid Flysch must have then formed the upper part of the mobile alpine allochthon, and thus would also correspond to the cordillera type source envisaged by Tercier.

V. Controls on Sedimentation

A. Relative Sea-level

The position of the shoreline on any margin is related to the rate of sea-level change and the rate of subsidence of the margin concerned (Pitman, 1978) (Fig. 2). Global high-stands and low-stands of sea-level have been elucidated (Vail *et al.*, 1977), together with their effect on the depositional pattern of terrigenous clastics.

This major control on detrital sedimentation played an important role during the accumulation of Flysch, particularly the TP and TE global cycles or the Paleocene-Eocene Ta global supercycle (Vail *et al.*, 1977). The widespread progradation of fan deposits of the Gurnigel Flysch occurs within the Danian-Thanetian stages, coinciding with the low-stand of sea-level at the beginning of the Ta supercycle (Van Stuijvenberg, 1979). Furthermore, fan progradation is halted during the Ilerdian-Cuisian stages (Ypresian), corresponding to the high-stand at the end of supercycle Ta. Evolution of sandstone composition also upholds this relationship, with abundant contemporaneous glauconite (outer shelf material) reworked at the onset of progradation, diminution of reworked neritic fossils (narrower shelf sea) during that time, and subsequent increase of neritic fossils (wider shelf sea) after the cessation of fan progradation (Van Stuijvenberg, 1979).

The same Danian-Thanetian low-stand left its marks on the Sardona Flysch (Ruefli, 1959) where lowering of sea-level caused the mature quartzarenite and sublitharenite sands of the Sardona quartzite to be fed into the Ultrahelvetic basin, probably from the Helvetic shoreline (B. Ferrazini, personal communication.).

B. Fan Growth Pattern

1. *Efficiency*

Following the conceptual breakthrough of the submarine fan model (Mutti and Ricci Lucchi, 1972), the abundance of case studies has led to a number of models for deep-sea fans (e.g. Mutti and Ricci Lucchi, 1975; Walker, 1978; Mutti and Ricci Lucchi, 1981). In particular, the pattern of growth of small, sand-rich systems frequently shows channellized sands superimposed immediately on non-channellized lobes ("inefficient"), whereas in larger, muddier systems, the progradational sandstone lobes are separated from the channel deposits ("efficient"). Efficient and inefficient depositional systems (Mutti, 1979; Johns and Mutti, 1981) may both be interpreted from Flysch deposits of the Alps. For example, many Ultrahelvetic Flysch sequences (Homewood, 1977) are "inefficient" whereas many sequences of the Gurnigel Flysch (Van Stuijvenberg, 1979) suggest "efficient" fans.

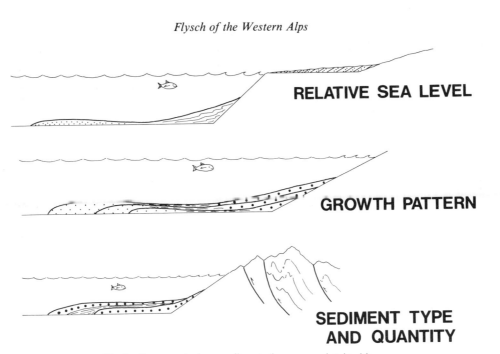

RELATIVE SEA LEVEL

GROWTH PATTERN

SEDIMENT TYPE AND QUANTITY

Fig. 2 Some controls on sedimentation were maintained by:
(a) Sea-level low-stands. Promotion of fan growth as clastics were fed over the shelf edge.
(b) efficient and inefficient growth patterns: governing fan morphology and vertical sequences.
(c) Type and quantity of sediment. The varying rate of sediment input, controlled fan growth morphology and vertical sequences.

2. *Maturity*

Depositional systems require some length of time to develop as well as a sufficient rate of sediment input to oppose the capacity of outside controls to redistribute the material (Fig. 3). Calculations have been made on frequency of turbidite events both in the Schlieren Flysch (Schaub, 1965) and in the Gurnigel Flysch (Van Stuijvenberg, personal communication) where litho- and biostratigraphy favour this sort of analysis. Figures obtained suggest one turbidity current event every 5000 to 10000 years, and both these Flysch accumulated over a 20 million year period. The well developed deep-sea fan nature of the deposits of the two Flysch groups, with numerous thickening-up progradational cycles, thinning-up channel-fill cycles and evidence of long-term fan growth governed by external controls (Ch. 1-5 A), suggests a "mature" depositional system. The use of fan models to interpret these deposits proves satisfactory (Van Stuijvenberg, 1979; Winkler, 1981b).

Some Flysch deposits, to the contrary, exhibit sequences less easily interpreted by direct application of fan models. Confrontation between the sediments and the models suggest that coarse clastics built out individual tongues or lobes, but that processes of channel avulsion and lateral wandering combined with progradation did not occur at a sufficient rate to shed the detritus out radially and thus produce an organized fan morphology (Fig. 4).

Local formations of the Ultrahelvetic Flysch (Col Zone) are suggestive of these "immature" depositional systems, for example the Orsay Flysch above Villars, and the Valerette Flysch above Monthey (Homewood, 1977).

C. Tectonics

Tectonics affecting the source area directly controlled the

MATURE FAN

TONGUES OF CLASTICS

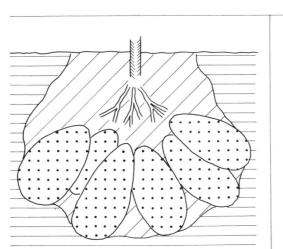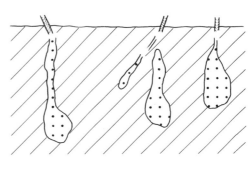

Fig. 3 Mature and immature fans. Mature fan only develops with a sufficiently high sedimentation rate compared to degradational processes. Insufficient clastic input results in isolated tongues or lobes of coarser material (immature fan).

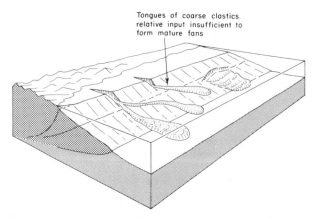

Fig. 4   An immature depositional system as envisaged for some Ultrahelvetic Flysch sequences.

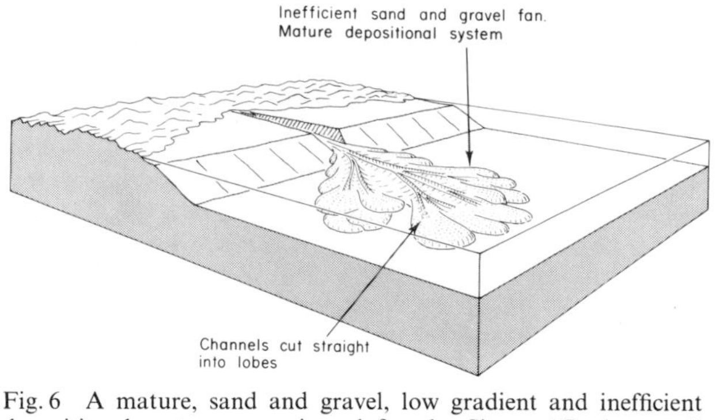

Fig. 6   A mature, sand and gravel, low gradient and inefficient depositional system as envisaged for the Simme "Rodomonts" Flysch, the Gets Flysch, the Crévoux Pic, and some Ultrahelvetic Flysch.

quality and quantity of sediment, and may therefore have been the direct cause of some thickening or thinning cycles.

1. *Sediment type*

Although the fan models predict the distribution of grain-sizes within a fan system in general, the sediments initially fed into the different Flysch basins were originally of widely varying grain-sizes. The Niesen Flysch contains a very high proportion of conglomerate and very coarse sandstone (Lombard, 1971), whereas the Gurnigel Flysch, containing roughly equal proportions of sandstone and shale, has only relatively minor conglomerates (Voirons Flysch, Van Stuij-venberg, 1980). Analysis of depositional processes, grain-size distributions and fan efficiency suggests that the mature fan systems found in Flysch deposits were of three kinds:

(a) steep gradient, coarse-grained boulder and gravel inefficient fans (e.g. Niesen) (Fig. 5).
(b) low gradient, sandy, inefficient fans (some Ultrahelvetic deposits; Simme "Rodomonts" Flysch; Gets Flysch) (Fig. 6).
(c) low gradient, sandy and muddy efficient fans (Gurnigel and Schlieren) (Fig. 7).

2. *Basin constriction*

Basin topography must also have played an important role during the accumulation of Flysch sequences. "Ponding" of deep-sea clastics is well known from oceanographical surveys, and the eastern Mediterranean turbidite traps have been proposed as analogues for the Helminthoid Flysch basins (Stanley, 1973). Ponding of deep-sea sands was also

suggested for Ventura Field (Hsü, 1977) and may be related to the growth of inefficient depositional systems (Johns and Mutti, 1981). Little direct evidence is available on basin constriction during deposition of Alpine Flysch, but isolated cases, such as the facies distribution of the Annot sandstones in the Peira Cave syncline (internal report IFP) strongly suggests that clastics were localized at times within structurally controlled basins, impeding the free growth of fan systems (Fig. 8).

VI. Flysch and Alpine Mountain Building

The rapid outline of Flysch facies, basins and source areas, together with the discussion of the controls on sedimentation given above, allow a somewhat more speculative discussion of the active (compressional) structural environments which simultaneously led to deposition of Flysch sediments and orogeny during the later phases of Alpine diastrophism.

A. Subduction

Evidence for a subduction event (Fig. 9) in the more customary sense of the word (as opposed to the original "crustal" subduction sense, see discussion in Trüpy, 1975a) comes from high-pressure low-temperature mineral parageneses of the upper Penninic units, and has been dated from between 130 and 100 M.Y. ("bibliography" in Homewood *et al.*, 1980). Mélange formations containing ophiolite olistholiths of the Perrières series (Gets nappe) and high proportions of chromite among the heavy minerals of the Turonian-early Senonian Simme Flysch all concur that the latter was

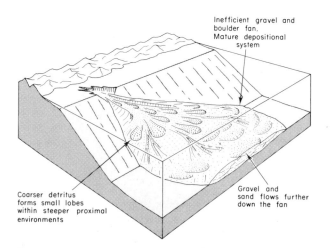

Fig. 5   A mature, coarse grained high gradient and inefficient depositional system as envisaged for the Niesen Flysch.

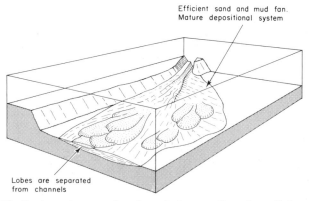

Fig. 7   A mature, sand and mud, low gradient but efficient depositional system as envisaged for the Gurnigel Flysch and the Schlieren Flysch.

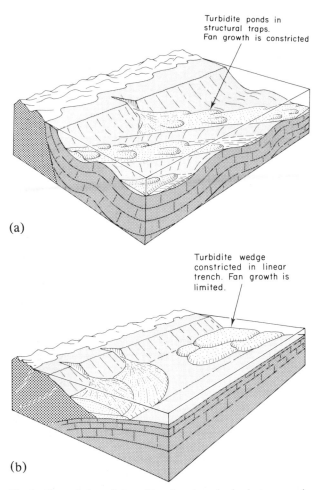

(a)

(b)

Fig. 8 Constriction of depositional systems by basin topography may have led to:
(a) ponded basins (Helminthoid Flysch, Annot Flysch) or
(b) linear wedges (Taveyanne and Val d'Illiez sandstones).

deposited during a Late Cretaceous subduction event in the Piemont-Ligurian ocean (Homewood *et al.*, 1980).

The recent work of Winkler (1981a) on the Schlieren Flysch suggests that the general environment of deposition was an east–west trench bordered to the south by a magmatic arc. The effect of subduction, structuring the Schlieren Flysch as an accretionary wedge before décollement (see also Hsü and Schlanger, 1971), would have been preponderent from middle Eocene to late Eocene (Winkler, 1981b).

B. Mobile Basement

After the subduction event controlling the deposition of the Simme Flysch, the Piemont-Ligurian ocean would appear to have undergone further narrowing during the Senonian and Paleocene (Fig. 10). Pre-Lepontine post-nappe deformations of the higher Penninic units may be invoked here, together with some radiometric evidence, to argue that Flysch sedimentation during these phases is represented by the Gets, Helminthoid and Gurnigel Flysch (Homewood *et al.*, 1980). This scenario could certainly explain the complex relationships between these various Flysch nappes from the Tethyan ocean, but further study is required. Further east, the Helminthoid Flysch is proposed to have filled an inactive trench overlying a major transiform zone (Hesse, 1981).

C. Collision

Progressive elimination of the deeper basins due to subduc-

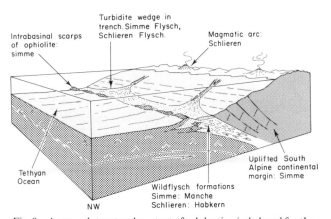

NW

Fig. 9 A general structural context of subduction is deduced for the Simme Flysch and the Schlieren Flysch. In the case of the Simme Flysch, coarse detritus was derived from an uplifted continental margin to the south. Clast types show this margin to have been similar to the present southern Alps. Finer grade clastics were derived from ophiolite scarps within the basin. The lack of shale within source areas led to the deposition of inefficient sandy fan systems. In the case of the Schlieren Flysch, detritus was fed from an andesitic/tonalitic arc to the south, and simultaneously from an uplifted margin (Corsica–Sardinia landmass) to the west. No scarps such as those of the Simme were located in the Schlieren basin.

tion and subsequent ductile deformation of basement inevitably led to collision between opposite margins. (Fig. 11). In this way, Flysch sediments invaded the Briançonnais or distal north-Tethyan margin, when expulsion of the Tethyan oceanic Flysch units furnished materials both to the Flysch and to the subsequent wildflysch. The same general scheme would hold for the inception of the Flysch of the proximal north-Tethyan margin (Ultrahelvetic).

D. Transform and Strike-slip Faulting

Trans-tensional movement has already been proposed as a possible control of the Valais trough during the Jurassic–Early Cretaceous period (Homewood, 1977) Fig. 12). Continued lateral movement would have accompanied Flysch deposition in fairly small basins of this trough during the late Cretaceous and Palaeogene, although some

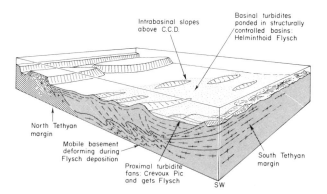

SW

Fig. 10 Helminthoid Flysch, Gets Flysch and perhaps earlier stages of Gurnigel and Schlieren Flysch were related to a progressively deformed mobile basement. Helminthoid Flysch was ponded in distal environments where intrabasinal lime-mud was also redeposited. Gets Flysch and Crévoux Pic facies of the French Helminthoid Flysch are more proximal, fan deposits. This mobile basement was related to later stages of consumption of oceanic crust and narrowing of the deeper Tethyan basins.

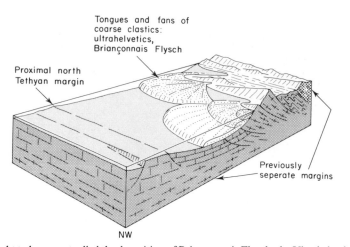

Fig. 11   Crustal collision is thought to have controlled the deposition of Briançonnais Flysch, the Ultrahelvetic Flysch and the Helvetic Flysch. Source areas were fairly complex, comprising uplifted margin sequences (Ultrahelvetics) or encroaching allochthons (Briançonnais and Helvetic Flysch). Detritus was localized in immature fans (Ultrahelvetics, Briançonnais) or constricted in an elongated wedge (Helvetics).

sort of shallower "crustal" subduction (Trümpy, 1975a) may have led to final closure of the trough.

Flysch such as the Aiguilles d'Arves, various external sequences of the Tarentaise zone (P. Antoine, personal communication) and the Niesen Flysch may well have been situated along a predominantly north-trending major transform, running south or south-south-west from the present Rhine graben, but now hidden under the lip of the French Alps (Plancherel 1979; Kerckhove, 1980).

All these basins would have experienced a peak of activity during the collision and subsequent locking of the crustal fragments of the Tethyan margins, whereas subsequently, depocentres were condemned to the shallower environments of the alpine foreland and Flysch deposits were succeeded by Molasse.

VII. Alpine Flysch In Space and Time

To sum up, alpine Flysch is shown to be predominantly deep-marine terrigenous turbidites laid down in basins formed by early diastrophism. Flysch sedimentation only started when clastic sources had been created by later orogenic movements. These phases of deformation can be correlated on a

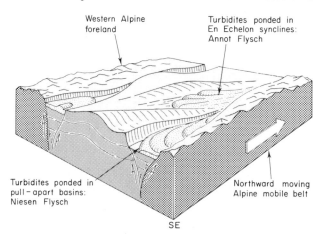

Fig. 12   Transform and strike-slip tectonics maintained during the deposition of Flysch from the Valais trough (e.g. Niesen), the Aiguilles d'Arves Flysch and perhaps the Annot Sandstones. The location of these Flysch sequences may be due to movement along a north-trending transform margin once separating the French alpine foreland to the west from the northward moving alpine mobile-belt to the east. Individual basins were either previously formed during trans-tensional movements, or caused by synsedimentary en-échelon folding or pull apart.

wider scale with the relative displacement of Africa and Europe as deduced from spreading rates and ages of the Atlantic Ocean (Hsü, 1971; Dewey et al., 1973).

Flysch basins differed from case to case. Those situated within the Tethyan Ocean were deep, below calcium compensation depth, and wide. Those in the Valais trough, within the north-Tethyan margin, were also deep, but were of more limited extent. Those either on the distal north-Tethyan margin (Briançonnais) or on the more proximal part (Ultrahelvetic and Helvetic) were of moderate extent and bathyal depth.

Clastics were supplied from several types of source area. Uplifted and emergent portions of the Tethyan margins, intrabasinal scarps and rises, magmatic arcs and volcanic fracture zones and lastly cordilleras all supplied detritus to one or the other Flysch sequence.

Earlier Flysch of the Western Alps accumulated in the Piemont-Ligurian Ocean when Late Cretaceous subduction initiated the consumption of Tethyan Ocean crust, as well as in the marginal Valais trough, possibly due to transform movements. Collision of Tethyan margins led to widespread Flysch sedimentation over the northern margin and within residual basins during Eocene times, but locking of the crustal elements led to uplift, and from Oligocene times no clastic depocentres were sufficiently deep to accommodate Flysch facies.

Flysch are thus shown in contrast to earlier scarp breccias and turbidites which were related to the tensional phase of alpine diastrophism, but also in contrast to petrographically similar Molasse which was laid down in shallow basins on the foreland.

Acknowledgements

Research was funded by successive grants from the Swiss National Science Foundation (2.1690.74, 2.783–0.77 and 2.283.79). The ideas expressed here have resulted from discussions within a team of Flysch geologists at Fribourg over several years. M. Schüpbach, J. Van Stuijvenberg, R. Morel, W. Winkler, T. Ackermann and J.M. Wicht have all contributed within the group, and M. Weidmann has provided additional help. From outside the team, valuable information has been given by A. Matter, R. Herb, B. Schwizer and B. Ferrazini, whereas the occasional reticence of some colleagues has helped to temper our views. We thank them all gratefully.

Dr P. Allen gave much useful advice when criticizing a first manuscript. Mrs F. Mauroux typed successive drafts and G. Papaux gave counsel on the figures.

References

Antoine, P. (1972). Le domaine pennique externe entre Bourg-Saint-Maurice (Savoie) et la frontière italo-suisse. *Géol. alp. (Grenoble)* **48**, 5–40.

Arbey, F., Clochiatti, R., Gigot, P., Gubler, Y., Le Tendre, L. and Rivière, M. (1976). Découvertes de cinérites dans les formations continentales carbonatées du Stampien, dans le bassin de Manosque-Forcalquier (Alpes de Haute-Provence). *C.R. Acad. Sci. Paris* **282**, sér. D, 1093–1095.

Argyriadis, I., de Graciansky, P.C., Marcoux, J. and Ricou, L.E. (1980). The opening of the Mesozoic Tethys between Eurasia and Arabia-Africa. *In* "Géologie des chaînes alpines issues de la Téthys". *B.R.G.M., mém.* **115** 199–214.

Badoux, H. (1962). Géologie des Préalpes valaisannes. Rive gauche du Rhône. *Matér. Carte géol. Suisse, n.s., no* **113**, 1–86.

Baudoin, B., Campredon, R., Franco, M., Giannerini, G., Gigot, P., Grandjaquet, C., Haccard, D., Lanteaume, M., Spini, H. and Tapoul, J.F. (1977). Age et modalités de plissement des chaînes subalpines méridionales. *In* "5e Réunion Annuelle des Sciences de la Terre, Rennes", 19–22.4.1977, p. 49.

Bernoulli, D. and Lemoine, M. (1980). Birth and early evolution of the Tethys: the overall situation. *In* "Geology of the Alpine Chains born of the Tethys". XXVIth Internat. Geol. Congr. Paris, colloque C5, pp. 168–177.

Bernoulli, D., Kälin, O. and Patacca, E. (1979). A sunken continental margin of the mesozoic Tethys: the northern and central Apennines. *Assoc. Sedimentol fr. Publ. spéc.* **1**, 197–210.

Beuf, S., Biju-Duval, B. and Gubler, Y. (1961). Les formations volcano-détritiques du Tertiaire de Thônes (Savoie), du Champsaur (Hautes-Alpes) et de Clumanc (Basses-Alpes). *Trav. Lab. Géol. Fac. Sci. Grenoble.* **37**, 143–152.

Blau, R.V. (1966). Molasse und Flysch im östlichen Gurnigelgebiet (Kt. Bern). *Matér. Carte géol. Suisse, N.F., NR.* **125**, 1–151.

Bourbon, M. (1980). Evolution d'un secteur de la marge nord-téthysienne en milieu pélagique: la zone briançonnaise près de Briançon entre le début du Malm et l'Eocène inférieur. Thesis Univ. Louis Pasteur Strasbourg, pp. 1–335, annexe.

Brousse, R. (1961). Recueil des analyses chimiques des roches volcaniques tertiaires et quaternaires de la France. *Bull. Serv. Carte géol. Fr.* **58 (263)**, 61 pp.

Brouwer, J. (1965). Agglutinated foraminiferal fauna from some turbiditic sequences I & II. *Proc. k. Nederl. Akad. Wetensch. (B)* **68**, 309–334.

Caron, C. (1966). Sédimentation et tectonique dans les Préalpes: "flysch à lentilles" et autres complexes chaotiques. *Eclogae geol. Helv.* **59**, no. 2, 950–957.

Caron, C. (1972). La Nappe Supérieure des Préalpes: subdivisions et principaux caractères du sommet de l'édifice préalpin. *Eclogae geol. Helv.* **65**, no. 1, 57–73.

Caron, C. (1976). La nappe du Gurnigel dans les Préalpes. *Eclogae geol. Helv.* **69**, no. 2, 297–308.

Caron, C., Charollais, J. and Rosset, J. (1967). Eléments autochtones et éléments allochtones du soubassement des Klippes des Annes et de Sulens (Haute-Savoie). *Trav. Lab. Géol. Fac. Sci. Grenoble* **43**, 47–62.

Caron, C., Hesse, R., Kerckhove, C., Homewood, P., Van Stuijvenberg, J., Tassé, N. and Winkler, W. (1981). Comparaison préliminaire des Flyschs à Helminthoïdes sur trois transversales des Alpes. *Eclogae geol. Helv.* **74**, no. 2, 368–378.

Caron, J.M. (1977). Lithostratigraphie et tectonique des schistes lustrés dans les Alpes cottiennes septentrionales et en Corse orientale. Thesis Univ. Louis Pasteur, Strasbourg.

Crimes, T.P., Goldring, R., Homewood, P., Van Stuijvenberg, J. and Winkler, W. (1981). Trace fossil assemblages of deep-sea fan deposits, Gurnigel and Schlieren flysch (Cretaceous-Eocene), Switzerland. *Eclogae geol. Helv.* **74**, no. 3, 953–995.

Dewey, J.F., Pitman III, W.C., Ryan, W.B.F. and Bonnin, J. (1973). Plate Tectonics and the Evolution of the Alpine System. *Bull. geol. Soc. Amer.* **84**, no. 10, 3137–3180.

Diem, B. (1981). Sedimentologie und Tektonik der subalpinen Molasse bei Schwarzenberg (Entlebuch). Lizentiatsarbeit Univ. Bern, pp. 1–161.

Elter, G., Elter, P., Sturani, C. and Weidmann, M. (1966). Sur la prolongation du domaine ligure de l'Apennin dans le Montferrat et les Alpes et sur l'origine de la Nappe de la Simme s.l. des Préalpes romandes et chablaisiennes. *Bull. Lab. Géol. etc. Mus. géol. Univ. Lausanne* **167**, 279–377.

Flück, W. (1973). Die Flysche der praealpinen Decken im Simmental und Saanenland. *Beitr. geol. Karte Schweiz, N.F. Nr.* **146**, 4–87.

Fontignié, D. (1980). Géochronologie potassium-argon: études théoriques et application à des matériaux de flyschs des Alpes occidentales. Thesis Univ. Genève, pp. 3–291.

Fontignié, D., Bertrand, J. and Delaloye, M. (1980). Nouvelles données sur des âges potassium-argon de diverses ophiolites au col des Gets (Haute-Savoie, France). *Schweiz. Mineral. Petrogr. Mitt.* **59**, no. 3, 422.

Furrer, H. (1962). Notice explicative de la feuille Gemmi no. 32 de l'Atlas géologique de la Suisse. Comm. géol. Suisse.

Gasser, U. (1968). Die innere Zone der subalpinen Molasse des Entlebuchs (Kt. Luzern): Geologie und Sedimentologie. *Eclogae geol. Helv.* **61**, no. 1, 229–319.

Gigon, W. (1952). Geologie des Habkerntales und des Quellgebietes der Grossen Emme. *Verh. Naturf. Ges. Basel* **63**, no. 1, 49–136.

Giraud, J.D. and Turco, G. (1976). Sur l'existence de laves à affinités calco-alcalines dans la région niçoise (district ligure). *C.R. Acad. Sci. Paris* **282**, sér. D, 2037–2039.

Graciansky, P.C., Bourbon, M., de Charpal, O., Chenet, P.Y. and Lemoine, M. (1979). Genèse et évolution comparées de deux marges continentales passives: marge ibérique de l'Océan Atlantique et marge européenne de la Téthys dans les Alpes occidentales. *Bull. Soc. géol. France* **7**, XXI/5, 663–674.

Gradstein, F.M. and Berggren, W.A. (1981). Flysch-type agglutinated Foraminifera and the Maestrichtian to Paleogene History of the Labrador and North-Sea. *Marine Micropaleont.* **6**, no. 3, 211–268.

Guillaume, H. (1957). Géologie du Montsalvens. *Matér. Carte géol. Suisse, n.s.* **no. 104**, 1–170.

Hendry, H.E. (1969). Sedimentary studies in the Nappe de la Brèche, French Prealps. Thesis Univ. Edinburgh, pp. 1–127.

Hesse, R. (1981). The significance of synchronous versus diachronous flysch successions and distribution of arc volcanism in the Alpine-Carpathian Arc. *Eclogae geol. Helv.* **74**, no. 2, 379–381.

Homewood, P. (1974). Le flysch du Meilleret (Préalpes romandes) et ses relations avec les unités l'encadrant. *Eclogae geol. Helv.* **67**, no. 2, 349–401.

Homewood, P. (1976). Sur les faciès des flyschs ultrahelvétiques dans les Préalpes Internes Romandes. *Eclogae geol. Helv.* **69**, no. 2, 281–295.

Homewood, P. (1977). Ultrahelvetic and North-Penninic Flysch of the Prealps: a general account. *Eclogae geol. Helv.* **70**, no. 3, 627–641.

Homewood, P. (1978). Exemples de séquences de faciès dans la Molasse fribourgeoise et leur interprétation. *Bull. Soc. fribourg. Sci. nat.* **67**, no. 1, 73–82.

Homewood, P., Gosso, G., Escher, A. and Milnes A. (1980). Cretaceous and Tertiary evolution along the Besancon-Biella traverse (Western Alps). *Eclogae geol. Helv.* **73**, no. 2, 635–649.

Hsü, K.J. (1971). The meaning of the word flysch: a short historical search. *In* "Flysch sedimentology in North America" (Lajoie, J. ed.) *Spec. Pap. geol. Assoc. Canada* **7**, 1–11.

Hsü, K.J. (1971). Origin of the Alps and Western Mediterranean. *Nature, London* **233**, no. 3, 44–47.

Hsü, K.J. (1977). Studies of Ventura Field, California; L.: Facies Geometry and Genesis of Lower Pliocene Turbidites. *Amer. Assoc. Petroleum Geol. Bull.* **61**, no. 2, 137–168.

Hsü, K.J. and Schlanger, S.O. (1971). Ultrahelvetic Flysch Sedimentation and Deformation related to Plate Tectonics. *Bull. geol. Soc. Amer.* **82**, 1207–1218.

Ivaldi, J.P. (1974). Origines du matériel détritique des séries "Grès d'Annot" d'après les données de la thermoluminescence. *Géol. alp. (Grenoble)* **50**, 75–99.

Johns, D.R. and Mutti, E. (1981). Facies and geometry of turbidite sandstone bodies and their relationship to deep sea fan systems. Abstracts, IAS 2nd Eur. Mtg. Bologna, pp. 89–96.

Kaufmann, F.J. (1886). Emmen- und Schlierengegenden. *Beitr. geol. Karte Schweiz* **24**, 608 pp.

Kelts, K. (1981). A comparison of some aspects of sedimentation and translational tectonics from the Gulf of California and the Mesozoic Tethys, Northern Penninic Margin. *Eclogae geol. Helv.* **74**, no. 2, 317–337.

Kerckhove, C. (1969). La "zone du Flysch" dans les nappes de l'Embrunais-Ubaye (Alpes occidentales). *Géol. alp. (Grenoble), t.* **45**, 5–204.

Kerckhove, C. (1980). Panorama des séries synorogéniques des Alpes occidentales. *In* "Evolutions géologiques de la France"

(Autran, A. and Dercourt, J., eds), *Mém. Bur. Rech. géol. min.* **107**, 234–255.

Ksiazkiewicz, M. (1977). Trace fossils in the flysch of the Polish Carpathians. *Paleontologia Polonica* **36**, 1–208.

Lemoine, M. (1980). Serpentinites, gabbros and ophicalcites in the Piemont-Ligurian domain of the Western Alps: Possible indicators of oceanic fracture zones and of associated serpentinite protrusions in the Jurassic-Cretaceous Tethys. *Arch. Sci. Genève* **33**, 103–115.

Leupold, W. (1933). Neue mikropaläontologische Daten zur Altersfrage der alpinen Flyschbildungen. *Eclogae geol. Helv.* **26**, 295–319.

Lombard, A. (1971). La nappe du Niesen et son flysch: *Matér. Carte géol. Suisse, n.s.* **141**, 13–252.

Lowe, D.R. (1976a). Subaqueous liquefied and fluidized sediment flows and their deposits. *Sedimentology* **23**, 285–308.

Lowe, D.R. (1976b) Grain flow and grain flow deposits. *J. sediment. Petrol.* **46**, 188–199.

Lugeon, M. (1896). La région de la Brèche du Chablais. *Bull. Serv. Carte géol. France* **7**, no. 49, 337–646.

Marthaler, M. (1981). Découvertes de foraminifères planctoniques dans les "schistes lustrés" de la pointe de Tourtemagne (Valais) *Bull. Lab. Géol. etc. Mus. géol. Univ. Lausanne* **254**, 171–178.

Martini, J. (1968). Etude pétrographique des Grès de Taveyanne entre Arve et Giffre (Haute-Savoie, France). *Schweiz. Miner. Petrogr. Mitt., Bd.* **48**, H. 2, 539–654.

Matter, A., Homewood, P., Caron, C. Rigassi, D., van Stuijvenberg, J., Weidmann, M. and Winkler, W. (1980). Flysch and Molasse of Western and Central Switzerland. *In* "Geology of Switzerland, a guide-book, Part B: Geological excursions (Exc. 5)". Schweiz. geol. Komm. (Ed.), Wepf and Co, Basel.

Middleton, G.V. and Hampton, M.A. (1976). Subaqueous sediment transport and deposition by sediment gravity flows. Marine Sediment Transport and Environmental Management (Stanley, D.J. and Swift D.J.P. eds). John Wiley, New York, pp. 197–218.

Moorkens, T.L. (1976). Palökologische Bedeutung einiger Vergesellschaftungen von sandschaligen Foraminiferen aus dem NW europäischen Alttertiär und ihre Beziehung zu Muttergesteinen. Compendium 75–76, Zeitschr. Erdöl u. Kohle, Erdgas Petrochemie, pp. 77–95.

Morel, R. (1976). Le contact Préalpes médianes-Préalpes externes entre Epagny et les Paccots (canton de Fribourg). *Eclogae geol. Helv.* **69**, no. 2, 473–480.

Morel, R. (1980). Géologie du massif du Niremont (Préalpes romandes) et de ses abords. *Bull. Soc. fribourg. Sci. nat.* **69**, fasc. 2, 99–208.

Mornod, L. (1945). Molasse subalpine et bord alpin de la région de Bulle (Basse-Gruyère). *Eclogae geol. Helv.*, v. 38, no. 2, p. 441–452.

Mutti, E. (1979). Turbidites et cônes sous-marins profonds. *In* "Sédimentation détritique". Cours de 3e Cycle romand en Sciences de la terre", (Homewood, P., ed.). Fribourg, p. 353–419.

Mutti, E. and Ricci Lucchi, F. (1972). Le torbiditi dell'Apennino settentrionale: introduzione all'analisi di facies. Mem. Soc. geol. it., v. XI, p. 161–199.

Mutti, E. and Ricci Lucci, F. (1975). Turbidite facies and facies associations. *In* "Examples of turbidite facies and Facies Associations from selected Formations of Northern Apennines: Guide of excursion 11", (Mutti, E., Parea, C.C., Ricci Lucchi, F., Sagri, M., Zanzucchi, G., Ghibaudo, G. and Jaccarino, S., eds). IX. int. Congr. Sedimentol. Nice, pp. 21–36.

Mutti, E. and Rucci Lucchi, F. (1981). Introduction to the excursions on siliciclastic turbidites. *In* "Excursion Guidebook with contributions on sedimentology of some Italian basins" (Ricci Lucchi, F. eds). IAS 2nd Eur. Reg. Mtg. Bologna.

Nilsen, T.H. (1980). Modern and Ancient Submarine Fans. Discussions of papers by R.G. Walker and N.R. Normark. *Amer. Assoc. Petroleum Geol. Bull* **64**, no. 7, 1094–1101.

Pettijohn, E.J. (1975). "Sedimentary Rocks", 3rd edn. Harper International Edition.

Pitmann, W.C. III (1978). Relationship between eustacy and stratigraphic sequences of passive margins. *Geol. Soc. Amer. Bull.* **89**, 1389–1403.

Plancherel, R. (1979). Aspects de la déformation en grand dans les Préalpes médianes plastiques entre Rhône et Aar. Implications cinématiques et dynamiques. *Eclogae geol. Helv.* **72**, no. 1, 145–214.

Ricci Lucchi, F. (1975). Depositional cycles in two turbidite formations of North Apennines (Italy). *J. Sediment. Petrol.* **45**, no. 1, 3–43.

Rigassi, D. (1957). Le Tertiaire de la Région Genevoise et Savoisienne. *Bull. Ver. Schweizer. Petrol. Geol. u. -Ing.* **24**, no. 66, 19–34.

Rüefli, W.H. (1959). Stratigraphie und Tektonik des eingeschlossenes Glarner Flysches im Weisstannental (St. Galler Oberland). Thesis ETH-Zürich, 195 pp.

Sawatski, G.G. (1975). Etude géologique et minéralogique des Flyschs à grauwackes volcaniques du synclinal de Thônes (Haute-Savoie, France). Grès de Taveyanne et grès du val d'Illiez. Thesis Univ. Genève.

Schaub, H. (1965). Schlierenflysch. *Bull. Ver. Schweiz. Petrol.-Geol. u. -Ing.* **31**, no. 81, 124–134.

Schroeder, J.W. and Ducloz, C. (1955). Géologie de la Molasse du Val d'Illiez (Bas-Valais). *Matér. Carte géol. Suisse, n.s.* **100**, 1–43.

Seilacher, A. (1967). Bathymetry of trace fossils. *Marine Geology* **5**, 413–428.

Siegenthaler, C. (1972). Die nord-helvetische Flysch-Gruppe im Sernftal (Kt. Glarus). Thesis Univ. Zürich, 73 pp.

Silver, E.A. and Beutner, E.C. (1980). Melanges. *Geology* **8**, no. 1, 32–34.

Stanley, D.J. (1973). Basin plains in the eastern Mediterranean: significance in interpreting ancient marine deposits. 1. Basin depth and configuration. *Marine Geology* **15**, 295–307.

Stanley, D.J. and Bertrand, J.P. (1979). Submarine slope, fan, and trench sedimentation. New concepts and problem solving. *Geology* **7**, no. 1, 49–52.

Stanley, D.G. and Bouma, A.H. (1964). Methodology and paleogeographic interpretation of flysch formations: a summary of studies in the Maritime Alps. *In* "Turbidites, Developments in Sedimentoloy 3", (Bouma, A.H. and Brouwer, A., eds). Elsevier, pp. 34–64.

Studer, B. (1827). Geognostische Bemerkungen über einige Teile der nördlichen Alpenkette. *Leonards Taschenbuch* **21.**.

Stuijvenberg, J. van (1979). Geology of the Gurnigel area (Prealps, Switzerland). *Matér. Carte géol. Suisse, n.s.* **151**, 5–112.

Stuijvenberg, J. van, (1980). Stratigraphie et structure de la Nappe du Gurnigel aux Voirons, Haute-Savoie. *Bull. Soc. fribourg. Sci. nat.* **69**, fasc. 1, 80–96.

Tercier, J. (1948). Le Flysch dans la sédimentation alpine. *Eclogae geol. Helv.* **40**, no. 2, 163–198.

Trümpy, R. (1973). L'évolution de l'orogenèse dans les Alpes Centrales. *Eclogae geol. Helv.* **66**, no. 1, 1–10.

Trümpy, R. (1975a). On crustal subduction in the Alps. *In* "Tectonic Problems of the Alpine System", (Mahel, M., ed.). Veda, Bratislava, pp. 121–130.

Trümpy, R. (1975b). Age and Location of Mesozoic scarp breccias in the Swiss Alps. *In* "Tectonique et Sédimentation". IXe Congr. Intern. Sédiment. Nice, thème 4, t. 2, pp. 313–319.

Trümpy, R. (1980). Geology and Switzerland. Part A: an outline. *In* "Geology of Switzerland, a guide-book". Schweiz. Geol. Komm. ed., Wepf and Co Basel, New York, pp. 7–80.

Vail, P.R., Mitchum, R.M. Jr. and Thompson, S. III, (1977). Seismic Stratigraphy and Global Changes of Sea Level, Part 3: Relative Changes of Sea Level from Coastal Onlap. *In* "Seismic Stratigraphy — applications on hydrocarbon exploration". *Mem amer. Assoc. Petroleum Geol.* **26**, 63–81.

Vuagnat, M. (1952). Pétrographie, répartition et origine des microbrèches du Flysch nordhelvétique. *Matér. Carte géol. Suisse, n.s.* **97**, 1–103.

Walker, R.G. (1978). Deep-Water Sandstone Facies and Ancient Submarine Fans: Models for Exploration for Stratigraphic Traps. *Bull. amer. Assoc. Petroleum Geol.* **62**, no. 6, 932–966.

Weidmann, M. (1967). Petite contribution à la connaissance du Flysch. *Bull. Lab. Géol. etc. Mus. géol. Univ. Lausanne.* **166**, 1–6.

Weidmann, W. (1972). Le front de la Brèche du Chablais dans le secteur de Saint-Jean-d'Aulph (Haute-Savoie). *Géol. alp., Grenoble* **48**, no. 2, 229–246.

Weidmann, M., Homewood, P., Caron, C. and Baud, A. (1976). Réhabilitation de la "Zone Submédiane" des Préalpes. *Eclogae geol. Helv.* **69**, no. 2, 265–277.

Wicht, J.M. (1979). Etude géologique de la nappe de la Brèche dans les régions de Saanen et de la Videmanette (Préalpes romandes). Diplom thesis, Univ. Fribourg.

Winkler, W. (1981a). Petrographical and sedimentological evidence for a dynamic control of the Schlieren Flysch (Swiss Alps). *In* "IAS 2nd Eur. Mtg. Bologna", Abstracts, pp. 208–211.

Winkler, W. (1981b). Die Sedimentologie und Sedimentpetrographie des Schlierenflysches (Zentralschweiz). Ph.D. Thesis Univ. Fribourg.

History and Deformation of the Alps

H. Laubscher and D. Bernoulli

Geologisch-Paläontologisches Institut der Universität Basel, Basel, Switzerland

Abstract

The Alps are a segment of the Alpine–Mediterranean system of mountain ranges that at present are characterized by an intricate arrangement of loops. These loops are not yet understood dynamically but seem to be linked with the fact that the Africa–Europa plate boundary has been oblique with respect to plate motions throughout most of its history, first sinistrally divergent, then dextrally convergent. Deformation and metamorphism first began in the eastern Alps probably in Albian times, apparently associated with an early loop; at that time motions in the northern and western margin of the Tethys sea were of an intraplate or sub-plate boundary nature, particularly along the Pyrenean-Northpenninic belt. From the Late Cretaceous to the Middle Miocene dextral convergence brought the Eastern Alps from their original distant position over a distance of several hundred, and possibly over one thousand, kilometers into their present position where they override (by "obduction") the European continent. At their western front they now appear squeezed into the tight arc of the western Alps. This tectonic development was fraught with numerous three-dimensional geometrical problems. Obliqueness of convergence caused a superposition of normal compression and strike-slip. Compression led to the successive formation of the Austroalpine, the Pennine, and the Helvetic nappes, of which the Jura is the frontal shallow decollement edge in the Tortonian. Dextral strike-slip is most prominently expressed in the Insubric fault zone but is distributed throughout the Alps. Earlier complexities are often hard to decipher because of subsequent deformations, but for the Tortonian Alps some revealing 3-D features emerge. Of these, axial stretching particularly in the domain of the "northern hinge" of the arc of the western Alps can be followed all across the Alps from the Jura in the northwest to the Insubric fault zone in the south-east. Where the northern limit of this hinge zone joins the Insubric fault a temporary Tortonian triple junction for the Central, the Western, and the Southern Alps "plates" is established. The most interesting part of the Southern Alps is the Ivrea zone of granulitic to peridotitic rocks which marks the collision zone between the "plates" of the Southern and the Western Alps. This zone has a long and complex history but its present position and "bird's head" shape is believed to be the result of Miocene obduction.

I. Introduction

The historian of the Alps and the Jura Mountains is confronted by an unusual wealth of information, collected by a large number of geologists over more than a hundred years, on one hand, and an exceedingly complex situation on the other hand. At present no unambiguous historical account is possible; instead, the authors offer a sequence of historical pictures, situations, or, in modern parlance, of "scenarios", some in more detail than others.

The history of a mountain range is that of the movement of rock masses, of kinematics. In this article we particularly endeavour to trace movements on both maps and cross-sections, with varying emphasis. Scenarios will be developed as a time sequence, beginning with the Middle Cretaceous, but occasionally geographical or tectonic units will be treated from a somewhat more encompassing time perspective, and this is especially true for the Ivrea zone in the southern Alps.

Historical documents are of a variety of types and qualities. In order to weave them into a coherent story they must be harmonized, and this is often difficult as they seem to lead to contradictory conclusions. These contradictions, of course, can only be apparent, due to our imperfect understanding of the processes fossilized in the documents. At times we are trapped by unquestioned traditions of interpretation. This is particularly true where radiometric data from the basement are at odds with stratigraphic information of the cover as in the Pennine realm. Here some attempts at reconciliation will be made, but too many uncertainties remain for unquestionable conclusions.

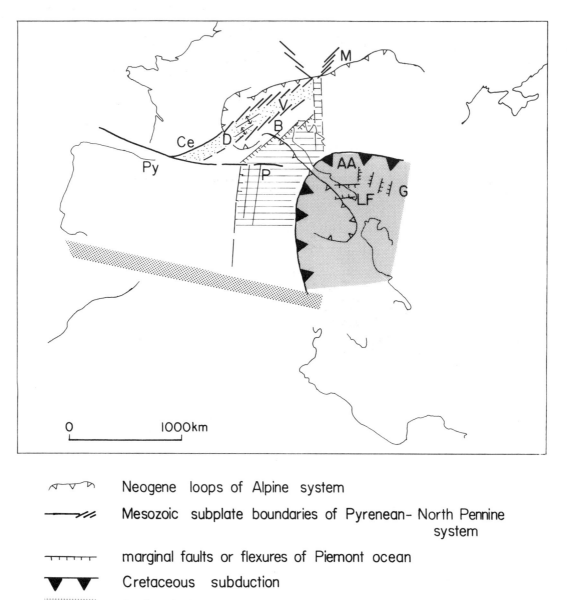

Neogene loops of Alpine system

Mesozoic subplate boundaries of Pyrenean- North Pennine system

marginal faults or flexures of Piemont ocean

Cretaceous subduction

Iberia - Africa plate boundary

Fig. 1 *The Mid-Cretaceous scenario*
AA: Austroalpine-Southalpine domain; P: South Pennine = Piemonte ophiolite trough; B: Central Pennine = Briançonnais high; V: North Pennine = Valais trough (including Ultrahelvetic zone); Py = Pyrenean subplate boundary; Ce = Cevennes fault; M = Mailberg fault zone; G = Gosau; LF = Lombardian Flysch. The location of the Austroalpine domain is uncertain, it depends on the amount of decoupling from Africa. In particular, it may have been somewhat north of the position shown.

The important points of this scenario are:
(1)   Cretaceous orogeny took place far from the Central and North Pennine domains. The latter is a complex intra-European subplate boundary branching off the Pyrenean subplate boundary in the southwest and joining the intra-European fault zones bordering the Bohemian Massif in the north-east: this may be the point where the Penninic domain as known in the Western and Central Alps ends. The fault zone as shown is that bordering the foundering part of the Helvetic domain. The internal faults of V are unknown, except in the Pelvoux (Gidon, 1979). We believe, however, that true oceanic pull-aparts are unlikely as neither in the Dévoluy-Pelvoux nor in the Fosse Vocontienne anything of the sort is observed. As a sub-plate boundary it probably ought to be compared with the High Atlas rather than with the Gulf of California, but even the High Atlas with its discontinuous extensional gashes (Studer, 1980) with basic intrusions in the Early Cretaceous seems to have had too violent a history.
(2)   The history of mountain building in the Western and Central Alps is the history of moving Cretaceous orogenic loops, so typical for the Africa–Europa plate boundary zone, to the north-west (or west–north-west) to finally wind up squeezed into the straitjacket of the arc of the Western Alps. This complex boundary dictated a whole set of constraints on the successive stress fields and fields of motion. Furthermore, in this scenario, it looks like the Apullian prong of the African plate moved in a counterclockwise gyration (Heller, 1980), in spite of general dextral tendency, into the arc of the Western Alps. Conditions responsible for this peculiar gyration (which is, however, typical for the Africa–Europa boundary zone) may have been similar to that for the Aegean and Calabrian arcs (cf. McKenzie, 1972; Angelier and Le Pichon, 1980): a receding (rolling back) of the subduction zone and a "beckoning of the void". These "hernias" of one plate infusing itself into another are further reminiscent, at a larger scale, of the West Indies and South Sandwich arcs which protrude into the Atlantic.

II. The Cretaceous orogeny

Mid-Cretaceous orogenic events are recorded in the Austroalpine domain (Fig. 1). Inasmuch as the history of Atlantic opening requires large subsequent strike-slip movements between the Africa and Europa plates it is necessary first to examine the location, with respect to Europe, of the scene of action. The Alps constitute a sort of collage, to use a now fashionable term. Segments from other plates have been rafted over large distances, both by convergent and by strike-slip motion, and have been welded to the European continent. The original breaks were inactivated, and subsequent breaks cut off the transported masses from their roots. This notion is different from the classical one of cross-sectional development (e.g. Dal Piaz *et al.*, 1972; Geyssant, 1980) and also from that of Dewey *et al.* (1973) who, by and large, favoured individual microplates that kept their individuality throughout most of Alpine–Mediterranean development. The notion is akin to that propagated by Biju-Duval *et al.* (1977).

A. The Location of the Austroalpine Domain in the Middle Cretaceous

The Austroalpine domain, being south of the Central Tethys ophiolite belt and, for all we know, continuous with the external Dinarids and Apennines, is conventionally considered a part of Africa (Channell and Horvath, 1976) or of an independent Apulian microplate (Biju-Duval *et al.*, 1977). By Late Cretaceous times, the central and southern Atlantic had opened to the extent that Africa was displaced sinistrally with respect to Europe on the order of 2000 km. It is, however, probable that the Austroalpine–Southern Alps domain was decoupled from Africa to some extent, though hardly as completely as assumed by Dewey *et al.* (1973: "Carnic plate"), and this would have reduced their displacement with respect to Europe (cf. Laubscher and Bernoulli, 1977, Fig. 8). In the absence of reliable criteria, we take an intermediate position as shown in Fig. 1. Evidently, these mid-Cretaceous events cannot be represented on one cross-section with those occurring in the Helvetic to Central Penninic parts of the central Alps at that time, although, for convenience, we have done that ourselves (e.g. Laubscher, 1974, Fig.–2).

B. The Nature of Cretaceous Orogenic Events

Information about Cretaceous events in this far-away region is scattered, and it is hard to form a concrete picture. The Gosau unconformity in the eastern Alps has been known for a long time; the significance of Cretaceous flysch in the western and central Alps has been recognized somewhat later (cf. Kerckhove *et al.*, 1980, for a recent overview), and even later is the discovery of chrome spinels (Gasser, 1967; Oberhauser, 1968) in some of these flysches and the realization that they ought to be attributed to ophiolite obduction. Radiometric

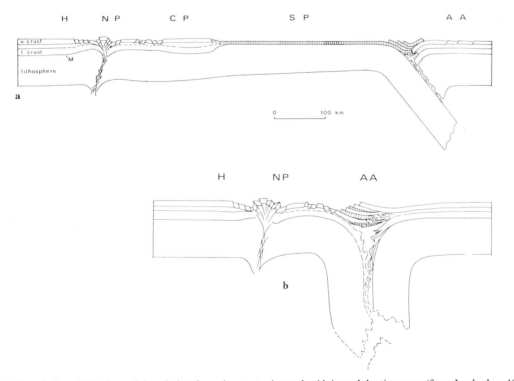

Fig. 2   The relation of Northpenninic subplate boundary tectonics to the Alpine subduction zone (from Laubscher, 1974).
a   A cross-section through the Alpine orogen in the Middle to Late Cretaceous. H = Helvetic domain; NP – Ultrahelvetic to Northpenninic d.; CP – Central Penninic d.; SP – South Penninic d.; AA = Austroalpine d. + Southern Alps. For this time the most important compression is indicated for the southern margin of the oceanic South Penninic trough. There is evidence for obduction of ophiolite on the southern continental margin. Detachment phenomena in the southern continental crust are also suggested. They may have been considerably stronger than shown, and may already have resulted in continental basement nappes.
A second, less severe zone of compression branches off from the Pyrenees — Gulf of Biscay active sub-plate boundary into the North Penninic domain. It gave rise to large positive and negative crustal displacements probably associated with oblique compression (strike-slip plus moderate compression). This is known to produce "flower structures" as shown in the figure (Harding and Lowell, 1979). The normal faults are due to Jurassic–Early Cretaceous oblique extension.
b   In the Late, possibly already in the Middle Eocene the whole South Penninic oceanic domain had been consumed, and the Central Penninic zone became covered with peels from the South Penninic (ophiolite) and Austroalpine domains. The North Penninic–Ultrahelvetic domain shortly afterwards became engulfed in the main subduction zone, and its shallow portions were peeled off to become part of the Alpine nappe system.

age data are even later and though in many instances they harmonize well with the stratigraphic information there are disturbing exceptions. Those radiometric data fitting within the stratigraphic framework date various types of metamorphism in the Austroalpine domain and its margin as Cretaceous. If we start with the base of the Oetztal basement nappe, the 100 m.y. given by Thöni (1980) for its mylonites would fit excellently a pre-Gosau (Cenomanian or more probably Albian) orogenic event. Although most cooling data around the Tauern window are somewhat younger (Satir, 1975) most of them easily fit pre-Coniacian deformation attended by greenschist metamorphism. There is a metamorphic gradient from west to east: the Ducan sediments on top of the Silvretta nappe are only anchimetamorphic (Dunoyer and Bernoulli, 1976), whereas the tectonically correlative Brenner sediments are in the greenschist facies (Miller *et al.*, 1967). Is this an indication of east–west thrusting? Such a simple conclusion is not warranted by the information. The subsequent large dextrally convergent displacements confused geometric relations, e.g. in the Austroalpine units in south-eastern Switzerland and adjacent Italy, to the extent that correlations are uncertain. Rotation of elements is probable, and, hopefully, one day paleomagnetism will help in working out a more substantial picture. As the Austroalpine domain occupied an African promontory with boundaries probably swinging from a northerly into an easterly and then south-easterly direction (Laubscher and Bernoulli, 1977), the orogeny may have had a sharply arcuate shape, it may have formed a loop similar to those characteristic for the present Mediterranean: the Aegean arc, the arc of the western Alps, the Calabro-Peloritan and the Gibraltar arc – not to forget the Carpatho-Balkanian contorsions. In this context one may even interpret the Gosau basins as the result of "back-arc spreading" like the basins of the Aegean or the Tyrrhenian; the Southalpine Lombardian Flysch basin apparently was far enough from these events that no unconformity marks the beginning of clastic sedimentation in the Late Cenomanian; it remained in the deep-sea situation that had obtained there since the Middle Liassic.

Other problems are posed by Cretaceous high-p metamorphism in lower Austroalpine units and adjacent ophiolites. That ophiolites are subducted as well as obducted is an old story; in some places they form the highest nappes, and usually they are the prime target for high-p metamorphism. More intriguing are the eclogitic gneisses of the Sesia zone, a continental basement mass. It is intriguing on two counts. First, low density continental crust is usually assumed to be non-subductable; second, subduction is generally viewed as oceanic lithosphere under continent, that is, of Tethys under Austroalpine basement.

The subduction of continental crust in the Sesia zone calls for a plausible explanation. Laubscher (1970) has advocated bivergent subduction, from the Tethys as well as from the Austroalpine side, whereas Dal Piaz *et al.* (1972) preferred two separate subduction zones, both directed towards Africa. The case for bivergence rests on two considerations. First, most surficially observable mountains are strongly bivergent, even the Pacific Cordilleras, and this requires at least delamination of low-density masses from their high-density lithospheric underpinnings; these then may be free to sink by their own weight. Second, bivergent sinking does not require a new break through the lithosphere as that at the already existing subduction zone is ready for use; it is energetically advantageous. At present, bivergent subduction is more fashionable than it was a decade ago: Panza and Mueller (1979) have presented a case for bivergent subduction under the Alps on the evidence of surface wave dispersion, and complex and occasionally bivergent Benioff zones are reported from the South-East Asian plate boundaries

which with their intricate loops to some extent resemble the Alpine situation (e.g. Cardwell *et al.*, 1980).

Cretaceous orogenic events are well documented by various techniques for the Austroalpine domain and its margins, although the picture is still fragmentary. The real trouble begins in what is usually considered central Penninic as it now underlies Austroalpine and ophiolite nappes. The central Penninic as defined in the sediments gives clear enough information: it was on the European side of the Tethys, and it was not affected by orogeny till the Middle or even Late Eocene. But since the sediments have been subject to universal decollement, correlation with basement units is an uncertain thing. Cretaceous events have been inferred on radiometric data for several "Penninic" basement nappes (Monte Rosa, Monte Leone, Suretta: Hanson *et al.*, 1969; Hunziker, 1970), but the situation varies from one to the other. For the Monte Rosa nappe, whole rock ages give a good 100 m.y. isochron (Hunziker, 1970), and there is disseminated kyanite in the nappe which predates the Paleogene metamorphism and may be Cretaceous (Dal Piaz, 1971). These interpretations, to us, require further clarification. For one thing, no clear picture has as yet been offered of the diffusion mechanisms operating in low-grade, albeit intensely deformed rocks, that in some cases would run to completion and reset the radiometric clock, whereas mostly they would merely succeed in inflicting partial loss of daughter nuclides. What kind of tectonic setting does this imply in each case? Assuming that the data imply true orogeny with nappe tectonics (compare p. 171), the far-off scene of Cretaceous orogeny all but forces us to give up the notion that the Monte Rosa nappe is Central Penninic basement and attribute it, as a piece of the collage, to some unidentified margin of the Austroalpine complex. Of course, more complicated scenarios might be envisioned as well, but for the moment there is not much point in that. The ophiolites of Zermatt-Saas Fee would then, to keep within the simple picture, without difficulty be attributable to Cretaceous "obduction", albeit at an initially considerable depth to account for the high p-metamorphism in both units. Moreover that obduction, with African vergence, would have resulted in a substitution of a large part of the original sedimentary cover of the Monte Rosa basement. The Antrona ophiolites below the Monte Rosa nappe in this view would have attained their position in the Tertiary by the thrusting of Austroalpine flakes in the European direction. Alternatively, if the Central Penninic origin of the Monte Rosa nappe were retained (i.e. its radiometric data were not taken at face value) substitution of its original sedimentary cover by the ophiolites would have taken place in the Tertiary, part of it would now lie on the St Bernhard nappe, and another part in the Préalpes decollement nappes. There is indeed much room for speculative association of facts, semifacts, and artifacts.

III. The Northpenninic Intracontinental Subplate Boundary — a Scenario

One of the difficulties in intricately deformed mountain ranges such as the Alps (Fig. 3) is that vestiges of deformation that happened at the same time but in distant regions and under different circumstances may now be intimately associated geographically. We think that this is the case with Cretaceous movements in the Northpenninic and Austroalpine domains. The misunderstanding has been and still is being helped by the classical notion of Swiss geologists that the Falknis-, Sulzfluh-, and Tasna nappes are Austroalpine (Gruner, 1980). French geologists had always maintained they were Central Penninic, and this view is now accepted by most Swiss geologists (Trümpy, 1960). For the authors there

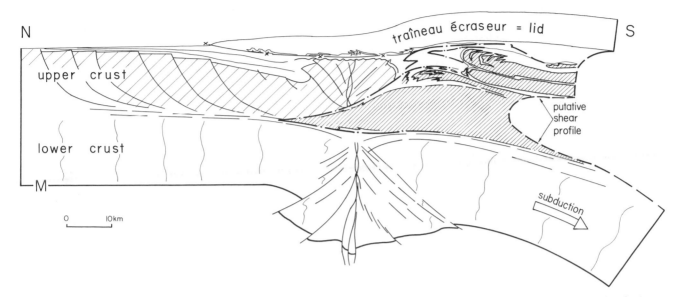

N

S

traîneau écraseur = lid

upper crust

lower crust

putative shear profile

M

subduction

0   10km

Fig. 3   The Penninic zone, Late Eocene situation. The detachment zone in the middle crust is reactivated again as the North Penninic sub-plate boundary enters the subduction zone. This time, upper and lower crust are split apart as high-T mobile masses (narrow ruling, lower-part) are wedged into the opening gap: the lower crust is bent down into the subduction zone. Widely ruled: upper crustal masses detached from lower crust. Narrow ruling, upper part: basement nappes usually attributed to the Middle Penninic realm. This type of mass displacements implies backthrusting under the "Traîneau écraseur" (= orogenic lid). See Laubscher (in press).

can be no reasonable doubt: the respective stratigraphies are explicit enough. They demonstrate that the Northpenninic or Valais trough in the Cretaceous was separated from the Austroalpine domain by a vast non-orogenic terrain. We shall consequently try to develop the scenario for the Cretaceous movements in the Northpenninic zone independently.

A.   The Development of the Northpenninic Subplate Boundary

Faulting that was synchronous with subsidence in the southern part of the Europa plate but north of the Central Penninic high began in the Early Jurassic and continued through the Middle Jurassic (Homewood, 1977). These faults are documented in several places and are partly outside the Alps (the Cevennes fault in the west and the Mailberg fault zone in the extraalpine Vienna basin in the east, Fig. 1; see also Laubscher, 1975), and partly in the Helvetic zone of the Swiss Alps (Trümpy, 1949; Schindler, 1959). Paleofaults of that age are widespread in the Central Penninic zone as well (Baud and Septfontaine, 1980; Bourbon et al., 1977), and it would seem a fair proposition to call the entire zone in between, and particularly the North Penninic zone, a fault trough. Details are not known. In particular it is still uncertain whether there were severe enough pull-aparts of the continental crust to introduce important amounts of mantle material: incoherent and badly tectonized ophiolites now found associated with Northpenninic cover nappes are usually interpreted as being Northpenninic in origin but may be enveloped Southpenninic material.

Faults in this Lower-Middle Jurassic fault zone tend to be arranged en échelon. The pattern is sinistral in the Torrenthorn embayment in northern Valais but dextral in the extraalpine Vienna basin. The latter is atypical inasmuch as it strikes north-north-east at a high angle with the general strike of the Europa-Africa plate boundary which moved sinistrally at the time. It would seem a fair assumption that the trough was segmented after the fashion of the Gulf of California (cf. Kelts, 1981) but with much less extension.

Along the north-western (Helvetic) border of this trough a new cycle of sedimentation began with the Cretaceous but

its significance in terms of movement along the subplate boundary remains obscure. On the other hand there is ample evidence that with the beginning of the Late Cretaceous the Northpenninic trough was reactivated as a branch of the Pyrenean sub-plate boundary. Of particular importance in that respect are the pre-Senonian compressive structures at the southern border of the Pelvoux massif (Dévoluy); Gidon (1979) points out that in both the sedimentary cover and the crystalline basement north-east striking bivergent structures overthrusting their foreland in both flanks were formed. As they seem to have been rather isolated structures, and as their character evokes that of a "flower structure" (Harding and Lowell, 1979), it is our guess that they were part of an obliquely compressive en échelon belt (Fig. 2; compare also Laubscher, 1970, 1974).

This scenario harmonizes with that of a branch of the Pyrenean zone. The details, however, are still far from clear. They depend on the rotational pole for the relative movement of the Central Penninic block with respect to Europe, and as that block was separated from the Iberian block, the opening history of the Gulf of Biscay and the developments in the Pyrenean zone are of limited help. It may well be that the strike-slip component had been sinistral until the Late Cretaceous and then became dextral as suggested by Atlantic opening history. As to the normal component, it probably was extensional up to the Cenomanian and then became compressional. However, in zones with oblique movement, extension and compression often go together and moreover depend on local changes in strike of the boundary.

Also in keeping with the notion that the Northpenninic zone in the late Cretaceous contained a number of en échelon "brachyanticlines" is the limited occurrence of the Niesen flysch, with its large masses of continental basement debris. It could have been derived from something like the Cretaceous Pelvoux (compare also Fig. 3). It is well known that in convergent strike-slip zones isolated slivers of basement may be locally pushed up by many kilometres (Habicht, 1960). Perhaps the several thresholds and basins postulated by Alleman (1956) for the Northpenninic flysch of Liechtenstein are an expression of a similar arrangement there.

This style differs substantially from that of a nappe mountain like the Alps. The difference is similar to that between the Ouachita and the Wichita mountains, or the Merida Andes and the Caribbean Coast Ranges, or the Atlas and the Rif. The Northpenninic zone of movement is neither a Cretaceous Northpenninic system of nappes, nor even of nappe embryos, although it may have produced some metamorphism (for the Atlas compare Studer, 1980). However, when in the Eocene the principal Europa–Africa plate boundary advanced across the Central Penninic High, and subduction began to engulf the Northpenninic zone, this pre-existing lithospheric break imposed important constraints on the formation of Alpine nappes. We believe that back-thrusting in the Central Alps is partly due to this inherited irregularity (Fig. 3, Laubscher, in press).

IV. The Paleogene Orogeny in the Penninic Realm

The Central Penninic high or Briançonnais zone (Fig. 3) is characterized throughout, from the Mediterranean to the Swiss–Austrian border, by sedimentation up to the Middle Eocene. There is synsedimentary faulting, there are stratigraphic gaps, but up to the Eocene this domain was never covered by nappes.

The general scenario leading to orogeny in the Late Eocene follows from the Middle Cretaceous situation. The Austroalpine–Southalpine domain was still far in the east at that time (Fig. 1). From the latest Cretaceous on it moved towards its present position by oblique dextral convergence.

In the Late Eocene, South Pennine and Austroalpine nappes overrode the Briançonnais zone (or this zone was subducted, which amounts to the same). This "traîneau écraseur", the "crushing sledge" (Termier, 1903), or, less dramatically, the orogenic wedge, detached the sedimentary cover from its basement, pushed it, sheared it, dragged it along by various amounts as far as the frontal Prealpes, in some places folding (shear-induced folds, particularly Falknis nappe), in other places stretching it ("boudinage", particularly Sulzfluh nappe). The sheared-away cover was substituted by masses moving in from the south. For these reasons it is not known, and sometimes hard to guess, which "Penninic" basement masses belong to which cover nappes. Are basement nappes like the Monte Rosa or the Suretta, commonly believed to be Central Penninic, really Penninic at all in the sense of their preorogenic history? This problem has been discussed on p. 172.

At a late stage of Penninic nappe emplacement regional backfolding to the south took place along the entire arc of the western Alps and the central Alps as far east as the Lower Engadine window (Fig. 3). This invariably affects the whole Penninic sequence, that is, it is of Tertiary age. Backthrusting in the Schams-Avers region has been much debated for several decades. Recently, Milnes and Schmutz (1978) and Milnes and Pfiffner (1980) have argued for a mid-Cretaceous age of backfolding in the Suretta nappe, taking their cue from the radiometric data of Hanson et al. (1969). This, and their whole reconstruction of the history of the area, lies like

an exotic block in the history of the Alps as sketched here. We have examined their data and found that they can be interpreted in a non-exotic way that harmonizes with developments in the rest of the Penninic realm. One of their central notions is that of the existence of the great recumbent Niemet fold; however, we have difficulties in seeing this fold on the maps or in inferring it from their structural data, and find that in spite of many uncertainties, smaller mistakes and weaknesses, the development as proposed by Streiff (1962), with modifications, fits the local and regional picture better.

V. Oligo-Miocene Developments in the Helvetic-Jura Domain

The Palaeogene Alpine nappes were thrust on the Helvetic domain which in the process was buried several kilometres deep (Laubscher, 1978) (Figs 4 and 5). However, this development apparently did not proceed smoothly. One irregularity has been mentioned: the northward displacement of the nappe system was probably halted, interrupted for a while, and a good reason for this interruption is seen in the interference of the Penninic basement nappes with the Northpenninic zone (Fig. 3; Laubscher, in press). A similar interruption may have occurred in the Northhelvetic domain of western Switzerland. It has been known for a long time that the early Oligocene flysch of the Morcles and Dolden-horn nappes contains basement material. The easiest explanation within the classical scenario would be to derive it from the approaching nappes, the Doldenhorn-Morcles domain at the time being in the foredeep. However, Künzi et al. (1979) have recognized in this basement material Gastern granite which occurs farther north, and if we accept this interpretation, then a new scenario for the foreland of the nappes advancing from the south must be invented. Topographically it would involve a steep cliff, facing south, towards the advancing nappes, instead of the gentle slope expected for the north flank of the foredeep. Normal faults are found along hinges of subduction zones (Ludwig et al., 1966; for the Alps see also Laubscher, 1978). However, they are associated with general subsidence and not with a drastic uplift exposing basement. On the other hand, such drastic foreland uplifts exist in the Rocky Mountains, where for instance the great basement uplift of the Wind River faces with its marginal thrust the Laramide decollement sheets piled up from the west (Royse et al., 1975). In the Alps this would require a repetition of the underthrusting or flaking postulated for the Northpenninic obstacle (Fig. 3; compare also Fig. 7); it is at least conceivable that the Early Jurassic fault zone here induced a similar development. However, information is too scant to go beyond these vague analogies. At any rate, it would have to be assumed that the obstacle was suppressed soon afterwards to permit passage of the higher nappes and the development of the Doldenhorn nappe.

Time of movement of the Helvetic nappes is controversial. Ever since from the Perwang area in Austria Helvetic

Fig. 4 *The northern hinge zone of the Tortonian western Alps.*
The divergence of motion between the east–west directed compressive movements in the western Alps and the north–south to north-west–south-east directed compression of the central Alps requires axial stretching all across the Alps. Evidence for this is particularly good in the north-west where south-west of the stippled boundary zone ("northern hinge" of the Tortonian western Alps) an abundance of complementary dextral and sinistral strike-slip faults have been mapped. As subsequent deformation affected particularly the metamorphic core of the Alps which among other things was subject to uplift and erosion, deeper levels of Tortonian tectonics are exposed there with a more ductile rheology, but a similar pattern of stretching. Figures indicate ages of closing temperature of biotite.

Fig. 5 *Cross-sections through the Helvetic nappes from opposite sides of the Kander valley zone* (from Herb in Masson et al., 1980). The obvious difference is due to a variety of factors not all of which are directly linked with Tortonian movements along the Kanger valley zone. However, the evident sinistral displacement of the front of the Wildhorn nappe, particularly with respect to the Gasternmassif, with the appearance of the Niederhorn nappe (TS = "Border Range" in this article) on the east side, requires sinistral motions that probably began before the Tortonian but had important late Tortonian components.

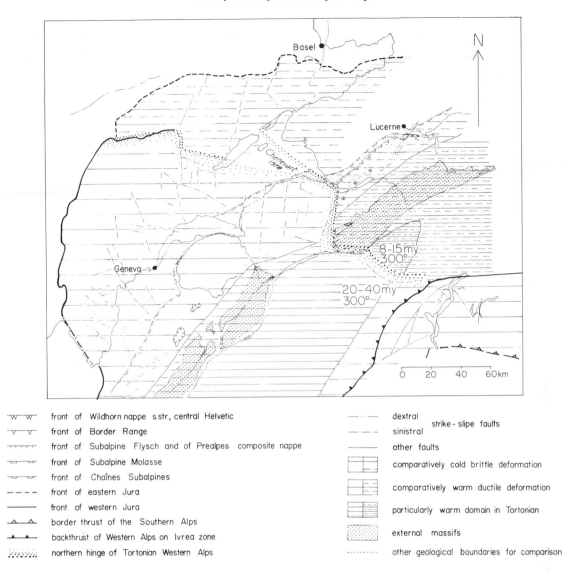

w—w front of Wildhorn nappe s.str, central Helvetic

v—v front of Border Range

т—т—т front of Subalpine Flysch and of Prealpes composite nappe

⌐—⌐ front of Subalpine Molasse

⌒—⌒ front of Chaînes Subalpines

- - - - front of eastern Jura

——— front of western Jura

△—△ border thrust of the Southern Alps

▲—▲ backthrust of Western Alps on Ivrea zone

.... northern hinge of Tortonian Western Alps

—·—·— dextral
—··—··— sinistral
} strike-slipe faults

——— other faults

comparatively cold brittle deformation

comparatively warm ductile deformation

particularly warm domain in Tortonian

external massifs

·········· other geological boundaries for comparison

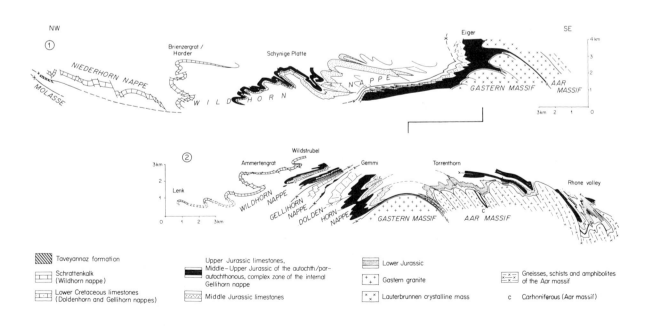

Taveyannaz formation

Schrattenkalk (Wildhorn nappe)

Lower Cretaceous limestones (Doldenhorn and Gellihorn nappes)

Upper Jurassic limestones, Middle–Upper Jurassic of the autochth./par-autochthonous, complex zone of the internal Gellihorn nappe

Middle Jurassic limestones

Lower Jurassic

Gastern granite

Lauterbrunnen crystalline mass

Gneisses, schists and amphibolites of the Aar massif

c Carboniferous (Aar massif)

olistholiths in Oligocene Molasse have been reported (Janoschek and Götzinger, 1969), the tendency has been to attribute an Oligocene age to the emplacement of some of the Helvetic nappes. This timing was corroborated by radiometric dating of the weakly metamorphic rocks in the Helvetic nappes of Glarus (Frey *et al.*, 1973). However, interpretation of radiometric results in such rocks is difficult, and if an Oligocene age is accepted, one has to find ways to reconcile it with the Miocene age — more than 10 m.y. later — of the large frontal thrusts of the Western Alps and the Jura, and with a 10 m.y. age of important movements in the Doldenhorn nappe (Frank and Stettler, 1979). It is conceivable that some tectonization and thrusting together with slight metamorphism took place before actual nappe transport at the time the Paleogene nappes were emplaced on the Helvetic domain while this was still foreland (cf. Laubscher, 1973). There are numerous other possibilities and instead of a general discussion we propose to assess but one factor contributing to the confusion: the possible role played by non-cylindric developments in the Helvetic nappes.

The most obvious place to examine is the Lake Thun–Kander Valley zone in the Bernese Oberland (Laubscher, 1982). The structure of the Helvetic nappes west of that zone is different from that east of it (Fig. 5), and this implies different kinematics with possibly different timing of some of the movement of units which, viewed in axial projection, might seem to correlate.

Laubscher (1982) argues that there is a "northern hinge zone of the arc of the Western Alps" of Tortonian age, and that the Lake Thun–Kander Valley zone is its most prominent feature; it also marks the north-eastern border of the hinge zone. Where a dextral displacement along Lake Thun terminates against a sinistral displacement of the Kander valley zone, at Merligen, a triple junction is required by elementary kinematics, with the Helvetic Border Range branching off to the north-east as the third, compressional branch of the junction. If the block kinematics is thought of in terms of distributed deformation, a horizontal deformation ellipse results with its long axis parallel to the Helvetic Border Range (south-west) and an extension of 9 km and the short axis striking north-west with a compression of 14 km. The Lake Thun zone crosses the Molasse basin to the north-west according to Chenevart (1978), and is postulated on kinematic grounds to somehow (precise information is lacking) connect with that prominent hinge zone of the arc of the Jura — the belt of complementary dextral-sinistral strike-slip faults — passing from the south end of Lake Neuchâtel in the south-east to the Faisceau Salinois in the north-west. Kinematics of the triple junction then imply, that a part of the compression of the south-west Jura is, at Merligen, transferred to the Helvetic Border Range: an outstanding example of non-cylindrical history.

The south-west end of the Aar massif lies in the south-eastern prolongation of this hinge zone, and in the Rhône valley is, after the work by Steck (1980) and Dolivo (1982) a zone of considerable east–west dextral shear, in the ductile domain. Laubscher (1982) thinks that the adjacent Rawil depression, a pronounced axial low in the nappe edifice, is part of the broader hinge zone as it exhibits the same NE–SW stretching as found at Lake Thun and on the south-west border of the Aar massif. Finally, this latter in the east connects with the Simplon-Centovalli fault zone (Steck, 1980; *et al.*, 1979; Bearth, 1972).

There is evidence that all these segments had a main activity about 10 m.y. ago though some show minor movements in the Quaternary.

The Centovalli fault is a branch of the Insubric fault zone which borders the domain of the Southern Alps. It is interesting to notice the kinematic — or historical — link between events at the marginal thrust of the Jura and the Southern Alps, all across the Alps. West of Locarno, where the "Northern hinge zone of the Western Alps" (Fig. 4) joins both the Insubric fault zone and the north-eastern end of the Canavese fault zone (which on the surface borders the Ivrea Body), we again have a triple junction of sorts where the blocks of the central Alps in the north, the southern Alps in the south, and the western Alps in the west join. The southern branch emanating from this triple junction, that bordering the western Alps, seem mostly compressional, if only because Miocene thrusting is conspicuous all along the western Alps (see also p. 170). But then there must exist, by the rules of kinematics, at least a component of dextral strike-slip along the eastern branch, the Insubric fault zone (Laubscher, 1971 a, b). The recent work of Steck (1980) extends dextral strike-slip of great importance far north of the Insubric line and thereby lends support to the kinematic role attributed to the Insubric line itself. We note further that the flat Miocene thrusts at the southern border of the southern Alps and the steep and straight Insubric fault zone fit quite well the division of roles often observed along obliquely convergent plate boundaries (e.g. strike-slip faults and thrusts along the southern border of the Caribbean plate, Mapa Geológico de Venezuela), the component normal to the boundary resulting in rather purely compressional features, whereas the parallel component produces predominantly strike-slip faults.

Thus, there is evidence that in the history of the Alps two types of deformation were superposed: convergent movements with decollement on various levels and the formation of nappes on one hand, and a pattern of strike-slip motions accommodating oblique convergence and divergence on the other hand. While the formation of nappes may, to some extent, be studied on a cross-section, the strike-slip pattern can be grasped only on a map, and even this is not sufficient as its aspect changes in the different structural levels. The strike-slip pattern defined a block mosaic, albeit often with diffuse block boundaries, for a limited time interval. The pattern seems to vary quite frequently as old boundaries are inactivated and new ones form, and kinematic relations between faults may change. We therefore have taken pains to try to define some such boundaries for a situation that prevailed 10 m.y. ago, and we insist that the pattern 20 m.y. or 30 m.y. ago was quite different although we have not presented the evidence in this paper.

The Southern Alps are a part of the "Insubric Plate" of Laubscher (1971,b). They develop their most conspicuous feature, the Ivrea zone, where they impinge on the arc of the Western Alps. The Southern Alps are characterized by compressive tectonics, again in the Tortonian. This is obvious in the sediments; however, little is known about what happened at that time in the basement which has yielded fission track ages of 10 m.y. (Wagner *et al.*, 1977). The most intriguing part of this basement is the Ivrea zone. Mapping thus far identifies it as the basal crust of the Southern Alps. It has been hunting ground mostly for petrologists, geochronologists, and geophysicists. Just about all the local historical information is due to their painstaking work. They found out something about the gross present configuration, and about pTt developments. As historians, however, we are supposed to put this into the frame of regional, mobilistic development. Accepting the Ivrea body as the basal crust of the Southern Alps, we think its history should be reflected in the stratigraphic history of the Southern Alps. We have attempted to combine the different lines of evidence on Fig. 6 (compare Oxburgh and England, 1980) which at least should provide a basis for discussion.

Radiometry dates the formation of the Ivrea granulites and basic intrusives as Caledonian. Conditions were about 800°C at a depth of perhaps 25–30 km, (Hunziker and Zingg, 1980). Since surficially deposited sediments are involved this would seem to imply subduction either then or during an earlier orogeny.

There are several radiometric check points that suggest slow uplift and cooling ever thereafter (Hunziker, 1974). How are granulites brought up from a depth of 30 km? There are several possible mechanisms, and the uplift branch of Fig. 6 is shown as composed of segments corresponding to those mechanisms suggested by the stratigraphic record.

In zones of tectonic convergence (convergent plate and subplate boundaries), reference is usually made to synorogenic and postorogenic isostatic uplift. These terms are shorthand for complex processes involving horizontal mass movements, buoyancy, and erosion. Compression with horizontal mass movement is necessary to produce the root of the mountain that in turn leads to buoyant uplift and erosion. The most efficient process for getting deep-seated rocks to the surface, however, is by detachment and thrusting, including obduction.

In zones of divergent movement near-surface masses subside along normal faults but deep-seated masses including the M-discontinuity move up by crustal stretching and by intrusion of warm mantle material. This is particularly well documented for continental margins but is also found in subsidiary rifts such as the Rhine graben or the North Sea grabens (Ziegler, 1977; Sclater and Christie, 1980). At the end of Caledonian orogeny we assume that the Ivrea granulites rose slowly by synorogenic and post-orogenic isostatic uplift, cooling somewhat in the process. They would have remained at a relatively stable depth as part of the lower crust of a stable shield, had not other events interrupted the process of stabilization. A first such event recorded in the Southalpine basement is the Variscan orogeny; its exact nature, however, is not known. From the studies of Zingg (1978) it seems clear that the Ivrea zone was not affected by major burial, heating, or uplift. We consequently interrupt the cooling process by a minor loop depicting modest burial by overthrust masses and subsequent small isostatic uplift. The abundant Early Permian intrusions in the upper crust and the associated volcanism must have heated the Ivrea zone somewhat, whatever the origin of the intrusives. But Permian volcanism was associated with uplift and probably rifting in the area, and thus this segment of the curve has a negative slope. The uplifted masses were eroded; the Ivrea zone, by this event pushed to a shallower level, entered a new cooling cycle which would have resulted in asymptotic

T-stabilization at a depth of perhaps 20 km had not other events again foiled the stabilization process. There was some Triassic burial, perhaps at continued cooling, but the great event must have been the thinning of the crust when the Tethys split took place in the Early Jurassic (cf. Bernoulli, 1964; Bally *et al.*, 1981). Heat advected by mantle intrusions nearby warmed up the crust, uplifting it and subjecting its Triassic cover and part of the basement to erosion. The Ivrea zone then underwent cooling typical for continental margins with subsidence and relatively modest burial by sedimentation. It again would have remained at that stable depth, like the continental margins of the Atlantic, had not Alpine orogeny intervened, thrusting it into the position where it is found now.

During the Jurassic-Cretaceous movements that lead to the development of the Tethys, the Ivrea zone along with parts of the African or near-African margin was carried away sinistrally by 1000–2000 km, depending on the amount of decoupling from Africa. At that great distance it witnessed the Cretaceous orogeny of the neighbouring rock masses from the Albian on. Later, beginning with the late Cretaceous, it was transported backward, dextrally, to its present position, where it has assumed its place in the "bird's head" of the geophysicists (Fig. 7B).

Is there anything in its history suggesting that this "bird's head" shape has been acquired previous to its being incorporated into the Western Alps? This configuration has been variously interpreted, but we think the scenario that naturally fits the picture is obduction (Fig. 7). Indeed, the likeness with any model of obduction is striking (Davies, 1968; Laubscher, 1970; Coleman, 1971; Oxburgh, 1972; Armstrong and Dick, 1974). It has been argued above that in order to bring

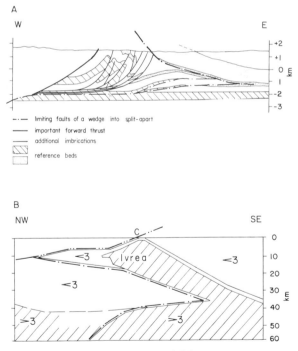

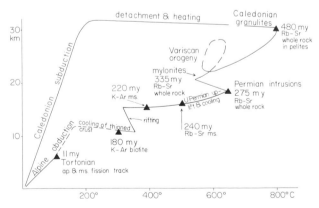

Fig. 6 *The p-T-t development of the Ivrea zone* (compare Oxburgh and England, 1980). This figure should be viewed as a first attempt at organizing the main lines of presently available information rather than a definitive statement of fact. Although this type of graph can be strictly valid only for small rock volumes, information obtained from many scattered points has been used. Furthermore, there is some probable error in all three, p, T, and t, and the stratigraphically recorded events entering the picture have been obtained from a larger region. Explanations in the text.

Fig. 7 *The Ivrea body as a product of obduction.*
A. Medium-scale "obduction" in the Alberta foothills, after Price (1981). Such features, called "wedge into split-apart" by Laubscher (in press) are common on different scales in many parts of the world. B. The Ivrea body (after Kaminski and Menzel, 1968) has the same shape as A, on a larger scale. Densities greater than 3 g cm^{-3} are cross-hatched. C is the Canavese fault, a backthrust of the western Alps onto the Ivrea body. The latter is interpreted as an obducted, flaked-off part of the south-eastern lithospheric plate here subducted to the north-west. Compare Fig. 2.

the basal part of the thinned crust of the continental margin into its present, anisostatic, elevated position, a special, anisostatic mechanism must have been at work. The case is similar to that of ophiolites obducted after detachment in the uppermost mantle. Would it be reasonable to expect this obduction to have occurred at a place other than the western Alps in exactly this form, and then to have been rafted into the arc of the western Alps to fit in this absolutely snug way? We think that to ask the question is to answer it.

We further propose that this is but a late chapter in a sequence of events that brought, in the Early Tertiary, flakes of African crust as Austroalpine nappes onto the European side of the Alpine orogen by obduction. These flakes were successively cut off from their hinterland by strike-slip motions due to the dextral component (which may have been on the order of 1000 km) of total transport. It is possible that the initial sinistral northern transform boundary of the Piemonte trough was reactivated in the reverse sense for this purpose. If so, it cannot be recognized any more as it has been deformed by subduction and nappe forming due to the compressive component.

Ahrendt (1980) presents information about the geometry of the Insubric fault zone. He comes up with an essentially fixist interpretation of its kinematics. We cannot see it his way for various reasons. First there is the Neogene scenario which, to us, precludes interpretation of the Insubric line as a system of essentially normal faults rimming the collapsed Po basin: there are sizeable thrusts along large tracts of both the northern and the southern margin of the Po basin. As we see it, association of thrusting and folding with steep strike-slip faults is typical for oblique convergence the world over. Then there is his arbitrary definition of an apparently normal fault of some 2000 m displacement between the Sesia gneisses and Oligocene conglomerates in the Biellese as "the" Insubric fault; this fault, however, is modest as compared with the geophysically intimated obduction which, unfortunately, at the surface is covered by backthrusting, and this, in some places, may be modified by subsidiary faults such as the Cremosina fault (Boriani and Sacchi, 1974). The Tertiary kinematics of the western part of the Southern Alps are being restudied at present, and further discussion will be deferred, except for a few words about total translation. Laubscher (1971a, b) has suggested a figure of 300 km to 400 km dextral displacement across the Alps (the entire plate boundary, not just the Insubric fault) in the Neogene, based on correlation of rocks of the southern margin of Tethys, of the ophiolite nappes, and on the position of the Monferrato if interpreted as an Apennine klippe (compare also Stein et al., 1978). Not all of this occurred along the Insubric line (some certainly inside the Alps as shown by Steck, 1980), and perhaps some Oligocene motions should be included as well. The geophysically indicated obduction alone suggests 60 to 100 km. The total dextral component of movement since the late Cretaceous is perhaps on the order of 1000 km, but as is well known from other, similar zones (e.g. California) the exact distribution of this movement on individual features in space and time is a complex matter for various reasons, not the least being that later movements tend to mask earlier ones. The history of the kinematic interpretation of the San Andreas fault zone is a case in point (Hill, 1981): though legions of first-rate earth scientists have worked on the problem there is still no consensus. Yet most would at least agree with the general dextrally transforming, somewhat oblique plate boundary scenario.

Conclusions

The Central Alps should be seen in the proper perspective: as a small part of one of the tight loops so characteristic for the Alpine–Mediterranean ranges. These loops have developed, and in many places are still active, in a complex, first obliquely (sinistrally) divergent, then obliquely (dextrally) convergent plate boundary zone. The obliqueness of motion requires special attention to map view kinematics: typical complications are the divergence and probably special rotations of more or less diffusely bounded segments, "blocks", or "plates" that accommodate the diverse tendencies of movements in such complex configurations. These block movements are superposed on subduction and detachment (which lead to nappe forming), and blocks change their shape and rheology with time and depth.

Earth movements have been distorted by subsequent deformations and dislocations to the extent that at present it is impossible to piece them together to any degree of precision; for the moment, at least, one has to settle for general scenarios. The situation is somewhat better though far from satisfactory for the latest datable large-scale movements in the Miocene, and some insight into what might have happened during earlier phases may be gained from them. It is this latest phase that exhibits clearly the confusing complications exacted by obliqueness of compression and the strait-jacket of loop geometry.

Acknowledgements

The authors acknowledge helpful discussions with several colleagues and particularly with André Zingg. They are indebted to the Swiss Nationalfonds for financial support of several projects bearing on the development of the Alps and the Jura.

References

Ahrendt, H. (1980). Die Bedeutung der Insubrischen Linie für den tektonischen Bau der Alpen. N. Jb. Geol. Paläont. Abh. **160**, 336–362.

Allemann, F. (1956). Geologie des Fürstentums Liechtensteins (Südwestlicher Teil) unter besonderer Berücksichtigung des Flysch-Problems. Jb. hist. Ver. Fürstentum Liechtenstein 56, 244 pp.

Angelier, J. and Le Pichon, X. (1980). La subduction hellénique et l'expansion égéenne: reconstitution cinématique et interprétation dynamique. C.R. somm. Soc. géol. France 158–161.

Arbenz, P. (1934). Die helvetische Region. In "Geologischer Führer der Schweiz", pp. 96–120. Wepf, Basel.

Armstrong, R.L. and Dick, H.J.B. (1974). A model for the development of thin overthrust sheets of crystalline rock. Geology **2**, 35–40.

Bally, A.W., Bernoulli, D., Davies, G.A. and Montadert, L. (1981). Listric normal faults. Oceanologica Acta, N° spéc. Actes 26ᵉ Congr. Internat. Géol., Coll. Géol. Marges Continentales pp. 87–101.

Baud, A. and Septfontaine, M. (1980). Présentation d'un profil palinspastique de la nappe des Préalpes médianes en Suisse occidentale. Eclogae geol. Helv. **73**, 651–660.

Bearth, P. (1972). Atlas géologique de la Suisse, 1:25000, feuille Simplon. Comm. Géol. Suisse.

Berggren, W.A. and van Couvering, J. (1978). Biochronology. In "Contributions to the Geologic Time Scale" (C.V. Cohee, M.F. Glaessner and H.D. Hedberg, eds). Stud. Geol. **6**, 39–55. Amer. Assoc. Petroleum Geol.

Bernoulli, D. (1964). Zur Geologie des Monte Generoso (Lombardische Alpen). Beitr. geol. Karte Schweiz, N.F. **118**, 134 pp.

Biju-Duval, B., Dercourt, J. and Le Pichon, X. (1977). From the Tethys Ocean to the Mediterranean Seas: A plate tectonic model of the evolution of the western Alpine system. In "Int. Symp. struct. Hist. Mediterranean basins. Split (Yugoslavia), 1976" (B. Biju-Duval and L. Montadert, eds), pp. 143–164. Ed. Technip, Paris.

Bourbon, M., Caron, J.M., de Graciansky, P.Ch., Lemoine, M., Mégard-Galli, J. and Mercier, D. (1977). Mesozoic evolution of the Western Alps: Birth and development of part of the spreading oceanic Tethys and of its European continental margin. *In* "Int. Symp. struct. Hist. Mediterranean basins, Split (Yugoslavia), 1976" (B. Biju-Duval and L. Montadert, eds), pp. 19–34. Ed. Technip, Paris.

Boriani, A. and Sacchi, R. (1974). The "Insubric" and other tectonic lines in the Southern Alps (NW Italy). *Mem. Soc. geol. ital.* 13, Suppl. 1, 327–337.

Cardwell, R.K., Isacks, B.L. and Karig, D.E. (1980). The spatial distribution of earthquakes focal mechanism solutions, and subducted lithosphere in the Philippine and north-eastern Indonesian islands. *In* "The Tectonic and Geologic Evolution of Southeast Asian Seas and Islands" (D.E. Hayes, ed.), *Geophys. Monogr.* 23, 1–35. Amer. Geophys. Union, Washington.

Channell, J.E.T. and Horvath, F. (1976). The African/Adriatic promontory as a palaeogeographical premise for Alpine orogeny and plate movements in the Carpatho-Balkan region. *Tectonophysics* 35, 71–101.

Chenevart, C.J. (1978). Seismic profiles as related to wrench-faulting in the Swiss Molasse basin. *Eclogae geol. Helv.* 71, 53–60.

Coleman, R.G. (1971). Plate tectonic emplacement of upper mantle peridotites along continental edges. *J. geophys. Res.* 76, 1212–1222.

Cook, F.A., Albaugh, D., Brown, L., Kaufman, S., Oliver, J. and Hatcher, R. (1979). Thin-skinned tectonics in the crystalline southern Appalachians. *Geology* 7, 563–567.

Dal Piaz, G.V. (1971). Nuovi ritrovamenti di cianite alpina nel critallino antico del M. Rosa. *Rend. Soc. ital. Mineral. Petrograf.* 27, 437–477.

Dal Piaz, G.V., Hunziker, J.C. and Martinotti, G. (1972). La zona Sesia-Lanzo e l'evoluzione tettonico-metamorfica delle Alpi nordoccidentali interne. *Mem. Soc. geol. ital.* 11, 433–460.

Davies, H.L. (1968). Papuan ultramafic belt. *Proc. 23rd Int. geol. Congr., Prague 1968*, 1, 209–220.

Dewey, J.F., Pitman, W.C., Ryan, W.B.F. and Bonnin, J. (1973). Plate tectonics and the evolution of the Alpine system. *Bull. geol. Soc. Amer.* 84, 3137–3180.

Dolivo, E. (1982). Nouvelles observations structurales au sud-ouest du Massif de l'Aar entre Visp et Gampel. *Mat. Carte géol. Suisse.* N.S. 157.

Dunoyer de Segonzac, G. and Bernoulli, D. (1976). Diagenèse et métamorphisme des argiles dans le Rhétien Sud-alpin et Austroalpin (Lombardie et Grisons). *Bull. Soc. géol. France (7)* 18, 1283–1293.

Eaton, G.P. (1979). A plate-tectonic model for late Cenozoic crustal spreading in the western United States. *In* "Rio Grande Rift, Tectonics and Magmatism" (R.E. Riecker, ed.), pp. 7–32. Am. Geophys. Union, Washington, D.C.

Frank, E. and Stettler, A. (1979). K-Ar and $^{39}Ar-^{40}Ar$ systematics of white K-mica from an Alpine metamorphic profile in the Swiss Alps. *Schweiz. mineral. petrogr. Mitt.* 59, 375–394.

Frey, M., Hunziker, J.C., Roggwiller, P. and Schindler, C. (1973). Progressive niedriggradige Metamorphose glaukonitführender Horizonte in den helvetischen Alpen der Ostschweiz. *Contr. Mineral. Petrol.* 39, 185–218.

Gasser, U. (1967). Erste Resultate über die Verteilung von Schwermineralen in verschiedenen Flysch-Komplexen der Schweiz. *Geol. Rdsch.* 56, 300–308.

Geyssant, J. (1980). Corrélations péri-adriatiques le long des Alpes orientales: rapports entre domaines austro-alpin et sudalpin et tectogenèse crétacée. *Bull. Soc. géol. France (7)* 22, 31–42.

Gidon, M. (1979). Le rôle des étapes successives de déformation dans la tectonique alpine du massif du Pelvoux (Alpes occidentales). *C.R. Acad. Sci. (Paris), (D)* 288, 803–806.

Gruner, U. (1980). Die Jura-Breccien der Falknis-Decke und die paläogeographischen Beziehungen zu altersäquivalenten Breccien im Bündner Querschnitt. *Diss. Bern.*

Habicht, K. (1960). La Sección de el Baño, Serranía de Trujillo, Edo. Lara. 3. Congr. Geol. venez., Mem. Tomo 1, Bol. Geol. (Caracas). *Publ. esp.* 3, 192–213.

Hanson, G.N., Grünenfelder, M. and Soptrayanova, G. (1969). The geochronology of a recrystallized tectonite in Switzerland — the Roffna Gneiss. *Earth Planet. Sci. lett.* 5, 413–422.

Harding, T.P. and Lowell, J.D. (1979). Structural styles, their plate-tectonic habitats, and hydrocarbon traps in petroleum provinces. *Bull. Amer. Assoc. Petroleum Geol.* 63, 1016–1058.

Heller, F. (1980). Paleomagnetic evidence for Late Alpine rotation of the Lepontine Area. *Eclogae geol. Helv.* 73, 607–618.

Hill, M.L. (1981). San Andreas fault: history of concepts. *Bull. geol. Soc. Amer., Pt 1.*, 92, 112–131.

Homewood, P. (1977). Ultrahelvetic and North-Penninic Flysch of the Prealps: a general account. *Eclogae geol. Helv.* 70, 627–641.

Hunziker, J.C. (1970). Polymetamorphism in the Monte Rosa, Western Alps. *Eclogae geol. Helv.* 63, 151–161.

Hunziker, J.C. (1974). Rb-Sr and K-Ar age determinations and the Alpine tectonic history of the Western Alps. *Mem. Ist. Geol. Mineral. Univ. Padova* 31.

Hunziker, J.C. and Zingg, A. (1980). Lower Palaeozoic amphibolite to granulite facies metamorphism in the Ivrea zone (Southern Alps, Northern Italy). *Schweiz. mineral. petrogr. Mitt.* 60, 181–213.

Janoschek, R. and Götzinger, K. (1969). Exploration for oil and gas in Austria. *In* "The Exploration for petroleum in Europe and North Africa" (P. Hepple, ed.), pp. 161–180. Institute of Petroleum, London.

Kaminski, W. and Menzel, H. (1968). Zur Deutung der Schwereanomalie des Ivrea-Körpers. *Schweiz. mineral. petrogr. Mitt.* 48, 255–260.

Kelts, K. (1981). A comparison of some aspects of sedimentation and translational tectonics from the Gulf of California and the Mesozoic Tethys, Northern Penninic Margin. *Eclogae geol. Helv.* 74, 317–338.

Kerckhove, C., Caron, C., Charollais, J. and Pairis, J.-L. (1980). Panorama des séries synorogénetiques des Alpes occidentales. *Mem. Bur. Rech. géol. min.* 107, 234–255.

Künzi, B., Herb, R., Egger, A. and Hügi, T. (1979). Kristallin-Einschlüsse im nordhelvetischen Wildflysch des Zentralen Berner Oberlands. *Eclogae geol. Helv.* 72, 425–437.

Laubscher, H. (1970). Bewegung und Wärme in der alpinen Orogenese. *Schweiz. mineral. petrogr. Mitt.* 50, 565–596.

Laubscher, H. (1971a). Das Alpen-Dinariden-Problem und die Palinspastik der südlichen Tethys. *Geol. Rdsch.* 60, 819–833.

Laubscher, H. (1971b). The large-scale kinematics of the western Alps and the northern Apennines and its palinspastic implications. *Amer. J. Sci.* 271, 193–226.

Laubscher, H. (1973). Jura Mountains. *In* "Gravity and Tectonics" (K.A. de Jong and R. Scholten, eds), pp. 217–227. Wiley, London.

Laubscher, H. (1974). The tectonics of subduction in the Alpine system. *Mem. Soc. geol. ital.* 13, suppl. 2, 275–283.

Laubscher, H. (1975). Plate boundaries and microplates in Alpine history. *Amer. J. Sci.* 275, 865–876.

Laubscher, H. (1982). A northern hinge-zone of the arc of the western Alps. *Eclogae geol. Helv.* 75, 233–246.

Laubscher, H. (in press). Detachment, shear and compression in the central Alps. *In* "Tectonics and geophysics of Mountain Chains" (R. Hatcher, ed.), Geol. Soc. Amerc. Mem.

Laubscher, H. and Bernoulli, D. (1977). Mediterranean and Tethys. *In* "The Ocean Basins and Margins. 4A: The Eastern Mediterranean" (A.E.M. Nairn, W.H. Kanes and F.G. Stehli, eds), pp. 1–28. Plenum, New York.

Ludwig, W.J., Ewing, J.I., Ewing, M., Murauchi, S., Den, N., Asano, S., Hotta, H., Hayakawa, M., Asanuma, T., Ichikawa, K. and Noguchi, I. (1966). Sediments and structure of the Japan Trench. *J. geophys. Res.* 71, 2121–2137.

Masson, H., Herb, R. and Steck, A. (1980). Helvetic Alps of Western Switzerland, Excursion No. 1, in Geology of Switzerland, a guidebook. (Schweiz. Geologische Kommission, ed.), pp. 109–153. Wepf and Co., Basel, New York.

McKenzie, D.P. (1972). Active tectonics of the Mediterranean region. *Geophys. J.R. astron. Soc.* 30, 109–185.

Miller, D.S., Jäger, E. and Schmidt, K. (1967). Rb-Sr Altersbestimmungen an Biotiten der Raibler Schichten des Brenner Mesozoikums und am Muskovitgranitgneis von Vent (Oetztaler Alpen). *Eclogae geol. Helv.* 60, 537–541.

Milnes, A.G. and Pfiffner, O.A. (1980). Tectonic evolution of the Central Alps in the cross section St. Gallen-Como. *Eclogae geol. Helv.* 73, 619–633.

Milnes, A.G. and Schmutz, H.-U. (1978). Structure and history of the Suretta nappe (Pennine zone, Central Alps) — a field study. *Eclogae geol. Helv.* 71, 19–34.

Oberhauser, R. (1968). Beiträge zur Kenntnis der Tektonik und der Paläogeographie während der Oberkreide und dem Paläogew im Ostalpenraum. *Jb. geol. Bundesanst. (Wien)* 111, 115–145.

Oxburgh, E.R. (1972). Flake tectonics and continental collision. *Nature, London* 239, 202–204.

Oxburgh, E.R. and England, P.C. (1980). Heat flow and the

metamorphic evolution of the Eastern Alps. *Eclogae geol. Helv.* **73**, 379–398.

Panza, G.F. and Mueller, S. (1979). The plate boundary between Eurasia and Africa in the Alpine area. *Mem. Sci. geol.* **33**, 43–50.

Price, R.A. (1981). The Cordilleran foreland thrust and fold belt in the southern Canadian Rocky Mountains. *In* "Thrust and Nappe Tectonics" (K.R. McClay and N.J. Price, eds), pp. 427–448, The Geological Society of London.

Royse, F., Jr., Warner, M.A. and Reese, D.L. (1975). Thrust belt structural geometry and related stratigraphic problems. Wyoming-Idaho-northern Utah. *In* "Symposium on deep drilling in the central Rocky Mountains" (D.W. Bolyard, ed.), pp. 41–54. Rocky Mtn. Assoc. Geol., Denver.

Satir, M. (1975). Die Entwicklungsgeschichte der westlichen Hohen Tauern und der südlichen Oetztalmasse auf Grund radiometrischer Altersbestimmungen. *Mem. Ist. Geol. Mineral. Univ. Padova* **30**, 84 pp.

Schindler, C. (1959). Zur Geologie des Glärnisch. *Beitr. geol. Karte Schweiz, N.F.* **107**, 135 pp.

Sclater, J.G. and Christie, P.A.F. (1980). Continental stretching: an explanation of the post-mid-Cretaceous subsidence of the central North Sea basin. *J. geophys. Res.* **85**, B7, 3711–3739.

Smithson, S.B., Brewer, J., Kaufman, S. and Oliver, J. (1978). Nature of the Wind River thrust, Wyoming, from COCORP deep-reflection data and from gravity data. *Geology* **6**, 648–652.

Spicher, A. (1980) Carte géologique de la Suisse, 1:500 000, 2ème éd. Common. géol. Suisse.

Steck, A. (1980). Deux directions principales de flux synmétamorphiques dans les Alpes centrales. *Bull. Soc. vaud. Sci. nat.* **75**, 141–149.

Steck, A., Ramsay, J.G., Milnes, A.G. and Burri, M. (1979). Compte

rendu de l'excursion de la Société Géologique Suisse et la Société de Minéralogie et Pétrographie en Valais et en Italie nord du 2 au 5 octobre 1978. *Ecolgae geol. Helv.* **72**, 287–311.

Stein, A., Vecchia, O. and Froelich, R. (1978). A seismic model of a refraction profile across the Western Po Valley. *In* "Alps, Apennines, Hellenides" (H. Closs, D. Roeder and K. Schmidt, eds) pp. 180–189. Schweizerbart, Stuttgart.

Streiff, V. (1962). Zur östlichen Beheimatung der Klippendecken. *Eclogae geol. Helv.* **55**, 77–132.

Studer, M. (1980). Métamorphismĕd'enfouissement dans le Haut Atlas central (Maroc). Essai sur l'évaluation de l'épaisseur des couvertures sédimentaires. *C.R. Acad. Sci. (Paris) (D)* **291**, 457–460.

Termier, P. (1903). Les nappes des Alpes orientales et la synthèse des Alpes. *Bull. Soc. géol. France (4)*, **4**, 711–765.

Thöni, M. (1980). Zur Westbewegung der Oetztaler Masse. Räumliche und zeitliche Fragen an der Schlinigüberschiebung. *Mitt. Ges. Geol.-u. Bergbaustud, Oesterr.* **26**, 247–275.

Trümpy, R. (1949). Der Lias der Glarner Alpen. *Denkschr. schweiz. natf. Ges.* **79/1**, 192 pp.

Trümpy, R. (1960). Paleotectonic evolution of the Central and Western Alps. *Bull. geol. Soc. Amer.* **71**, 843–903.

Wagner, G.A., Reimer, G.M. and Jäger, E. (1977). Cooling ages derived by apatite fission — track, mica Rb-Sr and K-Ar dating: the uplift and cooling history of the Central Alps. *Mem. Ist. Geol. Mineral. Univ. Padova* **30**, 27 pp.

Ziegler, P.A. (1977). Geology and hydrocarbon provinces of the North Sea. *Geojournal* **1**, 7–32.

Zingg, A. (1978). Regionale Metamorphose in der Ivrea Zone (Nord — Italien). Diss. ETH Zürich.

Deep Structure and Recent Dynamics in the Alps

St. Mueller

Institut für Geophysik (ETH), Zürich, Switzerland

Abstract

The Alps are a deep-reaching collision structure in Europe situated at the northernmost tip of the "Adriatic promontory", a spur-like microplate which has moved with the African plate since the early Mesozoic thereby eventually creating this spectacular mountain range. In this paper the most recent geophysical and geodetic observations are summarized which have led to a crust-mantle model of the Central (Swiss) Alps consistent with all the presently available data.

The crustal structure in the northern Alpine foreland is characteristic of tectonically active areas with an upper crustal low-velocity layer and a second zone of reduced velocity immediately above the crust-mantle boundary. A crustal flake consisting of a granitic core and gneissic envelopes apparently has been sheared off near the base of the upper crustal low-velocity zone and then been bent upward thus forming the present-day Aar Massif.

The Pennine Alps between the Rhine-Rhône Line and the Insubric Line are probably made up of two superimposed crustal blocks whose layers are intercalated in a complex manner. This central portion of the Alps, with the maximum crustal thickness of 53 km observed just north of the Insubric Line, must be considered as the transition region between the Eurasian and African plates. Beneath the Southern Alps the crust is relatively undisturbed with features still reflecting its "rift flank" character which presumably developed in lower Cretaceous time.

There are several sets of data which indicate that a considerable uplift must have taken place in the Alps during the past 40 m.y. The crustal block north of the Insubric Line has been vertically uplifted by isostatic movements relative to the Southern Alps and then subsequently been eroded by about 20 to 25 km. Repeated precise levellings show that the uplift is still going on today at rates of 1·0 to 1·5 mm per year in the Lepontine area. It could be demonstrated that the regions of highest uplift at present correlate extremely well with the most negative isostatic gravity anomalies.

The conspicuous thickening of the Alpine crust and the asymmetric shape of the crust-mantle boundary point toward a much deeper-reaching structural anomaly involving the entire lithosphere–asthenosphere system. Long-range seismic refraction measurements along the strike of the Alps as well as a detailed regional analysis of seismic surface-wave dispersion and P-wave travel time residuals have revealed a rather anomalous velocity-depth distribution within the uppermost mantle under the Alps. During the plate collision process south- and northward dipping slabs of lower lithosphere — characterized by higher P- and S-velocities — must have been subducted to a depth of 200 to 250 km, i.e. to the bottom of the asthenosphere. This zone of "Verschluckung" provides a reasonable explanation for the long-sought mode of deposition of the excess lithospheric material during the dramatic shortening of the Alpine crust-mantle system.

I. Introduction

A detailed analysis of the seismicity of the earth revealed that earthquakes do not occur randomly in space, but are restricted to narrow zones which coincide with the four basic structural elements of the global plate tectonic model, namely active ridge crests (in oceanic areas), transform faults, trench systems and (compressional) zones of orogeny. They clearly outline the extent of the major lithospheric plates which cover the earth's surface (Fig. 1, after Vine, 1969) and whose interior behaves roughly as a quasi-rigid medium, i.e. it is essentially aseismic and not subject to major internal

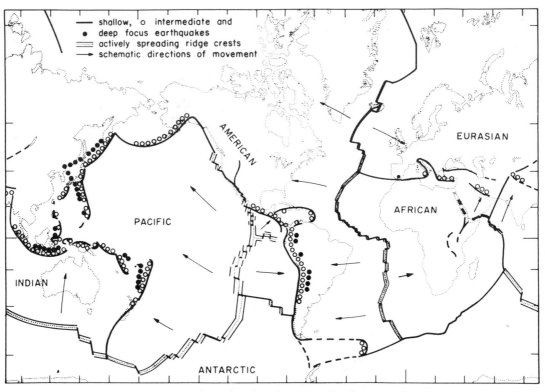

Fig. 1   Schematic summary of the earth's seismicity. The earthquake epicentres outline the extent of the lithospheric plates bounded by active ridge crests, transform faults, trench systems and zones of orogeny (after Vine, 1969). The Alps are situated at the northernmost tip of the Adriatic promontory ("spur") of the African plate.

deformations. Whereas earthquakes beneath ridge crests and transform faults appear to happen at depths of less than 20 km, shocks under trench systems and under some of the major mountain belts of the world occur at all depths up to a maximum of 720 km. It thus becomes clear that most of the earth's seismicity is a direct consequence of the relative movements of these quasi-rigid plates. The boundaries and marginal zones between different plates are therefore regions of particular interest.

In the present context of mountain building only zones of compressional plate contact (see schematic directions of plate movement in Fig. 1) are considered. Prime examples are the Andes, the Himalayas, the Caucasus and the Alps. While in the first case the small oceanic "Nazca" plate collides with the continental edge of the massive (South) American plate, the other three cases are of the continent–continent collision type. In particular, the Alps which are situated at the northernmost tip of the African plate (Fig. 1) apparently have been formed by a primarily north-west–south-east directed compression caused by the active sea-floor spreading in the North Atlantic and by the slow counter-clockwise rotation of the so-called "Adriatic promontory" (Channell et al., 1979) of the African plate as a consequence of the slightly higher spreading rate in the South Atlantic, as compared to the Central Atlantic. The seismicity of the Alpine–Mediterranean region summarized in Fig. 2 (after Lort, 1971) outlines the dimension of the Adriatic promontory which — as can be seen — extends all the way into the Alps.

At a first glance it may appear difficult to understand the complex present-day tectonic situation in the Mediterranean area and in the Alps (Mueller and Lowrie, 1980). The

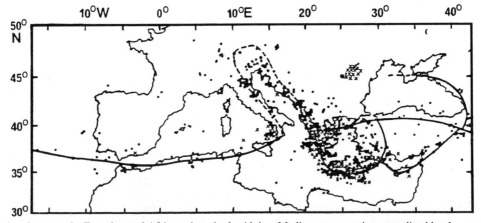

Fig. 2   The boundary between the Eurasian and African plates in the Alpine–Mediterranean region as outlined by the recent seismicity (after Lort, 1971). Black dots represent shallow-focus earthquakes (1962–1967) with depths less than 70 km, while crosses denote foci below 70 km depth since 1925. The dashed line indicates roughly the shape of the Adriatic promontory which extends all the way into the Alps.

reconstruction of plate positions at previous periods of time by shifting back the magnetic anomalies of the Atlantic ocean floor has, however, made it possible to re-establish the relative motions between Africa and North America on one hand, and between Europe and North America on the other hand (Pitman and Talwani, 1972). It could be shown that the separation of the former started approximately 180 m.y. ago, while the latter began to separate only about 80 m.y. ago. The predominant relative movement along the boundary between the African and Eurasian plates was first a right lateral shear motion which around 50 m.y. ago gradually changed into a thrust-type motion (Dewey *et al.*, 1973). A number of paleogeographic models have been developed based on either geological data (see e.g. Frisch, 1980) or tectonic observations (Illies, 1975) which have led to a surprisingly consistent picture of the geodynamic evolution of the Alpine–Mediterranean region since the Triassic (~200 m.y. ago).

In all these models the evolution of the Alps during this period of time is viewed as the result of an involved history with episodes of lithospheric rifting and shortening. The complex crustal structure — partially visible at the earth's surface — is only the "surficial" expression of a much deeper-reaching disturbance caused by the collision of the Eurasian plate with the Adriatic promontory of the African plate.

From the available evidence it must be surmised that the entire lithosphere–asthenosphere system is affected by this process and there are indications that the collision front may extend to even greater depths, i.e. well into the mantle transition zone. Multidisciplinary efforts have therefore been made over the past few decades to elucidate the deep structure, dynamics and evolution of the Alps. The most recent results of these various studies are summarized in this paper.

II. Crustal Structure

During the past 25 years a large amount of seismic refraction observations, a few deep reflection results as well as some detailed data on travel-time variations of seismic body waves and dispersion characteristics of seismic surface waves have been collected for the region of the Alps. The areas of main interest shifted with time from the Maritime Alps in the west to the anomalous Zone of Ivrea, the Dolomites and the Northern Calcareous Alps in the east and back to the central part of the Alps (Miller *et al.*, 1982). Technical details of the deep seismic sounding work, in particular the exact positions of the various profiles, the shooting and recording procedures as well as first interpretations were published by Closs and Labrouste (1963), Choudhury *et al.* (1971), Giese and Prodehl (1976), the Alpine Explosion Seismology Group (1976), and Miller *et al.* (1977, 1978) for the Western and Eastern Alps, by Ansorge *et al.* (1979) for the Southern Alps and by Mueller *et al.* (1976, 1980) for the Swiss Alps.

As part of the International Geodynamics Project multidisciplinary research aimed at a comprehensive study of the structure, the movements and deformations — past and present — of the Alpine lithosphere was initiated by the Swiss Academy of Natural Sciences in 1974. The geophysical results obtained for the central portion of the Alps in Switzerland will be illustrated in the form of a crust-mantle cross-section for the so-called "Swiss Geotraverse" across the Alps from the Rhinegraben in the north to the Po Plain in the south. The Swiss Geotraverse transects the main tectonic and geologic units of Switzerland as shown by the thickly dotted line in Fig. 3. It extends from the southern Rhinegraben near Basel across the tabular and folded Jura mountains through the Molasse basin, the Helvetic nappes, the Aar and Gotthard Massifs, the Penninic nappes of the Lepontine, and the

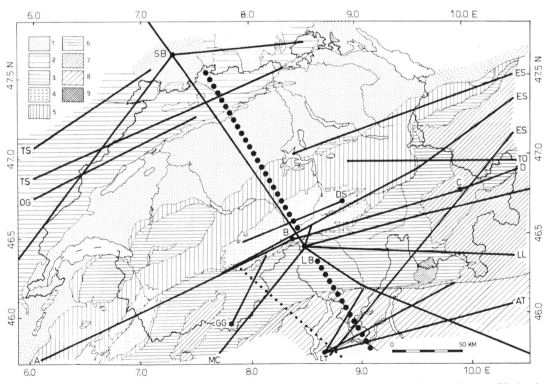

Fig. 3 Shotpoint locations and positions of seismic refraction profiles on a schematic geologic-tectonic map of Switzerland. 1 = Tertiary sediments, Molasse; 2 = Tabular Jura mountains; 3 = Folded Jura mountains; 4 = Crystalline massifs and basement, incl. the Gotthard Massif; 5 = Helvetic autochthonous sediments, Helvetic and Ultrahelvetic nappes; 6 = Penninic nappes; 7 = Austro-Alpine nappes; 8 = Southern Alps; 9 = Tertiary intrusives and volcanics.
A, B, C, D = Shotpoints of the Alpine Longitudinal Profile (ALP 75). Other shotpoints: AT = Albiano/Trento; DS = Disentis; ES = Eschenlohe; GG = Gornergrat; LB = Lago Bianco; LL = Lago Lagorai; LT = Lentate/Varese; MC = Mt-Cenis; OG = Orgelet; SB = Steinbrunn; TO = Osttirol; TS = Tournus. ●●● = Location of Swiss Geotraverse; ··· = location of traverse across the Zone of Ivrea.

Southern Alps to the Tertiary sediments of the Po Plain. Heavy dark lines in Fig. 3 mark the geographic position of the various seismic refraction lines used for the determination of crustal structure in Switzerland for which the Swiss Geotraverse is intended to give a representative cross section. Shotpoints for the refraction measurements within the area of Fig. 3 are indicated by full dots and letter codes. Lettering on the edges of Fig. 3 denotes shotpoints outside the schematic map. As can be seen in Fig. 3 within Switzerland the Molasse basin, the helvetic nappes and the Aar Massif are still poorly covered by refraction profiles, and hence the models of crustal structure deduced in these areas should be considered only as preliminary. The few data obtained from shotpoint DS in the Aar Massif indicate that the structure of the upper crust there differs considerably from the regions to the north and south of this highly deformed unit.

In order to demonstrate the high quality of the more recently obtained data from seismic refraction experiments carried out as part of the Swiss Geotraverse project and in order to document the key data for the crustal structure derived three record sections from the main tectonic units along the Geotraverse have been selected. A much larger number of profiles of similar quality has, of course, been evaluated in this study. Figures 4, 5 and 6 show the three seismogram assemblages. As the ordinate the absolute travel time (t) of each record trace is used, reduced by the quantity given as distance ($\triangle$) divided by 6, i.e. a velocity of 6 km/s has been used in this time reduction. The profiles selected are Steinbrunn-SW (shotpoint SB in Fig. 3) in the folded Jura mountains; the profile from the Nufenen-Pass eastward towards the Flüela-Pass in the Central or Penninic Alps (shotpoint B towards shotpoint C in Fig. 3); and in the Southern Alps a profile from the southern end of the Lago Maggiore to the east (shotpoint LT towards shotpoint AT in Fig. 3).

The most pronounced phases common to all seismogram sections and those which demonstrate important lateral variations of the crustal structure are correlated on the record sections of Figs 4, 5 and 6. Rather significant dif-

ferences in travel time and apparent velocity are obvious for the first arrivals near the shotpoints, i.e. the sedimentary phases P_s. The influence of the laterally variable thickness of Quaternary sediments is clearly visible on the record section of the Southern Alps (Fig. 6). These sedimentary phases are followed in all three cases by the P_g phase which propagates through the crystalline basement with velocities between 6·0 and 6·1 km/s. Another common feature on the three record sections shown are arrivals with a velocity between 6·1 and 6·3 km/s coming in about 1 s after the P_g phase. This phase is followed by a signal which has propagated with a velocity between 6·7 and 6·8 km/s under the folded Jura mountains (Fig. 4) and the Central Alps (Fig. 5). No clear arrivals with this velocity can be traced along the profile in the Southern Alps (Fig. 6) which indicates a less differentiated type of crust in this area as compared to the profiles further north.

Strong later arrivals identified as the refracted (P_n) and over-critically reflected (P_MP) signals from the crust-mantle boundary follow the high-velocity intermediate phase of the northern profiles after a variable interval of travel time, i.e. approximately 1 s under the Jura mountains (Fig. 4) and 4 to 5 s under the Central Alps (Fig. 5). This comparison should not be extrapolated to the Southern Alps, because in that area the high-velocity intermediate phase seems to be absent. The central and southern profiles show a few weak arrivals slightly earlier than the P_MP and P_n phases, which suggest a relatively thin high-velocity layer (with a P velocity of about 7 km/s) immediately above the crust-mantle boundary.

The dense coverage of the territory of Switzerland and its adjacent areas with seismic refraction profiles (Fig. 3) has made it possible to compile a depth contour map of the crust-mantle boundary as shown in Fig. 7. A recently completed map of the Mohorovičić discontinuity for Switzerland (Egloff, 1979) was combined with the results from the Rhinegraben (Edel *et al.*, 1975), the Bresse-Graben (Michel, 1978), Southern Germany (Emter, 1971; Giese, 1976), and from the Eastern Alps (Miller *et al.*, 1977). Additional data incorporated in this map were taken from the Alpine Explosion Seismology Group (1976), Miller *et al.* (1978) and Ansorge *et al.* (1979). The most conspicuous features in this

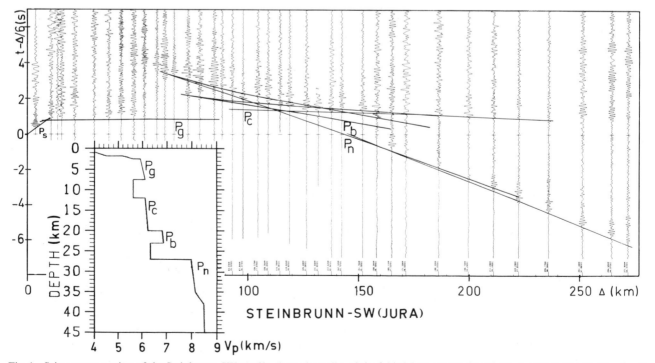

Fig. 4   Seismogram section of the Steinbrunn-SW profile along the strike of the folded Jura mountains (shotpoint SB in Fig. 3). The signal correlations were calculated on the basis of the P velocity-depth function shown in the inset (lower left corner).

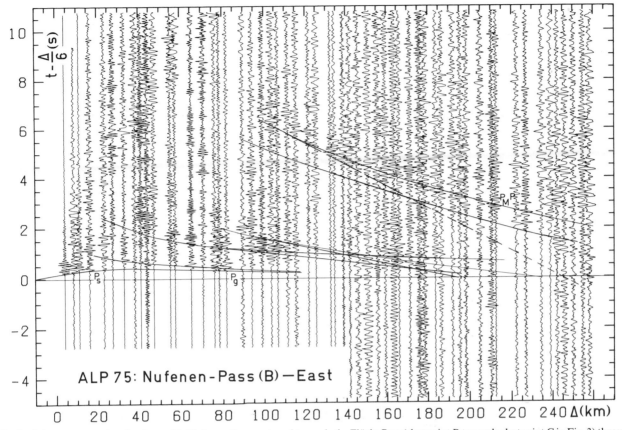

Fig. 5   Seismogram section for the profile Nufenen-Pass eastward towards the Flüela-Pass (shotpoint B towards shotpoint C in Fig. 3) through the Central Alps. Correlations were calculated based on the corresponding P velocity-depth function (Pennine Zone) in Fig. 9.

map are the diapiric mantle upwarp under the southern Rhinegraben (north of Basel) and the considerable thickening of the crust under the Alps due to the compressional stress which is directed in a north-west–south-east direction and which is causing a considerable crustal shortening. It can be seen in Fig. 7 that the depth pattern of the crust-mantle boundary exhibits an asymmetric shape with respect to the main axis of the Alps in agreement with the interpretation of gravity and earlier seismic data by Kahle *et al.* (1976a, 1976b). A more gentle decrease from about 24 km near the southern end of the Rhinegraben to about 54 km under the central part of the Canton Grisons contrasts to a rather steep rise to 35 km under the Southern Alps.

There is some evidence that the mantle upwarp under the Rhinegraben probably extends south-westward to the Bresse-Graben north of Lyon (Fig. 7) and eventually further west to the Central Massif of France as shown by Michel (1978). The complex structure of the Zone of Ivrea on the

inner arc of the Western Alps (north-west of Torino) has been omitted in Fig. 7, because it is not included in the discussion of the Swiss Geotraverse.

The described pattern of crustal thickness can also be clearly recognized in the new Bouguer gravity map of Switzerland which is reproduced in Fig. 8 (Klingelé and Olivier, 1980). As the axis of the Alps is approached, the gravity anomalies become more and more negative. Again the asymmetry mentioned is quite apparent with a relatively steep gradient under the Southern Alps. Superimposed on this regional anomaly is the pronounced positive gravity anomaly caused by the denser rocks in the Zone of Ivrea (German Research Group for Explosion Seismology, 1968). If corrections are made for this anomalous structure and for the Molasse basin (Kissling, 1980) the deep structure deduced for the Swiss Geotraverse can be considered to be more or less representative for the entire area under discussion.

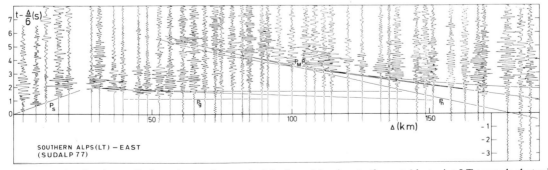

Fig. 6   Seismogram section for the profile from the southern end of the Lago Maggiore to the east (shotpoint LT towards shotpoint AT in Fig. 3). Correlations were calculated based on the corresponding P velocity-depth function (Southern Alps) in Fig. 9.

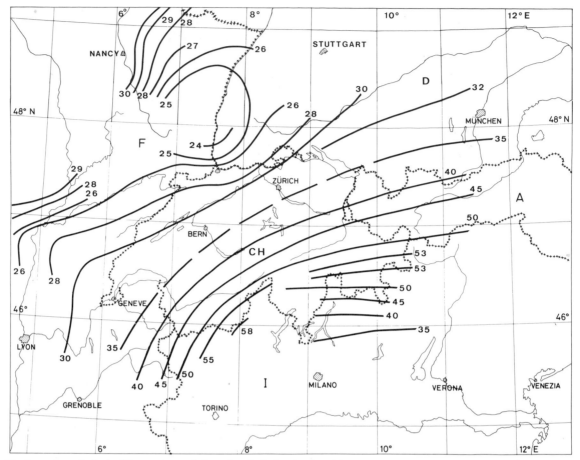

Fig. 7   Depth contours (in km) of the crust-mantle boundary in Switzerland and the adjacent areas after Egloff (1979), and Alpine Explosion
Seismology Group (1976), Ansorge *et al.* (1979), Edel *et al.* (1975), Emter (1971), Giese (1976), Miller *et al.* (1977, 1978).

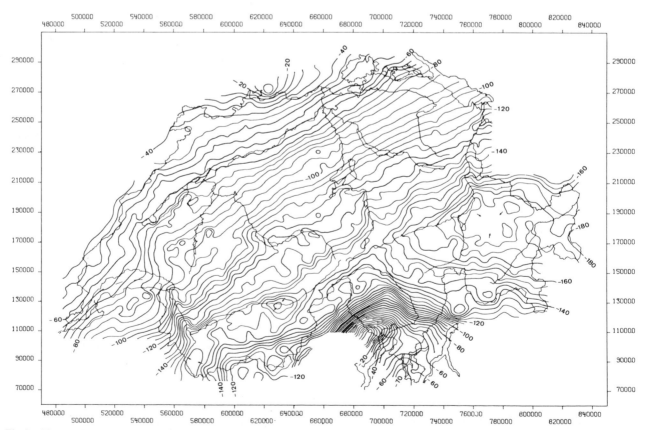

Fig. 8   The new Bouguer gravity map of Switzerland (after Klingelé and Olivier, 1980). It is based on measurements at over 2000 field stations.
The (negative) isolines more or less follow the strike of the Alps (cf. Fig. 7), except in the south where the effect of the high-density Ivrea body
is superimposed.

The interpretation of the main travel-time branches which have been correlated in Figs 4, 5 and 6 and which are also observed on most of the other profiles depicted in Fig. 3 showing the same consistent pattern (Egloff, 1979) led to individual velocity-depth functions for five of the main tectonic units along the Swiss Geotraverse (Fig. 9). The depth profiles for the Rhinegraben (solid line), the folded Jura mountains and the Helvetic zone of the Northern Alps show the same schematic velocity-depth distribution. Pronounced differences mark the transition from the rift system of the southern Rhinegraben (Mueller *et al.*, 1973; Prodehl *et al.*, 1976) to the normal type of crust under the Jura mountains (Egloff and Ansorge, 1976; Mueller, 1977). The thickness of the low-velocity zone in the upper crust decreases markedly whereas the depth to the crust-mantle boundary shows a pronounced increase towards the northern margin of the Alps.

The model for the northern margin of the Alps (Helvetic zone) was derived from the profile Eschenlohe-West terminating near Einsiedeln (northernmost profile from shotpoint Eschenlohe = ES in Fig. 3) and extrapolated along the Helvetic zone onto the Swiss Geotraverse. A thin shallow zone of low velocity within the sediments (depth range 3.5 km to 6.5 km) characterizes this segment of the Geotraverse. It is caused by the overthrust of the Helvetic nappes associated with higher velocities over the slower material of the folded foreland Molasse. This type of interpretation had been suggested by Will (1976) for the Northern Calcareous Alps east of the shotpoint Eschenlohe in Bavaria. It has been confirmed recently by the results from detailed seismic reflection measurements in the course of exploration work for hydrocarbon deposits (BEB, 1979) close to the Swiss Geotraverse (Fig. 12).

A low-velocity zone (with a velocity reduction of 3 to 10%) separates the upper part of the crystalline basement with velocities of about 6 km/s from the middle crust under all three northern velocity-depth distributions (Fig. 9). A zone with velocities ranging from 6·1 to 6·3 km/s is interrupted by a relatively thin high-velocity zone with values around 7 km/s which effectively produces a second low-velocity layer immediately above the crust-mantle boundary. This general type of continental crust for tectonically active areas has been discussed in detail by Mueller (1977). The depth to the crust-mantle boundary increases smoothly from 25 km under the southern Rhinegraben to slightly less than 40 km under the Helvetic zone of the Northern Alps.

In contrast to these first three models a very different crustal structure is found under the Pennine zone of the Central Alps (Fig. 9). If one takes the high-velocity layer ("tooth") with P velocities of about 7 km/s in the lower crust of the northern foreland as a reference horizon two alter-native correlations have to be discussed for the crustal structure under the Lepontine area. The high-velocity "tooth" at a depth of about 25 km must be considered to be characteristic of an original feature in the lower Alpine crust which has been uplifted by 20 to 25 km as indicated by the observed metamorphism of rocks exposed at the surface in that region (Fig. 16). More likely is an extrapolated correlation of the foreland "tooth" with the high-velocity step at a depth of 44 km under the Central Alps. This interpretation implies that the lower crust of the northern foreland extends under the Pennine zone, but has been separated from its upper part by a relatively thick layer of a "quasi-uniform", little differentiated structure with an average P velocity of not more than 6 km/s ranging from a depth of 26 km down to 44 km. It cannot be resolved in more detail with the presently available data. The crust-mantle boundary in this section of the Swiss Geotraverse lies at a depth of ~ 50 km.

The crustal structure changes again abruptly when reaching the Southern Alps as can be seen from the fifth model in Fig. 9 (right-hand side). The crustal thickness decreases sharply from 53 km under the Central Alps to 35 km under the Southern Alps, which is much less than the value of 42 km derived by Stein *et al.* (1978) for the same area. Except for the uppermost part of the crust no fine structure seems to exist within the crust. However, the average P velocity is slightly higher than that found in the northern foreland of the Alps. This structure with the thin high-velocity transition layer directly overlying the crust-mantle boundary is similar to what is normally found under rift flanks at an evolutionary stage shortly before the acute break-up of a continental plate sets in (Mueller, 1978). This structural feature would be in agreement with palinspastic reconstructions postulating a tensional phase in Lower Cretaceous time (Büchi and Trümpy, 1976; Trümpy, 1980) which must have led to extensive rifting.

By combining all available seismic refraction and reflection data along the Swiss Geotraverse a representative crustal cross-section could be constructed which is shown in Fig. 10. As mentioned before some features of the crustal structure had to be extrapolated or projected onto the Swiss Geotraverse. The depth countour map of the crust-mantle boundary in Fig. 7 and the Bouguer gravity map in Fig. 8 justify this procedure within certain limits. The proposed crustal structure is well documented for the northern foreland of the Alps, the Lepontine area (Penninic domain) and the Southern Alps, while the transition structures between these three major units are still somewhat uncertain.

Starting in the north-west close to the pronounced mantle upwarp under the southern Rhinegraben the entire crust dips down towards the south-east beneath the thickening sedimentary wedge of the Molasse basin. Only minor inter-

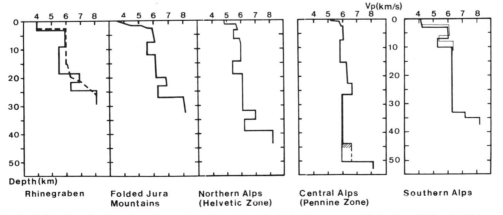

Fig. 9 P velocity-depth functions for five selected crustal sections along the Swiss Geotraverse (dashed model for the Rhinegraben after Edel *et al.*, 1975).

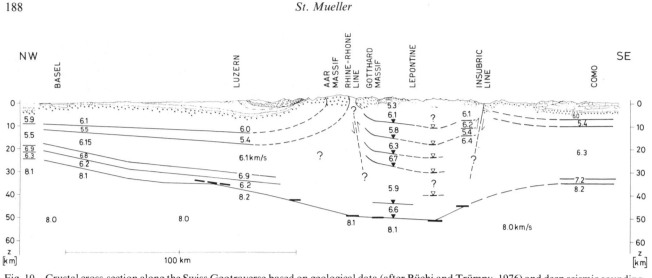

Fig. 10   Crustal cross-section along the Swiss Geotraverse based on geological data (after Büchi and Trümpy, 1976) and deep seismic sounding
results:
—— = Depth of the crust-mantle boundary after Egloff (1979)
▼ = Depth derived from near-vertical reflections (after Wehebrink, 1968).

nal variations of velocities and thicknesses of the crustal layers seem to occur with the crust-mantle boundary running roughly parallel to the contact between the Mesozoic formations and the basement. Heavy bars in Fig. 10 indicate the depth of the crust-mantle boundary as it has been determined by a standard evaluation of the wide-angle reflection observations (t^2, x^2 method).

The low-velocity layer in the upper crust which seems to exist throughout the northern segment of the Swiss Geotraverse is well documented also by additional observations from shotpoint Steinbrunn (SB in Fig. 3) towards the east as shown on the record section of Fig. 11. The P_g branch which is recorded over the entire range of observations of 90 km is followed by the near-vertical and wide-angle reflections from the top of the low-velocity zone indicating a rather abrupt decrease of the velocity at that boundary. Wide-angle

reflections from the bottom of the low-velocity layer were recorded about 0·7 s later than those from the upper boundary. The relative amplitudes of P_g and later following phases reflected from the low-velocity layer are crucially influenced by the velocity gradients in each layer and across the interfaces of the various layers (Egloff, 1979).

The following segment of the Swiss Geotraverse to the south-east, i.e. the crustal structure under the Aar Massif, seems to be rather complex and is not yet completely understood. This is partly due to the lack of sufficient information from deep seismic experiments in this area. The relatively low P_g velocities which were observed along the short profile through the Aar Massif (shotpoint DS in Fig. 3) (Ottinger, 1976) and the surface geology with the granitic outcrops in the axial core of the massif (see Fig. 14) suggests that in this area the upper crust has been sheared off at the base of the

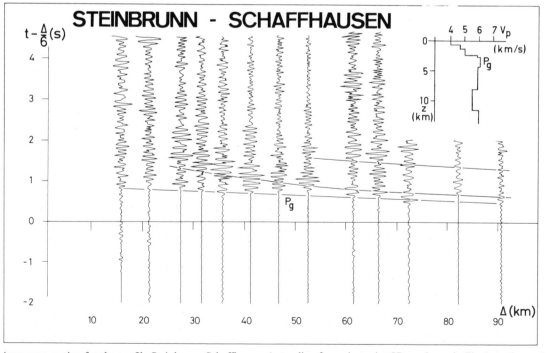

Fig. 11   Seismogram section for the profile Steinbrunn-Schaffhausen (extending from shotpoint SB, as shown in Fig. 3, to the east). Correlations were calculated based on the P velocity-depth function shown in the inset (upper right-hand corner) which illustrates the existence of a distinct low-velocity layer in the upper crust.

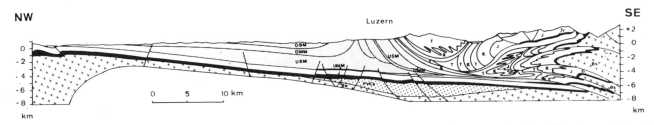

Fig. 12   Detailed geologic section along the Swiss Geotraverse from the Jura mountains (in the north) to the Aar Massif (in the south) based on seismic reflection work (after BEB, 1979). — OSM = Upper Freshwater Molasse; OMM = Upper Marine Molasse; USM = Lower Freshwater Molasse; UMM = Lower Marine Molasse; T = Tertiary (incl. Flysch); K = Cretaceous; J = Jurassic; Tr = Triassic; P-Ca = Permo-Carboniferous; Bs = Crystalline Basement.

low-velocity zone. The compressional shortening of the crust has caused these layers to be bent upward in a flake-type manner as indicated in Figs 10 and 13 (Laubscher, 1970; Oxburgh, 1972). The backward thrust of the geologic units observed near the surface seems to be restricted only to the upper portion of an otherwise relatively homogeneous crust without pronounced velocity variations down to a depth of at least 15 km under the central part of the Aar Massif according to the observations from shotpoint DS (Egloff, 1979). The grade of metamorphism (Fig. 16) observed in that part of the Alps (Frey *et al.* 1980) suggests that the

material of the exposed Aar Massif has once resided at depths of about 10 to 15 km. If the crustal flake in Fig. 10 is bent back into its original position it would fall into the appropriate depth range.

The geologic cross-section in the uppermost part of Fig. 10 is taken from Büchi and Trümpy (1976). Recently published data obtained from seismic reflection measurements (BEB, 1979) show a much more complex structure of the Mesozoic and Tertiary sediments and their interaction with the northern boundary of the Aar Massif than has been assumed so far. This new model is shown schematically in Fig. 12 where the outer part of the Aar Massif, i.e. the gneissic envelope of the granitic intrusive masses, has been thrust in slices over the Mesozoic sediments producing scaly intercalations. It seems as if these processes reach to a depth of about 8 km (see also Fig. 13). The interpretation of these new data does, however, not imply that the boundary between the sediments and the crystalline basement is the main shearing horizon along which the Aar Massif has been pushed upwards from the south-east over a distance of several hundred kilometres following the suggestion recently published by Hsü (1979). As pointed out above the central granitic core of the Aar Massif is more likely derived from the laccolithic zone of granitic intrusions which compose the sialic low-velocity zone in the upper crust of tectonically active areas (Mueller, 1977) and which here has been pushed upwards in a flake-type manner. An example of the present-day situation is shown in Fig. 14 where the granitic Bietschhorn (light grey colour) in the central Aar Massif surmounts the outer envelope to the south-east, which is composed of gneissic material (dark grey colour). A photograph of the summit

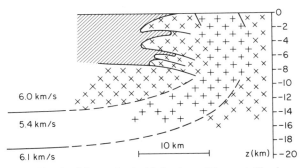

Fig. 13   Sketch of the mechanical behaviour of the crystalline basement beneath the northern part of the Swiss Alps. The section combines the near-surface structure as shown in Fig. 12 with the upper crustal structure deduced from seismic refraction measurements in the Aar Massif. In this model the granitic (flake-type) core of the Aar Massif is embedded in slivers of gneiss and linked with the low-velocity layer under the northern foreland of the Alps.

Fig. 14   The granitic Bietschhorn (3934 m) — light grey colour — in the central Aar Massif as seen from the south across the Rhine-Rhône Line. In front of it lies the dark gneissic envelope immediately to the north of the Rhône valley.

region of the Aletschhorn, a neighbouring peak, shows a cap of gneissic rocks resting on top of granitic masses demonstrating the sharp contact between the envelope and the core of the Aar Massif (Mueller, 1977).

The sketch in Fig. 13 incorporates the newly obtained data from the reflection measurements cited as well as the seismic refraction observations near the northern margin of the Aar Massif. The model proposed previously for the development of the Aar Massif (Mueller et al., 1976), i.e. the uplift of an upper crustal flake sheared off near the base of a low-velocity zone, is compatible with the structure of the upper basement derived from reflection measurements (Fig. 12). The actual relative position of gneissic and granitic portions in the Aar Massif varies from the simple sequence shown in Fig. 14 to alternate vertical sequences (Fig. 13) and in some places even to granitic slices thrust over gneissic ones with strong lateral variations. The thrust character of the northern boundary of the Aar Massif is also illustrated by the focal mechanisms of earthquakes in that region which contain a clear component of thrust motion (Ahorner et al., 1972).

A high-velocity layer (6·7 km/s) is normally found in the lower crust or in transition zones at the bottom of the crust, as for instance under the folded Jura mountains (Fig. 4) or in the Eastern Alps (Miller et al., 1977). As mentioned earlier, in the Penninic or Central Alpine segment of the Swiss Geotraverse this characteristic high velocity is found both at an intermediate depth followed by a pronounced layer of low velocity and in a normal type of transition (6·6–6·7 km/s) to the crust-mantle boundary (Figs 9 and 10). This sequence of velocities can be interpreted as an extension of the northern lower crust reaching southward approximately to the Insubric Line (Fig. 10) overlain by a different crustal block with its northern boundary near the Rhine-Rhône Line. The top of the low-velocity zone (i.e. the depth range of approximately 26 to 30 km) in the present-day middle crust of the Lepontine region would then be the horizon permitting the relative motion of these two crustal slabs. It is very likely that both processes, uplift and north-westward translation, occurred at about the same time. However, the amount of translation and the geologic history cannot be determined from the presently available seismic data.

This suggestion has some important implications for the Rhine-Rhône Line and the Insubric Line. It may be that the slope of the Rhine-Rhône Line as shown in Fig. 10 is too steep or not as deep-reaching judging from the crustal structure which is known very close to this fracture zone. The Insubric Line must be considerably younger than the still ongoing uplift of the Lepontine block (see Fig. 17) otherwise the zone of relative vertical movement could not be restricted to such a sharp boundary. As shown in Fig. 10 the rather steep rise of the crust-mantle boundary towards the south near the southern limit of the Lepontine region coincides with the position of the Insubric Line which may be another indication that this lineament is a rather deep-reaching (lystric ?) fracture zone as already suggested by Gansser (1968) and Laubscher (1970, 1974b).

The complex crustal structure of the Lepontine region as determined from seismic refraction measurements is supported by the observations of near-vertical seismic reflections which were obtained in an azimuth range from north-east to south-east from the explosions in the Lago Bianco 1964 (Wehebrink, 1968). Figure 15 presents an example of the reflections observed to the north-east (see inset in Fig. 15) which are marked according to their character and quality. Black triangles indicate the two-way travel times calculated for the intracrustal interfaces of the model shown in Figs 9 and 10. The strongly differentiated upper crust is very well confirmed. In addition reflections of minor quality suggest a less pronounced differentiation in the lower crust which is characterized by a surprisingly low average velocity of 5·9 to

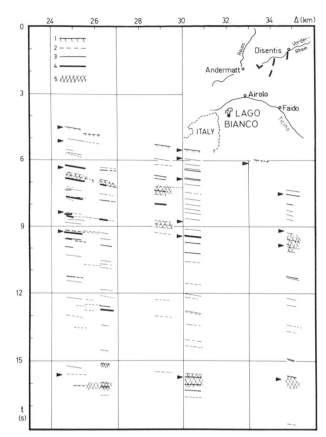

Fig. 15   Comparison of two-way travel times (t) from near-vertical deep reflection observations (after Wehebrink, 1968) north-east of the shotpoint Lago Bianco (LB in Fig. 3) with travel times calculated from the refraction-seismic model for the Central Alps in Fig. 9. The refraction horizons are marked by arrow points. Heavy bars in the inset map indicate the location of the reflection spreads. — 1 = first arrivals; 2 = weak reflections; 3 = normal reflections; 4 = good reflections; 5 = bands of reflections.

6·0 km/s as derived from seismic refraction observations.

The Southern Alps adjacent to the Insubric Line seem to consist of a relatively undisturbed stable crustal block of continental ("rift flank") type (Mueller, 1978) with little structural variations except for a minor zone of low velocity in the upper crust and a thin transition layer above the crust-mantle boundary (Ansorge et al., 1979). The rather abrupt change of the type of crustal structure across the Insubric Line may be explained by a model proposed by Laubscher (1974, a + b). According to this model (cf. Fig. 24) the Insubric Line represents the surface trace along which a stack of intercalated crustal layers was peeled off from a steeply descending lithospheric slab in a secondary, northward dipping subduction zone leaving behind the undisturbed continental block of the Southern Alps.

III. Recent Dynamics

The ongoing compressive shortening of the thickened crustal stack must have led to a sizeable uplift of the Central Alpine block. This process will also have caused a continuous downward motion of the lower portions of the lithosphere. The resulting zone of extension should be sought in the deeper Alpine crust where indeed lower P-wave velocities have been observed (see Figs 5 and 10).

There are several sets of data which confirm that a considerable uplift must have taken place in the Alps during the past 40 m.y. A schematic map of the Alpine metamorphism

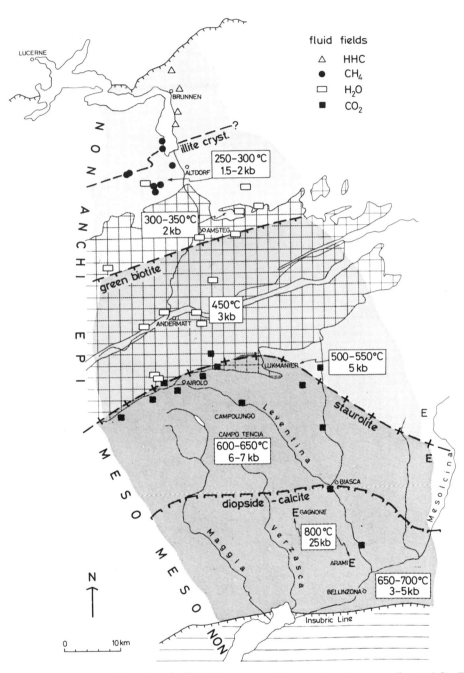

Fig. 16   Zonation map of Alpine metamorphism along the Swiss Geotraverse with temperature/pressure estimates (after Frey *et al.*, 1980). The composition of fluid inclusions in fissure quartz crystals is also indicated. E = eclogites of the Adula nappe and the Cima Lunga zone.

(Frey *et al.*, 1980) based on mineral zonation, the geothermometry and geobarometry as well as on a zonation of fluid inclusions in fissure quartz crystals (Fig. 16) demonstrates that the crust has been subjected to an asymmetric uplift with its maximum in the region north of the Insubric Line. As has been pointed out above (Fig. 9) the asymmetric crustal root of the Alps at present still has a maximum thickness of 53 km in the Penninic domain, but the original crustal thickness must have been much larger, since the block north of the Insubric Line has been vertically uplifted relative to the Southern Alps and then subsequently been eroded by about 20 to 25 km (Büchi and Trümpy, 1976; Werner, 1980).

Exactly the same uplift pattern has been observed as a result of geodetic measurements where repeated first-order precise levellings have been compared for different periods of time (Kobold, 1977). In Fig. 17 the observed uplift is depicted for three levelling campaigns along the profile Schwyz – Gotthard – Bellinzona – Mendrisio/Ticino. The curves for the periods 1919–1869 and 1919–1872, as well as the average for this 50 year interval, clearly show that there exists no direct correlation with topography and the maximum uplift (of about 3 mm per year) occurred at that time just north of the Insubric Line thus confirming the asymmetry mentioned above. During the past 50 years (1970–1919), however, the pattern seems to have changed; the uplift is now more symmetric with its maximum (near Biasca) amounting to less than half the rate of the preceding time period (1919–1870). This episodic nature of the most recent crustal movements has presumably prevailed during geologic times, and there is now ample evidence that various crustal blocks in the Alps have undergone different uplift histories (see e.g. Wagner *et al.*, 1977; Werner, 1980).

A more comprehensive picture of the present-day dynamics in the Alps is obtained if all the available measurements of recent crustal movements in Switzerland are analysed (Gubler *et al.*, 1981). Figure 18 shows the uplift rates determined from the first repetition of first-order levellings (between 1943 and 1978) as compared to the initial measurements (between 1903 and 1925) carried out by the Swiss Federal Office of Topography. The changes in elevation are all referred to a base station at Aarburg, located at the southern foot of the Jura mountains near Olten. From a closer look at Fig. 18 the following pattern emerges: at the northern margin of the Alps near Luzern/Schwyz where the Molasse submerges beneath the Helvetic nappes (cf. Fig. 12) an annual uplift of 0·3 mm is observed. Between Luzern and Andermatt the rates of recent vertical movements reach 1 mm per year. Relatively high uplift rates are found along the Rhine-Rhône Line with maxima (~ 1·7 mm per year) near Chur (Canton Grisons) and Brig/Visp (Canton Valais) and a saddle point in between around Andermatt/Hospental in the Gotthard region. Further south the most recent uplift reaches a secondary maximum (~ 1·4 mm per year) near Biasca, at a location within the Penninic nappes (about 15 km north of Bellinzona; see also Fig. 17). From there the uplift decreases gradually towards Chiasso/Como where a value of 0·8 mm per year is observed.

The question now arises if the increased thickness of the Alpine crust (see Fig. 7) is primarily responsible for the observed uplift. Three-dimensional isostatic anomalies have, therefore, been computed and projected onto the Swiss Geotraverse (Kahle *et al.*, 1976b, 1980). In the calculation of an Airy-type isostatic crustal model realistic corrections were made for the edge effects of the high-density Ivrea body and the low-density sedimentary fill of the Molasse basin in the north and the Po valley in the south. The average of the resulting anomalies indicates that the entire Alpine crust is characterized by an overall negative isostatic anomaly of − 20 mgal. This overcompensation must be due to the excessive depth of the M-discontinuity in the Alps and is the primary cause for vertical isostatic movements. In Fig. 19 the regional isostatic anomalies and the recent crustal uplift rates (see Fig. 18) in the Cantons of Grisons and Valais are presented. It can be seen that the area of highest uplift (~ 1·7 mm per year) near Chur is clearly associated with negative isostatic anomalies reaching a minimum of − 48 mgal. Moreover, it is interesting to note in Fig. 19 that the uplift rate decreases almost linearly from Chur to Andermatt whereas the isostatic anomalies increase proportionately.

A similar correlation is obtained in the Canton Valais.

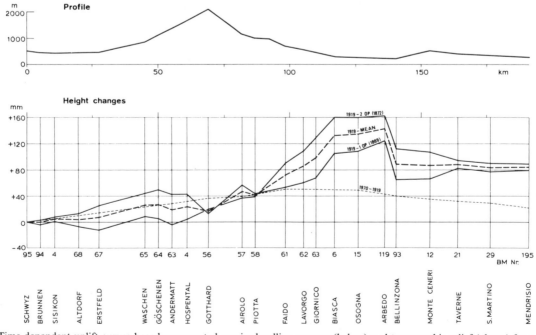

Fig. 17   Time-dependent uplift curves based on repeated precise levelling surveys (below) and topographic relief (above) for a north–south profile from Schwyz across the Rhine-Rhône Line (Andermatt/Hospental) and the Insubric Line (Arbedo/Bellinzona) to Mendrisio in the Canton Ticino (after Kobold, 1977). The pronounced asymmetric uplift between 1869/72 and 1919 (cf. also Fig. 16) has decreased in the recent past (1919 to 1970) and is now more symmetrical.

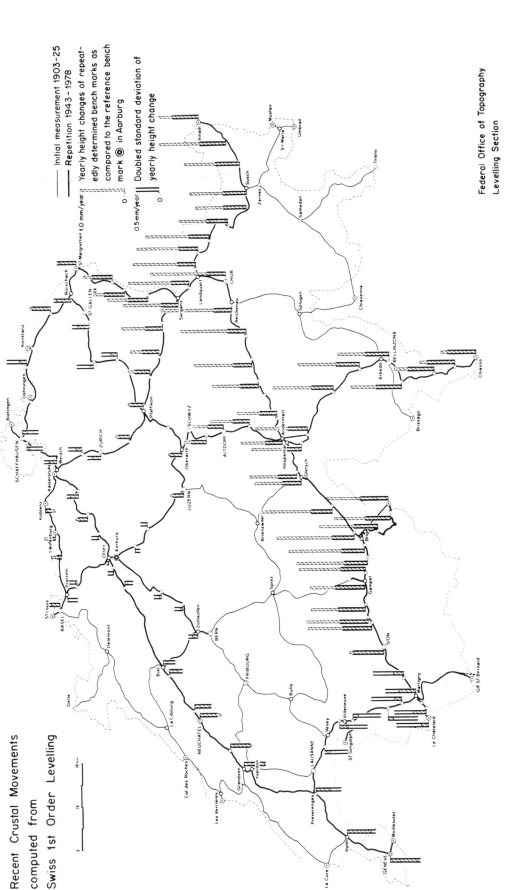

Fig. 18   First-order levelling net and annual height changes in Switzerland with respect to a reference bench mark in Aarburg (after Gubler *et al.*, 1981). The regions of highest uplift rates are located around Chur (Canton Grisons) and Brig/Visp (Canton Valais).

There, however, the complex structure of the near-by high-density zone of Ivrea through its positive edge effects masks the isostatic low near Brig/Visp. If proper corrections are made for the influence of the Ivrea body (Kissling, 1980) the isostatic anomaly would also decrease to values of about −40 mgal in a region where high uplift rates are observed. These facts in themselves may be considered as convincing evidence that the uplift in the Alps is predominantly controlled by isostatic rebound effects.

In Fig. 20 a synoptic representation is given summarizing the significant and characteristic features of the Swiss Geotraverse from Basel to Chiasso/Como (Rybach *et al.*, 1980) which relate the geologic structures as visible at the earth's surface (after Büchi and Trümpy, 1976) to the deep structure as determined by geophysical techniques along with geodynamic manifestations such as crustal movements, *in situ* stresses and gravity anomalies.

A summary of the observed uplift rates (Gubler, 1976) taken from the map in Fig. 18 (Gubler *et al.*, 1981) is presented in the second diagram (from the top) in Fig. 20. The wavelength of the uplift envelope is fairly large; it calls for a relatively deep-seated cause of the measured vertical movements. *In situ* stress determinations have revealed that a considerable excess *horizontal* compressive stress is present in the

upper crust of the Swiss Alps. Whereas low stress values (<5 MPa) prevail in the northern foreland, the excess horizontal stress increases from the margin of the Alps (near Luzern) to a maximum of about 25 MPa in the Lepontine area and decreases again towards the south-east. The shape of the stress curve corresponds rather well with the uplift pattern (Mueller *et al.*, 1976).

With the completion of the new gravimetric survey of Switzerland (Klingelé and Olivier, 1980) it is now possible to present a Bouguer anomaly profile between Basel and Chiasso (third diagram in Fig. 20). The asymmetric gravity minimum (−150 mgal) is located near the Rhine-Rhône Line (R.R.L.); the maximum just north of the Insubric Line (I.L.) is due to the pronounced edge effect (of about +40 mgal) of the Ivrea body to the west of the traverse. Another distorting influence (of about −30 mgal) must be attributed to the low-density sediments of the Molasse basin and the Po valley. If proper corrections for these effects are applied (see Kissling, 1980) the corrected Bouguer anomaly curve is a direct image of the crust-mantle boundary (M = "MOHO") under the Swiss Geotraverse. The crustal structure in the seismic section (Mueller *et al.*, 1980) as depicted in the fourth diagram (from the top) of Fig. 20 has already been discussed in conjunction with Fig. 10, the detailed

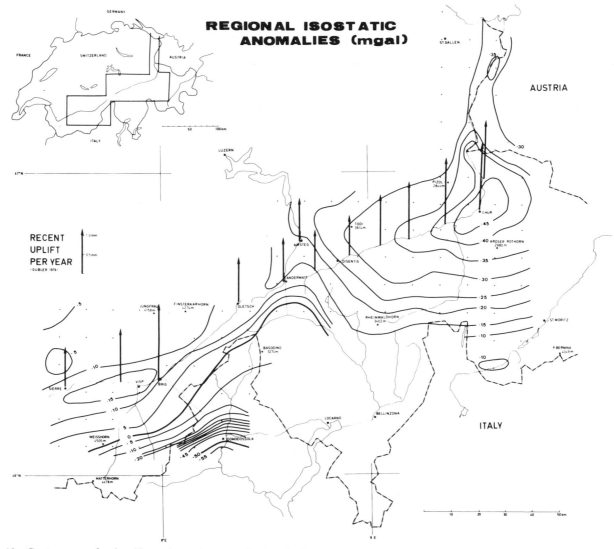

Fig. 19   Contour map of regional isostatic gravity anomalies (mgal) after Kahle *et al.* (1980). The arrows signify recent crustal uplift rates (per year) as shown in Fig. 18 (after Gubler, 1976). There is a perfect correlation between maximum uplift and the minima in the isostatic anomalies if the effect of the high-density Ivrea body (around Domodossola) is corrected for.

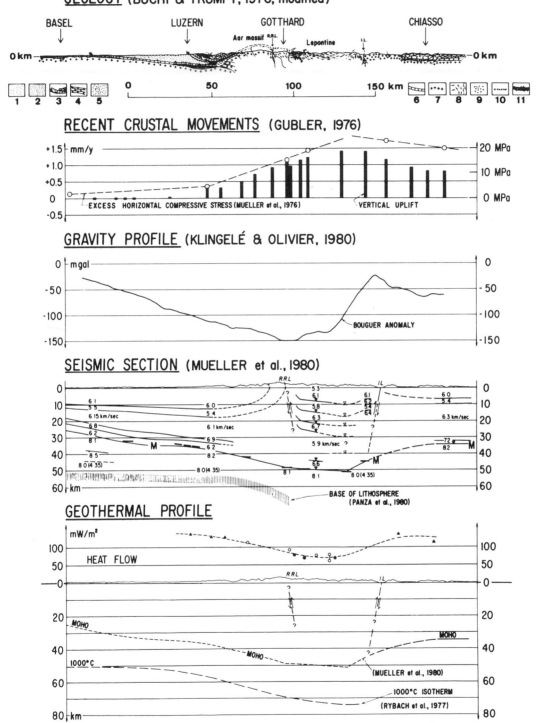

Fig. 20 Synoptic summary of the available geological, geodetic and geophysical data along the Swiss Geotraverse from Basel to Chiasso/Como (after Rybach *et al.*, 1980). For a detailed discussion of the various data sets see text.

Legend of the geologic section (top diagram):

1 = Molasse sediments; 2 = Flysch sediments; 3 = Mesozoic sediments of the Helvetic nappes; 4 = Mesozoic sediments of the Southern Alps; 5 = Mesozoic sediments of the Penninic units; 6 = Mesozoic sediments of the Jura mountains and of the autochthonous cover of the Aar Massif; 7 = crystalline basement including external massifs; 8 = intensely deformed basement of the Penninic zone; 9 = ultrabasic rocks of the Ivrea zone; 10 = Upper Paleozoic volcanites; 11 = Permo-Carboniferous sediments.

structure of the lower lithosphere as well as the anomalous structure of the entire lithosphere–asthenosphere system beneath the Alps will be dealt with in the following section.

Heat flow determinations near the Swiss Geotraverse have been compiled by Rybach and Finckh (1979) and are plotted in Fig. 20 (bottom diagram). Solid triangles indicate heat flow determinations in lake bottom sediments, and those from measurements in drillholes, shafts and tunnels are denoted by solid dots. The heat flow trend along the Swiss Geotraverse is characterized by lower values in the central part of the section. Approximately the same heat flow apparently prevailed at the time of peak metamorphism (Eocene/Oligocene) based on "geothermal gradients" as deduced from p/T data of metamorphic mineral reactions along the Geotraverse (Frey *et al.*, 1980) and by assuming an average thermal conductivity of 2·5 W/m.K for crustal rocks, heat flow values in the range of 63 to 112 mW/m² (open circles in Fig. 20, bottom diagram) are obtained which plot surprisingly close to the most recent heat flow determinations.

A characteristic feature of the geothermal field as observed along the profile of the Geotraverse Basel – Chiasso/Como is the decreasing geothermal gradient and the resulting heat flow as the Alps are approached from the northern foreland. Model calculations of the temperature field at greater depth based on deduced or assumed thermal parameters of the lithosphere (Rybach *et al.*, 1977) have revealed that beneath the Central Alps there are some indications of a thermal disturbance due to subduction processes ("Verschluckung", cf. Fig. 22). The downwarp of the 1000°C-isotherm which more or less coincides with the base of the lithosphere (see the "Seismic Section" above in Fig. 20) points towards a deeper reaching thermal "disequilibrium". It is possible that in the section with the thickest crust heat flow from deeper levels in the upper mantle will be lower than in the adjacent regions

to the north and south where crustal thickness is normal and the mantle structure appears undisturbed.

IV. Mantle Structure and Subduction

As has already been pointed out in the context with Fig. 10 that the thickening of the Alpine crust and the asymmetric shape of the crust-mantle boundary represent a clear indication of a much deeper reaching velocity anomaly beneath the Alps. Long-range seismic refraction observations in the northern Alpine foreland and along the strike of the Alps in addition to the detailed regional analysis of surface-wave dispersion and P-wave travel time residuals reveal a rather anomalous distribution of P- and S-wave velocities with depth.

North of the Alps an upper-mantle layer with a markedly high P-wave velocity of up to 8·5 km/s and a thickness of the order of 5 to 10 km (see Seismic Section in Fig. 20) lies between the crust-mantle boundary and the relatively shallow base of the lithosphere located at depths between 50 and 55 km (Ansorge *et al.*, 1979; Panza *et al.*, 1980). As the Alps are approached this layer of high velocity (8·6 km/s) is found at slightly greater depths. Following the Alpine chain from west to east, refraction seismic evidence (Miller *et al.*, 1979, 1982) shows that roughly between the Mont Blanc massif and the eastern end of the Tauern window the *mean P* velocity between the crust-mantle boundary down to depths of approximately 100 km amounts to about 8·5 km/s (Fig. 21). In contrast to the marginal regions of the Alps in the west and east, where in the same depth range of the uppermost mantle a distinct layering has been found no such structure could be detected beneath the central part along the axis of the Alps. The dimensions of this anomalous "block" of high-velocity material are estimated to be about 500 km in length

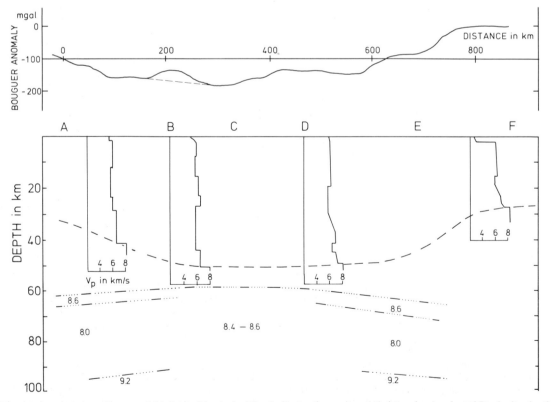

Fig. 21   Bouguer gravity anomaly, crustal thickness (the dashed line indicates the crust-mantle boundary), selected P velocity-depth functions and schematic structure of the uppermost mantle for the main line of the "Alpine Longitudinal Profile 1975" (after Miller *et al.*, 1978, 1981). The section extends along the axis of the Alps from Aix-les-Bains (A) in France to the Pannonian Basin (F) in Hungary. Note the high-velocity "block" under the central portion of the Alps which extends from a depth of 60 km to at least 100 km.

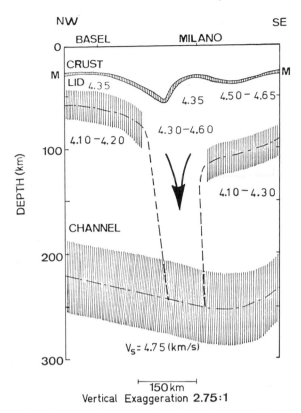

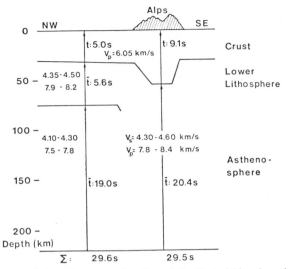

Fig. 23 Schematic cross-section through the Central Alps along the Swiss Geotraverse (cf. Fig. 22) after Panza and Mueller (1979). The one-way times of P waves travelling vertically from the bottom of the asthenosphere to the surface corroborate that the time delay caused by the low-velocity crustal root of the Alps must be compensated by the underlying high-velocity "block" in the asthenosphere (after Baer, 1980). In the model a ratio of $V_P/V_S = 1·82$ has been assumed.

Fig. 22 Crust-mantle cross-section from Basel to Milano as derived from the simultaneous inversion of all available dispersion data of seismic surface waves (after Panza and Mueller, 1979). S-wave velocities (V_S) are given in km/s. "Lid" = lower lithosphere, "Channel" = asthenosphere. Hatched areas indicate the range of uncertainty of the bottom of the crust (M), of the lithosphere and the asthenosphere. In the collision ("Verschluckung") process between the Eurasian and African plates the lower lithosphere seems to have been subducted to depths of about 200–250 km.

(east–west) and 100 to 150 km in width (north–south) extending to a depth of at least 100 km.

On a much larger scale the existence of a high-velocity block within the upper mantle under the Alps could be deduced from the dispersion of seismic surface waves by Panza and Mueller (1979). Figure 22 shows a schematic cross section of the lithosphere and asthenosphere system along a profile from Basel to Milano which coincides roughly with the Swiss Geotraverse. The hatched areas in this figure mark the range of uncertainty for the bottom of the crust, of the lithosphere and of the asthenosphere. The centre part is characterized by a high-velocity, subducted lower lithosphere reaching down to the bottom of the asthenosphere at a depth of about 200 to 250 km. This lithospheric block of higher velocity most likely corresponds to the two slabs of lower lithosphere subducted to the south and to the north during the plate collision process ("Verschluckung") forming the Alps (Panza and Mueller, 1979).

A crust-mantle model of this type not only provides a reasonable solution for the deposition of the excess lithospheric material (of 400 to 500 km in width) which must have been subducted during the shortening of the Alpine crust-mantle system, but it also gives an explanation for the apparently non-existing difference in the P-wave travel time residuals of teleseismic events observed at stations in the Alpine foreland and in the Alps (Baer, 1980). Figure 23 demonstrates that the proposed model with a high-velocity block in the uppermost mantle will provide the required compensation for the extra time delay caused by the much

thicker crust under the central portion of the Alps. It should be noted that the zone of near-vertical subduction or "subfluence" ("Verschluckungszone" after Ampferer, 1906) is not symmetrical with respect to the central zone of the Alps, but appears to be somewhat displaced towards the south-east (see Fig. 22), i.e. towards the inner side of the Alpine arc.

This new geophysical model of the crust-mantle system in the Alps is in full accord with an evolutionary scheme presented by Laubscher (1974a + b). In Fig. 24 several stages of Alpine evolution in this scheme starting at the end of Paleozoic times (230 m.y. ago — (a) in Fig. 24) through the Pliocene (5 m.y. ago — (f) in Fig. 24) are depicted in the form of cross-sections. During a pronounced spreading phase in the middle Jurassic (170 m.y. ago — (b) in Fig. 24) the South Penninic Ocean was formed associated with incipient rifting and graben formation also in the North Penninic realm.

In mid-Cretaceous times (90 m.y. ago — (c) in Fig. 24) — after the maximum extent of the South Penninic Ocean was reached — a southward directed subduction sets in, which causes compression of the entire stack of layers making up the lithosphere. The effects of compression are clearly seen at the southern margin of the South Penninic Ocean, where ophiolitic sequences are obducted onto the Austroalpine continental margin in the south. Detachment phenomena in the upper crust of this margin are also suggested. They may have been considerably stronger than shown in Fig. 24 and may already have resulted in the formation of continental basement nappes (Laubscher, 1974b). A secondary, less severe zone of compression is found in the North Penninic domain with large positive and negative crustal displacements whose contributions to crustal shortening in the Alps do probably not exceed 50 km.

The compressional shortening continues until the South Penninic Ocean has been completely consumed in the subduction process. At this point — in Lower to Middle Eocene times (about 50 m.y. ago — (d) in Fig. 24) — the continuing compression now leads to a continent–continent collision which results in the formation of a steeply northward dipping subduction zone in addition to the existing one formed in the Cretaceous. Further shortening of the crustal stack can only be accommodated if the two subduction zones penetrate deeply into the asthenosphere thus forming a nearly vertical

198 St. Mueller

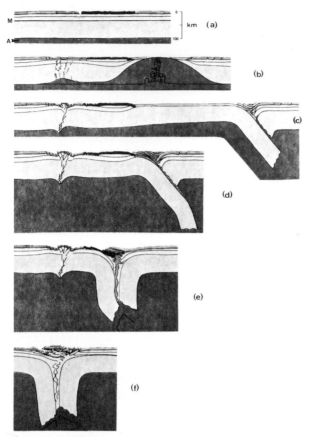

Fig. 24 Selected cross-sections through the Alpine orogenic system illustrating schematically the various stages of evolution since the end of the Paleozoic (after Laubscher, 1974a + b). M = crust-mantle boundary (Mohorovičić discontinuity), A = asthenosphere. (a) initial crust-mantle system, 230 m.y. ago; (b) pronounced spreading phase, middle Jurassic ∼ 170 m.y. ago; (c) maximum extension and onset of southward directed subduction, middle to upper Cretaceous ∼ 90 m.y. ago; (d) compressional shortening until the South Penninic Ocean is completely consumed, lower to middle Eocene ∼ 50 m.y. ago; (e) continent–continent collision accompanied by the formation of a "Verschluckungszone", upper Eocene ∼ 44 m.y. ago; (f) Continued shortening until the North Penninic domain is also engulfed in the vertical subduction zone, Pliocene ∼ 5 m.y. ago. The present-day situation is sketched in Fig. 22.

zone of "subfluence" (or "Verschluckungszone", cf. Fig. 22). In this process the Central Penninic zone is gradually covered with crustal peels and slices originating from the South Penninic (ophiolitic) and Austroalpine (continental) domains as shown in Fig. 24 for the Upper Eocene (44 m.y. ago — (e) in Fig. 24).

In the final stage of the Alpine orogeny the North Penninic–Ultrahelvetic domain becomes engulfed in the vertically dipping double-subduction zone. The deep structure of the Alps — as viewed now — was more or less completed in Miocene/Pliocene times. The lowest cross-section in Fig. 24 illustrates the situation in the Pliocene (5 m.y. ago — (f) in Fig. 24) where the crustal shortening has reached its maximum. As a consequence of the described deep-reaching lithospheric subduction slices of upper crustal material are peeled off and shoved into each other thus forming the complex nappe system and the crustal root of the Alps.

It thus becomes clear that a large-scale plate-tectonic mechanism, such as the north-west–south-east directed compression caused by the push of the African plate against the Eurasian plate through the Adriatic promontory (cf. Fig. 1) is the fundamental driving force ultimately responsible for the formation of the Alps. On this scale the still ongoing uplift of the Alpine mountain chain is a secondary effect due

to isostatic adjustment of the heavily deformed upper lithosphere which was considerably thickened in this severe plate collision process.

Acknowledgments

The results reported in this paper could not have been obtained without the help and support of a large number of individuals and institutions who — over many years — have cooperated unselfishly within several international research projects. The author wishes to acknowledge with gratitude all these contributions, in particular the financial assistance of the Swiss National Science Foundation which substantially subsidized the field experiments. Sincere thanks for many stimulating discussions are due to the author's colleagues and collaborators at the "Institut für Geophysik der ETH Zürich", especially to J. Ansorge, E. Kissling and L. Rybach. The author is also indebted to Mrs E. Hirzel for typing the manuscript and to M. Frey and H.P. Laubscher (Basel) for granting permission to reproduce Figs 16 and 24. Contribution No. 352, ETH Geophysics, Zürich, Switzerland.

References

Ahorner, L., Murawski, H. and Schneider, G. (1972). Seismotektonische Traverse von der Nordsee bis zum Apennin. *Geologische Rundschau* **61**, 915–942.

Alpine Explosion Seismology Group (H. Miller) (1976). A lithospheric seismic profile along the axis of the Alps, 1975, I: First Results. *Pure and Appl. Geophys.* **114**, 1109–1130.

Ampferer, O. (1906). Ueber das Bewegungsbild von Faltengebirgin. *Jahrbuch der kaiserlich-königlichen geologischen Reichsanstalt* **56**, 539–622.

Ansorge, J., Bonjer, K.-P. and Emter, D. (1979). Structure of the uppermost mantle from long-range seismic observations in Southern Germany and the Rhinegraben area. *Tectonophysics* **56**, 31–48.

Ansorge, J., Mueller, St, Kissling, E., Guerra, I., Morelli, C. and Scarascia, S. (1979). Crustal section across the Zone of Ivrea-Verbano from the Valais to the Lago Maggiore. *Bolletino di Geofisica Teorica ed Applicata* **21**, 149–157.

Baer, M. (1980). Relative travel time residuals for teleseismic events at the new Swiss seismic station network. *Annales de Géophysique* **36**, 119–126.

BEB Gewerkschaften Brigitta und Elwerath Betriebsführungsgesellschaft m.b.H. (1979). Auf der Suce nach Erdgas und Erdöl in der Schweiz. (Firmen-Prospekt), Hannover (B.R.D.).

Büchi, U.P. and Trümpy, R. (1976). Bemerkungen zum geologischen Profil längs der Geotraverse Basel-Chiasso. *Schweiz. Mineral. Petrogr. Mitt.* **56**, 589–603.

Channell, J.E.T., d'Argenio, B. and Horvath, F. (1979). Adria, the African promontory. *In* "Mesozoic Mediterranean paleogeography". *Earth Sci. Rev.* **15**, 213–292.

Choudhury, M., Giese, P. and de Visintini, G. (1971). Crustal structure of the Alps: Some general features from explosion seismology. *Bolletino di Geofisica Teorica ed Applicata* **13**, 211–240.

Closs, H. and Labrouste, Y. (1963). Recherches séismologiques dans les Alpes occidentales au moyen de grandes explosions en 1956, 1958 et 1960: Mémoire collectif du Groupe d'Etudes des Explosions Alpines, Année Géophysique Internationale, Série XII, Fascicule 2 (Séismologie), Centre National de la Recherche Scientifique, 241 pp.

Dewey, J.F., Pitman, W.C.III., Ryan, W.B.F. and Bonnin, J. (1973). Plate tectonics and the evolution of the Alpine system. *Geol. Soc. Amer. Bull.* **84**, 3137–3180.

Edel, J.B., Fuchs, K., Gelbke, C. and Prodehl, C. (1975). Deep structure of the southern Rhinegraben area from seismic refraction investigations. *J. Geophys.* **41**, 333–356.

Egloff, R. (1979). Sprengseismische Untersuchungen der Erdkruste in der Schweiz. Dissertation No. 6502, ETH Zürich, 167 pp.

Egloff, R. and Ansorge, J. (1976). Krustenstruktur unter dem Faltenjura (Zusammenfassung), Programm 36. Tagung der Deutschen Geophysikalischen Gesellschaft, Bochum (B.R.D.).

Emter, D. (1971). Ergebnisse seismischer Untersuchungen der Erdkruste und des obersten Erdmantels in Südwestdeutschland. Dissertation, Universität Stuttgart, 108 pp.

Frey, M., Bucher, K., Frank, E. and Mullis, J. (1980). Alpine metamorphism along the Geotraverse Basel-Chiasso — a review. *Eclogae geol. Helv.* **73**, 527–546.

Frisch, W. (1980). Plate motions in the orogen of the Alps and their correlation to the opening of the Atlantic Ocean. Berliner Geowissenschaftliche Abhandlungen, Reihe A, Band 19, pp. 51–53.

Gansser, A. (1968). The Insubric Line, a major geotectonic problem. *Schweiz. Mineral. Petrogr. Mitt.* **48**, 123–143.

German Research Group for Explosion Seismology (H. Berckhemer) (1968). Topographie des "Ivrea-Körpers" abgeleitet aus seismischen und gravimetrischen Daten. *Schweiz. Mineral. Petrogr. Mitt.* **48**, 235–246.

Giese, P. (1976). Results of the generalized interpretation of the deep-seismic sounding data. *In* "Explosion Seismology in Central Europe" (Giese, P., Prodehl, C., and Stein, A., eds). Springer, Berlin, Heidelberg, New York, pp. 201–214.

Giese, P. and Prodehl, C. (1976). Main features of crustal structure in the Alps. *In* "Explosion Seismology in Central Europe" (Giese, P., Prodehl, C., and Stein, A., eds). Springer, Berlin, Heidelberg, New York, pp. 347–375.

Gubler, E. (1976). Beitrag des Landesnivellements zur Bestimmung vertikaler Krustenbewegungen in der Gotthard-Region. *Schweiz. Mineral. Petrogr. Mitt.* **56**, 675–678.

Gubler, E., Kahle, H.-G., Klingelé, E., Mueller, St and Olivier, R. (1981). Recent crustal movements in Switzerland and their geophysical interpretation. *Tectonophysics* **71**, 125–152.

Hsü, K.J. (1979). Thin-skinned plate tectonics during neo-Alpine orogenesis. *Amer. J. Sci.* **279**, 353–366.

Illies, J.H. (1975). Interplate tectonics in stable Europe as related to plate tectonics in the Alpine system. *Geologische Rundschau* **64**, 677–699.

Kahle, H.-G., Klingelé, E., Mueller, St and Egloff, R. (1976a). The variation of crustal thickness across the Swiss Alps based on gravity and explosion seismic data. *Pure Appl. Geophys.* **114**, 479–494.

Kahle, H.-G., Klingelé, E., Mueller, St and Egloff, R. (1976b). Gravimetrie, Sprengseismik und Krustenmächtigkeit entlang der Schweizer Geotraverse. *Schweiz. Mineral. Petrogr. Mitt.* **56**, 679–684.

Kahle, H.-G., Mueller, St, Klingelé, E., Egloff, R. and Kissling, E. (1980). Recent dynamics, crustal structure and gravity in the Alps. *In* "Earth rheology, isostasy and eustasy" (Mörner, N.-A., ed.). John Wiley and Sons, Chichester, New York, Brisbane, Toronto, pp. 377–388.

Kissling, E. (1980). Krustenaufbau und Isostasie in der Schweiz. Dissertation No. 6555, ETH Zürich, 165 pp.

Klingelé, E. and Olivier, R. (1980). La nouvelle carte gravimétrique de la Suisse (Die neue Schwerekarte der Schweiz). Beiträge zur Geologie der Schweiz, Serie Geophysik **20**, 1–93.

Kobold, F. (1977). Die Hebung der Alpen aus dem Vergleich des "Nivellement de Précision" der Schweizerischen Geodätischen Kommission mit den Landesnivellementen der Eidgenössischen Landestopographie. *Vermessung, Photogrammetrie, Kulturtechnik* **75/4**, 129–137.

Laubscher, H.P. (1970). Bewegung und Wärme in der alpinen Orogenese. *Schweiz. Mineral. Petrogr. Mitt.* **50**, 565–596.

Laubscher, H.P. (1974a). Evoluzione e struttura delle Alpi. Le Scienze (ed. ital. di Scientific American), No. **72**, (Agosto).

Laubscher, H.P. (1974b). The tectonics of subduction in the Alpine system. *Memorie della Società Geologica Italiana, Supplemento* **2** al volume XIII, pp. 275–283.

Lort, J.M. (1971). The tectonics of the Eastern Mediterranean: A geophysical review. *Rev. Geophys. Space Phys.* **9**, 189–216.

Michel, B. (1978). La croûte entre Vallée du Rhin et Vallée du Rhône: Interpretation de profils sismiques et résultats structuraux. Thèse (3ᵉ cycle), Université Paris VI, 133 pp.

Miller, H., Gebrande, H. and Schmedes, E. (1977). Ein verbessertes Strukturmodell für die Ostalpen, abgeleitet aus refraktionsseismischen Daten unter Berücksichtigung des Alpen-Längsprofils. *Geologische Rundschau* **66**, 289–308.

Miller, H., Ansorge, J., Aric, K. and Perrier, G. (1978). Preliminary results of the lithospheric seismic Alpine longitudinal profile, 1975, from France to Hungary. *In* "Alps, Apennines, Hellenides" (Closs, H., Roeder, D. and Schmidt, K., eds). Schweizerbart, Stuttgart, pp. 33–39.

Miller, H., Ansorge, J. and Mueller, St (1979). Evidence of a high-velocity zone in the upper mantle under the central part of the Alps. *6th European Geophysical Society Meeting, Vienna (abstract)*, E⊕S **60**, 594.

Miller, H., Mueller, St and Perrier, G. (1982). Structure and dynamics of the Alps — a geophysical inventory: Final Reports of the International Geodynamics Project, Geodynamics Series, American Geophysical Union **7**, 175–203.

Mueller, St (1977). A new model of the continental crust. *In* "The Earth's Crust," Geophysical Monograph Series (Heacock, J.G., Keller, G.V., Oliver, J.E. and Simmons, G. eds) *Amer. Geophys. Union* **20**, 289–317.

Mueller, St (1978). Evolution of the Earth's crust. *In* "Tectonics and Geophysics of Continental Rifts" (Ramberg, J.B., and Neumann, E.R., eds). Reidel Publishing Company, Dordrecht (Holland), pp. 11–28.

Mueller, St and Lowrie, W. (1980). Die geodynamische Entwicklung des westlichen Mittelmeerraums und der Alpen. *Vermessung, Photogrammetrie, Kulturtechnik* **78/12**, 470–495.

Mueller, St, Peterschmitt, E., Fuchs, K., Emter, D. and Ansorge, J. (1973). Crustal structure of the Rhinegraben area. *Tectonophysics* **20**, 381–391.

Mueller, St, Egloff, R. and Ansorge, J. (1976). Struktur des tieferen Untergrundes entlang der Schweizer Geotraverse: *Schweiz. Mineral. Petrogr. mitt.* **56**, 685–692.

Mueller, St, Ansorge, J., Egloff, R. and Kissling, E. (1980). A crustal cross section along the Swiss Geotraverse from the Rhinegraben to the Po Plain. *Eclogae geol. Helvet.* **73**, 463–483.

Ottinger, T. (1976). Der Aufbau der Erdkruste unter dem schweizerischen Teil des refraktionsseismischen Alpenlängsprofils. Diplomarbeit, ETH Zürich, 166 pp.

Oxburgh, E.R. (1972). Flake tectonics and continental collision. *Nature, London* **239**, 202–204.

Panza, G.F. and Mueller, St (1979). The plate boundary between Eurasia and Africa in the Alpine area. *Memorie di Scienze Geologiche* **33**, 43–50.

Panza, G.F., Mueller, St and Calcagnile, G. (1980). The gross features of the lithosphere-asthenosphere system in Europe from seismic surface waves and body waves: *Pure Appl. Geophys.* **118**, 1209–1213.

Pitman, W.C.III. and Talwani, M. (1972). Sea-floor spreading in the North Atlantic. *Geol. Soc. Amer. Bull.* **83**, 619–646.

Prodehl, C., Ansorge, J., Edel, J.B., Emter, D., Fuchs, K., Mueller, St and Peterschmitt, E. (1976). Explosion-seismology research in the central and southern Rhine Graben — A Case History. *In* "Explosion Seismology in Central Europe" (Giese, P., Prodehl, C., and Stein, A. eds). Springer, Berlin, Heidelberg, New York, pp. 313–328.

Rybach, L. and Finckh, P.G. (1979). Heat flow data in Switzerland, *In* "Terrestrial Heat Flow in Europe" (Čermak, V., and Rybach, L., eds). Springer, Berlin, Heidelberg, New York, pp. 278–282.

Rybach, L., Werner, D., Mueller, St and Berset, G. (1977). Heat flow, heat production and crustal dynamics in the Central Alps, Switzerland. *Tectonophysics* **41**, 113–126.

Rybach, L., Mueller, St, Milnes, A.G., Ansorge, J., Bernoulli, D. and Frey, M. (1980). The Swiss Geotraverse Basel-Chiasso — a review. *Eclogae geol. Helvet.* **73**, 437–462.

Stein, A., Vecchia, O., Steinbeck, J. and Froehlich, R. (1978). A seismic model of a refraction profile across the western Po valley. *In* "Alps, Apennines, Hellenides" (Closs, H., Roeder, D., and Schmidt, K., eds). Schweizerbart, Stuttgart, pp. 180–189.

Trümpy, R. (1980). "Geology of Switzerland — a guide book". Wepf and Co. Publishers, Basel, New York, 334 pp.

Vine, F.J. (1969). Sea-floor spreading: new evidence. *J. Geol. Educ.* **27**, 6–16.

Wagner, G.A., Reimer, G.M. and Jäger, E. (1977). Cooling ages derived by apatite fission-track, mica Rb-Sr and K-Ar dating: The uplift and cooling history of the Central Alps. *Memorie degli Instituti di Geologia e Mineralogia dell'Università di Padova* **30**, 27 pp.

Wehebrink, F. (1968). Auswertung der reflexionsseismischen Messungen Lago Bianco 1964. Diplomarbeit, Universität Hamburg, 48 pp.

Werner, D. (1980). Probleme der Geothermik im Bereich der Schweizer Zentralalpen. *Eclogae geol. Helvet.* **73**, 513–525.

Will, M. (1976). Ergebnisse refraktionsseismischer Messungen im Nordteil der Geotraverse IA. *Geologische Rundschau* **65**, 733–748.

Land-Locked Oceanic Basins and Continental Collision: the Eastern Mediterranean as a Case Example

X. Le Pichon

Laboratoire de Géodynamique, Université P. et M. Curie, Paris, France

Abstract

The role played by the presence of a deep-sea basin within a continental collision zone is discussed, based on a study of the Hellenic subduction in the Eastern Mediterranean. The present tectonic framework of the Eastern Mediterranean area is dominated by subduction of the Mediterranean lithosphere along the Hellenic trench. It is this subduction which is responsible for the active extension north of the trench and the active compression south of it. As a result, the Aegean sea, north of the outer arc, is rapidly subsiding whereas the arc is being uplifted, in spite of extension, most probably because of underplating. To the south, the upper sedimentary cover is tectonically thickened, progressively forming the Mediterranean ridge. Thus a deep oceanic basin is progressively transformed into a shallow, narrow, tectonically thickened sedimentary belt while the continent to the north progressively founders and evolves into a deep basin into which oceanic accretion may eventually occur. This geodynamic evolution leading to a tectonic inversion can be considered to be characteristic of the last stages of closure of an oceanic basin within a collision belt. The different tectonic processes involved are dominated by the release of potential energy stored within the dense deep-sea lithosphere and within the adjacent thick continental crust, release triggered by the stresses applied at the boundaries of the collision zone. The different forces involved, slab pull and trench suction, are estimated. In addition, it is shown that stretching results in the formation of a "rift push" force which is of a magnitude comparable to the ridge push force.

I. Introduction

Argand (1922), considering the Alpino–Himalayan system within Eurasia, noted that the whole mass of the continent is affected "par un grand jeu où dominent les effets horizontaux". Large scale deformation is not confined to geosynclinal mountain belts, but rather is distributed in a coherent fashion over the whole continent. In a first approximation, one can consider continental crust as a continuous medium in which the displacement field can be theoretically completely described provided the stresses at the boundaries are known. This is the approach followed by Tapponier and Molnar in describing the deformation of a "plastic" Asia indented by a "rigid" India (see Taponnier, 1978). The same approach was extended by Tapponier (1977) to the evolution of the Alpino–Mediterranean region in the last 150 m.y. and has been used since by many authors. It is argued that this history can be understood as due to lateral flow of the continental lithosphere away from two rigid indenters, the Arab and Italian ones. In this perspective, the Alpine mountain belts indeed appear to be "les enfants illégitimes de la tectonique des plaques" (Tapponier, 1978).

Although the continuous medium approximation has given excellent insight into the continental collision process, it has some serious limitations. Strictly speaking, the discrete localization of mountain belts along suture zones is impossible to account for in this hypothesis. A more important limitation is that it is implicitly assumed that the totality of the orogenic energy involved comes from the stresses applied at the boundaries of the collision zones. In other words, there are no large sources of potential energy within the collision zone which existed prior to the collision and can be released during it, thus influencing its evolution. For example, the Tibetan plateau is now releasing potential gravitational energy stored within its very thick crust, but this energy was provided by the stresses applied by the collision with India and consequently can be accounted for within an Argand model.

The orogenic forces result from the heat dissipated by the Earth which is a thermal engine with a mechanical efficiency of about 1% (e.g. Turcotte, this volume). The thermal energy is used to store potential gravitational energy within the lithosphere under two principal forms: vertical density inversion and lateral density changes. The first one was discussed by Elsasser (1971) who recognized that subduction releases the large potential energy stored within the inverted density structure of the oceanic lithosphere. Forsyth and Uyeda (1975) and Chapple and Tullis (1977) have confirmed that sinking lithospheric slabs indeed are significant engines in geodynamics. Consequently, pieces of oceanic lithosphere trapped between the irregular boundaries of two colliding continents are the source of a large amount of energy as they are subducted.

Lateral density changes within the lithosphere produce the second type of potential gravitational energy available for work. The lateral density changes related to the cooling of the oceanic lithosphere (the "ridge push" force) have been shown to play an important role in the motion of the plates (Lister, 1975; Forsyth and Uyeda, 1975; Chapple and Tullis, 1977), although this role is probably smaller than the one played by sinking slabs (Carlson, 1981). But another important source of this type of energy lies within continental margins. With respect to the adjacent deep sea, each continent is a Tibet with a lot of stored potential gravitational energy. As pointed out by Jeffreys (1959) and more recently by McKenzie (1978), it is not generally available for work either because of the too high finite strength of the lithosphere or, more probably, because of the existence of compressive stresses applied on it. However, it will be shown that part of this energy is necessarily released when a trapped piece of deep-sea lithosphere is subducted within a continental collision framework.

The purpose of this paper then is to discuss the role played by the release of potential energy stored within trapped pieces of deep-sea lithosphere and within the adjacent thick continental crust, release triggered by the stresses applied at the boundaries of the collision zone. I shall rely on work done within the HEAT (*H*ellenic *A*rc and *T*rench) programme and published elsewhere (Le Pichon and Angelier, 1979; Angelier, 1979; Le Pichon and Angelier, 1981; Le Pichon *et al.*, 1982, b; Angelier *et al.*, 1982). I propose that this process has played a dominant role in the distribution of the deformation within the alpine mountain belt (Le Pichon, 1979). In a sense, then, these mountains result from plate tectonic processes although the lithosphere involved obviously is not undeformable.

II. Potential Gravitational Energy within Trapped Pieces of Oceanic Lithosphere

As the lithosphere can be considered, to a first approximation, to float on top of the asthenosphere, the elevation of its surface is a direct measure of its excess or deficit mass with respect to the asthenosphere (Le Pichon *et al.*, 1982, a, and in press). If its average density is equal to the average density of the hot asthenosphere, that is to say its excess mass is null, then its elevation is equal to the elevation which would be reached by hot asthenosphere in the absence of lithosphere. Le Pichon and Sibuet (1981) following Turcotte *et al.* (1977) have shown that this elevation is close to 3·6 km, this value being determined rather precisely by computing the change in level produced by the absence of oceanic crust in zero age oceanic floor.

Calling *B* (for buoyancy) this mass:

$$B = h_L(\rho_a - \rho_L)$$

where h_L is the thickness of the lithosphere, ρ_a the density of the asthenosphere and ρ_L that of the lithosphere. If *E* is the elevation of the lithosphere above the 3·6 km level:

$$E = B/(\rho_a - \rho_w)$$

where ρ_w is the density of water, assuming that the elevation is under water, and:

$$B = E(\rho_a - \rho_w)$$

In this paper, I adopt the following constants proposed by Le Pichon and Sibuet (1981), slightly modified from Parsons and Sclater (1977),

Parameters	Value
h_L	125 km
h_C	5·5 km
ρ_m	3·35 g cm^{-3}
ρ_c	2·78 g cm^{-3}
ρ_w	1·03 g cm^{-3}
α	3·28 × 10^{-5}°C^{-1}
T_a	1333°C
C_p	0·3 cal g^{-1}°C^{-1}

where h_C is the thickness of the crust (oceanic crust in the table), ρ_m the density at 0°C of the mantle, ρ_c the density of the crust, ρ_w the density of water, α the coefficient of thermal expansion, T_a the temperature of the asthenosphere supposed to be isothermal (compressibility is ignored) and C_p is the heat capacity.

When the water depth equals 3·6 km, the lithosphere is neutrally buoyant which means that an oceanic lithosphere is neutrally buoyant for an age of 10 m.y. using the depth-age curve of Parsons and Sclater (1977). If *E* is positive (the water depth is smaller than 3·6 km), *B* is positive and the lithosphere has a deficit of mass. If *E* is negative, the buoyancy is negative. There is gravitational instability. The excess mass is equal to − *B*:

$$B = 2·17E \, \mathrm{g\,cm}^{-2} \quad \text{with } E \text{ in cm}$$

Crough and Jurdy (1980) have used a similar reasoning to estimate the excess mass of an oceanic lithosphere 81 m.y. old. However, to do so, they assume that the ridge crest represents the hydrostatic level of the asthenosphere, thus ignoring the presence of crust (see the discussion by Le Pichon and Sibuet, 1981). Thus, as the water depth of a lithosphere 81 m.y. old is about 5·65 km, the increase in depth is 3·15 km and they find $B = 6·6 × 10^5 \, \mathrm{g\,cm}^{-2}$ (*B* = 6·8 × 10⁵ with the constants I have adopted). Actually, *B* = 4·4 × 10⁵ g cm^{-2} and they make an overestimate of about 50%. Similar overestimates are made by all those who ignore the presence of crust and just consider thermal cooling of the lithosphere (e.g. Molnar and Gray, 1979). Note that the maximum possible excess mass for an oceanic lithosphere 6·4 km deep is about 6 × 10⁵ g cm^{-2}.

Let us now consider the deep Eastern Mediterranean basin (Fig. 1). Its surface is roughly equivalent to a 1000 by 500 km rectangle and its average water depth is 3 km. Taking an average thickness of sediments of 8 km with an average density of 2·4 g cm^{-3}, the water depth of the Eastern Mediterranean basin in the absence of sediments would be 6 km (Angelier *et al.*, 1982). Thus the corresponding excess mass is 5·2 × 10⁵ g cm^{-2}. With the value of h_L chosen, it corresponds to an excess density of 0·04 g cm^{-3}, that is an average density ρ_L equal to 3·24 g cm^{-3} compared to 3·20 for the asthenosphere. We have noted above that in so doing, we ignore the compressibility of mantle material which would increase the estimates of density *in situ* but should not affect significantly the value obtained for the average excess density.

Let us now assume that the plate is able to sink in the asthenosphere without its cover of sediments which would be somehow incorporated within the subduction zone. This assumption is necessary because otherwise the buoyancy of

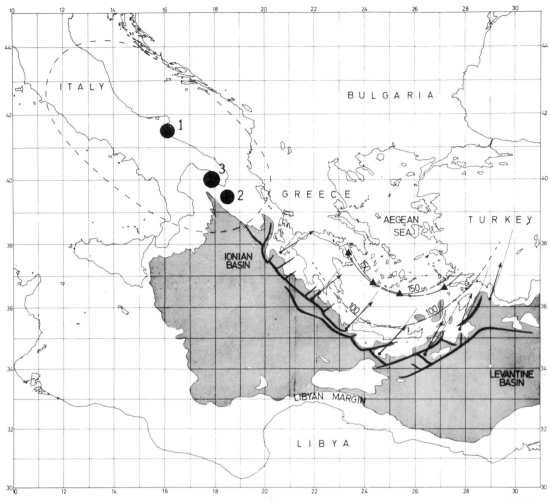

Fig. 1 The deep Eastern Mediterranean and the Aegean consuming boundary. Shaded, depths greater than 2000 metres; thick lines, schematic axes of main Hellenic trenches; dashed lines, 100 and 150 km iso-depths of intermediate earthquakes: triangles, main volcanoes; filled circles, computed poles of rotation governing the subduction of the Mediterranean sea-floor; arcs of small circles about the adopted pole of rotation (3) are also shown (after Le Pichon and Angelier, 1981).

the plate is positive and it cannot sink under its own weight. I shall come back later on this point. The total excess mass trapped in the Eastern Mediterranean basin is then 2.6×10^{21} g and the potential energy available there can be estimated by assuming that this excess mass can sink to an average depth of 500 km, at which depth it will have been resorbed by heating. The work which can be produced then would be 6.6×10^{31} ergs. If I now assume that the Mediterranean sea floor is subducted in 20 m.y., along a subduction zone 500 km long, at the geologically reasonable rate of 5 cm/year, this subduction can produce a work of 3×10^{24} ergs/year, which is about one tenth of the amount dissipated in earthquakes every year over the Earth.

Coming back to the present situation in the Mediterranean, it is known that the Mediterranean lithosphere is subducted to the north-west under the Hellenic trench (McKenzie, 1978). Using the estimates made by Le Pichon and Angelier (1979), the surface subducted, as indicated by intermediate depth earthquakes, is about 2.5×10^5 km² and the total length of trench is about 1000 km. However, 400 km of trench are nearly parallel to the motion so that one can approximate the situation by a 600 km long trench with a 400 km long slab. Le Pichon and Angelier (1981) and Angelier *et al.* (1982) show that the Mediterranean sediment cover most probably does not sink with the plate. Part of it is trapped within the accretionary Mediterranean ridge (Le Pichon *et al.*, 1982, b) and part underplates the continental

crust of the external arc (Angelier *et al.*, 1982). Consequently, assuming an excess mass of $5.2 \times 10^5 \mathrm{g\,cm^{-2}}$, a gravitational force of 10^{16} dyn/cm is exerted on the sinking slab — that is a total of 6×10^{23} dynes for the whole slab. Assuming that the subduction started about 10 m.y. ago, the average subduction rate is close to 4 cm/yr (Le Pichon and Angelier, 1979); thus the work is 2.4×10^{24} ergs/year, an estimate which is again quite comparable to the estimate made above. If the totality of the remaining 5×10^5 km² of Eastern Mediterranean sea floor are subducted (average length 830 km), the work done will be 5×10^{31} ergs, an estimate which confirms that the one made above is reasonable.

Of course, a large proportion of this work will be dissipated within the asthenosphere (e.g. Forsyth and Uyeda, 1975; Chapple and Tullis, 1977). For example, McKenzie (1977) estimates a maximum stress of only 100 bars due to the action of the sinking slab on the remaining lithosphere. As pointed out by Molnar and Gray (1979), this is equivalent to a surface force per unit length of only 10^{15} dyne/cm (assuming a thickness of about 100 km) which is an order of magnitude smaller than the one computed above. The part available for work on the surface plates then is about 10%. On the other hand, Davies (1981), on the basis of a discussion of the regional compensation of sinking slabs using altimetry results, indicates that about 30% of the maximum force transmitted up the slab reaches the surface plates.

I conclude that the excess weight of the sinking slab transmits up to the upper part of the plate a force of 10^{15} to 3×10^{15} dyn/cm which is available for orogenic work in the Hellenic subduction zone. The corresponding work over the whole subduction zone is now about 2 to 7×10^{23}ergs/year. The potential energy available in the present Eastern Mediterranean lithosphere is sufficient to maintain this work rate during an additional 20 m.y. at which time the totality of the lithosphere would be subducted. A very important point which I shall develop later is that the Upper Cenozoic rate of continental collision in the Mediterranean area is less than 1 cm/year (e.g. Minster and Jordan, 1978). At this low rate, which is four to five times smaller than the average present subduction rate, it would take 50 to 70 m.y. to eliminate the Mediterranean sea floor instead of 20 m.y. as computed above. Thus, the main part of the driving force responsible for the subduction of the Mediterranean lithosphere cannot result from the relative motion of Africa; rather, it must reside within the sinking slab itself.

Bird (1978), McKenzie (1978) and Bird and Baumgardner (1981) have pointed out that delamination of the mantle part of the continental lithosphere is another way of releasing pre-existing potential energy and that this is increasingly likely in regions of strong crustal shortening (Houseman *et al.*, 1981). However, I shall not discuss this process in this paper for lack of direct evidence.

III. Potential Gravitational Energy due to Lateral Density Changes

I now consider the forces due to the presence of lateral density changes from continental lithosphere to deep sea lithosphere. I first assume the juxtaposition of two pieces of lithosphere, an old oceanic one and a continental one, both at thermal equilibrium and without radiogenic heating. I choose a continental crust at sea level which, with the values previously adopted, gives a thickness of continental crust of 30 km and a water depth for the oceanic crust at equilibrium of 6·4 km. Figure 2 (curve a) shows the computed difference in lithostatic pressure as a function of depth between the two structures. The maximum difference in lithostatic pressure reaches a little more than 1·0 Kbar between 6·4 km (level of sea floor) and 11·9 km (oceanic Moho). It decreases to 0 at 30 km depth (continental Moho) with the thermal conditions chosen. These ignore radioactive heating and are thus unrealistic, but I am only interested in an order of magnitude discussion. The corresponding force F_1 acting from the continent toward the ocean has a value of about 2×10^{15} dyn/cm, using the hydrostatic approximation, which is equivalent to the force exerted by the sinking slab on the surface plates. The average difference in hydrostatic pressure over the thickness of continental crust is 650 bars. The actual stresses of course depend on the rheology of the mantle but are probably equivalent (Jeffreys, 1959; Artyushkov, 1973; Bott and Dean, 1979), if not larger (Bott and Kusznir, 1979).

Consider now a situation more representative of the northern Eastern Mediterranean margin next to the subduction zone, that is a continental relief of 1 km, 3 km of water and 8 km of sediments. The magnitude of the corresponding force is now $2·5 \times 10^{15}$ dyn/cm and the average difference in hydrostatic pressure over the thickness of continental crust is 700 bars. McKenzie (1977) has proposed that a stress of about 800 bars is necessary to initiate a trench. It is thus significant that the stresses due to lateral density changes are maximum in the first 20 km where the lithosphere has its maximum strength. An additional tectonic stress of moderate amplitude (a few hundred bars) is thus sufficient to initiate a subduction zone at the base of a continental margin.

Once the subduction zone is initiated, force F_1 acts in the

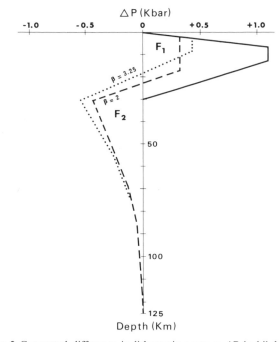

Fig. 2 Computed difference in lithostatic pressure ΔP in kilobars between a continental lithosphere at sea-level and at thermal equilibrium ($h_c = 30$ km, $h_L = 125$ km) and (a) in full line, a deep oceanic lithosphere at thermal equilibrium (water depth of 6·4 km), (b) in dashed line, the same continental lithosphere but instantaneously stretched by a factor β of 2, (c) in dotted line, the same continental lithosphere but instantaneously stretched by a maximum factor β of 3·25. Force F_1 is obtained by integrating the positive difference in lithostatic pressure over the corresponding depth. Force F_2 is obtained in the same way, but for the negative difference.

same direction as the gravity of the slab. Both tend to induce migration of the trench and its adjacent continental margin away from the European continent. This is the equivalent of the "suction" force of Elsasser (1971), Forsyth and Uyeda (1975) and Chase (1978). Large extensional stresses of several hundred bars should be present under the adjacent continent (Bott and Dean, 1979; Bott and Kusznir, 1979). However, these extensional stresses are maximum, not on the edge of the continent, below the continental margin, where compressional stresses actually predominate, but further away inside the continent. Consequently, if extension affects the continent, it should be maximum at some distance from its edge. This is known to to be the case for the Aegean landmass which is affected by widespread extension and consequent subsidence (McKenzie, 1978; Le Pichon and Angelier, 1981). Angelier (1981) has shown that this subsidence can be quantitatively explained using the homogeneous lithosphere stretching model of McKenzie (1978).

Let us consider the consequences of this homogeneous stretching. If stretching is done in a short time with respect to the thermal time constant of the lithosphere, the density distribution is not changed while the thickness is reduced by a factor β and the corresponding new elevation E_n above 3·6 km water depth is also divided by β. Thus the instantaneous subsidence:

$$Si = E - E_n = (1 - 1/\beta)E$$

E, being the elevation above 3·6 km, under water (see Le Pichon *et al.*, 1982 a, and in press, for a fuller discussion). The maximum measured stretching factor in the Aegean Sea is 2 (Angelier *et al.*, 1982).

But stretching produces considerable lateral density changes that can be easily computed, using the hypotheses and the constants given above. The corresponding lithostatic pressure difference between the adjacent unstretched continent and the bottom of the Aegean sea ($\beta = 2$) is shown in Fig. 2. This difference reaches a maximum of about 300 bars between 2 and 15 km, passes by 0 at 22 km and becomes negative, with a minimum close to -500 bars at 30 km (Moho's level). The -500 bars minimum is due to the presence of hot asthenosphere at shallow depths below the Aegean Sea. As a result, stretching activates two forces acting at different levels and in opposite directions. Force F_1 acts above 22 km from the unstretched continent toward the Aegean Sea and has a magnitude of 6×10^{14} dyn/cm. Force F_2 is about three times larger (1.5×10^{15} dyn/cm) and acts below 22 km within the mantle portion of the lithosphere from the Aegean toward the continent. Thus, the net force acting on the lithosphere has a magnitude of 0.9×10^{15} dyn/cm and contributes to the extension. In addition, force F_1 acts in such a way as to expand the zone of stretching by feeding new unstretched continental crust to the stretching area.

Figure 2 also shows the lithostatic pressure difference between the unstretched continent and a continent affected by a 3.25 stretching factor. A β of 3.25 is the one producing a subsidence of 2.5 km water depth if the starting altitude is at sea-level. It consequently generally corresponds to the transition from continental stretching to oceanic accretion and can be considered to be close to the maximum possible value of stretching within these conditions (Le Pichon and Sibuet, 1981). For $\beta = 3.25$, the lithostatic pressure difference reaches a maximum of 430 bars between 2.5 and 8 km and a minimum of -560 bars at 30 km (Moho's level). Force F_1 has now a value of 7×10^{14} dyn/cm and force F_2 2×10^{15}; the net force acting on the lithosphere has a magnitude of 1.3×10^{15} dyn/cm and contributes to the extension. This is equivalent to the ridge push force and it has the same order of magnitude. It will be called here the rift push force.

A first conclusion then is that thinning induces lateral density changes which amplify the initial stretching forces. This rift-push progressively grows from 0 for $\beta = 1$ to 6×10^{14} dyn/cm for $\beta = 2$ and to a maximum of 1.5×10^{15} dyn/cm for the maximum $\beta = 3.25$ extension (again assuming that $\beta = 1$ corresponds to sea-level). The actual force acting on the rifting zone is twice this value, taking into account the symmetry of the rifting zone; its magnitude is comparable to the slab force and the continental margin force discussed in the preceding section, as well as to the ridge push force. It may possibly be sufficient to drive the stretching process by itself once the stretching factor exceeds two.

A second conclusion is that large forces act in opposite directions above and below about 20 km; these may produce a zone of shearing within the lower continental crust which may eventually lead to inhomogeneous stretching as proposed by several authors; the upper force tends to expand the area of upper stretching with respect to the smaller area of deeper more intense stretching. One might find there an explanation for apparently extremely high thinning of the continental crust in some portions of lower continental margins (see for example Montadert *et al.*, 1979). However, Le Pichon and Sibuet (1981) have shown that the homogeneous stretching hypothesis is a good first approximation over most of the margin as it predicts the right subsidence and the proper amount of stretching within the upper crust. I consequently use this approximation for our discussion.

Coming back to Fig. 2, we see that the distribution of lithostatic pressure difference will progressively tend toward curve a, as the stretched lithosphere cools down, thickens and subsides. Consequently the upper compressional force F_1 grows while the lower extensional force F_2 diminishes and finally disappears. Consider for example the cooling of a

basin where the stretching factor reached the upper limit of 3.25 and the initial water depth was 2.5 km. The decrease in force F_2 is controlled by the thermal time constant of the lithosphere which is about 60 m.y. (Parsons and Sclater, 1977). Thus:

$$F_2 \simeq 20e^{-t/60} \quad \text{in } 10^{14} \, dyn/cm$$

where t is the time in m.y.

$$F_1 \simeq 7 + 13(1 - e^{-t/60})$$

which gives $t \simeq 30$ m.y. for $F_1 = F_2$. At this time, the net force acting on the lithosphere is null.

The thermal subsidence of a thinned basin can be approximated by:

$$S_{th} = 4.2(1 - 1/\beta)(1 - e^{-t/60})$$

(Le Pichon *et al.*, 1982a, and in press). Thus, 30 m.y. after stretching ceased, the depth of the thinned basin is about 3.6 km and the thinned lithosphere is beginning to acquire a negative buoyancy. The tectonic context becomes favourable for subduction while stretching becomes less and less likely. I conclude that successive episodes of stretching are unlikely unless the pause in stretching between two episodes is smaller than about 30 m.y. On the other hand, subduction of a highly stretched basin is quite likely within a context of continental collision, provided the age of the stretched basin is greater than 30 m.y., the exact value depending on the actual amount of stretching and on the value of the regional compressive tectonic stresses due to continental collision.

Berckhemer (1977) has discussed the amount of potential energy available due to the presence of a high and thick continental crust next to a deep basin with thin crust. The potential energy in the excess relief Z is:

$$U_1 = g(\rho_c - \rho_w)Z^2/2$$

where Z is the altitude above the basin floor (everything being under water), and the potential energy in the root is:

$$U_2 = g(\rho_m - \rho_c)Z'^2/2$$

where Z' is difference in depth of the Moho level.

Taking the case of the maximum stretching factor $= 3.25$ applied on a crust originally at sea-level, the final depth reached after an infinite time is:

$$Z = 7.8(1 - 1/\beta) = 5.4 \, km$$

(Le Pichon *et al.*, 1982a and in press). Thus $Z' = 15.3$ km and:

$$U = U_1 + U_2 = 8.8 \times 10^{14} \, ergs/cm^2.$$

This is significant although it is one order of magnitude smaller than the potential energy within the heavy Mediterranean lithosphere.

But thinning of the lithosphere forces the asthenosphere to rise and consequently brings a large amount of heat. This amount is very simple to compute. In the case of a 3.25 instantaneous stretching:

$$Q = 6.6 \times 10^4 \, cal/cm^{-2}$$
$$= 2.8 \times 10^{17} \, ergs/cm^{-2}$$

which is 300 times larger than the potential energy stored in the continental crust. Of course, most of this energy will not be converted into mechanical energy but even a low efficiency of 1% would still provide three times more mechanical energy than the simple thinning of continental crust. This thermal energy comes from below the lithosphere and consequently is of a different type than the others we have discussed up to now. *It is new potential energy which is brought into the system from the asthenosphere.* Note that energy brought by delamination would be of the same nature.

IV. Consequences on the Energy Budget of the Land-locked Eastern Mediterranean Basin

I now have the necessary background to discuss the recent evolution of the Eastern Mediterranean basin, a land-locked basin trapped within a continental collision zone. The rate of collision has been about 1 cm/yr for at least 20 m.y. (Chase, 1978) and is perhaps even smaller 0·7 cm/yr (Minster and Jordan, 1978).

Figure 3 shows a very schematic plan view of this land-locked deep-sea basin trapped within a collision zone. Figure 4 is a N–S schematic section across this basin. The basin and the A (Italy) and B (Arabia) indenters belong to the southern African plate which is moving toward Europe at 0·7 to 1 cm/year, the rate of motion increasing from west to east.

Consider what happens to the north of the B collision zone. The northern (European) continental lithosphere has to move away. Whether the deformation is continuous or not, part of the northern lithosphere (Turkey) moves westward and increases the stresses applied along the northern margin of the basin. In the absence of any collision, these are already of the order of 500 bars because of the lateral density changes discussed above. As a result, the margin fails. The exact location of failure depends on the pattern of motion of the continental lithosphere (Turkey). The initial point of failure is probably close to B, the fracture then propagating westward to a point P, at which the stresses applied by the action of the B indenter become too small to break the lithosphere. Once the lithosphere is fractured, underthrusting of the Mediterranean lithosphere starts and clockwise motion of the PC boundary about the P rotation pole becomes the easiest way to yield to the stresses applied.

However, the failure of the lithosphere along the continental margin now release the gravitational potential energy stored in the continental lithosphere under the form of lateral density changes (force F_1 in Fig. 4) and stored in the basin lithosphere as a reversal of density (force F_2 in Fig. 4). To simplify the discussion, let us assume that the collision velocity L_1 is small and can be neglected. Then, the southern and northern plates are locked and form a single reference frame. They can also be considered as fixed with respect to the asthenosphere. Component F'_2 of force F_2 along the underthrust plate cannot act. Component F_2 pulls the plate southward and the subduction zone migrates southward at a velocity L_2 typical for subduction (4 cm/year or larger) and consequently large with respect to L_1, thus justifying my hypothesis. Force F_1 then contributes to the extension of the

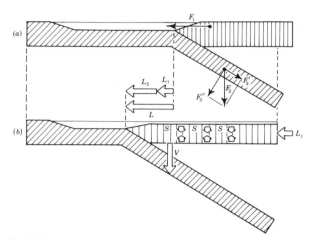

Fig. 4 Highly schematic S–N section of the Hellenic subduction zone with relative motions and gravitational forces.
(a) F_1, outward component of the gravitational force acting on the Aegean region, owing to the hydrostatic head with respect to the adjacent Mediterranean sea crust. F_2, negative buoyancy force acting on the sinking slab, with components F'_2 and F'', parallel and perpendicular to the slab, respectively.
(b) L_1, displacement of Eurasia relative to Africa; L_2, displacement of the Hellenic arc relative to Eurasia, due to the Aegean expansion (L_2 is approximately 3 or 4 times larger than L_1); L, total displacement of the Hellenic arc relative to Africa; S, subsidence of the Aegean region due to lithospheric thinning (double arrows); V, vertical motion of the sinking slab (after Le Pichon and Angelier, 1981).

northern (Aegean) continental lithosphere at a total velocity $L_1 - L_2$. This induces subsidence and progressively creates a new basin (the Aegean Sea) as the older basin is subducted.

We have seen that, using the reconstruction made by Le Pichon and Angelier (1981), $2 \cdot 5 \times 10^5$ km² of old basin have already been subducted in an amount of time of about 10 m.y. Out of these, about 5×10^4 km² correspond to the motion of Africa (L_1). An additional 5×10^4 km² surface may be due to the westward motion of Turkey. Thus, $1 \cdot 5 \times 10^5$ km² have been subducted at the expense of the creation of an equal amount of Aegean area by stretching of a surface which is now about 5×10^5 km², thus corresponding to an average β of 1·4. But the stretching is not uniformly distributed. De Bremaecker et al. (1982) have shown how the kinematic conditions imposed at the boundaries of Aegea result in a concentration of stretching to the south, near the sea of Crete where β reaches a value of 2.

Assuming that this process continues at the same rate until the remaining 5×10^5 km² of deep Mediterranean floor are subducted, the total time necessary would be about 20 m.y. During this time, shortening due to the northward motion of Africa will be 2×10^5 km² and consequently stretching should produce an additional 3×10^5 km². Thus, the original surface of the Aegean continent which was $3 \cdot 5 \times 10^5$ km² 10 m.y. ago should have expanded to 8×10^5 km², implying an average stretching factor of 2·3. Another possibility is to assume that this surface is produced by maximum stretching (β = 3·25) of an original surface of $1 \cdot 4 \times 10^5$ km². At this time, the $7 \cdot 5 \times 10^5$ km² pre-subduction Upper Miocene Mediterranean basin would be replaced by a $4 \cdot 5 \times 10^5$ km² basin due to stretching of continental crust which may or may not include oceanic lithosphere, although the first case is more probable. The total energy released by subduction of the Mediterranean lithosphere would have been 10^{32} ergs (of which 1 to 3×10^{31} ergs would have been released within the subduction zone and the remainder within the asthenosphere). The new thermal energy brought by the uplift of the asthenosphere within the stretched zone would

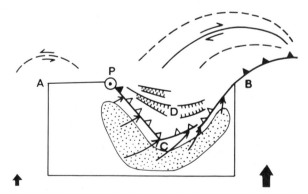

Fig. 3 Highly schematic Eastern Mediterranean basin. The European continent lies to the north. The African continent, to which the A (Italy) and B (Arabia) indenters belong, is moving toward the European continent at a velocity materialized by thick black arrows, which increases from the west to the east, PCB is the Hellenic subduction zone. The thin arrows give the velocity of subduction. The dotted zone corresponds to the accretionary Mediterranean ridge. D corresponds to the Aegean distension zone.

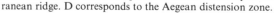

be 4×10^{32} ergs. Assuming for example an original unstretched zone 1000 km long and 140 km wide changing into one 1000 km long and 455 km wide ($\beta = 3.25$), the actual mechanical work done by force F_2 would be approximately 6×10^{30} ergs, or about 1.5% of the potential thermal energy. Finally, the potential energy lost by the continent, once cooling is completed, would be about 10^{30} ergs, thus being relatively minor with respect to the other two types of energy.

In summary, the largest component of the orogenic energy spent in the upper plates would come from the slab pull force; the rift push force would provide about half this amount and the loss of potential gravitational energy from the continent one tenth.

This energy will now be compared to the one involved in the continental collision process. Let us assume for example that, instead of subduction, we have pure continental shortening at a rate of 1 cm/year over the same original zone (1000 by 750 km) and over the same 30 m.y. At the end, the shortened crust would occupy an area 1000 by 450 km, which is a shortening factor β of 1.66. The instantaneous increase in elevation (assuming homogeneous shortening) would be:

$$Z_i = 2.45(\beta - 1) \text{ km}$$

assuming an original elevation at sea-level. After an infinite amount of time, it would become:

$$Z_t = 5.3(\beta - 1)$$

(Le Pichon *et al.*, 1982a and in press).
Thus $Z_i = 1.66$ km and $Z_t = 3.5$ km after the thickened lithosphere comes back to thermal equilibrium. The increase in potential energy then, after thermal equilibrium has been reached, would be due to an excess elevation of 3.5 km and an excess root of continent of 16.3 km. Thus:

$$U = 8.8 \times 10^{14} \text{ ergs/cm}^2$$

and for the whole surface of thickened crust:

$$U_{tot} = 4 \times 10^{30} \text{ ergs.}$$

This is equivalent to the force produced by a compressive stress of 100 bars acting over the whole thickness of the lithosphere during the shortening. This amount of energy can be considered to be a rough minimum estimate of the actual energy spent during this shortening. It is about one order of magnitude smaller than the total energy spent by the three other forces discussed above. I conclude that the energy budget of the Eastern Mediterranean basin is dominated by internal potential energy sources and that the external collision forces applied only play a subordinate role, acting mostly as a triggering device.

V. The Actual Geological Evolution: Role of the Sedimentary Cover

In this section, I briefly discuss the actual geological evolution of the Eastern Mediterranean area. The interested reader is referred to Angelier *et al.* (1982) and Le Pichon *et al.* (1982b) for a more detailed description. The preceding discussion concerned the different processes and was highly schematic as far as the geology is concerned. In particular, it had a major shortcoming as it ignored the role of the high rates of erosion on the surrounding tectonized continents which contribute large amounts of terrigeneous sediments to the basins which are progressively filled. That subduction occurs at all indicates that the sedimentary cover is not subducted. Otherwise, the plate would be buoyant and would not sink. Intermediate earthquakes indicate that it sinks.

What happens then to the sedimentary cover? Le Pichon *et al.* (1982b) have shown that the structure of the Mediterranean ridge, a large topographic bulge to the south of the

Hellenic trench, can be explained by sedimentary shortening of the middle and upper Mediterranean sedimentary cover. The Mediterranean ridge would thus be an accretionary ridge. The remaining lower part of the sedimentary cover underplates the Hellenic outer arc, thus quantitatively accounting for its progressive uplift (Le Pichon and Angelier, 1981; Angelier *et al.*, 1982). Consequently, the whole series of processes can be thought of as a complex way of progressively transferring material from the adjacent continental lithosphere into the sink which is provided by the basin until it is completely choked up.

Figure 1 shows in black the location of the remaining deep water Mediterranean basin (> 2000 m water depth) with respect to the Hellenic trench system where Mediterranean lithosphere is subducted below the Aegean landmass. Figure 5 shows the reconstruction of the same area at the start of subduction, probably 12 to 13 m.y. ago, after Le Pichon and Angelier (1979). The validity of this reconstruction based on seismic and neotectonic criteria has been reinforced by the paleomagnetic work of Lai *et al.* (1982) who find that Peloponnesus has rotated by 25° with respect to Europe since Uppermost Miocene, compared to 28° since Early Tortonian in the Le Pichon and Angelier's reconstruction. The reconstruction will not be discussed here and the reader is referred to Le Pichon and Angelier (1979, 1981) and to Angelier *et al.*, (1982). In Fig. 5, it is seen that the Aegean landmass has been spreading away in front of the westward moving Turkey mass and behind the rotating Hellenic arc. The progressive formation of the eastern Levantine branch of the trench also appears quite clearly by comparing Figs 1 and 5.

To understand the peculiar geometry of the trench, consider Fig. 3. Because of the initial geometry, the subduction zone has two contrasting sections. One (PC) is perpendicular to the motion and keeps a constant length through time. A second (CB) continuously lengthens at velocity $L_2 - L_1$ from a zero initial length; for reasons developed by Huchon *et al.* (1982), it is not exactly parallel but makes an angle of 30° with the subduction slip vector. Note that point P, which is the pole of rotation between the arc PC and the northern continent, does not coincide with the pole of rotation of the basin sea floor with respect to PC, unless the collision motion is negligible. However, if the collision velocity L_1 is small with respect to the total subduction velocity L, the two poles are quite close and can be considered to coincide for the present discussion. Thus PC is purely a thrust trench while CB is a mostly transform trench which has no steady state geometry but must continuously readjust itself to its lengthening.

Note on Fig. 3 that, although I have not discussed here the western portion, it is possible that a subduction zone develops between A and P, as a mirror image of the PB section, depending upon the patterns of motion of European continental lithosphere away from the A (Italy) and B (Arabia) indenters. In the Eastern Mediterranean, this AP section would be related to the formation of the Tyrrhenian basin which is not discussed in detail in this paper.

There is however a difficulty with this scheme when it comes to explaining the geometry of the present subduction zone, which is the amphitheatre shape of the intermediate earthquake zone. This shape has been explained by Le Pichon (1979) in the following way. Assuming that the asthenosphere is fixed with respect to the Africa–Europe frame of reference, the migration of the subduction zone to the south implies a flow of asthenospheric material from south to north. The easiest path for this flow is laterally, on each flank of the relatively short sinking slab which is then forced to take an amphitheatre shape.

Figure 6 shows the simplified distribution of the average surface strain pattern over the whole Eastern Mediterranean area based on neotectonic studies on land (Angelier *et al.*,

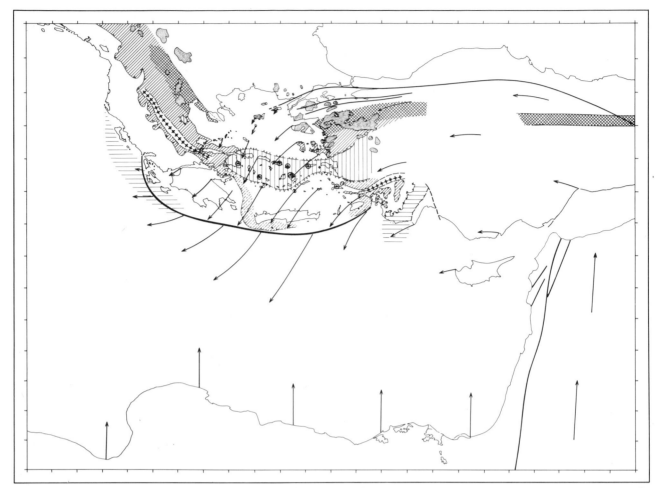

Fig. 5 Reconstruction of the Eastern Mediterranean in Upper Miocene, approximately 13–12 m.y. ago. Arrows are vectors of total motion since that time with respect to Europe (after Le Pichon and Angelier, 1979; see this reference for a discussion of the geology of the reconstruction).

1982) and on Sea Beam and submersible surveys at sea (Huchon *et al.*, 1982; Le Pichon *et al.*, 1982b). It confirms that the whole Aegean landmass is in extension. On the other hand, the Mediterranean sea-floor is under compression, the limit between the two strain patterns being the Hellenic trench. The shortening of the Mediterranean sea-floor is a superficial phenomenon which reflects the shortening of the upper two thirds of the sedimentary column (Le Pichon *et*

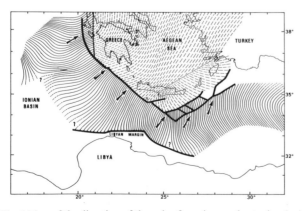

Fig. 6 Map of the direction of the axis of maximum shortening (σ_1) over the Mediterranean ridge in continuous lines and the axis of maximum extension (σ_3) over Aegea in dashed lines. Black arrows: horizontal motion vectors of the Mediterranean plate with respect to the Aegean plate. Note the effect of the increased shortening in front of the Libyan margin (after Le Pichon *et al.*, 1982, b).

al., 1982, b). Note that the shortening of the Mediterranean sea-floor is parallel to the subduction motion in front of the western branch of the Hellenic trench but oblique to it along the eastern branch as predicted by simple mechanical considerations (Huchon *et al.*, 1982). Over the Aegean continent, the extensional strain is governed by the rotation of the western branch except near the eastern branch where the lateral density forces act perpendicularly to the boundary, adding a north-west south-east component of extension.

Figure 7 is a section without vertical exaggeration from the Aegean landmass to the African continent which summarizes the main geological facts. The Mediterranean lithosphere is plunging to the north-east below the Aegean landmass to a depth of 150 km below the line of Quaternary volcanoes. Above it, the Aegean lithosphere is extended behind the retreating subduction zone. The stretching factor reaches a maximum of two immediately north of Crete in the Cretan Sea. Angelier (1981) and Angelier *et al.* (1982) have shown that the subsidence is quantitatively explained by the stretching, using the homogeneous stretching hypothesis. However, this is not true on Crete where the tectonically measured extension is 1·4 whereas the island is not subsiding but is actually actively uplifted at a rate of about 2–3 cm/century since about 10 m.y. ago (Angelier, 1979). Angelier *et al.* (1982) have shown that this uplift is due to the addition of a crustal root 6 km thick which corresponds to a volume of 400–500 km^3 per km of length of arc. This can be explained if the equivalent of a thickness of 2 km of sediments coming from the Mediterranean basin is underplating the Hellenic arc.

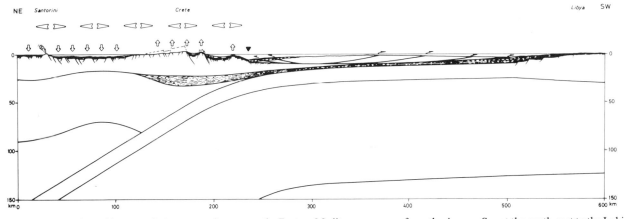

Fig. 7 NE–SW section without vertical exaggeration across the Eastern Mediterranean area from the Aegean Sea at the north-east to the Lybian continental margin at the south-west. The crust and lithosphere boundaries have been materialized. The Mediterranean ridge, due to shortening by thrusting, is shown in white. The lower part of the sedimentary column underplates Crete and is responsible for its uplift. The Hellenic trench is identified by a black arrow. Extension over the Aegean continent induces subsidence except over Crete where the effect of the underplating dominates. In the figure, it is assumed that underplating has migrated to the southwest as the plate increased its dip. Drawn by J. Angelier.

Thus, the lower 2 km of the sedimentary cover of the Mediterranean basin contribute to the underplating of the Aegean lithosphere and the consequent formation of the outer arc. The undeformed sedimentary section within the 4 km deep Ionian Sea is approximately 6 km thick. These values should be compared to the adopted average values for the whole Eastern Mediterranean basin, which are respectively 3 and 8 km. In both cases, the corresponding depth of the unsedimented basin is 6 km. Le Pichon *et al.* (1982, b) proposed that, as shown in Fig. 7, the upper 4 km of the undeformed sedimentary column are being shortened by a series of thrusts to form the Mediterranean ridge. This ridge is similar to an accretionary prism but it is much wider with respect to its height, probably because of the existence of a decollement over a level of overpressure (Ryan *et al.*, 1982). In a sense, then, the Hellenic trench is in the situation of a fore-arc basin. The average amount of shortening across the ridge is about 2, except in its narrowest portion, between Crete and Libya where it reaches 2·75 (Le Pichon *et al.*, 1982, b).

It is clear, then, that as subduction continues the Mediterranean ridge will grow in height and eventually will become subaerial. Taking the average present depth of 3 km for the basin, it will be completely filled up after receiving an additional 9 km thickness of sediments. This requires an average shortening factor of 3 within the Mediterranean ridge. Thus subduction of two thirds of the present surface of the deep Mediterranean would lead to a situation in which the basin is actually choked up. Although, this should not necessarily stop the subduction process, it will require more and more energy to shorten and uplift the sedimentary cover. One may eventually arrive at the situation of Fig. 8 where the accretionary ridge, about 12 km thick and 100–150 km wide, will be thrust upon the adjacent African continental margin. I further speculate that, if the African motion toward Europe continues, subduction of the stretched Aegean continental lithosphere, possibly containing oceanic lithosphere in its central portion, will start, thus leading to a complete inversion of the preceding tectonic set-up (Fig. 9). However, we have seen that this is unlikely in the first 30 m.y. after stretching has occurred.

A final point will be considered in Fig. 10 which is a schematic hypothetical structural history of the Eastern Mediterranean Sea. Up to now, I have assumed that all of the

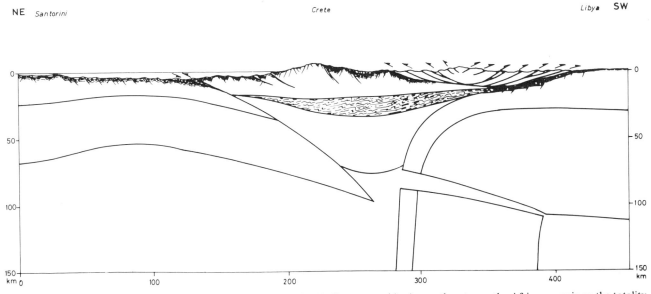

Fig. 8 Hypothetical tectonic evolution of the preceding figure. The Mediterranean ridge is overthrust over the African margin as the totality of the Mediterranean lithosphere has been subducted. Subduction of the thinned Aegean lithosphere is initiated. Drawn by J. Angelier.

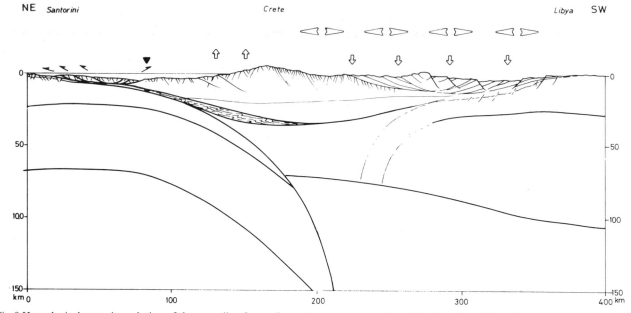

Fig. 9 Hypothetical tectonic evolution of the preceding figure. Complete tectonic inversion of the situation of Fig. 7 has now occurred. Drawn by J. Angelier.

Mediterranean lithosphere will eventually be completely subducted. However, this is not necessary. It is possible for example that the eastern Levantine portion will be filled up by sediments and transformed into a thick subaerial basin while only the western portion (Ionian basin) would be completely subducted. The purpose of these figures is not of course to predict the future, which is impossible, but rather to illustrate some possible geological situations which may have had analogues in the past evolution of the Alpine system.

Conclusions

There is no reason to think that the Eastern Mediterranean basin is an exceptional tectonic case. The irregularities of the continental boundaries necessarily imply that collision of two continents will produce numerous similar land-locked deep sea basins. The remarkable fact is that subduction of

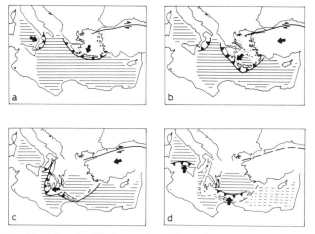

Fig. 10 (b) is a simplified tectonic configuration of the present Eastern Mediterranean area; (a) is the situation in Upper Miocene; (c) and (d) indicate a possible future evolution. In (d) it is assumed that the eastern Levantine basin has been filled up with sediments and transformed into a continental basin which is not being subducted, although this assumption is not necessary. Drawn by J. Angelier.

these land-locked deep-sea basins, because of the large slab-pull force, will in general occur much faster than the collision rate. As a consequence, subduction of the old deep-sea basin will be compensated by the formation of a young deep-sea basin behind the subduction zone. This formation occurs by stretching of the continental crust initially under the action of the trench suction force.

However, I have shown that as stretching proceeds and subsidence of the new basin begins, a rift-push force, similar to the ridge-push force, appears which eventually may be large enough to drive the stretching by itself. On the other hand, once stretching stops, this force decays by cooling as the basin subsides. After 30 m.y., the basin becomes both negatively buoyant and under the action of compressive forces. Thus subduction of the basin becomes more likely and tectonic inversion may then appear. Finally, I have shown that the collision forces applied from the outside of the basin only play a subordinate role, acting mostly as a triggering device.

I suggest that the processes described in this paper have dominated the evolution of the alpine mountain belt and probably of all other collision belts. The Tyrrhenian Sea and the Pannonian basin may be directly compared to the Aegean basin, the Tyrrhenian Sea being more developed and having reached the oceanic accretion stage whereas the Pannonian basin probably never reached this stage. I suggest that the present western and possibly also Eastern Mediterranean basins were formed by the same process. It seems also rather probable that the Ionian basin, within the alpine belt, was formed in the same way and was later destroyed by shortening, as argued by Le Pichon et al. (1982, a). In fact, the couple subduction-stretching should be a characteristic of collision belts as long as land-locked deep-sea basins exist. The tectonic polarities involved are clear and should be diagnostic although inversion may seriously complicate the situation.

Acknowledgements

This work was part of the HEAT program financed with the help of CNEXO, DGRST and CNRS. The Laboratoire de Geôdynamique is part of L.A. 215. I thank J. Angelier with whom many of these ideas were tested and elaborated. J. Angelier contributed directly the drawings of Figs 7, 8, 9 and 10. I thank K. Hsü who asked me to speak on the subject.

References

Angelier, J. (1979). Néotectonique de l'arc égéen. *Société Géologique du Nord, publication* No. 3, 418 pp.

Angelier, J. (1981). Analyse quantitative des relations entre déformation horizontale et mouvements verticaux: l'extension égéenne, la subsidence de la mer de Crète et la surrection de l'arc Hellénique. *Annales de Géophysique* **37**, 1–19.

Angelier, J., Lyberis, N., Le Pichon, X., Barrier, E. and Huchon, P. (1982). The tectonic development of the Hellenic arc and the sea of Crete: a synthesis, *Tectonophys.* **86**, 139–196.

Argand, E. (1922). La tectonique de l'Asie. 13e Congrès International, Bruxelles, 372 pp.

Artyushkov, E.V. (1973). Stresses in the lithosphere caused by crustal thickness inhomogeneities. *J. Geophys. Res.* **78**, 7675–7708.

Berckhemer, H. (1977). Some aspects of the evolution of marginal seas deduced from observations in the Aegean region. International Symposium on the structural history of the Mediterranean basins, Split, Technip, Paris, pp. 303–314.

Bird, P. (1978). Initiation of intracontinental subduction in the Himalaya. *J. Geophys. Res.* **83**, 4975–4987.

Bird, P. and Baumgardner, J. (1981). Steady propagation of delamination events. *J. Geophys. Res.* **86**, 4891–4903.

Bott, M.H.P. and Dean, D.S. (1972). Stress systems at young continental margins. *Nat. Phys. Sci.* **235**, 23–25.

Bott, M.H.P. and Kusznir, N.J. (1979). Stress distributions associated with compensated plateau uplift structures with application to the continental splitting mechanism. *Geophys. J. Roy. Astrom. Soc.* **56**, 451–459.

Carlson, R.L. (1981). Boundary force and plate velocities. *Geophys. Res. lett.* **8**, 958–961.

Chapple, W.N. and Tullis, T.E. (1977). Evaluation of the forces that drive the plates. *J. Geophys. Res.* **82**, 1967–1984.

Chase, C.G. (1978). Extension behind island arcs and motions relative to hot spots. *J. Geophys. Res.* **83**, 5385–5387.

Chase, C.G. (1978). Plate Kinematics: The Americas, East Africa, and the rest of the world. *Earth Planet. Sci. lett.* **37**, 355–368.

Crough, S.T. and Jurdy, D.M. (1980). Subducted lithosphere, hot spots and the geoid. *Earth Planet. Sci. lett.* **48**, 15–22.

Davies, G.F. (1981). Regional compensation of subducted lithosphere: effects on geoid, gravity, and topography from a preliminary model. *Earth Planet. Sci. lett.* **54**, 431–441.

De Bremaecker, J.C., Huchon, P. and Le Pichon, X. (1982). The deformation of Aegean: a finite element study. *Tectonophys.* **86**, 197–211.

Elsasser, W.M. (1971). Sea-floor spreading as thermal convection. *J. Geophys. Res.* **76**, 1101–1112.

Forsyth, D. and Uyeda, S. (1975). On the relative importance of the driving forces of plate motion. *Geophys. J.* **43**, 163–200.

Houseman, G.A., McKenzie, D.P. and Molnar, P. (1981). Convective instability of a thickened boundary layer and its relevance for the thermal evolution of continental convergent belts. *J. Geophys. Res.* **86**, 6115–6132.

Huchon, P., Lyberis, N., Angelier, J., Le Pichon, X. and Renard, V. (1982). Tectonics of the Hellenic trench: a synthesis of Sea-Beam and submersible observations. *Tectonophys.* **86**, 69–112.

Jeffreys, H. (1959). "The Earth." Cambridge University Press, London, 4th edit., 420 pp.

Laj, C., Jamet, M., Sorel, D. and Valente, J.P. (1982). First paleomagnetic results from Mio-Pliocene series of the Hellenic sedimentary arc. *Tectonophys.* **86**, 45–67.

Le Pichon, X. (1979). Bassins marginaux et collision intracontinentale: exemple de la zone égéenne. *Comptes Rendus des Séances de l'Académie des Sciences* **288**, sér.D, 1083–1086.

Le Pichon, X. (1981). The Aegean Sea. *Phil. Trans. Roy. Soc. Lond.* A **300**, 357–372.

Le Pichon, X. and Angelier, J. (1979). The Hellenic arc and trench system: a key to the neotectonic evolution of the Eastern Mediterranean area. *Tectonophys.* **60**, 1–42.

Le Pichon, X. and Sibuet, J.C. (1981). Passive margins: a model of formation. *J. Geophys. Res.* **86**, 3708–3720.

Le Pichon, X., Angelier, J. and Sibuet, J.C. (1982a). Plate boundaries and extensional tectonics. *Tectonophys.* **81**, 239–256.

Le Pichon, X., Sibuet, J.C. and Angelier, J. (in press). Subsidence and stretching. AAPG Proceedings of the Hedberg Research Conference, Galveston, Texas, 12–16 June 1981.

Le Pichon, X., Lyberis, N., Angelier, J. and Renard, V. (1982). Strain distribution over the East Mediterranean ridge: a synthesis incorporating new Sea-Beam data. *Tectonophys.* **86**, 243–274.

Lister, C.R.B. (1975). Gravitational drive on oceanic plates caused by thermal contraction. *Nature, London* **257**, 663–667.

McKenzie, D.P. (1977). The initiation of trenches: a finite amplitude instability. *In* "Island arcs, Deep sea trenches and Back-arc basins." (M. Talwani and W.C. Pitman, eds). American Geophysical Union, Maurice Ewing, ser. 1, p. 57.

McKenzie, D.P. (1978). Active tectonics of the Alpine-Himalayan belt: the Aegean sea and surrounding regions. *Geophys. J. Roy. Astrom. Soc.* **55**, 217–254.

Minster, J.B. and Jordan, T.H. (1978). Present-day plate motions. *J. Geophys. Res.* **83**, 5331–5354.

Molnar, P. and Gray, D. (1979). Subduction of continental lithosphere: some constraints and uncertainties. *Geology* **7**, 58–62.

Montadert, L. *et al.* (1979). North-East Atlantic passive margins: rifting and subsidence processes. *In* "Deep-drilling results in the Atlantic ocean: Continental margins and Paleoenvironment." (M. Talwani, W.W. Hay and W.B.F. Ryan, eds). M. Ewing serie 3, American Geophysical Union, Washington, D.C., pp. 164–186.

Parsons, B. and Sclater, J.G. (1977). An analysis of the variation of ocean floor bathymetry and heat flow with age. *J. Geophys. Res.* **82**, 803–827.

Richter, F.M. and McKenzie, D.P. (1978). Simple plate models of mantle convection. *Geophys. J.* **44**, 441.

Ryan, W.B.F., Kastens, K.A. and Cita, M.B. (1982). Geological evidence concerning compressional tectonics in the Eastern Mediterranean. *Tectonophys.* **86**, 213–242.

Tapponnier, P. (1977). Evolution tectonique du système alpin en Méditerranée: poinconnement et écrasement rigide-plastique. *Bulletin de la Société Géologique de France* **19**, 437–460.

Tapponnier, P. (1978). Les mécanismes de la déformation intracontinentale: exemple de la tectonique alpine en Asie et en Europe (Thèse). Université des Sciences et Techniques du Languedoc.

Turcotte, D.L. This volume.

Turcotte, D.L., Haxby, W.F. and OcKendow, J.R. (1977). Lithospheric instabilities. *In* "Island Arcs, Deep Sea Trenches and Back-arc basins," Maurice Ewing, ser., Vol. 1 (M. Talwani and W.C. Pitman III, eds). American Geophysical Union, Washington D.C., p. 63–69.

Vetter, U.R. and Meissner, R.O. (1979). Rheologic properties of the lithosphere and applications to passive continental margins. *Tectonophys.* **59**, 367–380.

The Indus Suture Zone: Paleotectonic and Igneous Evolution in the Ladakh-Himalayas

V. Trommsdorff, V. Dietrich and K. Honegger

*Department of Earth Sciences,
ETH Zentrum Zurich, Switzerland*

Abstract

During upper Carboniferous and Permian times a rifting phase lead to widespread formation of mildly alkaline volcanics in the Kashmere-Zanskar area of north India. Opening of a Thethyan ocean during the Triassic resulted in formation of an Indian continental margin and to corresponding variation in facies of sedimentation. Alkaline basaltic to trachytic volcanism accompanied pelagic sedimentation in the Lamayuru unit, the Triassic Indian forelands. Sea-floor tholeiites no older than Jurassic have been incorporated in tectonic melange zones north of the Lamayuru unit. North directed subduction then started in the middle Jurassic and lead to the formation of an island arc (Dras volcanics) in front of Eurasia. This upper Jurassic to Cretaceous island arc volcanism was basaltic and dacitic and grades northwards and laterally to the east into a volcano-sedimentary flysch-facies. Contemporaneous with and after the island arc volcanism, the voluminous Trans-Himalayan plutons intruded the island arc and the back arc basin. Low Sr-initial values point to oceanic mantle origin of these calc-alkaline gabbroic to granitic magmas. After continental collision, in post Paleocene times the first nappe movements were south-directed and comprised, from bottom to top: Lamayuru unit, Dras volcanics and dry harzburgitic back arc basin mantle that were emplaced as nappes on Indian platform sediments. An isostatic uplift mechanism caused by the intrusion of the Trans-Himalayan plutons is proposed for lifting the peridotites into the highest position. These movements were followed by molasse sedimentation and compressive folding probably contemporaneous with the Miocene tectonics and Barrovian type metamorphism in the Main Himalayas. Finally, steepening and north-directed movements occurred in the Indus zone. This sequence corresponds well to the sequence of orogenic events observed in the Alps.

I. Introduction

The upper Indus region in Ladakh, between the main Himalayan and the Karakorum mountain ranges (Fig. 1), provides a section across a Thethyan ocean basin from the Indian to the Eurasian continent. This section and its possible evolution will be discussed on the basis of a profile (Fig. 2), in which the following units (Frank *et al.*, 1977) are distinguished from south to north:

1. The Indian continental basement, overprinted by alpine metamorphism, with its prepaleozoic and paleozoic sedimentary cover. In upper Carboniferous and Permian times large eruptions of basaltic magmas (the Panjal Trap; Lydekker, 1883) occurred over wide areas along the northern rim of India (Bhat and Zainuddin, 1978)

2. The Mesozoic to Eocene (Gaetani *et al.*, 1980) Kashmere-Zanskar-Spiti synclinorium consisting mostly of platform-type sediments resting on the Indian continent (Fuchs, 1977 and 1979).

3. The Triassic to Jurassic and probably also Cretaceous Lamayuru unit (Frank *et al.*, 1977; Bassoullet *et al.*, 1981) comprised of pelagic and flysch sediments of the Indian forelands. Isolated lenses of serpentinite occur in this unit. In the lower Triassic there was a period of alkaline basaltic volcanism (Bassoulet *et al.*, 1978), producing mostly flows and pyroclastics within this unit.

4. The basaltic and dacitic (Honegger *et al.*, 1982) Dras and the volcano-sedimentary (Frank *et al.*, 1977) Dras-Nindam (Bassoulet *et al.*, 1978) units; Jurassic to

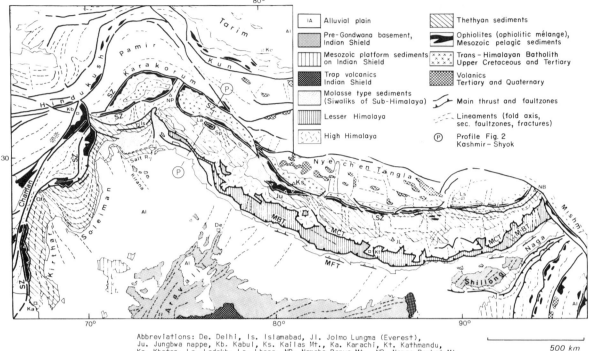

Abbreviations: De. Delhi, Is. Islamabad, Jl. Jolmo Lungma (Everest),
Ju. Jungbwa nappe, Kb. Kabul, Ks. Kailas Mt., Ka. Karachi, Kt. Kathmandu,
Ko. Khotan, La. Ladakh, Ls. Lhasa, NB. Namche Barwa Mt., NP. Nanga Parbat Mt.,
Qt. Quetta, Sp. Spongtang Klippe.

Main structural units: SZ. Suture Zone (Indus/Tsangpo), MCT. Main Central
Thrust, MBT. Main Boundary Thrust, MFT. Main Frontal Thrust.

Fig. 1   Tectonic map of the Himalayas (after A. Gansser)

Cretaceous in age (Wadia, 1937; Fuchs, personal communication) probably represent an island arc association in front of the Eurasian continent.

5. Ophiolitic mélange zones (Gansser, 1974), which occur on both sides of the Dras unit (Frank et al., 1977) contain intercalations of Upper Jurassic radiolarian cherts and limestones (Mac Mahon, 1901), Upper Cretaceous foraminifera limestones, and mid-ocean ridge type basalts (Honegger et al., 1982).

6. The Tertiary Indus Molasse zone (Tewari, 1964) partly transgressive on the rocks of unit 7 (Frank et al., 1977).

7. The Ladakh Intrusives ranging in age at least from Cenomanian gabbronorite (103 m.y) to Eocene granite (39 m.y.) (Honegger et al., 1982) and forming part of the Trans-Himalayan (Gansser, 1979) or Kangdese plutons (Chinese Acad. Sci. Cinidests., Tibet-Symposium, 1980). They intrude the Dras unit near Kargil (Frank et al., 1977) and dacitic volcanics north of the Indus valley near Leh. Ultramafic roof pendants (Srikantia and Bhargava, 1978; Kelemen and Sonnenfeld, in press) occur on top of these plutons.

8. The Shyok zone (Thakur et al., 1981), a still poorly known section consisting of crystalline basement slices mixed with serpentinite-sedimentary (? melange) zones. The young Karakorum batholiths (Desio, 1979) are thrusted southwards over this zone.

9. The Spongtang Klippe (Lydekker, 1883; Fuchs, 1977; Frank et al., 1977; Fuchs, 1979; Fuchs, 1981) consisting, from base to top, of rocks from the Lamayuru unit, from the Dras unit, and of huge ultramafic, unserpentinized, harzburgitic masses, forms a relic of a nappe overriding the Zanskar synclinorium.

A detailed account on the build up of zones 1–9 is given in Honegger et al. (1982). In this paper we shall discuss a possible model for the paleotectonic, igneous and metamorphic evolutions of the belt.

II. Paleotectonic Evolution of the Ladakh Area

The igneous evolution of the area is summarized in Fig. 3, and the paleotectonic evolution in the geophantasmograms of Fig. 4. The large eruptions of the Panjal Trap volcanics in Northern India during Upper Carboniferous and Permian times are interpreted as due to a rifting phase (Fig. 4). For this time span, the location of the southern Tibetan continental basement relative to the northern Indian basement is unknown. The fact, however, that only shallow water limestones occurred during Upper Carboniferous to Permian times in both units argues against the existence of a large open ocean during that period between India and South Tibet. In the Indus zone area between the Lamayuru unit and the Shyok units (Fig. 2) only exotic blocks of Permian have been found. This Thethyan zone and its formations are, therefore, younger than Permian (see also Bassoulet et al., 1982).

Considerable lateral differences in facies become evident in Triassic times. Platform-type sediments were deposited on top of the Indian continental sedimentary sequence in the Spiti-Zanskar-Kashmere area; pelagic sedimentation probably began during the Lower Triassic (Bassoulet et al., 1982) and certainly during the Middle Triassic (Frank et al., 1977) in the Lamayuru unit (i.e. just north of the Indian continent). Thus, in the Triassic, an Indian continental margin existed. Blocks of Permian limestones in the Lamayuru unit which contain subaerially weathered surfaces (Tewari and Pande, 1970; Bassoulet et al; 1982) were derived from the Indian continental margin or from oceanic islands.

With the development of this continental margin, the character of volcanism, which was mildly alkaline during Carboniferous and Permian times, changed to that typical of alkalibasaltic volcanic series. The rocks range from alkalibasalts to trachytes (Fig. 3) that occur as sills, flows and pyroclastics within the pelagic Triassic sediments.

The existence of Triassic oceanic crust has not yet been proven in the Indus zone. Jurassic to Cretaceous sea-floor

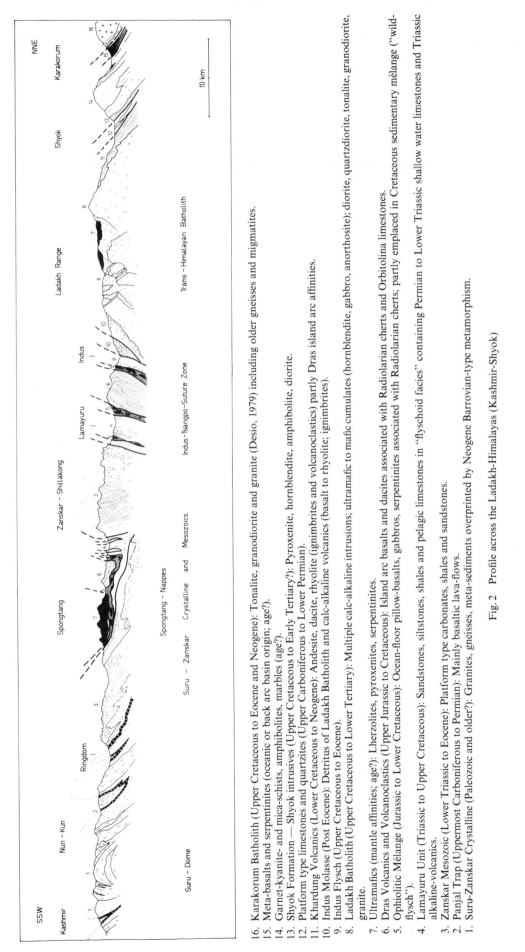

Fig. 2 Profile across the Ladakh-Himalayas (Kashmir-Shyok)

16. Karakorum Batholith (Upper Cretaceous to Eocene and Neogene): Tonalite, granodiorite and granite (Desio, 1979) including older gneisses and migmatites.
15. Meta-basalts and serpentinites (oceanic or back arc basin origin; age?).
14. Garnet-kyanite- and mica-schists, amphibolites, marbles (age?).
13. Shyok Formation — Shyok intrusives (Upper Cretaceous to Early Tertiary?): Pyroxenite, hornblendite, amphibolite, diorite.
12. Platform type limestones and quartzites (Upper Carboniferous to Lower Permian).
11. Khardung Volcanics (Lower Cretaceous to Neogene): Andesite, dacite, rhyolite (ignimbrites and volcanoclastics) partly Dras island arc affinities.
10. Indus Molasse (Post Eocene): Detritus of Ladakh Batholith and calc-alkaline volcanics (basalt to rhyolite; ignimbrites).
 9. Indus Flysch (Upper Cretaceous to Eocene).
 8. Ladakh Batholith (Upper Cretaceous to Lower Tertiary): Multiple calc-alkaline intrusions; ultramafic to mafic cumulates (hornblendite, gabbro, anorthosite); diorite, quartzdiorite, tonalite, granodiorite, granite.
 7. Ultramafics (mantle affinities; age?): Lherzolites, pyroxenites, serpentinites.
 6. Dras Volcanics and Volcanoclastics (Upper Jurassic to Cretaceous): Island arc basalts and dacites associated with Radiolarian cherts and Orbitolina limestones.
 5. Ophiolitic Mélange (Jurassic to Lower Cretaceous): Ocean-floor pillow-basalts, gabbros, serpentinites associated with Radiolarian cherts; partly emplaced in Cretaceous sedimentary mélange ("wild-flysch").
 4. Lamayuru Unit (Triassic to Upper Cretaceous): Sandstones, siltstones, shales and pelagic limestones in "flyschoid facies" containing Permian to Lower Triassic shallow water limestones and Triassic alkaline-volcanics.
 3. Zanskar Mesozoic (Lower Triassic to Eocene): Platform type carbonates, shales and sandstones.
 2. Panjal Trap (Uppermost Carboniferous to Permian): Mainly basaltic lava-flows.
 1. Suru-Zanskar Crystalline (Paleozoic and older?): Granites, gneisses, meta-sediments overprinted by Neogene Barrovian-type metamorphism.

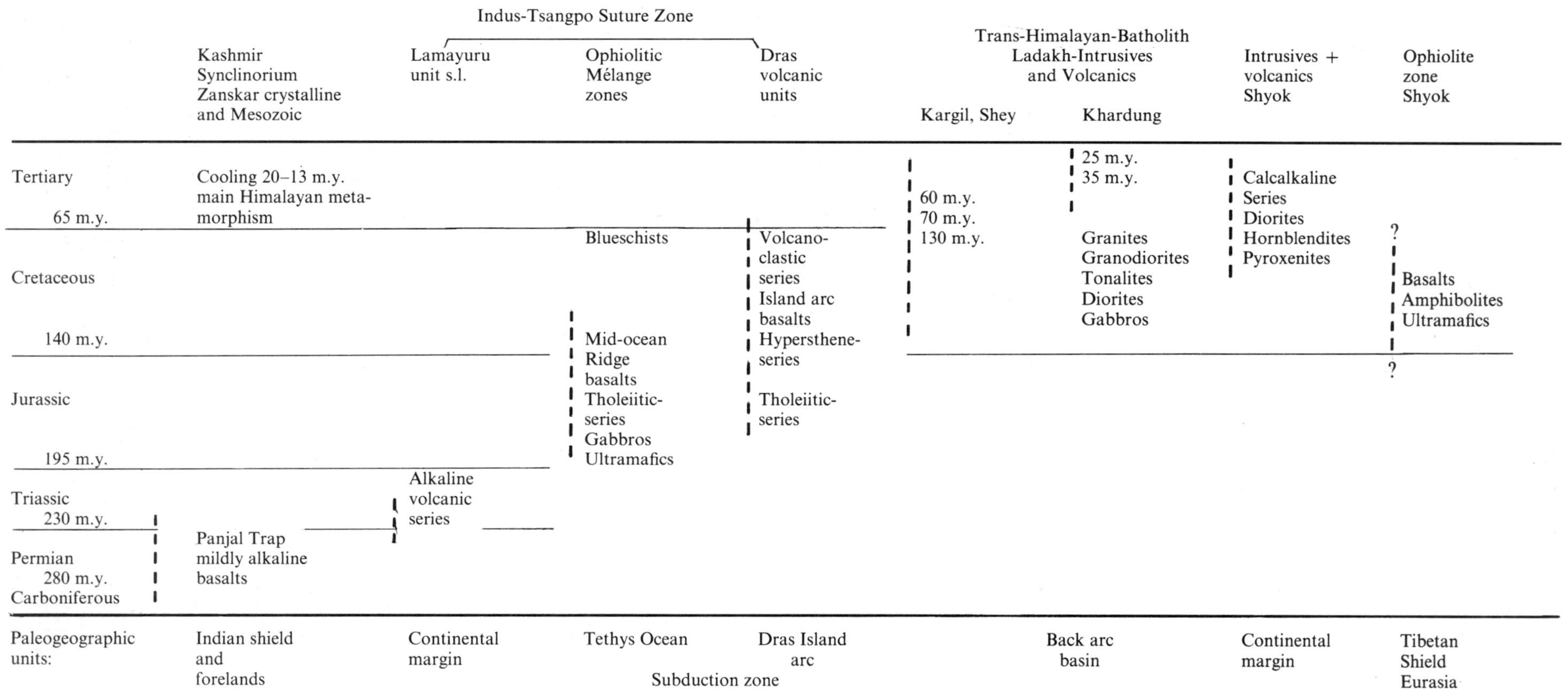
Indus-Tsangpo Suture Zone
Trans-Himalayan-Batholith Ladakh-Intrusives and Volcanics
Kashmir Synclinorium Zanskar crystalline and Mesozoic
Lamayuru unit s.l.
Ophiolitic Mélange zones
Dras volcanic units
Kargil, Shey
Khardung
Intrusives + volcanics Shyok
Ophiolite zone Shyok
Tertiary
65 m.y.
Cretaceous
140 m.y.
Jurassic
195 m.y.
Triassic
230 m.y.
Permian
280 m.y.
Carboniferous
Cooling 20–13 m.y. main Himalayan metamorphism
Panjal Trap mildly alkaline basalts
Alkaline volcanic series
Blueschists
Mid-ocean Ridge basalts Tholeiitic-series Gabbros Ultramafics
Volcano-clastic series Island arc basalts Hypersthene-series
Tholeiitic-series
60 m.y.
70 m.y.
130 m.y.
25 m.y.
35 m.y.
Granites Granodiorites Tonalites Diorites Gabbros
Calcalkaline Series Diorites Hornblendites Pyroxenites
?
Basalts Amphibolites Ultramafics
?
Paleogeographic units:
Indian shield and forelands
Continental margin
Tethys Ocean
Dras Island arc
Subduction zone
Back arc basin
Continental margin
Tibetan Shield Eurasia

Fig. 3 Time–space Diagram for Igneous and metamorphic activities in the Ladakh-Himalayas

PERMIAN
Panjal Trap volcanism

Indian shield north rim

S

N

TRIASSIC
Period of subsidence, stable continental margin

Lamayuru unit

— detrital and pelagic sediments

alkaline volcanism

Eurasian continental margin

LATE JURASSIC TO CRETACEOUS
Subduction / island arc phase

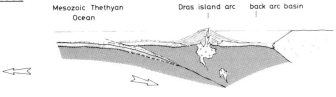

Mesozoic Thethyan Ocean   Dras island arc   back arc basin

India

LATE CRETACEOUS TO EOCENE
Intrusions into back arc basin

India

mélange   Dras   Ladakh intrusives

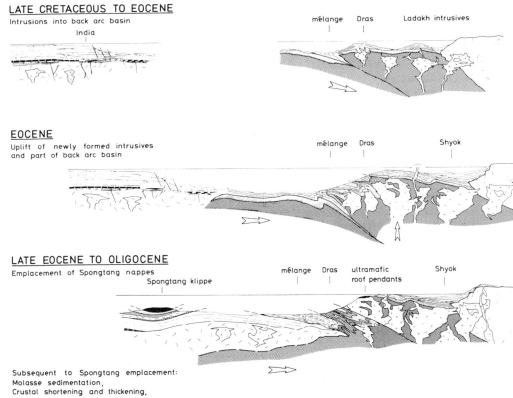

EOCENE
Uplift of newly formed intrusives
and part of back arc basin

mélange   Dras   Shyok

LATE EOCENE TO OLIGOCENE
Emplacement of Spongtang nappes

Spongtang klippe

mélange   Dras   ultramafic   Shyok
roof pendants

Subsequent to Spongtang emplacement:
Molasse sedimentation,
Crustal shortening and thickening,
steepening of units,
thrusting into present position

Fig. 4   Schematic paleotectonic evolution of the Himalayas in Ladakh

tholeiites have, however, been found in the southern mélange zone accompanying the Dras unit. Moreover the low $^{87}Sr/^{86}Sr$ initial ratios of the Dras volcanics and of most Ladakh intrusives argue for mantle derived melts.

The basaltic and dacitic Dras suite, which shows all the characteristics of an island arc, is intercalated with radiolarian cherts of Callovian to Tithonian age (Honegger et al., 1982). Thus, subduction may already have started during middle Jurassic times. On the other hand, inclusions of Orbitulina Limestones in the Dras volcanics and volcanosedimentary rocks (Gupta and Kumar, 1975; Fuchs, 1977; Bassoulet et al., 1982) yield Albian to Cenomanian ages. The Dras volcanism may therefore have lasted over a long time span. Rb-Sr isotopic data for Dras samples (Honegger et al., 1982) plot along a "pseudoisochron" of 264 m.y. which certainly does not represent a true age. The $^{87}Sr/^{86}Sr$ initial ratio is well established at 0·7035, which is characteristic of other island arc volcanics.

Zircons from a biotite-granodiorite that intrudes into the Dras volcanics of the Kargil area plot at 103 ± m.y., right on the Concordia curve (Honegger et al., 1982). Thus, there may be an overlap in time between the Trans-Himalayan plutonism and the Dras volcanism. In a Rb-Sr evolution diagram, early gabbroic to granodioritic Kargil intrusives align nicely with the Dras suite. The former are interpreted as intrusive counterparts of the latter (Fig. 4). Dras volcanics (Frank et al., 1977) and large peridotite masses outcrop near Dras (Srikantia and Bhargava, 1978) and in the Indus valley region (Kelemen and Sonnenfeld, in press), but no basement rocks of continental origin have been found as roof pendants on the Trans-Himalayan plutons. This situation suggests that the Trans-Himalayan plutons intruded into the island arc rocks and the back arc basin. Also, volcanics within the basin that have a Lower Cretaceous age (Thakur et al., 1981) are intruded by the Trans-Himalayan plutons near Leh (Khardung La area, Fig. 4). Isotopic data (Honegger et al., 1982) suggest that these intrusions lasted from late Cretaceous to Eocene times.

Sedimentation continued during Cretaceous times in the back arc basin, in the Dras volcano-sedimentary unit and in the Indian forelands. The paleogeographic origin of the Cretaceous flysch in the Indus valley (Fig. 2), (i.e. Indus Flysch s.s., Fuchs, 1979) is unknown, but must lie north of the Dras unit; i.e. according to our model, in the back arc region. The Middle to Upper Cretaceous Dras flysch was mainly deposited north of the island arc volcanic suite but also laterally replaces it towards the east (Fuchs, 1977; Frank et al., 1977).

The flysch section of the Lamayuru unit was derived from the Indian continental margin and probably reaches Middle Cretaceous age (see also Fuchs, 1979, p. 534). Shallow-water sedimentation continued to the uppermost Cretaceous and Paleocene on the Indian platform (Gaetani et al., 1980). In the Kangi La region (unit 3 in Fig. 2 between Spongtang and Ringdom) this sedimentation became flyschoid due to the Himalayan orogeny in the main Himalayas (Fuchs, 1979).

The first nappe movements are represented by the emplacement of the Spongtang nappes. This edifice rests upon the Paleocene of the Kangi La flyschoids and possibly on Eocene (Fuchs, 1981) and involves, from bottom to top, the Lamayuru unit, a melange zone, the Dras volcanics and a huge peridotite slab. Paleogeographically, these are successively more northerly units — the Peridotite nappe coming from north of the Dras zone. The sequence matches perfectly with that described by Heim and Gansser (1939) from the Jungbwa nappe in the Amlang La region of South Tibet.

A simple obduction mechanism does not satisfactorily explain such a succession, because it needs enormous shearing forces to emplace the peridotite masses on top of the whole Trans-Himalayan plutons as well as on the Zanskar-Spiti-synclinorium. On the other hand, an isostatic uplift of the marginal basin mantle as a consequence of the intrusions of the Ladakh batholith would provide an elegant mechanism to bring the Spongtang peridotites into their present positions, possibly by gravity gliding (Fig. 4). The roof pendants on top of the Ladakh Intrusives are interpreted as relics of the more southern Dras unit and of the more northern, marginal basin mantle corresponding to the upper two Spongtang units. Except for the mechanisms of emplacement, our tectonic interpretation of the Spongtang nappes agrees with that of Fuchs (1979) in his excellent contribution

and contrasts markedly with that of Bassoulet et al. (1982).

Only after the emplacement of the Spongtang nappe molasse sedimentation transgressed upon the Trans-Himalayan batholiths (Fig. 4). Lower Eocene pebbles within this molasse (Frank et al., 1977) provide an upper age limit.

The dramatic shortening and steepening in the Indus zone as a consequence of continental collision must then have occurred in post-molasse times. The shortening lead to the isoclinal folding of the Zanskar zone. These movements may have been synchronous with the Miocene tectonics in the Main Himalayas.

The latest movements in the Indus zone were north-directed, and lead to the overthrusting of the Hemis molasse on autochthonous molasse (Fig. 2) (Frank et al., 1977) and to an inversion of the whole Indus zone sequence (Fuchs, 1979).

The sequence of events is: 1. nappe movements; 2. shortening and isoclinal folding; 3. backfolding, which is equivalent to that observed in the Alps.

Acknowledgements

We are particularly grateful to Augusto Gansser, who introduced us into Himalayan geology. We thank K. Riklin and U. Eichenberger for drawing assistance and P.O. Koons for carefully reading the manuscript.

References

Bassoullet, J.P., Colchen, M., Marcoux, J. and Mascle, G. (1978). Une transversale de la zone de l'Indus de Khalsi à Phothaksar, Himalaya du Ladakh. C.R. Acad. Sc. Paris 286, 563–566.

Bassoullet, J.P., Colchen, M., Guex, J., Lys, M., Marcoux, J. and Mascle, G. (1978). Permien terminal néritique, Scythien pélagique et volcanisme sous-marin, indices de precessus tectono-sédimentaires distensifs à la limite Permien-Trias dans un bloc exotique de la suture de l'Indus (Himalaya du Lakakh). C.R. Acad. Sc. Paris 287, Série D, 675–678.

Bassoullet, J.P., Colchen, M., Marcoux, J. and Mascle, G. (1981). Les masses calcaires du flysch triasico-jurassique de Lamayuru (zone de la suture de l'Indus, Himalaya du Ladakh): Klippes sédimentaires et éléments de plate-forme remanies. Riv. Ital. Paleont. 86, 4, 825–844.

Bassoullet, J.P., Colchen, M., Juteau, Th., Marcoux, J., Mascle, G. and Reibel, G. (in press). Geological studies in the Indus Suture Zone of Ladakh (Himalayas).

Bhat, M.I. and Zainuddin, S.M. (1978). Geochemistry of the Panjal Traps of Mount Kayol, Lidderwat, Pahalgam, Kashmir, J. Geol. Soc. Ind. 19/9, 403 410.

Desio, A. (1979). Geologic evolution of the Karakorum. In "Geodynamics of Pakistan" (A. Farah and K.A. De Jong, eds). Geol. Survey Pakistan, Quetta, pp. 111–124.

Frank, W., Gansser, A. and Trommsdorff, V. (1977). Geological Observations in the Ladakh Area (Himalayas), a preliminary Report. Schweiz. mineral. petrogr. Mitt. 57, 89–113.

Fuchs, G. (1977). Traverse of Zanskar from the Indus to the Valley of Kashmir, a preliminary note. Jb. Geol. B.-A. 120 (2), 219 229, Wien.

Fuchs, G. (1979). On the Geology of Western Ladakh. Jb. Geol. B.-A. Bd. 122 (2), 512–540.

Fuchs, G. (1981). Outline of the Geology of the Himalaya. Mitt. österr. geol. Ges 74, 101–127

Gaetani, M., Nicora, A. and Premoli Silva, I. (1980). Uppermost Cretaceous and Paleocene in the Zanskar Range (Ladakh Himalaya). Riv. Ital. Paleont. Stratigr. 86, 1, 127–166.

Gansser, A. (1974). The ophiolitic mélange, a world-wide problem on Tethyan examples. Eclogae geol. Helv. 67, 479–508.

Gansser, A. (1979). Ophiolitic belts of the Himalayan and Tibetan region. In "Internat. Atlas of Ophiolites" 1:2.500.000. Geol. Soc. Amer. Map and Chart Series MC-33.

Gupta, V.J. and Kumar, S. (1975). Geology of Ladakh, Lahaul and Spiti regions of Himalaya with special reference to the stratigraphic position of flysch deposits. *Geol. Rdsch.,* **64,** 540–563.

Heim, A. and Gansser, A. (1939). Central Himalaya, geological observations of the Swiss expedition 1936. -*Mém. Soc Helv. Sci. nat.* **73 (1),** 1-245, Zuerich.

Honegger, K., Dietrich, V., Frank, W., Gansser, A., Thöni, M. and Trommsdorff, V. (1982). Magmatism and metamorphism in the Ladakh Himalayas (the Indus-Tsangpo suture zone). *Earth planet. Sci. Lett.* **60**.

Kelemen, P.B. and Sonnenfeld, M.D. (in press). Observations on Stratigraphy, Structure, Petrology and Tectonics from Traverses in Central Ladakh and Zanskar.

Lydekker, R. (1883). The geology of Kashmir and Chamba territories and the British districts of Khagan. *Mem. Geol. Surv. Ind.* **22,** 31–34.

MacMahon, C.A. (1901). Petrological Notes on some peridotites, serpentines, gabbros and associated rocks, from Ladakh, North-Western Himalaya. *Mem. Geol. Soc. Ind.* **31 (3),** 303-329, Calcutta.

Srikantia, S.V. and Bhargava, O.N. (1978). The Indus Tectonic Belt of Ladakh Himalaya; Its Geology, Significance and Evolution. Tect. Geol. of the Himalaya (Saklani, P.S., ed.) 1978, pp. 43–62.

Tewari, A.P. (1964). On the Upper Tertiary deposits of Ladakh Himalayas and correlation of various geotectonic units of Ladakh with those of the Kumaon-Tibet Region. *22nd Intern. Geol. Congr. Sect.* **11,** 37–58, New Delhi.

Tewari, B.S. and Pande, I.C. (1970). Permian fossiliferous limestone from Lamayuru, Ladakh. *Pub. Cent. Adv. Stud. Geol. Chandigarh* **7,** 188–190, Chandigarh 1970.

Thakur, V.C., Virdi, N.S., Hakim Rai and Gupta, K.R. (1981). A note on the geology of Nubra-Shyok area of Ladakh-Kashmir, Himalaya. *J. Geol. Soc. Ind.* **22, 1,** 46–50.

Wadia, D.N. (1937). The Cretaceous volcanic series of Astor/Deosai, Kashmir, and its intrusions. *Rec. G.S.I.* **72 (2)** 151–161, Calcutta.

The Morphogenic Phase of Mountain Building

A. Gansser

Geological Institute, Zurich, Switzerland

Abstract

The morphology of a high mountain which we admire is the result of recent vertical uplift, the morphogenic phase. It is the follow-up of the compressional phase of the orogeny. The causes of the uplift (thermal expansion, isostatic compensation, etc.) are still being disputed. The uplift rate can be measured in places and are estimated to amount to about one fifth of the value accepted for horizontal movements. The erosion factor has to be considered when such estimates are made.

Morphogenesis is not only a recent event and has been recognized in older orogenies. Frequently substantial plutonism (and volcanism) has preceded a morphogenic phase. Based on age of plutonic rocks and their presence as clasts in molasse sediments, one must assume very rapid uplifts, often raising an unroofed pluton to heights, surpassing the elevations of present mountain ranges. Examples from Alpine, Andean and Himalayan events are discussed.

Without a morphogenic phase of mountain building we could not have held this symposium today, since we could not have seen these mountains, or only a very rudimentary part of it. The outstanding three dimensional model we now admire and which has given us so many facts and many more theories is the result of this important event, which is still going on. Morphogeny is however not only a recent event. During the long and complicated history of mountain building older morphogenic phases have produced mountains which in volume and height may even have surpassed the present ranges.

The morphology of the high mountains on our globe is invariably related to substantial vertical uplifts, not yet compensated by erosion and which we find in various stages of development. Here we may distinguish such mountain ranges which are still developing as marginal ranges such as the Andes (Andean type), which are nearing their culmination such as the collision type ranges as the Himalayas (Himalayan type) and which have passed their culminating stage such as the Alps (Alpine type). Needless to say many mountain ranges fall between the above mentioned main types. All may finally die, overcome by erosion and subsidence until a new orogenic impulse prepares the way for a new morphogenic event.

It is important to realize that morphogeny is a follow-up of orogeny by a remarkable change from mostly horizontal compressional movements to vertical uplifts. Tentative estimates suggest that the yearly rate of uplift is approximately one fifth of the horizontal movement during the orogenic phase. The active orogeny related to mountain building passes through various stages: intense dynamic events are accompanied and mostly followed by metamorphism, first rather of the high pressure type, later with increasing temperatures. The latter phase is mostly syn- to postkinematic. The relations of the progressive metamorphism with the various deformational phases are still vaguely known. This is particularly the case in large and little known mountain ranges such as the Himalayas where the problem could be studied on superb exposures (Western Himalayas). In many cases the metamorphic peak is followed by leucogranite intrusions which postdate the progressive metamorphic event and are formed through anatexis in a deeper level of the continental crust. I may mention here the Novate granite of the Central Alps, the leucogranites of the Himalayas (tourmaline granites) and the Cordillera Blanca batholith of the Central Andes. They should be distinguished from earlier phases which produced the Bergell and Adamello in the Alps, the Trans-Himalayan plutons in the northern Himalayas as well as the Coastal batholiths of the Andes. They all originated from a similar, mostly oceanic basement source, the I-type granites of Pitcher (this volume) (Honegger *et al.*, 1982; Gansser, 1982).

The metamorphic peak and the related acid plutonism are the precursory "happenings" which trigger the important morphogenic event. The hot rocks are elevated and begin to erode and cool. The radiometric clocks are closed and the well displayed cooling ages of the regional metamorphism are convincing evidence for the beginning morphogeny. Fission track ages are particularly valuable in this connection (Wagner *et al.*, 1979). It is interesting to note that the high uplift

221

rates in the Simplon region of the Central Alps coincides with youngest alpine cooling ages of this region (Jäger, 1973). The remarkable metamorphic event is however not met in all mountain ranges in spite of the morphogenic follow-up. No regional metamorphism comparable to the young Alpine–Himalayan type exists in the Andes though some post-Andean acid plutonism is well developed (Cordillera Blanca), as well as extensive volcanism. Alpine type metamorphism is also missing in ranges like the Elburz and Caucasus. In the former, a remarkable leucogranite intrusion forms the highest non-volcanic peak, the 4900 m high Alamkuh, which with its 4 m.y. old intrusion age is one of the youngest granites known (Isler, 1977). It is interesting to note that the leucogranites of the Himalaya are concentrated within the highest peaks of the range, from Nanga Parbat in the west over Badrinath, Mustang, Manaslu, Shisha Pangma, Everest, Makalu to the 7000 m peaks in north Bhutan (Le Fort, 1973; Gansser, 1982).

I. The Rate and Type of Uplift of the Morphogenic Event

Only in the Alps do we have precision levelling which allows us to deduce the present rate of uplift. We still note an active rise in spite of the mature stage of the Alpine morphogenic phase, but this present uplift does not coincide with the morphological picture. The maximum uplift is clearly displaced to the south and coincides with the deepest Alpine exposures, the southern Lepontine rocks, which display the highest grade metamorphism. It also coincides with the deepest level of the Moho at 50 km (Gubler et al., 1981) (Fig. 1).

This picture is quite different from the Himalayas, where in spite of lack of precision measurements the distribution of elevated terraces suggests a coincidence of maximum elevation with the highest part of the range (personal observations, A.G.) (Fig. 2A). On the other hand this same distribution of the remarkable terraces in the higher

Himalayan ranges strongly suggests a shortlived but marked periodicity of the uplifts and we may expect similar differential movements also for the Alpine type ranges. This would show that the dates obtained through precision levelling are representative for this short interval but may give little information on the morphogenic phase as a whole.

The measured regional rise of the Central Alps does not reflect the present morphological picture which clearly shows that the Alps have passed the culmination of the morphogenic phase. The large alpine lakes, unknown in the Himalayas, as well as the subsided and deeply buried valleys (you can walk from the internal Alps all along flat alluvium into the Adriatic sea) show this fact clearly. The largest vertical movement was measured in the drowned and alluvium filled valleys of Rhône and Rhein in Brig and Chur respectively, with the reservation that the benchmarks were not selected by a geologist (Gubler et al., 1981). Furthermore, isostatic compensation subsequent to the removal of a considerable ice load could also explain the substantial rise along these wide valley floors. Such a possibility would change the regional picture considerably (Hantke, 1978, p. 395). A remeasured section through the Gotthard tunnel over an interval of 60 years shows clear reversals (Funk and Gubler, 1980) (Fig. 3).

In the Himalayas, where direct measurements of elevations in the central range do not exist, the present rate of morphogenic uplift can be deducted from direct geological evidence. Chinese scientists found in the high terraces of Southern Tibet along the north slopes of the Himalayas which have been elevated to 5000–6000 m a flora and fauna of subtropical origin and of late Pliocene to early Pleistocene age (Hsü, 1973). A post-Pliocene uplift of 4000–5000 m must be assumed. Some of these terraces were visited during the excursion of the Tibet symposium 1980. In the large Hundes basin of the Central Himalaya, half the size of Switzerland, Lydekker reported exactly 100 years ago rhinoceros bones of the tropical Siwalik type which have been uplifted to nearly 5000 m (Lydekker, 1881). These still perfectly horizontal

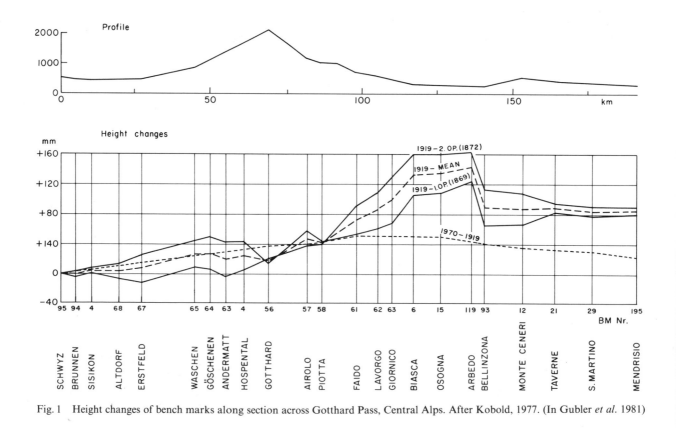

Fig. 1   Height changes of bench marks along section across Gotthard Pass, Central Alps. After Kobold, 1977. (In Gubler et al. 1981)

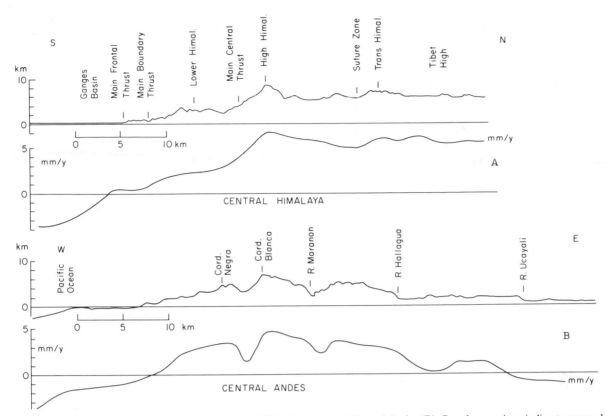

Fig. 2 Estimated morphogenic rise in mm/year of Central Himalaya (A) and Central Andes (B). Based on various indirect sources by A. Gansser.

gravel beds are cut by 1000 m deep canyons in which the oldest Bhuddistic remnants of Tibet were discovered. Well known are the tilted and uplifted Karewa lake beds of the Kashmir basin showing pre-Holocene elevations in the order of 3000 m (De Terra and Paterson, 1939). From all these facts a substantial uplift since earliest Pleistocene of over 4000 m seems to be a reasonable figure with an estimated present rate of uplift of at least 5 mm/year, nearly five times the measured amount of the Alps. More surprising seems however the fact, that not only have the Himalayas been affected by this latest morphogenic phase, but that with it the whole of Tibet has similarly risen, which amounts to an area

of 2 500 000 km² (Hsü, 1973). The effect of such an uplift on meteorology has been discussed during last years Tibet symposium (Akademia Sinica, 1980). The irradiation and its related climatic changes, apart from an increasing monsoon activity in the south and drying up of the main plateau in the north, shown by the reduction of the Tibetan lakes (Fig. 4), may even be responsible for the drying up of the Sahara! Large uplifted areas with high albedo and irradiation may have played a much more important role in the distribution of paleoclimates than so far realized (Barron, 1981).

The Andes present much more differentiated uplifts (Fig. 2B), with reversals along longitudinal valleys such as

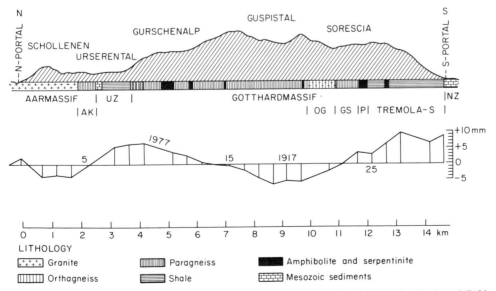

Fig. 3 Height changes determined in the Gotthard railroad tunnel between 1917 and 1977, after Funk and Gubler (1980).

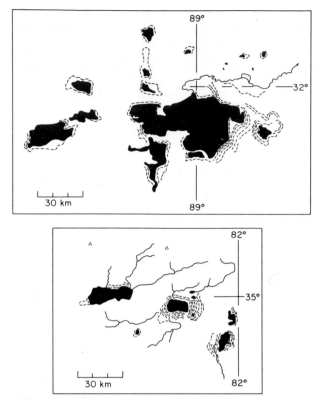

Fig. 4 The drying up of some Tibetan lakes with marked strand terraces and strand lines: – – – – – –. Landsat photo interpretation by A. Gansser.

the Chile "graben". During the large earthquake of southern Chile in 1960 the coastal strip dropped 2 m. Further to the north we note the famous Puna high plateau representing a late Neogene erosional peneplain, uplifted over 4000 m

(Aubouin, 1973). An extreme morphogenic effect is the rapid rise of the Cordillera Blanca in the Peruvian Andes. Along the eastern fault zone more than 4000 m of pre-Holocene and Holocene uplift must be assumed, and this above the Puna level. This young batholith was emplaced 10 m.y. ago and has a cooling age of less than 5 m.y., and must have had an overburden of at least 8000 m which has been completely removed while the present granite peaks are 6000 m high. The Recent movement is surprisingly well documented along the western fault zone, paralleling the range over 150 km and which has displaced Recent moraines with fresh scarps over 10 m high (Fig. 5). Similar scarps, produced by recent earthquakes were reported along the northern border of the range by Arnold Heim (1949), (Aubouin, 1973; Cobbing et al., 1981).

More differentiated are the morphogenic movements in the Northern Andes. Here we find the spectacular uplift of the Sierra Nevada de Santa Marta surrounded by the subsided regions of the Caesar, the Magdalena and Cauca Valleys, together with the 6000 m deep Ariguani graben. Along the Santa Marta fault zone the Sierra Nevada block has been separated from the northwards plunging (drowning) Central Cordillera (Fig. 6). The Sierra has been uplifted to its present height of the glaciated peaks of 5800 m which are only 45 km from the Caribbean shore, the highest mountain known so near the coast. The striking morphology of this triangular block is the result of this very young morphogenic uplift which rejuvenated the large faults bordering the massif on the west and north. Along the west side the Santa Marta fault zone coincides with the Ariguani graben which is filled by 6000 m of Neogene and younger sediments. Considering the 5800 m as a minimal elevation (one has to expect a considerable erosion in this tropical belt) one must assume an uplift since the Neogene of at least 12 000 m, much of which happened subrecently and recently. This young uplift is clearly reflected by the presence of only two main stages of glaciation, probably of the latest ice age (Würm type) (Gansser, 1955). The largest known present difference in elevations of

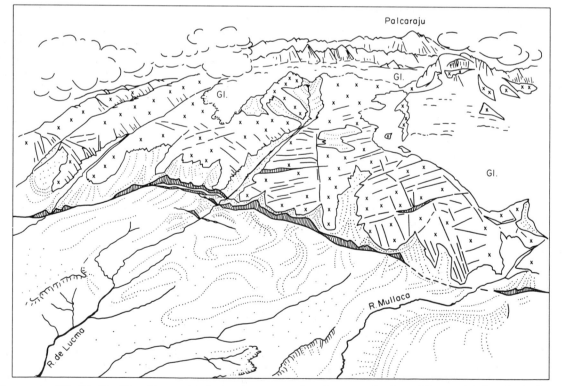

Fig. 5 The recent uplift of the Cordillera Blanca with displaced recent moraines. Interpretation from oblique aerial photo by A. Gansser. View to E.

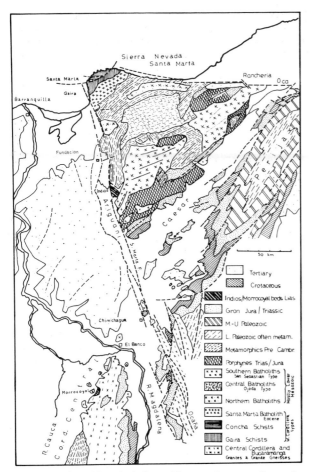

Fig. 6   The Sierra Nevada de Santa Marta and surrounding regions (N. Columbia). After Gansser, 1973.

the Andes, from the highest volcano to the deepest trench is 14 000 m (Aubouin, 1973).

The highest peaks of the Sierra Nevada consist of granodiorit and monzonitic batholiths of Mesozoic age (Jurassic and Lower Cretaceous) which have intruded Triassic porphyres as well as basement which gave an age of 1400 m.y. (Dibulla gneisses in the north-west corner of the range), probably the oldest basement of the Andes (Tschanz et al., 1969, MacDonald and Hurley, 1969). On the northern tip of the Sierra we note a thrusted relic of the Western Cordillera (Gansser, 1973) and a granitoid batholith of Eocene age.

In sharp contrast to the Sierra Nevada de Santa Marta are the drowned valleys of the Cauca, Lower Magdalena and Caesar rivers. All show signs of recent subsidence which is particularly well developed in the Caesar valley. The latter separates the Sierra Nevada from the Cordillera de Perijà. The Sierra is just surrounded by lowlands, only a few metres above sea level. This fact is responsible for the surprisingly isolated development of its flora, fauna and even human element such as the unique Aruaco Indians and the fascinating old Tyrona culture (Gansser, 1955).

II. Erosion

Any morphogenic phase is evidently counteracted by erosion. To calculate the amount of erosion is most difficult (Jäckli, 1958). Some data can be gathered by studying the foreland sediments. In Alpine ranges an amount of 1 mm/year has been calculated, which compensated the

present uplift rate of 1·5 mm/year. A comparable estimate is more difficult in the Himalayas. The foreland sediments are negligible compared to the visible volume of the range. This fact is already evident if we compare the Alpine and Himalayan molasses. The estimated volume of the Alpine molasse equals the visible volume of the present Alps, while the Siwaliks, the Himalayan molasse equivalent, represents only one tenth of this amount (rough estimate by A.G.). Not included are the large Indus and Ganges deltas. They are partly older than the Siwaliks. In most of the mountain ranges the present detritus is mostly coarser and less sorted than the respective molasses. Fanglomerates are the rule in the Himalayas and the Andes as well as along the steeper southern slopes of the Alps. Climatic changes due to the uplift (Monsoon of the Himalaya) and the human element (deforestation) are partly responsible. The Ganges river has at present the greatest amount of suspension known.

In the Himalayas the erosive detritus is partly trapped in large basins and terraces along the northern part and has not yet reached the foreland. The largest one is the Hundes basin, already mentioned. A peculiar fact is further manifested by the eroded remnants of lake sediments, often high along the valley slopes. They are well exposed in the dry western Himalayas, with the classical vestige of Lamayuru in Lakakh. From cursory observations they seem mostly of a similar composition, surprisingly rich in carbonates and often related to the last glaciation. Some still show signs of glacial loading well exposed in the large basin of Skardu along the Indus with intense cryoturbate folding. Field observations suggest that they may have emptied through catastrophic events and in a very short time, producing enormous fanglomeratic floods. Important morphological changes must have happened in a few days! The lakes have drained through the already existing largest rivers which have their sources north of the Himalayas. They have cut the highest tectonical and morphological culminations. The Indus at the Nanga Parbat high, the Arun between Everest (Chomolungma) and Kangchendzönga and the Tsangpo at the Namche Barwa culmination in the east (Gansser, 1964).

The Indus gorge at Nanga Parbat is of particular interest. Here we find the largest difference in elevation known (1100 m to 8125 m) over a distance of only 21 km. In the deepest part of the gorge outcrop clastic sediments of an Upper Siwalik facies transgressing the basement on the south side and gabbros of the Transhimalayan pluton on the north side. They are steeply folded up to 70° and transgressed by the lower Indus river terraces. Similar terraces have been uplifted on both valley slopes over 2000 m (Fig. 7). These enigmatic sediments have been named by Peter Miesch 45 years ago as Jalipur formation (Miesch, 1936). Why are they preserved in the deepest part of the young Indus gorge and not high on the slopes? Through the same spot passes the large thrust contact between the Precambrian Nanga Parbat gneisses and the Trans-Himalayan batholith, the southern Suture Zone. The thrust is outlined by a row of steaming hot springs (Fig. 7).

III. Recent Seismicity

An interesting fact of the morphogenic phase in mountain ranges of the collision type (the Andes are here excluded) is the apparently abnormal location of the present seismicity. We realize that frequently the distribution of the epicentres does not follow the major orogenic trends but shows a reactivation of older structural patterns. The present crustal unrest seems to have inherited trends reflecting alignments which may even predate the orogeny precursory to the actual morphogeny.

The earthquake clusters in the Swiss Alps at the lower

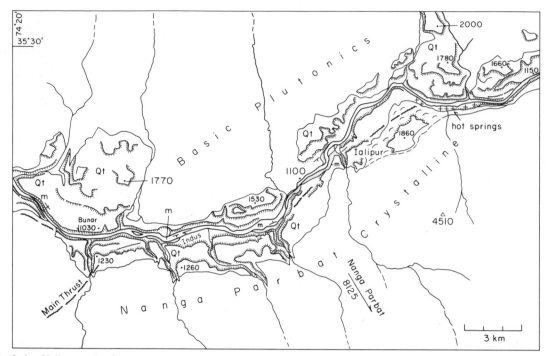

Fig. 7   The Indus Valley north of Nanga Parbat with the Jalipur Molasse(m) and uplifted terraces. Note main thrust and hot springs. Topography from Misch, 1936.

Valais and the Chur region do not seem to be related to the major east–west structures between the Helvetian and Pennine zones, the "Swiss Rocky Mountain trench". The important Tonale or Insubric Line is seismically dead. The Sarnen earthquake centre has not yet received any convincing explanation (Pavoni, 1977, 1979). A comparable lack of correlation between seismicity and major structures is more striking in the Himalayas, though admittedly, the data there are incomplete. The Main Central Thrust, studded with hot springs is not reflected by present seismic activities. Even the Suture Zone further to the north, the major Himalayan structural feature, again with hot springs, cannot be outlined by seismicity alone. Some of the epicentres falling on this line are rather related to north–south trending faults where they intersect the Suture Zone. Only the Main Frontal Thrust is reflected by some major quakes, but here again they seem not to follow the main trend. On the other hand active north–south features, such as faults and fractures, visible in landsat photographs, are reflected by present seismicity and can be followed far into Tibet (Molnar and Tapponnier, 1978). Depth and focal mechanism solutions (compression versus extension) give so far no convincing patterns. The rejuvenation of older trends is well documented near the famous syntaxis of the western Himalayas by the seismic investigations of the Columbia University team in connection with the Darbela Dam. They outlined a very marked SE–NW trend, cutting the Syntaxis. It also coincides with recent upheavals along the Indus/Kabul river alluvium. At the intersection of this trend with the southern Suture Zone, occurred in 1974 the large destructive earthquake of Patan (Gornitz and Seeber, 1981) (Fig. 8). Detailed microseismic investigations are certainly a most important tool in order to appreciate the structural pattern related to morphogeny.

IV. Older Morphogenic Events

Morphogeny is not only related to the last phase of present mountain building, but substantial phases of uplift must be assumed during the complex history of a mountain range.

Their effect is evidently no more visible in the form of spectacular peaks, which may have even surpassed the present summits in height. There is some evidence which indicates that the Alpine type mountains have passed through more earlier morphogenic phases than the Himalayas and the Andes. The Alpine history is more complex with more orogenic events compared to the Andes and the Himalayas. On the other hand the Alps are one of the best studied mountain systems in the world, and much remains to be done in the Andes and the Himalayas. We still do not know how extensive in time and space morphogenic events have been, but it seems most likely that they were short-lived.

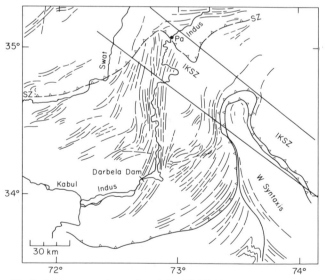

Fig. 8   The western Syntaxis and the Middle Indus Valley with the Indus-Kohistan Seismic Zone cutting the main structures. Situation of the IKSZ after Seeber (Gornitz and Seeber, 1981).
Pa = Patan site of the 1974 earthquake.
SZ = Suture Zone southern branch.
Structural trends interpretation by Gansser.

Products of plutonism, frequently a forerunner of a morphogenic phase, and its denudation products, such as conglomerates or fanglomerates may give us some hints of such past events. A striking example is the Alpine Bergell intrusion and its erosion products in the Como molasse. The Bergell is, together with the Adamello pluton, a later Alpine intrusion related to deep seated effects involving oceanic crusts similar to the coastal Andean batholiths and the Trans-Himalayan plutons. It may however present only the end phase of this longer process. The Bergell pluton was emplaced 30 m.y. ago into a well built alpine nappe edifice. Exposed is now a tonalitic rim, surprisingly similar to the Andean and Transhimalayan tonalites, and slightly older than the coarse granitic centre which gave the 30 m.y. date (Koeppel and Gruenenfelder, 1975).

Both must have crystallized under an overburden of at least 8000 m. This overburden was removed during the rapid morphogenic rise, while the tonalitic mantle and the granitic core were being eroded; the erosion products were deposited as large boulders in the upper third part of a coarse, 1000 m thick conglomerate of the Como molasse. The conglomerate unit is underlain by foraminiferal, well bedded silts of Middle Oligocene age deposited under open marine conditions and overlain by well bedded sandstones and banded clays with an Upper Oligocene to Lower Miocene fauna (Rögl *et al.*, 1975) (Fig. 9). Both the underlying and overlying sediments are not typical of normal Molasse section. Age and petrology of the Bergell boulders in the Como molasse are identical to the rock types exposed at present in the Bergell pluton and different from the more stressed southern and western tonalites. We have here the surprising fact that we must assume a rapid uplift over 10 000 m of the Bergell, a strong erosion, rapid transport and deposition of the large Bergell boulders in the Como molasse, within a few million years. All happened during the same geological epoch when there was no compressional nor substantial strike-slip movements as some authors (e.g. Trümpy, 1975; Laubscher, 1971) had assumed. The direct relation of the Bergell boulders in the Como molasse with the actual outcrops of the Bergell pluton is further corroborated by fission track ages, which suggest that the granite boulders of the Como molasse can be reassigned to a vertical position of 6 km above the present morphology of the Bergell massif (Wagner *et al.*, 1979).

Similar events, only in a more regional way, can be recognized in connection with the large Trans-Himalayan plutons which genetically have a similar origin than the Bergell and the Adamello batholiths of the Alps. For the Trans-Himalayan plutons we must assume a similar overburden as suggested for the Bergell. The most important and rapid uplift of this range followed the last and more acid intrusions about 40 m.y. ago, producing a relief exceeding the present height of about 6000 m. We find the detritus in the Shigatse-Kailas-Ladakh-molasses. The base is characterized by conglomerates containing large granitic boulders with Eocene clasts as the youngest components (Frank *et al.*, 1977). This fact is now observable at the present outcrop level.

The deeper beds, further away and exposed through an intense tectonic (Shigatse formation) still contain coarse conglomerates interbedded (curiously enough) with pelagic shales containing Upper Cretaceous ammonites, discovered during the excursion of the Tibet symposium in Shigatse in 1980. The morphogenic uplift of the Trans-Himalaya must have happened with various pulses, following successive intrusions changing from basic to acidic (Honegger *et al.*, 1982). The tectonic deformation of the molasse following the older morphogenic events has been intense, as indicated by the well exposed and folded Shigatse formation (Guidebook Tibet, 1980).

Much of the block faulting in the older history of mountain ranges may have been the effect of morphogenic phases, with many more ups than downs. This may have been the case during the Gondwana glaciation. Alpine-type mountains probably existed during the lower and middle Carboniferous in the Andean and Tasman belts (Martin, 1981). The Permian Verrucano has probably been related to a substantial Pre-Alpine morphogenic phase with a corresponding high relief. Many other major breccia deposits such as the Alpine Lias breccias, the spectacular giant breccias of the Cretaceous and some Oligocene molasse deposits suggest morphogenic phases with mountain ranges competing with the splendour of our present Alpine peaks.

References

Aubouin, J. (1973). In Géologie et géomorphologie de la Cordillère des Andes. Special volume. *Revue de Géogr. phys. et de Géol-Dyn.* **15/1–2**, 216 pp.

Akademia Sinica (1980). A Scientific Guidebook to South Xizang (Tibet) Organizing Committee, Symposium Tibet Plateau, p. 104, Beijing, China (with geol. map. 1:150′000).

Barron, E.J. (1981). Paleogeography as a climatic Forcing Factor. *Geol. Rdsch.* **70/2**, 737–747.

Cobbing, E.J., Pitcher, W.S., Wilson, J.J., Baldcock, J.W., Taylor, W.P., McCourt, W. and Snelling, N.J. (1981). The Geology of the Western Cordillera of northern Peru. *Inst. of Geol. Sci. Overseas Memoir*, **5**, London, 143 pp.

Chang, Cheng-Fa and Cheng, Hsi-Ian (1973). Some tectonic features of the Mt. Jolmo Lumgma area, southern Tibet, China. *Sci. Sinica* **16**, 257–265.

De Terra, H. and Paterson, T.T. (1939). Studies on the Ice Age in India and associated human cultures. Carnegie Inst. Washington. 354 pp.

Frank, W., Gansser, A. and Trommsdorff, V. (1977). Geological Observations in the Ladakh Area (Himalayas). A preliminary Report. *Schw. Min. Petr. Mitt.* **57**, 89–113.

Funk, H. and Gubler, E. (1980). Höhenänderungen der Fixpunkte im Gotthard Bahntunnel zwischen 1917 und 1977 und ihre Beziehungen zur Geologie. *Eclogae Geol. Helv.*, **73/2**, 583–592.

Gansser, A. (1955). Ein Beitrag zur Geologie und Petrographie der Sierra Nevada de Santa Marta (Kolumbien, Südamerika). *SMPM* **35/2**, 209–279.

Gansser, A. (1964). "Geology of the Himalayas". Wiley-Interscience, London, 289 pp.

Gansser, A. (1973 a). Orogene Entwicklung in den Anden, im Himalaya und den Alpen, ein Vergleich. *Eclogae Geol. Helv.* **66/1**, 23–40.

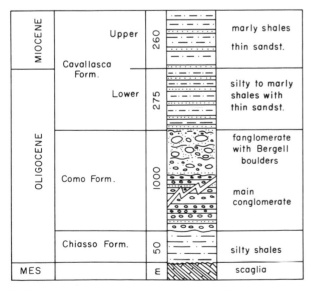

Fig. 9 Generalized section through the Como Molasse. Redrawn from Rögl *et al.*, (1975).

Gansser, A. (1973). Facts and theories on the Andes. *J. Geol. Soc. (London)* **129**, 93–131.

Gansser, A. (1982). The Geology of the Bhutan Himalaya. *Mem. Soc. Helv. Sci. nat.* (In print).

Gornitz, V. and Seeber, L. (1981). Morphotectonic analysis of the Hazara arc region of the Himalayas, North Pakistan and Northwest India. *Tectonophysics* **74**, 263–282.

Gubler, E., Kahle, H.G., Klingele, E., Müller, St. and Oliver, R. (1981). Recent Crustal Movements in Switzerland and their Geophysical Interpretation. *Tectonophysics* **71**, 125–152.

Hantke, R. (1978). Eiszeitalter, Bd. I, Ott Verlag AG Thun, 468 pp.

Heim, Arn., (1949). Observaciones geologicas en la région del terramotto de Ancash de Noviembre de 1946. *Soc. Geol. del Peru.* **2/6**, 28.

Honegger, K., Dietrich, V., Frank, W., Gansser, A., Thöni, M. and Trommsdorff, V. (1982). Magmatism and metamorphism in the Ladakh Himalayas. *Earth planet. Sci. lett.* **60**, 253–292.

Hsu, J. (1978). On the Paleobotanical Evidence for Continental Drift and the Himalayan Uplift. *The Paleobotanist* **25**, 131–142.

Isler, A. (1977). Die Geologie des West-Alamkuh Gebietes (Zentral Elburz/Iran). *Diss. ETH.* **6107**, 272 pp.

Jäckli, H. (1959). Der rezente Abtrag der Alpen im Spiegel der Vorlandsedimentation. *Eclogae Geol. Helv.* **51/2**, 354–365.

Jäger, E. (1973). Die Alpine Orogenese im Lichte der Radiometrischen Altersbestimmung. *Eclogae Geol. Helv.* **66**, 11–21.

Koeppel, V. and Gruenenfelder, M. (1975). Concordant U-Pb ages of monazite and xenotime from the Central Alps and the timing of the high temperature Alpine metamorphism, a preliminary report. *SMPM* **55**, 129–132.

Laubscher, H. (1971). Das Alpin-Dinariden Problem und die Palinspastik der südlichen Tethys. *Geol. Rdsch.* **60**, 813–833.

Le Fort, P. (1973). Les Leucogranites de l'Himalaya, sur l'example du granite du Manaslu (Népal central). *Soc. Geol. France. Bull.* **7**, 555–561.

Lydekker, R. (1881). Observations on the ossiferous beds of Hundes in Tibet. *Rec. Geol. Surv. India* **31**, 179–204.

McDonald, W.D. and Hurley, P.M. (1969). Precambrian gneisses from Northern Colombia, South America. *Bull. geol. Soc. Am.* **80**, 1867–1872.

Martin, H. (1981). The late Paleozoic Gondwana glaciation. *Geol. Rdsch.* **70/2**, 480–496.

Misch, P. (1936). Einiges zur Metamorphose des Nanga Parbat. *Geol. Rdsch.* **27**, 79–81.

Molnar, P. and Tapponnier, P. (1978). Active Tectonics of Tibet. *J. Geophys. Res.* **83**, No. B 11, 5361–5375.

Pavoni, N. (1977). Erdbeben im Gebiet der Schweiz. *Eclogae Geol. Helv.* **70**, 351–370.

Pavoni, N. (1979). Investigations of recent crustal movements in Switzerland. *SMPS* **59**, 117–126.

Pitcher, W.S. (1978). The anatomy of a batholith. *J. Geol. Soc. London,* **135**, 157–182.

Pitcher, W.S. (1982). Mobile Belts and Granite Types. This Volume.

Rögl, F., Cita, M.B., Müller, C. and Hochuli, P. (1975). Biochronology of conglomerate bearing Molasse sediments near Como (Italy). *Riv. Ital. Paleont.* **81**, 57–88.

Trümpy, R. (1975). Penninic-Austroalpine boundary in the Swiss Alps. A presumed former continental margin and its problems. *Amer, J. Sci.* **275–A**, 209–238.

Tschanz, C.M., Jimento, A. and Cruz, J. (1969). Mapa geologico de reconocimiento de la Sierra Nevada de Santa Marta, Colombia, 1:200 000. Inst. Nac. de Investig. Geologico-Minera. Bogotà.

Wagner, G.A., Miller, D.S. and Jäger, E. (1979). Fission track ages on apatites of Bergell rocks from Central Alps and Bergell boulders in Oligocene sediments. *Earth Planet. Sci. lett.* **45**, 335–360.

The Life History of a Mountain Range — The Appalachians

J. Rodgers

Yale University
Conn. U.S.A.

Abstract

The life history of the Appalachian Mountain range began in the late Precambrian with an episode of rifting within the body of an older mountain range, the Grenville orogenic belt. Divergence continued for perhaps 200 million years, establishing an oceanic realm and trailing edges. On the western trailing edge, a thick carbonate bank was built up on continental crust; the ocean itself was complicated by internal volcanic belts, whether simple island arcs or founded on older continental fragments.

Convergence took over at different times in different parts of the ocean. In a first orogenic climax (Ordovician), not only was some of the ocean destroyed and the sediments it contained deformed and metamorphosed, but also ocean crust was obduced onto the western continental margin in the form of ophiolite thrust sheets, beneath which are other far-travelled thrust sheets of sediments and also continental basement. In a second climax (Devonian), most of the rest of the ocean was closed and its sediments strongly deformed, metamorphosed, and intruded, completing the creation of a metamorphic core zone. In a third climax (Carboniferous and Permian), deformation though severe was largely confined to certain belts; the blocks between were moved laterally but not greatly deformed internally. In the northern Appalachians, strike-slip movement was important; in the southern, a very large part of the metamorphic core zone created by the earlier climaxes was thrust bodily up to 200 km north-westward on a deep sole fault. All the climaxes produced mountainous islands or highlands that shed vast amounts of debris westward to form clastic wedges or delta complexes on the continental margin. In the southern half of the range, these deposits and those of the underlying carbonate bank, which together constitute the classical Appalachian geosyncline, were caught in front of the advancing metamorphic thrust sheet, stripped off the basement on a décollement, and formed into the classical Appalachian folded belt.

In the early Mesozoic, divergence began again; out of several lines of rifts, one developed into the Atlantic Ocean. In the Appalachian range, left on one side of the ocean, there has since been only broad uplift and erosion. In the Atlantic, divergence has now continued for about 200 million years, and in due course one may expect . . .

I. Prologue

I strongly suspect my interest in the subject I am to discuss here was awakened when as a schoolboy I picked up in a second-hand bookshop a copy — the presentation copy to John M. Clarke — of James Geikie's book: *Mountains, Their Origin, Growth and Decay* (1913). I read it through fascinated, though of course not comprehending half of it, and despite disparaging remarks from members of my family, who dubbed it *Mountains, Their Cause and Cure*, I have been fascinated by the subject ever since.

Mountain ranges are of course not living organisms, but we geologists have long believed with Geikie that they go through a sequence of stages over geologic time, from a period when nothing hints that a range will develop in the future, through a stage of origin (the geosyncline) and a period in which mountains grow (the orogeny), to a stage of decay ending in their dissection and obliteration, often in their interment beneath a cover of younger sediment. In this talk, I shall not attempt a generic description of a life history applicable to all mountain ranges, but rather a specific one, that of the range best known to me, the Appalachians of eastern North America (Fig. 1), and at first I shall concentrate on their northern half, especially New England, beside which I grew up (reading Geikie's book) and in which I have spent the largest part of my own life history.

ward movement of this block was what compressed and deformed the rocks of the folded belt, producing all the folds and thrust sheets observed there, as a snowplough pushing over a smooth pavement forces wet sticky snow before it to slide and fold.

If an ocean was closed during any of this quite intense orogenic activity, its former site is not obvious in the presently exposed Piedmont province. The Coastal Plain and continental shelf sediments clearly overlie rocks much like those in the Piedmont, however, as at Cape Hatteras, 200 km east of the Coastal Plain border, where a well encountered them at about 3 km depth. Probably, moreover, rocks that are similar to and were once continuous with these also underlie the West African continental shelf and Coastal Plain, whose width ranges from 200 to 400 km. East of that, poorly dated crystalline rocks in the Mauritanide orogenic belt are thrust eastward over the Paleozoic sediments at the margin of the Sahara platform, affecting strata as high as lower Upper Devonian (Frasnian; in the Anti-Atlas of Morocco, lower Carboniferous — Viséan — rocks are folded). This thrusting *may* also belong to the third orogenic climax, though in Mauritania it could have been earlier, but if an ocean closed between here and the Piedmont, its trace is now hidden under one or the other Coastal Plain or the Atlantic Ocean itself.

C. Crystalline Belt: Earlier Orogenic Climaxes

The rocks that moved forward on the late Paleozoic sole fault already contained virtually all the structure and metamorphism that they now display but, as mentioned above, the age of that structure and metamorphism is controversial. The few fossil localities known in the Piedmont give us a little help. Close to the Coastal Plain overlap in east-central Alabama, within the Talladega thrust sheet at the north-west edge of the Piedmont province, a relatively thin chert unit (Jemison chert), well dated by a Lower Devonian (Siegenian ?) shelly fauna, lies near the top of a thick otherwise undated* clastic sequence (Talladega group), locally containing spectacular diamictite with pebbles and cobbles of a variety of older rocks, probably including basement. Disconformably (possibly unconformably) beneath are carbonates (now marble) resting in turn on clastics; these strata resemble the Lower Ordovician to latest Precambrian sequence of the folded belt, and there seems little reason to doubt the correlation, though no fossils are known. The disconformity could thus be the ubiquitous post-Lower Ordovician disconformity, and the diamictite an even more poorly sorted equivalent of the conglomerate in the Blountian clastic wedge. The rocks are somewhat metamorphosed, reaching greenschist facies, so that here at least some metamorphism is post-Lower Devonian. The diamictite tells of an earlier climax, which could be Middle Ordovician or somewhat younger. The Talladega sheet is separated from the rocks on either side by post-metamorphic thrust faults, however; that on the north-west side cuts Lower Carboniferous strata (of the Ouachita-related clastic wedge), whereas that on the south-east brings in middle-grade metamorphic rock (with kyanite) of typical Piedmont aspect. The thrust faults are thus clearly late Paleozoic, Alleghanian, and post-metamorphic, so that the fossils date only the low-grade metamorphism in the Talladega rocks and tell us nothing about the metamorphism in the rest of the Piedmont. (Furthermore, the Talladega rocks, despite their metamorphism, have much more in common, both structurally and stratigraphically, with the rocks in the Valley and Ridge province than with those in most of the Piedmont.)

The "Avalonian" Carolina slate belt contains a thick sequence of volcanics and volcanogenic sediments, in the

*Carboniferous fossils have also been reported from this sequence, but I do not regard them as authenticated.

upper part of which a very few Cambrian fossils have been found. The rocks here are metamorphosed only to greenschist facies or less, but they grade laterally into rocks at medium grade; thus the major metamorphism in central North and South Carolina is at least post-(Middle)Cambrian. Nevertheless, Glover and Sinha (1973) have adduced isotopic evidence for a very late Precambrian orogenic episode within the slate belt (called by them the Virgilina phase), which probably interrupted volcanic and volcanogenic deposition in several parts of the belt.

The most instructive evidence comes from two synclines of slaty rocks in north-central Virginia (the Arvonia and Quantico "slates"), both of which contain well attested marine Upper Ordovician fossils (probably about Maysville, late Caradoc). The rocks in the synclines lie with angular unconformity on older metavolcanic and metaplutonic rocks belonging to the Avalonian belt and dated isotopically, but not by fossils, as probably latest Precambrian but possibly reaching into the Cambrian. The slaty rocks themselves are tightly folded (possibly in two phases, one recumbent) and metamorphosed, locally to kyanite grade. Thus here again there is unequivocal evidence of two episodes of orogeny, one before and one after marine sedimentation during the Late Ordovician.

Beyond that, one must rely on isotopic age determinations. They have been interpreted by some (Butler, 1972; Rodgers, 1971, p. 1169) as indicating that the main Piedmont metamorphism, certainly accompanied by isoclinal or recumbent folding, was mainly or entirely Ordovician, Taconic; by others that it was later, presumably Acadian. Probably both groups are at least partially right, yet in most parts of the region the data do not require us to choose only an Ordovician or a Devonian age or to postulate a sharp separation; indeed the fixed categories Taconic and Acadian imported from the north may be preventing us from seeing a truer picture. In the past, I have been reluctant to accept a true Acadian orogenic phase in the southern Appalachians because the absence in the folded belt of any major Devonian clastic wedge centred south of Pennsylvania suggests the absence of any mountainous uplifts in the belts to the east. (Indeed even the Blountian delta is small compared with the Queenston delta.) But if, as the new geophysical evidence tells us, most of the crystalline southern Appalachians is a great, far-travelled, late Paleozoic thrust sheet, then the rocks we now see in the Piedmont and probably in the Blue Ridge, at least from Roanoke south, were some 200 km farther away from the folded belt than they are now, so that there could well have been Acadian orogeny in the eastern Piedmont that was never reflected by sedimentation within the Valley and Ridge province.

Evidence for Ordovician or at least Early Paleozoic orogeny seems best along the western side of the crystalline Appalachians, especially in and near the Blue Ridge of North Carolina, where also are found the major pre-metamorphic thrust faults mentioned above; for example, the Greenbrier (Hadley and Goldsmith, 1963, p. 79–81, 96) and Hayesville (Hatcher et al., 1979) faults. Here also lies the most prominent and extensive line of ultramafic bodies, recognized long ago by Hess (1939, pl 279, Fig. 13) and assigned by him to the Taconic orogeny; it seems to have the same position here as the line of ultramafic fragments in New England though no ophiolitic thrust sheets are known (except perhaps in Maryland). Yet ultramafics are also present in belts farther east within the Piedmont (Misra and Keller, 1978, p. 406 ff.); whether they are Taconic or Acadian is simply unknown. Evidence for Devonian or at least mid-Paleozoic orogeny seems strongest in northern Virginia near the Coastal Plain overlap, in the region east of the Upper Ordovician slate synclines (which could be regarded as providing confirming evidence). Evidence for Late Paleozoic orogeny, as we have seen, is strongest in the folded belt and adjacent Blue Ridge on the one side and in the far eastern Piedmont on the other side of the visible Appalachian orogenic belt. Thus, aside from the well dated folded belt, the scanty evidence in the southern half of the Appalachians is tantalizingly like the much stronger evidence in the northern half where the Taconic, Acadian, and Maritime climaxes were displaced successively eastward, though of course with large overlaps. The major difference between the two halves, as we understand them so far, seems to be the grandiose north-westward horizontal displacement and accompanying uplift of the southern metamorphic zone over its sole fault and the resulting large-scale deformation of the folded belt.

V. Decay

The mountains that formed in the Appalachian region at several times during the Paleozoic were obviously attacked by erosion as soon as they arose, as recorded by the voluminous clastic wedges and deltaic complexes still preserved in the western belts of the range and on the continental platform beyond. The record of events between Early Permian and Late Triassic is lost, however, except that at this time non-marine redbeds spread over large parts of the *western* continental platform, interfingering with marine beds in the eastern part of the Cordilleran geosyncline. The absence of any deposits in eastern North America suggests that that Appalachians then stood high and were being vigorously dissected, though orogeny and its accompanying processes were over. One must remember, moreover, that at this time North America, Europe, and Africa were contiguous parts of a single great continent, no ocean intervening, so that the mountainous region also took in western and north-western Africa and large parts of Europe.

In Late (possibly late Middle) Triassic time, rifting began to cut through this continent along several lines, generally following the trend of the Appalachian Mountains (and the then still adjacent mountains in Morocco and Iberia), just as rifting had cut through the "Grenvillian" continent and mountain range in the late Precambrian. As before, debris from the range accumulated in the rift depressions as variable but in places very great thicknesses of clastic sediments, ranging in age through the Late Triassic and Early Jurassic. In the earliest Jurassic there was basaltic volcanism; then and somewhat later swarms of dikes were intruded. Finally, in about Middle Jurassic time, one of the lines of rifts passed into a Red Sea stage, the others ceased to grow, and the Atlantic Ocean was born. Thus if the late Precambrian rifting had been the birthpangs of the Appalachian range, the Early Mesozoic rifting was a sort of Caesarian section in that range to permit the birth of the next generation.

In the Appalachian range, left on the west side of the widening ocean, there has since been, besides unceasing erosion, only broad archlike, presumably isostatic uplift of its central portion and accompanying subsidence of its eastern and southern margins. The uplift is attested most clearly around the south end of the range where the Cretaceous and Cenozoic sediments of the Coastal Plain dip a degree or two away from the mountains (and dip less the younger they are); their dip direction swings smoothly from south-east in the Carolinas to south at the Georgia–Alabama line, south-west in western Alabama and central Mississippi, and west in west Tennessee. The margins of the range have gradually been buried under these sediments, beginning (in the subsurface) already in the Jurassic, and indeed today's epicontinental shelf sea encroaches more and more onto the roots of the chain from Georgia northward into Canada, where in the Gulf of Saint Lawrence it extends all the way across and laps onto the roots of the old Grenville range.

The timing and character of the uplift has been debated for a long time. It has been maintained that the Appalachians were worn down to a peneplain, perhaps several times, and that in the Cretaceous at least the sea covered them completely. That any part of the present land surface in the central part of the mountains represents such a peneplain is improbable, however, as shown by Cooper (1944, pp. 213–214) for a supposed remnant in the mountains of south-west Virginia. The discovery of old sinkholes containing early Eocene, Paleocene, and even Late Cretaceous plant fossils (Bridge, 1950, p. 194; Pierce, 1965) on erosion surfaces hundreds of metres below the present-day mountain crests also strongly suggests that at no time has the relief been much less than that. Whether uplift and erosion have been relatively steady or relatively spasmodic is also not known, though the evidence to decide the question, and perhaps to estimate quantitatively the Cretaceous and Cenozoic erosion history, can presumably be found in the clastic sediments under the Atlantic Coastal Plain and the continental shelf, slope, and rise. In any case, though past their prime, the mountains are still there; the highest peaks still reach 2 km above the sea, and local relief passes 1 km in several regions.

In the meantime, Atlas' Ocean has been steadily widening and extending itself north and south for about 200 million years now, with little sign that mountains will some day grow out of it. To be sure, we could have said the same thing for Iapetos' Ocean in the Late Cambrian. Moreover, deformed Cretaceous and early Cenozoic strata on the eastern Canary and Cape Verde Islands off West Africa suggest at least one brief episode of convergence and orogeny along the eastern side of the ocean. Perhaps somewhere in the global system what had been easy subduction became blocked (could it be when the North American plate and the subduction zone along its Pacific margin collided with the East Pacific rise?), and the accumulating stresses sought relief elsewhere, but if so, after a short-lived attempt to start something off Africa, they found and started to use an easier place, and the Atlantic returned to placid divergence. The next generation of mountains here is still in embryo.

VI. Epilogue

Is the life history of the Appalachian range typical of mountain ranges generally? I suspect so, as Tuzo Wilson apparently did (1966) when he deduced from it the Wilson cycle. During a preparatory period of divergence, rifts open and oceanic crust forms; sediments accumulate upon it and also as continental rise, slope, and shelf deposits along the trailing edges of the fragmented continents. When convergence begins, probably irregularly at first and only in some areas, volcanic island arcs form that migrate sometimes toward, sometimes away from the continents, opening and closing marginal seas and deforming their contents. As convergence becomes more general, not only these arcs but continental fragments and even large continental masses arrive at subduction zones and try to go down them. The first time or times this happens in a mountain range, ocean crust may be obducted onto the edge of the continental block to form the great ophiolite thrust sheets; in later episodes — and there generally seem to be several — the ocean crust is mostly pulled down into the mantle, the sediments upon it being scraped off and piled up as accretionary wedges against the arcs or continental blocks. Moreover, "exotic" terrains may arrive, pushing straight in or sliding in from one side, and fragments of oceanic crust may get stuck along the boundaries of the different elements that are thus being pushed or slid together, though generally they are less easily decipherable than the obduced ophiolites. If the volcanic arcs are already strongly curved, as in Indonesia today, and marginal seas and small continental fragments abound, the resulting pattern can become very complex; thus to guess what Indonesia will look like after its post-Cocacolazoic climax when Australia collides with Asia, we can look at the mess that Paleozoic convergence of the Russian and Siberian platforms (Kropotkin, 1961, Fig. 1) has made of the geology of the Sayan-Altay region and central Kazakhstan. The Appalachians have been luckier; though their history is also complex and successive orogenic episodes overlapped and overprinted each other, the resulting orogenic belts were at least not bent into hairpins but only anastomose. In each orogenic climax, mountains are built, to be attacked at once by erosion but often to be further uplifted, perhaps to even greater heights, in later spasms. After several climaxes, the relatively mobile and "disposable" oceanic crust is largely used up by being subducted or converted into continental crust, the region becomes more resistant to convergence, and the blocks involved get bigger. Then convergence and uplift wane and erosion takes over; orogeny is done with and soon subsidence and divergence start in again, quite possibly beginning in some regions while convergence is still continuing in others. After its dissection by erosion, the mountainous cadaver can then be partly or wholly buried beneath newer sediments, or it can be cut up into blocks ready for the next round of the cycle. Again the Appalachians were luckier than, say, Hercynian Europe, so fragmented by later events; though somewhat cut up in the Carboniferous in the north and in the early Mesozoic throughout, they still stand fairly high and they have retained much of their original continuity, meriting perhaps Philip King's epithet: "the most elegant mountain range on Earth."

References

Arkle, T., Jr. (1974). Stratigraphy of the Pennsylvanian and Permian systems of the central Appalachians. *Geol. Soc. America Spec. Paper* **148**, 5–29.

Arthaud, F. and Matte, P. (1977). Late Paleozoic strike-slip faulting in southern Europe and northern Africa: result of a right-lateral shear zone between the Appalachians and the Urals. *Geol. Soc. America Bull.* **88**, 1305–1320.

Autran, A. and Cogné, J. (1980). La zone interne de l'orogène varisque dans l'Ouest de la France et sa place dans le développement de la chaîne hercynienne. Internat. Geol. Congress, 26th, Paris 1980, Colloque C 6, pp. 90–111.

Belt, E.S. (1968). Post-Acadian rifts and related facies, eastern Canada. In "Studies of Appalachian geology: Northern and Maritime" (Zen, E-an, White, W.S., Hadley, J.B. and Thompson, J.B., Jr., eds). (Billings v.), pp. 95–113.

Boucot, A.J. (1968). Silurian and Devonian of the Northern Appalachians. In "Studies of Appalachian geology: Northern and Maritime" (Zen, E-an, White, W.S., Hadley, J.B., and Thompson, J.B., Jr., eds). (Billings v.) pp. 83–94.

Boucot, A.J., Field, M.T., Fletcher, Raymond, Forbes, W.H., Naylor, R.S. and Pavlides, L. (1964). Reconnaissance bedrock geology of the Presque Isle quadrangle, Maine. *Maine Geol. Survey Quad. Mapping Ser.* **2**, 123 pp.

Bridge, J. (1950). Bauxite deposits of the Southeastern United States. In "Symposium on mineral resources of the Southeastern United States, 1949 Proc." (Snyder, F.G., ed.). Knoxville, Tenn., Univ. Tennessee Press, pp. 170–201.

Bridge, J. (1955). Disconformity between Lower and Middle Ordovician series at Douglas Lake, Tennessee. *Geol. Soc. America Bull.* **66**, 725–730.

Butler, J.R. (1972). Age of Paleozoic regional metamorphism in the Carolinas, Georgia, and Tennessee Southern Appalachians. *Am. J. Sci.* **272**, 319–333.

Cook. F.A. and Oliver, J.E. (1981). The Late Precambrian-Early Paleozoic continental edge in the Appalachian orogen. *Am. J. Sci.* **281**, 993–1004.

Cook, F.A., Albaugh, D.S., Brown, L.D., Kaufman, S., Oliver, J.E. and Hatcher, R.D., Jr. (1979). Thin-skinned tectonics in the crystalline southern Appalachians; COCORP seismic-reflection profiling of the Blue Ridge and Piedmont. *Geology* **7**, 563–567.

Cooper, B.N. (1944). Geology and mineral resources of the Burkes Garden quadrangle, Virginia. *Virginia Geol. Survey Bull.* **60**, 299 pp.

Dineley, D.L. and Williams, B.P.J. (1968). The Devonian continental rocks of the lower Restigouche River, Quebec. *Canadian J. Earth Sci.* **5**, 945–953.

Fullagar, P.D. and Butler, J.R. (1979). 325 to 265 m.y.-old granitic plutons in the Piedmont of the southeastern Appalachians. *Am. J. Sci.* **279**, 161–185.

Geikie, J. (1913). Mountains, their origin, growth and decay. Edinburgh, Oliver and Boyd, 311 pp.

Glover, L. III, and Sinha, A.K. (1973). The Virgilina deformation, a late Precambrian to Early Cambrian (?) orogenic event in the central Piedmont of Virginia and North Carolina. *Am. J. Sci.* **273-A** (Cooper v.), 234–251.

Hadley, J.B. and Goldsmith, Richard (1963). Geology of the eastern Great Smoky Mountains, North Carolina and Tennessee. *U.S. Geol. Survey Prof. Paper* **349-B**, 118 pp.

Hatcher, R.D., Jr. and Zietz, I. (1978). Thin crystalline thrust sheets in the southern Appalachian Inner Piedmont and Blue Ridge: interpretation based upon regional aeromagnetic data (abs.). *Geol. Soc. America Abs. with Programs* **10**, 417.

Hatcher, R.D., Jr., Howell, D.E. and Talwani, P. (1977). Eastern Piedmont fault system: speculations on its extent. *Geology* **5**, 636–640.

Hatcher, R.D., Jr., Acker, L.L., Bryan, J.G., and Godfrey, S.C. (1979). The Hayesville thrust of the central Blue Ridge of North Carolina and nearby Georgia; a pre-metamorphic, polydeformed thrust and cryptic suture within the Blue Ridge thrust sheet (abs.). *Geol Soc. America Abs. with Programs* **11**, 181.

Hess, H.H. (1939). Island arcs, gravity anomalies and serpentinite intrusions. A contribution to the ophiolite problem: Internat. Geol. Congress, 17th, Moscow 1937, Rept., v. 2, pp. 263–283. (Russian edition, pp. 279–300.)

Jacobi, R.D. (1981). Peripheral bulge — a causal mechanism for the Lower/Middle Ordovician unconformity along the western margin of the Northern Appalachians: *Earth Planet. Sci. lett.* **56**, 245–251.

Kindle, C.H. and Whittington, H.B. (1958). Stratigrahy of the Cow Head region, western Newfoundland. *Geol. Soc. America Bull.* **69**, 315–342.

Kish, S. Fullagar, P.D., Snoke, A.W. and Secor, D.T., Jr. (1978). The Kiokee belt of South Carolina (Part I): Evidence for late Paleozoic deformation and metamorphism in the southern Appalachian Piedmont (abs.). *Geol. Soc. America Abs. with Programs* **10**, 172–173.

Kreisa, R.D. and Bambach, R.K. (1973). Environments of deposition of the Price Formation (Lower Mississippian) in its type area, south-western Virginia. *Am. J. Sci.* **273-A** (Cooper v.), 326–342.

Kropotkin, P.N. (1961). Paleomagnetizm, paleoklimaty i problema krupnykh gorizontal'nykh dvizheniy Zemnoy kory. *Sovetskaya Geologiya, 1961,* **no. 5**, 16–38. (English translation: *Internat. Geol. Review,* **5**, 1214–1234, 1962.)

Misra, K.C. and Keller, F.B. (1978). Ultramafic bodies in the southern Appalachians: a review. *Am. J. Sci.* **278**, 389–418.

Naylor, R.S. (1971). Acadian orogeny; an abrupt and brief event. *Science* **172**, 558–560.

Pierce, K.L. (1965). Geomorphic significance of a Cretaceous deposit in the Great Valley of southern Pennsylvania. *U.S. Geol. Survey Prof. Paper* **525**, C152–C156.

Piqué, A. (1981). Northwestern Africa and the Avalonian plate: relations during late Precambrian and late Paleozoic. *Geology* **9**, 319–322.

Rankin, D.W. (1975). The continental margin of eastern North America in the southern Appalachians: the opening and closing of the proto-Atlantic Ocean. *Am. J. Sci.* **275-A**, 298–336.

Rankin, D.W. (1976). Appalachian salients and recesses: late Precambrian continental breakup and the opening of the Iapetus Ocean. *J. Geophys. Res.* **81**, 5605–5619.

Rast, N. (1980). The Avalonian plate in the northern Appalachians and Caledonides. *Va. Polytech. Inst. Dept. Geol. Sci. Mem.* **2**, 63–66.

Rast, N. and Currie, K.L. (1976). On the position of the Variscan front in southern New Brunswick and its relation to Precambrian basement. *Canadian J. Earth Sci.* **13**, 194–196.

Rast, N. and Grant, R. (1973a). Transatlantic correlation of the Variscan-Appalachian orogeny. *Am. J. Sci.* **273**, 572–579.

Rast, N. and Grant, R. (1973b). Trip A-2, the Variscan front in southern New Brunswick. *In* "Geology of New Brunswick" (New England Intercoll. Geol. Conf., 65th Ann. Mtg., Fredericton, N.B., 1973, Gdbk.) (Rast, Nicholas, ed.), pp. 4–11.

Rast, N. and Grant, R. (1977). Varsican-Appalachian and Alleghenian deformation in the northern Appalachians. *In* "La chaîne varisque d'Europe moyenne et occidentale." *Centre Natl. Rech. Sci., Colloques Internat.* **243**, 583–586.

Ratcliffe, N.M. (1969). Structural and stratigraphic relations along the Precambrian front in southwestern Massachusetts, Trip 1: New England Intercoll. Geol. Conf., 61st Ann. Mtg., Albany, N.Y., 1969, Gdbk., Trip 1, 21 pp.

Ratcliffe, N.M. and Harwood, D.S. (1975). Blastomylonites associated with recumbent folds and overthrusts at the western edge of the Berkshire massif, Connecticut and Massachusetts — a preliminary report. *U.S. Geol. Survey Prof. Paper* **888**, 1–19.

Robinson, P. and Tucker, R.B. (1982). Discussion — The Merrimack synclinorium in northeastern Connecticut. *Am. J. Sci.* **282**, 1735–1740.

Rodgers, J. (1965). Long Point and Clam Bank Formations, western Newfoundland. *Geol. Assoc. Canada Proc.* **16**, 83–94.

Rodgers, J. (1971). The Taconic orogeny. *Geol. Soc. America Bull.* **82**, 1141–1177.

Rodgers, J. (1981). The Merrimack synclinorium in northeastern Connecticut. *Am. J. Sci.* **281**, 176–186.

Rogers, W.B. and Rogers, H.D. (1843). On the physical structure of the Appalachian chain, as exemplifying the laws which have regulated the elevation of great mountain chains, generally. *Assoc. Am. Geologists and Naturalists Repts.*, pp. 474–531. Reprinted *in*

Rogers, W.B., 1884, A reprint of annual reports and other papers on the geology of the Virginias: New York, Appleton, pp. 601–642.

Rowley, D.B. and Kidd, W.S.F. (1981). Stratigraphic relationships and detrital composition of the medial Ordovician flysch of western New England: implications for the tectonic evolution of the Taconic orogeny. *J. Geology* **89**, 199–218.

Secor, D.T., Jr., Snoke, A.W., Kish, S. and Fullagar, P.D. (1978). The Kiokee belt of South Carolina (Part II): Tectonic implications of late Paleozoic deformation and metamorphism in the southern Appalachian Piedmont (abs.). *Geol. Soc. America Abs. with Programs* **10**, 197.

Thomas, W.A. (1965). Ouachita influence on Mississippian lithofacies in Alabama. *In* "Alabama Geol. Soc. 3rd Ann. Field Trip, 1965", Gdbk., pp. 23–28.

Thomas, W.A. (1966). Late Mississippian folding of a syncline in the western Appalachians, West Virginia and Virginia. *Geol. Soc. America Bull.* **77**, 473–494.

Thomas, W.A. (1974). Converging clastic wedges in the Mississippian of Alabama. *Geol. Soc. America Spec. Paper* **148**, 187–207.

Wilson, J.T. (1962). Cabot fault, an Appalachian equivalent of the San Andreas and Great Glen faults and some implications for continental displacement. *Nature, London* **195**, 135–138.

Wilson, J.T. (1966). Did the Atlantic close and then re-open? *Nature, London* **211**, 676–681.

Wynne-Edwards, H.R. (1972). The Grenville Province. *In* "Variations in tectonic styles in Canada." *Geol. Assoc. Canada Spec. Paper* **11**, 263–334.

Zen, E-an (1967). Time and space relationships of the Taconic allochthon and autochthon. *Geol. Soc. America Spec. Paper* **97**, 107 pp.

Crustal Faults in North America: a Report of the COCORP Project

S. Kaufman

Department of Geological Science, Cornell University, N.Y. 14, U.S.A.

Abstract

Deep crustal reflection profiling by the COCORP group has produced data which has solved several fundamental geologic problems, both of an academic and of a practical nature. The importance of overthrusting and large-scale thin-skin tectonics has been demonstrated; the crust has been shown to be complex and the pervasiveness of the classic layered system must be re-examined; and other structural forms in several geologic terranes have been noted.

The operations of the Consortium for Continental Reflection Profiling (COCORP) represent the most concerted effort to date to apply the seismic reflection profiling technique to the study of the continental basement. The objective is to adapt and apply the most sophisticated reflection techniques to map the basement rocks of the United States and to focus on specific geologic problems. Seismic crews are hired from the petroleum exploration industry and scientists from industrial, governmental, and academic institutions advise as to the best areas to work, the equipment and techniques to use, and to review the results. Cornell University is the operating institution and the prime contractor. The project is sponsored by the U.S. National Academy of Sciences as part of the U.S. Geodynamics Project, and is funded by the National Science Foundation.

To date over 3000 line km of reflection profiling have been done in 11 areas within the U.S. The traverses are shown in Fig. 1, covering a variety of geological terranes and attacking a variety of geologic problems. The widespread occurrence of reflecting horizons in the continental crust, combined with the structures observed, indicates a complexity much greater than that expected from the classical simple division of the crust into a "granitic layer" overlying a "basaltic layer" with one or more pervasive midcrustal discontinuities. The layering is seen to be variable and complex, and the seismic horizons in the deep crust often appear different than those characteristic of the sedimentary section, being complex transition zones, possibly "laminated", probably with layered structures, and of limited continuity. The "laminations" may be discontinuous vertically and horizontally, with sporadic structural "tuning" of the reflected signals possibly accounting for the high amplitudes observed. The seismic signatures can be interpreted in a variety of ways. They could be explained by a crust composed of metamorphic complexes caused by small or large scale folding of, or intrusion into, part of an originally layered crust. The original layering could have been sedimentary, or volcanic, or gneissic banding.

The present COCORP practice is to run long profiles over areas of geological interest, typically 50–200 km long. Data are usually recorded to between 18 and 20 seconds, two-way travel time, a second of two-way travel time being equal to about 3 km depth in the crystalline basement. The VIBROSEIS* system is used as a source because it offers high quality while maximizing efficiency and array flexibility, yet with minimum environmental impact. Five vibrators are used, with linear upsweeps of 8–32 Hz or 8–40 Hz, arrayed in an optimum array, as are the 24 geophones at each of the 96 stations. Spread length is usually over 10 km, but may vary either way depending on local conditions. Data are collected and processed generally in a manner to produce a 24-fold common-depth-point stacked seismic section.

Surface geological control, where it exists, is an important aspect of the method in that it may then be possible to follow identifiable features to depth. Sometimes long lines are required for this purpose, and some of the most successful COCORP results have been so obtained. In the Wind River Mountains, Wyoming, data critical for the interpretation of Laramide structure have been obtained. The Laramide orogeny, which occurred from the late Cretaceous to early Eocene, is characterized in Wyoming by large uplifts of Precambrian basement, commonly flanked by reverse faults. The attitude of these faults at depth has been a major tectonic problem and is very important for deciding whether horizontal or vertical crustal movements were primarily responsible for the basement uplifts. COCORP has run 158 km of deep seismic reflection profiles across the south-eastern end of the Wind River Mountains, the largest of these Laramide uplifts. Reflections from the thrust fault flanking the Wind River uplift can be clearly traced on the profiles to

---

* Registered trademark of Conoco Inc.

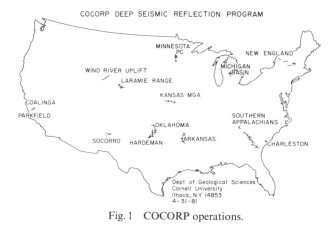

Fig. 1   COCORP operations.

at least 24-km depth and possibly as deep as about 36 km with a fairly uniform apparent dip of 30°–35°. Other reflection events subparallel to the main Wind River thrust are present in the seismic profiles and may represent other faults. There is at least 21 km of crustal shortening along the thrust. There is no evidence in the reflection profiles for large-scale folding of the basement; the Wind River Mountains were formed predominantly by thrust movements. Gravity anomalies in the Wind River Mountains can be modeled by a thrust that displaces dense material in the lower crust. If the thrust ever cut the Moho, the effect is not observed in the gravity today. A proposed model for the presence of uplifted basement in Wyoming invokes a shallow dipping, subducted Farallon plate beneath the North American continent; drag between the two plates localized compressional stresses in an area over 800 km into the North American plate causing large thrusts to develop. The earth's crust seems to have fractured as a fairly rigid plate.

COCORP seismic-reflection profiling in Georgia, North Carolina, and Tennessee and related geological data indicate that the crystalline Precambrian and Paleozoic rocks of the Blue Ridge, Inner Piedmont, Charlotte belt, and Carolina slate belt constitute an allochthonous sheet, generally 6 to 15 km thick, which overlies relatively flat-lying autochthonous lower Paleozoic sedimentary rocks, 1 to 5 km thick, of the proto-Atlantic continental margin. Thus, the crystalline rocks of the southern Appalachians appear to have been thrust at least 400 km to the west, and they overlie sedimentary rocks that cover an extensive area of the central and southern Appalachians. The hydrocarbon potential of these sedimentary rocks is unknown. The data show that the Brevard fault is the surface expression of an eastward-dipping splay off the main sole thrust, and they show, or imply, that other major faults of this region have similar origins. A southward extension onto the Coastal Plain confirms the large-scale, thin-skinned thrusting of crystalline rocks of the southern Appalachians. Most of the reflectors can be interpreted as either fault surfaces or as metamorphosed strata of Late Precambrian/Early Paleozoic age and are consistent with the hypothesis that a major detachment extends eastward beneath this part of the orogen, although other interpretations with a more complex pattern of detachments of sutures are also possible. This large-scale overthrusting provides a mechanism for incorporating sedimentary rocks into the lower crust and may help to explain many of the layered features on crustal seismic data. Reflections from deep beneath the Coastal Plain indicate that the structural configuration of the rocks is complex and that the remains of a collision zone are being observed. Several east-dipping horizons, which bear strong similarities to thrust faults in Valley and Ridge sedimentary rocks, are seen in the basement at shallow and mid-crustal levels beneath the Coastal Plain. The Augusta fault, for example, displays a reflection which extends at a low angle some 80 km or more south-east of its surface position. In conjunction with surface geologic information, these new data demonstrate that Late Paleozoic compressive deformation was pervasive and resulted in lateral movements in the upper crust extending from the Valley and Ridge to the crystalline rocks beneath the Coastal Plain.

OKLAHOMA LINE I

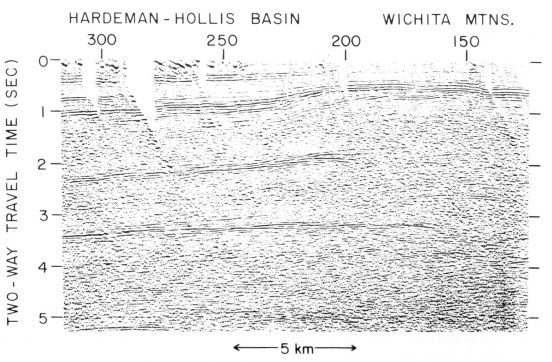

Fig. 2   Truncation of deep basement layering against bounding fault on south side of Wichita mountains.

An interesting antiformal structure is also observed far to the east, beneath the coastal plain of Georgia. As seen in Fig. 3, the east-dipping limb of this structure is of considerable extent, with an event of stronger east dip beneath the apex of the structure. Migration of this time section would place the latter in a position appropriate for a bounding fault plane. Fig. 4 shows the cross line over the antiform. A possible interpretation of these data is that the west-directed compressive deformation, previously referred to, also affected rocks this far to the east.

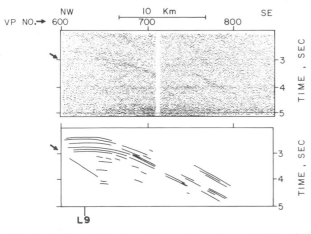

Fig. 3   Antiformal structure observed beneath coastal plain of Georgia.

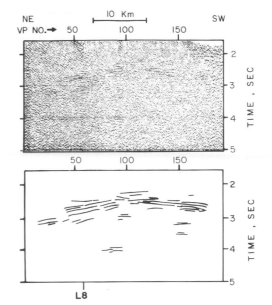

Fig. 4   Cross line over antiformal structure beneath coastal plain of Georgia.

In the southern mid-continent a Protoerozoic basement has been revealed. The seismic profiles in south-western Oklahoma show strong, persistent, continuous and undeformed layering in the basement over an area at least as great as, and probably very much greater than, 2500 km². Such layering is very unusual, judging by COCORP experience with basement rocks elsewhere in the United States. The data can be interpreted as representing a Protoerozoic basin filled with clastic and/or felsic volcanic rocks 7–10 km thick, whose base lies 10–13 km deep. These rocks are believed, on the basis of sparse evidence from regional geology, to have been deposited or extruded about 1100–1300 m.y. ago. This basin lies on the south side of the Wichita mountains, under the Paleozoic Hardeman basin, and is of similar depth to the Paleozoic Anadarko basin north of the mountains. The deep basement layering is truncated on the south side of the Wichita mountains as seen in Fig. 2, probably by Precambrian faults in conjunction with granitic intrusions. Pennsylvanian compression probably reactivated these Precambrian trends. Extensive Precambrian basin deposits in this area were unexpected, based on the evidence from sparse well control, and indicate a much more complex geological history than could previously be determined without the COCORP data. Simple models for the evolution of southwestern Oklahoma as an aulacogen must be reformulated in the light of these new data.

The Michigan Basin is a classic example of a cratonic basin. The Precambrian surface underlying it is an approximately circular depression (about 500 km in diameter) filled with Phanerozoic sediments that reach their maximum thickness of 4·5 km west of Saginaw Bay. The object of the profiling here was to investigate the deep underlying structure of the basin, and to try to determine what caused its formulation.

The COCORP seismic profiles show strong subhorizontal reflections from the sedimentary rocks of the basin. Below these, and truncated by them, is a prominent trough-shaped event approximately 60 km wide, with about 3 km of relief and lying about 9 km below the surface at its deepest point. A conformable series of reflections underlie the trough-shaped event. The curvature of these events and discontinuities in the events suggest normal faulting of these and underlying horizons. Deeper reflections are sparse, consisting largely of discontinuous segments. These seismic data, together with gravity and magnetic data, strongly support the suggestion that the Michigan basin is underlain by a north-west–south-east trending rift, probably closely related to the Keweenawan rifting event (about 1100 m.y. ago). However, the relationship, if any, between this and the Phanerozoic basin is not clear. Not only did the basin start forming much later (late Cambrian–early Ordovician), but it is also circular, as opposed to the relatively linear Precambrian structure. It is difficult to see the connection between radially symmetric models of basin formation and the rift structure.

The Rio Grande Rift Area, New Mexico, was the site of the first full scale COCORP investigation of a specific geologic problem. Crustal extension along this rift began about 32–27 m.y. ago and much diverse evidence indicates that rifting is continuing today. The data show a crustal seismic response different from other COCORP areas. Events which appear to be diffractions are localized, and the deeper part of the crust show short, discontinuous reflecting segments of variable concentration with generally low dip. Several zones of few reflectors exist, most noticeably just below the top of the basement, towards the base of the crust, and a steeply dipping transparent zone beneath the surface expression of the east-flanking fault. If this steeply dipping zone does represent the eastern rift boundary, then it indicates that the boundary was not formed by listric faulting but might have been caused by a pervasively sheared fault zone, or a pre-existing area of weakness along which faulting was localized; or by intrusions which developed during rifting.

A major feature in this region is a high amplitude complex group of events at a depth of about 18–20 km. These appear to confirm the existence of a magma body previously inferred from other geophysical data. Whether the magma represents *in situ* melting of the crust, or migration from deeper levels, is not known at present.

In conclusion it can be stated that the continental crust is indeed worthy of detailed study in three dimensions, and seismic reflection profiling has the capacity to do this. The data are as yet limited, and it would be premature to state their ultimate impact on problems such as the genesis and evolution of the crust, or whether they uphold the ideas of plate tectonics in continental crust or not. Structures such as the Wind River mountains and the southern Appalachians allochthon suggest that horizontally directed stresses are important, as might be generated by horizontally moving plates. It may well be that examples of horizontal movements, such as large allochthonous masses, are much more widespread than previously thought.

These data demonstrate the utility of the method for providing information on possible hydrocarbon and mineral provinces. They strongly suggest the nature of the dominant tectonic regimes involved in the formation of the Rocky Mountains of Wyoming and in the southern Appalachians, in the former by indicating that basin sequences might extend under the flanks of some of the Laramide basement uplifts, and in the latter by suggesting that Lower Paleozoic sediments of the Valley and Ridge might extend for hundreds of kilometres under the southern Appalachians allochthon. The Rio Grande rift data have enhanced the area as a prospect for future geothermal energy studies.

References

Allmendinger *et al.* (1982). COCORP profiling across the northern Rocky Mountain front, Part II: Precambrian basement structure and its influence on Laramide deformation. (Submitted to *Bull. GSA*).

Ando *et al.* (1982). Crustal geometry of the Appalachian Orogen from seismic reflection studies. (Submitted to *GSA Memoir*).

Brewer, J.A. and Oliver, J.E. (1980). Seismic reflection studies of deep crustal structure. *Ann. Rev. Earth Planet. Sci.* **9**, 205–230.

Brewer, J.A., Smithson, S.B., Oliver, J.E., Kaufman, S. and Brown, L.D. (1980). The Laramide Orogeny: evidence from COCORP deep crustal seismic reflection profiles in the Wind River Mountains, Wyoming. *Tectonophysics* **62**, 165–189.

Brewer, J.A., Cook, F.A., Brown, L.D., Oliver, J.E., Kaufman, S. and Albaugh, D.S. (1981). COCORP seismic reflection profiling across thrust faults. Proceedings of Thrust and Nappe Tectonics Conference. Geological Society of London, pp. 501–511.

Brewer *et al.* (1981). A Proterozoic basin in the southern mid-continent of the U.S. revealed by COCORP deep seismic reflection profiling.

Brewer *et al.* (1982). COCORP profiling across the northern Rocky Mountain front, Part I: Laramide structure of the front in Wyoming. (Submitted to *Bull. GSA*).

Brown, L., Brewer, J., Cook, F., Kaufman, S., Krumhansl, P., Long, G., Oliver, J. and Schilt, S. (1978). Mapping the continental lithosphere by seismic reflection profiling. *Arabian Jr. Sci. Eng.*, special issue, 32–40.

Brown, L.D., Krumhansl, P.A., Chapin, C.E., Sanford, A.R., Cook, F.A., Kaufman, S., Oliver, J.E. and Schilt, F.S. (1979). COCORP seismic reflection studies of the Rio Grande Rift, Rio Grande Rift: Tectonics and Magmatism (R.E. Riecker, ed.). AGU Special Pub. **23**, 169–184.

Brown, L.D., Kaufman, S., Oliver, J., Chapin, C.E., and Sanford, A.R. (1980). Deep structure of the Rio Grande Rift from seismic reflection profiling. *J. Geophys. Res.* **85**, No. B9, 4773–4800.

Brown *et al.* (1981). Deep crustal structure: Implications for continental evolution.

Brown *et al.* (1982). Adirondack-Appalachian crustal structure: The COCORP northeast traverse. (Submitted to *Bull. GSA*).

Brown *et al.* (1982). Intra-crustal complexities of the U.S. mid-continent: Preliminary results from COCORP surveys of northeast Kansas.

Brown *et al.* (in press). Magma bodies, transverse faulting, and deep crustal structure from COCORP surveys across the Socorro cauldron, New Mexico.

Brown *et al.* (1982). Rift structure beneath the Michigan Basin from COCORP profiling.

Cook, F.A., Albaugh, D.S., Brown, L.D., Kaufman, S. and Oliver, J.E. (1980). The Brevard Fault: a subsidiary thrust fault to the southern Appalachian sole thrust, in The Caledonides in the U.S.A., I.G.C.P., Blacksburg, VA, 205–213.

Cook, F.A., Albaugh, D.S., Brown, L.D., Kaufman, S., Oliver, J.E. and Hatcher, R.D., Jr. (1979). Thin-skinned tectonics in the crystalline southern Appalachians: COCORP seismic reflection profiling of the Blue Ridge and Piedmont. *Geology* **7**, 563–567.

Cook, F.A., Brown, L.D. and Oliver, J.E. (1980). The southern Appalachians and the growth of the continents. *Sci. Amer.* **243**, No. 4, 156–168.

Cook *et al.* (1981). COCORP seismic profiling of the Appalachian orogen beneath the coastal plain of Georgia. (To appear in the *Bull. GSA*, September, 1981).

Cook *et al.* (1981). The Late Precambrian-Early Paleozoic continental edge in the Appalachian orogen. (To appear in November, 1981 issue of *Amer. J. Sci.*).

Cook *et al.* (1982). COCORP seismic reflection profiling of the southern Appalachians. (Submitted to *AAPG*).

Oliver, J. and Kaufman, S. (1976). Profiling the Rio Grande Rift. *Geotimes* **21**, 20–23.

Oliver, J., Dobrin, M., Kaufman, S., Meyer, R. and Phinney, R. (1976). Continuous seismic reflection profiling of the deep basement, Hardeman County. *Texas, Geol. Soc. Amer. Bull.* **87**, 1537–1546.

Oliver, J. and Kaufman, S. (1977). Complexities of the deep basement from seismic reflection profiling. *In* "The Earth's Crust" (J. Heacock, ed.), *Geophys. Mono.* **20**, American Geophysical Union, Washington, DC, 243–253.

Oliver, J. (1978). Exploration of the continental basement by seismic reflection profiling. *Nature, London* **275**, 485–488.

Oliver, J. (1980). Exploring the basement of the North American continent. *Amer. Sci.* **68**, No. 6, 676–683.

Oliver, J.E. and Allmendinger, R.W. (1981). Deep seismic reflection profiling of the continental basement: examples from North America and possible applications in China. *J. Geophys. Prospect. Petrol. P.R. China*, **20**, No. 2, 61–76.

Schilt, S., Oliver, J., Brown, L., Kaufman, S., Albaugh, D., Brewer, J., Cook, F., Jensen, L., Krumhansl, P., Long, G. and Steiner, D. (1979). The heterogeneity of the continental crust: results from deep crustal seismic reflection profiling using the Vibroseis technique. *Rev. Geophys. Space Phys.* **17**, 354–358.

Schilt *et al.* (1982). Crustal structure near Charleston, SC from seismic reflection profiling.

Schilt *et al.* (1982). Subsurface structure near Charleston, SC: Results of COCORP reflection profiling in the Atlantic coastal plain.

Schilt, Kaufman, and Long, (1979). A 3-dimensional study of seismic diffraction patterns from deep basement sources. (To appear in December, 1981 issue of *Geophysics*).

Smithson, S.B. (1978). Modelling continental crust: Structural and chemical constraints. *Geophys. Res. lett.* **5**, No. 9, 749–752.

Smithson, S.B., Brewer, J.A., Kaufman, S., Oliver, J. and Hurich, C. (1978). Question of the Wind River thrust, Wyoming, resolved by COCORP deep reflection data and by gravity data. Wyoming Geological Association Guidebook, pp. 227–234.

Smithson, S.B., Brewer, J., Kaufman, S., Oliver, J. and Hurich, C. (1978). Nature of the Wind River thrust, Wyoming, from COCORP deep reflection data and gravity data. Geology **6**, 648–652.

Smithson, S.B., Brewer, J.A., Kaufman, S., Oliver, J.E. and Hurich, C. (1979). Structure of the Laramide Wind River uplift, Wyoming, from COCORP deep reflection data and from gravity data. *J. Geophys. Res.* **84**, 5955–5972.

Smithson, S.B., Brewer, J.A., Kaufman, S., Oliver, J.E. and Zawislak, R.A. (1980). Complex Archean lower crustal structure revealed by COCORP crustal reflection profiling in the Wind River Range, Wyoming. *Earth Planet. Sci. lett.* **46**, 295–305.

Mountain Building and Metamorphism: a Case History From Taiwan*

W. G. Ernst

Department of Earth and Space Sciences,
Institute of Geophysics and Planetary Physics,
University of California,
Los Angeles, California U.S.A.

Abstract

The main part of Taiwan consists of an Upper Paleozoic–Mesozoic basement complex and an unconformably overlying Cenozoic cover series; this terrane is juxtaposed along the Longitudinal Valley on the east side of the island against the Coastal Range, the northern extension of the Neogene Luzon volcanic arc and Luzon trough forearc basin. Accumulation of miogeoclinal sandstones, shales, limestones and intercalated basaltic units along the eastern, rifted margin of Asia in Late Paleozoic and Early Mesozoic time was interrupted by a major dynamothermal event which produced the Tananao Schist composite terrane. This complex consists of a westerly Tailuko belt, separated from the Yuli belt on the east by an hypothesized fault. The Tailuko belt is characterized by biotite zone greenschist facies assemblages except in the northern portions where amphibolite facies assemblages occur, associated with the emplacement of S-type granitic rocks. The Yuli belt lacks marble layers and granitic intrusions, and instead contains rare serpentinite plus epidote amphibolite and barroisitic amphibolite tectonic lenses. This Late Mesozoic Tananao complex evidently was produced by subduction beneath the Asiatic margin. Mafic tectonic blocks in the Yuli belt show partial conversion to glaucophane-bearing assemblages; radiometric apparent ages are 8–14 m.y. The Cenozoic cover sequence was deposited following renewed Early Tertiary rifting and sea-floor spreading. It consists of largely sedimentary strata (plus basalts) laid down on the Asiatic continental margin and seaward in the South China Sea as slope deposits. An accretionary wedge was constructed adjacent to the approaching Luzon arc, which marked the non-subducted western margin of the Philippine Sea plate. During Plio-Pleistocene collision of the Coastal Range with the Chinese sialic crust, the Cenozoic continental slope units were imbricated and thrust westward; increased pressure and temperature during this loading evidently attended recrystallization of the basement plus passive margin sedimentary cover. Metamorphism ranged from diagenetic and zeolite facies in the Western Foothills to upper greenschist facies in the basement terrane. In contrast, the exotic terrane lying east of the Longitudinal Valley seems to be virtually unmetamorphosed. However, the East Taiwan Ophiolite, occurring as clastic debris and slide blocks in unmetamorphosed olistostromal deposits of the Coastal Range, carries the effects of an early Miocene (?) oceanic ridge recrystallization of actinolite hornfels facies, overprinted by a late Miocene–Early Pliocene ocean-floor zeolitization.

Mountain building in Taiwan thus involved at least two principal convergent episodes: (1) a westward-directed Late Mesozoic paleopacific lithospheric plate underflow which produced paired high-temperature and high-pressure belts; and (2), following a cryptic subduction event 8–14 m.y. ago, a Plio-Pleistocene collisional event during eastward descent of the South China Sea lithosphere beneath the Philippine Sea plate which generated a diagenetic to low-grade metamorphic sequence. Impaction of an outboard calc-alkaline volcanic arc provided further complications. Time–space relationships exhibited by the parageneses of this young orogenic area indicate that the processes of metamorphism and mountain building are intricate and complex.

* Institute of Geophysics and Planetary Physics publication no. 2357.

I. Introduction

Mountain building and the formation of orogenic igneous and metamorphic rock suites are complicated functions of lithospheric plate interaction. Mobile belts are characteristic of convergent and continental transform plate boundaries, so we turn to such settings to investigate relationships between petrology and tectonics. To a considerable extent, mountain building is a consequence of the volume and nature of crustal material delivered to the plate junction, and the rate at which it is supplied, whereas orogenic igneous and metamorphic rocks reflect both attendant lithologies and imposed thermal regime.

Twenty years ago, Miyashiro (1961) called attention to paired metamorphic belts in the Circumpacific region. It is now clear that high-pressure metamorphic terranes mark the suture zones of convergent lithospheric plates, and the more or less coeval high-temperature belts form in the environs of the calc-alkaline volcanic/plutonic arc (e.g. California, Japan). In regions where small amounts of closure have occurred due to a subsequent change in relative plate motions, the high-temperature belt may have failed to develop within the stable, non-subducted slab (e.g. the Southern Alps); this phenomenon apparently reflects less extensive advective heat transfer (accompanying the rise of magmas) because of limited plate descent. Intracratonic mountain building, on the other hand, may provide broad high-temperature metamorphic + calc-alkaline volcanic/plutonic complexes, apparently without generating blueschist belts (e.g. Panafrican orogenic belts). Archean mountain building must have been even more different from modern orogeny, judging by the contrasts in lithologic assemblages and styles of deformation (Ernst, in press).

Clearly, one cannot identify *the* relationship between mountain building and metamorphism, for the thermotectonic nature of the continental and oceanic crust — and the upper mantle as well — have evolved over the course of geologic time. Furthermore, the nature and timing of orogeny is very much a function of specific geographic dispositions of the interacting plates. Even during the Phanerozoic, any orogenic episode must have been a complicated function of the attendant P-T regime, the dynamics of lithospheric plate interactions, the geometric "accidents" of continental collision, terrane migration or oceanic ridge and trench obliteration, and so forth.

Accordingly, let us examine the metamorphic-tectonic history of a small, reasonably intact post-Paleozoic mountain belt, with the hope of being able to correlate mineral parageneses and large-scale geologic structures with inferred lithospheric plate motions. It will be difficult to generalize regarding the relationships between metamorphism and orogeny, but hopefully, the local complexities of recrystallization will provide a partial illumination of the specific tectonic history. The example chosen is Taiwan.

II. Current Plate Tectonic Setting of Taiwan

As illustrated in Fig. 1, Taiwan occupies a prominent salient along the leading edge of the Asiatic lithospheric plate (Biq, 1971; Chai, 1972; Bowin *et al.*, 1978; Hamilton, 1979). Present-day differential motions of the impinging plates are well documented by earthquake hypocentre locations (Tsai, 1978). The more easterly Philippine Sea plate is moving relatively north-westward (Seno, 1977). Convergence is accommodated along its northern boundary by subduction of the Philippine Sea plate beneath the Ryukyu volcanic arc which has been constructed on oceanic crust directly seaward from the Asiatic continental margin. The Tatun volcanic field at the northern tip of Taiwan probably represents the

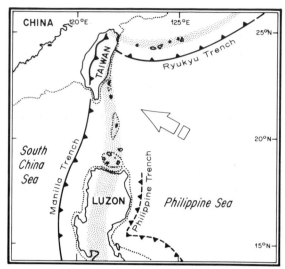

Fig. 1. Regional setting of Taiwan at the intersection of Ryukyu and Manila trenches with the continental margin of Asia. The arrow indicates the approximate motion of the Philippine Sea plate relative to Asia (7 cm/year according to Seno, 1977). Note that the Philippine Sea plate is descending obliquely beneath the Ryukyu arc, but is being thrust over the South China Sea and Chinese continental margin. Thus, relative to the Asiatic plate, the Manila trench is moving westward with time.

western termination of the Ryukyu arc. Because of curvature of the surface expression of this convergent plate boundary, the western part of the Ryukyu trench currently appears to be experiencing chiefly right-lateral transform motion. Convergence is accommodated along the western boundary of the Philippine Sea plate by eastward underflow of the South China Sea and incipient subduction of the Chinese continental margin. The northern part of the Philippine Islands, a northward extending bathymetric high and the Coastal Range of eastern Taiwan, constitute the Luzon calc-alkaline volcanic arc which has been produced by this eastward subduction of the Asiatic lithospheric plate. The island of Taiwan marks a sector where the Chinese continent adjacent to the South China Sea mantle lithosphere in large part refused to follow the latter as it descended beneath the Luzon arc. Instead, the edge of the continent collided with the arc and was structurally compressed, thickened and uplifted.

Taiwan therefore consists of portions of two major tectonic entities, (a) the Asiatic sialic crust including Mesozoic basement, and (b) the impacted Philippine Sea Luzon arc. Overlying the basement of the continental margin lies an imbricate, westward verging, accretionary prism of Cenozoic age. In part deposited on the Asiatic continental margin, and in part on the now consumed South China Sea oceanic crust, this section is largely allochthonous, having been thrust westward towards the mainland during continued convergence (Suppe and Wittke, 1977). Its contact with the Luzon volcanic arc occurs along the Longitudinal Valley of eastern Taiwan, a modern intraorogenic left-lateral strike slip vertical fault (Allen, 1962). General relations are sketched in Fig. 2.

Prior to the collision of the Coastal Range and the Asiatic continental margin which commenced about 4 m.y. ago (Chi *et al.*, 1981), oceanic crust of the South China Sea lay along the eastern edge of the Asiatic lithospheric plate. Consumption of this intervening oceanic crust allowed (1) impaction of the Chinese sialic crust, initially in north-easternmost Taiwan, with the northern end of the calc-alkaline Luzon arc, (2) incipient subduction of the Asiatic continental crust, and (3) imbrication and westward thrusting of the accretion-

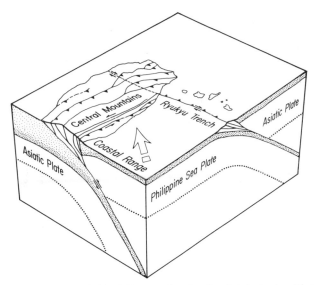

Fig. 2. Schematic block diagram showing the plate tectonic setting of Taiwan. Note that whereas the convergent plate junction which surfaces along the Ryukyu arc is a well defined linear feature, the eastward underflow of the Asiatic plate beneath the Philippine Sea and the surmounting Coastal Range is being choked off due to the imbricated accretionary wedge and distributory thrust faults present throughout the main part of Taiwan. The Longitudinal Valley marks the juxtaposition of exotic Coastal Range, accretionary wedge; and Asiatic basement; a minimum of 150 km left-lateral slip has taken place along the break since the onset of the collisional event according to Tsai (1978).

ary wedge. Distributory shear has moved westward with time, tending to transfer the accretionary wedge and underlying pre-Cenozoic basement complex to the overriding Philippine Sea plate. As convergence continued, the zone of continental impaction extended south-westward as more sialic material became involved in the eastward underflow and the South China Sea was progressively consumed. Ultimately, buoyancy forces should choke off the Manila trench subduction zone, and a new west-dipping convergent plate junction will be initiated, probably, as conjectured by Bowin *et al.*, (1978), as a northward extension of the reactivated Philippine trench (see also Cardwell *et al.*, 1980). This process should result in transference of the entire Luzon arc to the then stabilized Asiatic plate, and the westward underflow of the Philippine Sea lithosphere.

III. Lithotectonic Terranes of Taiwan

The various structural belts of Taiwan are illustrated in Fig. 3. From west to east they are: (1) the Coastal Plain; (2) the Western Foothills; (3) the Hsuehshan Range; (4) the Backbone Range; (5) the Basement Complex; and (6) the Coastal Range. Units (2)–(4) comprise the imbricated allochthonous Cenozoic cover strata and minor intercalated mafic volcanics, (5) represents chiefly the pre-Cenozoic Asiatic continental crust, and (6) is the Neogene Luzon calc-alkaline arc plus associated sediments as well as the Luzon trough forearc basin fill. With the exceptions of the Coastal Plain and the Coastal Range, all sections have been at least weakly recrystallized; moreover, the Coastal Range contains the East Taiwan Ophiolite which has been subjected to oceanic metamorphism prior to incorporation in the Luzon arc.

Various diatrophic events have been previously documented in Taiwan. Ho (1979) referred to three principal mountain building phases: (1) the Late Mesozoic multistage

Nanao orogeny involving the pre-Tertiary basement terrane; (2) the problematic Mid-Tertiary Puli orogeny, allegedly affecting strata lying to the east of the Western Foothills; and (3) the Plio-Pleistocene Penglai (= Taiwan) orogeny, resulting in the deformation, weak recrystallization and uplift of most of the island. As shown in Table I, Yen (1976; personal communication, 1981) in addition has divided the pre-Tertiary deformation into earlier and later Mesozoic stages and has distinguished between the Neogene orogenies in the Coastal Range on the one hand, and the rest of Taiwan on the other.

We will now consider the mineral parageneses developed within portions of the various structural terranes in order to elucidate the petrotectonic history of the island.

IV.   Metamorphism of the Basement Complex, Central Mountain Range

A. Tananao Composite Terrane

The pre-Cenozoic basement of Taiwan, called the Tananao Schist (Yen, 1954a, b, 1960, 1967; Ho, 1975) crops out as a narrow belt immediately west of the Longitudinal Valley. It bears evidence of multiple deformation and recrystallization events (Wang, 1979). As indicated in Fig. 3, two principal lithotectonic zones have been recognized, separated by the problematical Shoufeng fault (Yen, 1963). At least in the vicinity of the Southern Cross-island Highway, this conjectural break appears to be an east-dipping low-angle thrust fault (Stanley *et al.* 1981). On the west lies the Tailuko belt, consisting of Upper Paleozoic and Lower Mesozoic pelitic schists, quartzofeldspathic gneisses, platform carbonate units, intercalated mafic and tuffaceous metasediments, greenschists and amphibolites; in the north, this belt has been locally intruded by granitic rocks (Wang-Lee, 1981) of Mesozoic age. This terrane appears to represent a pre-existing (Atlantic-type) rifted margin, which was converted to an island or continental margin volcanic/plutonic arc in Late Mesozoic time. The occurrence of exclusively plutonic calc-alkaline rocks indicates that relatively deep levels of this igneous arc are exposed. East of the Tailuko belt lies a monotonous melange of pre-Cenozoic pelitic and mafic plus ultramafic schists of oceanic affinities (Liou, 1981a) — some containing glaucophane (Yen, 1966) — collectively termed the Yuli belt; carbonate strata and granitoids are conspicuous by their absence in this terrane. Judging from the lithologic assemblage, this seems to have been a Late Mesozoic argillite trench (?) deposit.

The so-called Shoufeng fault, which in most places has not been recognized in the field, has been compared with the Median Tectonic Line of south-western Japan (Miyashiro, 1961), and similarly juxtaposes a continentalward calc-alkaline magma-intruded thermally recrystallized section against a more seaward lithotectonic zone lacking plutonic igneous rocks other than "cold" alpine-type bodies such as serpentinized peridotites. In general, open folding appears to characterize the Tailuko belt, whereas oceanward vergence is typical of the Yuli terrane (Yen, 1967; Biq, 1971; Stanley *et al.*, 1981). Thus these two Mesozoic belts possess some of the contrasts which characterize Circumpacific volcanic/plutonic arcs and outboard subduction complexes (Ernst, 1977a).

B. Tailuko Metamorphism

Much of the landward portion of the Tananao Schist terrane has been subjected to high rank greenschist facies metamorphism, with dark green or red-brown biotite stable

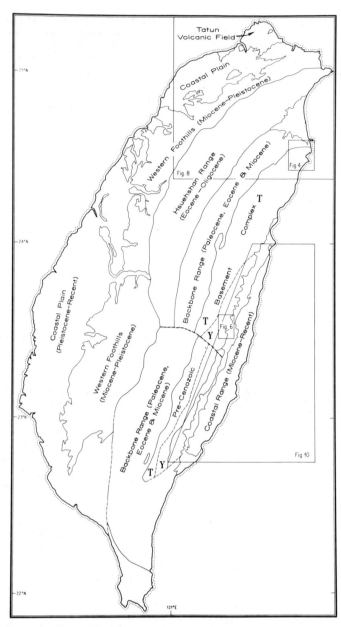

Fig. 3. Lithotectonic belts of Taiwan, after Ho (1975). The Coastal Range of eastern Taiwan is separated from the pre-Cenozoic basement terrane by the Longitudinal Valley. The Tananao Schist terrane is divided into two belts by the hypothetical Shoufeng fault; these are the Tailuko terrane (labeled T), and the Yuli terrane (labeled Y). The locations of Figs. 4, 6, 8 and 10 are also indicated.

Table I Mountain building phases in Taiwan after Yen (1976; personal communication, 1981)

Name of orogeny	Time of event	Area involved	Description
Nanao	Early-Mid Mesozoic	Tananao composite belt	Folding, faulting, regional greenschist facies metamorphism
Taiping	Early Cretaceous-Eocene	Central Ranges	Folding, faulting, production of slate, intrusion of granitoids and pegmatites
Puli	Eocene-Miocene	Central Ranges, Coastal Range	Uplift, folding, faulting, production of slate, calc-alkaline plutonism
Coastal Range	Miocene-mid Pliocene	Coastal Range	Uplift, folding, faulting
Penglai (= Taiwan)	Plio-Pleistocene-Recent	All of Taiwan	Folding, faulting, production of slate

throughout. In the author's experience, there is a tendency for grain size to increase eastward, but this apparent progradation is not mirrored by contrasts in mineral assemblages. However, in the northern part of the Tailuko belt (e.g. the Nanao-Suao area), amphibolites, quartzofeldspathic paragneisses and metagranitic rocks attest to more intense physical conditions of metamorphism (Fuh, 1962; Ho, 1975; Liou *et al.*, 1981; Ernst *et al.*, 1981). The local occurrence of sillimanite (Chu, 1981) also reflects this increase in grade.

The geologic map of a high-grade portion of the Tailuko belt is presented as Fig. 4. This Nanao-Suao area contains two pre-Cenozoic amphibolite units, as well as metadiabasic dikes and metabasaltic layers which also occur within the Tertiary cover sequence. The various mafic units were studied in detail and mineral parageneses are shown in Fig. 5. Amphibolites and neighboring small lenses of serpentinite are associated with marbles, pelitic schists and paragneisses, and have been metasomatized and thermally upgraded (locally producing clinopyroxene) during emplacement of granitic melts. The latter contain both biotite and muscovite, and appear to be of the S-type (White and Chappel, 1977). These granitoid rocks are gneissic, indicating a stage of subsequent metamorphism. They contain late pegmatites which yield K-Ar and Rb-Sr radiometric ages of 86 ± 5 m.y. (Yen and Rosenblum, 1964; Shih, 1971, unpublished data). If, as seems probable, the Late Cretaceous apparent age records the time of deformation and/or subsequent back-reaction, the granite intrusion must have taken place during an earlier Mesozoic event. The Tertiary cover series contains mafic intercalations, and the strata are transection by diabasic dikes as well; all units have been overprinted by a post-Miocene greenschist facies metamorphism. Liou *et al.* (1981) and Ernst *et al.* (1981) have estimated the physical conditions attending the various stages of recrystallization. Pre-Cenozoic amphibolite facies assemblages seem to have been produced at $600 \pm 50°C$ and $P_{fluid} \approx P_{total} \approx 5$ kb. The thermal event during granitic intrusion locally reached

Pre-Cenozoic Basement Complex

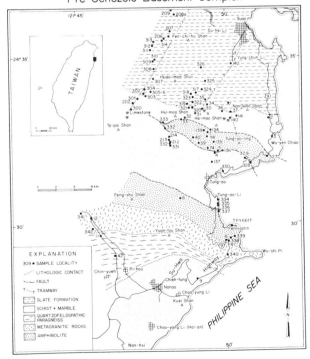

Fig. 4. Geology of the Nanao-Suao area, after Liou *et al.* (1981), and Ernst *et al.* (1981). The Slate Formation overlies an angular unconformity (Suppe *et al.*, 1976) and is probably of Eocene or Miocene age; the other mapped units are Tailuko belt rocks of pre-Cenozoic age.

Nanao-Suao Basement Complex

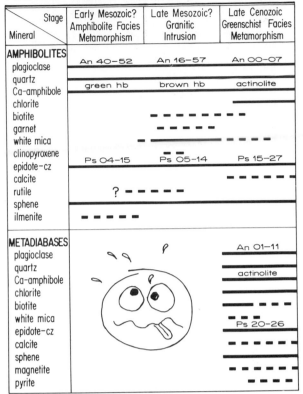

Fig. 5. Mineral parageneses developed in the basement complex (and the Tertiary cover series) after Liou *et al.* (1981) and Ernst *et al.* (1981). The abscissa represents time. The Early Mesozoic ? metamorphism may correspond to the Nanao movement of Yen (1976), the Mid Mesozoic to the Taiping, and the Late Cenozoic to the Penglai (= Taiwan).

$700 \pm 50°C$ at about 5 kb P_{fluid}. The Late Cenozoic overprint took place at $350-475°C$ and at similar or slightly lower lithostatic pressures.

Thus within the Nanao-Suao area, petrologic evidence exists for at least four distinct episodes of recrystallization: (1) Early Mesozoic (?) amphibolite facies metamorphism; (2) Mid or Late Mesozoic (?) upper amphibolite facies metamorphism accompanying calc-alkaline granitoid intrusion, (3) Late Cretaceous cooling, deformation and retrograde metamorphism; and (4) Plio-Pleistocene greenschist facies metamorphism. The first three perhaps accompanied construction of a volcanic/plutonic arc at the Asiatic continental margin, whereas (4) probably reflected collision of this margin with the far traveled Luzon arc.

C. Yuli Metamorphism

Metabasaltic epidote amphibolites and mafic, Mn-rich garnet plus glaucophane schists associated with serpentinites occur as large tectonic blocks in the Juisui area (Yen, 1966; Liou *et al.*, 1975; Liou, 1981a). Geologic relationships are illustrated in Fig. 6. This locality has provided important evidence supporting the postulated existence of a contemporaneous, relatively high-pressure, low-temperature Yuli terrane cropping out to the east of the Late Mesozoic granitoid-bearing Tailuko belt. It must be emphasized however, that the Yuli lithotectonic belt is characterized by a nondistinctive series of metapelitic and mafic greenschists and serpentinites; metagabbros, amphibolites and blueschists are of only local occurrence and are typified by sheared or faulted contacts.

Juisui Area

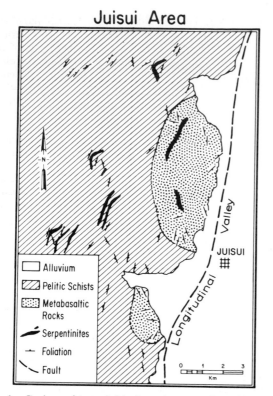

Fig. 6. Geology of tectonic blocks and surrounding schists of the Yuli belt, modified after Liou *et al.* (1975).

Juisui Tectonic Blocks

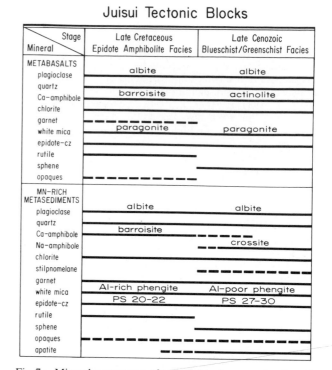

Mineral \ Stage	Late Cretaceous Epidote Amphibolite Facies	Late Cenozoic Blueschist/Greenschist Facies
METABASALTS		
plagioclase	albite	albite
quartz		
Ca–amphibole	barroisite	actinolite
chlorite		
garnet		
white mica	paragonite	paragonite
epidote–cz		
rutile		
sphene		
opaques		
MN–RICH METASEDIMENTS		
plagioclase	albite	albite
quartz		
Ca–amphibole	barroisite	
Na–amphibole		crossite
chlorite		
stilpnomelane		
garnet		
white mica	Al-rich phengite	Al-poor phengite
epidote–cz	PS 20–22	PS 27–30
rutile		
sphene		
opaques		
apatite		

Fig. 7. Mineral parageneses of tectonic blocks exposed at Juisui in the Yuli belt, simplified from Liou *et al.* (1975, 1981a) and Jahn *et al.* (1981). The abscissa represents time. A final stage of chloritization (not distinguished on this figure) has been correlated by Liou (1981a) with the Plio-Pleistocene low-grade recrystallization accompanying collision of the Asiatic margin with the Luzon arc. The Late Cretaceous metamorphism may correspond to the Taiping movement of Yen (1976), and the Late Cenozoic to the Penglai (= Taiwan).

The Juisui amphibolites display the effects of later crystallization as a greenschist facies overprint on the precursor epidote plus barroisitic hornblende assemblage. Intimately associated manganiferous deep-sea sediments (red clays or mafic tuffs?) are garnet-rich, and have developed late-stage blue amphibole and stilpnomelane. The mineral paragenesis is shown in Fig. 7. A final stage of chloritization recognized by Liou (1981a) is not illustrated in this diagram. Precursor amphibolites are estimated by Liou *et al.* (1975) to have formed at temperatures approaching 500°C, the later blueschist-type compatibilities at 400 ± 50°C, with both assemblages having been produced by relatively elevated lithostatic pressures. The presence of barroisitic hornblende suggests values on the order of 4–7 kb (Ernst, 1979).

Although the epidote-bearing Yuli barroisitic amphibolites apparently crystallized 79 ± 7 m.y. ago, radiometric data for associated sodic amphibole-bearing schists and greenschists yield much younger model ages, of the order of 8–14 m.y. and 5 m.y. respectively (Jahn and Liou, 1977; Jahn, *et al.*, 1981). Too few data are available to determine whether these are disturbed apparent ages or accurately reflect times of recrystallization. High $^{87}Sr/^{86}Sr$ ratios (>0·707) and spatial association of the Mn-rich glaucophane schists with Late Cretaceous epidote amphibolites suggest that the blueschists were derived from a precursor older than the Cenozoic South China Sea oceanic crust (Suppe *et al.*, 1981). As will be discussed later on, fragments of relatively young oceanic crust, perhaps derived from the South China Sea, are present in the Coastal Range as the East Taiwan Ophiolite.

The Pacific margin of Asia and yet more easterly South China Sea constitute the old sialic and young oceanic crust capping the Asiatic lithospheric plate. Currently and during Neogene time, this unit has been approaching and descending beneath the Philippine Sea plate (Biq, 1971; Chai, 1972; Ho, 1979; Suppe *et al.*, 1981). However, present-day seismicity indicates that north-easternmost Taiwan is characterized by northward subduction of the Philippine Sea plate (Tsai,

1978), the western extension of the convergent junction marked by the Ryukyu island arc and trench; thus, on the north, the eastward descent of the Asiatic plate is terminated by the Ryukyu subduction system. This truncation apparently has been migrating west-south-westward with time, and hence was evidently far to the east of the present location 8–14 m.y. ago during the eastward underflow which produced the Juisui blueschists. Presently active eastward-dipping thrust faults in central and southern Taiwan testify to the continuing underflow of the Asiatic plus South China Sea plate beneath the Luzon calc-alkaline arc in this region, and to a complex, imbricate suture zone. Accordingly, it seems plausible that the Juisui blueschists and related rocks are products of Neogene subduction zone metamorphism associated with descent of the South China Sea and associated older Yuli epidote amphibolitic and Mn-rich protoliths beneath the roughly coeval Coastal Range of Eastern Taiwan. Presumably this high-pressure, predominantly mafic section of pre-Cenozoic original age was tectonically included within the accretionary prism during convergent plate motion.

The Neogene glaucophane schists appear to have been generated by a tectonic regime more nearly analogous to the Alpine setting than to that of the Circumpacific subduction belts, for Taiwanese blueschists were generated due to consumption of the relatively small intervening South China Sea basin — not as a result of thousands of kilometres of underflow of paleopacific oceanic crust. Perhaps their limited occurrence in Taiwan is due to the recency of high-pressure metamorphism. The regional exposure of a deeply buried blueschist belt probably would require 30–40 million years of uplift and erosion whereas small samples of high-pressure rocks could be transported more rapidly to the Earth's surface as tectonic inclusions in low-density, buoyant serpentinite diapirs.

The age of recrystallization of the autochthonous Yuli schists is known to be post-Paleozoic, but otherwise is not closely constrained geologically. Yen and Rosenblum (1964) reported at 6 m.y. K-Ar mica age from an amphibole-bearing Yuli schist, but this might be a cooling date; the occurence of the specimen is not well known — it could be an *in situ* schist or a tectonic block. The Yuli belt may have been metamorphosed during the Late Cretaceous event that produced the allochthonous epidote amphibolites of Juisui, and the roughly contemporaneous, parallel, granite-invaded Tailuko terrane. If so, the barroisitic nature of the hornblende in the tectonic blocks would seem to suggest relatively high pressures for the Yuli Schists, in accord with the paired metamorphic belt model of earlier workers (Yen, 1963; Ho, 1975). The several Neogene recrystallization ages, and particularly those of sodic amphibole-bearing manganiferous metasediments at Juisui, however, attest to a much younger subduction event. Thus the possibility exists that a westward-directed underflow of a paleopacific lithospheric plate was responsible for the Late Mesozoic development of both Tailuko and Yuli belts, whereas a Neogene eastward descent of the South China Sea (the leading edge of the Asiatic plate) beneath the approaching Coastal Range andesitic arc produced the young blueschists. If so, it is an irksome coincidence that the Juisui blocks represent protoliths subjected to two distinct periods of high-pressure metamorphism (Jahn *et al.*, 1981), perhaps followed by a chloritic overprint reflecting the Plio-Pleistocene collisional event.

V. Metamorphism of the Cover Series

The diagenesis and very low-grade regional metamorphism of the basement complex plus Cenozoic cover sequence (passive margin deposits) has recently been documented for northern Taiwan by Liou (1981b; see also Lo and Chen, 1972; Yen, 1973). Areal distribution of the various diagenetic-metamorphic facies in the northern part of the Central Ranges based on this reconnaissance work is presented in Fig. 8. A gradual increase in grade from the incipiently zeolitized and chloritized Western Foothills to the biotite-bearing schists and gneisses of the Tailuko terrane is evident. Both basement and cover series have been penetratively deformed during the recrystallization (e.g. see Suppe *et al.*, 1976; Stanley *et al.*, 1981), and discontinuities in the mineral zonation are not obvious. The diagenetic-metamorphic facies boundaries appear to be subparallel to — but independent of — the tectonic contacts between adjacent lithotectonic belts, hence recrystallization seems to have outlasted deformation. Although pre-Cenozoic basement rocks have been affected as well, the involvement of strata as young as Pliocene and even Pleistocene draped over the Asiatic margin suggests that this metamorphic event occurred in Plio-Pleistocene time.

Paragenetic relationships for roughly metabasaltic and metapelitic bulk compositions are illustrated schematically in Fig. 9. Physical conditions inferred as appropriate for the generation of prehnite-pumpellyite facies mineral assemblages instead have developed clay mineral, illite and calcite-bearing assemblages in the northern part of the Central Ranges. The direct transition from diagenetic and zeolite facies rocks in the Western Foothills to lowest greenschist facies-type phase compatibilities in the Hsuehshan Range is a function of relatively high μ_{CO_2} which inhibits the formation of low-grade calcium-aluminium hydrous silicates characteristic of the prehnite-pumpellyite facies (Zen, 1961; Thompson, 1971; Zen and Thompson, 1974; Seki, 1973). Physical conditions attending this progressive metamorphism deduced by Tan and Lee (1977), Liou (1981b) and the present author from mineral assemblages, experimental and theoretical work, indicate a high proportion of CO_2 in the

Northern Taiwan Transect

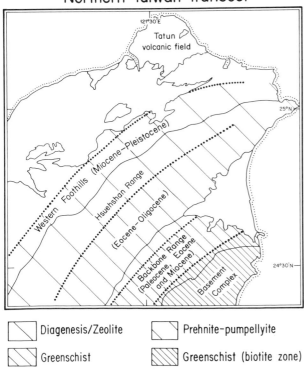

Fig. 8. Regional geology and diagenetic-metamorphic facies boundaries in lithotectonic belts of the northern Central Ranges, after reconnaissance studies chiefly by Liou (1981b).

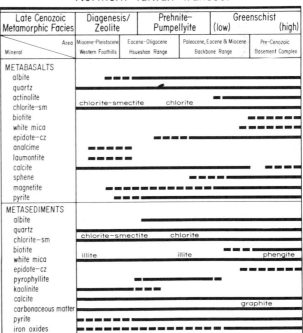

Fig. 9. Progressive mineral parageneses established in lithotectonic belts of the northern Central Ranges during Plio-Pleistocene metamorphism, after reconnaissance studies chiefly by Liou (1981b). The abscissa represents a geologic traverse from north-west on the left to the south-west on the right. This feeble metamorphism probably corresponds to the Penglai (= Taiwan) movement of Yen (1976).

aqueous fluid phase, fluid pressures less than but approaching lithostatic, and P-T values as follows: Western Foothills = 150 ± 50°C, 1–2 kb; Hsuehshan Range = 260 ± 40°C, 2–3 kb; Backbone Range = 300 ± 50°C, 4 kb; and the Nanao-Suao area = 350–475°C, 5 kb.

The Neogene progressive metamorphism of Taiwan seems to have been a consequence of the Plio-Pleistocene mountain-building, which in turn was caused by collision of the Asiatic continent and the Luzon calc-alkaline arc (Bowin et al., 1978; Chi et al., 1981). The deformed but virtually unmetamorphosed Cenozoic rocks of the advancing accretionary wedge, which accumulated along the western edge of the Philippine Sea plate, and were thrust westward accompanying 160–200 km of horizontal shortening (Suppe, 1976, 1980, 1981), loaded the descending Chinese continental rifted margin (Wu and Lu, 1976). The P-T regime imposed on this underlying imbricated, passive margin section and Asiatic basement by the advancing Luzon arc thus provided the observed Plio-Pleistocene metamorphic overprint. Uplift and erosion, progressively more pronounced in the more deeply buried eastern portion of the underlying rifted continental margin terrane, has now exposed this tectonically loaded section.

Perhaps the reason that the northern portion of the Tailuko belt exhibits a higher pre-Cenozoic metamorphic grade than the rest of the basement terrane to the south-west reflects more profound — but now recovered — burial depths during the Neogene convergence. As previously described (see section dealing with the current plate tectonic setting of Taiwan), this area was the site of first impact during Late Cenozoic collision, and it is not unreasonable that here the underflow and ultimate decoupling began earliest — thus there has been longer time for sustained, rapid uplift, as is well documented to be presently on the order of 5 km per million years (Peng et al., 1977). Accordingly we see deeper into the pre-Cenozoic basement in the north than farther to the south-west.

VI. Metamorphism in the Far Traveled Coastal Range, Eastern Taiwan

Andesitic volcanism and the construction of the Luzon arc reflects the eastward subduction of the South China Sea — the eastern, oceanic periphery of the Asiatic lithospheric plate — beneath the Philippine Sea plate. A geologic map of the Coastal Range is presented in Fig. 10. The oldest andesitic volcanics and volcanogenic sediments in the Coastal Range (base unexposed) are middle Miocene in age (Page and Suppe, 1981; Chi et al., 1981), hence initiation of the eastward underflow of the Asiatic plate must have began at that time or slightly earlier. As previously discussed, consumption of the South China Sea allowed impaction of the volcanic arc and accretionary wedge and the Asian rifted sialic margin and passive margin section (Wang, 1976) approximately 4 m.y. ago. This ongoing collision has driven the Paleogene and Neogene continental margin section westward over the Asiatic foreland, with the attendant metamorphism described in the previous section. Zeolitic alteration of the structurally higher calc-alkaline volcanics and tuffaceous sediments, and hornfelsic aureoles surrounding epizonal plugs of the Chimei igneous complex (not distinguished from the Tuluanshan Volcanics in Fig. 10) may be widespread, but have not been studied in detail.

Although most of the South China Sea oceanic crust lying in the path of the approaching Luzon arc was subducted, and has therefore disappeared, fragmentary portions were added to the Pliocene Lichi Mélange as detritus and slide blocks, collectively termed the East Taiwan Ophiolite (Liou et al., 1977; Ernst, 1977b; Suppe et al., 1977, 1981). In aggregate, this unit appears to represent a submarine plutonic breccia

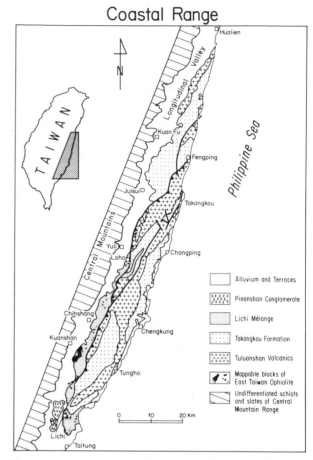

Fig. 10. Regional geology of the Coastal Range, modified from Liou et al. (1977).

composed of peridotites and gabbros, overlain by thin, middle Miocene deep-sea red shales (Huang et al., 1979) and intercalated glassy, pillowed tholeiites. The breccias are regarded as submarine talus which accumulated along a South China Sea fracture zone (ridge–ridge transform fault), whereas the overlying basalts represent spill-over supplied by spreading-centre volcanism. The plutonic breccias display the effects of ocean ridge metamorphism of probably early Miocene age (Liou and Ernst, 1979), and both talus and superjacent basalts have been subjected to a period of feeble late Miocene-early Pliocene sea-floor alteration (Liou, 1979). Stages in this metamorphism of the East Taiwan Ophiolite are illustrated in Fig. 11. Liou and Ernst have estimated the physical conditions during recrystallization as follows: pre-breciation (oceanic ridge) stage = 300–500°, >1 kb; ocean floor (off-axis) metamorphic stage = 150–250°C, 0–1 kb. Although not strictly a paragenesis accompanying mountain building, this sequence documents the general type of changes which take place in oceanic crust prior to its delivery to, and incorporation in, an accreting orogenic belt.

The manner in which the East Taiwan Ophiolite was supplied to the Coastal Range in Pliocene time is obscure; it is fittingly referred to the process termed obduction. Possibly the inferred transform fault along which the East Taiwan Ophiolite accumulated acted as a zone of weakness and bathemetric high such that, during subduction, a surficial segment peeled off from the descending lithospheric slab and was thrust up towards the east into the accretionary wedge. As it emerged above wave base, slide blocks and clastic debris moved down submarine slopes into the catchment basin of the Lichi olistostromal deposit (Ernst, 1977b; Page and Suppe, 1981; Suppe et al., 1981). The surficial nature of this

East Taiwan Ophiolite

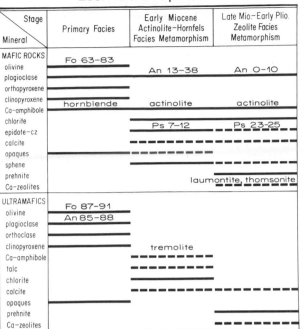

Fig. 11.   Mineral parageneses in mafic and ultramafic rocks of the East Taiwan Ophiolite, after Liou and Ernst (1979) and Liou (1979). The abscissa represents time.

process is attested to by the complete lack of metamorphic recrystallization of the scaly Lichi Mélange.

Summary

Post-Paleozoic geologic history recorded in the lithotectonic belts of Taiwan involves several recognizable events. These include:

(1) Mid and/or Late Mesozoic production of Tailuko and Yuli paired metamorphic belts at the eastern (rifted) edge of the Asiatic sialic crust (related to westward underflow);

(2) Paleogene-Miocene rifting and production of the South China Sea oceanic crust;

(3) Cenozoic deposition of miogeoclinal continental slope strata along the Asiatic passive margin and more eugeoclinal rocks progressively eastward; and

(4) eastward descent of the South China Sea beneath the Philippine Sea plate during Neogene time, resulting in the growth and imbrication of the passive margin section at and continentalward from the convergent plate junction, and construction of the Luzon andesitic arc and accretionary wedge yet farther to the east.

Episode (4), the Neogene event, is still in progress, and has had a profound influence on the geology of Taiwan, obscuring and obliterating evidence for the earlier history. Neogene production of blueschist mineral assemblages in portions of the pre-existing Yuli belt and Plio-Pleistocene regional metamorphism of the tectonically transported rifted margin strata and its Asiatic basement complex, are two of the manifestations of the young mountain building process. The contemporaneous Coastal Range, which formed on the stable non-subducted Philippine Sea plate, bears exotic block remnants of oceanic metamorphism, but this recrystallization had no direct relationship to orogenic events recorded in Taiwan.

Tawian is a very small island and represents a collisional belt in the formative stage. It provides excellent exposures for petrotectonic study, reflecting a unique position at the present intersection of two convergent plate junctions of opposite polarity (Fig. 1 and 2). Transcurrent faulting provides an additional complication. This small, well exposed natural laboratory documents the complicated interrelationships among plate tectonics, mountain building and metamorphism; moreover, these intricacies are subject to rapid evolution. What has been reasonably well demonstrated here can be only surmised for many less well preserved, more ancient orogenic belts.

Acknowledgments

This work was supported by the University of California, Los Angeles, and by the U.S. National Science Foundation, most recently through grant EAR 80–17295. Earlier U.S.–Taiwan cooperative science projects were supported by the NSF and by the National Science Council of Taiwan. I have drawn heavily on the extensive prior investigations of my collaborators performed during this international effort, particularly those of J.G. Liou (Stanford University) and John Suppe (Princeton University). The manuscript has been reviewed by Liou, Suppe, C.S. Ho (Mining and Research and Service Organization), Y. Wang (National Taiwan University) and T.P. Yen (National Central University). My deep appreciation is extended to the above-named scientists and institutions.

References

Allen, C.R. (1962). Circum-Pacific faulting in the Philippines-Taiwan region. *J. Geophys. Res.* **67**, 4795–4812.

Biq, C. (1971). A fossil subduction zone in Taiwan. *Proc. Geol. Soc. China 14,* 146–154.

Bowin, C., Lu, R.S., Lee, C.S. and Schouten, H. (1978). Plate convergence and accretion in Taiwan-Luzon region. Amer. *Assoc. Petrol. Geol. Bull.* **62**, 1645–1672.

Cardwell, R.K., Isacks, B.L. and Karig, D.E. (1980). The spatial distribution of earthquakes, focal mechanism solutions, and subducted lithosphere in the Philippine and northeastern Indonesian islands. *Amer. Geophys. Union Monog.* **23**, 1–35.

Chai, B.H.T. (1972). Structural and tectonic evolution of Taiwan. *Amer. J. Sci.* **272**, 389–422.

Chi, W.R., Namson, J. and Suppe, J. (1981). Stratigraphic record of plate interactions in Coastal Range, eastern Taiwan. *Memoir* **4**, Geological Society of China, 155–194.

Chu, H.T. (1981). The discovery of sillimanite in northern Taiwan. *Memoir* **4**, Geological Society of China, 491–496.

Ernst, W.G. (1977a). Mineral parageneses and plate tectonic settings of relatively high-pressure metamorphic belts. *Fortschritte der Mineralogie* **54**, 192–222.

Ernst, W.G. (1977b). Olistostromes and included ophiolitic debris from the Coastal Ranges of Eastern Taiwan. *Memoir* **2**, Geological Society of China, pp. 97–114.

Ernst, W.G. (1979). Coexisting sodic and calcic amphiboles from high-pressure metamorphic belts and the stability of barroisitic amphibole. *Mineralog. Mag.* **43**, 269–278.

Ernst, W.G. (in press). The early Earth and the Archean rock record: Chapter 3. *In* "Origin and Evolution of Earth's Earliest Biosphere: An Interdisciplinary Study" (J.W. Schopf, ed.). Princeton Univ. Press.

Ernst, W.G., Liou J.G. and Moore, D.E. (1981). Multiple metamorphic events recorded in Tailuko amphibolites and associated rocks of the Suao-Nanao area. *Memoir* **4**, Geological Society of China.

Fuh, T.M. (1962). Metamorphic rocks of the Nanao district, Taiwan, with special reference to the origin of orthogneiss. *Memoir* **1**, Geological Society of China, pp. 113–132.

Hamilton, W. (1979). Tectonics of the Indonesian Region. U.S. Geological Survey Professional Paper, No. 1078, 345 pp.

Ho, C.S. (1975). An introduction to the Geology of Taiwan: explanatory text of the geologic map of Taiwan. Ministry of Economic Affairs, Republic of China, Taipei, 153 pp.

Ho, C.S. (1979). Geologic and tectonic framework of Taiwan. *Memoir* 3, Geological Society of China, 57–72.

Huang, T.C., Chen, M.P. and Chi, W.R. (1979). Calcareous nannofossils from the red shale of the ophiolite-melange complex, eastern Taiwan. *Memoir* 3, Geological Society of China, 131–138.

Jahn, B.M. and Liou, J.G. (1977). Age and geochemical constraints of glaucophane schists of Taiwan. *Memoir* 2, Geological Society of China, 129–140.

Jahn, B.M., Liou, J.G., Nagasawa, H. and King, B.S. (1981). High-pressure metamorphic rocks of Taiwan: REE geochemistry, Rb-Sr ages and tectonic implications. *Memoir* 4, Geological Society of China, 497–520.

Liou, J.G. (1979). Zeolite facies metamorphism of basaltic rocks from the East Taiwan Ophiolite. *Amer. Mineral.* **64**, 1–14.

Liou, J.G. (1981a). Petrology of metamorphosed oceanic rocks in the Central of Taiwan. *Memoir* 4, Geological Society of China, 291–342.

Liou, J.G. (1981b). Recent high CO_2 activity in Taiwan; geological and petrological evidence. *Memoir* 4, Geological Society of China, 551–582.

Liou, J.G. and Ernst, W.G. (1979). Oceanic ridge metamorphism of the East Taiwan Ophiolite. *Contributions Mineral. Petrol.* **68**, 335–348.

Liou, J.G., Ernst, W.G. and Moore, D.E. (1981). Geology and petrology and some polymetamorphosed amphibolites and associated rocks in northeastern Taiwan. *Geol. Soc. Amer. Bull.* **92**, Part I, 219–224, Part II, 609–748.

Liou, J.G., Ho, C.O. and Yen, T.P. (1975). Petrology of some glaucophane schists and related rocks from Taiwan. *J. Petrol.* **16**, 80–109.

Liou, J.G., Lan, C.Y., Suppe, J. and Ernst, W.G. (1977). The East Taiwan Ophiolite, its occurrence, petrology, metamorphism and tectonic setting. Special Report No. 1, Mining Research and Service Organization, 212 pp.

Lo, H.J. and Chen, C.H. (1972). Composition and genesis of analcime from the Kungkuan tuff, northern Taiwan. *Proc. Geol. Soc. China* **15**, 123–126.

Miyashiro, A. (1961). Evolution and metamorphic belts. *J. Petrol.* **2**, 277–311.

Page, B.M. and Suppe, J. (1981). The Pliocene Lichi mélange of Taiwan: its plate tectonic and olistostromal origin. *Amer. J. Sci.* **281**, 193–227.

Peng, T.H., Li, Y.H. and Wu, F.T. (1977). Tectonic uplift rate of the Taiwan island since the early Holocene. *Memoir* 2, Geological Society of China, 57–70.

Seki, Y. (1973). Metamorphic facies of propylitic alteration. *J. Geol. Soc. Japan* **79**, 771–780.

Seno, T. (1977). The instantaneous rotation vector of the Philippine Sea plate relative to the Eurasian plate. *Tectonophysics* **42**, 209–226.

Stanley, R.S., Hill, L.B., Chang, H.C. and Hu, H.N. (1981). A cross section through the southern Central Mountains of Taiwan. *Memoir* 4, Geological Society of China, 443–474.

Suppe, J. (1976). Décollement folding in southwestern Taiwan. *Petrol. Geol. Taiwan* **13**, 25–35.

Suppe, J. (1980). A retrodeformable cross section of northern Taiwan. *Proc. Geol. Soc. China* **23**, 46–55.

Suppe, J. (1981). Mechanics of mountain-building and metamorphism in Taiwan. *Memoir* 4, Geological Society of China, 67–90.

Suppe, J. and Wittke, J.H. (1977). Abnormal pore-fluid pressures in relation to stratigraphy and structure in the active fold-and-thrust belt of northwestern Taiwan. *Meng Volume, Petrol. Geol. Taiwan* **14**, 11–24.

Suppe, J., Wang, Y., Liou, J.G. and Ernst, W.G. (1976). Observations of some contacts between basement and Cenozoic cover in the Central Mountains, Taiwan. *Proc. Geol. Soc. China* **19**, 59–70.

Suppe, J., Lan, C.Y., Hendel, E.M. and Liou, J.G. (1977). Paleogeographic interpretation of red shales within the East Taiwan Ophiolite. *Petrol. Geol. Taiwan* **14**, 109–120.

Suppe, J., Liou, J.G. and Ernst, W.G. (1981). Paleogeographic origins of the Miocene East Taiwan Ophiolite. *Amer. J. Sci.* **281**, 228–246.

Tan, L.P. and Lee, C.M.W. (1977). Quartzite and quartz veins. *Acta Geologica Taiwanica* **19**, 74–78.

Thompson, A.B. (1971). P_{CO2} in low-grade metamorphism: zeolite, carbonate, clay minerals, prehnite relations in the system $CaO-Al_2-SiO_2-CO_2-H_2O$. *Contributions to Mineral. Petrol.* **33**, 145–161.

Tsia, Y.B. (1978). Plate subduction and the Plio-Pleistocene orogeny in Taiwan. *Petril. Geol. Taiwan* **15**, 1–10.

Wang, C.S. (1976). The Lichi formation of the Coastal Range and arc-continental collision in eastern Taiwan. *Bull. Geol. Survey Taiwan* **25**, 73–86.

Wang, Y. (1979). Some structural characteristics of Tertiary basement on Taiwan. *Memoir* 3, Geological Society of China, 139–145.

Wang-Lee, C. (1981). Field trip guide to eastern section of the cross-island highway. *In* "Field Guidebook, Seminar Plate Tectonics Metamorphic Geology", 9–22 Nat. Sci. Council. Taipei, 71 pp.

White, A.J.R. and Chappell, B.W. (1977). Ultrametamorphism and granitoid genesis. *Tectonophysics* **43**, 7–22.

Wu, F.T. and Lu, C.P. (1976). Recent tectonics of Taiwan. *Bull. Geol. Survey Taiwan* **25**, 97–112.

Yen, T.P. (1954a). The gneisses of Taiwan. *Bull. Geol. Survey Taiwan* **5**, 1–100.

Yen, T.P. (1954b). The green rocks of Taiwan. *Bull. Geol. Survey Taiwan* **7**, 1–46.

Yen, T.P. (1960). A stratigraphic study on the Tananao Schist in northern Taiwan. *Bull. Geol. Survey of Taiwan* **12**, 53–66.

Yen, T.P. (1963). The metamorphic belts within the Tananao Schist terrain of Taiwan. *Proc. Geol. Soc. China* **6**, 72–74.

Yen, T.P. (1966). Glaucophane schist of Taiwan. *Proc. Geol. Soc. China* **9**, 70–73.

Yen, T.P. (1967). Structural analysis of the Tananao schist of Taiwan. *Bull. Geol. Survey Taiwan* **18**, 110. pp.

Yen, T.P. (1973). The Eocene sandstones in the Hsuehshan Range terrain, northern Taiwan. *Proc. Geol. Soc. China* **16**, 97–110.

Yen, T.P. (1976). Geohistory of Taiwan. *Proc. Geol. Soc. China.* **19**, 52–58.

Yen, T.P. and Rosenblum, S. (1964). K-Ar ages of micas from the Tananao Schist terrains of Taiwan — A preliminary report. *Proc. Geol. Soc. China* **7**, 80–81.

Zen, E-an (1961). The zeolite facies, an interpretation *Amer. J. Sci.* **259**, 401–409.

Zen, E-an, and Thompson, A.B. (1974). Low-grade regional metamorphism: mineral equilibrium relations. *Ann. Rev. Earth Planet. Sci.* **2**, 179–212.

Index